GROUNDWORK
of
SKILL ACQUISITION
and
DEVELOPMENT

Jacob B. Oroks MISM, PMP, CISM, CTS

CHIEF EXECUTIVE OFFICER
IBOTO EMPIRE LLC AND HRS ACADEMY
CALIFORNIA, UNITED STATES OF AMERICA

NEWMAN SPRINGS PUBLISHING
320 Broad Street
Red Bank, NJ 07701

First originally published by Newman Springs Publishing 2023

ISBN 978-1-68498-932-4 (Paperback)
ISBN 978-1-68498-931-7 (Hardcover)

Printed in the United States of America

To Christiana Nkiru, Esther and Asuquo

Contents

Foreword xv
Preface xvii
Acknowledgments xix

Chapter One: Meaning and Scope of Skill Acquisition 1
    1.0 Introduction 1
    2.0 Catalogue of Definitions of Skill Acquisition 2
    3.0 Circle of Definitive Terms 5
    4.0 Analysis of Entries 5
    5.0 Selected Differentials 6
         5.1 Skill and Talent 6
         5.2 Skill and Entrepreneurship 7
         5.3 Skill and Knowledge 7
         5.4 Skill Acquisition and Skill Development 8
    6.0 Summary and Conclusion 9

Chapter Two: Road Map to Skill Acquisition and Training 10
    1.0 Introduction 10
    2.0 Learning and Behavioral Objectives 10
         2.1 Behavioral Objectives 12
    3.0 Preparation of Training Notes 15
         3.1 Importance of Training Notes 15
         3.2 Constituent Parts of a Training Plan 16
         3.3 Training Notes Preparation Format 16
    4.0 Instructional Materials and Equipment 20
    5.0 Creating a Suitable Training Environment 23
         5.1 Communication Skills 23
         5.2 Feedback 25
    6.0 Training Management 25
    7.0 Evaluation of Skills Performance 27
         7.1 Evaluation Methods 28
    8.0 Summary and Conclusion 30

Chapter Three: The Language of Skill Acquisition 31
    1.0 Introduction 31
    2.0 Overview of the English Language 31
    3.0 English for Specific Purposes 32

4.0 How Language Is Used in Communication 33
    4.1 Features of Language in Aid of Communication 34
    4.2 Linguistic Creativity and Choices 34
    4.3 Flexibility for Stylistic Variation 35
    4.4 Registers 35
5.0 Functions of Language for Deployment in Skill Acquisition 35
6.0 Language Choice for Skill Acquisition 36
7.0 Selected Dimensions of Language in Use 37
8.0 Words/Phrases List in Skill Acquisition 39
9.0 Summary and Conclusion 39

Chapter Four: Psychology of Acquiring a Skill 42
1.0 Introduction 42
2.0 Perception and Training 42
3.0 Stimulus and Responses 43
4.0 Learning and Thinking 44
5.0 Problem Solving and Attitudes to Learning 47
6.0 Motivation and Personality Adjusted 48
7.0 Competency and Performance 51
8.0 Repetition of Activities 55
9.0 Peak Efficiency and Performance 55
10.0 Summary and Conclusion 56

Chapter Five: Skill Acquisition: Theories and Approaches 57
1.0 Introduction 57
2.0 Cognitive Learning Theories 58
3.0 Theoretical Competency Theory 64
4.0 Dreyfus Model of Skill Acquisition 66
5.0 Dekeyser's Skill-Learning Theory 69
6.0 Adam's Closed Loop Theory 71
7.0 Fitts and Posner's Stage Theory 73
8.0 A Constraints-Led Approach to Skill Acquisition 76
9.0 Summary/Conclusion 77

Chapter Six: Typology of Skills 78
1.0 Introduction 78
2.0 General and Specific Skills 79
    2.1 General Skills 79
3.0 Personal and Social Skills 80
    3.1 Personal Skills 80
    3.2 Social Skills 80
4.0 Soft and Hard Skills 80
5.0 Low and High Domain Skills 81
    5.1 Features of High Skills 81
    5.2 Selected Low Skills 82
6.0 Digital and Manual Skills 84

 7.0 8 Checklists of Careers and Skills 85
 8.0 Conclusion 87

Chapter Seven: Stages of Skills Acquisition **88**
 1.0 Introduction 88
 2.0 The Kaufman's Four Stages 88
   2.1 Ten Principles of Speedy Skill Acquisition 90
 3.0 The Pretraining, Training, and Post Training Stages 90
 4.0 Three Dimensions of Skill Acquisition Module 104
 5.0 The 4 Stages Pattern 112
 6.0 Conclusion 113

Chapter Eight: Role Playing in Skill Acquisition **115**
 1.0 Introduction 115
   1.1 How Role Playing Works in Skill Acquisition 116
 2.0 The Role of the Trainer in Skill Acquisition 116
 3.0 The Role of the Trainee in the Skill Acquisition Process 118
 4.0 The Role of the Sponsor in Skill Acquisition 120
 5.0 Role of the Management in Skill Acquisition 120
 6.0 Conclusion 121

Chapter Nine: Management Strategies for Skill Acquisition **122**
 1.0 Introduction 122
 2.0 Planning and Feasibility Analysis 123
 3.0 Organizing and Production 124
 4.0 Directing 125
 5.0 Controlling 125
 6.0 Communication 126
 7.0 Monitoring 126
 8.0 Evaluation 127
 9.0 Conclusion 127

Chapter Ten: Evaluation of Skilled Performance **128**
 1.0 Introduction 128
   1.1 Characteristics and Facts about Evaluation 129
 2.0 Evaluation and Assessment Processes 129
   2.1 Processes Involved in Evaluation 130
   2.2 Questions that Guide the Conduct of an Assessment 131
 3.0 Types of Evaluation: Formative/Summative 131
   3.1 Formative Evaluation 131
   3.2 Summative Evaluation 132
   3.3 The Purpose, Goals, Focus, and Results of the Formative and
     Summative Evaluation 133
 4.0 Monitoring and Evaluation 133
   4.1 The Importance of Monitoring and Evaluation 134
   4.2 Types of Monitoring 134
   4.3 Components of the Monitoring Systems in Education 135

5.0   The Cognitive, Affective and Psychomotor Domains 135
      5.1 The Cognitive Domain 135
      5.2 The Affective Domain 136
      5.3 The Psychomotor Domain 137
      5.4 The Importance of the Taxonomy in Educational Objective 137
6.0   Continuous Assessment Approach 138
      6.1 Characteristics/Benefits of the Continuous Assessment 138
7.0   Measurements in Education 138
8.0   Conclusion 139

Chapter Eleven: Skill Development Advisory Dynamics **140**
1.0   Introduction 140
2.0   Nature of Skill Development 140
2.0   Key Issues in Skills Development 142
3.0   Why Skill Development Is Necessary 142
4.0   Ten Benefits of Skill Development 144
5.0   The Skill Development Advisory 144
6.0   Conclusion 146

Chapter Twelve: Ethical Issues in Skill Acquisition **147**
1.0   Introduction 147
2.0   What Is Ethics and What Are Its Values 147
3.0   Ethics as Legal Code of Conduct 150
4.0   Ethics as Moral Codes of Conduct 150
5.0   Ethics in a Learning Environment 151
      5.1 Ethical Features of Learning 151
6.0   Ethics in a Business Environment 152
7.0   Addressing Some Unethical Issues in Skill Acquisition 153
8.0   Conclusion 154

Chapter Thirteen: Economic Basis of Skill Acquisition **155**
1.0   Introduction 155
2.0   Generation of Personal Income 156
3.0   Fighting Hunger and Lack 156
4.0   Eliminating Extreme Poverty 157
5.0   Job and Wealth Creation 158
6.0   Skilled Labor and Technicians 158
7.0   Scaling Down Unemployment 159
8.0   Improved Standard of Living 159
9.0   Increase in Literacy Rate 160
10.0 Industrial/Sectoral Growth 160
11.0 Mobility of Capital 161
12.0 Harnessing of Informal Sector 161
13.0 Empowering Vulnerable Populace 161
14.0 Conclusion 162

Chapter Fourteen: Skill Acquisition as Business 163
    1.0   Introduction 163
    2.0   Business Principles in Skill Acquisition 163
          2.1 Mindset 164
          2.2 The Business Plan 165
    3.0   Knowledge of the Industry 166
    4.0   Operational Guides 167
    5.0   Equipment, Modules and Materials 167
    6.0   Strategic Planning 168
    7.0   Ethical Considerations 168
    8.0   Conclusion 169

Chapter Fifteen: Skill Acquisition, Entrepreneurship, and Enterprise: A Symbiotic Relationship .. 170
    1.0   Introduction 170
    2.0   Features of Skill Acquisition 171
    3.0   Entrepreneur as a Labor Factor 171
    4.0   Functions of an Entrepreneur 174
    5.0   Enterprise: Forms of Business 174
    6.0   Skillful Entrepreneur in Business 176
    7.0   How to Become a Skillful Entrepreneur 178
    8.0   Conclusion 178

Chapter Sixteen: Achieving Career Growth Through Skill Acquisition 179
    1.0   Introduction 179
    2.0   Making Findings for Career Opportunities 179
    3.0   Growing a Career Through Volunteering 181
    4.0   Upgrading Knowledge through Further Education 181
    5.0   Adapting New Technologies to Work 182
    6.0   Setting New Goals in Career Development 183
    7.0   Seek Specialization in a Skill Area 184
    8.0   Undergo Higher Performance Tasks in Skills 185
    9.0   Engage in Professional Partnerships 186
    10.0   Leverage on More Practice/Practicals 187
    11.0   Get Mentorship under a Pro: 187
    12.0   Conclusion 188

Chapter Seventeen: Government's Role/Impact in Skill Acquisition 189
    1.0   Introduction 189
    2.0   Registration of Skill Trainers 190
    3.0   Sponsorship of Trainings 192
    4.0   Regulation of Skill Training 193
    5.0   Harnessing the Informal Sector 195
    6.0   Provision of Facilities for the Skill Acquisition Program 198
    7.0   Approval of Institutional Curricula 198
    8.0   Enacting Ethical Order 200
    9.0   Conclusion 201

Chapter Eighteen: Empowerment Through Skill Acquisition 202

    1.0   Introduction 202

    2.0   The Concept/Meaning of Empowerment... 202

    3.0   Empowerment: A Global Phenomenon 203

    4.0   Purpose of Empowerment through Entrepreneurship Education.................. 204

    5.0   Types of Empowerments 204

    6.0   Factors that Promote Empowerment 205

    7.0   Benefits of Empowerment 207

            7.1 The Benefits of Youth Empowerment 207

    8.0   Challenges to Empowerment Programs 208

    9.0   Overcoming the Challenges of Empowerment.. 209

    10.0   Recommendations 210

    11.0   Conclusion 211

Chapter Nineteen: Curriculum Development for Skills Programs 212

    1.0   Introduction 212

    2.0   Curriculum: Knowledge, Experience and Content... 212

    3.0   Curriculum Development and Planning.. 215

    4.0   Tools for Developing Curriculum 221

    5.0   Curriculum Development Process and Organization 222

    6.0   A Sample Curriculum for Skill Acquisition Context 224

    7.0   Evaluation as a Curriculum Context... 227

    8.0   Conclusion 229

Chapter Twenty: Practical Issues in Skill Acquisition and Development.. 230

    1.0   Introduction 230

    2.0   Mental Setting: Purpose Driven 230

    3.0   Awareness of Approaches 231

    4.0   The Time Factor 232

    5.0   Leveraging on Potentials.. 232

    6.0   The Money Factor 233

    7.0   A Matter of Priority 234

    8.0   Networking and Marketing... 234

    9.0   Technological Resources 235

    10.0   Conclusion 236

Chapter Twenty-One: Designing Modules for Skill Acquisition Programs 237

    1.0   Introduction 237

    2.0   Vision/Mission Statements.. 237

    3.0   Aims and Objectives 238

    4.0   Philosophy of Learning.. 238

    5.0   Contents Description 238

    6.0   Equipment, Facilities, and Raw Materials 239

    7.0   Modes of Evaluation 248

    8.0   Conclusion 249

Chapter Twenty-Two: Instructional Materials and Resources in Skill Training............................ 250

    1.0   Introduction 250

    2.0   The Importance of Instructional Materials 251

    3.0   General Learning Resources 252

    4.0   Reading Materials, Handbooks, and Syllabuses 253

    5.0   Multimedia Components 255

    6.0   Tools and Equipment 257

    7.0   Customized/Improvised Resources 260

    8.0   Consumables and Machinery 263

    9.0   Conclusion 266

Chapter Twenty-Three: Inclusive Skill Training... 268

    1.0   Introduction 268

    2.0   Philosophy of Inclusiveness: Skill Is a Right 268

    3.0   Dynamics of Inclusive Learning 270

    4.0   Value of Inclusiveness 272

    5.0   Relevant Methodologies in Inclusive Skill Training (Instructional Principles) P. 91 273

    6.0   Inclusiveness, Integration and Mainstreaming: Similarities and Differences.................... 274

    7.0   UN Convention on the Rights of Persons with Disabilities (Un, 2006): A Review 275

    8.0   Inclusive Practices or Approaches (P. 89 of Text)....................... 284

    9.0   Conclusion 287

Chapter Twenty-Four: Setting Up a Skill Acquisition Center.................................... 288

    1.0   Introduction 288

    2.0   What Is Skill Acquisition Center? 288

    3.0   Types of Skill Acquisition Centers 289

    5.0   Preparing the Training Curriculum 299

    6.0   Raising Capital for the Skill Acquisition Center......................... 302

    7.0   Certifying and Graduating Trainees 304

Chapter Twenty-Five: Online Skill Training... 305

    1.0   Introduction 305

    2.0   Definition and Scope of Online Skills... 305

    3.0   Online Training: Background Issues 305

    4.0   Merits of Online Training... 306

    5.0   Demerits of Online Training.. 307

    6.0   Use of Technology in Online Training.. 308

    7.0   Approaches to Online Training 309

    8.0   Online and Offline Training: A Contrast 312

    9.0   Challenges of Training Online 312

    10.0 Pedagogical Factors in Online Training 313

    11.0 Role Playing in Online Training.. 315

    12.0 A Survey of Online Applications (APPS)................................... 316

    13.0 Assessment of Performances Online.. 319

    14.0 Psychological Factors in Online Training 320

    15.0 Conclusion.. 321

Chapter Twenty-Six: Skill Development in Sports 322

    1.0   Introduction 322

    2.0   Developing Skills in Sports... 323

    3.0   Types of Skills to Master in Sports 324

    4.0   The Role of Effective Practice... 327

    5.0   Role Playing in Sports 328

    6.0   Kinetic and Physiological Issues 329

    7.0   Stages of Skill Acquisition in Sports 329

    8.0   Conclusion 331

Chapter Twenty-Seven: Communication Skills Development 332

    1.0   Introduction 332

    2.0   Receptive Skills.. 333

    3.0   Expressive Skills 335

    4.0   Verbal Communication Skills 336

    5.0   Nonverbal Communication 337

    6.0   Benefits of Effective Communication Skills 339

    7.0   Barriers to Communication 341

    8.0   Maximizing Communication Skills 343

    9.0   Conclusion 344

Chapter Twenty-Eight: Selected Skills in Arts and Humanities............................ 345

    1.0   Introduction 345

    2.0   Broad Components of Skills.. 345

    3.0   Values of Arts-based Skills 346

    4.0   Prevalence of Communication Skills 347

    5.0   Basics of Lawyering Skills 362

    6.0   Conclusion 364

Chapter Twenty-Nine Selected Skills in Sciences.. 365

    1.0   Introduction 365

    2.0   Features of Skills in Sciences 366

        2.1 Objectivity 367

        2.2 Verifiability... 367

        2.3 Ethical Neutrality.. 368

        2.4 Systematic Exploration 368

        2.5 Reliability.. 368

        2.6 Precision 369

        2.7 Accuracy 369

        2.8 Abstractness 369

        2.9 Predictability.. 369

        2.10 Empirical Observation 369

        2.11 Provisional Results 370

    3.0 Science Process Skills.. 370

        3.1 Observation 371

        3.2 Communication 371

        3.3 Measuring Skill 372

    3.4 Sorting/Classification 372

    3.5 Inference 372

    3.6 Prediction 373

    3.7 Innovative Skills 374

    3.8 Experimenting 374

    3.9 Forming Conclusions 374

  4.0 Technical Issues in Sciences: Challenges and Perspectives 374

    4.1 Falling Enrolment and Increasing Gender Gap 375

    4.2 Contradictory and Optimistic Trends 378

    4.3 Public Understanding of Science and Technology: An International Concern 379

    4.4 Ways Forward 379

  5.0 Social Dimensions of Scientific Development 380

  6.0 Careers in the Sciences 382

    6.1 Environmental Science 382

    6.2 Pharmacy 382

    6.3 Medical Laboratory Science 382

    6.4 Science Education 383

    6.5 Geology, Geophysics and Hydrogeology 383

    6.6 Veterinary Science 383

    6.7 Life Sciences 384

    6.8 Agricultural Science 384

    6.9 Chemistry 384

    6.10 Forestry Science 385

  7.0 Templates/Models for Developing Skills in Sciences 385

    7.1 Visual Models 385

    7.2 Mathematical Models 387

    7.3 Computer Models 388

  8.0 Conclusion 389

Chapter Thirty: Selected Skills in Technology **390**

  1.0 Introduction 390

  2.0 Selected Skills in the Technology Sector 391

    2.1 Strong interest in Technology/IT/Computing 391

    2.2 Problem Solving 391

    2.3 Good with Numbers 391

    2.4 Commercial Awareness 391

    2.5 A willingness and Openness to Learn 391

    2.6 Ability to Work Independently and in a Team 391

  3.0 Difference between Science and Technology 392

    3.1 Definitions of Science and Technology 392

  4.0 Deployment of Technology in the Production Sector 395

    4.1 Maximizing Efficiency 395

    4.2 Managing Data 395

    4.3 Increasing Productivity 396

  5.0 Types of Manufacturing and Production Technologies 396

    5.1 Smart Factories 396

    5.2 Cyber-Physical Systems 396

5.3 Additive Manufacturing 397
5.4 Big Data 397
5.5 Augmented Reality 397
5.6 Numerical Control 397
5.7 Robotics in Manufacturing Technology 397
6.0   Economic Values of Technology 398
6.1 The impact of Technology Economy 398
6.2 Technology's Role in Economic Development 399
7.0   Patterns of Learning Technology 400
8.0   Templates on Teaching and Learning Information Communication
and Technology ICT Skills 402
9.0   The Future of Technology 404
9.1 Lab-Made Dairy Products 404
9.2 Digital Twins Health Tracker 405
9.3 Bio-Cremation and Green Funerals 405
9.4 Artificial Eyes 406
9.5 Airports for Drones and Flying Taxis 406
9.6 Energy Storing Bricks 406
9.7 Sweat powered smart watches 407
9.8 Self-Healing "Living Concrete" 407
9.8 Living Robots 407
9.10 Internet for Everyone 407
9.11 Heart Monitoring T-shirt 408
9.10 Drown Forest Fires in Sound 408
9.11 The Artificial Intelligence (AI) Scientist 408
9.12 Car Batteries that Charge in 10 Minutes 408
9.13 Self-Driving Trucks 409
9.14 Artificial Neurons on Silicon Chips 409
9.15 Floating Farms 409
10.0   Conclusion 409

3.4 Sorting/Classification..372

3.5 Inference 372

3.6 Prediction 373

3.7 Innovative Skills...374

3.8 Experimenting 374

3.9 Forming Conclusions..374

4.0 Technical Issues in Sciences: Challenges and Perspectives 374

4.1 Falling Enrolment and Increasing Gender Gap...375

4.2 Contradictory and Optimistic Trends 378

4.3 Public Understanding of Science and Technology: An International Concern...........379

4.4 Ways Forward 379

5.0 Social Dimensions of Scientific Development 380

6.0 Careers in the Sciences...382

6.1 Environmental Science 382

6.2 Pharmacy..382

6.3 Medical Laboratory Science 382

6.4 Science Education..383

6.5 Geology, Geophysics and Hydrogeology...383

6.6 Veterinary Science 383

6.7 Life Sciences 384

6.8 Agricultural Science 384

6.9 Chemistry..384

6.10 Forestry Science 385

7.0 Templates/Models for Developing Skills in Sciences 385

7.1 Visual Models..385

7.2 Mathematical Models...387

7.3 Computer Models..388

8.0 Conclusion..389

Chapter Thirty: Selected Skills in Technology...**390**

1.0 Introduction 390

2.0 Selected Skills in the Technology Sector..391

2.1 Strong interest in Technology/IT/Computing..391

2.2 Problem Solving...391

2.3 Good with Numbers 391

2.4 Commercial Awareness 391

2.5 A willingness and Openness to Learn 391

2.6 Ability to Work Independently and in a Team 391

3.0 Difference between Science and Technology..392

3.1 Definitions of Science and Technology 392

4.0 Deployment of Technology in the Production Sector 395

4.1 Maximizing Efficiency 395

4.2 Managing Data...395

4.3 Increasing Productivity...396

5.0 Types of Manufacturing and Production Technologies 396

5.1 Smart Factories 396

5.2 Cyber-Physical Systems..396

       5.3 Additive Manufacturing 397

       5.4 Big Data.. 397

       5.5 Augmented Reality... 397

       5.6 Numerical Control 397

       5.7 Robotics in Manufacturing Technology.. 397

6.0   Economic Values of Technology... 398

       6.1 The impact of Technology Economy 398

       6.2 Technology's Role in Economic Development 399

7.0   Patterns of Learning Technology.. 400

8.0   Templates on Teaching and Learning Information Communication
       and Technology ICT Skills 402

9.0   The Future of Technology... 404

       9.1 Lab-Made Dairy Products... 404

       9.2 Digital Twins Health Tracker 405

       9.3 Bio-Cremation and Green Funerals... 405

       9.4 Artificial Eyes 406

       9.5 Airports for Drones and Flying Taxis 406

       9.6 Energy Storing Bricks 406

       9.7 Sweat powered smart watches.. 407

       9.8 Self-Healing "Living Concrete"... 407

       9.8 Living Robots 407

       9.10 Internet for Everyone 407

       9.11 Heart Monitoring T-shirt 408

       9.10 Drown Forest Fires in Sound 408

       9.11 The Artificial Intelligence (AI) Scientist... 408

       9.12 Car Batteries that Charge in 10 Minutes 408

       9.13 Self-Driving Trucks.. 409

       9.14 Artificial Neurons on Silicon Chips 409

       9.15 Floating Farms 409

10.0   Conclusion.. 409

Foreword

BY

PROFESSOR NDEM AYARA
DEPARTMENT OF ECONOMICS
UNIVERSITY OF CALABAR
NIGERIA

Man's survival on earth depends on the satisfaction of wants which is largely driven by production as a means of creating wealth for individual and community/national economic welfare in the circle of the variables of poverty, wealth and income. Production thrives on three key factors: Land, Labor and Liquidity (Capital). To this tripartism needs to be added the emerging factor called entrepreneur. The equation will therefore appear in the ratio of 50:50 (Land and Capital VS Labor and Entrepreneur).

Development as a governance goal around the world centers on the matrix of maximizing people's potentials to pursue and attain the level of life they desire. In democratic regimes, governments engage in social contracts of ensuring the security of lives and properties owned by the citizens and states as well as making efforts to fight poverty which underpins insecurity, avoidable mortality and social conflicts.

For example in 2015, the Indian Government launched the Skill India initiative with the vision to create an empowered workforce by 2022 with the help of various schemes and training courses that link the skill development with industry.

On 31st July 2018, the American President, Donald Trump while signing the workforce Training Bill into Law said the law would boost apprenticeships, job training and the re-skilling of U. S. workers. And on 1st July 2020, Trump added that emphasis on employability should be shifted from College degree and placed on applicants' job skills and competence based qualifications.

Also the Social Development Goals at 4.3 states thus: "Ensure equal access for all women and men to affordable quality technical, vocational and tertiary education, including university" and 4.4 "By 2030, increase by X% the number of youth and adults who have relevant skills, including technical and vocational skills, for employment, decent jobs and entrepreneurship.

The above scenarios point to a global agenda to improve world's economic welfare through production by using technology and education (Skill training and development) to leverage on and increase labor and entrepreneur which have the capacity to enhance the available land and capital.

This book will facilitate this need of humanity to attain higher development through better production of wealth, slashing of poverty and creating optimal economic welfare. The comprehensive approach to the book makes it an effective tool for skill trainers around the world, especially where skill acquisition and development need to be properly structured in terms of contents and techniques for maximum outcomes. This should be the exact manual in this dimension of education!

Preface

Groundwork of Skill Acquisition and Development conveys a broad spectrum of researched theories, practical guides, principles, and directions in the field of skill training and career development across diverse biases. The contents have been carefully selected to serve the needs of skill instructors and practitioners, students and trainers, academics and scholars, as well as general readers who require some grounding in the dynamics of skill acquisition, career growth, and college-industry change demands.

It appears the world started giving attention to skill development at the birth of the millennium when it started becoming clear that the normal education largely informed the mind without impacting the hands. Gaps were noticed between the colleges and the industries, especially with the blossoming of technology in almost all fields. Managing technology and managing projects, among other things, required turning labor into entrepreneurs and reskilling them for higher efficiency and productivity to match the global population increase and demands for the basics of life.

Skill tooling and quest for "pros" in various fields needed a third arm of education: formal, informal, and skilling. Skill acquisition and development has emerged as a different form of education for both the less educated and the highly educated. This calls for a new set of approaches and principles in offering skilled knowledge to mixed groups. Compared to the informal and formal sectors, there are only a few publications on this subject. This has motivated us to put up this compendium as a groundwork that covers the field considerably as demonstrated in these thirty chapters with over three hundred themes.

The book comes in five sections of six chapters each, outlined as follows:

Section A	Background Issues
Section B	Skill Acquisition Processes
Section C	Benefits of Skill Acquisition
Section D	Materials and Approaches to Skill Acquisition/Development
Section E	Description of Selected Skills

Section A of the book comprises six chapters under the heading "Background Issues." Indeed, the matters thrashed here constitute the first and tone setting elements of the entire collection. As a groundwork text, it is important to define and border the subject matter of the text. The book is primarily concerned with skill acquisition as a learning process for gaining abilities to carry out trade, vocational and professional practices, as explicated in chapter 1.

In chapter 2 under "Road map to Effective Skills Acquisition," we isolated seven (7) dimensions of the skill architecture under "Learning and Behavioral Objectives": preparation of training notes; instructional materials and equipment; creating a suitable training environment; training management and evaluation of skill performance.

The theories and practices of skill acquisition are examined in chapter 3. This chapter brings to the fore field concepts and classifications in the skill practice as a framework for constituting the necessary guides and specifications in the field.

Chapters 4–6 encapsulate issues that deploy insight from other fields that inform skill acquisition and development. Chapter 4 proffers the realities of the means of communication, instruction, and sharing of meaning and information in skill acquisition and development. No meaningful learning can take place without the linguistic and communication skills that motorize the memory facilities for the internalization and comprehension of the ideas and processes. This chapter is therefore very useful in the spectrum of the text.

In chapter 5, the focus is on the psychological dimensions of learning with emphasis on skill acquisition and development. The learning processes and factors are explicitly considered as the basis of aligning the mind with specific operational and conceptual activities in skill acquisition. In the last chapter in this section, we have provided the typology of skills to enable the text reader and user to know the diverse skills domains, their nature, prerequisites, engagements, and expected outcomes.

Section B skillfully portrays the stages of skills acquisition, roles played by participants in the processes, the management of skill trainings, as well as the evaluation, assessment, and ethical issues. This section is very useful to practitioners of skill development advisors.

Section C provides the economic and social benefits of skill acquisition and development in the light of entrepreneurship, enterprise, career growth, and empowerment, which lead to business growth, economic stability, and poverty alleviation in line with the United Nations Social Development Goals.

Section D is a manual for the materials, principles, and approaches required to carry out a skill training effectively. Issues of curriculum, syllabuses, lifestyle, modules, instructional tools, and business settings are laid out for ease of comprehension by all practitioners, instructors, and trainees.

Section E focuses on skilling and reskilling in selected fields: online learning, sports, communication, lawyering, science, and technology. These areas have been carefully selected to reflect the majority of interests in major world activities.

The other features of this text include the following:

- ❖ The three-dimension chapter layout of introduction, body, and conclusion. Thus in each chapter, there is a bird's eye view of the content and specification of the perspective deployed in the research and composition.
- ❖ Deployment of graphics, tables, graphs, and diagrams to add clarity to the issues under discussion.
- ❖ Reference to specific scenarios for adequate illustrations and reflections in similar contexts.
- ❖ Wide references to existing sources and academic due diligence in bibliographical citations and documentations.
- ❖ Simple expressions for easy comprehension bearing in mind the mixed audience
- ❖ Index compilation for easy reference to specific terms, concepts, ideas, and information considering the volume of the work.

In all, a lot of intellectual energies have been deployed in this project to stand the test of time and prompt future researches into the domain of skill acquisition and development.

Acknowledgments

I return all glory to God, the source of providence who dropped into me the idea of producing suitable material on the subject of skill acquisition and development. I thank the research team driven by Bassey Ekpenyong, a professorial associate, legal practitioner, researcher, and eclectic writer who worked with an array of great writers: Esther, Ibah, Cally, Agnes, and Savior. I appreciate the dexterity of the stenographer, Esther, who produced this volume in a matter of weeks.

I thank the team of editors who combed the work and skillfully organized and recognized the contents and structure in this final form. My thanks also go to Professor Ndem Ayara, a renowned economist who wrote the foreword so professionally and admirably. I appreciate the kind words from the blurbs at the back cover of the book.

I appreciate Christiana Oroks, Eno E. Uti, Barrister Janet Obong, and Emmanuel Nsemoh, Adetunji Robert for their encouragement and support.

Thanks, too to the librarian, who produced the index to ease reference to specifics in work. As the author and patent proprietor, I take responsibility for all critiques of the work and promise the necessary additional editions in the future.

Chapter One

Meaning and Scope of Skill Acquisition

1.0 Introduction

A groundwork on a subject matter as phenomenal as skill acquisition should commence with an attempt at defining the constituent terms and limiting the scope of usage. This background will set the search light into the issues, concepts and discourses developed in the book. A reader or user of this text who does not comprehend the term "skill acquisition" and the context of its usage in this exposition may not be able to apply the text in the most effective manner.

This chapter will offer explanations on such terms as skill, acquisition, entrepreneur, enterprise, trade, vocation, craft, talents, and the related phrases such as skill acquisition, skill development, skill development advisor, skill and entrepreneurship development, etc.

The *Oxford English Dictionary* defines *skill* as "the ability to do something well" or "a particular ability or type of ability." A person who is skilled is defined as one "having enough ability, experience, and knowledge to be able to do something well"; for example, skilled engineer/negotiator/craftsman.

In the same vein, *acquisition* is defined as "the act of getting something, especially knowledge, a skill, etc." "To acquire" denotes "to gain something by your own efforts, ability, or behavior." A composite reading of the above elementary definitions posits that skill is "a performing ability, experience, or knowledge that is learnt or acquired"—internalized, assimilated, committed to memory, formed as a habit and deployed for efficient solving of problems.

The motivational basis for this process of acquisition was hinted in the psychology of learning espoused in Sperling and Martin (1967), as the prevalence of learning:

> Learning is certainly a universal experience. Everyone must always be learning, at every stage of life… Adults must learn how to perform their jobs, and how to meet the responsibilities of family. Daily life is a succession of major and minor problems that have to be solved by learning. (P. 52–53)

Like learning, skill acquisition follows a tripartite process of discovering or inventing based on the necessity to fill a gap or solve a problem; committing the dynamics of the solution to memory and attaining efficiency through a habitual pattern of structured repetitions in performance of an act or sets of acts. Once a person perceives a problem such as lack of income, inability to pay bills, boredom of joblessness, unemployment, etc., he/she will first begin to engage in thinking or reasoning to invent or discover a way to solve the problem such as obtaining knowledge of creating garments (tailoring) to sell and obtain funds to pay bills.

1

Thinking will result in having an awareness of an array of solutions; skills, trades, vocations, services, etc., to engage for outcomes. Once a particular option is settled, he/she proceeds to acquire the knowledge, experiences, abilities, processes, systems, attitudes and functions involved in the performing the specific act (skill) through a training or learning structure. These acts are then repeated until a mastery sets in and results in an efficiency.

2.0   Catalogue of Definitions of Skill Acquisition

Webster Encyclopedia Dictionary 1994
—an ability coming from ones
knowledge, practice, aptitude to…

Prezi—com>skill-acquisition
—the ability to learn, develop
and control skills to perform better
in our sports

en.m.wikipedia.org>wiki>skill
—an ability and capacity
acquired through deliberate, systematic,
and sustained effort to smoothly and
adaptively carryout complex activities
or job…

eltvoices.inEVI-26-5
—a specific form of learning, in
which a number of events are
associated together, association
strengthened through similar
stimuli with particular responses,
or practice under the right conditions

www.kofastudy.com>lessons>topic
—the learning and mastering of
special abilities in any type of
profession. A skilled worker is one
who is highly proficient or expert in
his/her trade or a person who has
attained excellence in a particular trade or vocation

Oxford Advanced Learners Dictionary
Skill is the ability to do
something well, usually gained
through training or experience.
It is the special ability acquired

2

or developed as a result of training
to do something well.

passnownow.com>basic-science-jss…
Skill acquisition is the science that
underpins movement learning and
execution and is more commonly
termed motor learning and control
(Williams and Ford, 2009). Each stage
embodies unique characteristics
relative to an athlete's level of
performance of a skill or activity

psychology.irsearchnet.com>skill…
—a type of learning in which repetition
results in enduring changes in an
individual's capability to perform a
specific task. With enough repetition
performance of the task eventually
may become automatic, with little
need for conscious oversight

classhall.com>lessons
—the art of learning to do
something in order to earn a living
and or to survive

www.igi-global.com>dictionary>s …
—a process through which a
prisoner attains mastery of the
basics of a task with the aim to
render service(s) for financial freedom.

    2. The development of new skills through
practice or repetition
3. How players learn to use the tools
and abilities available in the game
4. A specific form of learning as the
representation of information in
memory concerning some environment
or cognitive event

topwintersden.com>skill-acquisition
—a specific form of learning
it is the ability to be trained on a

particular function or task till you
become an expert on the skill

decnigeria.com>bulletin
—the ability to be trained
on a particular task or function
and become expert in it.

www.indeed.com>career-advice
Acquired skills are talents
or expertise often obtained
through education or experience

discover.hubpages.com>business
—the ability to be trained on
a particular task

core.ac.uk>download>pdf
—the ability to do something
well, usually gained through training
or experience…
—a complex, intential action involving
a whole chain of sensory, central and
motor mechanisms which through the
process of learning have come to be
organized and coordinated in such
a way as to achieved predetermined
objectives with maximum certainty.
                    Morris and Whiting (1971)

Morris, P. and Whiting, H. T. A (1971) Motor
Impairment and Contensatory Education
London: Bell

—the ability to acquire knowledge
in new conditions and on the basis
of the abilities and experiences, a
person had previously.

—the process of mastering
Skills characterized by applying them
In particular situations.

3.0   Circle of Definitive Terms

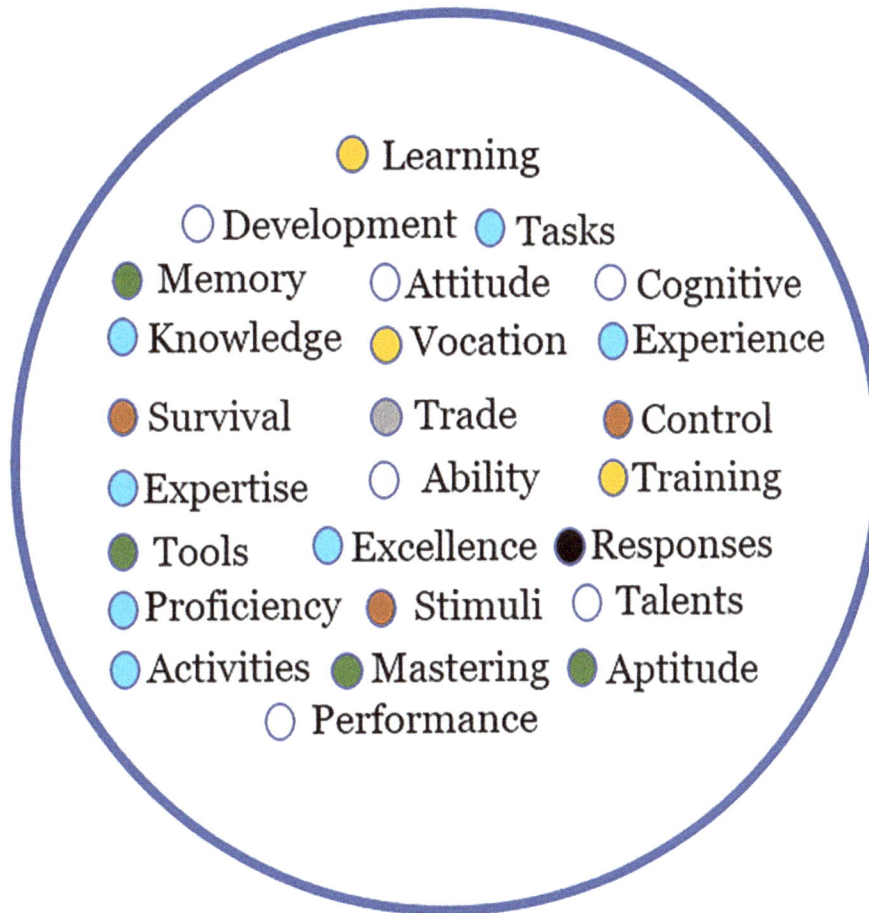

Learning

Development   Tasks

Memory   Attitude   Cognitive

Knowledge   Vocation   Experience

Survival   Trade   Control

Expertise   Ability   Training

Tools   Excellence   Responses

Proficiency   Stimuli   Talents

Activities   Mastering   Aptitude

Performance

4.0   Analysis of Entries

A community reading of the collated definitions will result in a workable definition or comprehensible meaning explication of the subject, skill acquisition. The definition will be formed by considering the following highlights or components of the definitions.

4.1   "The ability to learn, develop and control skills." Here skill acquisition is seen as a process that the ingredients of a particular task are learnt (committed to memory), developed (practiced), and controlled (mastered).

4.2   "The learning and mastering of special abilities…" Skills are presented here as "special abilities," proficiencies, expertise, or "wellness" involved in the execution of tasks. The abilities are embodiments of experiences attained through guided repetitions that do result in sometimes "involuntary" capability to perform or automatic effect.

4.3   "The art of learning to do something to earn a living or to survive." This is a utilitarian approach to defining skill acquisition based on the needs or available values that can bring about more impactful changes in a person's life. Sometimes, the survival instinct may lead to a mastery that produces financial freedom and wealth creation to employ others.

4.4 "A process of learning to become organized and coordinated to achieve objectives with maximum certainty." The key words in this definition are very strategic. Sometimes acquiring a skill is simply becoming better organized or more coordinated in an act or set of acts. These coordination and organization which are products of experiences can lead to "maximum certainty"—avoidance of errors, dependable precision and peak performance.

4.5 "The ability to acquire knowledge in new conditions based on experiences a person had previously." This definition extends the scope of skill acquisition to situations where a skilled person can raise the standard in his field or get into new conditions that demand more knowledge or experience. It amounts to skill development if a computer operator proceeds beyond the computer basics to seek mastery in more technical areas such as programing, graphics or web-development.

5.0 Selected Differentials

5.1 Skill and Talent

It appears that the simplest difference between skill and talent is that the former must be learnt or acquired while the latter is innate or inborn. Skills leads to consummated progress in mastery while talent comes with a natural ability to carry out a task. It can be said that while everyone can acquire or learn a skill, not everyone is talent. Talents are manifest in the way people do things effortlessly. For example, a person irrespective of gender may express a high level of competence in cooking by combining an array of recipe to achieve the right taste. Another person who intends to reach this level of performance may need to be taught either formally or informally.

Skill	Talent
• Learnable	• Inborn
• Progressive mastery	• Automatic feat
• Efforts assertion	• Effortlessness
• Habitual	• Intuitive
• Transferable knowledge	• Innate disposition
• Repetitive experience	• Autonomous function
• Acquired	• Derived
• Dependent adjustment	• Independent adjustment
• Objective	• Subjective

5.2 Skill and Entrepreneurship

This differentiation can be achieved by a juxtaposition of the community definitions of the twin terms, entrepreneurship and intrapreneurship on the one hand and skill on the other hand.

According to Etuk and Mbat (2010, p. 1),

> entrepreneurship could be defined as a process through which individuals and/or government either on their own or jointly exploit available opportunities without being scared by associated risks or inadequate resources under their control.

Relatedly, Bassey, U. (2014, p. 14) defines an intrapreneur as "someone who utilizes his or her skills, passion and innovation to manage or create something useful for someone else's business with entrepreneurial zest."

From the above, it is clear that while skill is the acquired or learned ability to execute an action or task based on practiced art or mastery of processes/techniques, holistic competences and positive adjustment, entrepreneurship involves the deployment or management of skill (embodied in personnel) to exploit opportunities for profit. The entrepreneur must have the relevant skill to engage the production/distribution/service demands or employ a skilled labor.

5.3 Skill and Knowledge

This differentiation is very important in our exposition of skill acquisition. It is very easy to equate skill with knowledge. But they are different.

While knowledge is the aggregate or totality of information; concept, principles, language, that a person has internalized concerning a subject or group of subjects or field of endeavor; skill is the application of this knowledge in solving problems within a particular context of need.

This table further explicates the difference

Skill	Knowledge
• Practical	• Theoretical
• Not fully transferable	• Generally transferable
• Tangibly manipulate	• Intangible
• Applied	• Residual

Mastery

For example, Mr. A. (an entrepreneur) may decide to build a special cancer treatment center in a remote village near Bakassi Islands to manage patients from both Nigeria and Cameroon. He will need to first of all assemble a team of architects, engineers, and artisans to build the physical structure. If he is a skilled medical practitioner, he will still require skilled medical laboratory personnel, accountants, secretaries, drivers, boat operators, etc., to handle the diverse tasks involved in running a medical facility.

It therefore means that entrepreneurship feeds on skill while skill drives entrepreneurship. Both attributes demand intellectual motives for success. Obviously, there will be more skilled labor than entrepreneurs because in most situations, an entrepreneur requires the inputs and skills of diverse experts to help him realize his vision.

An experience became obvious when the CEO of Harvest Resources Academy (USA) had a vision to establish a College of Empowerment (a skill acquisition center) to train skill aspirants. After fixing the accommodation and equipment, the skill trainers became a paramount requirement to fully implement the vision.

Though these terms have been differentiated, their goals are identical. A person who reads for a degree in Engineering desires to gain mastery of the field in solving relevant problems. The same goal applies to a skill learner who intends to use the knowledge of the skill to solve practical problems. Taking the engineering knowledge further, it appears the engineer cannot work alone or in isolation. He needs to combine his knowledge with the skill of the technician/artisan; mason, bricklayer, concrete mixer, iron-bender, carpenter, electrician, aluminum, formulator, etc., in the practice of his trade.

However, in some professional fields like engineering, medicine, law, mass communications, etc., where mastery is achieved by a combination of theoretical knowledge and applied skill, there are productive programs in the training syllabus or curriculum and no professional can be certificated without successfully passing the practical experiences. A doctor must pass through the residency. A lawyer must undergo court and chamber attachments and an engineer must go through a mandatory industrial attachment.

The complimentarity of knowledge and skill is expressed in the need for further studies, continuous training and retraining that occur in career growth, sometimes called "skill development."

5.4 Skill Acquisition and Skill Development

Skill acquisition and skill development are outcomes of learning through a patterned process that leads to continuous improvement in an individuals' practical behavior especially in the performance of trade, vocation or profession. Both activities are reasonable investments in the faculty and functions of a person in the course of survival experiences.

Despite the above similarities, acquisition can be further contrasted with development in the context of skill propagation. While acquisition is the practical learning of a habit or quality, development entails the identification or realization of "gaps" in the aspiration and sustenance of peak performance capabilities of a person and ensuring that such gaps are filled through continuous training, retraining and advanced learning of the skill. Skill development will help a skilled laborer or a professional to keep abreast with development in the field and introduction of new equipment, tools, principles and processes.

A medical practitioner who has acquired a surgical skill will need to take more training in the practice to key into a new development in bloodless surgery.

A legal practitioner in Nigeria who knew rudimentary issues in the profession up to the early 2000s may drop out now unless he goes ahead to hone his lawyering skills with compositional or writing techniques. This is because modern legal practice demands "front loading" or filing of briefs prior to trial sessions.

An architect of the 1990s who has not learnt "AutoCAD technology" may not go far in the practice today. This applies to so many professional practices, especially where materials and processes have changed. An old carpenter who merely knew how to fix rafters and put on the old model corrugated iron sheets should now progress in the roofing craft by learning the technology of roofing with aluminum long span sheets with wood and iron rafter options, combining solar panel in roofing technology. An outline blogger opines:

> Skills development is where we turn from beginner to novice, to intermediate, to senior, to expert. (personalexcellence.co>blog>skills)

The above perspective can be diagrammatically represented in the upward progress in a field as follows:

Iconoclast

↑

Professional

↑

Expert

↑

Novice

↑

Beginner

It appears that while skills can be acquired as an outcome of choice and decision, skill development may be a mandatory learning experience which is condition precedent to career growth or promotion. For example, a skilled university teacher at the level of graduate assistant must go through research skills in the masters and PhD programs, to be able to go up the scale to senior lecturer/professor. Some skill development programs may be self-advised based on individual aspiration.

After *acquiring* a skill, a person may need to study the diverse *branches* of the trade and if he chooses to become a *pro*, then he needs to take up a skill development program. A lawyer may learn mediation and arbitration skills so as to use the legal methodology in settling disputes outside litigational technique.

While skill acquisition is more from an individual's volition, skill development may proceed from a professional advice by a skill development advisor who understands the dynamics of skill advancements, the benefits, the options, the durations, the costs of training, locations of training and admission or induction protocol.

6.0 Summary and Conclusion

In this chapter, we have reviewed a number of definitions of skill acquisition as a concept. We went further to analyze some of the definitions and perspectives by situating them within the context of this exposition. We proceeded to differentiate skill/skill acquisition from some of their synonyms or identical words or expressions; talent, entrepreneurship, knowledge, skill acquisition, and skill development.

In this book, our working definition of skill acquisition is a process of learning the patterns in trade practices with the view of gaining functional mastery for effortless, effective and productive performances. Skill development entails professional growth, advancement and value-addition to an acquired skill. Talent differs from skill because talent capabilities may be inborn. Knowledge is the theoretical information which constitutes part of skill acquisition. Entrepreneurship is the economic application of skill(s) to create problem-solving outcomes and to take risks in managing time and resources for income, livelihood, and survival.

Chapter Two

Road Map to Skill Acquisition and Training

1.0 Introduction

Skill acquisition and training road map will not just be useful as a step-by-step guide for training and learning program, it also comes in a compact, handy information pact volume which covers everything trainee/trainer needs to know. It will aid structure the set of values, enlighten you about the taste of acquiring intellectual training and implementation of spring up and develop you to an entrepreneur.

Follow every steps in this chapter to guide you as a trainer and trainee when designing your learning objectives and aspiring toward a certain skill. This chapter has been systematically outlined in logical steps to guide you.

Step two: Learning and behavioral objectives consist of knowledge, facts, theories, principles, and skills of the training. The learning and behavioral goals created must be in line with the training strategies, goals, and values.

Step three: Preparation of training notes, here, you choose the training notes format suitable for the type of skill training and best for your school or company in achieving its set goals.

Step four: Instructional materials and equipment introduces both the trainer and the trainee to new innovations and how they can be used effectively during training.

Step five: Creating a suitable training environment helps the trainer to adequately train in a conducive environment, or atmosphere, manage the class, and receive constructive feedback (objectives).

Step six: Training management provides adequate guide for the program manager and the trainers on various types of training and the most suitable one that should be adopt during training process.

Step seven: Evaluation of skills performance enable the trainer to carefully assess the trainer and award scores. It also introduces the trainer on the best evaluation method to be used.

2.0 Learning and Behavioral Objectives

This section outlines what is meant by the terms' aims and learning objectives or outcomes and how they relate to training delivery and assessment.

An institution should have reflected on the aims of the courses which it provides, and articulated those aims clearly both to trainees/learners (in course materials) and also to the outside world through its program specifications. Aims can be set at any level: for the entire tripos, or part of the tripos, or a major subdivision such as a module, option, or paper.

Aims articulate should:

- enable prospective learners/trainees, their advisers and external examiners to understand the ethos and purpose of the course;
- provide the institution and internal review committees with a benchmark against which to consider wither courses are meeting their purposes;
- represent the intentions of the teacher (whereas outcomes are concerned with the achievement of the learner).

The term *learning experience* is the interaction between the learner and the external conditions in the environment to which he can react (Tyler, 1949). Learning takes place through the action behavior of the learner, it is what he does, and he learns not what the teacher does. Learning experiences involve the interaction of the student/learner and his learning environment. This implies that the student is an active participant, that some features of his environment attract his attention and it is to these that he reacts.

The problem of selecting learning experiences is the problem of determining the kind of experience likely to produce given educational or training objectives and also the problem of how to set situations which will evoke or provide within in students the kinds of learning experiences desired.

General principles in selecting learning experiences

Tyler (1949) had suggested five guiding principles to be able to select appropriate experience and there are certain general principles that the curriculum worker must be familiar with. The first of these principles is that for a given objectives to be attained a student must have experiences that give him an opportunity to practice the kind of behavior implied by the objectives.

Second principle is that the learning experiences must be such that the student obtains satisfaction from carrying on the kind of behavior implied by the objective.

A third guiding principle in respect of learning experience is that the reaction desired in the experience is within the range of possibility for the student involved (i.e., the experience should be appropriate), to the student's present achievement in his interest, his predisposition, etc.

A fourth guiding principle is that there are many particular experiences that can be used to attain the same education/training objectives; in other words, learning occurs through various channels. This means that the teacher/trainer has wide range of creative possibility in planning and particular work.

A fifth guiding principle is that the same learning experience will usually bring about several outcomes.

Therefore, all learning is multiple though focus may be on one particular desired outcome, other learning takes place simultaneously.

Learning objectives are integral determining factor of strategies, instructional design model, methods, pedagogical scenarios, and lesson plans. It also refers to statements that define the expected goal of a curriculum, course, lesson or activity in terms of demonstrable skills or knowledge that will be acquired by a student as a result of instruction (edutechwiki.unige.ch/en/learning…).

Objectives of the school have no simple source of information to provide wise and comprehensive decision about the school curriculum. Sources should be given consideration in planning comprehensive curriculum program.

The studies of the learner is one of the appropriate objectives that can be included in the curriculum; this is because education is a process of changing and molding the behavior patterns of learners/trainers.

Education should be view by using behavior in the broad sense to include thinking and feelings as well as overt action. When education is viewed in this way, it is clear that educational objectives represent the kind of change in behavior that an educational institution seeks to bring about in his student/learner.

Investigation of students' interest is another importance of learner's objective. Education is an active process and involves the active participation of the learners themselves. The curriculum incorporates matters of interest to the learner will actively participate in them and thus learn to deal very effectively with those situations. It is essential for selected objectives to permit the learner to enter wholeheartedly with the things in which he is deeply involved and to learn particularly how to carry on such activities effectively.

A study of contemporary life outside the school is another source for selecting educational objective. Focusing on educational efforts as a critical aspects of this complex life and treating it a matter of importance in acquiring a skill today will bring about continual change in life because the society is so complex. This will prevent wasting the learner's time in learning things that were significant some decades ago but are no longer tenable at present, while neglecting areas of life that are important and for which the curriculum provides no preparation. Transfer of training has supported the importance of considering contemporary life.

Suggestions from subject specialists selected is another source for selecting educational objectives. Most of the reports of subject specialists do not stop with objectives and many of them do not list objectives specifically of them begin with some outline indicating their conception of the subject field itself and then move to indicate ways in which it can be used for purposes of general education.

The objectives with psychology of learning consistencies should also be put in to consideration in selecting and stating educational objectives. Educational objectives are results to be achieved from learning and they are educated ends.

- Knowledge of the psychology of learning enables us to distinguish changes in human being that can be expected to result from learning process from those that cannot, this is at the lowest extreme.
- Knowledge of the psychology of learning enables us to distinguish goals that are likely to take a very long time or are almost impossible of attainment at the age level contemplated, this is at higher level.
- Another use of the knowledge of psychology is in connection with grade placement for objectives which are educationally attainable
- Psychology of learning has to do with the conditions requisite for the learning of certain types of objective and the time required to bring about a certain types of changes in learners.
- Psychology of learning also guides curriculum planner to discover that most learning experiences produce multiple outcomes.
- Psychology of learning involves a unified formulation of a theory of learning which helps to outline the nature of the learning process, how it take place, under what conditions what sort of mechanism it operate and like.

Thus, it is helpful to apply the important elements of a defensible psychology of learning and then to indicate the connection with each main point what possible implications it might have for educational objectives.

2.1 Behavioral Objectives

Behavioral objective can be defined as a desire outcome of what the learner should be able to achieve at the end of every training experiences. Here, the learner should be able to demonstrates changes in his behavior. When one observes that there is change in behavior, that means that learning has taken place.

The behavioral change can be shown or demonstrated in three ways, which include knowledge (cognitive), attitude (affective), or skills (psychomotor). These three ways are also known as elements or taxonomy of educational objectives to effective planning which are meant for the learners, to explain the result of the learner and how he is likely to be after the experiences in learning.

The classification of behavioral objectives according to Bloom (1956) and Krathwohl (1964) is that "the taxonomy consists of a set of general and specific categories that encompass all possible learning outcomes that might be expected from instruction. These three taxonomy is divided in three as mentioned above. They are significance in the definition of aims, objectives and goals as well as selecting content and learning experiences." All the objectives stated by the teacher in schools and our educational literature fall into the three domains.

> **The Cognitive Domain:** This type of domain deals with different group of individuals using it as a technique to modify or solve issues like behaviors, thought, emotions, etc.; these individuals include psychologists, counselors, and therapists. It also lay emphasis on remember (previous knowledge)—that is, the process of thought to absorb the original strategies and also create new ways for combining new ideology and techniques or materials.
>
> **The Affective Domain:** This type of domain deals with awareness of one's emotion, feelings, tone and accepting or rejecting them. They consist of characters and conscience which is based internally structure (i.e., from simple to complex). It expresses interest, emotion, and attitudes among others in educational literature.
>
> **The Psychomotor Domain:** This type of domain relates to speech order, handwriting, physical movement (education), etc., when found on literature related work. It utilizes body movement activities and manipulations of objects to optimize behavior of movement.

Aptitude Test

Collins Dictionary (accessed July 2021) describes aptitude "as the ability to learn and do it well." It also describes it as the condition or quality of being apt (BE). In addition to the aforementioned explanation of aptitude, the same dictionary explains in American English (AME) as "the readiness or quickness in learning; intelligence." "Test is a procedure intended to establish the quality, performance, or reliability of something, especially before it is taken into widespread use." It is also known as a short written or spoken examination of a person's proficiency or knowledge."

Aptitude test

Aptitude test is a type of test administered to either the learners or employees to assess their ability to perform or react to tasks or situations in what they are about to be engaged in for—it may be work or school. Aptitude test is a tool used to check-mate the challenges the candidates/learners might face in their perspective role. This test can take place via online platform, office, schools, etc., depending on the reasons of the aptitude test.

Aptitude test questions comes in different forms depending on the role type an individual is applying for. The test comes in written and oral (verbal) form. The verbal aptitude tests questions are organized in "yes or no" and "true or false" formats as the answers, while written form deals with a series of written scenarios which an individual should answer by writing down the answers; it may come in objective form (choosing a or b as an answer), subjective (filling the blank spaces), or theory (explaining the whole scenarios in a paper or using your devices like phone, computer, or tablet).

Components of Behavioral Objectives

- **Knowledge:** Refers to mastery, skill proficiency, expertness, understanding of experience or something. According to Merriam Webster Dictionary (accessed July, 2021), "knowledge is the fact or condition of knowing something with familiarity gained through experience or association. It is also the fact or condition of being aware of something." "Knowledge represents the lowest level of learning outcomes in the cognitive domain" (Bloom, 1956). It deals with remembrance of series of subject matter and empirical, from specific facts to complete hypothetical set of principles.

- **Comprehension:** It is the process of understanding the sense or meaning of materials. This may be shown by interpreting material (explaining or summarizing), future trends (predicting consequences or effects). These learning outcomes go one step beyond the simple remembrance of material, and represent the lowest level of understanding in cognitive domain.

- **Application:** This refers to the ability to use learned material in new and concrete situations. This may include the application of such things as rules, methods concept, principles, laws, and theories. Learning outcomes in this area require a higher level of understanding than those under comprehension.

- **Analysis:** This refers to the ability to breakdown material into its component parts so that it organizational structure may be understood. This may include the identification of the parts, analysis of the relationships between parts, and recognition of the organizational principles involved recognitions of higher intellectual level than comprehension and application because they require an understanding of both the content and the structural form of the material.

- **Synthesis:** This is the ability to put parts together to form a new whole. This may involve the production of a unique communication (theme or speech), a plan operations (research proposal), or a set of abstract relations (scheme for classifying information). Learning outcomes in this area stress creative behaviors, with major emphasis on the formulation of new patterns or structures.

- **Guided response:** It is concerned with the early stages in a learning a complex skill that includes imitation (to perform again an act demonstrated by the trainer) and trial and error (applying different response approach to identify an appropriate response). Adequacy of performance is achieved and judged by the trainer by practicing. This stage deals or is associated in the psychomotor domain (Sampson, 1966).

- **Mechanism:** This stage is concerned with various types of skills performance but the series of organized activities working toward the patterns (movement) are less complex than at the next higher level. "It is concerned with performance acts where the learned responses have become habitual and the movements can be performed with some confidence and proficiency."

- **Organization:** This refers to the creating of new movement patterns to fit a particular situation or specific problem; learning outcomes emphasize creativity based upon highly developed skills.

- **Organization:** It is concerned with putting and building together different values, information, ideas, resolving conflicts between the trainees and accommodating them. Here, learning outcome is concerned with the organization of a value system, the student is comparing, relating, and elaborating on what has been learned (affective domain of taxonomy of education objective; Krathwohl, 1964).

- **Evaluation:** It involves the presenting and defending opinions by making judgments about the value of material, information, the validity of ideas, or quality of work based on definitive criteria. These maybe judgment in terms of internal evidence (organization) or external criteria (relevant to the purpose). "Learning outcomes in this area are highest in the cognitive domain because they contain elements of all the categories, plus conscious value judgment based on clearly defined criteria.

3.0 Preparation of Training Notes

Training online is strange or not well known to many people. Before a teacher trainer and manager trains the learners, he should discover the effectiveness of a particular skill and work toward the level of competencies and must be confidence.

One way this training can be achieved to arrange a regular weekly class for the trainees. Zoom, Skype or Microsoft teams (real time) platform can be used for training. The trainer should use a micro training technique to prove his/her confidence and competency by allowing colleagues to contribute ideas that they have used and achieved well for them. Someone should take notes and record, then summarize and share it in their already created platform or online folder for corrections.

There should be feedback and positive learning environment should be created. Every answers should come with experimentation and observation and others should learn from the mistakes made.

Steps to achieving a successful training online course

- Trainers should rehearse primarily online classroom management with colleagues.
- Trainer should rehearse muting microphones and permit someone to express his/her opinions at a time
- Trainer should practice receptive skills (practical and listening tasks) during training time, to see how it can affect the flow of the training

Training/lesson notes preparation form an important part of a formal training program. The training notes serve as a guide to the trainer, it is also used to improve the quality of task to be performed during and after the training program. It is a step-by-step plan to train. Every training manager should make it compulsory for trainers to know how to plan their online classes ahead. Training note explains all the steps outlined in a training plan. Trainers can present their training plans weekly or daily. This is the reason every trainers should know how to arranged their training notes and plans together.

Training notes show what is expected to be trained, how to train a particular team and what the trainees are expected (learners outcome) to have learned at the end of the training. It shows the influence of training on the trainees and increase the trainer's progress during the training. It ensure harmony of conduct in presentation of content, putting together every tasks, information on skill training, processes and other relevant requirement can be achieved through training notes preparation.

3.1 Importance of Training Notes

It serves as

- a preliminary treatise to training subject matter
- a preliminary account to be followed at a point of training
- a relation to subject matter after training
- a concerned reference to portray realistically training
- a functional unit of information

3.2 Constituent Parts of a Training Plan

This is one of the important parts of what a trainer will do to have a successful training or set goals. It is effective when a trainer applies it during training. This constituent parts include

- training objectives
- activities
- methods of comprehension

- **Training objectives:** The trainer should determine the taxonomic position (training objective) of the class is required to train. This can be effectively achieved by emphasizing on the topic (skills) to be trained, a skinning what you want to see trainees accomplish or achieve by the end of the training (inquire yourself as a trainer) and what you want them to be able to do with the skill they will be trained on.
- **Activities:** This part is trainer-centered and is the largest section. A trainer should apply method of using different method of teaching/training to explain the skill lesson. Here, the trainer can train comprehensively using training styles, applying different learning and training styles, the training class should be fund, it should also be applied to actual events occurring in reality and it should be reciprocally active.
- **Methods of comprehension:** This part is trainee-centered and trainer-centered. Here, the trainer will be able to know what the trainees learned or achieved from the training and how much of it they were able to keep in their memory. The trainer can apply an evaluation method to assess the trainees, it can be formal or informal method of assessment.

3.3 Training Notes Preparation Format

Training notes show how a training class is to be trained and the trainees' outcome (i.e., what is expected from them at the end of the training). It shows the effect of training on the trainees after training class.

Steps to create or produce a good training notes

1. Have understanding of your intention.
2. Form or compose your outline.
3. Design your timetable.
4. Have understanding of your trainees.
5. Apply different trainee rapport patterns.
6. Apply eclectic training methods.

Training Notes Sample

Training notes on shoemaking skill acquisition

Subject: Practical skill acquisition
Lesson: Leather goods manufacturing and repairs
Class: Adult
Date: August 20, 2021

Time: 12:10–2:10 p.m.
Duration: 2 hours
Gender: Mixed
Average age: 20+

Specific Objectives: By the end of the training, the trainees should be able to:

a.   Identify the components used in shoemaking.
b.   Discuss the various functions of shoemaking tools.
c.   Know all the techniques involve in producing quality shoes and produce them (practice).

Instructional materials: The trainer should present different kinds of shoemaking tools and leather
Entry behavior: The trainer asks the trainee questions based on the type of shoes they have seen or wore before.
Set-induction: The trainer captures the trainees' attention by asking them questions or telling them stories related to shoemaking.
Instructional procedure: This level come in steps for clarity.

Step I: The trainer introduces the topic and the components used in shoemaking. The components includes animal leather, evostic gum, fibre, macco sole, shoe polish, shoe leather dye, among others.
Step II: The trainer explains various functions of shoemaking tools.

Functions of shoemaking

Sewing machine: Is to stitch and design the upper work of the shoe
Shoe last: Is used to form and to determine the shape and size of shoes
Scissor: Used for cutting of materials
Shoe brush: For applying gum and other liquid.
Deigning puncher: For boring of holes and designs, etc.

Step III: The trainer explains the techniques and steps of producing quality shoes. Here, the trainer will practically show the trainees the methods involve in producing quality shoes for the masses.

Evaluation: The trainer assess the trainees based on the training lesson/topic by asking the following questions about what was being trained.

a.   Identify the components used in shoemaking? This can be achieve by showing different components previously discussed about on the screen for the trainees to see (i.e., online training) correctly in two (2) minutes correctly without any help.
b.   Discuss the various functions of shoemaking tools in three (3) minutes correctly without any help.
c.   Knowing all the techniques involve in producing quality shoes and produce them (here, the trainee should be able to give details on every steps needed for production).

Conclusion: The trainer picks out the key facts from the lesson and laid emphasis on them.

Summary: The trainer summarizes the topic/lesson by going through it again by discussing that shoemaking as one of the skills can be a selling and productive entrepreneurial skills that does not require big capital for a start. The trainer should encourage the trainees to practice more and make it big because people wear different patterns and designs of shoes in today's world.

TABULAR FORMAT OF TRAINING NOTE

Training Notes Sample

Training notes on shoemaking skill acquisition

Subject:	Practical skill acquisition
Lesson:	Leather goods manufacturing and repairs
Class:	Adult
Date:	August 20, 2021
Time:	12:10–2:10 p.m.
Duration:	2 hours
Gender:	Mixed
Average age:	0+

Specific Objectives: By the end of the training, the trainees should be able to:

a. Identify the components used in shoemaking
b. Discuss the various functions of shoemaking tools.
c. Know all the techniques involve in producing quality shoes and produce them (practice).

Instructional materials: The trainer should presents different kinds of shoemaking tools and leather.

Entry behavior: The trainer asks the trainee questions based on the type of shoes they have seen or wore before.

Set induction: The trainer captures the trainees' attention by asking them questions or telling them stories related to shoemaking.

S/N	CONTENT	TRAINERS' ACTIVITY	TRAINEES' ACTIVITY	TRAINING METHOD	EVALUATION	SUMMARY	CONCLUSION
1.	Components used in shoemaking	The trainer introduces the topic and the components used in shoemaking. The components includes animal leather, evostic gum, fibre, macco sole, shoe polish, shoe leather dye, among others.	Listen attentively to the trainees and jot down notes	Class approach	The trainer assesses the trainees based on the training lesson/topic by asking the following questions about what was being trained. Identify the components used in shoemaking? This can be achieved by showing different components previously discussed about on the screen for the trainees to see (i.e., online training) correctly in two (2) minutes correctly without any help.	The trainer summarizes the topic/lesson by going through it again by discussing that shoemaking as one of the skills can be a selling and productive entrepreneurial skill that does not require big capital for a start. The trainer should encourage the trainees to practice more and make it big because people wear different patterns and designs of shoes in today's world.	The trainer picks out the key facts from the lesson and laid emphasis on them.
2.	Functions of shoemaking tools.	The trainer explains various functions of shoemaking tools. **Functions of shoemaking Sewing machine:** Is to stitch and design the upper work of the shoe **Shoe last:** Is used to form and to determine the shape and size of shoes **Scissor:** Used for cutting of materials **Shoe brush:** For applying gum and other liquid. **Deigning puncher:** For boring of holes and designs, etc.	Listen attentively to the trainees and jot down notes	Discussion approach	Discuss the various functions of shoemaking tools in three (3) minutes correctly without any help.	The trainer emphasizes on the importance of affording personal tools for shoemaking as a would-be entrepreneur.	The trainer picks out the key facts from the lesson and laid emphasis on them.
3.	Techniques involve in producing quality shoes and produce them (practice).	The trainer explains the techniques and steps of producing quality shoes. Here, the trainer will practically show the trainees the methods involve in producing quality shoes for the masses.	Listen attentively to the trainees and imitates the trainer by practicing (doing what the trainer is doing) how to make shoe	Demonstration approach	Knowing all the techniques involve in producing quality shoes and produce them. (here, the trainee should be able to give details on every steps needed for production).	The trainer summarizes the lesson/training of techniques involve in producing quality shoe in steps or giving an overview of the procedures.	The trainer picks out the key facts from the lesson and laid emphasis on them.

4.0 Instructional Materials and Equipment

Instructional materials are those necessary ingredients used by a trainer in the development of any training curriculum. According to Esu (1995), "ordinary word of verbalization has been known to be inadequate for effective teaching because it has failed to deliver the needed objective instruction in schools hence the instructional materials which may be used by the learner to facilitate the acquisition and evaluation of knowledge and skills." They are training materials that aid trainees in concretizing a training experience so as to make training more exciting, interesting and interactive. These group of materials includes animate (full of life) and inanimate (lacking power of motion) resources that a trainer may use in training and learning situations to help achieve desired learning objectives. The effectiveness of these materials is that it can be used both in online classrooms and in a regular (face-to-face) classrooms; hence, it must be redesigned to be used for online setting.

Instructional materials should be accurate so as to come into correct relative position with all other rudiments in a particular skill or course, including the learning objectives, assessments, activities and evaluations.

Instructional materials have moral and intellectual power related with curriculum, and this intellectual power is pivotal and crucial in transforming and interpreting curriculum in a practical manner at the training situation or classroom situation.

Hence, it is important to design or plan for instructional material that trainee and the trainer will use to ease the acquisition of skill and knowledge in any venture when developing training curriculum.

Importance of Instructional Materials for Skill Training

1. Instructional materials arouse the trainee's interest and have significant purpose during and after training.
2. It aimed at enriching training effectiveness and put in a proper state of mind in the trainee for mental accountability for the future.
3. It is used to assist trainees understanding of the training and the trainee's effective training.
4. It provides the arrangement of skill information of training that combines under basic topics material that trainees will encounter, train/learn and apply during training.
5. Online training rely on a meditative and having all necessary instructional materials that trainees will have ability to obtain or make use of them, analyze, learn, and reference as they continue in a training.

"The planning and selection of instructional materials should be taken into consideration, both the breadth and depth of content so that trainee learning is optimized. Instructional materials must be carefully planned, selected, organized, refined and used in a course of training for the maximum effect" (design-teachengage.wisc.edu/instruction…).

Questions to Pose when Selecting Instructional Materials for Online Training

Consider these questions as a trainer when selecting instructional materials for training:

• Is the intention and the insurance available to meet the target compatible?
• Do the materials and media support in line with the fixed learning objectives?
• What will trainees/learners view/hear?
• What will trainees/learners read/explore?
• Will you find or create this material?

- What could learners experience/create
- Is there enough involvement and engagement?
(same reference)

Types of Instructional Materials

There are two types of instructional materials namely:

a.   Textual materials (i.e., prints materials)
b.   The nontextual materials

➢ **TEXTUAL OR PRINTS MATERIALS:** These types of materials are mostly used in schools. They include, manuals, pamphlets, textbooks, reference, workbook, and mimeographs.
    According to Esu (1995, p. 75), "there are two broad areas of printed materials that can be effectively utilized in teaching. These are the textbook and the supplementary reading materials. Developing a text for use in school follows almost the same process of curriculum development."

➢ **NONTEXUAL MATERIALS:** These are materials that can be combined with the use of textbooks to provide high value or quality in training/learning experience. They are classify into five groups, namely
  - The visuals
  - The audios
  - Audio-visuals
  - Phenomenal
  - Manipulative

i.   The Visual Materials: They are material that appeal to the sense of sight and possibly touch. The provide the trainee with direct first-hand experience necessary for concept information. They provide models and specimens which trainers use to facilitate training by seeing, touching and testing. These type of materials are flannel boards, bulletin board, globes, maps, charts, graphs among others.

ii. The Audio Materials: These are material that appeal to the sense of hearing. It is necessary to use instructional audio materials that are relevant to the sense of hearing especially while training online, discussion that involves listening. These types of audio materials include audio card, compact disc, cassette (audio tape), micro cassette and phonograph record.

iii. The Audio-Visual Materials: These are materials that incorporate both the audio and visual characteristics. They stimulate both the auditory and visual senses which depends on each other. Examples includes, videotapes, audio-slides, CDs, television, DVDs, microforms (microfilm and microfiche). They give accurate means of training and learning.

iv. The Phenomenals: Are the kinds of materials that the trainer uses in training which learners/trainees can immediately understand in their natural or semi-natural setting. These materials are things, festivals, events, settings and resources. These materials help to bring the trainees in direct contact with training environment (Inyang-Abia and Esu 1990, p. 76).

v.   The Manipulatives: These are materials that the trainee actually handles skillfully and manages expertly to bring about the desired behavioral changes. These type of instructional materials enable the trainee to be able to hear, see, feel, and adjust both conceptually and in a learning skill.

Examples of Instructional Materials

Instructional Resources	Uses
Animation	Animation can create an illusion of movement when shown in sequence. It visually and dynamically presents concepts, models, processes, or phenomena in space or time.
E-portfolio	A collection of electronic materials assembled and managed by a user. These may include text, electronic files, multimedia, blog entries, images, and links. E-portfolios are both demonstrations of the user's abilities and platforms for self-expression, and, if they are online, they can be maintained dynamically overtime. An e-portfolio can be seen as a type of training/learning record that provides actual evidence of achievement.
Illustration/Graphic	Visual concepts, models, or processes (that are not photographic images) that visually present concepts, models, or processes that enable trainees to learn skills or knowledge. These can be diagrams, illustrations, graphics or infographics in any file format including photoshop, illustrator and other similar file types.
Simulation	Approximates a real or imaginary experience where users' actions affect the outcomes of tasks where they have to complete. Users determine and input initial conditions that generate output that is different from and changed by the initial conditions.
Assessment Tool	Forms, templates, and technologies for measuring performance.
Collection	A meaningful organization of training/learning resources such as websites, documents, apps, etc., that provides users' an easier way to discover the materials.
Open Journal-Article	A journal or article in a journal that is free of cost from the end user and has a creative commons, public domain or other acceptable user license agreement.
Quiz/Test	Any assessment device intended to evaluate the knowledge or skills of trainees/learners.
Video-Instructional	A recording of moving visual images that show real people, places and things that enable trainees/learners to learn skills or knowledge.
Open Text Book	An online textbook offered by its author(s) with creative common public domain, or other acceptable use license agreement allowing use of the e-book at no additional cost.
Workshop and Training Material	Materials best used in a workshop setting for the purpose of professional development.
Reference Material	Material with no specific instructional objectives and similar to that found in the reference area of a library. Subject specific directories to other sites, texts, or general information are examples.

(support.skillscommons.org/hom/com…accessed July, 2021)

5.0 Creating a Suitable Training Environment

You will be able to retain skills and knowledge better when your workplace is an effective training environment. Tips for creating an effective/suitable training environment and becoming an ultimate trainer include the following:

- Embrace the Distractions: When providing on-the-job training, treat the distractions for the workplace as opportunities to reinforce training. For example, if a customer issue demands your attention during training, demonstrate exceptional service while still sticking to the task at hand.
- Create a Positive Atmosphere: Having positive energy impacts everyone around you. If you work hard, treat everyone with respect, and enjoy your work, your trainees will follow suit and training will be more effective. New trainees, especially, will find information easier to learn when they feel they are in a supportive and positive training environment.
- Foster Open Communication: To encourage ongoing learning, all your trainees should feel comfortable asking and answering questions. You won't always be available to answer questions that come up, so empower veteran employees to coach new hires, through open communication. Remember, effective communication requires listening as much, if not more than you talk. Take the time to really listen to trainee questions so you can provide complete answers.
- Provide Praise Frequently: Trainees need a boost to help them stay motivated. Praise trainees when they do a good job, and do it in front of others. Be sure to spread out your praise evenly between all your trainees. Everyone needs encouragement and can benefit from a well-placed "great job."
- Offer Constructive Feedback: For learning to thrive, trainers and coaches need to provide constructive feedback as well as praise. Trainees will make mistakes sometimes, that's just part of learning process. When this happens, avoid using phrases such as "That's not how you do it," or "I already told you that." Instead use a phrase such as "I noticed something wasn't quite right here. Let's take a look."

Ongoing learning can't happen in a vacuum. When you create an effective training environment based on positive open communication, praise, and feedback, trainees will be more open to learn new things and improve their performance.

5.1 Communication Skills

Communicating effectively is one of the essential life skills to learn, and *communication* itself is defined as transferring information to produce greater understanding.

It can be done vocally (through verbal exchanges), through written media (books, websites, and magazines), visually (using graphs, charts, and maps), or nonverbally (body language, gestures, pitch of voice, and tone). All of these means of communication skills are essential soft skills that are vital for a successful career.

Having strong communication skills aids in all aspects of life—from professional to personal life and everything that falls between. From a business standpoint, all transactions result from communication. Good communication skills allow others and yourself to understand information more accurately and quickly.

In contrast, poor communication skills lead to frequent misunderstandings and frustration. In a 2016 LinkedIn survey conducted in the United States, communication topped the list of employers' most sought-after soft skills.

Improving Communication Skills

Here are some pointers to look out for when looking to improve group or personal ability to communicate effectively.

1. Listening: To become a good communicator, it is important to be a good listener. It is important to practice active listening—pay close attention to what others are saying and clarify ambiguities by rephrasing their questions for greater understanding.
2. Conciseness: Convey the message in as few words as possible. Do not use filler words and get straight to the point. Rambling will cause the listener to tune out or be unsure of what the key points were. Avoid speaking excessively and do not use words that may confuse the audience.
3. Body language: It is important to practice good body language, use eye contact, utilize hand gestures, and watch the tone of voice when communicating with others. A relaxed body stance with a friendly tone will aid in making the speaker look approachable. Eye contact is important in communication—look the person in the eye to indicate that you are focused on the conversation, but make sure not to stare at the person as it can make him or her uncomfortable.
4. Confidence: Be confident in what you say and in your communication interactions with others. Being confident can be as easy as maintaining eye contact, maintaining a relaxed body stance, and talking with concision. Try not to make statements sound like questions and avoid trying to sound aggressive or demeaning.
5. Open-mindedness: In situations where one disagrees with what someone else has to say—whether with an employer, a coworker, or a friend—it is important to sympathize with their point of view rather than try to get your message across. Respect the opinion of others and never resort to demeaning those who disagree with your point.
6. Respect: Respecting what others say and acknowledging them are important aspects of communication. Respectability can be as simple as paying attention to what they have to say, using the person's name, and not being distracted. The other person will feel appreciated by respecting others, leading to a more honest and productive conversation in career development.
7. Using the correct medium: There are several different forms of communication to use—it is important to choose the right one. For example, communicating in person about serious matters (layoffs, salary changes, etc.) is more appropriate than sending an email regarding the matter.

Good Communication Skills for a Great Career

Succeeding in a career requires good communication skills. You need to know what you want and how you will attain it. Being an excellent communicator can help propel your career.

Good communication skills can aid you in landing an interview and passing the selection process. Being able to articulate well provides a significant advantage. To do your job effectively, you must discuss problems, request information, interact with others, and have good human relations skills—these are all part of good communication skills. They help in being understood well and in helping understand the needs of those around you.

Poor Communication in the Workplace

Communication drives workplace success. Although the detriments of poorly communicating with others may not be apparent in the short term, it has a crippling effect on the workplace in the long term. Here are some signs of poor communication:

- Lack of specific communication
- Using the incorrect mediums to convey essential messages
- Passive-aggressive communication
- Lack of follow-through and consideration
- Blaming and intimidating others
- Failing to listen

An example of poor communication would be the RadioShack layoff notices in 2006. The electronics chain laid off four hundred employees by notifying them through email. The company faced significant backlash following the move, with many surprised that it used email instead of face-to-face meetings.

Bad communication by RadioShack resulted from using the incorrect communication medium with its employees. The company's employees felt dehumanized and subsequently resented the company.

5.2 Feedback

Feedback is a reaction or information that occurs due to actions or behavior undertaken by an individual or group. Positive and negative feedback is crucial in a learning and development context. Feedback provides a sense of engagement and interactivity and allows learners to take ownership of their learning. Effective feedback shows learners their current level of performance and lets them know what they need to do to reach a higher level.

In today's world, eLearning offers a range of opportunities to give feedback to the learner. On a basic level, questions inserted into the learning can act as a "knowledge check," with the feedback offered reinforcing learning points covered in the content so far.

Alternatively, questions can be asked before new information is introduced. This enables learners to think critically about a learning point and "discover" the correct answer using their common sense and existing knowledge. The feedback then expands on the learning point once interest has been firmly established. Be sure to make it clear to the learner that they will not be penalized for incorrect answers.

Assessment topics featuring several questions can offer opportunities for feedback in several ways. Used as "end of learning" tests, assessments can measure the learner's retention of the learning and direct them to specific areas of the learning that they may need to repeat.

Alternatively, used as a diagnostic tool, these topics can pretest the learner's existing knowledge, then cater to the content they need to access based on their performance.

6.0 Training Management

Training is an action or process of developing or teaching and learning a person on a particular skill for the purpose of being useful for a job and applying the knowledge, skills when needed. The importance of training is to improve and develop self-confidence. It makes an individual independent (entrepreneur). It is employees' competent booster. Training improve quality in an organization.

There are various types of training namely:

1. Job instruction training
2. Refresher training
3. Vestibule training
4. Induction training
5. Apprenticeship training

> Job Instruction Training: This training gives overview about the job and experienced trainers instructs and demonstrates the entire job. After evaluating the trainee to assess his competencies, additional training is being offered if need be.
> Refresher Training: This type of training is to impart and upgrade the skills of employees or an individual. It can also be used for promotion (i.e., military officer that embarks on a course for promotion). "This type of training is offered in order to incorporate the latest development in a particular field."
> Vestibule Training: This type of training is that is being attended and learned far from an individual place of work or company. It is centered on the employee.
> Induction Training: This type of training serves as a guide to new members in the school, companies, etc., to make them understand the requirement and the nature of their job. The learners/trainees get to understand the dos and don'ts, rules and regulations existing in their new domain.
> Apprenticeship Training: This is a system for job training that is associated with trainees following the instructions given to them by their instructors on-the-job training to attain professionalism in the trained-job. Examples of these skills includes carpentry, welding, among others.

Managers are responsible for the maintaining and enhancing an existing set of products and services, and possibly creating and developing new ones, enough people with the right skills are needed to get all these jobs done. If there is no manager, the company or group of individuals (team) will collapse from being overworked or under-skilled.

Management's primary job is maintaining and over-seeing that the team he is managing finished their tasks with low cost and low risk. He enhances the abilities of the new members through a good skills acquisition process and with proficiencies, he coordinates the team members to get the work done that requires doing. The team will become confident that anything can be accomplished with a good trained management for acquiring new skills.

Training management control the risk and try to reduce it over time while positioning a team to keep pressing on despite the difficult task and huge challenge. Training management must try to anticipate the skills a team needs to deliver assigned and anticipated projects/work. Training management is an activity that works on changing an individual's skills, mindset as a manager.

Training management is the act of putting tools, skills/ideas, techniques, knowledge to training an individual or team to accomplish the result of training. A skeletal structure to training include planning, implementation and evaluation.

Training Management Planning: This is the act of determining goals and to be able to see things as they really are, select a group or team for a particular tasks for attaining those goals.

Training Management Implementation: This is process of executing important actions and plans arranged to proficient or skillfully done with necessary planned objectives and goals.

Training Management Execution: This involves arrangement on how the process will be achieved for each number of the result (evaluation) and making sure that they are accomplished well.

There should be workshops for trainers to follow-up with. This workshop will consolidate understanding and how new ideas can be applied to have a successful training and learning online. Before a training manager assigns a skill to an instructor/trainer, he should ask or evaluate the trainer on the following questions:

1. What skills do they have and test (practically) their competencies
2. Which one do they need help with to train learners online.
3. Which expedient and skills do they need support with for effectively training achievement. (**www. yourarticlelibrary.com/hum**)

7.0 Evaluation of Skills Performance

Evaluation is seen by Oyedgi (1992), as the examination and judgement of the worth, quality, significance, amount, degree or condition of something. This definition focuses on the assigned value of any activity. This definition recognize the fat that except the given activity is assessed, its value would not be determined.

Bloom *et al.* (1956) regard evaluation as the systematic collection of evidence to determine whether in fact certain changes are taking place in the learner as well as to determine the amount of degree of change in individual learners.

Evaluation according to Merriam-Webster's Dictionary is the determination of the value, nature, character, or quality of something or someone.

Curriculum evaluation involves a culture of judgement that individuals, groups, institution and governments pass on judgment about appropriateness, inappropriateness, goodness or badness of a situation. The term evaluation connote test and examination.

When it comes to the evaluation of training programs, its best to start at the beginning. Before you decide what to measure, how to measure it, choose the evaluation technique that is most helpful. We must know the meaning of evaluation of training or skill evaluation since our focus is on skills acquisition.

What is training evaluation? (corehr.wordpress.com/training…)

Training evaluation is the systematic process of analyzing if training programs and initiatives are effective and efficient. It is also an attempt to obtain relevant information whether the goals or objectives were met and what impact the training had on actual performance on a particular skill. There are four kinds of standard training evaluation namely:

1. Formative
2. Process
3. Outcome
4. Impact

➢ Formative evaluation provides ongoing feedback to the curriculum designers and developers to ensure that what is being created really meets the needs of the intended trainees/learners.
➢ Process evaluation provides information about what occurs during training. This includes giving and receiving verbal feedback.
➢ Outcome evaluation determines whether or not the desired results (e.g., what participants are doing) of applying new skills were achieved in the short-term.
➢ Impact evaluation determines how the results of the training affect the strategic goal.

7.1 Evaluation Methods

Evaluation methods can be either qualitative (e.g., interviews, case studies, focus groups) or quantitative (e.g., surveys, experiments). Training evaluation usually includes a combination of these methods and reframes our thinking about evaluation in that measurements are aimed at different levels of a system.

- Formative Evaluation: May be defined as "any combination of measurements obtained and judges made before or during the implementation of materials, methods, or programs to control, assure or improve the quality of program performance or delivery." This type of evaluation is also be seen as guidance oriented.
- It answers such questions as, "Are the goals and objectives suitable for the intended learners/trainers?" "Are the methods and materials appropriate to the training?" "Can the training be easily replicated?"
- Formative evaluation furnishes information for program developers and implementers.
- It helps determine program planning and implementation activities in terms of
  a. Target population
  b. Program organization and
  c. Program location and timing
- It provides "short-loop" feedback about the quality and implementation of program activities and thus becomes critical to establishing, stabilizing, and upgrading programs.
- Process Evaluation: It answers the question, "What did you do?" It focuses on procedures and actions being used to produce results.
- It monitors the quality of training or project by various means. Traditionally, working as an "onlooker," the evaluator describes this process and measures the results in oral and written reports.
- Process evaluation is the most common type of training evaluation. It takes place during training delivery and at the end of the training.
- Outcome Evaluation: This type of evaluation answers the question, "What happened to the knowledge, attitudes, and behaviors of the intended population?"

  This training would produce both "outcomes" and "impacts" outcome evaluation is a long-term undertaking. It answers the question, "What did the participants/learners do?"

  Outcome evaluation data is intended to measure what training participants were able to do at the end of training and what they actually did back in the class as a result of the training.
- Impact Evaluation: This type of evaluation takes even longer than outcome evaluation and you may never know for sure that your training helped bring about the change. Impacts occur through an accumulation of outcomes.

What are the Methods of Skill Training Evaluation?

There is a long list of skill training evaluation techniques to choose from. Different authors come up with their skill training models techniques. But there are five techniques that are most often trusted by different establishments today. These skill training evaluation models include the following:

1. Kirkpatrick's Four-Level Training Evaluation Model
2. The Philips Roi Model
3. Kaufman's Five Level of Evaluation

4.   Anderson's Model for Learning Evaluation
5.   Summative vs Formative Evaluation

Explanation of Kirkpatrick Model:

The model below explains different levels of analyzing and evaluating the result of training programs.

Level 1
Reaction: Measures how participants react to training (e.g., satisfaction?).

Level 2
Learning: Analyzes if they truly understood the training (e.g., increase in knowledge, skills or experience?).

Level 3
Behavior: Looks as if they are utilizing what they learned at work (e.g., change in behaviors?).

Level 4
Results: Determines if the material had a positive impact on training.
Furthermore, the model can be implemented before, throughout and following training to show the value of training.

Kirkpatrick's four-level training evaluation model:

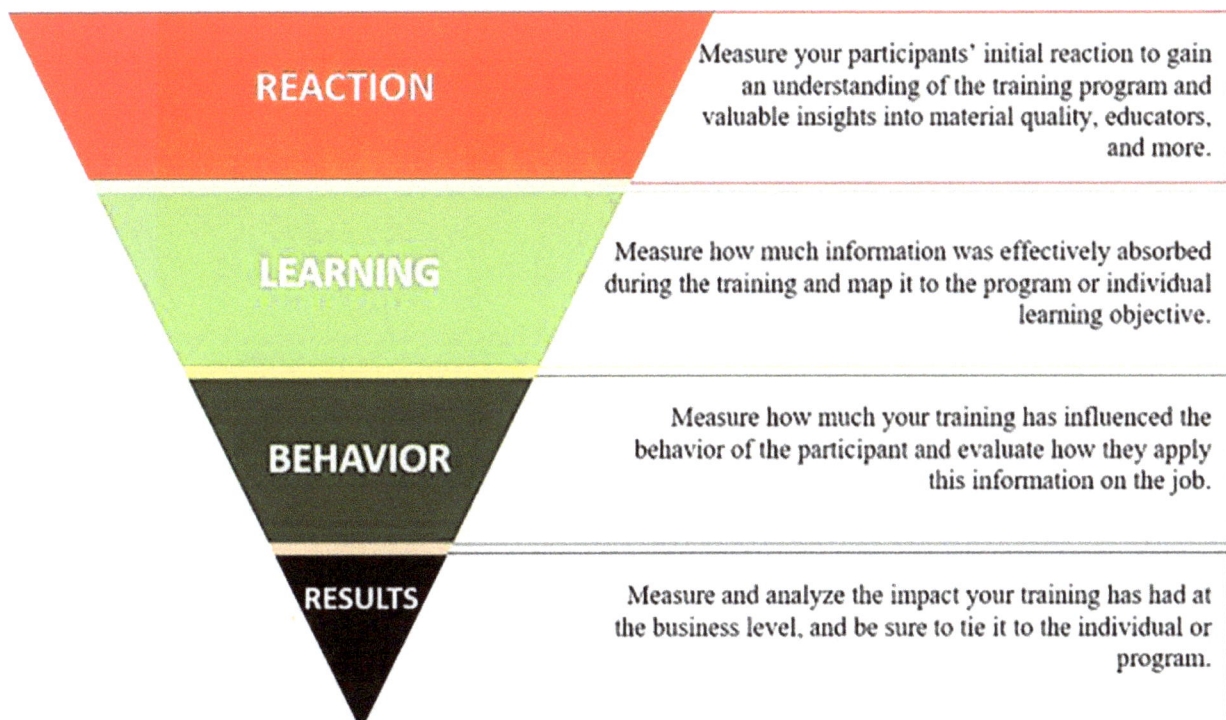

REACTION — Measure your participants' initial reaction to gain an understanding of the training program and valuable insights into material quality, educators, and more.

LEARNING — Measure how much information was effectively absorbed during the training and map it to the program or individual learning objective.

BEHAVIOR — Measure how much your training has influenced the behavior of the participant and evaluate how they apply this information on the job.

RESULTS — Measure and analyze the impact your training has had at the business level, and be sure to tie it to the individual or program.

Dr. Donald Kirkpatrick (1924–2014)
(educationaltechnology.net/Kirkpatrick-model-four-levels-learning-evaluation assessed July, 2021.)

8.0 Summary and Conclusion

Road map to effective skill acquisition has been a challenge in the society and world. Illiterate or quack trainers are known to flood in different aspects of training skills without a formal setting, training note, learning and behavioral objectives, and instructional material, among others.

Often times, these instructors are confused in their orderly arrangement and management of the training class. Because of these facts, the trainees end up not being able to comprehend what was taught or trained, and become training-dropouts (i.e., not being able to complete their training).

However, some trainee-dropouts lamented that paucity of instructional materials for their inability to perform well during training and assessment of their skills. Based on this, road map to effective skill acquisition introduces the trainer on a wheel of a successful and effective ladder to help pose and repackage them to reabsorb and engage this chapter into practice.

In conclusion, the type of training that should be received by the trainees should have direct impact on their lives and society. Since this chapters are in split formats, which is to help the readers to explore different activities that should be focus on while acquiring new skills. It is condensed in form to provide you with a detailed plan to guide your progress toward an expected goal of training and learning.

Chapter Three

The Language of Skill Acquisition

1.0 Introduction

Language is a tool for thinking, speaking and writing ideas, instructions, requests and information. It comprises words and expressions which are used according to the context (role of the user, purpose, subject matter and circumstance of communication). These factors give rise to strands of language or varieties which are functionally identifiable and characterized according to the dominant features. Thus, the language of a subject matter or field is the aggregate of the words and expressions most commonly and appropriately used in that field. These conventional choices serve as a linguistic banner for the field and the players therein.

The technical view of the above exposition is captured under the sociolinguistic phraseology, context of situation which suggests the features of participants and their verbal actions, nonverbal actions; relevant objects and effect of the verbal action. Specifically, when humans come across a particular situation or subject, they draw resources from the language to express themselves and communicate the issues in that domain.

Advancements in humanity, inventions, discoveries and practices have resulted in the emergence of a "language program" or range of usages that meets the communicative needs of the time and place. This emergence has given rise to two identifiable levels of language, namely the "general" level and the "specialized" level.

In this chapter, we will establish the reality of a specialized language used in skill acquisition based on the principles of registers, idiomicity, and English for specific purposes. The impost of this discourse is to portray the fact that skill acquisition is advancing into a distinct field of activities and study with resources from the linguistic norms of entrepreneurship, technology, economy, management, administration, education, culture and artisanship, among others.

2.0 Overview of the English Language

Current rankings place English at the top of the chart as the language with the highest population of users in the world. In the comity of native speakers, it comes third to Chinese and Spanish. It is spoken officially in over sixty countries and used in the business of over twenty global and regional organizations. Since the fifth Century when Anglo-Saxons brought the language to England, it has passed through distinct phases of Old English, Middle English to Modern English characterized by

i.   Wide usage across the word
ii. Lingua franca status in many multilingual settings

iii.   Language of international discourse
iv.   Flexible inflectional morphology and syntax
v.   Second language status in many bilingual settings
vi.   Mutually intelligible varieties/dialects
vii. Global and regional variation
viii. Online media communication across cultures
ix.   A great variety of dictionaries
x.   Hundreds of thousands of growing vocabularies
xi.   Flexible phonological systems

3.0   English for Specific Purposes

The expansion of the English vocabulary to accommodate new dimensions of communications in diverse domains has given rise to the concept of English for specific purpose with offshoots in:

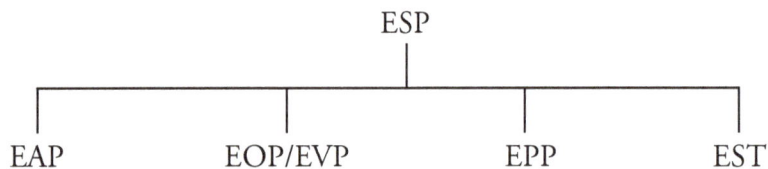

```
                        ESP
                         |
      _____|_____
     |             |              |          |
    EAP        EOP/EVP           EPP        EST
```

EAP—English for Academic Purposes
EOP/EVP—English for Occupational or Vocational Purpose
EPP—English for Professional Purposes
EST—English for Science and Technology

English for specific purposes is the teaching/learning of English as a way of attaining communicative competence in a discipline such as academics, ICT, teaching, engineering, law, preaching, etc. (**Error! Hyperlink reference not valid.**)

> Since the language people speak or write varies from context to context considerably, ESP provides the platform to direct language to meet identified needs or interest. The target of ESP is to meet learners at the point of their needs. This is why the ESP enterprise cuts across the academic, professional and vocational. At the vocational level, we have English for occupational purposes. (Egbe, G. B. 2014 *Patterns of Est Writing*, Kraft, p. 21).

A tree of explication can be constructed thus, to show the drawdown from English as a language through ESP to other subtypes:

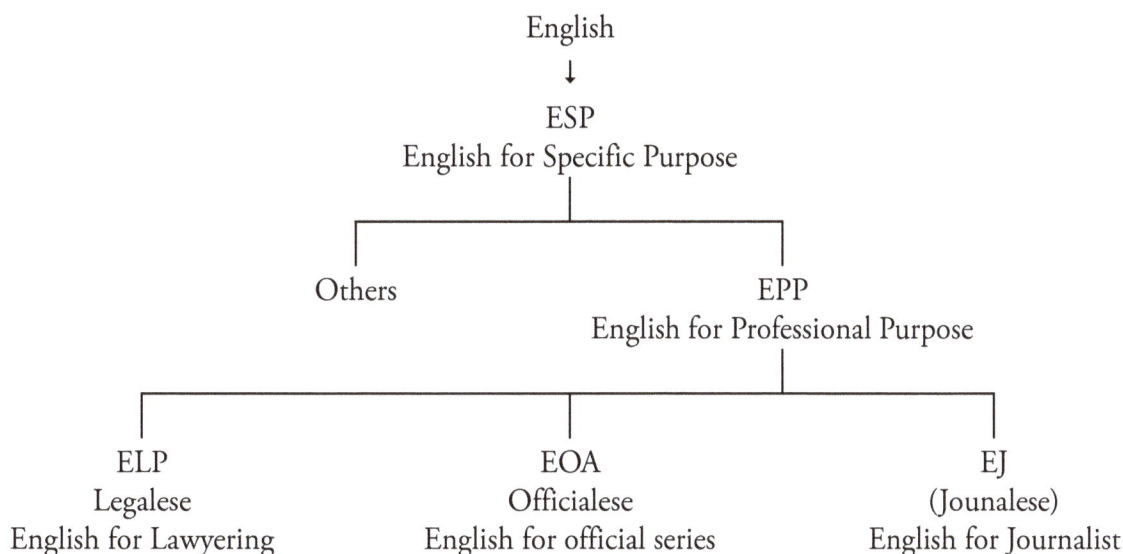

```
                            English
                               ↓
                             ESP
                    English for Specific Purpose

              Others                        EPP
                                 English for Professional Purpose

    ELP                      EOA                         EJ
  Legalese                Officialese               (Jounalese)
English for Lawyering   English for official series   English for Journalist
```

4.0 How Language Is Used in Communication

Most times people take the existence of language for granted until it is done on them that they are only able to do things by using language. How would humans reason, socialize, inform and teach/learn a skill without language. It would be an uphill task that may end in confusion. Communication can take place at the general level on the one hand and technical level on the other hand as this table illustrates:

General	Technical
• Mixed audience	• Target audience
• Use of general words	• Use of jargon
• No specific format	• Determined pattern
• Mostly oral	• Oral and written

Both levels can occur as interpersonal exchange of information between persons (sender/receiver(s)), organizational level such as industrial settings, and mass communication through the media.

33

4.1 Features of Language in Aid of Communication

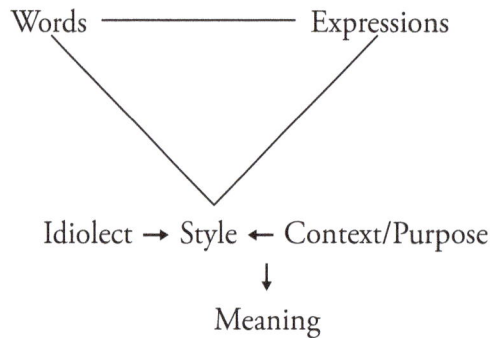

Words —————————— Expressions

Idiolect → Style ← Context/Purpose
↓
Meaning

Three aspects of language make for effective communication. Since the goal of communication is to share meaning by transferring information from the source (speaker, writer) to the target (listener, reader), the language user explores three dimensions to achieve this: Words, Expressions and Style

Gutb, Hans P. (1977), American English Today New York: McGraw-Hill Book Company, explains the power of words thus:

> Men and women are set apart from the rest of creation by their mastery of words. They use words to put a label on what they see in the world around them. They use words as a way of mapping their environment. Once they can out a label like "school" or "home" or "service station" on a place, they know where they are and what they are supposed to do. Part of what makes us human is that human beings use language for orientation.

4.2 Linguistic Creativity and Choices

A key feature of language that makes it ideal for multipurpose communication is the wide range of resources to choose from. For example, English has approximately 470,000 words. Many more can be created through the processes of invention, morphological processing, borrowing, neologism and adaptation.

Also, novel sentences are created based on the normal word order (subject-predicate-compliment) and transformations
Okon goes to school (Basic sentence)
Will Okon go to school? (Question)
Okon, go to school (Command)

The guiding principles for the choice of words and expressions are

➢ clarity in relation to meaning
➢ precision in achieving the purpose
➢ relevancy to the context of usage
➢ potency in conveying meaning
➢ simplicity to aid compression
➢ impressiveness through appeal
➢ acceptability through convention

4.3 Flexibility for Stylistic Variation

Language can be sent to match the personality of the user, the situation of usage, the target audience, the location and subject/topic of discussion. The aggregate of a style realities constitutes a stylistic variety which is comparable in shift in time and place. In pronunciation and semantics, it is important that varieties retain mutual intelligibility semantic/lexical field.

Words and expressions collocate or exist as a family or a system of meaning relationship. For example, in the field of economy the words demand, supply, export, import, inflation, etc., are related and can be said to constitute a lexical voice or idiom. Other dimensions of word families are synonymy and antonymy.

4.4 Registers

In most general meaning in language, register refers to the total characteristics of a sample of language (text/discourse) in relation to the purpose and context of usage. A conversation among a group of young men about beer, a report to a council meeting, an account of a football match, a family discussion between husband and wife; a student making a request from his father will also show different characteristics of usage.

Register refers to the words/expressions that suit the subject matter, communication situation/context, the interlocutors, profession, tone and mode of communication. Register follows the degree of formality: intimate, casual, consultative, formal, technical, instructive, informative, reflective, complaining, encouraging, promotional, fastidious, narrative, descriptive, argumentative, etc.

Another description of register is the dialect of a profession or field of discourse bearing distinctive features of the contents. It comprises the common core vocabulary with their collocations and phraseologies.

5.0 Functions of Language for Deployment in Skill Acquisition

Four major functions of language are usually identified, though same researchers have stated more functions. A community reading of any functions of language will always like zero on these four:

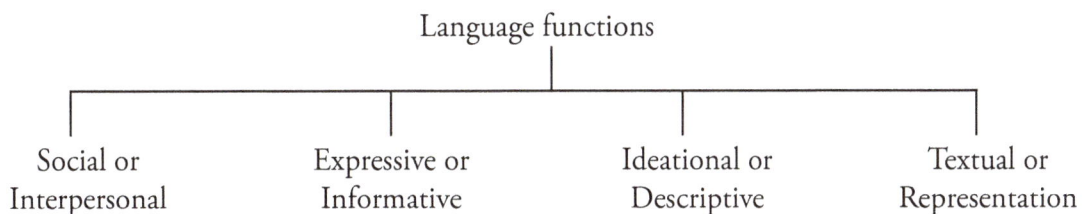

Language functions

| Social or Interpersonal | Expressive or Informative | Ideational or Descriptive | Textual or Representation |

The ideational function relates to the linguistic formation of our experiences, knowledge, perceptions, observations, and imaginations in an organized and describable form that can be conveyed as meaning or messages to the world. For example, in a skill acquisition scenario, the interlocutors use language to constitute the training concepts, principles, processes, materials, outcomes, etc., in their minds.

The expressive function allows language users to convey their ideas, experiences, observations, thoughts, opinions, prejudices and preferences across to their communication targets (listeners, readers, viewers, etc.). For example, a trainer can express his findings in a question form:

Do you understand this process?

The trainee will also express his response linguistically with a yes or no answer. This function helps the training to progress effectively through questions and answers, call and responses, enquiries and information, complaints and solutions, etc.

Through the social function, further interpersonal and group relationships are sustained such as greetings, phatic communication, religious activities, counselling, mediations, etc. Without this social functions, congenial atmosphere cannot be created for the skill acquisition activities to go on social function of language allows for emotional interactions that depict humanity: love, admiration, encouragement, appreciation, criticism, etc.

Textual function, though also expressive and ideational, specifically allows creative use of language either in speech or writing. It is a more formalized form of communication with language based on set standards and structures. With textuality, it is possible to have a written manual for skill acquisition process statements and analysis. This book is a good example of the textual function of language because if it is used as a creative conveyance of information about skill acquisition.

The three functions of language are operational in skill acquisition field. For example, the expressive function of language allows the trainee to reflect on the need to learn a skill and this choice also leads to classifying the skills and choosing the most preferred to adopt. This decided trainee then proceeds to explore the social function of language in searching for the ideal trainer with whom interaction takes place.

6.0 Language Choice for Skill Acquisition

Skill acquisition cuts across all classes of people: the professionals, the school leavers, regular students, school dropouts, etc. Some skills are constituted in the language in which the tools are named. In some cases, there could be translations across the languages or varieties. As stated earlier, registers refer to the various usages of language based on the contexts.

Thus:

> There are cases in which a person using different varieties of language for different uses will in fact use different languages. In Kenya, it is not uncommon to hear a student speak to a lecturer in English, to a friend in Kikuyu and to the hall-porter in Swahili all within the space of five to ten minutes. J. F. Wallwork. (Languages and Linguistics, p. 110, London 1955 Heinenmann Educational Books)

The above scenario suggests multilingualism: the knowledge and use of different language by a speaker. One feature of multilingualism is the reservation of diverse functions for particular languages. For example, in Nigeria, English places the role of an official language for education, legislation, judiciary and administration while also serving as a lingua franca. The Nigerian Pidgin English exists side by side with English and the indigenous languages. Therefore a Nigerian trainee in skill acquisition can shift from English with his trainee, to NPE with his co-trainee and to indigenous language with his parent who visits the training center at that moment, all within ten to twenty minutes.

This scenario was recorded in a skill acquisition center (College of Empowerment) at Akpabuyo, near Bakassi Pennisula, Calabar Area, Cross River State. A young school leaver came to the college with his friends and parents to make findings on the available skills and training charges and the following conversation ensured:

Trainee:	Good morning, sir.
College Provost:	Yes, young man, welcome. How can I help you?
Trainee:	Thank you, sir. Please, I am here to purchase a tailoring enrollment form. How much is it, sir?
College Provost:	The tailoring enrollment form is $275.00, and the tailoring manuals for training are $200.
Trainee (turning to the friends):	da, this is a serious case; the cost is well too high!
Trainee (getting to the parent):	Father, etc., requesting $755.00.
Trainee's Parents:	That is too expensive. Can't we negotiate (for $500.00)? This is too expensive for poor fellows like me. Whom can I talk to?
College Provost:	No, father. It is even less because of the subsidy from Iboto Empire. We have no option. It would have been more expensive if not for the subsidy provided by Mr. Oroks of Iboto Empire. Iboto Empire decided to pay for the training fees as a scholarship for the locals in an attempt to improve the professionality and develop the skills of the locals.

7.0   Selected Dimensions of Language in Use

In this section, we are explicating basic linguistic concepts that feature in skill acquisition and training:

1.   Reference to materials, substances, and objects

Generally, these three classifications refer to things which are expressed by nouns and noun phrases (nominal groups). Nominals come in these binarities:

> Singular: 1
  Plural: 2 and above

> Part of a group: a cake
  Group (collection) pastry

> Some: part
  All: whole

> Abstract: knowledge
  Concrete: wood

> Count: tools
  Noncount: water

> Specific: Etim, Okon
  General: Boys

2. Verbs express the following notions:
   ➢ Time Reference
   ➢ Nonpast: Present and Future (Speaking, hill speak)
      Past: Past (spoke)

   ➢ Presentness
      Temporary: progressive (cutting trees)
      Habitual: repetitive (cuts trees)

   ➢ Voice
      Active: subject + action (Okon kicked the ball)
      Passive: object + was/by (The ball was kicked by Okon)

   ➢ Transivity
      Transitive: subject + objects (He cuts the wood)
      Intransitive: subject - object (He laughed)

3. Adverbials and prepositionals express place, direction, distance, and manner
   Place: Here, there, anywhere
   Direction: away, across, around
   Distance: far, near,
   Manner: Fast, slow, smart, dull

4. Other conceptual issues expressed linguistically which may relate to skill acquisition settings are as follows:
   ➢ Cause, reason and purpose
   ➢ Actions and reactions
   ➢ Conditions and degrees
   ➢ Qualities and quantities
   ➢ Additions and restrictions
   ➢ Requests and responses
   ➢ Questions and answers
   ➢ Agreement and disagreement
   ➢ Liking and disliking
   ➢ Obligation and permission
   ➢ Volition and compulsion
   ➢ Invitations and prohibitions
   ➢ Offers and prohibitions
   ➢ Vocatives and affirmations
   ➢ Position and reinforcement

8.0 Words/Phrases List in Skill Acquisition

Skill
Acquisition
Training
Empowerment
Career
Entrepreneurship
Sensitization
Mobilization
Enrollment
Enablement
Enhancement
Vocation
Participant
Tool kits
Goals setting
Counselling
Guidance
Advisory
Extrinsic feedback
Schema theory
Efficiency
Instance theory
Adaptive components of thought
Declarative knowledge
Procedural knowledge
Implicit representation
Memory representations
Patterns of coordination
Animation

Outcomes
Performance
Employment
Volunteering
Task
Expertise
Mastery
Process
Earn a living
Learning
Mastering
Cognition
Job creation
Soft skills
Motivation
Crafts
Economic value

9.0 Summary and Conclusion

Language use is explicated under four categories: context of situation (appropriate choices based on subject matter, users, and circumstance), purpose-determined variation, practical/functional usage, and the linguistic elements and forms (words and phraseotogies).

We started by providing an overview of English language tailored to the emergence of a language program tagged "English for specific purposes." We proceeded to analyze how language is deployed in communication and the relevance of registers as a set of choices. We then examined how language is used in skill acquisition with specific emphasis on the preferred choices of words and expressions under diverse dimensions of usage.

The chapter is concluded with a check list of words and phrases that occur in the skill acquisition conceptualization, environment ant process. Our conclusion is that awareness of the language and linguistic choices used in particular contexts (skill acquisition training and development) is an integral and major part

of the learning process because language is used for conceptualization, classification, identification, instruction, declaration, interrogation and explication.

Skill	Skillfulness	Dexterity
Handiness	Ambidexterity	Style
Elegance	Deftness	Adroitness
Ease	Facility	Proficiency
Competence	Faculty	Capability
Capacity	Ability	Versatility
Adaptability	Flexibility	Mastery
Wizardry	Virtuosity	Excellence
Prowess	Goodness	Strong point
Métier	Forte	Attainment
Accomplishment	Skills	Seamanship
Airmanship	Horsemanship	Marksmanship
Experience	Expertise	Professionalism
Specialism	Know-how	Technique
Knowledge	Deft fingers	Craftmanship
Art	Artistry	Finish
Execution	Perfection	Ingenuity
Resourcefulness	Craft	Craftiness
Cunning	Cleverness	Sharpness
Worldly	Wisdom	Savoir faire
Finesse	Discrimination	Feat of skill
Trick	Dodge	Contrivance
Sleight of hand	Aptitude	Innate ability
Good head for	Bent	Natural
Tendency	Faculty	Endowment
Gift	Flair	Knack
Green fingers	Talent	Natural
Genius	Genius for aptness	Fitness
Masterpiece	Chef-d'oeuvre	A beauty
A creation	Piece de resistance	Master-work
Magnum opus	Stroke of genius	Masterstroke
Coup	Feat	Exploit
Hat	Trick	Deed
Smash hit	Tour de force	Ace
Trump	Exceller	Work of art
Objet d'art	Collector's piece or item	**Adj.** Skillful
Good	Good at	Top-flight

Top-notch	First-rate	Ace
Excellent	Skilled	Crack
Handy	Dexterous	Ambidextrous
Deft	Slick	Adroit
Agile	Nimble	Nimble-fingered
Green-f	Sure-footed	Cunning
Clever	Quick	Quick-witted
Shrewd	Smart	Ingenious
Intelligent	Politic	Diplomatic
Statesmanlike	Wise	Flexible
Resourceful	Versatile	Sound
Able	Competent	Wizard
Masterly	Accomplished	Gifted
Of many parts	Talented	Endowed
Well-e	Expert	Experienced
Veteran	Seasoned	Tried
Versed in	Up in	Well up in
Au fait	Skilled	Trained
Practiced	Well-p	Prepared
Finish	Specialized	Matured
Proficient	Qualified	Competent
Up to the mark	Professional	**Vb.** Be skillful, deft, etc.
adj.; be good at	do well	Be good
Shine	Excel	Be superior
Have a gift for	Show aptitude	Show a talent for
Have the knack	Be on form	Be in good f.
Have one's eye or hand in	Play one's cards well	Not put a foot wrong
Know what one is about	Live by one's wits	Know all the answers
Know what's what	Have one's wits about one	Be wise
Be expert	Be at the top of one's profession	Be good at one's job
Be a top-notcher	Know one's stuff or one's onions	Have the know-how
Have experience	Be an old hand	Know the ropes
Know all the ins and outs	Know backwards	Display one's skill
Adv. Skillfully	Craftily	Artfully, etc.
adj.; well	With skill	With aplomb
Knowledgeably	Expertly	Faultlessly
As to the manner born		

Psychology of Acquiring a Skill

1.0   Introduction

The two parts of an individual are traceable to the psychological (intangible) and the physiological (visual) dimensions. Incidentally, the former drives the later. In this chapter we take a look at the psychological basis of the skill acquisition and development processes. We presume that the motivation to learn a skill and the impetus to stay on the habit formation through repetition will come out of perception: an action and reaction or stimuli and responses going on in an individual.

Perception lends to learning, thinking and the problem-solving attitude that feeds the behavior toward an effective personality adjustment or accurate perception of positive results. The repetition of the performances adjudged to be efficient produces competencies in performances. This sustained repetition and habitual successes ultimately produces the peak performance, which represents the highest aspiration of the human personality.

Skill acquisition is defined as intentional control over the processes of joints and body fragments to enable an individual to find a solution to a motor skill challenge and to attain a desired aim. This explanation leads us to what is skill acquisition in psychology?

Acquisition of skill is a type of learning in which repetition results in enduring changes in an individual's capability to perform a specific task. Any behavior that needs to be learned and that is improved by practice can be considered to be a skill.

An individual that has competence to accomplish an expected work that has a result continually in different ways and usually associated little physical or involving conscious intellectual effort than a little accomplished act is known as skilled performer.

"With enough repetition, performance of the task eventually may become automatic, with little need for conscious oversight. Any behavior that needs to be learned and that is improved by practice can be considered to be a skill" (psychology.iresearchnet.com/sports-psychology/motor-development/skill-acquisition).

Implementation can be accomplished at the time of characteristic or skill being brought together that enables an individual practice the skill and the manner in which an individual performs.

2.0   Perception and Training

Training is an interplay of our psychology and physiology because our senses first receive stimuli in the form of sensations and send them to our minds as raw information for identification, organization, analysis and interpretation. As humans, we go through this process, sometimes in seconds or minutes without a deliberate consciousness. Our five sensory receptors that relate to taste, touch, sight, smell and audio (hear-

ing) form the instruments for collecting the stimuli and converting them into percepts or impressions from the environment. With this process, we take decisions about things around us.

Training which includes learning information helps in achieving a goal such as assimilating a skill. It promotes the ability to capture and process information in a skill acquisition and development situation.

According to Christian Balkenius, perception plays three major roles in learning, training and behavioral adjustment:

- Characterizing the situation
- Taking a decision about it
- Relating with the motivational system

These roles accordingly project the need for the learner to have a positive attitude toward the learning climate, milieu and tasks.

Experience is considered a major element of perception as it represents the apprehension of a present situation in terms of our past activities. The other elements include the sensory nature of the stimulus, the background or setting; personal feelings, attitudes, drives and goals. The outcomes of the aggregate of these elements are comparative judgements which could lead to accuracies or errors. It can be put in a way that just as the setting, previous occurrence and nature of the stimuli affect perception and results, so do the background, setting and nature of the individual affect perception.

Therefore, aside from motivation which foregrounds perception, the adjustment into a habitual repetition of experiences can lead to acquisition and development of a skill. Thus, an individual who is positively adjusted to capacity development pattern and builds a concept of success will succeed in learning a skill (**Error! Hyperlink reference not valid**).

Also, skill development can build a positive perception in the minds of the "laborers." For example, Dr. Shalini Garg, Anu Lather and Sona Vikas carried out "Study of Employee Perception Towards Training and Development (in travel agencies in India)" and concluded training leads to a higher quality of work and builds positive perception in the minds of employees who believe that because of training they have acquired further skills to perform their jobs more effectively and have a greater awareness in the industry (www.researchgate.net, January, 2013).

3.0 Stimulus and Responses

Stimulus Response theory is a concept in psychology that refers to the belief that behavior manifests as a result of the interplay between stimulus and response. Psychologists belief that a subject is presented with a stimulus, and then in response to that stimulus, produce "behavior." It is noted that behavior cannot exist without a stimulus of some sort (www.psychologistworld.behavior/stimulus-response-theory, accessed July 2021). The theory states that learning occurs through the contiguity principle of ideas or events. The theorist of stimulus and responses include Thorndike, Pavlov, Skinner, Guthrie, Hall, and Miller, among others.

"Ivan Petrovich Pavlov (1849–1936) was the first person to carry out an experimental study of conditioned reflexes" (R. A. E. Iheanacho, psychology-of-learning pg. 19, ISBN-978-2142-11-5). Pavlov's classical conditioning represents the concept of stimulus and response. Pavlov used chemical composition of animal digestive system and secretion control of neural mechanism in his discoveries. He used dogs to adopt a devised apparatus to measure his experiments. He conditioned a group of dogs to salivate when they heard sound of bell ring. This bell was an attention-giver between the dogs and food. He observed that the dogs started salivating before the food was presented to them whenever they heard the sound of the bell. The salivation is a conditioned response (CR) to the conditioned stimuli(cs) of the ringing bell.

"Stimulus response to stimulate and influence what and how trainees do things including how they learn." It also encourages trainees to learn any skill they are engaged to do with continuous incentives and support (reinforcement) and the trainers should make the introductory topics in brief.

In classical conditioning (C-C), repeated parings of the conditioned stimulus (CS) and the unconditioned stimulus (UCS) ultimately lead to acquisition. The unconditioned stimulus naturally evokes the unconditioned response (UCR). The conditioned stimulus will elicit the response after paring the conditioned stimulus with the unconditioned stimulus again and again.

Conditioned and unconditioned stimulus are repeatedly paired to create circumstance during acquisition. The response can be acquired when there is association between conditioned stimulus and unconditioned stimulus. Here, reinforcement to strengthen the association of behavior is still needed.

Factors that Influence Acquisition of Skill

1. Time: If there is too much of a delay between the presentation of the conditioned stimulus and the unconditioned stimus, the trainer might not form an association between the two. Presenting the conditioned stimulus and then quickly introduce the unconditioned stimulus so that there is an overlap between the two is the effective approach to be used. As a rule, the greater the delay between the unconditioned stimulus and conditioned stimulus, the longer acquisition of skill will take.
2. The salience of the conditioned stimulus can play an important role. If the conditioned stimulus is too subtle, the trainee may not notice it enough for it to become associated with the unconditioned stimulus, stimulus that are more noticeable usually lead to better acquisition of skill.

"For example, if you are training a dog to salivate to a sound, the acquisition will be more likely if the sound of a bell will produce a better result than a quiet tone or a neutral sound that the animal hears regularly" (www.verywellmind.com/whatisacquisition-2795219-accessed July 2021).

4.0   Learning and Thinking

Learning is a change in behavior, influenced by the environment. In our everyday living, we experience diverse things that make us to constantly react to the environment. The result of learning is characterized by the following attributes: interest, skills, habits, knowledge, among others.

Learning is defined as "any relatively permanent change in behavior that occurs as a result of practice and experience." The important elements in this definition include the following:

a. Learning is a change in behavior. It can be better or worse.
b. Learning is a change that takes place through practice or experience, but changes because of growth or maturation are not learning.
c. This change in behavior must be relatively permanent, and must last a fairly long time.

An activity learned by the individual to different types of learning. It may be complex, simple mental activities, involving various muscles, bones, etc. For example, facts, skills, habits, etc.

Types of Learning

i. **Attitude Learning:** Attitude is inborn (i.e., people are born with it). Sometimes, we develop different attitudes from early stage of life. It maybe from the people, objects and everything we know. It is a predisposition which determines and directs our behavior. Our behavior can be positive or negative depending upon our attitudes.

ii. **Discrimination Learning:** Learning to differentiate between stimuli and showing the appropriate response to these stimuli is called discrimination learning.

iii. **Verbal Learning:** This type of learning involves the language we speak, the communication devices we use, signs, symbols, pictures, sounds, figures, etc., are tools used in such activities. We use words for communication.

iv. **Learning of Principles:** Individuals learn certain principles related to science, grammar, mathematics, etc., to manage their work effectively. These principles always show the relationship between two or more concepts.

v. **Motor Learning:** Motor learning is our daily life activities. Here, the individual has to learn them to maintain his regular life. Example, walking, driving, running, climbing, etc. All these activities involve the muscular coordination.

vi. **Problem Solving:** This learning requires the use of cognitive abilities—such as thinking, reasoning, observation, generalization, imagination, etc. This is a higher order learning process. It is used to solve or overcome difficult problems an individual encountered by people.

vii. **Concept Learning:** This learning is used in recognizing, identify things. It requires higher order mental processes like reasoning, thinking, intelligence, etc. Learning concept involves two processes, viz, abstraction and generalization. The learning concepts begins from childhood.

TRIAL AND ERROR LEARNING

This theory was propounded by EL Thorndike (1974–1949). The theory stated that learning takes place through trial and error method. According to him learning is a gradual process where the individual will make attempts to learn.

According to this theory when an individual is placed in a new situation, he makes a number of random movements. The essence of this theory is-as the trial increase, the errors decrease. Among them, those which are unsuccessful are eliminated and the successful ones are fixed. Improvement takes place through repetition. Gradually, the individual learns to avoid unnecessary movements and reaches the goal.

Thorndike studies the character of trial and error learning in a number of experiments on cats-using a box which he called 'puzzle box'. In one of the experiments a hungry cat was placed in the box and the door was closed which could be opened by pressing a Latch. A fish was placed outside the box in a plate. The cat could see the fish and was given one hundred trials—ten in the morning and ten in each afternoon for five days. The cat was fed at the end of each experimental period and then was given nothing more to eat until after the next session. If succeeded in opening the door in any trial by chance, he went to eat food (fish). A complete record was made of the cat's behavior during each trial.

In the beginning the cat made a number of random movements like biting, crawling, dashing, etc., gradually, in subsequent trials the cat reduced the incorrect responses (errors), as it was in the position to manipulate the latch as soon it was put in the box.

This experiment revealed that the random movements were decreased gradually, that is as the trail increased the errors decreased. As the trials increased the solution to open the door (pressing the latch) was discovered

and at the end the cat could open the door with zero error. The time taken in each trial was eventually reduced (www.phycologydiscussion.net/learning/learning-meaning-nature-types-and-theories-of-learning1652).

Thinking can be referred to as thought that are categorized (as of a period, group or person). It is the action of using one's mind to produce thoughts (Merriam Webster Dictionary, accessed July 2021). The APA Dictionary of Psychology defines *thinking* as "cognitive behavior in which ideas, images, mental representation and other such hypothetical elements of thoughts are experienced or manipulated." Thinking is both a covert and a symbolic process that allows to form psychological associations and create models to understand the world. It is considered a covert process seeing as our thoughts, and the processes behind their formation are not directly observable. It is understood as symbolic because thinking operates using mental symbols and representation (APA Dictionary of Psychology, n.d.).

"Reasoning is that form of thinking in which the possible solutions are tried out symbolically." What differentiate us (human race) from other species (animals) is the ability to think. The three primary elements of thought are: concept, signs/symbols, and brain functions.

Concepts: These are ideas that arise in the mind when we are presented with information or objects.

Signs/Symbols: These represent objects or idea, example a red traffic signal, flags, etc., are signs/symbol that convey information to our brain.

The Brain Function: These is the organ that performs the act of thinking. Objects, language, signs, and symbols in our environment conveys signal to the brain by our sensory organs to create thoughts.

Types of Thinking

- **Perceptual or Concrete Thinking:** This is the simplest form of thinking that primarily utilities our perception-interpretation of the information absorbed by our senses-to create thoughts. For example: children play with toy, they form thoughts about the size of the toy. They cry when the toy is taken away, and forget (stop thinking) about the toy when another object is being replaced, this is because that object get their attention. Children form thoughts about objects only when the objects are presented to them. It is also known as concrete thinking because thought reflect our perception of concrete objects, exact interpretations or meaning of language rather than applying other concepts or ideas to transmit the same information.

- **Conceptual or Abstract Thinking:** This refers to an individual's ability to form thoughts about the information presented to them using complex concepts and ideas. It is a critical aspect of social interactions and communication as it allows individuals to study nonverbal cues, comprehend humor, analogies, and other symbolic representations. Abstract thinkers are able to form complex thoughts about theories, emotions, and language.

- **Reflective Thinking:** Here, learning occurs when an individual reflects upon past events/experiences and learn from them. It can be utilized when we are trying to solve complex problems. Our brain reorganizes all of our experiences pertinent to a specific situation in an attempt to relate experiences and ideas to find viable solutions to the challenges we face.

- **Critical Thinking:** This type of thinking processes requires higher cognitive skills and abilities such as reflection and reconstruction of thoughts and experiences so that we may interpret, analyze, evaluate and make inferences in a purposefully self-regulatory manner that is unbiased. It is one of the most complex thinking processes.

- **Creative Thinking:** This is one of the most important components of one's cognitive behavior because it is an entirely internal mental process. It allows individuals to interpret their surroundings in narrative ways and arrive at innovative solutions for the challenges faced by their environment. B. F. Skinner, an American psychologist defined creative thinking as the ability of an

individual to draw new, original, ingenious, and unusual inferences from and predictions about their environment.

- **Divergent and Convergent Thinking:** This is a process during which a thinker studies infinite solution to a problem, to develop an innovative answer that is a product of free-flowing, flexible cognitive process that creates connections between these infinite solutions. It involves finding solutions to problems by exploring a vast array of ideas and possibilities and encourages individuals to take creative risks that may or may not have the desired outcome.
- **Linear and Nonlinear Thinking:** This type of thinking processed information sequentially. It is useful when solving problems that require a step-by-step approach that has a clear starting and ending point. While nonlinear thinking is a type of abstract thinking that does not follow a single line progression and instead connects ideas and concepts from multiple sources to approach a problem.

The development of thinking requires that individuals be presented with adequate opportunities to participate in healthy and stimulating environments that foster creative, analytical, and critical thought.

"Thinking is fundamental to the process of problem-solving and learning. Individual's must acquire relevant knowledge and experiences in order to develop the various types of thinking discussed above" (www.sociologygroup.com/types-of-thinking/).

5.0 Problem Solving and Attitudes to Learning

Problem-solving is a mental process that involves discovering, analyzing, and solving problems. To overcome obstacles and finding lasting solution to any problem faced is the best resolves issue.

Steps in Solving Problem-Solving

a. **Identifying the Problem:** In an attempt to solve a problem, an individual should firstly, identify the problem, the causes of the problem and then find a lasting solution to the problem.
b. **Defining the Problem:** Define the problem, so that it can be solved after you have identified the problem.
c. **Forming a Strategy:** Forming a strategy depends on the kind of problem/situation and the individual's unique preferences to develop.
d. **Organizing Information:** As a problem-facer, you need to first organize the available information. What do you know about the problem? What do you not know? These questions should be asked before coming up with a solution.
e. **Allocating Resources:** Before you begin to solve a problem, you need to determine how important it is. If it is an important problem. It is probably worth allocating/channeling more resources to solving it.
f. **Monitoring Progress:** Individuals must monitor the progress of finding solution to their problems. If they are not making good progress toward reaching their goal, they have to look for new strategies by re-evaluating the approaches used.
g. **Evaluating the Results:** The evaluation is important to determine the results, after reaching the solution. This evaluation can be immediately or it can be delayed, such as evaluating the success of a therapy program after several months of treatment.

Subsequently, "it is important to remember that problem-solving in real-world situations requires a great deal of flexibility, resourcefulness, resilience, and continuous interaction with the environment" (www. verywellmind.com/what-is-problem-solving-2795485, accessed July 2021).

6.0 Motivation and Personality Adjusted

"Motivation is the process that initiates, guides, and maintains goal-oriented behaviors. It simply refers to what causes you to act, whether it is getting a glass of water to reduce thirst or reading a book to gain knowledge" (www.verywellmind.com).

"Motivation is the internal urge or external condition or need that arouses action, sustains the activity in progress and regulates the pattern of that activity in order to attain the desire goal" (Onyejiaku and Onyejiaku, 2011 p. 115).

Motivation simply means a driving force or some unspecified or extraordinary thing that drive energetically that activate behavior in an individual. It propels pattern of action of using one's mind to produce thoughts, generalized bodily consciousness and deeds.

Brophy (1998), assert that there are a number of motivational theories which includes behavior theories, goal theories, need theories, and intrinsic motivational theories.

He explains that the emphasis of the behaviorists is on reinforcement which they consider as the primary mechanism for establishing and maintaining behavior. Behaviorist set up the conscious impulse through modifying and uninterrupted succession is sustained through contingent of sufficient reinforcement.

Thus, more emphasis should be on trainee's subjective experiences rather than relying on the manipulation of trainees through the action of strengthening them. "Motivation involves the biological, emotional, social, and cognitive forces that activate behavior" (www.verywell).

Cognitive force or model of motivation include reinforcement, they accept that the act of administration of reinforcer is based on preponderance of cognitive factors. These factors comprise the relative intensity of importance the trainees attach to the reinforcer, in what degree or extent do they consider it delivery when the assigned task is concluded, trainee's optimism of terminating in success of the task, in what manner do the trainees accept that the state of having reinforced will prove the amount of duration, hard work, and previous favorable opportunities in terms of expressing a choice of courses of conduct.

Goal theorists lay emphasis on learning goals which consist the learner in learning all the necessary skill for accomplishment of a complete tasks. The act of preservation of self-perception and the method the trainee is viewed or seen as a person that is successful, instead of acquiring knowledge about the task.

Need theories were the first alternative theories to behavior reinforcement theories that emerged according to Brophy. The need theorist believes that behaviors are merely responses to felt needs that are either inborn or universal, such as self-preservation, thirst and hunger, or learned through cultural experiences, developing to different levels in different people, such as achievement, affiliation, and power. The theoretical problems with need concept, include circuitous principle, as source of perplexity of procreating diligent research investigation to assist their catalog of needs.

Abraham Maslow hierarchical needs of motivation model remained suitable or popular and influential. The displayed this model ranging from physiological needs, through safety needs, love needs, esteem needs, to needs for self-actualization, it is in ascending order of magnitude.

A Diagram showing Hierarchical Needs

(en.m.wikipedia.org/Maslow's-hierarchy-of-needs)

(Maslow's hierarchy of needs, represented as a pyramid with the more basic needs at the bottom) 1970.

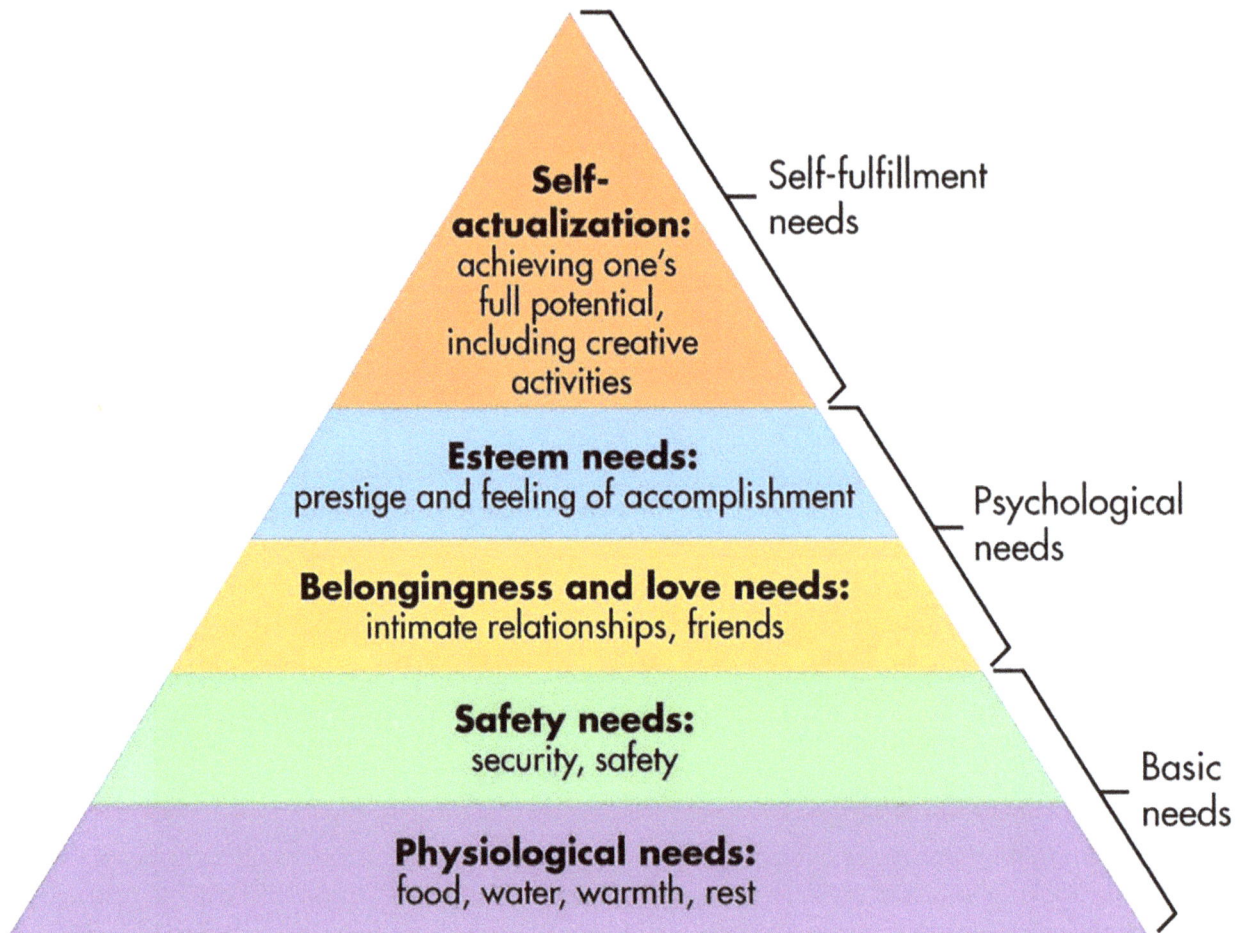

Self-actualization: achieving one's full potential, including creative activities — Self-fulfillment needs

Esteem needs: prestige and feeling of accomplishment

Belongingness and love needs: intimate relationships, friends — Psychological needs

Safety needs: security, safety

Physiological needs: food, water, warmth, rest — Basic needs

When the lower needs have been satisfied that the next need in the hierarchy surfaces to start motivating behavior. This means that, hunger, tiredness, rejection, and anxiety, amongst others, impede training, once each becomes deficient as the higher needs become inconsequential. Motives that go beyond the deficiency needs or lower need differentiate humans from animal (Maslow, 1968).

Intrinsic Motivation theories involves a move or change from replication to felt pressures to motivation that is supporting on self-determination of purposes and self-regulation of actions. Here, trainees learn because they want to do so, not because of any felt desirable. These theories involve an individual being marked by desire to investigate and learn. It calls for natural tendency or interest and satisfaction that is experienced in the act of performing it.

Different types of motivation are classified as being either extrinsic or intrinsic:

- Extrinsic motivations are those motivation that exist from independent mind (outer) of the individual and frequently envelop with recompense which includes money, social acknowledgement, among others.
- Intrinsic motivations are those motivation that exist from inwardly (i.e., in the mind of an individual).

Uses of Motivation

- It helps to guide and strengthen human behavior.
- It aids to enhance the quality of individuals as they work near the goals.
- It assists individual to act.
- It helps people handle and control their lives.
- It urges individual refrain from unwholesome behaviors.

PERSONALITY ADJUSTMENT

Personality is a set of distinctive traits and characteristics. It is the complex of characteristics that distinguishes an individual or a nation or group (Merriam Webster Dictionary, accessed July 2021).

"Personality is defined as an individual's unique pattern of thoughts, feelings, and behaviors that persists over time and across situations" (opentext.wsu.edu/motivation-claffin/chapter/module-7-personality-and-motivation, accessed July 2021).

Personality can be referred as the whole quality of an individual's character.

Adjustment, in psychology, the behavioral process by which humans and other animals maintain an equilibrium—a state of intellectual or emotional balance) among their various needs and the obstacles of their environment (www.britannica.com/science/adjustment-Psychology, accessed July 2021).

An adjustment can be an act of practicing technique to win interruption or cessation, reaching the end, gratifying motives, being free from discouragement, and persevere a state of emotional balance.

ATTRIBUTES OF AN ADJUSTED INDIVIDUAL

- Full development in thinking
- Comfortably established comprehension or understanding in relation to different people
- Not looking to others for one's opinions or guidance in determination making
- Enjoying personal freedom from a state of latent hostility appropriate to a regular course of procedure occurrence

In general, the adjustment process involves four parts:

i. A need or motive in the form of a strong persistent stimulus
ii. The thwarting or nonfulfillment of this need
iii. Varied activity, or exploratory behavior accompanied by problem solving
iv. Some response that removes or at least reduces the initiating stimulus and completes the adjustment (www.britannica.com/science/adjustment-psychology).

Personality Adjustment is described as a personal adequacy, self-fulfillment, and psychological maturity. Yet the term is one-sided, since it implies the individual's "coming to term" with society, but not his active involvement (**Error! Hyperlink reference not valid.**). When an individual acquires various kinds of habits to make effort to meet their motives, this is called adjustment mechanisms. Personality adjustment is a ranking ingredient when it involves an individual choice of career (i.e., your character traits must fit with the choice of skill you venture). For example, a person whose personality is typically gregarious and unreserved (extrovert) is more likely to flourish or succeed in a social, customer-oriented independently while a person

who tends to be quiet (introvert) succeeds not relying on others, uses analysis especially in thinking about what to be done. This can help in predicting the trainee's performance either negative or positive.

THE IMPORTANCE OF PERSONALITY ADJUSTMENT FOR SKILL ACQUISITION

- It helps to attract enlightenment and excellence of taste acquired by intellectual and personal training competence.
- It helps improve specific duty and role implementation.
- It aids in advancement of fulfil task needed.
- It fixes conclusively an individual strengths and weaknesses.

The importance of personality adjustment is not limited. This is because those with responsive and openly friendly personality will likely have a good time learning with those who exhibit the same attitude. While those who are not open and showing a desire for freedom may decide to choose a skill they can learn in petty or small team or online.

In summation, personality is a set of psychological processes which emerges from our brain, which defined as ongoing natures that crafts the characteristic patterns of interaction with individual's environment (Goldberg, 1993; Oliver and Mooradian, 2011; Parks and Guay, 2009).

7.0   Competency and Performance

Competencies is the practice of psychologists that is based on the acquisition and application of knowledge, skills and behaviors that are often conceptualized.

Within the discipline of psychology, focus has shifted from demonstrating discrete learning to acquiring competencies through psychology training programs (Kaslow, 2004; Lichtenberg *et al.*, 2013). In the applied setting, this shift has been realized via assessments of competencies that reflect real-world practices (e.g., via simulations) (Leigh *et al.*, 2007; Lichtenberg *et al.*, 2007).

Competencies have been defined as "a measurable pattern of knowledge, skill, abilities, behaviours, and other characteristics that an individual need to perform work roles or occupational functions successfully" (Rodriguez *et al.*, 2002, p. 310). Thus, competencies specify what individuals need to do and the behaviours they should undertake for certain activities, tasks or roles to perform their professional responsibilities effectively (Schippmann *et al.*, 2002). Competencies are often combinations of the knowledge, skills and abilities necessary to perform a given role (Campion *et al.*, 2011). Competencies cannot be acquired or achieved without hard work or laboriously, it has something in common while acquiring skills or undergoing skill training programs.

MODELS OF COMPETENCY

A competency model is a framework for defining the skills and knowledge requirements of an occupation. It represents a collection of the requisite skills, and the combination of these, that jointly define successful job performance (Baczyriska *et al.*, 2016). An organizational psychologist first introduced the term competency modeling in the mid-1970s (McClelland, 1973). Subsequently, organizations have been using competency-based methodologies and approaches for many years over the last 40 years, to describe the characteristics necessary for effective performance have become increasingly popular (Dai and Liang, 2012; Sliter, 2015).

Researchers and educators within psychology have proposed various competency models (Rodolfa *et al.* (2005) outlined six foundational (first dimension) and six functional (second dimension) competencies in their "competency model." A third dimension (i.e., stage of professional development) depicts foundational and functional competency development over the career of the professional psychologists. However, while the cube model offers a structural representation of competency domains within psychology, it has been criticized for failing to reflect the fluidity or the various pathways of developing the competencies (Nash and Larkin, 2012). Rodolfa *et al.* (2014) later identified a number of deficiencies in the much-cited cube model, including the general complexity of the model.

Clearly, the more that is understood about competencies, the better the profession (skill acquisition) will become at identifying, assessing, and managing incompetence (Kaslow *et al.,* 2007). Given the obvious link between competencies and assessments for both educators and regulators, it is important that a psychology competency model be established that reflects real-world practice.

PERFORMANCE

Performance is the action or process of performing a task or function. Performance is the ability to perform efficiency. It can also be referred to as the manner of reacting to stimuli (Merriam Webster Dictionary, accessed July 2021).

A skill performer can be defined as a person with the ability to achieve an intended outcome. This outcome can be done repeatedly using cognitive or physical effort. The performance achievements can be temporary or permanent.

Performance can be assessed after the completion of task depending on the type of task. Some can be assessed during practice.

The Effect of Acquisition of Skill on Performance

Before acquiring a skill, there must be development of skill and a number of variables which modern skill is created. These variables include, personal characteristics to such a degree as confidence, ability and genetics. Skill acquisition is also affected by the environment. This environment includes the type of skill itself, as well as the types of feedback provided and practice/training method chosen.

Of the utmost importance to acquiring a modern skill is feedback and evaluation/assessment in performance to identify improvements in performance and success of coaching approaches. Assessment of a skill can be objective or subjective though, and the validity or reliability of a performance measure is crucial in deciding how to respond.

How does the acquisition of skill affect performance?

These can be seen in:

i.   The stages of skill acquisition
ii. Characteristics of the learner
iii. The learning environment
iv. Assessment of skill and performance
     (www.pdhpe.net/factors-affecting-performance/how-does-the-acquisition-of-skill-affect-performance/characteristics-of-the-learner/)

The Stages Model of Skill Acquisition

There are three compulsory stages every individual must pass through. You must be enlightened by the fact that, as an individual that wants to acquire a skill, you must be conversant with the stage you are in so as to enable you speed up in your learning by months or years. These stages include

- Cognitive (early) stage
- Associative (intermediate) stage
- Autonomous (late) stage

➤ **Cognitive (Early) Stage:** This is the first stage of skill acquisition. This stage requires the trainee to be intellectually aware of what you are being trained and do. It needs total focus, working base on instructions or repetitions (i.e., the trainer do this, then the trainee do that…). This is the most difficult stage, it is a stage of confusion, where you do not really know what you are doing. It is chiefly guided by intellect rather than emotion or by experience. This stage can function in any skill with the help of a trainer or instructor.

➤ **Associate (Intermediate) Stage:** This is the stage of flexibility and pain. It is a stage of practical. Here, task are given to trainees to test or assess their performances. The trainee begins "try" and "error" "(first I did this, then this happened so maybe if I change x…)." He/she begins adjusting his/her approach based on the feedback. The trainee should begin to notice environmental feedback. This stage requires deliberate practice, and working right at the limits of your powers.

➤ **Antonomous (Late) Stage:** This is the stage of proficiency. It is the final stage of skill acquisition. Paying attention to practical works is not necessarily needed here. Effective and efficient skill can be done without having a second thought or thinking about it. This stage is characterized by danger while continuing skill acquisition.

ii. Characteristics of the Learner

The characteristics of the learner area as varied as any personal characteristics. These characteristics of a person affect their capacity to and speed at which they learn a new skill. The characteristics include personality traits, such as a willingness to learn and accept criticism. They also hereditary factors, such as your height or body type.

Confidence levels will also affect the rate at which a new skill is learnt. Other characteristics of the learner such as their prior experiences and natural ability will also affect skill learning. Examples of characteristics of the learner includes

- personality
- heredity
- confidence
- prior experience
- ability

➤ **Personality:** It is referred to the characteristic way that someone behaves, thinks and feels. These characteristic aspects of the person influence their work efforts and mentality toward skill development, which greatly influences skill acquisition.

Acquiring a skill requires hard work and dedication. Someone who is characterized by a good work, ethic and punctuality will develop a skill faster than someone who is not. If someone has

a personality that frequently has negative thoughts about skill development and personal ability, this will diminish their ability to acquire skills. However, positive self-talk and self-confidence will positively influence skill acquisition.

Willingness to try something new, dedication, determination, attitude (positive), enthusiasm, patience, and cooperation are traits within a personality that aid in the acquisition of skill.

➢ **Heredity:** Gender is heredity and affects levels of hormones, particularly testosterone, responsible for muscle growth and development. As such, males tend to be more muscular, stronger, and more powerful than females.

➢ **Confidence:** Confidence is a belief in one's own ability and positively influences skill execution will in turn increase confidence. Faster success in the easier skill will increase confidence and result in faster acquisition of the new harder skill.

Conversely, if skills are not learnt and frequent failure occurs, belief levels will decrease and the rate and level of skill acquisition will decrease with it. Also, over confidence results in poor skill acquisition.

➢ **Prior Experience:** Prior experience is the transfer of skills from one context to another. Skill transfer can be lateral or vertical. Lateral transfer is easy and is the transfer of a similar skill from one context to another. Vertical transfer is the transfer of a skill from a lower order skill to a similar higher order skill.

➢ **Ability:** It is used to describe people who are skilled in various areas. A person can have a great ability in many things. Most often the term is used to refer to the person's natural talent.

iii. The Learning Environment

The learning environment affects the acquisition of the skill. The learning environment refers to the nature of the skill and whether it is an open or closed skill, gross or fine skill, discrete, serial or continuous skill and if it is self-paced or externally paced. The nature of the skill affects how the skill should be taught and which practice/training method is best suited to the skill.

The learning environment is not so much the natural environment in which the skill is learnt, but refers to the variables around skill acquisition, many of which can be managed or adapted by the trainer to ensure the skill is acquired quickly and to a high degree.

The performance elements will also influence skill acquisition and are part of the environment in which skills are learnt. These performance elements are essentially skills themselves, but are more skills of the mind than of the physical sense. Finally, the nature of the feedback, including the speed at which it is given are part of this learning environment.

iv. Assessment of Skill and Performance

Assessment of skill and performance is very vital for monitoring progress and providing guidance for future training. Knowing the characteristics of skilled performers helps to guide the trainer in skill assessment to ensure performance is moving toward mastery of the particular skill.

Assessment of skill and performance often uses objective and subjective measures to determine how well the skill or performance was executed. However, even at the basic level, most people watch a performance with a particular bias and person expectation, which they use as criteria in judging a performance.

Finally, you are required to apply this knowledge and create your own subjective and objective performance measures, which you can evaluate. (Medium.com/self-starter/the-three-stage-model-of-skill-acquisition, accessed July 2021).

8.0   Repetition of Activities

New skills require a considerable amount of practice to learn and master (Ericsson *et al.,* 1993; Magill and Anderson, 2013).

Repetition simply means to do a particular thing over or again. Repetition can also be known as "redo." Repetition refer to implicit short-term memory phenomena that facilitate the processing of a stimulus as a result of exposure to this same stimulus in the preceding trial (Schwartz and Hashtroudi, 1991).

Several studies have investigated the short-term consequences of repeating the same action from trial to trial. Effects of the preceding trail have been shown across a diverse range of paradigms and measures of performance; reaction times are shorter on repeated trials when the time lag between the stimulus presentation and response is short (Bertelson, 1961) and when stimulus features such as color to position are repeated (Maljkovic and Nakayama, 1994, 1996; Tanaka and Shimojo, 1996).

Trial-to-Trial priming effects are present when we observe the actions of another person before performing the same action ourselves (Edward *et al.,* 2003; Griffiths and Tipper 2009; Hardwick and Edwards, 2011). Taken together, repetition on a trial-to-trial level has been shown to modulate and enhance performance in the short term.

Thus, recent work has shown beneficial effects of trial-to-trial repetition (Ariani *et al.,* 2019; Mawase *et al.,* 2018). These studies used single group, within-subject approaches; as such, they were not designed to examine whether varying the amount of repetition a participant completes during training affects their overall learning. "Notably, many training protocols involve presenting different trial types in a [pseudo] random order without controlling for the amount of trial-to-trial repetition that occurs, despite the effects of such repetition being largely unexplored. Therefore, manipulating the amount of trial-to-trial repetition that occurs when a task is learned has considerable potential as an easily implemented, purely behavioral approach to augment the learning process."

The present study investigated the effects of switching between and repeating the same response as participants learned an arbitrary visuomotor association (Hardwick *et al.,* 2019). Subsequently, any team of trainees that includes trial-to-trial techniques frequently, will experience less challenge during practical than those without repetition practice.

9.0   Peak Efficiency and Performance

Efficiency is (often measurable) ability to avoid wasting materials, energy, efforts, money, and time in doing something or in producing a desired result. Efficiency is the ability to do things well, successfully and without waste (en.m.wikipedia>wiki>Efficiency).

Part of the desire in skill acquisition and development is to scale up abilities to the point of conserving energy, materials and efforts while attaining higher results in performance. For example, an athlete at a competition will do the meterage in lesser time by putting in special capabilities that is derived from experiences during rehearsals and training.

Skill training is similar to coaching and through it, a trainer builds commitment and confidence through a relationship of trust and support to reduce the possibility of performance fluctuations.

In all situations of training and skill development, trainees and skilled performance require help to control their minds efficiently and consistently in the drive to achieve their goals. Mind control, concentration, high self-esteem and stress management are some of the psychological tools in achieving peak performance and success in skill higher accomplishments.

Improving skills and competences, trainees and performance must be encouraged with positive and reinforcing self-talk and conversations. Drawback should be de-emphasized and negative thoughts should be avoided especially in challenging moments.

Generally, peak performance is based on creating a road map to the top through measurable short, medium- and long-term outcomes that are adjustable through cognition, visuality (imagery), stable mindset, reinforced positives, and concentration.

10.0 Summary and Conclusion

This chapter proceeded from the significance of perception in training for a skill or harnessing capabilities. The gamut of the sustenance of training for a skill derives from a motivation which is based on perception. Stimuli and responses constitute the two-way interface of human psychology and physiology. Thus, the urge for success, food and life-stability can stimulate the need to learn a trade or upgrade learned skills.

Learning depends on thinking and reasoning which helps individuals to solve problems such as ignorance, indolence, lack and low performance. The drive to solve these problems can serve as a motivation which produces a behavior or personality adjustment.

Competency can be gained through a repetition of pattern activities such as using the machine to sew daily or training daily in a football pit. Therefore, efficient and repeated performances will ultimately culminate in peak performance which represents the maximum aspiration of any individual who is involved in an activity.

Skill Acquisition: Theories and Approaches

OUTLINE

1. Introduction (Dimensions of Acquisition Theory)
2. Cognitive Learning Theories
3. Theoretical Competency Theory
4. Dreyfus Model of Skill Acquisition
5. Dekeyer's Skill-Learning Theory
6. Skill Development Theory
7. Adam's Closed Looped Theory
8. Fitts and Posner's State Theory
9. A Constraints-Led Approach
10. Summary/Conclusion

1.0 Introduction

This chapter aims to describe a theoretical framework of acquiring knowledge and skills that aid the trainer and trainee in applying it on training processes.

Skill acquisition theory accounts for how people progress in learning of a variety of skills, from initial learning to advanced proficiency. Skills studied include both cognitive and psychomotor skills in domains that range from classroom learning/training to application in sports and industry. The scientific roots of skill acquisition theory are found in various branches of psychology (Dekeyser, R., 2007).

From the late 1800s to the early 1960s, research into skilled performance and skill acquisition was largely devoid of any clear direction, theory, or results. The research was mainly applied in nature and concerned motor skills almost exclusively. The focus was typically on discovering the best methods for training motor skills, where the best methods were those that enabled the fast learning and the greatest transfer to different situations and tasks (Adams, 1987).

Research on complex skills really began with the work of Bryan and Harter (1899). They trained subjects in the sending and receiving of Morse code signals and examined the learning curves of these two tasks.

Theories of skill acquisition are based on a formulated thought or opinion that require mastery or of skill in behavior in any field being inherently able or designed to become routinized and even act or done

unconsciously under fixed state of physical readiness or conditions by way of repeated paring of stimuli and responses (source ?).

Dekeyser defined "practice" as "specific activities in the second language, engaged in systematically, deliberately, with the goal of developing knowledge of and skills in the second language" (Dekeyser, 2007, p. 1).

A number of researchers, scholars and exponents have lent their voices to create theoretical formulations in guiding formal knowledge and practice directions for skill acquisition. This chapter is designed to bring up the key proponents of these bodies of knowledge as a basis of enhancing our understanding of what skill acquisition entails.

2.0   Cognitive Learning Theories

Jean Piaget was born in Switzerland in the late 1800s and was a precocious student, publishing his first scientific paper when he was just eleven years old. His early exposure to the intellectual development of children came when he worked as an assistant to Alfred Binet and Theodore Simon as they worked to standardize their famous IQ test.

He was the first psychologist to make a systematic study of cognitive development in the year (1936). He created and studied an account of how children and youth gradually become able to think logically and scientifically (i.e., a theory of child cognitive development), detailed observational studies of cognition in children, and a series of simple but ingenious tests to reveal different cognitive abilities.

The goal of this theory is to explain the mechanisms and processes by which the infant, and then the child develops into an individual who can reason and think using hypotheses.

Piaget's methods (observation and clinical interviews) are more open to based interpretation than other methods. His theory of cognitive development suggests that children move through four different stages of mental development. His theory focuses on understanding the nature of intelligence and also on understanding of how children acquire knowledge.

Stages of Cognitive Development

i.   Sensorimotor stage: From the cradle to 2 years
ii. Preoperational stage: ages 2 to 7
iii. Concrete operational stage: ages 7 to 11
iv. Formal operational stage: ages 12 and up

I. The Sensorimotor Stage (from the cradle to 2 years):

Here, major characteristics and Developmental changes occur. These could be observed when:

* The infant knows the world through their movements and sensations.
* Children learn about the world through basic actions such as sucking, grasping, looking, and listening.
* Infants learn that things continue to exist even though they cannot be seen (i.e., object permanence).

The theorist believed that the child understand that objects continue to exist even when they cannot be seen.

* They are separate beings from the people and objects around them.
* They realize that their actions can cause things to happen in the world around them.

At this earliest stage of cognitive development, infants and toddlers acquire knowledge through sensory experiences and manipulating objects. It is during this stage that children go through period of dramatic growing and learning. The cognitive development that occurs during this period takes place over a relatively short period of time and involves a great deal of growth, learning that occur during this period is that the children learn how to perform physical actions such as crawling and walking; they also learn a great deal about language from the people with whom they interact with on daily basis.

II. Preoperational Stage (2 to 7 years):

In this stage, the major characteristics and developmental changes children involve with are:

- Children begin to think symbolically and learn to use words and pictures to represent objects.
- Children at this stage tend to be egocentric and struggle to see things from the perspective of others.
- While they are getting better with language and thinking, they still tend to think about things in very concrete terms.

Children learn through pretend play but still struggle with logic and taking the point of view of other people at this developmental stage. They also often struggle with understanding the idea of constancy.

III. The Concrete Operational Stage (7 to 11 years):

The major characteristics and developmental changes include the following:

- Children beginning to think logically about concrete events.
- They begin to understand the concept of conservation; for instance, that the amount of liquid in a short, wide cup is equal to that in a tall, skinny glass.
- Their thinking becomes more logical and organized, but still very concrete.
- They begin to use inductive logic, or reasoning from specific information to a general principle.

Children in this stage begin to understand that their thoughts are unique to then and that not everyone else necessarily shares their thoughts, feelings and opinions.

IV. The Formal Operational Stage (12 and up):

Major characteristics and developmental changes include these:

- The adolescent or young adult begins to think abstractly and reason about hypothetic problems at this stage.
- Abstract thought emerges.
- Teens begin to think more about moral, philosophical, ethical, social, and political issues that require theoretical and abstract reasoning.
- They begin to use deductive logic, or reasoning from a general principle to specific information.

At this point where people involves in an increase of logical reasoning the ability to use deductive reasoning, and understanding of abstract ideas, they become capable of seeing multiple potential solutions to problems and think more scientifically about the world around them (July 2021).

COGNITIVE LEARNING THEORIES

The cognitive learning theory explains how internal and external factors influence and individual's mental processes to supplement learning.

When cognitive processes are not working regularly, delays and difficulties in learning appear. These processes are attention, observation, retrieval from long-tern memory and categorization. Cognitive learning theory can be categorize into two; namely: social cognitive theory and behavioral theory.

▪ Social Cognitive Theory

This theory helps the trainee or an individual to understand how people are influenced and their influence on the environment.

Observation learning is one of the major components of social cognitive theory. It is the process of learning other desirable and undesirable behaviors through observation.

It is the fastest way of acquiring information when a trainee individually take action. A person who demonstrates behavior for another person is known as a model. These 'mode' may be real people such as teachers/trainers, our peers, and supervisors/instructors, or symbolic models, they are also known as fictional characters that influence an observer's behavior.

Observational learning teaches people both positive and negative behaviors. For example, a manager within a company can teach the employees how they are supposed to have ethically and be socially conscious when interacting and dealing with rude customers. Moreover, the manager can also train his/her employees on the different procedures that they can take in case of fire or other low probability hazardous scenarios.

COGNITIVE LEARNING

Cognitive learning is an active style of learning that focuses on helping a trainee to learn how to maximize his/her brain's potential. It makes it easier for a trainee to connect new information with existing ideas hence deepening his/her memory and retention capacity.

Cognition is the ability of the brain's mental processes to absorb and retain information through experience, senses and thought. These are the things going on in one's brain; thinking, attention, learning, problem-solving, and perception, among others.

Components of Cognitive Learning

Traditional learning mainly focuses on memorization instead of trying to achieve mastery in a particular subject comprehension, memory and application are the fundamental aspects of cognitive learning.

a. **Comprehension:** Here, the trainee must understand the reason he or she is learning a specific skill in the first instance. This will make cognitive learning efficient and beneficial for trainees.
b. **Memory:** Here, cognitive learning discourages cramming of information, which is very ineffective in education. Once a trainee have a deep understanding of the job/skill, improves his or her ability to relate new knowledge with previous experiences or information.
c. **Application:** Cognitive learning strategies help the trainees to apply new information or skills in life situations. They encourage the trainees as they continue to develop problem-solving skills (http://www.valamis.com/documents/10197/783138/cognitive-learning-loop.png, accessed July 2021).

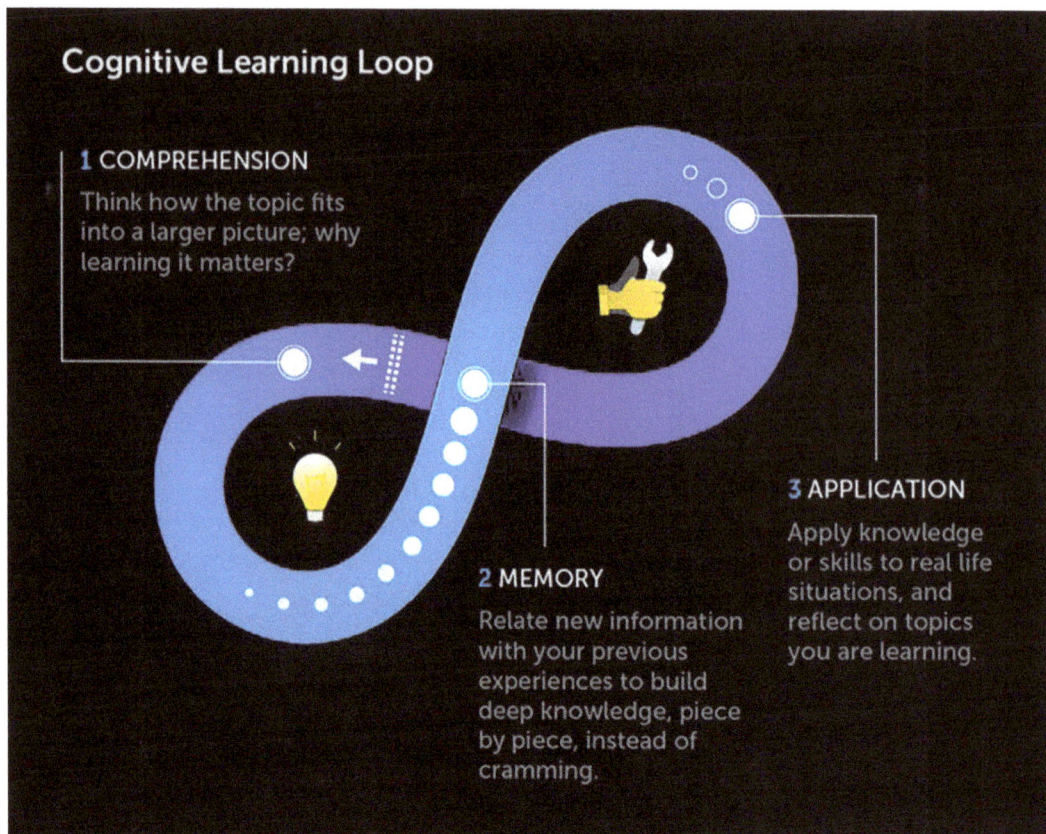

Cognitive Learning Loop

1 COMPREHENSION
Think how the topic fits into a larger picture; why learning it matters?

2 MEMORY
Relate new information with your previous experiences to build deep knowledge, piece by piece, instead of cramming.

3 APPLICATION
Apply knowledge or skills to real life situations, and reflect on topics you are learning.

▪ **Cognitive Behavioral Theory:**

This theory refers to our mental process, such as our thoughts and interpretations of life events. It explains how the thoughts, feelings, and behavior of a person interact with each other. Thoughts lead to particular emotions, which in turn lead to specific behavioral responses.

When an individual changes his or her thoughts, he or she can change his or her emotions and then his/her behaviors. It also works in reverse where changing how we behave leads to changes in our feelings and ultimately our thoughts.

For example, a developer who encounters a problem in a particular sphere and automatically believes that the task is difficult for him/her right away. The employee is automatically likely to have a negative attitude toward this particular task, and his performance will likely be poor.

Benefits of Cognitive Learning

a. **It enables learning:** Cognitive learning theory enhances lifelong learning. Trainees can build upon previous ideas/knowledge and apply new concepts to already existing knowledge.
b. **It boots confidence:** Trainees becomes more confident in approaching tasks/job as they get a deeper understanding of new topics and learn new skills.
c. **It enhances comprehension:** Cognitive learning improves trainee's comprehension of acquiring new information. They can develop a deeper understanding of new learning materials.

d. **It improves problem-solving skills:** Cognitive learning equips trainees with the skills they need to learn effectively. They are thereby able to develop problem-solving skills they can apply under challenging tasks.

e. **It helps trainees learn new things faster:** The trainees will be able to recycle and use the same training methods that worked previously, through the experience of learning. This will help them learn new things a lot, and faster as they already know what works for them when it comes to obtaining new knowledge.

f. **It teaches to form concept formation (think abstract):** Cognitive learning can also teach trainees to form a range of different concepts such as easily perceiving and interpreting information that could boost creativity and lead to innovations at the training school/classroom.

Cognitive Learning Strategies

Several psychologist came up with theories and learning strategies that can be implemented in a corporate learning environment. These strategies include learner-centered strategy, meaningful experiences strategy, learning through discovery strategy, and personalized learning strategy.

1. **Learner-Centered Strategy:** Jean Piaget posited that learning relates information to an already existing knowledge. And that each trainee/learner starts with their own knowledge and experience. According to his theories, learning begins with the accumulation of some basic knowledge and advancing deeper into the field with time Piaget suggested three vital components of learning:
   - **Accommodation:** Taking new information into account by modifying what we already know.
   - **Assimilation:** The arrangement of new knowledge inside our heads beside what we know.
   - **Equilibration:** Balancing what we already know with the new information that we are trying to acquire

Every training center should develop their training programs with a personalized learning approach to make it engaging for their trainees to achieve something better results.

How to Achieve

To achieve that L and D, professionals should focus on the following points:

a. Develop and introduce their programs based on already existing knowledge.
b. Provide more analogies to connect new knowledge with already existing knowledge.
c. Divide learning materials into stages and maintain a logical flow of lessons taught or trained.
d. Provide examples of practical tasks that show how new information or principles can connect with previous knowledge, or enhance it.
e. Encourage questions and comments from trainees.

2. **Meaning Experiences Strategy:** David Ausubel made a clear distinction between meaningful learning and role learning. According to him, material that was closely related to what the learner/trainee knew was meaningful and always turned out to be effective.

Trainees with relevant background knowledge find it easier to add new information. During the training of learners/trainees in an organization or training centers:

- There should be am emphasis on the meaningfulness of each section to the task at hand.
- Background information on new material is essential.
- New information should be instiled in trainees in a sequence to build on what is already understood.

3. **Learning Through Discovery Strategy:** Jerome Bruner is a psychologist who built his theory on top of Piaget's theory of cognitive development that was focusing on learning through discovery.

His theory identified three stages of cognitive representation which are enactive, iconic and symbolic. Enactive defining the representation of knowledge through actions, iconic being the visual summarization of images, and symbolic which is the use of words and symbols to describe experiences.

Through his study of cognitive learning in children, he suggested that they should be allowed to discover information for themselves. He believed that learners review previously learned material even as they gain new knowledge.

His interpretation of cognitive learning theory in a corporate environment can be put by:

- Allow trainees to learn new skills and get new knowledge through new tasks and challenges.
- Challenge trainees to solve real-world problems your organization faces.

4. **Personalized Learning Strategy:** A common practice in recent years create personalized learning in the use of modern technologies: AI recommendations, learning paths, machine learning, natural language processing L and D professional should try to organize a learning environment, to allow trainees to learn at their own pace, and with a variety of learning opportunities.

Creating learning experiences that fit each trainee based on their own knowledge that is meaningful for their role which encourages them to discover new solutions can drive great results and improve their overall performance. Each trainee is unique and has their own experiences, knowledge, and perception. Which can greatly influence the way they interpret and consume new information.

Examples of Cognitive Learning

1. **Explicit Learning:** This happens when an individual intentionally seek knowledge to attempt and learn a new skill or process that may be vital to his/her work. It requires an individual to be attentive and take action to acquire knowledge.
2. **Implicit Learning:** This type of learning may occur when an individual is working, talking, or going about his/her normal life. Sometimes a trainee or an individual passively gain new knowledge and learn some new skills. It is known as implicit learning, where an individual is unaware of the entire process until he/she realize that he/she have retained something new.
3. **Meaningful Learning:** This occurs when an individual is capable of acquiring new information and relating it to past experiences. This is because cognitive learning approach teaches trainees to build transferable problem-solving skills that can be applied in other areas.
4. **Discovery Learning:** This happens when an individual actively seek new knowledge by researching new concepts, processes, and subjects.
5. **Receptive Learning:** This type of learning outcomes in handy where an individual get a deeper understanding of a new information by being active and responsive to the speaker. It requires the trainee to be active by asking questions and taking down short notes.

6. **Nonassociative Learning (Habituation and Sensitization):** This type of learning enables humans to adapt to something by facing it frequently. When you get a new job at a factory where there are many machines making noise, it irritates for the first few days, but you later learn how to live with it. This is known as habituation.

   Sensitization is the vice versa whereby your reaction toward something increases as you get frequent exposure toward it. This type of learning happens in your typical situations in life and work. Working in an office teaches you to be more responsive to things like telephone calls.

7. **Emotional Learning:** Emotional learning helps people to learn how to take charge of their emotions and also understand others. Developing emotional intelligence is crucial to help an individual maintain friendly relationship with friends at work and in life.

8. **Experiential Learning:** Our experiences in life are our best lessons. An individual interactions with other people always teaches persons some precious life lessons. What an individual learn depends on how he/she interpret it.

9. **Observation Learning:** One of the significant components of the social cognitive theory is observational learning. It is handy among trainees since it mainly involves imitation of skills from colleagues and superiors. A manager at work can help an individual to improve his/her leadership qualities as he/she embrace and practice his habits.

10. **Cooperative and Collaborative Learning:** Cooperative learning helps to bring out one's best skills and deepens the collaboration between a group of people. However, for an individual to learn this way, he/she has to be an active and equal participant and interact with fellow group members.

"Some companies select individuals to train on new strategies that improve the success of an organization. The trained employees are then encouraged to pass on this knowledge to their team members."

The types of cognitive learning above are vital in using your brain's features as much as possible. They make it easier for you to acquire new skills and knowledge in life (www.valamis.com/hub/cognitive-learning, accessed July 2021).

3.0 Theoretical Competency Theory

This theory has its roots firmly in the behaviorist tradition popularized in the United States during the 1950s by educators such as Benjamin Bloom. It became popular in the U.S during the 1970s where it was used in vocational training programs. The approach spread to Europe in the 1980s and by the 1990s, it was being used in Australia to measure professional-skills. Throughout its evolution, this theory has been known by a variety of names including performance-based learning, criterion-referenced learning, and capabilities-driven instruction (Bowden, 2004).

This theory focuses on what learners/trainees can do rather than on what they know. This is because there is no conclusive evidence showing a link between knowledge about a subject or skill and the ability to use that information in context (Smith and Patterson, 1998). The basic idea is to focus on objective and observable outcomes which can be easily measured. The approach requires that trainees demonstrate value-added skills which are assessed by looking at outcomes rather than process (Bowden, 2004; Guskey, 2005).

A competency approach is a HRM systematic procedure that concentrates on the skills and mental power required to enable the trainees to perform a specific task to a certain standard.

This technique depends on applying a series of assessment tools that connect or identify not only the technical skills a trainee possesses, but his behavioral competences as well.

A competency refers to "critical work functions" or task in a defined setting (Learning Design Inc., 2011; Richards and Rogers, 2001). A set of skills and knowledge must be applied accurately for a successful completion of each specific task.

Competency is referred to as possession of sufficient knowledge or skill (Merriam-Webster Dictionary, accessed July 2021).

Components of Competencies

i. They describe the specific knowledge and skills that can be applied to complex situations: This means that the knowledge and skills must have value beyond the classroom or training centers because if a trainer trains the principles and how to learn, that knowledge acquired by the trainees will be useful for a whole lifetime.

ii. Each competency must have clear performance criteria that allow trainees to know where they are and what they need to work on to improve: Here, each task requires its own specific rubric identifying specific weaknesses and strengths.

iii. The competency must be personalized (Sturgis, 2012): poorly designed, nonexplicit criteria, and tasks will likely lead to probable failure since it would be difficult or even impossible to specify what needs to be done and to determine whether or not such competencies have been achieved.

Importance of Competency Theory to Skill Acquisition

- It makes clear implementation of skill standards.
- It develops a profession for which trainer trains and which he/she undertakes it as a permanent calling by supervising trainees to accomplish any given task.
- It helps in the assessment of trainers contrary to the competency-based approach standards.
- It makes clear the experiences acquired by trainer that trains and the state of development and identifying trainee's needs.
- It aids in the process of adding trainees or admitting fresh-trainees to a population and assessing the skills, competence, or abilities in carrying the required task and distinguishing personal character needed when admitting fresh-trainees and granting the trainer services.

Trainer's Role

The role of the trainer is to provide adequate materials, the arrangement of activities and the practice opportunities or juncture of circumstances to their trainees. The trainer is an information giver and also execute the informations' in diverse ways.

Trainers need to consecrate large quantity of time to producing activities connected to the accurate skills required to execute the competency requirements. Significant time will also be required to assess trainees and provide specific, directed and personalized feedback (Richards and Rogers, 2001).

Trainers must identify each competency and divide the parts of competencies into several parts of relevant skills. This is because the central part of training process solely depends on planning. "Modules must then be developed which allow trainees the opportunity to learn and practice whose skills." Trainers must determine exactly what and how well trainees must perform to master the competency. Trainers must develop specific rubrics, give trainees the ability to make use of each competency or approach from the origin of the lesson (Auerbach, 1986; Richards and Rogers, 2001).

The role of trainees will become apprentices. Their role will be to integrate, produce and extend knowledge. This is because they will no longer rely on the trainer and training-class to be the primary sources of information (Jones *et al.,* 1994). They will automatically become active participants in their own training and work toward being autonomous trainees. The expectations and standards are clear and precise, so trainees must learn to think critically and to adapt and transfer knowledge across a variety of settings. They have to be committed to continuing to work on each competency, mastering it, and then progressing to another level (Richards and Rogers, 2001; Sturgis, 2012).

In conclusion, trainees are rewarded only for successful completion of authentic tasks. At the beginning of every training, they should be given test determining the level of proficiency.

4.0   Dreyfus Model of Skill Acquisition

Dreyfus model of skill acquisition was developed by Stuart and Hubert Dreyfus in 1980, and it is today still a frequently used model to assess the level of experience of an individual.

The Dreyfus model of skill acquisition is a model that can be used to assess the level of development of competencies and skills of people who are learning something new (trainees).

According to the Dreyfus Model of skill acquisition, trainees learn from direct instructions and practice. The model assumes that the longer on individual practice by following rules and procedures, he or she becomes more experienced and more competent in a particular job or skill or task. When a trainee becomes more proficient, the direct rules and procedures will not be mandatory for him or her.

The Dreyfus brother's research found that one who practices a job or task will go through the following phases. These five phase include

- novice
- advanced beginner
- competent
- proficient
- expert

Dreyfus Model of Skill Acquisition Phases

  i.   Novice:

The novice phase of the Dreyfus model of skill acquisition is a preliminary stage. Here, every is new to the trainees and their chances of being creative is low. This is because they have no experience in the field (amateur).

It is expected that the trainee has no background knowledge of the skill or task which they ventured into. It is mandatory for trainees to follow direct orders, rules and procedures. This model believes that the trainee is unable to make its own decisions yet, and for this reason, the trainee must be trained and learn by following the basic orders from the trainers or instructors.

The most important part of this phase is that the trainee must obtain a thorough understanding of the context of the information that is shared.

Example: A trainee who wants to learn or to be train on how to drive a car and has never driven a car before, must first learn automobile and road theory such as speed limits, priority rules and special maneu-

vers. After acquiring this knowledge, the trainee has to practice by putting the theory into practice. However, driving on the real road is different than learning how to drive from a theory aspect.

Adequate time is needed during practice to enable the trainee to know exactly what to do in every situation. To achieve this, the trainee must first of all follow direct orders from the instructor or trainer until the trainee thoroughly understands what to do in every step during her driving period.

ii.   ADVANCED BEGINNER:

The advanced beginner phase believes that the trainee has obtained some background knowledge of the skill or task, he or she is expected to have more confident in the execution of a task that is being assigned to him or her.

This model perceive that the trainee has seen and practiced the various samples of a task. This would create an enabling opportunity for the trainee to deal with different scenarios because the trainee will recognize those from previous experiences.

According to the Dreyfus model of skill acquisition, if the trainee faces any challenges, or something goes wrong, the likelihood that the trainee will blame the high rules. This is because the trainee might believe that guiding principles or rules can be applied in every context, so the trainee might have a lower sense of reasoning and responsibility, thus, still needs the assistance of the instructor or trainee in this level.

Example: This is a follow-up phase on the previous example. As the trainee understands how to handle the wheel, he or she knows the rules, it happens that the trainee approach an intersection where the trainee has priority. However, another motorist who also approach the intersection and who has no priority takes the initiative to take priority.

Here, the trainer if forced to apply the brakes to prevent an accident. The trainee and trainer are in shock, and as a consequence, the trainee argues that the other motorist had no priority and that it is the motorist's fault.

You will agree with me that this is one of the examples of an advanced beginner because the trainee understands the rules and knows how to apply them during the driving context, the trainee must also be responsible for identifying other motorist's mistakes and anticipate on those.

iii.   COMPETENT:

According to the Dreyfus model of skill acquisition, it is expected that a trainee needs approximately 2 to 3 years before he or she becomes competent. The time needed to acquire competent performance varies the type of skill to be trained on. For instance, it might take more than three years to be a professional surgeon. But it could take a marketer these three years to learn skills, competencies and knowledge in different fields of life. The required time to have competent performance solely depends on the type of job/task.

The level of competence speed in which a trainee reaches is determined in the complexity of a task. Moreso, a trainee with a competent performance can work efficiently, must be organized, and have an understanding of what he or she is doing based on the foundation.

Trainees at this level of Dreyfus model of skill acquisition expected to be acquainted with many rules and procedures and should have sense of responsibility to proffer solutions. They should make appropriate choice in selecting rules and procedures required to solve problems. These can be difficult because some rules and procedures cannot be applied to all situations and it can be challenging when they are working under exigency.

Example: This example can be seen in a scenario where a manager of brand XY2, Mr. Steve, was offered a local opportunity by an entrepreneur to contribute to sponsoring an event that attracts thousands of vis-

itors and that might positively influence the brand on the local market. Mr. Steve got excited, but he knew that if he had to pay the sole entrepreneur directly, it would involve a lengthy legal process.

As a solution, Steve asked his PR agency to put the entrepreneur on their payroll so he could avoid the legal process and sponsor the event on short-term. He knows the rules and procedures, but he managed to proffer a solution for a short-term. In this way, he could sponsor the event, and the amount sponsored would be deducted from his PR budget.

iv. PROFICIENT:

Dreyfus model of skill acquisition posited that when a trainee is proficient in a task, he or she can effectively prioritize and fast in decisions making because the trainee has seen the critical aspects of situations.

Furthermore, a proficient trainee must understand its extent or boundaries, but the medium to manage specific circumstances occasionally remains uncertain when a trainee reaches this phase. This is because it is proficient trainee that is experienced with the task can proffer solutions when problems arises.

E.g.: An example of a nurse who is under the supervision of a gynecologist. As an expectant mother is about to be delivered of a child, the nurses in the hospital take care of the pregnant mother. However, the patient is in terrible pain and request medication for a smoother process of labor. The nurse next provides explanations of the possibilities, but they still have to consult with the gynecologist before a final decision is taken into consideration.

The illustrated example shows that the nurses knew what to do. They are proficient in the job, but before considering the final decision, they have to consult with the expert, who is the gynecologist.

v. EXPERT:

The Dreyfus model of skill acquisition expects that the trainees should use its analytical skills to assess the situation and identify which elements he or she is experienced with as an expert. The trainee does not need directions, rules, guidelines and procedures to execute a task.

Because of a broad exposure and extensive experience in the field, the expert unconsciously applies appropriate rules and guidelines to any situation if a new task occurs.

An expert is a trainee that applies personal intuition to achieve the most significant results. However, it is hard to identify an expert because they (experts) do not see themselves as experts. The find difficulties in explaining their specialties or area of specialization. They are always acknowledged by the coworkers.

An example of an experienced motorcycle mechanic: a motorcyclist bought a second-hand motorcycle a year ago. During the year, the motorcyclist did not notice anything wrong with the bike. However, after an interval of one year, he experienced some vibrations, and he thinks that the horsepower of the bike is diminished. As a consequence, the motorcyclist decides to go the motorcyclist mechanic for a checkup.

Subsequently, the motorcycle mechanic started the engine and plays with the throttle in neutral gear. He additionally smelled the motor oil reservoir and was able to tell the motorcyclist that the clutch plate is worn out and that the valves must be reset.

Here, the motorcyclist mechanic plays the expert role that is embedded in him during his years of training and his years of experiences after acquiring the training. He did not need to follow guidelines to identify the problem with the motorcycle. He could detect the challenge with the sound and the smell that comes out of the bike.

In conclusion, the model claims that the more experiences a trainee acquire in a task, the less dependent he or she can apply the rules and guidelines to execute a task.

The different states of the Dreyfus model of skill acquisition require time and practice. It is crucial for every trainee to follow direct rules and guidelines to learn a task in any type of skill or job.

The model is useful to understand the level of development of any trainee in any job. It also enables trainers to identify which elements a trainer or trainee can apply to improve to reach a higher level of competence.

After the trainee gets more experience, he or she will reach higher stages in the model such as becoming proficient or an expert. It is expected that the more experienced a trainee is, the better the person can deal and cope with unexpected events.

It is very pivotal and crucial to understand the fact that no one can be a beginner or an expert in everything. For this reason, it is best to use the model to assess a trainee's performance and how this correlates with required skills and competences of a task (Zeeman, A. [2019]. Dreyfus Model of Skill Acquisition. Retrieved [accessed July 2021] from Toolshero: https://www.toolshero.com/human-resources/reyfus-model-of-skill-acquisition).

5.0 Dekeyser's Skill-Learning Theory

Robert Dekeyser (born October 7, 1964) is a Belgian German entrepreneur and former football goal-keeper. He is also a professor of second Language Acquisition. He has publish different books. His research interests concern primarily cognitive aspects of second language acquisition.

Dekeyser's skill-learning theory claim that "the learning of a wide variety of skills shows a remarkable similarity from initial representation of knowledge through initial changes in behavior to eventual fluent, spontaneous, largely effortless, and highly skilled behavior, and that this set of phenomena can be accounted for by a set of basic principles common to the acquisition of all skill" (p. 97).

The theory includes declarative, procedural, power of learning curve, acquisition to skill-specific.

➢ Declarative:
  • "Knowledge about a skill without ever even trying to use it" (p. 98)
  • Acquired through direct instruction or observation and analysts.

➢ Automatic:
  i. "Relevant behavior is consistently displayed with complete fluency and spontaneity, rarely showing any errors" (p. 98).
  ii. Requires a large amount of practice.
  iv. Marked by decreased reaction time, error, rate, and interference from other tasks.

➢ Procedural:
  • "acting on [declarative] knowledge" (p. 98).
  • Once knowledge is proceduralized, it is accessible in a "program" (or "ready-made chunk") rather than "bits and pieces" of information.

POWER OF LEARNING CURVE

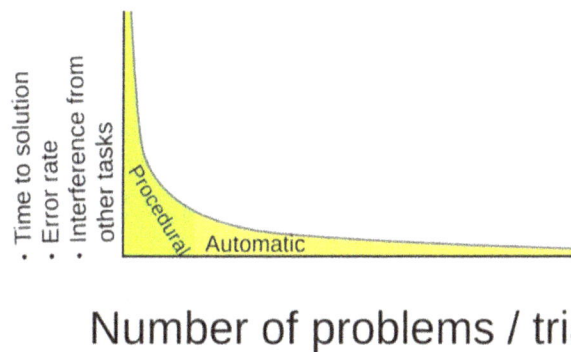

Number of problems / trials

(https://www.prezi.com/ozzgozm4igljl/dekeyser-skill-acquisition-theory1?frame=97e16f1b-8f7789a131e96b0179941, accessed July 2021)

- Time to solution
- Error rate
- Interference from other tasks
- Procedural
- Automatic

➤ Acquisition is skill-specific:
  - Knowledge at later stages of development is more specific.
  - Because knowledge becomes more specific, it does not transfer well to other tasks.

Implication for Training

Two kinds of knowledge are necessary:

a. Automatized procedural knowledge for immediate use.
b. Abstract declarative knowledge that can be used for adapting to new contexts.

Limit of Application

Primarily applies to:

"(a) High-attitude adult learners engaged in
(b) The learning of simple structures at
(c) Fairly early stages of learning in
(d) Instructional contexts." (p. 103)

Exemplary Study

Dekeyser (1997) (see Ortega pp. 85–87)

- Supported power of learning curve as a representation of fast proceduralization followed by slow automatization and underlined skill-specificity of procedural knowledge.
- Robinson (1997) suggested that "knowledge required from exposure to samples alone without a rule being available is completely memory-based and therefore limited in its generalizability."
- Indicated that the frequency of specific examples in the input does not influence the power curve (refuted Logan's theory of automaticity as retrieval of instances).

Implication for SLA

- All three stages (descriptive, procedural, automatic) are necessary, and must occur in this order, for skills to be acquired.
- Different learning outcomes occur because of:
  1. Different levels of ability to grasp declarative knowledge.
  2. Different amounts of practice of specific kinds for specific structures.
  3. Different sequencing of various kinds of explicit information, implicit input and practice.

- Although trainers may still follow predictable stages in their order of acquisition of target structures, the speed and systematicity with which they learn them should increase. (https://www.prezi.com/ozzgozm4igljl/dekeyser-skill-acquisition-theory1?frame=97e16f1b-8f7789a131e96b0179941, accessed July 2021)

Dekeyser's skill-learning theory (1998) states that to develop true fluency in an L2 proficiency, learners must have opportunities to create pragmatic meaning. Accordingly implicit knowledge arises out of explicit knowledge, when the latter is proceduralized through practice (Ellis, 2009).

Speelman and Krisne (2005, p. 26), posited that "skill acquisition is a specific form of learning. It will be sufficient to define learning as the representation of information in memory concerning some environmental or cognitive event." They see learning as an organism of storing something about its past in memory. "Skill acquisition refers to a form of prolonged learning about a family of events." Through many pairings of similar stimuli with particular responses, a person can begin to develop knowledge representations of how to respond in certain situations. These representations have some form in certain situations. These representations have some form of privileged status in memory because they can be retrieved more easily and reliably than memories of single events. Thus skill behaviors can become routinized and even automatic under some conditions.

6.0   Adam's Closed Loop Theory

This theory was proposed by J. A. Adams in 1971. It is a cognitive theory of skill acquisition which emphasizes the role played by feedback in the modification of a performer's movements. The theory has two-key neutral components: a memory trace, which selects and initiates an appropriate response; and a perceptual trace, which acts as a record of the movement made over many practices. During and after an attempt of the movement, feedback and knowledge of results enables the performer to compare the movement with the perceptual trace. The trace acts as a reference of correctness so that appropriate error adjustments can be made for subsequent attempts of the movement (https://www.oxfordreference.com/view/10.1093/oi/authority.20110803095618867, accessed August 2021).

Accordant to closed-loop theory, feedback should help people (trainees) perform tasks more effectively. In generally, feedback aid skill acquisition. Trainees acquiring new tasks who are explicitly told about their

performance usually do better-than those who are not told how well they have done. Such explicit, verbal feedback is called "knowledge of results [KR]".

Challenges with Adam's Closed-Loop Theory

1. The theory ultimately reduces to a response chaining theory. Each component of a movement is assumed to be triggered by a perceived error. Yet many movement sequences can be performed effectively when feedback is removed. Complex movements can often be performed effectively without proprioceptive, visual, or other forms of feedback.
2. The theory applies in a much more straight forward way to simple, one-dimensional movements than to more complex movements. For example, in bringing one's hand toward a glass, it is plausible that the distance between the hand and the glass is reduced between the hand and the glass is reduced over-time through an error-correction strategy. But if the task is to say "happy birthday," it is hard to see how each utterance is initiated for the sake of correcting an error. Thus, the scope of the theory is limited (Schmidt, 1988).
3. The closed-loop theory is that it predicts incorrectly that the knowledge of result a trainer receives, the more effectively he or she will perform.
   (https://www.sciencedirect.com/topics/engineering/loop-theory, accessed August 2021).

The key feature of this theory is the role of feedback.

i. Analyze the reference model actions, the result of those actions and the desired goals.
ii. Refine the reference model to produce the required actions to achieve the desired goals.

Elements of Adam's Closed-Loop Theory

This theory consists of two elements:

a. Perceptual trace: a reference model acquired through practice.
b. Memory trace: responsible for initiating the movement (Mackenzie, B., 1997; Skill Development, https://www.brianmac.co.uk/tech.htm, accessed August 2021).

A DIAGRAM FOR ILLUSTRATION

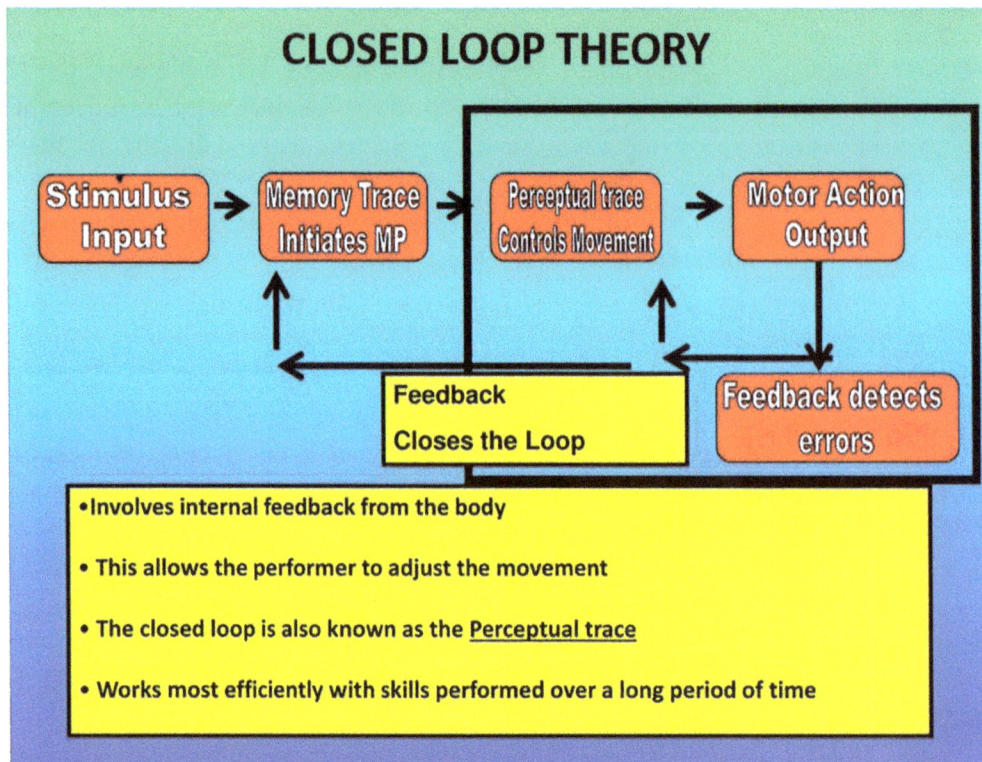

(https://slideplayer.com/slide/5812428/19/images/7/Closed+Loop+Theory+Stimulus+Input+Memory+Trace+initiatest+MP.jpy, accessed August 2021)

7.0 Fitts and Posner's Stage Theory

Fitts and Posner proposed a model of skill acquisition that centered on three stages. Fitts and Posner's (1967) model of skill acquisition as a function of the cognitive demands Working Memory (WM) placed on the leaner/trainee and his/her level of experience. Working Memory (WM) are those mechanisms or processes that are involved in the control, regulation and active maintenance of task-relevant information in the service of complex cognition, skill tasks, etc. It consists of a set of processes and mechanisms and is not a fixed "place" or "box" in the cognitive architecture. It is not a completely unitary system in the sense that it involves multiple representational codes or different subsystems. Its capacity limits reflect multiple factors and may even be an emergent property on the multiple processes and mechanisms involved. Working Memory is closely linked to LTM (Miyake and Shah, 1999, p. 450).

Performance was characterized by three sequential stages termed the cognitive, associative and autonomous stage in their now-classic theory (fig. 1B).

The cognitive stage marks the period in which the task goals are established and use to determine the appropriate sequence of actions to achieve the desired goals. Learning/training at this stage generally involves the use of explicit knowledge. The learner enters the associative stage, once the action sequence has been determined. This is to determine the appropriate subparts transitions. This stage may require some exploration of the solution space, with one segment being overhauled to ensure that the overall action is executed in a smooth and coordinated manner. The autonomous stage action is practiced to hone performance into

an automatized routine (Fitts and Posner, 1967; http://www.ncbi.nlm.nih.gov/pmc/articles/PMC4330992/, accessed August 2021).

a. **Cognitive Stage:** Schmidt and Lee (2005) posited that for the new leaner, the problem to be solved in this stage is understanding what to do. An individual must find it extremely difficult to learn a skill without receiving any prior knowledge about the skill, whether that knowledge is visual or verbal.

    The cognitive stage is of great interest to cognitivists because this stage involves information processing. It is also called the verbal-motor stage (Adams, 1971), this stage is verbal-cognitive in nature (Schmidt and Lee, 2005) because it involves the conveyance (verbal) and acquisition (cognition) of new information. In this stage, the person is trying to process information in an attempt to cognitively understand the requirements and parameters of motor movement. For example, "consider several young children taking beginning golf lessons. They might arrive early for their first golf lesson. Having never seen any golfers in action, they are excited and eager to see what golf is all about; each child is a mini tabula rasa ready to learn. They watch the preceding class of golfers and immediately begin collecting visual information. Next, the instructor explains the golf swing, beginning with the grip of the club and stance. Now they are gathering verbal information about the sport. In other words, they do not simply show up and begin golfing. Every words, begins with the acquisition and cognitive processing of newly presented information. During this stage, the beginning athlete ingests information and organizes it into some meaningful form that will ultimately lead to the creation of a motor program."

    The cognitive stage is characterized as having large gains in performance and inconsistent performance. During this stage, instruction, guidance, slow-motion drills, video analysis, augmented feedback, and other coaching techniques are highly effective (Schmidt and Lee, 2005). During the cognitive stage, it is important that the learner is provided with the necessary information, guidance and time to establish sound fundamentals of movement. Making errors and taking a constructivist approach to coaching and learning can sometimes be useful.

b. **Associative Stage:** This stage is characterized as much less verbal information, smaller gains in performance, conscious performance, adjustment making, awkward and disjointed movement, and taking a long time to complete. During this stage, the athlete works at making movement adjustments and stringing together small movement skills. This stage is also called the motor stage (Adams, 1971) because the problem to be solved in the associative stage is learning how to perform the skill (Schmidt and Lee, 2005).

    For instance, "As a trainee, a new athlete is recently transferred from another program to your program. The reason for the transfer is that he has hit a plateau. In fact, his level of performance has begun to decrease. After observing him, you realize that the reason for his lack of progress is that some of his fundamentals are badly in need of remedial work. Where do you begin with this adopted athlete with a host of bad habits? Given what you now know about motor acquisition, the best approach is to first explain that if he wants to improve his performance, he will have to make changes, and to make changes means letting go of old bad habits and learning new fundamentals by revisiting the three stages (cognitive, associative, autonomous) of motor learning. This relearning process means acquiring new information (cognitive stage) and then going through the frustrating associative stage."

c. **Autonomous Stage:** According to Fitts's and Posner's paradigm, this is the final stage of motor acquisition. It often requires years of training to arrive at the autonomous stage. But this stage is where it's at for elite athletes, where motor performance becomes largely automatic, where cogni-

tive processing demands are minimal and athletes are capable of attending to and processing other information, such as the position of defensive players, game strategy, or the form or style of movement (Schmidt and Lee, 2005) in sports such as ice-skating, dance and synchronized swimming. It is the stage where they can now respond and not think (or think minimally), where they can grip it and rip it, look and automatically react, and enter a state of flow.

Both good outcomes and bad outcomes are associated with the autonomous stage. The good is that performance requires much less attentional and cognitive demand, which thereby frees the performer to engage in secondary tasks, such as the concert pianist who is able to follow random digits or perform arithmetic while simultaneously playing the piano (Shaffer, 1980), or the quarter back who is capable of surveying the defense and detecting an eminent blitz while simultaneously calling the signals and changing the play at the line of scrimmage.

The bad is that since less cognitive demand exists during performance, it leaves ample room for irrelevant and distracting thoughts to sneak into the workshop (working memory) of the mind. Examples of this occurrence are the elite athletes at the Olympic trials who get caught thinking about making the Olympic team instead of focusing exclusively on performance during the last moments of a gymnastics routine, swimming race, or wrestling match. Think of the gymnast who puts together a stellar routine only to make a silly mistake at the end; or the swimmer who swims magnificently but does not finish the race and gets touched out at the wall, etc. This may be so because those experience used some of their available attention capacity to suddenly begin thinking about reaching the peak; the outcome rather than focusing on what got them to that part in the first place and the process.

The three stages of motor learning are summarized in the table below:

Stage	Process	Characteristics	Other name
Cognitive	Gathering information	Large gain, inconsistent performance	Verbal-motor stage
Associative	Putting actions together	Small gains, disjointed performance, conscious effort	Motor stage
Autonomous	Much time and practice	Performance seems unconscious, automatic, and smooth	Automatic stage

Fitts and Posner's (1967)
(http://www.researchgate.net/figure/Fitts-and-Posners-1967-model-of-skill-acquisition-as-a-function-of-the-cognitive_fig3_233446680, accessed July 2021).

Types of Skill

There are several different types of skills, namely,

- cognitive or intellectual skills that require thought processes
- perceptual-interpretation of presented information
- motor movement and muscle control
- perceptual motor—involve the thought, interpretation, and movement skills.

Methods of Teaching/Training

This can be achieve through

- verbal instruction
- demonstration
- video
- diagrams
- photo sequences

The learning/training of physical skills needs the important process of movements to be brought together, ingredient by ingredient, applying feedback to shape and burnish them into an uninterrupted action. A private performance of the skill must be done on a regular basis and without errors.

8.0   A Constraints-Led Approach to Skill Acquisition

A constraints led approach is a teaching/training/coaching method based on the principles of nonlinear pedagogy. It advocates a more 'hands-off' approach to teaching and learning within physical Education. Through the manipulation of certain constraints, different information is presented to the learner/trainee. The learner in turn is then challenged and channeled to find their own movement solutions to be problems faced or the goals needed to achieved. These constraints are the boundaries in which the trainees can search for those solutions.

The constraints that can be manipulated can be classified into three distinct categories, namely,

(i)   performer
(ii) environment
(iii) task constraints

➢ **Performer Constraints:** These are individual to the trainees as they are being trained. They can be physical such as somatotype, weight, height, fitness levels, muscle type or genetic make-up. Two trainees in a PE class may have a height difference over a foot. Therefore movement solutions for the two trainees maybe very different. Along with physical aspect. There are also functional. These can include affective state of a trainee can have a big impact on the learning of a trainee, especially within PE. There is also the prior skill level of the trainee on top of the physical and functional aspects, which is an important variable to take into consideration when designing an activity within a training lesson. Many of these constraints we have limited control over, but awareness of then can aid the trainers with their expectations of trainees within their various classes.

➢ **Environmental Constraints:** This is assumed to be physical in nature and are made-up of the immediate surroundings where the training/learning takes place. Things like the surface of play, light, noise, temperature or altitude. However, in a player Development Webinar, Jimmy Vaughan made the point that this could also be socio-cultural as well as physical environment. That the culture the trainers create within the classrooms or PE programs can act as a constraint in the trainees learning and development. It is influenced by other factors such as parental/guidance support, peer groups, expectations, values and cultural norms.

> ➢ **Task Constraints:** This is the easiest one for PE trainers to manipulate and therefore, probably the most important. Task constraints are rules, equipment, playing areas, goals, players, and therefore the information that is presented to the trainees.

Control over task constraints can direct trainees to acquire certain movement solutions. By manipulating task constraints as a PE trainer, an individual can direct his/her trainees to acquire specific equipment such as wider bats, shorter rackets, bigger playing balls and lighter projectiles. Changing these task constraints can allow the trainees in the classes the potential that take in to consideration their own variations in performer constraints as well as how they interact with the environmental and task constraints.

In conclusion, a constraint led approach is about situational learning for the trainees, through manipulation of constraints, ensuring lots of variability in practice when learning/training. By designing good learning environments the trainers ensure to focus less on the amount of practice and more on the quality of practice and how representative it is of the environment it is to be performed, in (https://drowninginthe-shallow.wordpress.com/2016/03/14/what-is-a-constraints-led-approach/, accessed August 2021).

9.0   Summary/Conclusion

This chapter presents an overview of theories and approaches to skill Acquisition theory. Skill acquisition is explained as a gradual transition from effortful use to more automatic use. (https://www.jbe-platform.com/content/books/9789027272225-aals.9.07ch4, accessed August 2021).

Theories need mastery of skills and execution of practiced skill during training. It requires progression, and proficiency during and at the end of training. The theories entail that learning/training can be done through physical actions. Trainees are required to increase their logical and deductive reasoning to enable them understand what they have never seen or learnt before.

Theories enhance and stipulate conceptualized information and acquire new development in training. It focuses on what an individual can do and not what he/she knows. It provides methods of applying specific knowledge and skill in a complex situation. It gives the trainers' direction in the execution of the training. It is also used to assess competency in diverse field of skills.

Typology of Skills

OUTLINE

1. Introduction
2. General and Specific Skills
3. Personal and Social skills
4. Soft and Hard Skills
5. Low and High Domain Skills
6. Digital and Manual skills
7. Check List of Skills and Careers
8. Conclusion

1.0 Introduction

This chapter introduces the attempts by researchers and writers on skill acquisition, to categories skills, careers and domains of knowledge and information that create or enhance special capabilities or growth through practical learning.

These disclosures create awareness of available opportunities for skill aspirants to make choices based on personal interests, aptitudes, and set goals. This is because people decide to acquire skills based on diverse reasons: boost ego, earn a living, climb the ladder of professional expertise and fame, get renowned in their practices or careers and attract higher pays and promotion.

This chapter also reveals that skills are not only the physical activities that people engage in but also some intangible tools such as problem solving, creativity, adaptability, and emotional intelligence, which make for employability and greater performance of the hard skills.

Another dimension of this chapter is the inclusion of a microencyclopedia of skills and careers on the one hand and the short profiles of selected skills. Our specific expose on the inclusive skill typology is also a useful guide to understanding the prerequisites for effectiveness in skill acquisition, skill development and excellence in productive work and workplace relationships.

2.0   General and Specific Skills

Skills have been categorized into general or fundamental on the one hand, and specific or applied on the other hand. The general skills are domain nonspecific while the specific skills are operative in particular domains. Both general and specific skills function as ethical realities or principles that enhance effective delivery in skills acquisition and development.

2.1 General Skills

2.1.1 Literacy

Ability to read, write and enumerate. This sub-category entails the following:

Receptive Skills	Expressive Skills
• Listening	• Speaking
• Reading	• Writing
• Creativity	• Problem solving
• Reasoning	• Interpretation
• Comprehension	• Decision making
• Thinking	• Actions

2.1.2 Socializing

This is a set of behavioral skills that proceed from personal qualities to demonstrations of convictions (experiences).

Pathos	Ethos
• History	• Citizenship
• Geography	• Science
• Language	• Communication
• Religion	• Teaching
• Cognition	• Charity
• Self-management	• Cooperation
• Empathy	• Teamwork
• Adaptability	• Responsibility
• Humility	• Conflict resolution
• Self-respect	• Mutual respect
• Organization	• Leadership
• Culture	• Negotiation
• Aspiration	• Planning

3.0   Personal and Social Skills

Personal skills are those characteristics, values, attitudes and aptitude that an individual must cultivate to be positively disposed to acquiring and developing a skill. Social skills on the other hand enhance behavioral and interactive modes at skill performance situations where a group is involved.

3.1 Personal Skills

- Self-confidence is considered a vital attitude for all aspirants to skill acquisition and development. It has to be developed first. It is the "I can do it" assertiveness.
- Reliability is another personal skill that must be inculcated in the skill performance place. It leads to dependability and dynamism. Little acts of prudence, sound judgement and integrity build up a reliable skill performance.
- Initiativeness and creativity are keys to efficiency in the skill place. These are needed skills for problem solving. A skill aspirant should be bold to initiative creative possibilities than promote skill performance.
- Orientation and concentration are also great assets to be possessed for as skills for further skill development. Orientation relates to understanding of frameworks, templates, instructions, accuracy in calculation of time and speed, etc. Concentration applies to focusing on goals, physical handling of items, memorization of information, and paying attention to relevant details.

3.2 Social Skills

- Intercultural awareness skills enable a person to understand and respect diversity of cultures and prevalent group behavioral patterns and laws to avoid distractions.
- Environmental concerns in the areas of public health, safety at work, mutual protective attitudes and respect for personal data are germane dimensions of social skills.
- Effective communication skills enable individuals to fit into teamwork, social dynamics, cooperation and group deliveries. Effective communication enhances empathy, leadership, and coordination in planning and executive with minimal conflicts.

4.0   Soft and Hard Skills

Soft skills differ from hard skills because they are transferable and universal in nature. They serve as enhancers for the acquisition, performance and development of hard skills.

While hard skills are abilities that are learnt based on structured systems like schooling, training or in-service training, soft skills help in the performance of duties and tasks associated with the hard skills.

Soft skills relate to the personnel and the work involvements while hard skills are things to do in specific jobs that can be done. Soft skills include problem solving capabilities, teamwork, creativity, persuasion, collaboration, adaptability, emotional intelligence, and other virtues that make for employability.

With adequate soft skills, hard skills such as cloud computing, analytical reasoning, affiliate marketing, video production, etc., can be done effectively and efficiently.

Selected Hard Skills
Office and Administrative

- Data entry
- Answering phones
- Billing
- Scheduling
- Microsoft office skills
- Office equipment
- Quick Books
- Shipping
- Welcoming visitors
- Sales force
- Calendar management

Sales, Retail and Customer Service Jobs

- Product knowledge
- Lead qualification
- Customer Needs Analysis
- Referral Marketing
- Contract Negotiation
- Self-motivation
- Increasing customer lifetime value
- Pos skills
- Cashier skills

Management and Project Management

- Agile
- Scrum
- Performance trading
- Financial modeling
- Ideation leadership
- Feature definition
- Forecasting
- Profit and loss
- Scope management
- Meeting facilitation
- Project life cycle management
- Managerial skills
- Organizing skills

5.0 Low and High Domain Skills

There are low and high profile skills which exist in the professional domains. While the low skills fall majorly under domestic skills, most high skills demand formal training and intellectual impartation in classroom situations with mandatory practical exposures.

5.1 Features of High Skills

- Data and information collation, extracting, evaluation, synthesis, analysis, assessing, transformation, management, and development.
- Professionalism in use of technological applications, facilities, tools, machines equipment and materials.
- Supervision, management and maintenance of equipment and outcomes.
- Commitment to excellence in services and products.
- Efficiency in management of human and financial resources.
- Teaching, guiding, and supporting subordinates to acquire good levels of skills.

5.2 Selected Low Skills

We have adopted verbatim here, the descriptions of selected low skills which Nwokike, F. (2021) has tagged "Top Profitable Skills to Acquire that can sustain you without a job after school." A preview of these skills discloses the fact that they do not demand high skills obtainable via and university degrees. They are cross-sectoral in nature and anybody with the right aptitude can acquire them for subsistent sustenance.

Selected Low Domain Skills: A Nigerian Perspective

1. **Fashion Design**
    The fashion industry does not know the meaning of recession. This industry grows yearly and as well the profit margins. If you are creative and the trendy type, you will make it in this industry. Also, in Africa, we are good at organizing/attending occasions in uniform and there is no week in Nigeria that people are not celebrating or mourning. When you are good at designing or sewing, you will be overwhelmed with job orders. A friend once said that if you can survive the disappointment of a Nigerian tailor, you can survive any disappointment. What this implies is that they hardly keep up with delivery date; this could be out of too much job order or just another lazy tailor (many of them are). So if you are good, creative, and keep up with the latest design in vogue as well as keep to time, then this industry is definitely a go for you.

2. **Makeup/Manicure/Pedicure**
    This is another industry that is profitable and does not require a degree to startup. All you need is acquire the skills, be good with color and know how to pamper your customers and I bet you will never lack money if you are good at it. Many students, male and female alike are already in this niche. On a weekly basis, most females, professionals, and students wear new nails. They pamper their face to look good especially during ceremonies. It is worthy to note that males in this industry make it faster than their female counterparts it they know the skill very well, want to know the reasons? Male touch up is definitely irresistible to most female clients who love to be pampered at all times.

3. **Hair Dressing/Barbing**
    Looking good is good business that every individual loves. Men always cut their hair to look smart and tidy, while the women folks dress their hair to look gorgeous. Many individuals cut/dress their hair on a weekly basis. If you can learn how to cut or dress men or ladies' hair respectively, you can earn a steady income for yourself. This remains one of the most profitable and lucrative businesses that also do not require huge capital depending on how you want to start and location. I have an idea for people that wish to venture into this business. Because of viability of the business, almost every street corner has a hairdressing salon or barbing shop. Once you acquire this skill, try to engage your customers in conversation while cutting their hair, this has been proven to bring repeat customers. Also location matters, you should look for a corner without a barber's shop to set up yours or looking for developing areas to start.

4. **Photography**
    During my days in higher institutions, I was not the picture type but every day I pass the picture stands, the traffic flow remains intimidating. People love keeping memories and the best way to do this is through picture documenting. Go to ceremonies, eateries, school, and even funerals,

etc., photography abound, both invited and uninvited. To get ahead in the photography business, you need to understand the art of digital photography, be creative, canvass your client's work and give them great designs that will keep them coming back to you or referring you to their family and friends. Some photo studios will also engage you to just take pictures and get paid. Also, be up to date with new technologies to spice up your work and keep you ahead of your game.

5. **Web Design**

Web designing remains very lucrative and businesses now understand the need to showcase their products/services online. Acquiring this skill and being creative with your design can put food on your table. Once you learn how to design a website, go out there, make your research and look out for small businesses that are yet to have online presence, offer them an opportunity to have their business online at a limited cost, do a great job, have a professional website about your business and link back to your site indicating you designed the site, do this for few other businesses and showcase your works in your site, if you are good and have lovely designs, you will start getting job orders that can be paying your bills.

6. **Graphic Design**

This is another profitable skill that can sustain an individual if he or she is good at it. Most acclaimed graphic designers even with the help of available software do messy jobs. Acquire this skill and you may not wish to work for anyone in your lifetime. Graphic designers are good at telling stories in images and texts. The best of comics are created by graphic designers. This skill can easily be outsourced and on a daily basis, novelists, writers, columnists, bloggers, magazines require the services of graphic designers to better buttress their stories.

7. **Banking**

If you learn how to bake cake, make chin-chin, meat-pie, fish-rolls, etc., you could be earning a small but steady income to sustain you during and after school. But if you are very good at those, why not, you could work for big eateries and hotels that are willing to pay for your services. This business is stressful but if you are good at it, you could generate a moderate income that can sustain you. You could bake for your friends during their parties, and if your work is good, they could recommend you to their family and friends during their wedding and big ceremonies. You can also be baking chin-chin and pies to supply supermarkets, stores and school canteens on a daily basis.

8. **Cobbler/Bag Maker**

Making foot wares and bags can be very profitable. Africans love wearing matching outfits, some fashionists could design/create foot wares to match with your outfit using your clothing material. You could learn this skill while in school and be making shoes and bags for your fellow students and friends. If you are creative and have interest in designing shoes and bags, you should consider acquiring this skill.

9. **Driving**

Yes, you can drive for cash. Taxi industry is booming according to statistics by UBER. You can raise money and get a car that you could use for part-time taxi business. You could also register with taxi companies or have a relation/friend get you a car as a loan and I bet you, before 6 months, if you are diligent, you would have paid back. From a little unofficial personal survey I conducted in FCT, Abuja, and Enugu in Nigeria, taxis in Enugu makes an average of N4000 to N7000 daily

JACOB B. OROKS MISM, PMP, CISM, CTS

while their counterparts in Abuja make even higher. A taxi man I met in Abuja who was formerly an automobile mechanic told me that he didn't know how profitable the business was until one of his customers paid him N4,000 to please take him to the airport and on his way back, he got another passenger to town. He said he drove town for roughly 2 hours and spent a total of 3 hours driving that day but made N9,000 after all expenses. He is now a full-time taxi driver. If your car is still very neat and in good shape, you could also register as an Airport taxi and that is more money.

10. **Cable TV Installer**

This is another profitable skill that will cost you almost nothing to learn if you love Engineering or like playing with electronic tools. You can do this business on the side while you do other things. Cable TV Installation is not so hard to learn and you could meet with Satellite Cable companies or their distributors and ask them to refer you to mount cable for new customers, this way you do not only install it that once but big changes are you will be maintaining it.

11. **Blogging**

This remains a profitable business if done right. Some bloggers make as much as a six-figure income monthly, others make less or more. When you are knowledgeable enough in a particular niche, that you alone can decide what your earning potential could be. But for you to monetize well, you need to register your own domain name and host your own blog, that way, you will be limitless with options to monetize with, either through affiliate marketing, ad networks, or sale of e-materials.

6.0 Digital and Manual Skills

The invention of electronic gadgets and application of mathematical index in solving problems have resulted into two classes of schools viz the skills that demand live hands-on operations and the button-pressing skills. The difference between these two categories is palpable in the error-prone results of the former and the precision achievable with the later (though computation is said to be garbage in, garbage out). Also both categories of skills still demand human interventions and motor index for performance. However, the difference in the use of machines in the manual skill is the fact that while such machines are used to produce results the digital machines are largely automated.

Manual Skills	**Digital Skills**
• Fashion designing	• Video editing
• Auto repairs	• Sound editing
• Painting	• Graphics design
• Tiling	• Photoshop
• POP installation	• Web design
• Hardware engineering	• Software development
• Catering	• Cyber security
• Script writing	• Networking
• Tailoring	• Microsoft office
• Plumbing	• Database management
• Welding	• Auto card

- Block molding
- Carpentry
- Photography
- Auto repairs
- Hairdressing
- Electrification
- Masonry

- Content development
- Excel
- Telecommunication
- Teleconference
- Page making
- Cartooning

7.0   8 Checklists of Careers and Skills

- Fishing
- Forestry
- Horticulture
- Lang control
- Land reclamation
- Building crafts and trades
- Technical grades
- Other staff
- Supplies
- The mining industry
- Oil and natural gas
- Quarries
- The Army
- The Royal Air Force
- The Royal Marines
- The Royal Navy
- Government departments
- The structure
- The brick, fireclay and refractory goods
- Pottery manufacture
- Cement
- The pharmaceutical industry
- Coal production
- The electricity supply industry
- The gas industry
- The oil industry
- The banking industry
- The brewing industry
- The dairy industry
- Fish
- Meat processing
- The tea and coffee trades
- Wines and spirits
- Britain's steel industry
- The foundry industry

- Paper making
- The printing industry
- The textile industry
- The aerospace industry
- The motor industry
- Other, smaller industries
- Teaching
- Ancillary and clerical staff
- Courts
- Legal executives
- Other occupations
- The Christian churches
- Christian missionary work overseas
- The Jewish community
- Computing
- Operational research
- Patent agents and officers
- Work study
- Community work
- Medical social workers
- Probation officers
- Psychiatric social workers
- Voluntary agencies
- Youth workers
- Education and training
- Demand for social workers
- Interpreting
- Translating
- Food preparation and cooking
- Food service
- Front office and reception
- Housekeepers
- Licensed trade
- Toastmasters
- Uniformed staff

- Beauty care, culture or therapy
- Children's nurses
- Hairdressing
- Laundry and dry cleaners
- The fire services
- The police
- The prison service
- Private security operations
- The telecommunications service
- The postal services
- Air travel
- Railways
- Road transport
- Travel agencies and tour operators
- Lifelong careers
- Archaeology
- Art
- Classics
- English
- History
- Drama
- Languages
- Music
- Philosophy
- Regional studies
- Religious studies and theology
- Aeronautical engineering
- Agricultural engineering
- Automobile engineering
- Biomedical engineering
- Chemical engineering
- Civil and structural engineering
- Control and measurement engineering
- Electrical and electronic engineering
- Environmental engineering
- Fuel and gas engineering
- Heating, air conditioning and ventilating engineering
- Marine engineering
- Mechanical engineering
- Metal working, foundry and welding engineering
- Mining and mineral engineering
- Municipal engineering
- Naval architecture, marine engineering and shipbuilding

- Nuclear engineering
- Production engineering
- Public health engineering
- Structural engineering
- Water engineering
- Welding engineering
- Building technology
- Ceramics
- Draughtsmanship
- Ergonomics
- Food science and technology
- Glass technology
- Industrial design
- Leather and leather goods technology
- Maritime studies
- Materials science and technology
- Nautical science
- Plastics, polymer and technology
- Printing and paper technology
- Textile technology
- Architecture
- Building technology
- Earth and environmental sciences
- Estate management and agency
- Geography
- Geology
- Landscape architecture
- Planning
- Surveying
- Astronomy
- Applied sciences
- Atomic research
- Bacteriology
- Biochemistry
- Biological sciences and biology
- Botany
- Chemistry
- Computer science
- Earth sciences
- Geology and earth sciences
- Genetics
- Mathematics
- Medical sciences
- Meteorology
- Microbiology
- Oceanography

- Ophthalmic optics
- Pharmacology and pharmacy
- Physics
- Physiology
- Statistics
- Veterinary science
- Zoology
- Accountancy
- Anthropology
- Applied social sciences
- Business and management studies
- Economics
- Education
- Law
- Librarianship and information science
- Politics
- Psychology
- Sociology
- Accountancy
- Company secretaries
- Legal services
- Management consultancy
- Personal management
- Secretarial, office and clerical work
- Advertising
- Market research
- Public relations
- Accountancy
- Banking
- Building societies
- Insurance
- Other financial institutions
- Buying, purchasing and supply
- Retailing and distribution
- Selling
- Trading in trade
- Wholesaling and warehousing
- Architecture
- Design
- Graphic design
- Fine art
- Photography
- Broadcasting
- Film industry
- Archive work
- Library and information work
- Museum work
- Acting
- Dancing
- Light entertainment
- Modeling
- The newspaper industry
- Periodical publishing
- Publishing books
- Writing
- Cricket
- Football
- Golf
- Horse racing
- Other sports
- Coaching, instructing and learning
- Gamekeepers
- Work with animals

8.0   Conclusion

The purpose of this chapter, to provide an array and characterization of diverse skills under appropriate categories, has been achieved. The necessary awareness through typologies has been created.

Aspirants of skill acquisition and development have a wide range of choices with knowledge of the implications for their preferences. This typology has thrown up the skills that are prerequisites to other skills. For example, personal, soft, and social skills are sine qua non for performance in specific and hard skills.

The differentiation between digital and manual skills also means people without digital skills in this age stand at a great disadvantage and may be required to acquire such digital skills for capacity to engage other levels of skills acquisition and development.

Stages of Skills Acquisition

OUTLINE

1.0   Introduction
2.0   The Kaufman's Three Stages
2.1   Ten Principles of Speedy Skill Acquisition
3.0   The Pretraining, Training, and Post-Training Stages
4.0   Three Dimensions of Skill Acquisition Module: The Theorization, Practice, and Assessment Stages
5.0   The 4-Stage Pattern
6.0   Conclusion

1.0   Introduction

Stages of skill acquisition sit along a continuum of skill learning. Since learning comes in stages, this chapter introduces the step-by-step learning from an enthusiasm stage to proficiency stage and how to learn different skills with speed.

This chapter also explains pretraining as an aspect of training that trainees should pay more attention to or focus on. It serves as motivation or primes trainees for an optimized training experience. It makes the trainer to understand that trainees had prerequisite knowledge before choosing a particular skill.

Training is another important aspect of skill acquisition stages and it is the first step toward perfection, which provides adequate help for both trainers and trainees post-training on the other hand explains assessment, certification, licensing, start-off, and establishment of skill practice that would assist the reader to function well in the society.

Dimensions of skill acquisition module explain key points of skill acquisition. The 4-stage pattern sort solutions to problems faced by trainers and trainees.

2.0   The Kaufman's Four Stages

Josh Kaufman is the author of books on business, entrepreneurship, skill acquisition, productivity, creativity, applied psychology, and practical wisdom. Kaufman shares how he learns anything from scratch. He opined that there are four elements for rapid skill acquisition.

How to Learn Anything from Scratch

1. **Deconstruct the Skill:**

   The driving force for the novice to acquire a new skill is often to accomplish a specific task: "This task could be to play a specific song or to learn enough calculus to finish the assigned math homework."

   Deconstructing a skill into smaller particles or bundles allows trainee to adjust for distinct understanding on what would help him/her achieve the desired outcome. Focus on the desirable and leave the left-over or others for another day.

   The learning curve is set up in such a way that novice or beginners can derive gains quickly at the start. To take advantage of this, it is advisable for an individual to study and understand the core principles behind the specific skill. Exploit it by knowing/understanding the 80/20.

2. **Spend the Actual 20 Hours:**

   20 hours is very achievable. Josh Kaufman posited that major barrier to skill acquisition is emotion and not intellectual. He stated that starting is often the hardest part. There will be resistance, no matter how simple something can appear to be. There are all sorts of reasons an individual can give to his/her self when he/she begin to learn any skill. Majority will quit before they even really begin.

   This period is known as a "frustration period," when an individual first start out. This is because he/she is unrefined incompetent or unsuitable for a particular purpose. The trainee would feel stupid.

   No one individual wants to feel stupid, or wants to feel scared. It does not feel tendency. But all of this occurs when an individual begin to acquiring any skill. It happens to every individual while trying to do something new.

3. **Learn Enough to Self-Correct:**

   Here, Kaufman explains that all the trainee really need is enough information to self-correct. This simply means that he/she needs the ability to recognize his/her own errors, mistakes and then make adjustments when this inevitably occurs. Mistake free can become part of the trainee over time.

   It is crazy to know that learning/training has become a new form of putting off intentionally and habitually: The act of acquiring information becomes more initials than the actual act of mastery. Every individual believe that they must know all that is involve in the skill they are about to learn before they begin, lest they make mistakes or be inefficient in their learning. When a trainee makes a mistake, it is advisable for him/her to rise and repeat, and he/she will eventually get to his/her desired level of proficiency.

4. **Remove Practice Barriers:**

   This is a simple idea but difficult to practice. Will power is not to be trusted, it ebbs and flows, giving individuals inspiration at one moment and leaving them at the next. Plenty excuses occur when it comes to getting work done.

   Focusing on mastering our behavior is a bad idea. Instead, focus on improving their environment and making it conducive for practice would be better. It is better also to remove the distractions that prevent them from focusing and practice. An individual will come up with all sorts of excuses to remain comfortable. But do not give up that opportunity, press on (https://louischew.medium.com/josh-kaufman-how-to-learn-anything-from-scratch-cb53d70c36ec, accessed August 2021).

2.1 Ten Principles of Speedy Skill Acquisition

Here are the ten principles of rapid skill acquisition:

- Select freely and consider an adorable scheme.
- Direct your attention and capacity of being active on a particular skill at a suitable moment.
- Identify your goal efficiency or competence level.
- Examine and separate the skill into a skill that is part of and necessary to other more complex skills.
- Acquire sufficient machines.
- Remove something that impedes progress to perform the necessary task.
- Construct devoted duration to perform or train by repeated exercises.
- Produce conducive transmission of evaluation loops.
- Perform near the time clock briefly to spring suddenly.
- Stress on the estimated amount and move swiftly.

Select a particular skill you desire to learn or procure, apply all your spare attention and strength into gaining that skill and position the former skills on temporary hold.

3.0   The Pretraining, Training, and Post Training Stages

Pretraining is an engagement technique the teacher or instructor put in to motivate would-be professionals or learners for an upcoming training course. It is what encourages the learners or trainees to optimize learning experience. Before we discuss the stages of pretraining, let us know the principles of pretraining.

Pretraining principle according to (Mayer, 2005a; Mayer and Moreno, 2003) is an instructional principle proposing that learners learn more deeply when they are made aware of the names and behaviors of main concepts in the lesson before they are presented with the main lesson itself.

The Importance of Pretraining

Pretraining gets trainees excited and wants to learn more when they absorb the behaviors of main concept or most of what they would learn. Trainees are going to understand everything about the skills they are going to learn. These are approaches to pretraining concept.

Approaches to Pretraining Concept:

Aptitude test, orientation, career choice, influence, interest, sponsorship, identification of objectives, and evaluation.

   i.   **Aptitude Test:** This is a type of test given to an individual to access that he have skill competency to succeed in any given training he undergoes. It is a test to assume an individual strengths and weaknesses using the innate capability in some specific areas or a particular skill.

It is used to examine one's knowledge and how they are likely to react or perform in an area of skill acquisition which they have no knowledge of the skill. It also determines the kinds of careers that are best for the trainees' interests.

90

ii. **Orientation:** "This measures the tendency or habit of seeking to increase one's knowledge and skills; toward valuing the learning process as a means to accomplish mastery over a task; toward being interested in challenging activities; and toward using information seeking as a personal strategy when problem solving."

iii. **Career Choice:** Before choosing the right career, an individual must assess his/her self, make lists of different kinds of skills on the list by creating a short list, conduct survey informational interviews by meeting with people who are already engaged in that skill, make your career choice from the most satisfying information gathered, identify your goals-either long-term or short-term goals (long-term goals takes about three to five years to be proficient, while a short-term goal takes about six months to three years), state a career action plan by writing down the steps to be taken before reaching your goals.

iv. **Influence:** Is an act of having an effect on the development of pretraining. The dynamics of change on trainees can influence pretraining in organization level (trainees may be motivated to participate in pretraining when they see it as mandatory or compulsion corroborated by training management), in team/social level (designing features to build positively or negatively influence on trainee's motivation for their pretraining). Supervisors/trainers can positively influence pretraining by providing interpersonal support to trainees during pretraining.

v.   **Interest:** This is something an individual prefers or likes to do. It can also be seen in this context of skill acquisition as something or a particular skill/task that a trainee prefers to learn. It is what an individual has determine to expend his/her energy to do in his/her spare time that will be valued-added for life-long. For example, trainee A may have interest in fashion and designing, trainee 'B' may have interest in cake baking, etc., interest varies depending on what each trainee would like to learn.

vi. **Sponsorship:** A systematic pretraining activities can be achieved with the assistance of sponsoring organizations. Sponsoring organizations like the NGOs, government and private establishments undertake a number of pretraining activities before the regular training program commences. Some of these activities include funding, scrutinizing proposals, promotion of skill acquisition in terms of the location of the program, target group, etc., among others.

vii. **Identification of Objectives:** According to https://www.ncbi.nlm.nih.gov/pmc/articles/pmc5024935/ (accessed August 2021), learning objective is a written statement outlining the goal the trainer wishes the trainees to achieve. It usually comes in verb form and focus on one of three areas; knowledge, skills and professional practice attitudes. It must be measurable and be SMART (i.e., learning objective should be specific [S], it should be measurable [M] as it quantifies the goal; achievable, it must have the ability to be accomplished [A], realistic [R] as the resources to achieve the goal are available and achieved in an appropriate time frame [T]. The SMART tutor skill is aided by the use of educational tools to assist the writing process. Bloom's taxonomy is one of the useful tools to aid develop written learning objectives.

viii. **Evaluation:** It is crucial to focus on how effective the pretrainings are at improving trainee's task performance. Evaluation can be achieved by identifying what trainees need for their task, craft learning objectives that will suit with the task requirements, assessing trainee's performance during and after pretraining and evaluating the trainee's effort after completion of task.

Pretraining Phase

Pretraining phase refers to the activities and preparatory work made before the actual conduct of training. Actual preparation is made to introducing program in this phase. It involves the following activities:

i.   The choice of geographical region or area.
ii.   Selection of career coordinator.
iii. Arrangement of resources or infrastructure.
iv.   Conducting the market survey to identify good business opportunities.
v.   Develop the program which includes training program organization, trainer selection and training syllabus finalization, etc.
vi.   Getting support from various agencies such as NGOs, private fames and government establishment, etc. (https://www.ecoursesonline.iasri.res.in/mod/page/view.php?id=49598, accessed August 2021).

Recommended Approaches or Techniques to Apply During Pretraining

All techniques need to be tested, as they vary based on the trainees, the trainer is about to train and the application of the knowledge or information. These approaches are stated below:

- **Incentives:** A certificate of completion should be offered to the trainee as a reward of participating in the pretraining program to enhance the trainee's carrier.
- **Surveys:** Let the trainees understand that you are thinking about them as a trainer, weighing their thoughts and opinions, and making them feel a part of the pretraining experiences by giving trainees a survey. Pretraining survey is a great way to make trainees feel like they are being given more options, or are parts of decision making.
- **Skills and Knowledge Assessments:** Present-questions to find out what trainees already understand about the topics to be taught in an upcoming training (tests on previous knowledge). This will motivate the low-scorer to be anxious to learn more and the good-scorer will feel proud.
- **Training Preferences Assessment:** Conducting a training preferences assessment with the trainees will create self-examination of thoughts and feelings as well as remind trainees which aspect of the training they may need to focus more on (written, audio, visual). This can also provide adequate information on which aspects of the course the trainee should improve on. It is also applicable to the trainers, trainers can have good idea to reformat their text documents into videos, etc. if he/she was training mostly virtual group of trainees. (https://www.shiftelearning.com/blog/the-importance-of-pretraining-engagement-Accessed August, 2021).

Benefits of Pretraining

a.   **Focused Training:** Here, the trainee will develop a more positive attitude toward his/her training requirements. When the trainees are provided with a personal learning direction, they develop a greater trust for the skill program and become more serious.
b.   **Foundation of Previous Knowledge:** The foundation of previous knowledge makes it easier on the trainer who can train a more intellectually homogeneous people. Pretraining makes the trainers to and provides them with the foundation that they need to be successful. "Knowledge is associative, and it is easier to learn new information when trainees link knowledge to their previous knowledge.

c. **Priming Increases Retention:** Priming refers to a general memory phenomenon which exposes an individual to stimulus influences and response to another stimulus. Pretraining can 'prime' the trainee and make it more likely that he/she will retain information. Priming, in the context of training refers to events that make an individual more likely to learn and retain essential information (https://www.learningsolutionsmag.com/articles/1570/brain-science-pre-training-is-essential-to-a-complete-training-package, accessed August 2021).

Subsequently, pretraining enables the trainees to have the prerequisite knowledge when the first walk in the door of training. It also saves funding from organization when applying it in a working environment. It helps the trainees to develop a more positive attitude toward their training requirements.

Training

Training is an action or process of developing or teaching and learning a person on a particular skill for the purpose of being useful for a job and applying the knowledge, skills when needed (pg. 49). Dale S. Beach defines training as "the organized procedure by which people learn knowledge or skill for a definite purpose." It can also be referred to as the teaching and learning activities carried on for the primary purpose of helping members of an organization acquire and apply the knowledge, skills, abilities, and attitudes needed by a particular job and organization. Edwin Flippo sees 'training as the act of increasing the skills of an employee for doing a particular job'.

Importance of Training

1. Training gives a lot of benefits to the employees/trainees such as improvement in efficiency and effectiveness, development of self-confidence and assists everyone in self-management.
2. Training of employees and managers is absolutely essential in this changing environment because it helps in improving trainee's and employee's competency.
3. It improves the quality and reduces the wastages to the minimum.
4. Training and development is very essential to adapt because of changing environment because the stability and progress of the organization solely depends on the training imparted to the employees. It becomes mandatory under every step of expansion and diversification.

Types of Training

Different types of training can be given to the employees/trainees which include induction, training, refresher training, job instruction training, vestibule training, and apprenticeship training.

- **Induction Training:** This type of training is given to the new recruits to make them familiarize with the internal environment of an organization. It helps the employees to understand the procedures, code of conduct, and policies existing in that organization. It is also known as orientation training.
- **Refresher Training:** This type of training is offered to incorporate the latest development in a particular field. This training is imparted to upgrade the skills of employees. It can also be used for promoting an employee.
- **Job Instruction Training:** This training provides an overview about the job and experienced trainers demonstrates the entire job. Addition training is offered to employees after evaluating their performance if necessary.

- **Vestibule Training:** It is the training on actual work to be done by an employee but conducted away from the place of work.
- **Apprenticeship Training:** Apprentice is a worker who spends a prescribed period of time under a supervisor.

```
                    ┌─────────────────────┐
                    │  Methods of Training │
                    └─────────────────────┘
```

On-the-job Training Methods	Off-the-job Training Methods
1. Job Rotation 2. Coaching 3. Job Instruction 4. Committee Assignments 5. Internship training	1. Case Study Method 2. Incident Method 3. Role Play 4. In Basket Method 5. Business Games 6. Grid Training 7. Lectures 8. Simulation 9. Management Education 10. Conferences

Reasons/Need for Training

Specific need for training arises because of the following reasons:

a. **Environmental Changes:** The organization should train the employees to enrich them with the latest technology and knowledge. An individual should also acquire training because of these facts. Mechanization, automation and computerization have resulted in many changes that require an individual or trained staff to possess enough skills to function in today's world.

b. **Employees Specifications to meet with the Job Requirements and Organizational Needs:** An employee's specification may not exactly suit to the requirements of the job and the organization, irrespective of past experience and skills. There is always a gap between an employee's present specifications and the organization's requirements. Training is required for filling this gap.

c. **Humans Relations:** Every management has to maintain very good human relations, and this has made training as one of the basic conditions to deal with human problems.

d. **Change in the Job Assignment:** Training is required to equip the old employees with new techniques and technologies. Training is also necessary when the existing employee is promoted to the higher level or transferred to another department.

e. **Organizational Complexity:** With modern inventions, technological upgradation, a diversification most of the organizations have become very complex. This has aggravated the problems of coordination. So to cope with complexities, training has become mandatory (www.yourarticlelibrary.com/human-resource-development/training-meaning-definition-and-types-of-training/32374, accessed August 2021).

Ten Principles of Effective Training

a. Investigate the skill and discoverable relation to the subject of a discourse.
b. Leap forward beyond your emotional control.
c. Determine the ideological patterns and ideological holds to attract and ensnare.
d. Guess the alternative or reverse of what you need.
e. Convey information to those who practice a profession to deliberate on purpose expected.
f. Get rid of mental confusion in your environment.
g. Apply spaced repetition and encouragement for the process of learning by heart.
h. Design a supporting framework and comprehensive lists.
i. Construct and characterize in advance.
j. Regard or give special recognition to your life processes especially every organism that aids in the acquisition of skills

Acquiring a skill is important and it is as a result of careful decisions, regular rehearsals and quality speed. Improvement of skill requires diligent practice or rehearsals.

The Essential Skills for Trainers

Every trainer needs to have specific skills as well as training and development tools to be effective.

1. **Strong Communication Skills:** The ability to communicate with each other in a direct manner differentiates human being from other living organisms. Communication is very essential during training and can break the trainee's experience. A trainer that is not a good listener and not also good at explaining concepts, will definitely disappoint his/her trainees. This is because a trainer that does not pay attention to their trainee's concerns is a bad trainer. All these are barriers to training. The responsibility of trainers is to deliver responsible training to trainees.

   As a trainer, one should adapt at listening, questioning, explaining and giving feedback. Communication is very pivotal and crucial during training. Trainers need to learn how to communicate effectively. It is a give-and-take scenario—the more you train people, the better communicator (and trainer) you would be.

2. **Enthusiasm for Lifelong Learning:** A trainer must develop lifelong learning habits so that he/she can keep up with all the advancements in a market/job that keeps changing. A trainer should invest in lifelong learning/training to be able to emphasize with his/her trainees and put his/her self in their shoes (i.e., trainers sometimes build courses on a daily basis and tend to forget what it really feels like to be learning something new). The trainees faces a lot during training which causes fear, fatigue, excitement, boredom, frustration among others in their minds. More so, trainer should be effective by seeing through the trainee's eyes and creating engaging fascinating courses.

3. **Advanced Research Skills:** Research is an important aspect of training and it is the most hardest. Since the world is evolving and global with the internet exploration, a trainer can access relevant and reliable content for both online/classroom training courses in half the time. Every effective trainer will be able to find websites that he/she may have not heard or use before that contain feature information and content which might be useful even in the long run.

Searching on Google has a lot of secrets, some which a trainee is going to find out in a bit. For instance, knowing how to use Boolean operators and symbols in your searches.

4. **Organizational Skills:** In learning, training and development, trainers need to complete various tasks before they deploy a training program. From collecting all the materials required to delivering training efficiently, mastering organization is vital. Strong organizational skills always take an individual far. Managing time will also help the trainer stay on track. This is applicable to both the trainers and trainees.

5. **Problem Solving:** This is a critical skill for trainers that is associated or related to organization. An organized trainer can proffer solution when need arises. He/she will have the capacity to solve proactively. This will lead to an excellent trainer experience since the trainer/instructor has taken care of everything before it escalates (**Error! Hyperlink reference not valid.** https://www.talentlms. com/blog/essential-skills-training-tools-for-trainers/, accessed August 2021).

Training Tools for Trainers

Training tools are all those programs, platforms, or templates that help trainers deliver their training to their trainees/learners. These tools help the trainer to perform proficiently by doing better training. They are categorized into four and are recommended that every trainer should have them in his/her toolbox. These tools include the following:

a. **Social Media:** A trainer can connect with learners/trainees on their favourite platforms and it is an excellent way to personalize the learning experience. Social media can be really powerful for training since there is an over whelming surge in popular social media platforms like Twitter, TikTok, YouTube, Instagram, Facebook, and Pinterest, among others. This means that this is where potential trainees hangout when they have some time to spare.

Social media are also great course marketing tools to reach potential trainees who might be looking for courses the trainer is offering. Integrate a social media tool with your Learning Management System (LMS) to encourage trainees to connect with others who might have taken the same course. Also, create Facebook groups or other social media micro-communities, to allow trainees to share ideas with each other and engage in their conversations about their training.

b. **Learning Management System (LMS):** LMS is the best training tool for trainers who want to create courses, manage users, and track the performance of their online training and trainees. It is use for both trainer and trainee, a trainer can have a course up and running in minutes, and go live two times faster than the category average so he/she achieve a much shorter ROI.

Trainers should not only know how to use an LMS. They should know how to make the best out of it without the hassle.

c. **Video Editing Software:** A corporate trainer, expert in creating subject matter courses should learn how to use video tools. This will help the trainee's experience and add extra touch to the courses they would to train and learn.

Video editing software is the most overlooked training tools for trainers. Videos are powerful because they offer a vivid and engage learning experience. A complete video can be edited on smart phone for free, so the trainer can use various video types to train on his/her course.

Here are the common formats recommended for usage:

- Screen recordings
- Documentary-like videos
- Talking head videos
- Video presentation, among others

For instance, if a trainer is 'camera-shy', screen-recording apps such as screencast-O-Matic can prove really handy when he/she wants to record his/her screen and explain complicated topics clearly.

d. **Content Authoring Tool:** Authoring tools are software platforms that let trainers add a variety of media and multimedia files to create engaging training. An eLearning authoring tool can help a trainer to build interactive courses.

More so, a proficient trainer needs to do his/her research, spend some time learning and mastering the training tools, interacts with his/her trainees, must not forget to be understanding and adaptable, never stop learning (i.e., play around with some eLearning tools for trainers) (https://www.talentlms.com/blog/essential-skills-training-tools-for-trainers/, accessed August 2021).

Post-Training

Issues and activities that follow a training to ensure that the skills are put to use in justification of the rationale for choosing to engage in the skill acquisition in the first instance.

There are three key dimensions of the post training template, namely: Evaluation/Assessment, Certification/Licensing and Start-off/Practice. Each of these has vital components for effectiveness.

1. Evaluation/Assessment
2. Certification/Licensing
3. Start-off/Establishment of Skill Practice

- **Assessment**

Assessment is the process of gathering and discussing information from multiple and diverse courses to develop a deep understanding of what trainees know, understand and can do with their knowledge as a result of their training experiences; the process culminates when assessment results are used to improve subsequent training/learning (Learner-Centered Assessment on college campuses: shifting the focus from teaching to learning by Huba and Freed, 2000).

Assessments are an important part of every training course or module. This is because they assist trainers understand how their trainees are progressing. For trainees' satisfactory completion of an examination or assessments as they have gotten nothing to show for it in the point where training ceases to exist or end if the trainees' are not awarded with a certificate that is.

Learning Centered Assessment

```
                    Formulate Statement of
                    intended learning outcome

    Discuss and use assessment          Assessment          Develop or select
    result to improve learning           Process          assessment measures

                    Create Experiences
                    leading to outcome
```

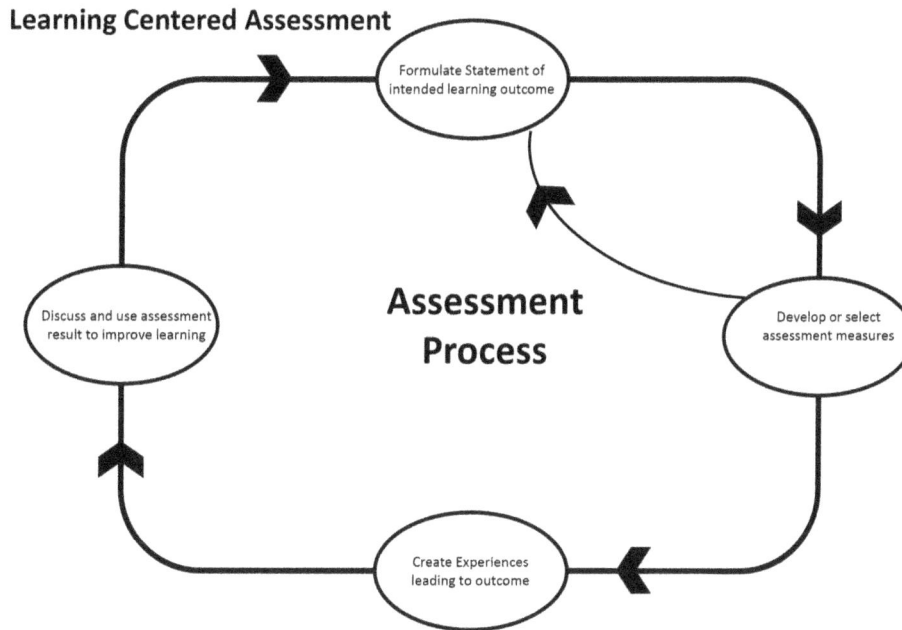

Four rudiment elements of learner-centered assessment:

i. **Formulating Statements of Intended Learning Outcomes:** Statements describing intentions about what trainees should know, understand, and be able to do with their knowledge when they graduate.

ii. **Developing or Selecting Assessment Measures:** These are to assess whether or not the trainees training outcomes have been achieved. It includes:
   • Direct Assessments: Projects, productions, paper/theses, exhibitions, performances, case studies, clinical evaluations, portfolios, interviews, and oral exams—which ask trainees to demonstrate what they know or can do with their knowledge.

iii. **Creating Experiences Leading to Outcomes:** Ensuring that trainees have experiences both in and outside their courses/target skills/tasks that help them achieve the intended training outcomes.

iv. **Discussing and Using Assessment Results to Improve Training and Learning:** Using the results to improve individual trainee performance.

These rudiment elements have been translated into an assessment cycle that includes four stages.

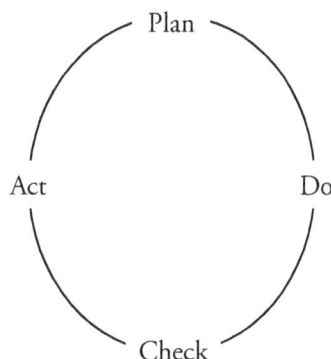

```
                    Plan

        Act                    Do

                    Check
```

a. Plan—What do trainers want trainees to learn?
    This stage includes the first fundamental component of assessment: Formulating statements of intended training outcomes.

b. How do trainers train effectively?
    This stage includes the second and third fundamental components: Developing or Selecting Assessment Measures and creating Experiences Leading to outcomes.

c. Check—Are trainer's outcomes being met?
    This stage involves evaluation of assessment data (part of the fourth component).

d. Act—How do trainers use what they have learned?
    This stage involves reinforcing successful practices and making revisions to enhance trainee training (part of the fourth component) (https://www.westminister.edu/about/accreditation-assessment/definition.cfm, accessed August 2021).

Certification

Certification is described as a document containing a certified statement especially as to the truth of something. It is also a document certifying that a trainee has fulfilled the requirements of and may practice in a field. While certification is the act of certifying and certified statement (Merriam Webster Dictionary, accessed August 2021).

Skill certification forms the basis for a credentialing program in a particular trade or profession. An industry or a government agency establishes the qualifications, requirements and standards to be met for granting certification to practitioners of a particular occupations.

To be eligible for certification, a trainee should typically go through several steps which includes

- obtaining the relevant education or training,
- completing the prerequisites and apprenticeship or internship,
- earning a passing grade in the qualifying examination,
- working the required number of years of relevant experience,
- demonstrating competence on the job at par with performance standards.

Benefits of Skill Certification for Organizations and Trainees

a. Cost-effective and objective recruitment and selection process.
b. Higher probability of hiring qualified personnel.
c. Standardized performance across the organization.
d. Motivated and qualified workforce.
e. Positive organizational image.
f. Enhanced productivity and competitiveness.
g. Professional recognition of trainees.
h. Useful tool to integrate immigrants into workforce.
i. Accurate, consistent verification of trainee's skills and experience.
j. Appropriate career placement.

k. Excellent method to promote and acknowledge cross-training.

l. Career mobility with portable credentials (https://www.thecompetencygroup.com/competency-services/skill-certification, accessed August 2021).

Licensing:

Licensing can be defined as a contract or agreement between two companies, where one company permits another company to manufacture its products under specified conditions and for a specified payment. It can also be seen as an agreement or contract between two companies where the owner of one company let the other company use its property under predecided specific parameters. The feature can be real estate property, personal professions, or intellectual properties like trademarks, patents, and copy rights.

Licensing is defined as a business arrangement, where in a company authorizes another company by issuing a license to temporarily access its intellectual property rights (i.e., manufacturing process), brand name, copyright, trademark, patent technology, trade secret, and the likes for adequate consideration and under specified conditions.

The firm that permits another firm to use its intangible assets is the licensor and the firm to whom the license is issued is the licensee. A fee or royalty is charged by the licensor to the licensee for the use of intellectual property right:

For example, "under licensing system, Coca-Cola and Pepsi are globally produced and sold by local bottlers in different countries."

In finer terms, it is the simplest form of business alliance, where in a company rents out its product based knowledge in exchange for entry to the market.

Types of Licensing

1. Mass licensing for software
2. Character and artwork
3. Academia
4. Brand and trademark
5. Vehicle licensing
6. Patent licensing

- **Mass Licensing for Software:** Mass licensing is a licensing that is used by individuals to be able to apply for software on personal computers. A user can install the software on the number of devices for which he/she has bought the license. For instance, on individual is required to purchase the license to be able to use its operating system.
- **Character and Artwork:** The character and artwork licensing are licensing that created to permit people to use and copy the copyrighted artwork and characters. For example, many famous cartoon characters like Mickey Mouse, Tom and Jerry, and Scooby-Doo are all licensed under character and artwork licensing.
- **Academia:** Academia is a licensing that a person requires becoming eligible to teach in a university. For example, a person must have a doctorate in a subject that he/she wishes to teach in a university.
- **Brand and Trademark:** Brand and trademark licensing is a type of licensing in which a licensor permits the licensee to distribute his/her products using his/her brand name. This type of licensing depends on specific contractual forms. For example, the brand and trademark licensing allow the

license to use it in specific geographical regions or for a specified period. The brand and trademark licensing can also be of two types.

In the first type, the fee of the license is independent of the sales and profits made by the license. While in the second type, the fee of the license is dependent on the sales and profit generated by the licensee. That means the licensing fee will increase with the increase in the profit.

A licensor can also grant permission to the licensee to manufacture and distribute its products. This type of licensing is called licensed production.

- **Vehicle Licensing:** Vehicle licensing is a licensing which is necessary to acquire to drive certain types of vehicles in several countries. That means, if a person wants to drive a specific type of vehicle, then he/she is required to have a particular kind of license. For example, an average driving holder person cannot drive heavy vehicles like trucks.
- **Patent Licensing:** Patent licensing is a licensing that a licensor gives to the license to grant permission to conduct patent activities. Several companies get patent their technology and other products that they do not want anyone else to use without their consent. Patent licensing is one of the most expensive licensing. A licensee is required to pay a considerable amount of money to obtain permission to be able to do business using patent products, processes, or services (https://www.marketing91.com/licensing, accessed August 2021).

Importance of ensuring your company for properly registered and licensed

There are a whole range of businesses that require the owner to buy a license, ranging from childminding businesses, taxi companies, restaurants, hairdressers, and hotels, among others. These importances are listed below:

a. **Privacy:** An individual ensures his/her personal information remains private when he/she obtain a license for business. This includes everything from his/her address to the finances as they will not be associated with the business and will guarantee his/her retain a level of personal privacy.
b. **Good for the Economy:** It ensures the businesses sector is thriving, as well as strong and protected. Small businesses can also only gain funding or protection by the law once they are registered and licensed. With so many new businesses appearing every day, ensuring your businesses is registered and licensed helps to formalize the economy.
c. **Protection for you:** Having the correct license will ensure your personal assets are protected in case of a lawsuit as well as providing protection for you if your business is damaged. A licensed business is completely separate from yourself, meaning your company's taxes are not filed with your own.
d. **Protection for your employees and customers:** A license will ensure your employees are protected if they are injured as well as protecting your customers (https://bmmagazine.co.uk/in-business/advice/importance-business-registration-licensing/, accessed August 2021).

Benefits and Limitations of Licensing

In licensing, the licensor gets the advantage of entering the international market at little risk. However, the licensor has little to no control over the license, in terms of production, distribution and sales of the product. In addition, if the license gets success, the firm has given up profits and whenever the licensing agreement expires, the firm might find that it has given birth to a competitor. As a prevention measure, there

are certain proprietary product components supplied by the licensor itself. Although, innovation is considered as the appropriate strategy so that the license will have to depend on the licensor.

On the other hand, the license acquires expertise in production or a renowned brand name. It expects that the arrangement will increase the overall sales, which might open the doors to the new market and help in achieving the business objectives. However, it requires a considerable capital investment, to start the operations, as well as the developmental cost is also borne by the license (https://businessjargons.com/licensing.html, accessed August 2021).

Start-Off

Starting a business takes a lot of preparation, and an individual have to do the work. So many entrepreneurs have great ideas, yet what they need is an actionable plan for getting to the next level. Here are questions that will help individuals to a successful business start-off. These questions will force an individual to turn his/her ideas into actionable next steps of business planning process:

- Why do you want to start a business?
- Is your business idea new, or can you follow someone else's blueprint?
- Is there actually a market for your business?
- How will you support yourself while starting this business?
- Who do you know that can help you?
- Should you have a partner or outside investors?
- How will you market and sell your products and services?

Where will you find your first customers?

- How will you brand your business?
- How patient are you?
- How do you feel about failure?

Taking time to thoroughly answer these questions and prepare yourself will help your business start off on the right foot (https://articles.bplans.com/11-questions-to-help-your-business-start-off-on-the-right-foot/, accessed August 2021).

These days, almost everyone has the dream of starting their own company. Jumping into the entrepreneurial world can be a bit intimidating, especially if you fall for the myth that go percent of startups fail. If you use the right tactics to start off strong, the better and successfully you would be. This is because startup failure rates are not nearly that high.

Methods that Will Get You Started on the Right Path

1. **Find your Passion:** The most successful startups are found by people who are passionate about what they do. The things you are most interested in can serve as a great source of inspiration for entrepreneurial ideas. When you base your ideas off something you truly love, you will be more focused and motivated. Bringing your own knowledge and personal experiences are the key ingredients that can assist you find a unique angle that helps you succeed.
2. **Understand your Market:** If you want any chance of success, you need to thoroughly research your target market before launching your business. Failure to understand your market is one of the

top reasons new businesses fail. This will help you identify important attributes such as the price point and marketing messages that will appeal to your target audience, as well as if there is even a need for your big idea in the first place. The better you understand your target market, the easier it will be to avoid costly misfires.

3. **Get your Finances in Order:** Many entrepreneurs need to use their own funds to start their company/business, which means you should do everything you can to improve your financial situation. While many startups enlist the help of angel investors to get up and running, you cannot assume you will get that type of financial help. As a trainee, start building credit as early as you can, and pay off trainee loans and other debts. This will make it significantly easier to get an affordable loan to help you fund your startup.

4. **Prepare to make Sacrifices:** To become a successful entrepreneur, an individual requires an intense level of dedication to his/her dream and this means sacrificing both time and money to make it happen. There is no such thing as an overnight success. Even the multimillion-dollar startups that seem to pop out of nowhere were the results of countless hours of hard work before they started making headlines.

5. **Find a Mentor:** Finding a mentor is one of the most important things a young entrepreneur can do. Mentors have taken this path before and bring knowledge and experience to help you move forward to make smarter business decisions. Running a business requires a wide range of skills and expertise that you likely have not mastered yet. Use alumni networks, conferences and other resources to form these valuable connections.

6. **Tune up your Business Knowledge:** Successful businesses require more than an innovative product; they also require a competent team to manage finances, operations, manufacturing, marketing and all the other things that go into the production and sale of a product. You may be passionate about your big idea, but this creative energy is not enough. Take the time to improve your business IQ and look for likeminded individuals who can join your team and make up for your deficiencies. You will lay the foundations for a startup that lasts by paying just as much attention to the business side of things as the creative side.

7. **Be a Planner:** You need the ability to plan ahead to be a successful entrepreneur. Use your overarching goals to set realistic milestones for the growth and development of your company (https://www.business.com/articles/7-tips-for-young-entrepreneurs, accessed August 2021).

Establishment of Skill Practice

Skill practice is described as the practice of psychomotor skills and techniques by trainees in the skills laboratory and training environments until they are proficient in basic techniques as applicable.

Personal development skills are qualities and abilities that help trainees grow both personally and professionally. In other words, they are skills that help a trainee nurture his/her personal development.

Reasons for Personal Development Skill

Personal development skills are important because they allow a trainee to create strategic and tactical plans for personal and professional growth toward his/her goals. A trainee can naturally work them into his/her daily routines and use them to

- achieve personal and career goals,
- better him/her,

- improve his/her strengths and talents,
- advance in his/her career.

Personal development skills can be traits/qualities that an individual have or had gain through education and training. Individuals will value different personal development skills depending on their goals.

Ways to Improve your Personal Development Skills

An individual can enhance his/her personal development skills by taking classes, learning from the people around, gaining new talents and improving upon existing ones. The guidelines to improve and develop oneself include

- overcoming fears
- reading
- learning something new
- asking for feedback
- keeping a journal
- meditating
- observing others
- getting a mentor
- Network (https://www.indeed.com/career-advice/career-development/improve-your-personal-development-skills-Accessed-August,2021).

4.0 Three Dimensions of Skill Acquisition Module

Motivation/Theorization

- **Conceptualization:** In skill acquisition, conceptualization is the abilities that allow a trainee to better understand complex scenarios and develop creative solutions. These skills are valuable from management perspective because those who have them can approach complicated training situations in various ways.
  Conceptual leader can think through their ideas, transforming thoughts into action-driven solutions. Leaders with conceptual skills are seen as strategic leaders, because of their ability to strategize potential situations and how to resolve them.

Types of Conceptual Skills

Conceptual skills are proven useful in various area of skill acquisition; it comes in categories and has its own benefits.

- **Technical Skills:** These types of skills are measurable, it helps to develop technical skills in diverse areas and the ability to market and come up with different ways to sell the organization's products and services. Most technical skills require experience and training to master, which sets them apart from softer conceptual skills.

To achieve and secure a leadership role, a trainee or trainer should fully understand their environment and what each member of the team does to further the goals of the organization.

- **Decision-Making Skills:** These involve the ability to solve problems quickly and efficiently. To develop these skills, an individual must have good attention to detail, the ability to analyze and show resourcefulness when facing a problem. Excellent trainee members can often identify problems that could impact the organization before they are apparent to every individual, which may require them to make a decision that leads to long-term benefits.
- **Interpersonal Skills:** These type of conceptual skills deals with any number of abilities associated with interacting with other people. It is associated with different types of skills that are relevant to an accomplished leader. These include
- the ability to motivate others,
- an innovative approach,
- professionalism in an individual role.

Methods to Develop Conceptual Skills

i. Communicate well with others.
ii. Work on developing your negotiation skills.
iii. Embrace leadership opportunities.
iv. Learn the essentials of project management.
(https://www.indeed.com/career-advice/career-development/conceptual-skill, accessed August 2021).

Classification

Classification is a systematic arrangement in groups or categories according to established criteria. (Merriam Webster Dictionary, accessed August 2021) (**Error! Hyperlink reference not valid.**).

Skills can be classified into three main types: Transferable/functional, personal traits/attitudes, and knowledge-based.

SKILL TYPE	DESCRIPTION
1. Transferable/Functional	• Actions taken to perform a task, transferable to different work functions and industries. • Based on ability and aptitude. • Expressed in verbs Examples: ▪ Organize ▪ Write ▪ Analyze ▪ Promote

2. Personal Traits/Attitudes	• Traits or personality characteristics that contribute to performing task. • Developed in childhood and through life experience. • Expressed in adjectives Examples: ▪ Patient ▪ Diplomatic ▪ Results-oriented ▪ Independent
3. Knowledge-based	• Knowledge of specific subjects, procedures, and information necessary to perform particular tasks. • Acquired through education, training, and on-the-job experience. • Expressed in nouns Examples: ▪ Personnel administration ▪ Contact management ▪ Accounting

Identification

Merriam Webster Dictionary (accessed August 2021) defines *identification* as a largely unconscious process whereby an individual models thoughts, feelings, and actions after those attributed to an object that has been incorporated as a mental image. Identification is also an act of identifying or the state of being identified.

Identification learning is a form of perceptual learning that refers to the ability to improve the identification or categorization of stimuli following a learning experience. Perceptual learning is a general term that refers to be improvement in performance on a variety of sensory tasks (e.g., discrimination, detection, identification) that occurs following practice. Identification learning in the auditory domain can be refers to the practice-dependent improvement in the identification of nonnative speech contrasts, or, in the visual domain, to performance gains in the identification of letters. Identification learning is a skill (i.e., procedural knowledge) and thus slowly acquired in an implicit manner; it requires many repetitions, multiple practice sessions, and results in long-lasting gain (Karni, 1996).

Most skills used in jobs are learned in school, skills learned at home or on the street are rarely applicable to a job. Everyone is aware of his/her talents and skills. Most people war blinders when they look at themselves, these are all myths about skills. The fact is that skills learned not only in school but also in personal life are applicable to many jobs. Identification of skills is intended to open an individual's eyes to the skills he/she have acquired either in school or on the street which will assist him/her to recognize his/her innermost talents.

Recognizing and identifying your skills is important in deciding what career you would like to try. Try also to identify other unique experiences that might give you a special background that others have not had. Decide which three areas you are strongest in, put it on check before you possess each skill. Think of career experienced by members of your family or friends from whom you have learned a great deal or perhaps you have been part of special projects that other people have not experienced. Use a career finder or your imagination and knowledge of the outside world to detect jobs which would be applicable to the skills that you already know.

Think of unusual people you have known, books that you have read and have taught you special things. List each experiences, try to define the skill that you feel you have obtained as a result of that experience, list the career, and note what is required and whether the conditions and requirements of the job is accepted by you (https://www.employmentcrossing.com/article/9000218971/skill-identification/, accessed August 2021).

Description

Description is an act of giving a vivid or mental picture/image of something experienced. Description in skill acquisition is referred to as having a step by step image of your potential skill. A trainee cannot venture into any field without knowing what it takes to accomplished his/her task. Without having a vivid picture of the right skill, an individual will not only frustrate his/herself but will waste time dealing with rudimentary issues caused by lack of foundation of knowledge and experiences.

Description will help potential trainees to start their skill training with core skills (i.e., starting from zero ground or imitating), break into little steps, learning from the best (having knowledge from the people who have done/know or are experienced in the skill), research and attending trainings will go a long way in giving mental pictures or describing any skill.

Personality

Personality is a distinguishing trait or means that an individual conducts reasons and believes. These distinguish trait of a particular exposure of an individual emanate his/her ability to function and operate according to plan or design and using the mind in the direction of skill development, which greatly sway skill acquisition.

Principles

Principles can be defined as rules or code of conduct. It is a comprehensive and fundamental law. (Merriam Webster Dictionary, Accessed August, 2021). In skill acquisition, principle is described as a peculiar or absolute training policy to checkmates irregularities during or in training. Some of the important principles of training include principle of training policy, principle of learning period. Principle of organized material, principle of practice, principle of feedback, principle of result, and principle of assessment, among others.

PRACTICE/INSTRUCTION

- **Analysis**

    This refers to detailed examination of anything complex to understand its nature or to determine its essential features: a thorough study. It can also be referred to as a separation of a whole into its component parts (Merriam Webster Dictionary, accessed August 2021).

    In skill acquisition, analysis of skills identifies the major responsibilities of a job/task and breaks down each major responsibility into its specific skills or tasks.

- **Interpretations**

    Interpretation is the process of discovering, determining, or assigning meaning. Interpretation skills can be applied to anything, e.g. written messages, charts, diagrams, maps, graphs, memes, and verbal and nonverbal exchanges. People apply their interpretive skills to behaviors, events, and

social interactions when deciding what they think something means in a given context (https://www.insightassessment.com/article/interpretation, accessed August 2021)

- **Activities**

    It is a similar process actually or potentially involving mental function. It is also an organizational unit for performing a specific function or duties (Merriam Webster Dictionary-Accessed August, 2021).

    Activities under skill acquisition are known as training activity or activities. A training activity is an abstract term for any planned undertaking that improves a trainee's qualifications, knowledge or expertise. A training activity is prepared in advance by the trainer to train specific abilities to specific trainees (https://docs.oracle.com/cd/A60725_05/html/comnls/us/ota/ota05a.htm, accessed August 2021).

- **Formations**

    Formation is an act of giving structure or shape to something or of taking form. The manner in which a thing is formed (Merriam Webster Dictionary, accessed August 2021).

    In skill acquisition, skill formation is the process by which trainees achieve and develop innate or acquired skills to cope with everyday life challenges. Besides heredity, it includes formal or informal training activities and life experience (https://www.igi-global.com/dictionary/is-entrepreneurship-a-bio-social-phenomenon/92105, accessed August 2021).

- **Quantification**

    Is the operation of making explicit to determine, express, or measure the quantity of something. Quantification of key skills is referred to a particular set of skills that are commonly needed in a range of activities in education and training, work and life in general (https://www.nidirect.gov.uk/articles/key-skills-qualifications, accessed August 2021).

- **Combinations**

    Combination is described as a result or product of admixture. It is any subject of a set considered without regard to order within the subset. (Merriam Webster Dictionary-August, 2021). Skill combinations are the results of combining multiple skills in outward (https://outward.fandom.com/wiki/skill-combinations, accessed August 2021).

- **Patenting**

    Patenting is an official document conferring a right or privilege. In education, there are patent teaching/training kits. The patent teaching/training kit is a valuable resource that will help raise awareness of the key issues surrounding patents.

- **Control**

    This can be described as the exercise restraining or directing influence over people or something. It can also be seen as skill in the use of a tool, instrument, technique, or artistic medium or power or authority to guide or manage (www.merriam-webster.com/dictionary/control, accessed August 2021).

- **Performance**

Performance is defined as the action or process of carrying out or accomplishing an action, task, or function. In skill acquisition, performance training system is a private sports training facility that uses the most effective training and nutrition protocols to achieve one's goals.

ASSESSMENT/CERTIFICATION

- **Testing**

    In general, testing is finding out how well something works. In terms of human beings, testing tells what level of knowledge or skill has been acquired. In computer hardware and software development, testing is used at key checkpoints in the overall process to determine whether objectives are being met (**Error! Hyperlink reference not valid.** https://searchsofwarequality.teachtar-get.com/definition/testing, accessed August 2021).

    In skill acquisition, a skill test is an assessment used to provide an unbiased, validated evaluation of a candidate's/trainee's ability to perform the tasks listed in the job/skill description. Typically, a skill test asks a variety of questions in different formats to see how trainees perform their day-to-day activities. A good skill test includes questions that are capable of being answered by someone already performing the task and can accurately measure key performance metrics.

    A personality assessment varies from a skills test in that it predicts how a person will behave in a specific scenario, rather than their ability to complete a task.

How to Apply Skill Testing

Skill testing is best applied when the questions being asked are specifically crafted to the role and needs of the team hiring the new trainee/candidate. In designing a skill test, combine different types of questions to get a 360^0 view of how a trainee will perform in different scenarios.

Deloitte suggests this sample process for selecting and implementing skill testing questions:

i. Define the "human elements" needed to perform the task.
ii. Compile questions that will measure and predict these human elements.
iii. Use the data gathered by the skills assessments to empower the next round of the screening process.
iv. Post-hiring, evaluate the efficacy of the hiring assessment to ensure the questions delivered the best result.

Ultimately, the best use for a skills assessment is to assist trainer's move away from the resume and allow trainees to prove they are the real deal (https://vervoe.com/skill-testing/#1, accessed August 2021).

Measurements

It is defined as an estimate of what is to be expected (as of a person or situation). It can also be referred to a step planned or taken as a means to an end (Merriam-Webster Dictionary, accessed August 2021).

In skill acquisition, measuring skills is the knowledge of how to measure the physical attributes of objects including how to appropriately use measurement tools and proper techniques. Measuring skills encompass all the skills required for a child to effectively measure something.

Importance of Measuring Skills in Skill Acquisition

Teaching/training measurement of ten requires a lot of new vocabulary as well as learning how to use new tools. Here are some measuring skills often developed in early education:

- Comparing objects by size (big, bigger, biggest).
- Comparing objects by length, height and weight.
- Comparing groups of objects and understanding that a lesser number is also a lesser quantity.
- Understanding basic concepts of time, such as this morning, or yesterday, or in a minute.
- Using nonstandard forms of measurement.

Tips for Training/Teaching Measuring

Here are tips for success training/teaching measurement:

a. Provide authentic and real-life experience whenever possible.
b. Allow for practice.
c. Use new arithmetic language frequently.
d. Allow trainees to move and use their newest skills.
e. Encourage trainees to talk about arithmetic and explain their thinking, even if their answer is wrong.
f. Teach multiple strategies, allowing trainees to choose the strategy that makes the most sense to them.
g. Allow time for trainees to compare their task and work with others (encouraging teamwork).
h. Provide manipulative for problem solving, rather than pencils/pen and paper.
i. Ask leading questions when training/teaching (https://thekindergartenconnection.com/secrets-developing-measuring-skills/, accessed August 2021).

Regulation

Is the act to given or direct according to rule, or to fix or adjust the time, amount, degree, or rate of something. It can be seen to bring order, method, or uniformity to one's habits (Merriam-Webster Dictionary, accessed August 2021).

In science, self-regulation theory (SRT) is a system of conscious personal management that involves the process of guiding one's own thoughts, behaviors, and feelings to reach goals. Self-regulation consists of several stages and individuals must function as contributors to their own motivation, behavior and development within a network of reciprocally interacting influences (https://en.w.wikipedia.org/wiki/self-regulation-theory, accessed August 2021).

In skill acquisition, self-regulation is a skill that allows people to manage their emotions, behavior, and body movement when they are faced with a tough situation. It also allows them to do that while staying focused and paying attention. It is a skill that develops over time (https://www.understood.org/articles/en/trouble-with-self-regulation-what-you-need-to-know, accessed August 2021).

In education, the appeal of self-regulation and its positive effects on behavior and educational outcomes has promoted much research in this area. Zimmerman 2001, posited that "self-regulation refers to the self-directive process through which learners/trainers transform their mental abilities into task related skills."

This is the method or procedure that learners use to manage and organize their thoughts and convert them into skills used for learning/training.

Zimmerman 2001, assert that for trainees/learners to be self-regulated, they need to be aware of their own thought process, to be motivated to actively participate in their own learning process.

Reasons for Using Self-Regulation

i)   Self-regulation is desirable because of the effects that it has on educational and behavioral outcomes.

ii) The use of self-regulation techniques are a way to actively engage otherwise passive learners/trainees in their academic instruction.

iii) Learners/Trainees need to view learning as an activity that they do for themselves in a proactive manner, rather than viewing learning as a covert event that happens to them as a result of instruction (Zimmerman, 2001).

iv) Allowing learners/trainees take a more active role in their education puts them in the driver's seat and in charge.

Qualification

Is described as knowledge, skill, or some other characteristic that gives a person the ability or the right to do or have something. It is also a level of skill or ability that an individual have to achieve to be allowed to do something or an ability, characteristic, or experience that makes an individual suitable for a particular job or activity (https://dictionary.cambridge.org/us/dictionary/english/qualification, accessed August 2021).

Professional qualifications are vocational training courses that relate to a specific industry or career path. They are typically regulated and awarded by relevant professional bodies, and are designed to ensure that everyone employed in a particular job meets the minimum required standards of professional expertise.

Some vocational training can be taken directly after completing university, while others are aimed at professionals with several years of experience who are looking to develop their career further. While in some jobs, a professional qualification is essential, and as an individual work as a qualified solicitor, for example, he/she must take a Legal Practice Course (LPC), and to become a chartered accountant, he/she will need to pass the relevant exams. In some areas of employment, professional qualifications are not required, but nevertheless it look great on an individual's curriculum vitae and resume and improve his/her changes of success by demonstrating his/her skills and knowledge.

The length of vocational training courses duration can range from a few weeks to a few years, depending on the qualification and whether the trainee study full or part time. On the other hand, some professional bodies simply offer an examination and it's up to an individual to determine how many hours of preparation he/she do before hand, either through independent study or by attending a course run by a training provider.

Reasons for a Professional and Vocational Qualification

1. It will help trainees to meet their employer's expectations of continuing professional development (CPD) by keeping their skills and abilities up to date.

2. It can be the first step toward achieving professional status, which will see a trainee registered as a member of the professional body and a recognized professional in his/her area of work.

3. A trainee will gain skills, recognition, and contacts through improving his/her specialist knowledge, demonstrating his/her ability to employers, and giving him/her greater opportunity to progress or change careers.

4. Many professions require an individual to possess specific qualifications, meaning that if he/she is serious about forgiving a career in one of these area, he/she will have to take the course (https://www.prospects.ac.uk/postgraduate-study/professional-qualifications, accessed August 2021).

Evaluation

Evaluation is concerned with assessing the effectiveness of teaching/training, teaching/learning strategies, methods and techniques. It provides feedback to the trainers/teachers about their training/teaching and the trainees/learners about their training/learning.

It is a systematic process of collecting, analyzing and interpreting information to determine the extent to which trainees are achieving instructional objectives.

Evaluation has its four different aspects, namely:

i) Objectives
ii) Learning experiences
iii) Learner appraisal
iv) Relationship between the three

Characteristics of Evaluation

i. **Evaluation is a continuous process:** Here, it is certainly a wrong belief that the evaluation procedure follows the teaching-learning process. Teaching-learning process on the one hand and the evaluation procedure on the other hand, they go together ideally.

ii. Evaluation always assumes that educational objectives have previously been identified and defined. For this reason, trainers/teachers are expected not to lose sight of educational objectives while planning and carrying out the teaching-training-learning process either in the classroom or outside it.

iii. Evaluation implies a systematic process which omits the casual uncontrolled observation of pupils.

iv. Evaluation emphasizes the broad personality changes and major objectives of an educational program. Therefore, it includes not only subject-matter achievements but also attitudes, interests and ideas. Ways of thinking work habits and personal and social adaptability.

Results

Results according to Merriam Webster Dictionary (accessed August 2021) is described as to proceed or arise as a consequence, effect, or conclusion. It can be a beneficial or tangible effect.

Acquisition of skill is a type of learning in which repetition results in enduring changes in trainee's capability to perform a specific task (https://www.psychology.iresearch.com/sports-psychology/motor-development/skill-acquisition/, accessed August 2021).

5.0 The 4 Stages Pattern

A pattern refers to a generalized set of a stage in a process that find a solution to a particular problem or accomplish the end toward which effort is directed.

Stage I: Unconscious Incompetence

This is the first stage in the model. It is the part of mental life that does not ordinarily enter the trainee's awareness yet may influence behavior and perception. In this stage, an individual lacks the qualities needed for effective action, he/she does not understand much about the skill. Furthermore, the trainees have only a fundamental comprehension of what ascendancy of the skill potency to impose or entail. The trainees will at an unspecified later time discover that understanding is insufficient. Individuals are likely unconsciously or unacquainted and unsuitable for a particular purpose in any sphere/arena where they inexperience whatsoever.

Stage II: Conscious Incompetence

In this stage, trainees have mental faculties or awake and have acquired sufficient knowledge about the skill to realize how diminutive they apprehend. The trainees' sophistication or elaborateness has augmented somewhat, but so has their knowledge and understanding of what it would grasp to obtain and bring to a level of genuine sophistication. This stage can be stupor or discomfortable to enter, because the trainees realize both how little they understood in the premature stage and how much task it will require to advance to farther stages.

Stage III: Conscious Competence

Conscious competence is the stage where the trainees have sufficient knowledge of the skills or tasks and are able to carry out the task to an increasing degree, but it requires much attention and diligent to achieve or attain the required goal. The trainees must exhibit admiration for what it would require to become an expert or master, and while their implementation relevant to the skill/task prolong to enhance in quality, they are also sensible of the obligation to succeed at the skill as well as the fact that they are executing the task in a different manner from the previous way they used to carryout.

Stage IV: Unconscious Competence

This stage is where the trainees' capacity to execute the task/skill has become entirely another disposition. The trainees must enhance nevertheless to a greater extent at their performance of task and have to apply little awake or conscious labor to do so.

Every trainee can presumably conceive multiple domains in which they are in each of these stages. Being in the conscious stages can be a bit dull/uncomfortable. But that also stipulates a favorable juncture for them to enhance their awareness or metacognition about learning dissimilar skills, and to broaden their horizons in general.

6.0 Conclusion

Skill acquisition and training describes the building blocks of cognitive, motor, and teamwork skills, and the factors to take into account in training the learners/trainees. The fundamental proceeding of concept or observation, cognition and the method of performing an action that stipulate the underlying basis for understanding skilled performance are extremely crucial. Human resource development is a basic concept

that constitutes training. A highly useful tool that can bring an employee or an individual into position and enable him/her to do their job/task effectively, correctly and conscientiously is training.

The use of self-regulation techniques assists trainees in performing tasks more effectively and independently. For example, successful trainees will constantly check their comprehension, when reaching a passage and realize that they do not understand what they have read, they will go back and reread, and question or summarize what is that they need to understand.

Role Playing in Skill Acquisition

OUTLINE

1.0   Introduction
2.0   Role of the trainer
3.0   Role of the trainee
4.0   Sponsor's role
5.0   Management role
6.0   Conclusion

1.0   Introduction

Role playing is an important aspect in the skill acquisition process also known as the active learning approach. Role playing is a student centered method of leaning or acquiring a new skill. Roles refer to the responsibilities of each and every participant in the skill acquisition process that promotes and accelerates the success of the performance.

Since role playing is a learner-centered approach, it therefore involves the activities that encourage or arouse the interest of the trainee in the process. "Role play is a technique that allows students to explore realistic situations by interacting with other people in a managed way, in order to develop experience and different trial strategies in a supported environment" (Role-play: An Approach to Teaching and Learning, 2014).

Sogunro (2004:367 as quoted in Elmore) explains that role play is essentially the practice of having students take on specific roles-usually ones in which they are not familiar and act them out in a case-based scenario for the purpose of leaving course content and understanding complex ambiguous concepts.

Swell (2013:1) asserts that "life, and reality is multi-dimensional… 'therefore'…living examples must be brought to the classroom because the subject taught is a living thing; moving and in process, rather than encapsulated on paper." Creative use of traditional teaching methods supplemented by use of audio-visual aids and role playing adds a new dimension to the classroom—that of feeling and experiencing." Newell and Rosenbloom (1981 as cited in Dekeyser, 2007) views practice as "the subclass of learning that deals only with improving performance on a task that has already been successfully performed. In skill acquisition, it is expected that the trainees acquire the skills in a procedural nature. Such skills require trainees to employ properly a sequence of actions that when taken together, constitute the entire task."

1.1 How Role Playing Works in Skill Acquisition

In skill acquisition, role playing involves assigning responsibilities to students or trainees to carryout practically with the least or no supervision on the part of the trainer. The trainee is encouraged to apply the theoretical knowledge acquired in a practical setting. Role play can be done individually or within a group. The trainee(s) is/are assigned a role(s), and they perform them. The students are as well given an opportunity to appraise the performance of one another. Role playing is usually short and goal oriented.

2.0   The Role of the Trainer in Skill Acquisition

A trainer is one whose duty is to impart knowledge within a specified field into the trainees. The Merriam Webster Dictionary (n.d.) defines a trainer as "one whose occupation is to guide or instruct people in a particular skill." The trainer plays a very important role in this learning process. Despite the fact that the student plays a major role in this learning process, all the events that take place during the period of the leaving process must align to the lesson plan of the trainer and the trainer tries to achieve this purpose which he or she has set out to do within the shortest possible time.

Personal/Developmental Strategies that Promote the Trainer Role Play

A trainer should be one that has a good knowledge of the skill he or she is training others on. A good trainer must be one that practices the skill which he is training others into and is well versed with the possible challenges that arise in the course of practicing that skill. This knowledge will help the trainer to guide the trainee(s) during the role-playing on what to do when any challenge arises.

The trainer should possess some interpersonal skills that enables a positive trainer-trainee relationship. The trainer can either make the learning process easier or 'appear' harder to the trainee. A lot of individuals confirm the fact that a trainer can either encourage or discourage the trainee. It is also worthy to note that in a skill acquisition, the participants (students) are not people who can be bullied around. They, in most cases, are people who are mature physically and psychologically but may not be emotionally mature to handle some bad emotions. In such persons, the trainer has to be a friend and must be down to earth. Any negative statement made by the trainer can put off such a student and may permanently kill the drive of that skill acquisition. A research from the Economic Policy Institute reveals that good teachers (trainers) are the most important factor that contributes to student's achievement in the classroom, more important than facilities, school resources, and even the school leadership.

1. **A good trainer must be a strong communicator:** A strong communication skill is very important in any skill acquisition process. A good trainer who is also able to communicate with his trainees will gain their trust. Good communication has a way of motivating the trainees into doing better.

2. **A Good Trainer must be a Good Listener**

    As important as communication is to the teacher (trainer), it is necessary for a trainer to develop good listening skill. In the role-playing process where the students have to practically perform what they have learned theoretically, they may encounter different challenges. A good trainer who is also a good listener, will understand the situation from the angle of the student and this will make it easier for the trainer to put the student through.

3. **A Good Trainer must be able to Adapt to Change**

   It is usually said that the only thing that is constant is change. "An effective trainer needs to be able to work in a constantly evolving environment and their teaching methods based on the age of their students, the resources available and the changing curriculum, practices and requirements" (Gagnon, 2019). With the invasion of the internet and the social network, a good should be able to take-his lessons beyond the physical to the virtual world. Gone are days when the trainer was the hub of knowledge. The trainer should encourage his trainees to access the internet for more ideas. As part of the role-playing process, the trainer can share out the topics outline and each trainee is made to source for materials and deliver a lesson on that topic. This will make the student work very hard so as to present well.

4. **A Good Trainer Must Have a Good Sense of Humor**

   A good skill acquisition trainer should develop a good sense of humor. This part, enables the trainer to captivate and sustain the interests of the trainees. The trainer should not be scared of talking about his past, most especially as a trainee too. He should share some of the challenges which he/she had at that time and how he/she was able to overcome it. Such approach promotes the interests of the trainees. This makes them believe in themselves and they will be encouraged by the fact that if the trainer could do well, then they can as well do better.

5. **A Good Trainer Should Be Patient**

   In the educational world, it is a generally known fact that students perform at different speed rates. There are students that are exceptionally intelligent and therefore learn at a more faster rate than the others. The teacher should be able to patiently groom the 'slow' learners and also encourage them to do better. In a situation where a particular aspect in the skill acquisition process is not well understood by the trainees, the teacher should patiently go over the lesson again and make sure that all the trainees understand the lesson. The trainer should be accommodating as well. Some of the trainees may put forth bad behaviors, and some may be out rightly insolent. The trainer should learn and apply the methods of managing such behaviors and in some cases ignore them so as to achieve his/her purpose for that class.

   Therefore one who desires to play the role of a trainer must first of all, develop himself or herself psychologically and emotionally so as to cope with the pressure and challenges that arise in the course of the training.

Awards and Incentives

It is no gainsaying that award and incentives play a vital role in the encouragement of the trainees. When trainees are assigned roles, those who perform better should be awarded. This will encourage the award winner to perform better and it will develop that competitive spirit among the trainees. Apart from awards, the trainer should encourage trial. There are some individuals that are so afraid of failure so much that they would not even want to try. The trainer should encourage such persons and make them understand that it is okay to make mistakes. Mistake making opens our eyes to ways in which things cannot be done. The trainer should encourage them to try again, rather than nailing them for failing.

Tips for Using the Role Playing Technique

1. The trainer should divide the trainees into manageable groups. This largely depends on the initiative of the trainer. If the trainees are many, they can be grouped in twos, threes or as the case may be but if the class is small, the trainer might decide to share the roles individually.
2. The teacher should prepare and share the roles to each of the groups. The roles should be achievable. The trainer should explain what he/she expects from each group and the rules guiding the performance should be student friendly. The teacher should attach a time frame for the performance. The trainer can as well provide the resources for the performance of a particular task where necessary.
3. The trainer should fix a time when all the groups will gather to explain the process which the members of the groups passed through to arrive at the final presentation. The trainee(s) should be able to explain too what each individual learned in the course of the performance of the task. The other members of the class should be given an opportunity to appraise their final presentation and correct where necessary.

3.0   The Role of the Trainee in the Skill Acquisition Process

The trainee is one who requires the skill to improve upon him/herself and be more relevant to the society where he/she resides. Since role-playing method of skill acquisition is student centered, therefore the bulk of the work has on the part of the trainee. As earlier explained, "this technique is an excellent tool for engaging students and allowing them to interact with their peers as they try to complete the tasks assigned to them in their specific role" (Role-Playing, 2020).

Personal Qualities that Promote a Good Trainee Role Playing

Every trainee at any skill acquisition venture expects to master that skill at some point in his/her life. However, this dream is sometimes cut short as some individuals tend to get discouraged too soon. Every individual needs these qualities to succeed at any venture one sets out to.

1. **Inner Drive or Self-Motivation**
    Motivation is that drive that pushes us out of our comfort zone to new 'territories'. It is a force that drives us to attempt something different or try to do better at what we do. There are two types of motivation, the internal and external motivation. The external motivation could be through the trainers, parents/guardians, friends, achievers, in that field or the prospect of making more money in that area. All these motivations are good but the best type of motivation is the internal motivation. This is the type of motivation that encourages one to move on, even in the face of difficulties. Coleman, a motivational speaker and writer identifies elements that make up self-motivation.
    a. **Personal Drive to Achieve:** When we think of drive, we think of desire that is backed up by some unseen force to achieve. This greatly depends on the individual's mindset. According to Coleman, there are two types of mindset, the fixed mindset and the growth mindset. The fixed mindset is one that believes that only those with the talent in a particular area can actually succeed in that skill and as such, no amount of learning can improve one who does not have that talent. Individuals with such mindset find it hard to succeed even when they have everything they need to succeed at such a skill.

The second mindset, the growth mindset is one that believes that through diligence and effort, one can improve at whatever one sets out to do. There is a known quote that says "He who says I will try climb to the highest top but he who says I can't, will remain at the bottom." Research has shown that those who believe that they can improve are far more likely to actualize their dreams.

b. **Resilience:** Resilience is the ability to remain positive despite the challenges that one faces. The ability to look on the bright side after a setback at a venture. Such individual's with resilience do not allow the negative emotions to control them when they seem to have failed at any point in the skill acquisition process. Such individuals are not afraid of asking questions and they aim at becoming better. They see their challenges as stepping stones to the height of their dreams.

2. **A Sense of Responsibility**

A sense of responsibility is an awareness or a consciousness of oneself and what one is expected to do. "A strong sense of responsibility gives birth to innovation, resilience, courage, achievement and generosity. Those who see themselves as responsible to life" (Markston, 2020). An enduring progress at any skill is a product of a strong sense of responsibility.

3. **Obedience**

Any trainee who is willing to succeed at any skill acquisition must be obedient. There are rules that guide the operation and activities of any setting or establishment. Any trainee who does not obey the rules will not anything. As one who is playing a particular role, you are expected to play by the rules.

Apart from these, there are other qualities that promote playing on the part of the trainee. One of such is social and emotional skills. An individual who keeps to himself or herself may not function properly within a group during the role playing process. Innovation, willingness to show forth and the ability to carry out researches in a particular area, beyond what is obtainable from the trainee.

Possible Hindrances to Success on the Part of the Trainee

There are many factors that can hinder an individual from playing his role effectively. The following are some of the hindrances.

1. **Trainee Personality:** Psychology has revealed that individuals have different temperaments. Trainees who are naturally introverts may not perform very well during role play. They may feel very shy among their peers and even when they have the best ideas, they tend to be quiet. Such individuals tend to perform less better if they are given roles that have to do with presentation.

2. **Inability to Communicate:** Any trainee who is unable to communicate will find it difficult to perform during a role play. In a situation where the role is to be presented in a foreign language and the trainee does not have the ability to do so, it will act as an impediment to the individual. In a research by Zaidi *et al.* (2017), the following are some of the comments of the respondents. "I was afraid that the examiner could not understand what I was going to say." "I did not know some words that I wanted to use in my sentences." "I had ideas to speak but I could not translate them in English." "I was not sure whether my performance fulfilled the given task." "I could not think clearly during the role performance," etc.

3. **Finance:** In a situation that requires the students to perform roles where finance is required, any trainee who cannot finance his/her part of the role may end up not fulfilling his/her part. This can hinder the success of the individuals or group which the individual is a member of.

However, these hindrances can be overcome if the trainee makes a conscious effort at performing better. Toister (2015 in Zaidi 2017) suggests using that students or the trainees practice the role play performance before proper performance with the examiner. This he calls "experiential learning." In the aspect of finance, the student can source for finance from family and friends or better still, get a student's loan to fund the project. The main element in making sure role playing is effective is that the trainee must have enough time to carry out researches, rehearse and effectively plan the performance process.

4.0   The Role of the Sponsor in Skill Acquisition

The sponsors have a great role to play in the trainee's performance. Research has shown that students (trainees) whose parents and sponsors are involved in their education or skill acquisition process tend to do better than their counterparts.

Sponsors are people who represent the outer community. The make the funding of individuals and institutions their priority. Such funding include scholarships for students, construction in skill acquisition centers. They can as well provide the facilities with tools and equipment for both the management and the trainees use. Aside this, the sponsors can as well bring in experts in the field to motivate the trainees. Some trainees need people to allay their fears and encourage them to succeed, for them to do well. Sponsors should organize workshops where some of the experts practically present to the students what is expected of them in the outside world. Sponsors should also provide awards to best performing trainees. This will make their efforts in the skill acquisition process worthwhile and will also act as an encouragement to others.

5.0   Role of the Management in Skill Acquisition

The management also have a part to play in skill acquisition.

1. The management should ensure at all the facilities and the equipment are in place before they venture into the business.
2. The management should ensure that the trainers are experts in the field and are people who also have an experience for a specified number of years.
3. The management should organize retraining programs and workshops for the trainers, to get them acquainted with recent developments in that field.
4. The management should collaborate with the trainers in developing an improved curricula, lesson plans and management of the trainees. The management should also develop new strategies for a better leaving experience.
5. They should set goals for the trainers in the different areas, such as daily, weekly, monthly or yearly. They should also provide the trainers with the means for achieving these goals.
6. The management should provide a proper anonymous feedback line from the student. This way, they can monitor the performance of the trainers through the eyes of the trainees. This way, they can observe the lessons and identify the trainers' strengths and weaknesses.

6.0 Conclusion

Role playing as an approach in skill acquisition is an exercise which gives students an opportunity to act in a given situation or capacity. Everyone has a part to play in this method. The teacher initiates the plan, divides the class into smaller groups and shared the roles. The trainees plan and prepare adequately and then present. The role play approach has a lot of benefits. It motivates and engages the students effectively. Role playing enhances the teachers' performance as it exposes the students to real-life scenarios and makes the lesson well understood. Role play also helps to bring out either the best or the worst in a trainee. In a situation where the trainer does well, he/she is applauded but if he/she does not perform the trainer will understand where the trainee needs help and correct appropriately.

Role play as an approach also gives the trainees an opportunity to brainstorm and tackle contingencies in the course of acting out then acquired skills. It also gives other students an opportunity to judge the performance and constructively criticize their colleagues.

Chapter Nine

Management Strategies for Skill Acquisition

OUTLINE

1.0   Introduction
2.0   Planning and Feasibility Analysis
3.0   Organizing and Production
4.0   Directing
5.0   Controlling
6.0   Communicating
7.0   Monitoring
8.0   Evaluation
9.0   Conclusion

1.0   Introduction

Skill Acquisition: Project or Program?

Before adopting any standard management model for this essay, it is important to establish if whether skill acquisition should be viewed as a project or a program. Ndebbio, J. (2007:2) asserted that a project can be defined as the use of one or more scarce resources (human, financial, and related material) during a specific time for the goal of producing economic and social benefits at a later time. He continued to state that a program, no matter its magnitude is also a conceived as an outfit that is expected to develop facilities that provide goods and services to the individuals as well as society or community.

Thus, one can evidently state that skill acquisition can be viewed as a project or a program. It is also important to note that project can be private or public. Ndebbio (2007:3) stated clearly that difference between a public project and a private project. Thus, projects/programs planned and owned by government (Federal, State and Local) are public projects. Whereas, private projects are planned and owned by private investors with the motive (aim) of making profit. The benefits or social returns of a project, whether public or private depend largely on the efficiency with which the project is managed. Hence, this chapte3r seeks to address management strategies for skills acquisition.

Management is a process of planning, decision making, organizing, leading motivating and controlling human resources, financial, material resources of an organization to reach its goal efficiently and effectively (What is Management? Definition, Concept, Features n.d.]). An economist, an administrator, and a sociol-

ogist may have different views about management, but the purpose of management remains static—to reach the goal of the organization effectively and efficiently.

The basic managerial functions or activities are planning, organizing, directing, controlling. These activities are undertaken by the managers to combine all resources (human, financial and material) efficiently and effectively to work toward achieving the goals of the organization. Strategy is an action that managers take to attain one or more of the organization's goals. Strategy can also be defined as general direction set for the company and its various components to achieve a desired state in the future. Strategy results from the detailed strategic planning process (Prach, 2015).

Amesi, Akpomi, and Okwuanaso (2014) argued that strategy is all about competitive position, about differentiating yourself in the eyes of the students or customer as the case maybe, about adding value through a mix or activities from those used by competitors.

From the above definition, it can be said that anything that a manager does, or consciously chooses not to do, to achieve the organization's goals is a strategy. It provides the blueprint for what the organization will do, how it will optimize its strengths and reduce the impact of its weaknesses and how it will behave toward its customers, employees and stakeholders, among other things.

From the above point of view also, there are three features that all management strategies have in common—which are long-term objective, providing a clear road map and taking in to account the behavior of competitors., customers and employees (Thompson, 2019).

Management strategies can therefore be viewed as techniques that are used to direct and control an organization to achieve a set of goals (Irukaku, O. and Mary N., 2018). Management strategy is sometimes wrongly used as a synonym for strategic management. The former has to do with plan for victory in competition with other companies while the latter is a process for formulating and implementing a strategy (Thompson, S. [n.d.]).

The concepts and activities of management Is applicable to all levels of management, as well as to all types of organizations or programs of which skill acquisition is included.

Afeti (2009), as cited by Solesi *et al.* (2014), affirms that skill acquisition has emerged as one of the most effective development strategies that African countries need to embrace to train and modernize the technical workforce for rapid industrialization and national development.

This awareness calls for a better collaborative effort among stakeholders, Federal, State and Local agencies like National Directorate of Employment (NDS), National Poverty Eradication Program (NAPEP), etc., private individuals as well as Faith Based Organizations. Apart from the collaboration, adaptive managerial strategies should be adopted toward achieving the goals of skill acquisition programs.

2.0 Planning and Feasibility Analysis

The process of planning involves the establishment of standards, objectives and goals against which actual performance will be based and compared. Planning is done to keep to targets and control, to prevent deviation. Planning involves developing the "Road Map," which will help the management to decide for specific course of action among several alternatives (Mgbekem, 2004).

Planning can also be defined as the systematic selection of goals and objectives for implementation over time for the overall development of an organization, a community, a society and a country at large (Ndebbio, 2000). Both definitions emphasized that planning involves developing goals/objectives and identifying targets that will help to achieve the goals.

Planning is also conceived as a mental process of deciding in advance the direction an organization intends to follow to achieve it stated objectives (Ndebbio, 2007). These decisions include who is to do a task when it is to be done, where it is to be done and how it is to be done.

On the other hand, Feasibility Analysis is the process of confirming that a strategy, plan or design is possible and makes sense. This can be used to validate assumptions constraints, decisions, approaches and business cases (Spacey, J. 2017).

According to Ndebbio (2007:89) Feasibility Analysis is designed to project the cost of a conceived project, the demand for the product the project is expected to produce, revenue, cash flow, profits/benefits, etc., of the project under consideration. He also stated that an ideal Feasibility report must include the following analyses:

1. Economic Analysis
2. Locational Analysis
3. Staff/Personal Analysis
4. Technical/Production Analysis
5. Demand and Market Analysis
6. Revenue and Cost Analysis
7. Financial Analysis
8. Cash Flow Analysis
9. Statement of Projected Profit and Loss Analysis
10. Projected Balance Sheet Analysis

From the above ideas on views of planning and Feasibility Analysis, one can evidently state that careful planning and feasibility analysis when undertaken can resolve issues bordering skills acquisition programs.

3.0 Organizing and Production

Organizing is the function of management that involves developing an organizational structure and allocating human resources to ensure the accomplishment of objectives (Principles of Management, 2010).

The organizing function consistently attempts to arrange three components of any unified effort, namely—human, resources and materials, which are necessary for putting plans into operation. Thus, the purpose of the organizing function is to correlate these components so that they will follow the plans and achieve the organization's objectives (Ndebbio, 2007).

Similarly, organizing means building material and human resources of business, arranging both people and materials into a good working team (Basil, 2004). The following steps have been proposed by Ndebbio (2007), to aid managers in organizing successfully:

1. They must establish objectives for the company.
2. They must identify the tasks which are necessary to accomplish these objectives.
3. They must group tasks according to some logical arrangement.
4. They must group staff efficiently so as to achieve the desired returns.

One of the values of organizing is the enhancement of productivity and reduction of waste. Production deals with the creation of goods and services through the application of management or business concept.

Production management involves using resources judiciously to create acceptable products. In this case raw materials are being transformed into value added products efficiently. Every successful organization has a line function which production comes under, and this has a direct impact on the customers. Hence, it dictates customer experience which is critical for the survival of any organization (Understanding of Production and Operations Management [n.d.]).

Skill acquisition programs should be organized successfully so as to achieve desired returns.

4.0 Directing

Directing has to do with supervision of employees as they perform their task. In directing, managers must adopt the style of Leadership which will encourage efficient work (Ndebbio, 2007). If managers are effective leaders, their employees or subordinates will be enthusiastic about exerting effort to attain organizational objectives. On this note, the manager has to develop capacity to motivate workers to greater achievement through his leadership.

Mgbekem (2002:3) noted that organizational leaders can motivate employees to work harder by behaving in conformity with the desires, expectations and preferences of employees. This means that they must do things which employees desire, expect or prefer them to do. And this will in turn change their negative behavior toward doing desirable things for the organization, making them to work enthusiastically and committedly to achieve organizational goals.

The author also stated that employee task, motivation is an essential element for production because maximum production is dependent on the level of employee's willingness and dedication to produce. If the level of their willingness is high, production will be correspondingly high. And if the level of their willingness to produce is low, production will be low (Mgbekem, 2002).

Directing or Leading which involves the social and informal sources of influence that managers use to inspire actions taken by subordinate should be implemented in skill acquisition programs. There should also be availability of incentives which will motivate trainers as well as trainees to work harder.

5.0 Controlling

Controlling involves seeing that everything is done in accordance with the rules which have been laid and the instructions which have been given (Basil, 2004). The managerial function of control is basically to ensure that plans already developed are carried through to successful completion (Ndebbio, 2007). Controlling indicates that actual performance is guided toward set of goals with the main purpose of correcting lapses and errors (mgbekem, 2004).

Pickle and Abraham (1974), as cited by Ndebbio (2007) highlighted the basic steps in the control cycle which include the following:

i.   Establishing standards of performance
ii. Checking on performance at regular interval
iii. Determining if any deviations from established standards of performance exist
iv. Taking corrective action if there are deviations from standards, otherwise continue the activity

From the above steps, a manager has to establish standards of performance for employees such as how much each worker is expected to produce. Thereafter, he has to continually educate and compare work-

125

er's output to these standards. If deviations occur, corrective action should be taken to achieve standard (Ndebbio, 2007).

The managerial function of controlling should not be ignored in skill acquisition programs. Controlling provides answer to questions like what is going on? Or what is happening here? The purpose of controlling is to measure actual performance as a guide toward predetermined goals. It is emphasized that what should be controlled should be activities that would have significant impact on the achievement of objectives and allow for remedial action (Mgbekem, 2004).

6.0   Communication

Communication is a process of exchanging information between two persons or among many people. In communication, words, ideas, feelings, emotions, perceptions and opinion are expressed and transmitted to other people in an organization (Mgbekem, 2004). The manager uses the following media to communicate or convey information to the target persons, he wishes to reach through: letters, memos, circulars, telex, telephone, notice board, radio, newspaper, television, etc.

Communication is seen metaphorically as the "nervous system" of business (Mgbekem, 2004). Communication is central to the entire management process especially in the way managers conduct the managerial functions of planning, organizing, directing and controlling.

Managers spend a great deal of time communicating, planning, controlling, coordinating, directing and it is done through communication. Communication is, therefore, seen as an integral function of management, as the proper operations of organization cannot be successful without communication (Damiola, 2007).

There should be effective communication in skill acquisition programs. Communication strengthens the organization and also enhances the achievement of objectives and goals of the program.

7.0   Monitoring

Project monitoring is a continuous or periodic review or surveillance of an activity by management at every level of project implementation, aimed at comparing the actual with the planned, analysis impact and make adjustment where necessary. Project monitoring is also describe as the provision of data or information and the use of that information by management to access progress or implementation (Ndebbio, 2007).

The following are reasons why management should embark on monitoring exercise as highlighted by Ndebbio (2007):

1. to access information on the performance of development projects;
2. to access the impact of the projects and programs on the beneficiaries and determine the success rate;
3. to assess the impact of policies associated with project implementation and the various attendant objectives, and
4. to give project planners direct exposure to the practical environment or project implementation, and a sense of direction for future planning.

From the above reasons, it is important for the management of skills acquisition programs to adopt a monitoring technique that will help to achieve the objectives of the program. Skills acquisition centers

should be adequately monitored so as to enable stakeholders establish the exact position of training in these centers.

8.0 Evaluation

Evaluation is a powerful public management tool that can be used to help policy makers and decision makers track progress and demonstrate the impact of a given project/program or policy (Zall, J. and Ray C., 2004).

Project evaluation involves comparing the expected benefits with the resources to be committed. And also comparing benefits or otherwise of a particular project with other competing projects of comparable sizes or magnitudes (Ndebbio, 2007).

The concept of project evaluation varies with the type of project conceived and the complexity of the problem involved. Some of these concepts include cost effectiveness, cost-benefit, budgeting program-ming, etc. Cost-benefit analysis is most appropriate for public projects. This analysis is a systematic way of evaluating a public project (possibly by discounting costs and benefits of a project to arrive at its present value) to determine whether the expected benefits outweigh costs or, vice versa. While in private project, the techniques of accounting and the time value of money are used for analysis. The time value of money is an important concept in which capital has value (Ndebbio, 2007).

Evaluation is essential to ensure that limited resources are efficiently utilized. In skill acquisition pro-grams, evaluation should be given serious attention and action. Evaluation of training programs enables management of organizations to determine how much should be expended on training and whether the money is actually producing results or not.

9.0 Conclusion

This chapter addresses management strategies in Skills Acquisition Programs. These programs are mak-ing positive impact in our nation, though, there is still room for improvement. To attain the required status in Skills Acquisition Programs, managers must perform their roles or functions effectively and efficiently. In addressing these managerial functions which are planning, organizing, directing (leading) and controlling; other processes were also considered which are feasibility study/analysis, production, communicating, moni-toring and evaluation which are used to track progress and demonstrate the impact of the program or project.

Chapter Ten

Evaluation of Skilled Performance

OUTLINE

1. Introduction
2. Evaluation and Assessment Processes
3. Formative and Summative Evaluations
4. Monitoring and Evaluation
5. Cognitive, Affective and Psychomotor Evaluations
6. Continuous Assessment Approach
7. Measurements in Evaluation
8. Conclusion

1.0 Introduction

Evaluation is defined as "an instrument for systematic measure of a sample of behavior" or as "as systematic procedure for observing a person's behavior and describing it with the aid of a numerical scale or category system" (Joshua, 1998; and Brown, 1983 as cited in Joshua, 2005). Evaluation is further defined as "the process of ascertaining the decision areas of concern, selecting appropriate information and collecting and analyzing information to report summary data, useful to decision makers in selecting among alternative and is aimed at choosing the most appropriate form of given situation or activity for the decision maker (Esu, Enukoha, and Umoren, 2016). Okeem simply views evaluation as "the process in determining the degree to which aims and objectives of an educational activity are achieved" (Okeem, 1992 in Esu, Enukoha and Umoren, 2016). Ellington, Percival and Race (1998) view evaluation as "a collection of analysis and interpretation of information about any aspect of a program of education or training as part of a recognized process of judging its effectiveness, its efficiency and any other outcomes it may have" (Ellington, Percival and Race 1998 in Crompton [n.d.]). Crompton (n.d.) asserts that "evaluation is concerned at the macro or holistic level of the learning event, taking into account the context of learning and all the factors that go with it." Evaluation is very important in skill acquisition and in every sphere of human endeavor. Without evaluation, one cannot ascertain his or her achievement in any skill acquisition venture. It forms the basis of the judgment of any activity. In skill acquisition and education generally, evaluation is not just a one stop activity but a continuous process.

1.1 Characteristics and Facts about Evaluation

The following are some of the facts and features of evaluation, according to Uche, and Enukoha (1995) and Disha (n.d.).

1. Evaluation implies a systematic process which omits the casual uncontrolled observation of the trainee.
2. Evaluation is a continuous process. In an ideal situation, the teaching-learning process on the one hand and the evaluation procedure on the other hand, go together. It is certainly a wrong belief that the evaluation procedure follows the teaching-learning process. The continuous nature of evaluation demands that the teacher/trainer appraises or judges the performances, progress and achievement of each trainee on a minute, hourly, daily, weekly, or monthly basis as may be appropriate.
3. Evaluation emphasizes the broad personality changes and major objectives of an educational/skill acquisition program. It therefore includes not only the subject-matter achievements but also attitudes, interests and ideals, ways of thinking, work habits and personal and social adaptability. The overall result of improved teaching and learning is a more positive and accurate perception of self and consequently a greater level of confidence with which the learner/trainee handles his learning responsibilities. Therefore evaluation involves the assessment of students based on the developments brought about through education.
4. Evaluation is more result-oriented when each individual apprentice is considered in terms of growth and development as a person rather than a member of a group. In this regard, the tendency on the part of the teachers to describe the achievement of the whole class of learners rather than those of specific individual learners is consistent with the concept of individual differences.
5. Evaluation serves to accumulate data on the instructional activities of a trainer and the learning gains recorded by trainee. Such a comprehensive program of evaluation involves the use of many procedures and other necessary techniques. The result of this may be used as an evidence for ascertaining whether trainee are progressing along certain desirable lives. Objectivity is the hallmark of the data gathering process.
6. Evaluation is not limited to the teacher. Learning is more effective if the trainees can accurately appraise their individual progress and make appropriate adjustments in terms of their strategies for learning. Training has no value if it does not result in learning on the part of the trainees. It is therefore expected that teachers impart self-appraisal skills to trainees and aid them in identifying their strengths and weaknesses in terms of instructional mastery.

2.0   Evaluation and Assessment Processes

Assessment, according to Erwin (1991), is "the systematic basis for making inferences about the learning and development of students. It is the process of defining, selecting, designing, collecting, analyzing, interpreting and using information to increase students' learning and development." Palomba and Banta (1999) view it as "the systematic collection, review and use of information about educational programs undertaken for the purpose of improving student learning and development." Assessments often include various tests, both standardized or criterion-referenced, which reveals a students' aptitude in a particular area" (The Importance of the Assessment Process 2013). The assessment process is a continuous cycle of data garnering with the sole aim of improving upon an activity, program, or venture.

2.1 Processes Involved in Evaluation

According to Disha (n.d.), the following are the steps that are involved in the process of evaluation.

i. **Identifying and Defining General Objectives**

In the evaluation process, the first step is to determine what to evaluate (i.e., to set down educational objectives). What kind of abilities and skills should be developed when a trainee studies a particular skill for a period of time? What type of understanding should be developed in the pupil who learns his mother tongue? Unless the trainer identifies and states the objectives, these questions will remain unanswered.

The process of identifying and defining educational objectives is a complex one. There is no simple procedure which suits all teachers some prefer to begin with the course content, some with general aims, and some with lists of objectives suggested by curriculum experts in the area.

While staking the objectives, therefore, we can successfully focus our attention on the product i.e., the trainee's behavior at the end of a course of study and the state in terms of his knowledge, understanding, skill, application, attitudes, interests, appreciation, and so on.

ii. **Identifying and Defining Specific Objectives**

It has been said that learning is the modification of behavior in a desirable direction. The trainer is more concerned with the trainee's learning than with anything else. Changes in behavior are an indications of learning. These changes, arising out of classroom instruction, are known as the learning outcome.

What type of learning outcome is expected from a student after he has undergone the teaching-learning process is the first and foremost concern of the teacher. This is possible only when the teacher identifies and defines the objectives in terms of behavioral changes (i.e., learning outcomes).

These specific objectives will provide direction to teaching-learning process. Not only that, it will also be useful in planning and organizing the learning activities, and in planning and reorganizing evaluation procedures too.

Thus, specific objectives determine two things; one, the various types of learning situations to be provided by the trainer and two, the method to be employed to evaluate both-the objectives and the learning experiences.

iii. **Selecting Teaching Points**

The next step in the process of evaluation is to select teaching points through which the objectives can be realized. Once the objectives are set up, the next step is to decide the content (curriculum, syllabus, course) to help in the realization of the objectives. For trainers, the objectives and courses are the skills to be acquired.

iv. **Planning Suitable Learning Activities**

In the fourth step, the teacher/trainer will have to plan the learning activities to be provided to the pupils and, at the same time, bear two things in mind—the objectives as well as teaching points. The process then becomes three dimensional, the three co-ordinates being objectives, teaching points and learning activities.

The teacher gets the objectives and content readymade. He is completely free to select the type of learning activities. He may employ the analytic-synthetic method; he may utilize the induc-to-deductive reasoning; he may employ the lecture method; or ask the trainers to divide into

groups and try to do a sort of group work followed by a general discussion and so on. One thing the trainer has to remember is that he should select only such activities as will make it possible for him to realize his objectives.

v. **Evaluating:** In this fifth step, the trainer observes and measures the changes in the behavior of his pupils. This step adds one more dimension to the evaluation process. While testing, he will keep the three aims in mind but his focus will be on the attainment of objectives. The teacher will construct a test by making the maximum use of the teaching points already introduced in the class and the learning experiences already acquired by his pupils. He may plan for an oral test or a written test or a practical one.

vi. **Using the Results as Feedback:** This is the last stage of the steps involved in evaluation process. If after testing the trainees, the trainer find out or realizes that he has not attained his objectives, he will use the results in reconsidering the objectives and in organizing the learning activities. He will retrace his steps to find out the drawbacks in the objectives or in the learning activities he has provided for his students. This is known as feedback. Whatever results the teacher gets after testing his pupils should be utilized for the betterment of the trainees.

2.2 Questions that Guide the Conduct of an Assessment

i) What do we want our students to learn at the course level, skill acquisition or program level?
ii) What is the performance of our students? How do we determine the performance of our students?
iii) What evidence do we need to know or determine how well our trainees are learning?
iv) How do we use the data to confirm or improve on our teaching and learning practices?
v) What impacts do our improvement actions have on student learning?
vi) How are we documenting the assessment and improvement activities and outcomes?

3.0   Types of Evaluation: Formative/Summative

There are two major types of evaluation: The Formative and Summative. Both perform distinct functions and sometimes the line between the two can be very thin that one may mistake the use of one for the other. However, both aim at generating data that determines the trainee's performance in the course of the skill acquisition program.

3.1 Formative Evaluation

This is "an on-going method of evaluation that helps the teacher/trainer to monitor the learner/trainee's progress and identify any challenges that students are facing as they learn. It includes a series of quick-fire tests that provide on time feedback on students' performance." (Formative vs. Summative Assessment). Esu, Enukoha and Umoren (2016:80) explain formative evaluation "to as guidance oriented, because it is meant to identify the child's need for help and guidance in working within the curriculum. In terms of evaluating a trainee's achievement, it carries the least load of threat and it operates on the basic predisposition to make the child succeed." The objective of formative assessment is to find out how much students' know as they move from one learning phase to another. There are no high stakes attached to formative evaluation and the students' performances are not measured against a rubric or standardized benchmark. The teacher/trainee

cannot be an objective outsider but must become deeply involved with the trainer and the skill acquisition process. Esu, Enukoha and Umoren (2016:80) further explain that in the curriculum development center, this type of evaluation goes through a variety of stages before the final product. For instance, ideas are tried out, modified and retried until the curriculum developer is reasonably satisfied with the product (i.e., a stage where the program is now ready for introduction into schools on a large scale).

In the skill acquisition center, formation evaluation takes place almost on a daily basis. It could include daily, weekly, practical performance test, among others. Yambi (2020:4) explains that the formative assessment is designed to assist the learning process by providing feedback to the learner, which can be used to identify the strengths and weaknesses and hence improve future performance.

3.1.1 Advantages of Formative Evaluation

The following are the advantages of the formative evaluation as summarized by Esu, Enukoha and Umoren (2016).

i.   The formative evaluation serves as an indicator as to whether the trainer is moving in the right direction, as regards the stated objectives.
ii.   It provides immediate feedback to the trainee, trainer and the curriculum expert as regards the learning successes and failure. If the information obtained from the formative evaluation is encouraging, the teacher has a strong feeling that he/she is working toward the right direction but if it is not encouraging, then it calls for modification.

3.2 Summative Evaluation

The summative assessment is used primarily to make decisions for grading or determine readiness for progression. Typically, summative assessment occurs at the end of an educational activity and is designed to judge the learner's overall performance. In addition, it provides the stakeholders, e.g. administrators, information about students' abilities (Darling-Hammond, 2006 as cited in Yambi 2020).

Summative assessment is a traditional method of evaluation where the teacher measures the students' performance using a standardized benchmark. It is done at the end of the course or instructional unit and it focuses on the program's outcomes. The summative evaluation has a high point value which is why it is used to determine whether the student gets a promotion, passes a course or moves to the next level in learning. The teacher can solely rely on the results of an end-of-term examination to grade the students' and promote them.

The summative assessment methods are not spontaneous. They however follow defined processes with controlled conditions that limit inconsistence. One of the strong points of summative assessment is that it produces similar results when it is done in a controlled context. The following are the examples of the summative assessments: end of term examinations, presentations, etc.

3.2.1 Advantages of the Summative Assessment

One major strong point of summative assessment is that is motivates the students to learn and pay attention in class. Unlike the formative, students known that their grades depend on how well they perform in summative evaluations and this boosts their commitments to the training. It produces consistent results and this is why it is best for grading (Formative vs. Summative Assessment).

3.3 The Purpose, Goals, Focus, and Results of the Formative and Summative Evaluation

The purpose of the summative assessment is to evaluate the students' understanding of the course and the course materials within a specific period. On the other hand, the primary purpose of the formative assessment is to observe the students as they learn and get real-time feedback on their knowledge and experiences. Formative assessments use different tools and methods to monitor knowledge and skill acquisition at different points in the learning curve. Summative assessment, on the other hand, is all about grading the quality of the students' knowledge based on his performance.

The goal of the formative evaluation is improving the teaching and learning process based on the feedback from students while the goal of summative evaluation is to grade a students' performance with a performance marker like a clearly defined benchmark. This means that while formative assessment evaluates learning and knowledge progression, summative assessment collects evidence as proof of a students' proficiency in the course.

Summative assessment pays attention to the outcome as measured by a performance marker while the formative assessment focuses on the on-going learning process. Because of its focus on the on-going learning experience, formative assessment encourages changes and modifications to the learning process based on the feedback from the program participants.

The summative assessments as the name implies, produce quantitative data as results while formative assessment results in qualitative data. Quantitative data has statistical value because it is measured in the form of numbers while qualitative data is the type of data that describes information using groups and categories (Formative vs. Summative Assessment).

4.0 Monitoring and Evaluation

Monitoring is a continuous function that uses the systematic collection of data on specified indicators to provide management and main stakeholders of an on-going development intervention with indications of the extent of progress and achievement of objectives and progress in the use of allocated funds (Organization for Economic Co-operation and Development (OECD) 2002 as cited in Nyirenda 2018).

Evaluation is the systematic and objective assessment of an on-going or completed project, program, or policy, including its design, implementation, and results. The aim is to determine the relevance and fulfillment of objectives, development efficiency, effectiveness, impact and sustainability. An evaluation should provide information that is credible and useful, enabling the incorporation of lessons learned into the decision-making process of both recipients and donors (OECD 2002 as cited in Nyirenda 2018).

When viewed together, monitoring and evaluation are distinct yet complementary. Monitoring provides routine, descriptive information on where a policy, program, or project is at any given time (and over time) relative to the respective targets and outcomes. Evaluation gives evidence of why targets and outcomes are or are not being achieved and involves making judgments and reaching conclusions (Kuse K. and Rist, 2004 as cited in Nyirenda 2018).

In the educational sector, the purpose of monitoring and evaluation (M and E) is to ensure that equitable and quality education is being provided to all the population at all levels. Quality education is a multi-dimensional concept that takes into account the quality aspects on input (human, material and financial) process (teaching-learning and effective management practices), and outputs and outcomes (IIEP:2007 as cited in UNESCO, 2016). Monitoring and evaluation give the basis for both questioning and testing

assumptions. Monitoring and evaluation should be an integral component of any particular school since it helps in planning (Miller, 2017).

4.1 The Importance of Monitoring and Evaluation

The importance and benefits of monitoring and evaluation in the educational sector cannot be underestimated. Miller (2017) summarizes the importance of monitoring and evaluation thus:

i.   **Accountability:** Through monitoring and evaluation in schools, good leadership is put into practice and accountability which leads to a positive improvement. Effective monitoring and evaluation can best be achieved through record keeping and proper reporting systems. This helps in figuring out whether the teaching method in the school is delivering to the desired educational results. Any school management team will have better means to learning and improve from past experiences; improve planning, and better allocation of resources if they put the best monitoring and evaluation practices. Through this, the school can be accountable to the stakeholders.

ii. **Performance:** Monitoring and evaluation systems have enhanced the performance of both the teachers and the students. Through the use of technology, the school management and the teachers can be used to give guides on how to improve the performance of the students.

iii. **Planning:** Monitoring and evaluation plays a major role in planning. It helps the management to plan on the future of the school. The school management plan on the areas to fill the gaps and cover, appropriately balance between attained targets and future assessment opportunities.

4.2 Types of Monitoring

Different activities take place within the school system or the skill acquisition center. The following are the types of monitoring as explained in UNESCO (2016).

i.   **Compliance Monitoring—Focusing on Inputs**

This is a bureaucratic type of monitoring to ensure that the educational institutions comply with predetermined standards and norms set by the rules and regulations. It is mainly focused on the teachers, textbooks, classrooms, teaching equipment, etc.

ii. **Diagnostic Monitoring—Focusing on Processes**

This type of monitoring focuses on the instructional processes relating to what happens in the classroom and whether the students are actually learning what they are supposed to learn. Since the teaching-learning process is equally as important as input variables in education, having such monitoring would give insightful information on explaining the quality of education provided by the educational institutions.

iii. **Performance Monitoring—Focusing on Outputs**

The emphasis of this kind of monitoring is on the academic achievement of the students through testing and to see what results have been yielded by the investments made in education.

4.3 Components of the Monitoring Systems in Education

The following are the components of the monitoring systems in education as explained in UNESCO (2016).

i. **School Record Keeping System:** This aims to keep information at the school level. This typically includes data on students (school entrance, attendance, academic achievements, etc.), teachers (individual profile), finance (school budget and expenses), and physical facilities (quantity and quality of school building, classrooms, furniture, equipment, etc.).

ii. **Statistical Data System:** This is also known as Educational Management Information System and analyze school level data (students, teachers, facilities, finance, etc.) for policy and program formulation, implementation and monitoring at different administrative levels.

iii. **Resource Management Systems:** These could include the following:
  a. Teacher management (or Teacher Management Information System—TMIS), which is designed to support the management of teachers' recruitment and deployment, and
  b. Financial resource management (of Financial Management Information Systems—FMIS), which is conducts the transactions and monitors the financial status of education institutions.

iv. **Performance Evaluation System:** This includes
  a. A school inspection and Evaluation System which is carried out by the Ministry of Education to observe and inspect whether schools comply with the rules, regulations and standards set by the relevant authorities, and
  b. A teacher evaluation system whose function is carried out by relevance education institutions to evaluate the performance of teachers.

v. **Student Evaluation System:** This may include the following:
  a. An examination system designed for the purpose of certifying or selecting students, usually covering the main subject areas in the school curriculum, and
  b. A student assessment system designed to provide an estimate of the achievement level in the education system as a whole at a particular age or grade level.

Therefore, a good monitoring system for a partnership combines information at all levels to give the management team, and ultimately, the governing body, a picture of performance, and helps facilitate decision-making and learning by the partners. The stakeholders in the educational system are the learners, teachers and facilitators, technicians, parents or guardians, curriculum developers, teacher trainers, educational administrators, education officials, employers and community based organizations.

5.0   The Cognitive, Affective and Psychomotor Domains

The knowledge of the three domains in education plays a vital role in the preparation, delivery and evaluation of the learners or trainees. The three domains are attributed to the following scholars Benjamin Bloom—Cognitive domain; David Krathwohl and Anita Harrow—psychomotor domain.

5.1 The Cognitive Domain

Gray (2021) explains that "the cognitive domain is where the intellect is developed. Within the cognitive domain, trainees possess new information, store knowledge and retrieve it to apply to new circum-

stances. According to Gray (2021), Bloom has developed a hierarchy of cognitive skills that guides teachers as they move students to more rigorous thinking.

The first level is recalling information. While there is a certain amount of remembering facts that trainees need to develop schema, teachers should be careful not to limit trainee's to low-level skills. The majority of instructional time should be spent working in higher cognitive levels.

The second level is comprehension. The third level requires students to apply information they have learned. Applying information may include making classifications or teaching others what they have learned.

The fourth is the analysis which involves making references and drawing conclusions. Trainees at this level compare and contrast two elements within the learning experience and further investigate a concept.

The fifth is the synthesis, which includes developing or creating a new product. The fifth level is evaluation in which trainees are able to critique others or defend a position through debate.

5.2 The Affective Domain

This domain yields emotions, values and attitudes. Student motivation and engagement are tied to the affective domain. The following are the domain of taxonomy in the affective domain as explain in Esu, Enukoha and Umoren (2016).

- **Receiving:** This refers to the students' willingness to attend to particular phenomena or stimuli. From a teaching standpoint it is concerned with getting, holing and directing the trainee attention. Learning outcomes in this area range from the simple awareness that a thing exists to selective attention on the part of the leaner. Receiving represents the lowest level learning outcomes in the affective domain.

- **Responding:** Responding refers to an active participation on the part of the trainee. At this level, he not only attends a particular phenomenon but also reacts to it in some way. Learning outcomes in this area may emphasize acquiescence in responding (reading assigned materials) willingness to respond (voluntarily reads beyond assignment), or satisfaction in responding (read for pleasure or enjoyment). The higher levels of this category include those instructional objectives that are commonly classified under interests; that is they stress the seeking out and the enjoyment of particular activities.

- **Value:** This is concerned with the worth a student attaches to a particular object, phenomenon or behavior. These range in degree from the simpler acceptance of value (desires to improve group skills) to the more complex level of commitment (assumed responsibility for the affective functioning of the group. Learning outcomes in this area is concerned with behavior that is consistent and stable enough to make the value clearly identifiable. Instructional objectives that are commonly classified under attitudes and appreciation fall into this category.

- **Organization:** Organization is concerned with bringing and building together different values, resolving conflicts between them, and beginning the building of an internally consistent value system. Learning outcomes may be concerned with the conceptualization of the value or with the organization of the value system (that satisfies his needs for economic security and social service).

- **Value Complex:** At this level, the individual has a value system that has controlled his behavior for a sufficiently long time for him to develop a characteristic lifestyle. Thus, the behavior is pervasive, consistent and predictable. Learning outcomes at this level cover abroad range of activities but the major emphasis is on the fact that the behavior is typical or characteristic of the trainee. Instructional objectives that are concerned with the trainee's general pattern of adjustment (personal, social, emotional) would be appropriate here.

5.3 The Psychomotor Domain

This domain governs the motor skill development. All the activities within the psychomotor domain improve fine motor, gross motor or perceptual skills. Such objectives when found on our educational literature are related to handwriting, speech, physical education as well as technical courses. Major categories in the psychomotor domain include the following:

- **Perception:** This is concerned with the use of the sense or skills to obtain cues that guide motor activity. This category ranges from sensory stimulation (awareness or stimulus, through one selection to translation (i.e., selecting task-relevant cues to relating the cue to perception), to action in a performance.
- **Set:** Set refers to readiness to take a particular type of action. This category include mental set (mental readiness to act), physical set (physical readiness to act), and emotional set (willingness to act). Perception serves as a prerequisite for this category.
- **Guided Response:** Is concerned with the early stages in learning a complex skill. It includes initiation (repeating an act demonstrated by the instructor) and trial and error (using multiple response approach to identify an appropriate response. Adequacy in performance is judged by an instructor or by a suitable set of criteria.
- **Mechanism:** Is concerned with performance act where the learned responses have become habitual and the movements can be performed with some confidence and proficiency. Learning outcomes at this level are concerned with performance skills of various types but the movement patterns are less complex than at the next higher level.
- **Complex Overt Response:** This is concerned with muscle response. Learning outcome at this level include highly coordinated motor activities.
- **Origination:** Origination refers to the creating of new movement patterns to fit a particular situation or specific problem. Learning outcome at this level emphasizes creativity based upon highly developed skills.

5.4 The Importance of the Taxonomy in Educational Objective

The following are the values of taxonomy of the educational objective as summarized in Esu, Enukoha and Umoren (2016:53).

i.   It makes for a tightening of the languages of educational objectives such that the objectives give direction to the learning process and determine the evidence to be used in appraising or evaluating the effect of the learning experience.
ii. It would enable authors of educational objectives to know exactly what they mean and the learners to equably have a clear view of what is intended.
iii. It provides a convenient system of describing and ordering test items and examination techniques and evaluation instrument.
iv. It will make possible for the studying and comparison of educational problems as well as serve as a tool for clarifying and organizing educational research result.
v.   It envisions the possibility that we might select the principles of classifying educational outcomes, such an order among those outcomes would be relevant to complex as well as simple types of human learning.

6.0   Continuous Assessment Approach

Joshua (2015) defines the continuous assessment as "the systematic collection of mails or grades over a period of time and their aggregation into a final grade. The Federal Ministry of Education (1985 Handbook as cited in Joshua, 2005) defines the continuous assessment as a mechanism whereby the final grading of a student in the cognitive, affective, and psychomotor domains of knowledge takes into account in a systematic way all of his performances during a given period of schooling.

6.1 Characteristics/Benefits of the Continuous Assessment

There are four major features of the continuous assessment, as explained in Joshua (2005).

i.   **It is systematic:** Continuous Assessment requires some plans, well laid out for effective implementation. Such plans will show what and when measurements are to be made, after what content materials have been covered; what measurement instruments will be applied, etc.

ii.   It is Comprehensive: CA does not focus on cognitive domain alone. It covers the entire three domains of learning. As the child is expected to be trained or educated holistically in the three domains, assessments should be done comprehensively. This also requires a wide variety of measurement instruments, like the test and nontest instruments like questionnaires, observation techniques, checklists, rating scales, anecdotal records, projects, assignments, etc.

iii.   **It is cumulative:** CA provides data for decision-making. This information is addictive. Any decision made on or about a child takes into account all previous decisions taken about him or her. The activities of the child from the first day he/she begins school till the day of graduation combine to determine his/her final grade or level of pass. These "measurements" will then reveal the child's true ability and will average out the subjective, imprecise, invalid and unreliable aspects of that measurement.

iv.   **It is guidance-oriented:** CA provides data or information that are not only used for giving appropriate grade to the learner or school child, but data can be used for guiding and counseling the child in educational and vocational areas. Data from CA constitute feedback to both the learners and teachers, and also parents/guardians. Learning disabilities can be discovered and corrected early enough. Patterns can emerge through the data that could lead to advice on career choice, placement, and early timely withdrawal from wrongly chosen careers/courses, etc.

7.0   Measurements in Education

Measurement is the process of obtaining a numerical description of the degree to which an individual possesses a particular characteristic (attribute, construct or variable). It is a process employed to obtain a quantified representation of the degree or level to which a person reflects a characteristic, attribute, trait or behavior" (Gronhund, 1985; Brown 1983 as cited in Joshua, 2005). Generally, measurement is a broad term for any activity and method that is used in assuming an individuals' level of competence in a particular level of knowledge acquisition. Test is an instrument of measurement in the educational and in any skill acquisition venture. There are components of the test as explained in Joshua (2005).

i.   **Measurement Instrument:** The test is a yardstick that a trainer requires to ascertain the level of understanding in a trainee.

ii. **A Systematic Procedure:** The test provides a systematic and perhaps a standard measure for a thing. The standard procedure of the test minimizes the possible influence of irrelevant factors such as emotional influences on the test scores and creates an enabling environment for everyone to be tested with the same procedure.

iii. **Behavior:** A test measures only the output (behavior or response) of the trainee and not what is not put forth. An individual's knowledge level is only known by his/her responses to the test items.

iv. **Sample:** A test usually contains only a sample of all possible items. No test can include all possible items that might be developed to measure a domain of characteristics.

8.0 Conclusion

Evaluation is as important as the activities one participates in, in the actualization of one's or any organizational goal. Evaluation judges the effectiveness of any skill acquisition venture to ascertain the level of achievement in such a program. Evaluation is useful to all the parties involved in the skill acquisition program; the trainee, trainer, management and the sponsors. To the trainee, evaluation allows for the individual to judge his/her performance within that skill acquisition venture. To the trainer, it serves as a feedback system that aids the trainer to modify or improve on the methods applied. It also serves as a basis for the counseling of a trainee, on the part of the management whether to continue in the program or not. Also on the part of the management, it creates room for the assessment of the level of the actualization of the organizational aims and objectives.

Skill Development Advisory Dynamics

OUTLINE

1. Introduction
2. Nature of Skill Development
3. Why Skill Development Is Necessary
4. Benefits of Skill Development
5. The Skill Development Advisory
6. Conclusion

1.0 Introduction

In this chapter, we have described the nature of skill development as a furtherance of basic or already high skill that a person obtains. We have stated the rationale for a higher degree of skill acquisition as a way of honing capabilities, being aware of new developments in the field and attracting their pay. Major part of this chapter focuses on the unique role of the skill development advisor or facilitator in the industry.

2.0 Nature of Skill Development

Skills cut across the regular education, vocational training and career growth. At all levels, individuals and groups have the need to enhance employability and productivity by undergoing hands-on and advance training toward improving capabilities.

Thus the two dimensions of skill development mandate entails identification of needs or gaps and taking counsel or advice on the best ways to fill the gap based on the need to obtain optimal productivity index.

```
                        ┌──────────┐
                        │  Skill   │
                        └──────────┘
                       ╱            ╲
                      ╱              ╲
      ┌───────────────┐  ◄──────  ┌──────────┐
      │ Knowledge gap │           │ Training │
      └───────────────┘           └──────────┘
                      ╲              ╱
                       ╲            ╱
                   ┌─────────────────┐
                   │ High productivity │
                   └─────────────────┘
```

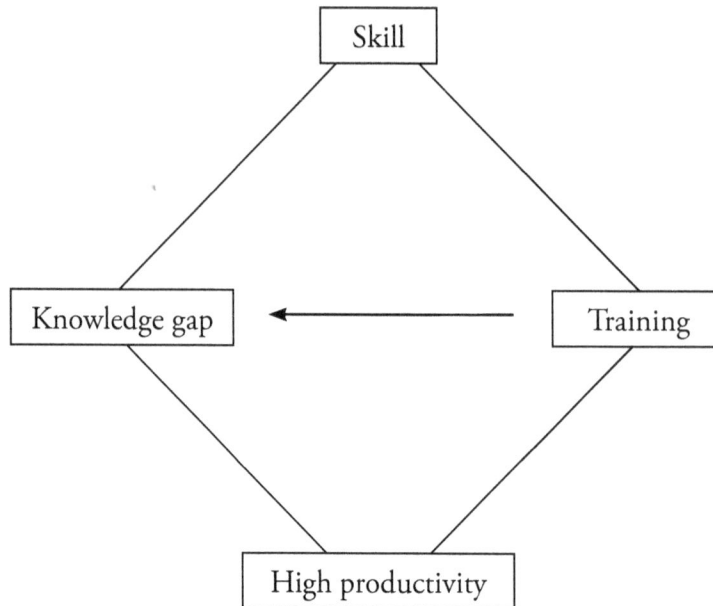

Skill development leads to evolution of talents into customized mastery that constitutes an asset to the organization based on the need of a particular time or season in a sector.

Generally, skill development hinges on four parameters which can result in a comprehensive value index that sets one apart as a twenty-first-century industry labor complaint. The workforce efficiency in both public and private systems becomes more competitive through education and training systems. Inversely, there are higher chances of employability and productivity in current future work situations.

The four skill development parameters and their correlates in skill set are as follows:

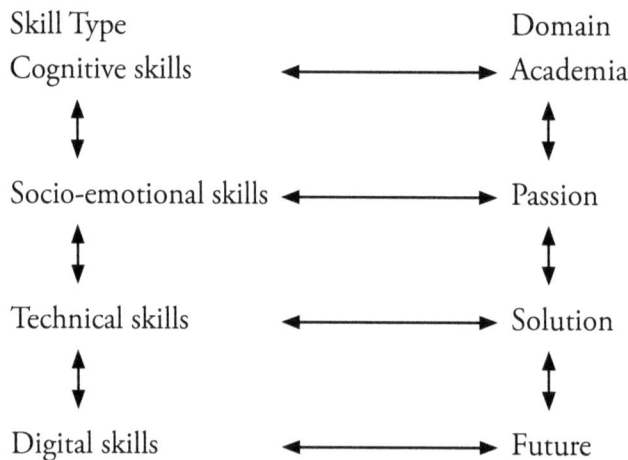

Skill Type	Domain
Cognitive skills ◄──────►	Academia
↕	↕
Socio-emotional skills ◄──────►	Passion
↕	↕
Technical skills ◄──────►	Solution
↕	↕
Digital skills ◄──────►	Future

There is a tight interrelatedness among these four sets to produce a total expert that holds the capability for effective delivery.

Emanating from the regular school curricula, a person learns from experience, reason, creativity and criticism such problem solving strategies like literacy and numeracy. He will proceed to obtain exposure in handling interpersonal and team relationships which also demand leadership and ethical grit.

The technical and digital skills set the educated and socially savvy person higher into new dimensions of advance knowledge, high-demanding tasks and mastery of technological, management, and communicative tools.

2.0 Key Issues in Skills Development

There are a number of challenging issues in the world of skill development as noticeable globally and are subject of study by experts in the skill acquisition and development sector.

Identification of Need and Access

A trainee and his sponsor must first identify a need for further out-or-in-service training based on perceived benefits, among which is the procurement of additional qualifications, earning of higher wages and return in investment. Once a need is identified, the next issue is if the potential trainee will be given access or opportunities. Experiences have confirmed that in most organizations or systems, the low or middle level workforce do not have easy access to training opportunities and their rise to the top positions in the industry turns out to be very slow.

There is also the question of aptitude and flexibility on the part of persons who need the upward talent movement especially when the training demands technical contents which contrast sharply with the regular educational qualifications.

Quality

Undoubtedly, skill gaps exist based on the need for improvement in performance, delivery and productivity. As against the simple information in the general, secondary and post-secondary education, the technical, vocational or institute trainings demand quality assurance for proper control. Quality assurance is part of the higher regulatory system put in place to ensure sustainability of the training.

Relevance

The idea of matching additional training with the existing expertise is key and can at times post challenges to the candidates for skill development. When driven by labor market career elevation, some candidates need to adjust to the new terms of engagement in curriculum, time, space, tools and methodologies of delivery in the new training.

Efficiency

Every skill development draws on the desire for increased efficiency in input and output or training processes and outcomes. This expectation can give rise to financing, sustenance and corporate governance. In less developed countries where corruption thrives, systems may be compromised and the training processes can fail to produce the desired result of more efficient personnel and workforce.

3.0 Why Skill Development Is Necessary

There are many reasons why careerists need to advance their skills and capabilities through establishment capacity building or personal skill development initiatives.

- **Commitment to Success**

    Career growth and skill development undoubtedly up employees interest in uplifting their job abilities rather than merely belonging to the corporate world. Success in professionalism is an attraction that gets deliberate pursuit through career/skill development. This is so because professionalizing is like climbing to a height using a ladder. The rungs are there as handlers of steps. Success rings at the higher rungs and only a commitment to deliberate skill development can take an individual there.

- **Motivation for Upgrading**

    Skill development training offers trainees the drive to learn new skills and grasp the niche of professional trends. A key dimension of professionalism is the motivation to maintain progressive growth in matching new developments in the profession. In some professions, inability to adjust to new technologies can create career extinction. A stenographer who refuses to train upwards from manual typing to the current direct imaging and computerized document production may be heading for irrelevance.

TYPEWRITER	COMPUTER OPERATOR

- **Beating Competitiveness**

    The laisse faire capitalist economy thrives on neck breaking, cutting edge competition. Any stagnant careerist will be thrown out of the industry and production market by the trendists.

To rise above personal or organizational tide of competition, both new and old employees must strive to hone their skills and aim at the stars in the profession and have something extra, to remain the lead. A talented footballer who refuses to attend a Football Academy may soon hang his boots.

- **Problem Solving**

    Life presents a lot of challenges generally. The workplaces and industries also pose their set of difficulties and challenges that demand high intellectual capacity, creative thinking and technical know-how to solve. In some situations, regular skills levels and knowledge do not suffice in solving such problems. Skill development and advanced capabilities are needed. This is more so in the area of handling new equipment. Fortunately every human civilization has ensured skills are deployed to handle the changes that bring about new challenges and difficulties. For instance, to avoid the danger of losing lives in a military operations, the drone facility maybe deployed.

4.0 Ten Benefits of Skill Development

1. It helps in increasing employee engagement so that employees can work toward their goals and accomplish them.
2. It creates a culture that's backed by accountability and ownership.
3. It increases employee motivation by helping them be updated with latest trends in the industry.
4. It reduces employee turnover and increases the adaptability toward accepting new technologies and policies.
5. It transforms organizational cultures to high performing cultures.
6. It enables leaders to shape up their experiences and beliefs of the people they are leading to help them achieve their goals.
7. It helps in risk management by training employees about topics like sexual harassment, diversity training, etc.
8. It helps in persistent and long term change-related problems as well.
9. It enhances company's image and brand value by conducting targeted ethical training.
10. It increases productivity and morale of employees which leads to overall growth of the organization.

5.0 The Skill Development Advisory

An SDA or SDF is a skill development advisor or skill development facilitator who specializes in identifying skill gaps, planning advisory policies, implementing them, and reporting their outcomes in an organization. Detailed functions of an SDA can be outlines as follows:

- Advising employees and employers on skill development plans based on needs, suitability, strategic plans and career requirements.
- Developing, drafting and implementing Workplace Skills Plan (WSP) as a skill development policy for an organization.
- Liaising between trainees and training centers by promoting integrated vocational services.
- Assisting training agencies (private and government) by providing operational and consultancy services.

- Analyzing and deploying skill development legislations in the workplace and individuals aspirations.
- Developing strategies for effective skill development for persons and institutions.
- Serving as a resource person in key aspects of skill development.

Professional Aspects of SDAs

The question that is often asked in the industry is: Does a skill development advisor or facilitator need to be a professional or a trained and licensed practitioner in the field?

It appears that for an SDA to effectively perform his task, he needs to go through an accreditation assessment and tested on the standards of the practice against latest developments in the field. These standards include

- organizational training and developmental plan;
- sustaining a learning culture for an organization;
- coordinating skill training interventions;
- establishing a quality assurance for training templates;
- upholding ethical values in skill development, selection, financing, and delivery;
- providing updated information and counseling in skill development issues;
- handling evaluation and registration processes in professionalism and career growth;
- maintaining a code of conduct and observing disciplinary requirements.

The Use of Training Committees

Most institutions establish committees to handle skill development matters in terms of recommendations, consultations and actual training. The committee comprises trade unions' representatives, employee representatives and Human Resources Managers. The committee meets regularly to carry out the following businesses.

- Consultations with relevant stakeholders in the skill development process
- Assessment of grants to suitable applicants
- Supporting the decisions by the skill development advisor or facilitator
- Improving the quality of life and productivity in the workplace through investment in training and up-skilling
- Providing guidelines on skill development with recommendations from the relevant Acts and legislations
- Analyzing internal procedures for skill development policies and practices
- Compiling reports to the relevant employment and training agencies
- Encouraging employees to take advantage of incentives, mobility, and training opportunities in the industry
- Assisting employees to hone competencies and up performance, especially in technological processes

Role of the Training Committee

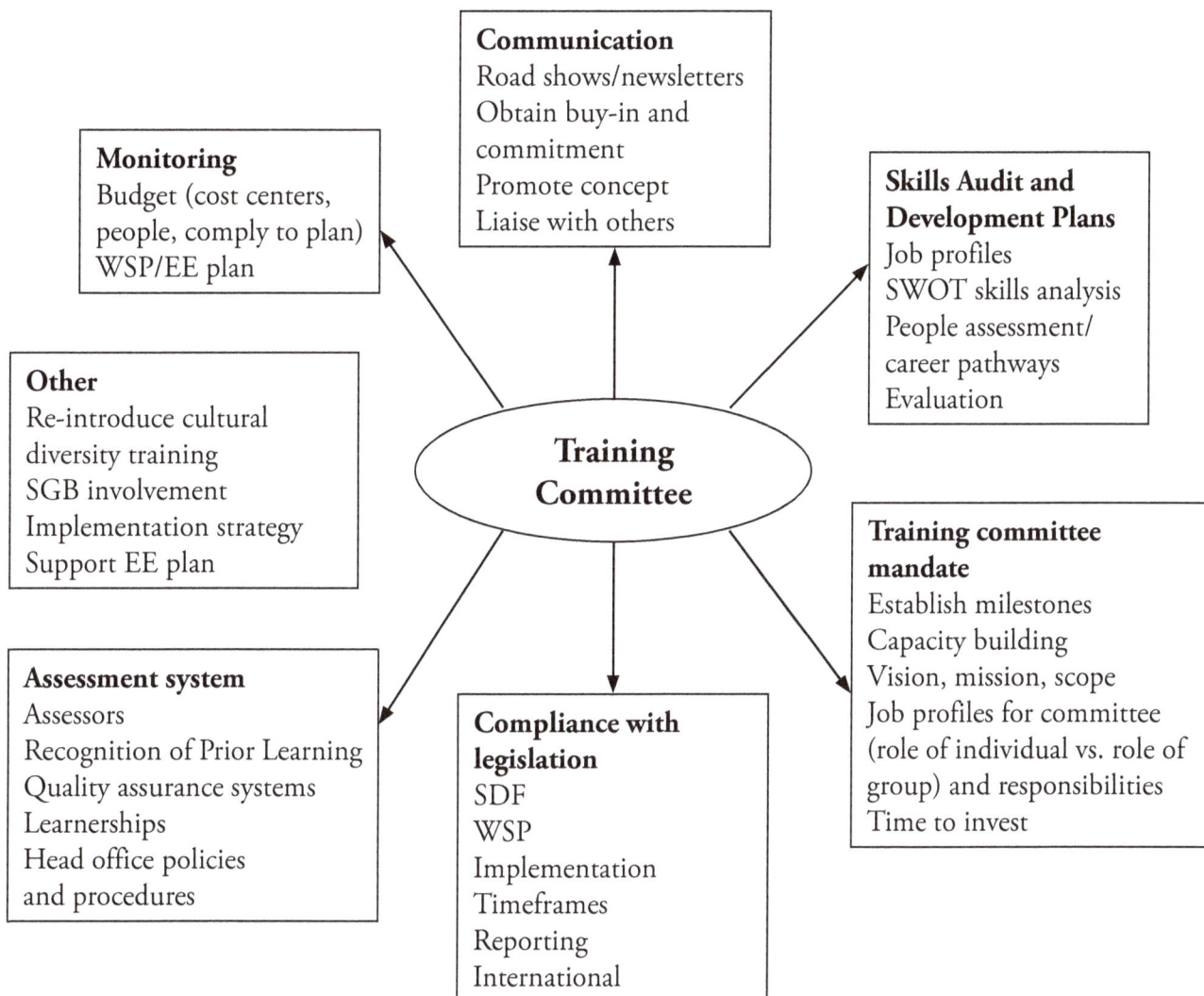

Communication
Road shows/newsletters
Obtain buy-in and
commitment
Promote concept
Liaise with others

Monitoring
Budget (cost centers,
people, comply to plan)
WSP/EE plan

**Skills Audit and
Development Plans**
Job profiles
SWOT skills analysis
People assessment/
career pathways
Evaluation

Other
Re-introduce cultural
diversity training
SGB involvement
Implementation strategy
Support EE plan

Training Committee

**Training committee
mandate**
Establish milestones
Capacity building
Vision, mission, scope
Job profiles for committee
(role of individual vs. role of
group) and responsibilities
Time to invest

Assessment system
Assessors
Recognition of Prior Learning
Quality assurance systems
Learnerships
Head office policies
and procedures

**Compliance with
legislation**
SDF
WSP
Implementation
Timeframes
Reporting
International

6.0 Conclusion

We examined the inter-relatedness the four domain types of skills cognitive, socio-emotional, technical and digital. We conclude that skill development, in addition to filling knowledge gap through high training, also leads to high productivity, quality of products/services, relevance in the field and efficiency. We realized that upgrading, problem-solving and beating competition are some of the motivating factors for skill development. We also x-rayed the duties of the skill development individual and committee advisory. Our conclusion is that skill development is indispensable for the growth of the economy and higher productivity.

Ethical Issues in Skill Acquisition

<small>OUTLINE</small>

1.0   Introduction
2.0   What Is Ethics and What Are Its Values
3.0   Ethics as Legal Code of Conduct
4.0   Ethics as Moral Code of Conduct
5.0   Ethics in a Learning Environment
6.0   Ethics in a Business Environment
7.0   Addressing Some Unethical Issues
8.0   Conclusion

1.0   Introduction

This chapter is dedicated to defining and stating the role of ethics in skill acquisition as a learning, working and socializing environment. Ethical codes portend great values pedagogically and business wise. Both as legal code of conduct and moral compass to behavior, the rules system molds proper standards of human relationships and enhance corporation and efficiency.

The chapter also proffers specific tasks in addressing palpable unethical practices such as harassment, discrimination, corruption and cyber criminalities.

2.0   What Is Ethics and What Are Its Values

Ethics is rooted in human behavior or reactions (responses) to given situations in the environments. These responses which are voluntary and involuntary result in four types of behavior or personality patterns: optimism, pessimism, trust, and envy.

| Optimistic | Pessimistic | Trusting | Envious |

Four Personality Types

| Passive-aggressive | Aggressive | Assertive | Passive |

Another Four Personality Types

| Purely practical | Theoretical-practical | Purely theoretical |

Three Types of Behavioral Patterns

Behavior types also manifest seven systemic patterns in relation to mental productions. These are planned behavior, playful, reflexive, instinctual, exploratory, driven and emotional.

A research by Universidad Carlos II de Medrid (**Error! Hyperlink reference not valid.**) affirms that of the four behavioral patterns, "envy" is the most common. The study classified the envious subjects as "those who don't actually mind what they achieve as long as they are better than everyone else.

Envy is a feeling of discontented or resentful longing aroused by someone else's qualities, possessions, asserts, gifting or talents. It connotes a feeling of unhappiness or inferiority over another person's fortune or advantage coupled with a desire to have same or better.

The above scenario implies that in every group, there are bound to be the envious personalities who will be bent on interpreting life and responding to situations based on the eye of envy. This has both positive and negative consequences. The positive reaction may be for the person to work as hard or be as smart as the subject of envy. The negative outcome is when the envious person thinks of nefarious or hurting ways to get equal. There is therefore a moral burden or code of conduct constraining envious persons from inflicting pains on their victims in their drive to achieve.

Ethics is therefore, a body of moral principles that govern a person's behavioral responses or conducts or activities especially in a group. It extends to attempts at classifying human actions as good and bad, right or wrong, charitable or evil. An ethical conduct is the standard of behavior prescribed for human decisions and their effects on others and the society. Ethical templates are systematically created to defend and recommend concepts of right behavior. They are presented as a system of tacit control over beliefs and convictions that should guide behavior.

Ethics are encoded from morality, social norms, religious creeds, cultural practices and traditions. Ethical contents tend to separate acceptable from unacceptable behavior as are applicable in religions, professions, meeting, institutions, establishments and systems.

Values of Ethics

The following constitute some of the reasons ethics must be applied to guide human behavior.

- **Restricting Ideologies:** In a workplace or group, some persons allow their beliefs to guide their decisions both internally and externally and in some situations, such decisions can undermine professionalism and decrease productivity.
- **Personal Value and Goal Setting:** Since individuals will create their preferences and set their goals according to their personal preferences, it is important to subject them to ethical guidance or codes so that their preferences do not disconnect or affect group goals or generally accepted group values.
- **Effective Leadership:** When both leaders and followers abide by a respectable code of ethics, the team works well confidently as each actor's actions and reactions/responses are predictable and consistent with laid down rules. Additionally, followers enjoy following trustworthy leaders who act credibly and ethically.
- **Progress and Good Decisions:** Persons and groups make progress based on sound decisions arising from strong ethical foundations and set standards of behavior. Therefore, supported with the right motivation and exclusion of fears of ego, whims, and caprices of the leader, the participants in a process can easily align with set mileages and accomplish tasks that lead to future achievements.
- **From Personal to Professional Codes:** Ethics start from individual's mindsets and conscience qualities and proceeds to the group aggregate conduct. A person who has personal integrity easily fits into a professional code of zero-stealing. A trustworthy person can maintain loyalty in an organization. A respectful person will uphold the rights and interests of others without discrimination. A selfless and responsible person will be loyal and committed to organizational vision and mission.

In concluding this segment, it should be stated that skill acquisition and development will depend largely on the ethical values or contents of the process participants: trainees/trainers, students/instructors, and learners/teachers.

3.0 Ethics as Legal Code of Conduct

Codes of conduct are rules or behavioral standards by which individuals organizations, industries private and public sectors of the society all abide. Codes of code help us to know and assess what is right and wrong. Hence doing the right and rejecting doing the wrong.

Business ventures or establishments make rules depending on what characteristic behaviors they want their employees to exhibit for proper functioning of such business organization. After making such rules/ codes of conduct, they encode them upon which the violation of such attracts penalties and sanctions.

With regard to the above entrepreneurial skill acquisition, specific standards that are law oriented to guide, direct, and control such human activities as maintaining good human relationship through peaceful coexistence among its workers, noninvolvement in unsocial activities such as quarrelling as well as employee's regard for his employer and for his fellow employees. Skills acquisition in vocations such as carpentry, tailoring, upholstery, electric repairs and installation, hair dressing, auto repairs and mechanics, roofing work, computer application and repairs, catering must as a matter of compulsion and necessity be carefully and cautiously learned.

Rules of conduct as regard skill acquisition, however, vary from one organization to another, but the following items could be very common among them:

1. Arriving early at work/being dedicated to duty.
2. Paying attention/being focused on the vocation.
3. Being humble and willing to learn.
4. Practicing what they are taught.
5. Being obedient and submissive to employer.
6. The employee must have good behavior and integrity so that their employers wouldn't get angry at them. This would imply that good behavior should be embraced by the apprentice/skill learner.

4.0 Ethics as Moral Codes of Conduct

Another ethical issue that is commonplace to skill acquisition is moral codes of conduct. By moral codes of conduct we mean rules and regulations that guide the moral behavior of an individual, organization, industry, or societies. Moral codes of conduct tend to control, direct, advise and supervise particular behavioral and attitudinal pattern of a person or community. Ethics as moral codes of conduct involves the do's and don'ts of a given socio-cultural, religious, political, institutional and even economic environments.

As moral codes of conduct, ethics of a business or working environment is of the warning that one who involves himself in skill acquisition should shy away from the following:

1. Bribery and corruption.
2. Dishonesty and untruthfulness toward employer and toward customers/clients.
3. Deviation from working standard and rules: This will involve going to work late on a regular basis.
4. Lying and gossips: This may not seem to be an extreme violation of ethics but can produce a very unfriendly and unsociable working environment.

Morally speaking, stealing is also considered an unethical vice. It involves embezzlement of money, misappropriation of funds, stealing office equipment or supplies or intentionally delaying to execute/complete a project within the orbit of the vocation in question, stealing and sharing of confidential information personally or with other workers.

Also, appealing for, and accepting or offering a bribe is unlawful and morally unethical and can breed lack of trust by the employer. This in turn often breeds moral decadence on the part of the practitioners/apprentices/workers who are involved in it. Therefore, if you are a worker or an apprentice who is offered a gift, ensure that you consider the cost, timing, and type of gift that is offered to you as well as the relationship between you, the receiver and the giver.

Ethics as moral codes of conduct imply that an employee must have some sort of consciousness of self; a consciousness that is propelled by his conscience to deviate from doing wrong to doing his job well, a consciousness that is capacitated by goodwill to create a conducive skill acquisition/entrepreneurial environment by creating good and friendly interpersonal relationship with his employer, with his co-workers and with the clients/customers of the company/business in question; by being honest and sincere to his employer and others and by being focused in the learning of the skill he intends to acquire. These and more are behavioral patterns the employee/apprentice must exhibit is he must succeed in acquiring a great amount of skill which would in turn enable him to be self-sustainable in the Nigerian society.

Ethics as moral codes of conduct additionally imply that individual apprentices/learners of skills should imbibe good behavioral pattern in terms of their mood of dressing to work place. Workers should adhere strictly to moral codes of conduct concerning dressing, appearing in a way that is typical of the company he is operating under. For the men, there is no room for indecent putting on of trousers, a term culturally referred to the Nigerian context as sagging, while for the young ladies, flaunting of cleavages and other indecent forms of exposing their bodies are morally unethical hence are liable to be frowned at by their establishments, organizations or companies.

Moreover, vocational centers/companies must include ethics in training from the start, and they cannot assume that their employees know the nitty gritty of what is right and wrong in any particular situation based on the personal standards of behavior.

Skill acquisition training is a parameter for guiding employees greatly through the organization's mission statement and the situation that may arise during the period of daily operations. Work learners through business organization practices for these tough situations, and allow them to listen to calls and practice various pathways to deal with these moral circumstances.

It is as well important to point out that all parties employer/employees are responsible and accountable for certain moral behavior they exhibit, as unethical choices cannot be rationalized or justified by another's action. Employees must understand the implications of their decisions but feel supported and enabled to do operate rightly as defined by the company. The moral conducts of employer and employee must tally.

5.0   Ethics in a Learning Environment

Every learning situation such as skill acquisition and development comprising students and teachers, primarily requires ethical awareness and rules that lead to mutual respect, obedience to instructions, academic responsibility, diligence, integrity, and self-discipline.

5.1 Ethical Features of Learning

- **Knowledge:** The trainer must demonstrate adequate knowledge of the subject through properly enacted principles and practicalities.
- **Empathy:** The trainer or instructor must share the needs of the trainee in terms of "why has this trainee come to put in time, resources and energy in learning a particular trade or vocation?" This feeling will ensure openness in the transfer of knowledge.

- **Reasoning:** Most training situations pose problems which can only be solved through proper reasoning or critical thinking. Both trainers and trainees must believe in using their brains and creative hones to solve problems.
- **Courage:** Nothing can be achieved in an atmosphere of fear and pessimism. While learners must hunger after knowledge and boldly pursue it, trainers must believe in themselves and manifest the dignity of confidence and trust in their capacity to deliver.
- **Interpersonal Skills:** These relate to mutual respect, charity and communicative capacities. Integrants in skill acquisition process must be able to communicate effectively through verbal and nonverbal media. Impeded communication, sincere alterations and held back expressions can affect learning negatively.
- **Justice:** Wherever human activities such as skill acquisition and development are carried out based on set or generally accepted rules, then the ethical question of fairness and justice comes to play. Despite individual beliefs, learners and teachers are obliged to explore ethical responsibilities of abiding by the rules or being made to face punishments for immoral or illegal conducts.
- **Fiduciary Duty of Care:** In a training environment, the teacher must care about his personal interest as well as the interests of his students and must strike a balance especially in the exercise of power. The students or trainees must obey their trainers who in turn should act in a way to earn their trust by acting ethically, confidently and professionally.
- **Moral Bannering:** Every teacher, instructor, and trainee is accountable to the training system in moral standard and behavior made manifest in interactions with students, colleagues, parents and administrators. A trainer cannot live carelessly and in serial breaches of rules and codes and go ahead to breach morality or integrity to the students or learners.

6.0 Ethics in a Business Environment

Business components are the other side of skill acquisition as opposed to learning. During training, materials and equipment are part to use within an acquired land and the learners provide the labor. The products in a skill training may be sold out for profit-All these involve business processes similarly to what is obtained in a regular industry. Therefore, it is undeniable that there are ethical business dimensions in skill training.

Michael Josephson, the CEO of Josephine Institute, outlined in Global Leadership Bulletin (A Journal of Leaders, by Leaders, and for Leaders), twelve ethical principles for business executives as follows:

1. **Honesty:** Be honest in all communications and actions.
2. **Integrity:** Maintain personal integrity and trust.
3. **Promise-Keeping:** Keep promises and fulfill commitments.
4. **Loyalty:** Be loyal within the framework of other ethical principles by advancing the lawful and legitimate interests of the organization.
5. **Fairness:** Strive to be fair and just in all dealings and in exercising power, tolerating diversity of opinions, admitting wrong and being flexible in positions.
6. **Caring:** Demonstrate compassion and a genuine concern for the wellbeing of others by being kind, benevolent and good and avoiding harm.
7. **Respect for Others:** Treat everyone with respect acknowledging human dignity, autonomy, privacy and interests of stakeholders in the decision process.

8. **Law Abiding:** Obey the Law by abiding by the rules, regulations, acts and codes of business conducts.

9. **Commitment to Excellence:** Pursue excellence all the time in all things in the performing duties, handling information, increasing proficiency and taking responsibility.

10. **Leadership:** Exemplify honor and high moral standards by playing role models and helping to create an environment where principles, logical reasoning and prudence inform decisions.

11. **Reputation and Morale:** Build and respect the organization's reputation and boost the morale of participants by taking affirmative actions and preventing inappropriate conducts that could tarnish personal and corporate image.

12. **Accountability:** Be accountable by owning up mistakes and taking correction and improving the quality of processes leading to decisions.

7.0 Addressing Some Unethical Issues in Skill Acquisition

There are key ethical breaches that occur in skill acquisition trainings and development both from the dimensions of teaching and learning, and the business enterprise or entrepreneurship. Here are some of them and approaches in dealing with them.

1. **Harassment**

   This unethical act relates to hostilities in words and actions, leading to intimidation, irritation, torment, doubts and lack of confidence. Harassment can be verbal, written, physical and visual, leading to humiliation and unfriendliness.

   Harassment can arise from racial prejudice, origin, nationality, skin color, impairments and disabilities, religious and political or cultural believes, sex-related issues (gender, abuse, forceful relationship, undue influence, etc.), age, physical characteristics, stigmatization, marital, and other personal history.

   Organizations need to build ethical codes that discourage all forms of harassment to avoid financial and reputational impact in can exert on the training program or process.

2. **Discrimination**

   This is another very inimical issue in a skill acquisition setting. The US Equal Employment Opportunity Commission (EEOC) represents a good codification of the types of discrimination common in professional settings and the way they affect performance fluency: age, disability, equal pay, pregnancy, race, religion, and sex (gender).

   Discrimination manifests in unjust or impartial or prejudicial treatment of people based on certain parameters like race, age, sex, or disability. When this happens, people are not allowed to enjoy equal human or legal rights on equal basis or they are untreated unfavorably by having their dignities violated.

   Discrimination is often carried out by persons who secretly take advantage of others. The victims should be protected and emboldened to make reports and complaints when they are made to suffer any form of discrimination.

3. **Health and Safety**

   Where there are no binding ethical regime in a training situation, the participants' health and safety can be largely compromised, especially in professions where chemicals and certain harsh

conditions prevail. Occupational Safety and Health Administration protocol stipulates peoples' right to safe working conditions.

Measures recommended to minimize hazards in organizational settings include provision of firefighting equipment, respiratory protection, regulated ladders, electrical protection, machine guarding, fall protection, etc.

4. **Corrupt Accounting System**

This is a vampire that sucks lifeblood from every system. It manifests largely in poor financial reporting by dishonest accounting personnel or dearth of records where figures are merely conjectured. Sometimes, there is no transparency in financial data and funds are easily misappropriated amidst heavy fraudulent racketeering. Quality materials may be substituted with inferior and cheaper ones thereby compromising quality of learning, products and services.

Sometimes, confidential information maybe stolen and used to compromise the financial security diligence. To avoid the above dangers, accounting policies and practices must be very stringent as to punishing violations with heavy penalties.

5. **Bribery**

Bribery of all forms are very destructive to any program. It could result in frustration as a result of compromised choices of personnel and materials, where unfit trainers are preferred and the trainees are denied their due. Bribery blinds the eye from excellence and imposes undue advantage to the perpetrators.

6. **Cyber Activities**

The internet of things and cyber operations have brought in a lot of abuses in processes and systems. Ranging from deceptions, harassments, insecurity, fraud, whistle blowing, unauthorized disclosures and privacy violations of hacking of all sorts, a system can be brought down where ethical measures are not strengthened to protect the operators, the brand and the beneficiaries.

8.0 Conclusion

Every member of an organization, industry or business firm has particular roles to play. Whatever their roles may be, it is incumbent on them to operate based on laid-down ethics which would guide their functions toward efficient and viable productivity. Employees should abide by specific standard as placed by the organizations they are acquiring their skills from, while the employer must avoid the imposition of any form of harassment and discrimination against their employees. They should not unduly psychological effects on their employees.

Health and safety devices and conditions should be given to employees for proper operation while employees should be morally upright, transparent and be honestly accountable to their employers in their services to them. While technological gadgets should be properly utilized for effective work operations and not to be used indiscriminately to divulge information.

Chapter Thirteen

Economic Basis of Skill Acquisition

1.0   Introduction
2.0   Generation of Personal Income
3.0   Fighting Hunger and Lack
4.0   Eliminating Extreme Poverty
5.0   Job and Wealth Creation
6.0   Skilled Labor/Techniques
7.0   Scaling down Unemployment
8.0   Improved Standard of Living
9.0   Increase in Literary Rate
10.0   Industrial/Sectoral Grown
11.0   Mobility of Capital
12.0   Harnessing Informal Sector
13.0   Empowering Vulnerable Populace
14.0   Conclusion

1.0   Introduction

In this chapter, we will situate skill acquisition within the economic scope of intellectual and social appreciation. The central goal here is to elucidate the economic factors that inform skill acquisition as well as the expected outcomes. The hub of economics is the reality that business constitutes a major part of living through specialization in narrow fields of the economy.

This specialization makes it possible for production and exchange of goods and services based on money as the medium of exchange for the basic needs of life (food, clothing and shelter). The web of specialization based on diverse skills for labor as a key factor of production, drives the entire complex economic system.

An economic system practically leads to the science of production and distribution of wealth which entails a long chain of differently skilled, semi-skilled and high skilled people engaging in diverse activities that bring about results and for which they get paid and make wealth and livelihoods.

Thus, labor which is the application of skill is a medium of exchange of services for personal income. While levels of income vary, every income learner can at least attempt to obtain food and ward off hunger and extreme lack that can result in death. Higher skills can lead to greater wealth creation that can create streams of enterprises that can employ other needed skills and this will scale down unemployment, reduce crime rate and improve standard of living.

Most skills are so structured that in the process of acquiring them, the trainees learn to write and speak simultaneously, thus improving their literacy and reasoning. And as skilled practitioners expand their knowledge in the field, the industrial growth increases, investments and banking are promoted he populace are empowered socially, economically and technologically.

2.0 Generation of Personal Income

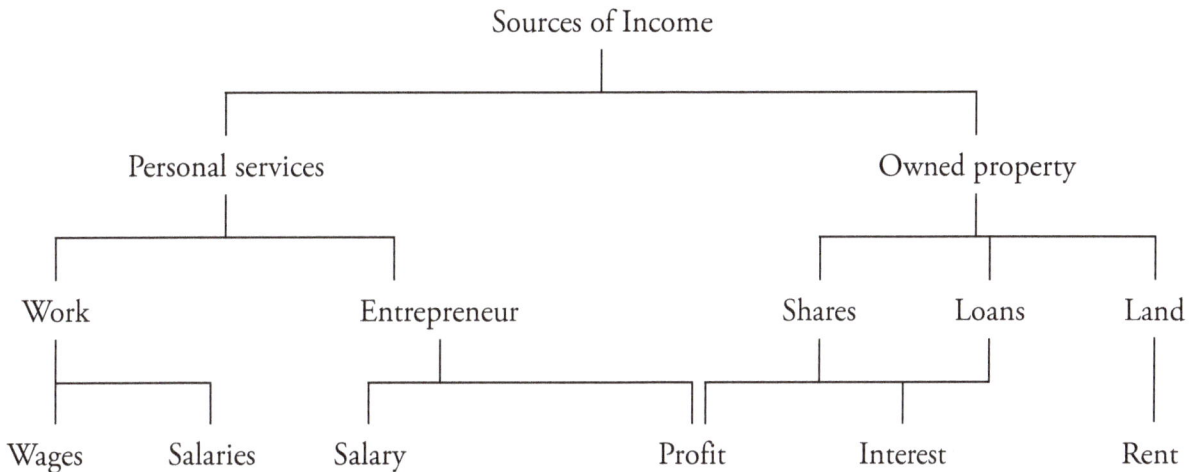

Income is what a person earns as a reward for engaging in labor or work as a factor of production. The earnings come in the form of wages, salaries, allowances, etc., for the worker, then profit, salary and interest for the investor or entrepreneur. Personal income as against national or institutional income is generated either through active work in providing services or serving as an entrepreneur on the one hand or through passive returns on property such as land, loans and shares (profit, interest and rent).

The economic motivation for skill acquisition in relation to the sources of income is that a skilled person can strandle the two legs of the income table. A skilled person, say a carpenter, can work in an aluminum roofing company where he receives salaries on monthly basis. He can proceed to provide part time repair services to estate owners and receive wages. He can also run an entrepreneurial outfit where he organizes a group of carpenters and hire them to different clients while he retains part of the labor costs for his franchise.

A multi-skilled person can attract a multistream of income and proceed to own property through savings that are converted into shares, lendings and land, to produce profit, interest and rents.

3.0 Fighting Hunger and Lack

Livelihood outcomes are important in revealing the rationale for peoples' actions and in actions. Lack of food as basic human need has been a known reason for many human actions and in actions. Hunger stimulus results in the stomach contracting rhythmically and the empire body of the person becoming restless. Some human beings are compelled to beg for food when the hunger stimulus is aroused. Avoiding the shame of begging can drive a person to seek ways of earning money to obtain food and abate lack which can result in more shame.

Hunger has also been known to be at the core of vulnerability to some segment of the population and the direct consequence of poverty associated with unemployment. Therefore as a skilled person is economi-

cally empowered to apply his skill and earn money, he goes ahead to procure food for and others who are yet to obtain skill, education, work or inheritance.

As one of the major Millennium Development Goals (MDGs) is the eradication of extreme poverty and hunger with a target of a proportion of people earning at least a dollar a date by engaging in skills acquisition, creating avenue for wealth creation, sufficiency and self-reliance becomes an economic basis for engaging in skills training.

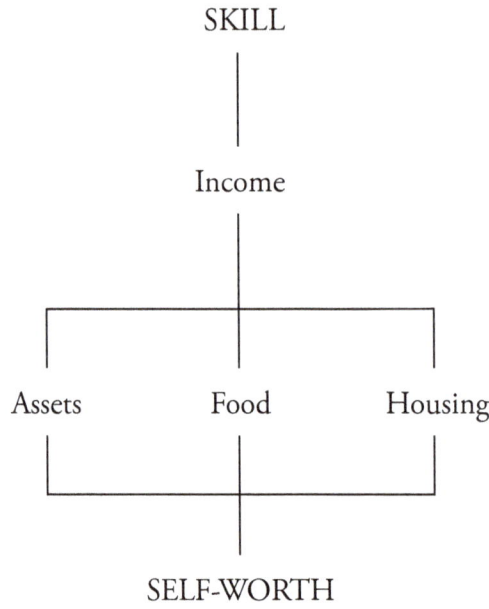

SKILL

|

Income

|

Assets   Food   Housing

|

SELF-WORTH

4.0 Eliminating Extreme Poverty

A major economic index in the world today is the proportion of the population living in extreme poverty, unable to afford the basic necessities of life, facing harsh economic conditions, illiteracy, and poor quality of life and poor health.

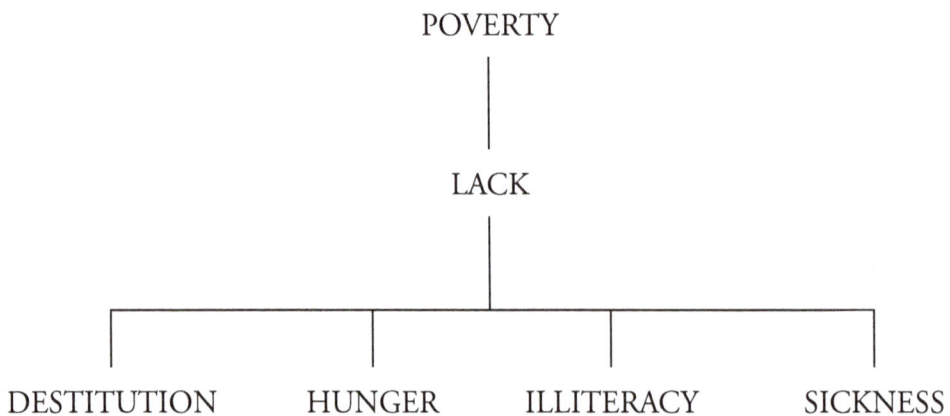

POVERTY

|

LACK

|

DESTITUTION   HUNGER   ILLITERACY   SICKNESS

157

For about a century now, the world has adopted the poverty alleviation dynamics to drive accelerated development, integrated rural development and sustainable community development. All these parameters have yielded a focus on how people can be lifted out of the dungeon of poverty by engaging in skill acquisition and development.

In a long run, poverty which may constitute a life cycle experience with shortage of resources, can be broken by the covering of the poverty gap.

Ndiyo, N. (2008) asserts that employment creation through skill acquisition can transfer income and asserts to the households of poor people and increase earnings, more education and self-reliance. As more households become lifted from poverty, the community as a whole experiences high productivity and can therefore partner government in the provision of basic amenities such as water, sanitation, and health services which will promote the health system and break the poverty circle.

5.0   Job and Wealth Creation

Indolence, joblessness and destitution are considered highly undesirable in every normal society. The human stimulus to satisfy needs and wants is a strong and undeniable reality. As people envy others for their gifting, labor rewards, and sometimes inheritance, the urge to have a similar experience or be in a similar status in life drives people to look for ways and means of earning income and having money to buy what they need and possibly own the factors to produce what they want, in the quality and quantity they want and sometimes to sell the excess or give out as charity.

From the five means of obtaining income (inheritance, gift, luck, crime, and earning), the last option appears to be the most legitimate, enduring and dignifying. Thus, people desire to earn their income by engaging in production of goods and delivery of services, both of which result in financial rewards and psychological satisfaction.

Jobs are pieces of work, tasks, and services done for the payment of agreed prices. People find jobs to have an occupation, build prospects for a greater future, run a family, pay their bills and be in business to boost their personality. Very specially, people search for jobs to practice a skill they have learnt or to obtain a skill while on the job. It is therefore a strong economic reason to seek a skill training so as to have a job of one's dream.

Also, people desire to have a skill to have a means of creating and possessing personal wealth which comprises belongings such as clothes, watches, books, cars, furniture and jewels wealth has money value and are transferrable. This is an additional value. There are also business wealth such as land and machinery which can be used to create further wealth and also build social or communal wealth for the good of all.

The desire to create various levels of wealth also creates impetus to train for skill or hone a talent that progresses into unique capabilities to possess money and use it to procure wealth for personal satisfaction.

6.0   Skilled Labor and Technicians

Labor or work is generally classified into skilled and unskilled. While unskilled labor refers to work that does not require much skill content or formal training, skilled labor is a product of specialized training, probably combined with or in addition to, or preparatory to formal or semi-formal education. Electricians, lawyers, accountants, administrators, marketers, teachers, etc., are skilled practitioners. A key dimension of being a skilled worker is the ability to adapt creative knowledge and technology to the work. This extra quality distinguishes a skilled worker from the unskilled who does not use any demanding reasoning or

intellectual means to do work. For example, sweepers, seed planters, buttom fixers, etc., do not require any expertise to perform their duties.

On the other hand, skilled labor workers or technicians work with practical skills and scientific equipment which sometimes demand special training in a particular field. Skilled workers and technicians contribute specially to the economy by using their special skills to build amenities and infrastructures. They are found in engineering (civil, mechanical, environmental, acronomtics, industries, broadcasting, electricity, computing), medicine, genetics, nuclear power, chemistry, etc.

It is unimaginable how the world would be without the vital role of the people of skill and technology. This is why this group of persons are highly respected in different sphere of life. Their status also attracts many people into the domain of skill and the desire to train as a specialist with a technical capability.

7.0   Scaling Down Unemployment

There is a direct link between lack of skill and lack of job (employment). Since industrial revolution, most jobs demand skills and technical capabilities, for beyond the mere zeal to work. A lot of work now demand technology and equipment that require mechanical know-how to operate. In fact, the emergence of the machine-based industry has thrown out a lot of manual labor. This scenario has become worse as more advances are being made in the world of technology. Experts have found out that machines can deliver 100 percent over what man can do with bare hands.

Robots have also emerged on the industrial scene and have shown far reaching capabilities devoid of human limitations and attitudinal drawbacks. The implication is that those who seek employment, even after formal education, need to obtain skills. The more unskilled people in an economy, the higher the rate of unemployment.

While it may be argued that skills and machines can increase unemployment as more jobs can be done by fewer persons, this argument can be debunked by the fact that skill comes with creativity and higher productivity.

With diverse machinery, more goods can be invented and designed to meet man's unending needs and wants. These new machines required skill training for their operations and deployment. Therefore the need to provide more employment opportunities in an economy effectively drives skill acquisition system.

8.0   Improved Standard of Living

Standard of living is the aggregate of the level of economic goods, services, income and livelihoods available in a system. Individual's quality of life provide the matrix for a standard of living. This quality of life is subject to same variables such as social, political, environmental and cultural indices. The outcomes of these variables are the volume of employment, housing, leisure time, access to health, educational opportunities, security/safety measures, personal freedom and liberty, access to justice, etc.

The average and acceptable standard living is referred to Decent Living Standard which most people aspire to attain by obtaining food, shelter, water, medication and safety. Article II (2) of the Universal Declaration of Human Rights has largely ventilated this human natural aspiration as a benchmark.

Since standard of living is tied to the duality of the individual lifestyle and community's provisions via a viable economic atmosphere, individuals will require to acquire skills that will put food on their table, create income which will be used to obtain shelter, water, healthcare and mobility which are basic to a good

living. Whereby, these provisions cannot be solely obtained by an individual, then people come together to constitute with the objective of providing large economic amenities and social infrastructures.

At the second leg of social or public works, skilled labor are also needed either as employment, paid jobs or ex-gratia services as volunteering. Every community can only attain an improved standard of living when these are enough skilled hands to drive the economy.

9.0   Increase in Literacy Rate

An important motivation for basic and higher skills is not only employment prospects and higher pay but also the social status the society puts on those who are literate. And skill acquisition and development also adds up to literacy.

The sum total of the human capital (creative skills and knowledge of laborers) obtained through regular and technical or technological or specialist training is a great motivation for skill from the economic perspective.

The tripartism of the labor market from the basic skills, middle-level skills and higher skills come with appropriate level of literacy. While a standard school graduand may be able to operate the computer basically, he/she will require more education/training/literacy to demonstrate a technical knowledge of software applications. Definitely, higher skills and training in the field of engineering will be needed to operate at the level of building both hardware and software for the computer. Inversely, the higher a person aspires in the world of skill, the brighter the chances for higher literacy, higher pay, and better standard of living.

10.0   Industrial/Sectoral Growth

The premier knowledge of division of labor stipulates that everyone cannot do the same job as many other jobs will suffer and human/industrial growth will be stalled. Industrialization thrives on division of labor, multiple specialization and sectoral growth. Division of labor entails the dividing of a work among members of a family, with extension in the specialization of individual trades occasional by growth of towns and splitting up of production processes in industries and different sectors of human economic activities.

In carrying out of any piece of work, the performance of separate tasks needs its own particular skill. This specialization saves time, increases productivity and lessens fatigue. It depends on sectoral growth as each worker acquires greater skill at their jobs. An economist put it thus: "by reducing every man's business to some simple operation, and by making this operation the sole employment of his life, necessarily increases very much the dexterity of the workman."

It is therefore the zeal for sectoral relevance through divided task and specialization in keeping the chain of production and economic activities going that an individual would need a skill to acquire. For example, to produce a book, there must be a creative author who puts the ideas into writing. The manuscript will be typed by a specialist in stenography after a professional editor has assessed the writing. An efficient proof—reader will be needed to match the typed script with the manuscript. A negative photo developer will have to put the plates if the and rotary printer will be used. After printing, a finishing technician (for binding, sewing, and cover attachment) will be required. Each of these processes is sine-quo-non if the book must be put on the shelf. The industry is grown by skilled workers with specialized capabilities in their deliveries within the chain.

11.0 Mobility of Capital

Capital is a key factor in any economic system. No skilled person can function with his personal or entrepreneurial capital. Therefore, the economic value of capital constitutes a basis for aspirants to skill acquisition to factor in this third leg of production, even during their training. The more people that go for capital, the greater the economy.

Since capital comprises buildings, tools, machines, raw materials, some finished goods, means of transportation, etc., skill acquisitioner must mobilize capital both for the pretraining, training, and post-training.

A skill acquisition aspirants will need a means of transportation to get to the location of the training. Sometimes, he needs to pay training charges and fees either by self-effort or sponsorship. The training itself demands materials, some finished goods as component, machines and tools. After training, the skilled person must be settle for the trade practice. All these stages require some form of capital. Therefore, skill acquisition and development is a key domain for the mobilization and utilization of capital.

The skilled worker also contributes to the building of human capital that can be deployed in diverse settings of the economy. Even in the extractive industry comprising farming, hunting, fishing, mining, etc., capital has a role to play to complement land and labor.

12.0 Harnessing of Informal Sector

In some economies, the informal sector provides most of the employment opportunities, significantly impacts inflation and contributes to economic growth. This sector constitutes the major workforce in the production of goods and services. Though the operators in this sector are easily identified by exclusion from taxation and less regulations if any, they control a significant portion of the outcomes in the economy.

Though this may be stigmatizing, no economy is known to run without these somewhat low skill workers who serve in restaurants, cleans the offices, repairs tires, weeds farms, and count monies in the black market.

The informal economy still requires an optimum skill to function as an effective complement to the formal and highly regulated sector. Within this sector, there is the palpable need for in-house supervisors. Usually, this supervisor may be exposed to a slightly higher skill than the colleagues. For example, an engineer may choose to train one of his masons in the art of measurement so as to empower him to supervise other masons. This extra needs also provide impetus for skill acquisition as some members of the informal sectors will aspire to be first among equals.

13.0 Empowering Vulnerable Populace

There are segments of the society or population that suffer some form of social exclusion and economic disadvantages. For example in some economics, women, people with disabilities, illiterates can be easily marginalized economically and even politically. Some ethnic/racial victims, HIV victims, low-income children, the elderly and shelterless people may suffer social exclusion, same for persons with some forms of mental illness who are denied access to information and the labor market. The skill acquisition opportunities provide economic windows to assist these vulnerable to have access to education, employment and healthcare.

In Education India Project #3754, Dream A. Dream calls for out "Empower Vulnerable Young People with Life Skills." With critical life skills and tools, thousands of young people are given a hope. The UNICRI also aims at preventing crime through protecting and empowering of vulnerable groups.

The world over has come to the realization that special focus must be given to a segment of the society that are easy targets of crime, violence, abuse and exploitation within the ranks of youths, minors and women. In some African countries, the Skill Acquisition Programs are tagged "Empowerment Programs" or "Empowerment Projects" because usually after elections where arms were used freely by the youths to rig the process to their sponsors, the actors become stranded as their masters do not have enough job opportunities to settle them. They resort to crimes and general lawlessness which affect all.

Based on outcries, government agencies will be called upon to organize skill trainings to "empower" such youths so that the society will experience peace.

14.0 Conclusion

It was discovered in this chapter that economic consideration is at the core of the need for skill acquisition. We identified about a dozen factors that inform the drive for skill acquisition and development from the economic perspective. This is not surprising because "skill" is inseparable from labor of production in economics, after land and capital.

Land comes from nature. Capital and labor come from man. Capital and labor and closely interrelated as human phenomenon that require creativity, capability and stability in thoughts and actions. People, who build human communities to sustain livelihood and good standard of living, must not be "imbeciles" but people of knowledge and compliant tendencies who are able to conduct productive activities on their own or function under supervision.

Skill Acquisition as Business

OUTLINE

1.0   Introduction
2.0   Business Principles in Skill Acquisition
3.0   Knowledge of the Industry
4.0   Operational guides
5.0   Equipment, Modules, and Materials
6.0   Strategic Planning
7.0   Ethical Considerations
8.0   Conclusion

1.0   Introduction

It appears two dimensional activities go on simultaneously in a skill training setting, production/service provision and teaching/learning. In both scenarios, business ingredients are obvious. The small and Medium Scale Enterprises which constitute the hub of the low and middle level skill acquisition comprises both learners, employees and employers.

Skill acquisition systems emanate from business or economic choices, based on mindsets, through decision-making processes in planning, management, finance, expertise, market and legal regimes.

Land, capital and labor come into play. The skill acquisition center must be located on land. The equipment, tools, machinery, accommodation and transportation must be procured. The center and the actors must be directed, managed and supervised. Costs must be paid. All these require different cadres of labor as even in a sole proprietorship, the sole proprietor cannot afford to do everything by himself. In this chapter, we shall portray how skill acquisition constitutes a business place.

2.0   Business Principles in Skill Acquisition

There are many parameters for making business from any concept, activity or structure. They can be outlined as follows:

- Product/service
- Knowledge of the industry

- Awareness of the market
- Competitiveness
- Promotion of business
- Personnel expertise and training
- Organizational structure
- Capital and cash flow
- Accounting systems
- Value of clientele
- Ethical principles/compliance
- Diversification
- Risk-taking and management
- Innovation and creativity
- Effective communication
- Creating peer relationships
- Strategic networking
- Strong leadership
- Written business plan
- Flexibility in approach
- Passion for purpose.
- Time management.

The above principles can be discussed under few subheadings:

2.1 Mindset

Since human actions emanate from the mind in terms of thoughts, decisions, choices, actions, and reactions, the most important principle in business will be the state of mind of the protagonist—the arrowhead, the visioner, the entrepreneur, and the unction carrier.

In setting up a skill acquisition center or program, the promoter must first think about the PURPOSE, the goal or objective as the driving force. Once the reason for the decision is made and the passion to achieve the purpose is ignited, then the first note has been struck.

The questions to ask and answer include, Why do I need to set up a skill acquisition program? Is it to provide training services? Do I intend to make it a profit-making or nonprofit organization? What do I want to achieve? Do I want to invest in money making or human capital development?

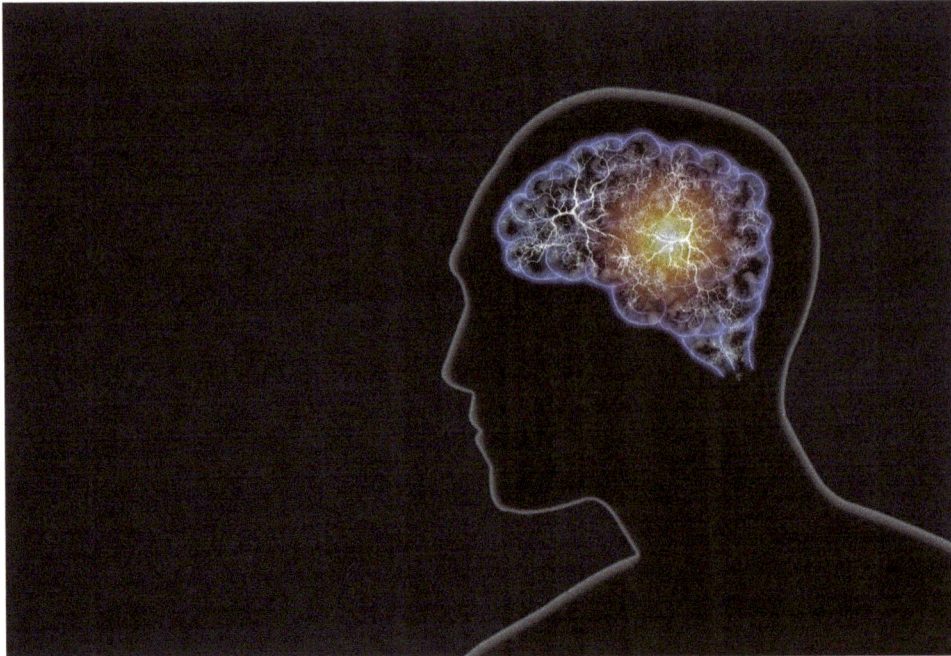

2.2 The Business Plan

Once a decision is made to engage in skill training as a business plan, a plan must be drawn up. A business contains the following entries, among others:

- The background
- Executive summary
- Structural description
- The prospects
- Potential market
- Strategic techniques
- The workforce
- Marketing plan
- Financial plan
- General operational guide
- Products and services
- Organogram
- Competitive analysis
- Modems and templates
- Any addendum

The importance of a business plan is that it serves as a feasibility report with highlights of the strengths, weaknesses (challenges/risks), opportunities, and threats. This preknowledge of the risk factors can help the business promoter to guard against frustration and failure.

The business plan also serves a compass for the navigation of the business through the turbulent economic waters that are sometimes unpredictable and filled with sharks. Most importantly, a business plan

flips up a market survey which is a determinant of business sustainability and expansion. The goals of the business as stated in the business plan also become measurable while the resources are better accounted for.

The executive summary of a business plan is a microcosm of the business operations, spelling out highlights on the core aspects of the plan such as nature of business, location, purpose, mission and vision statements, goods and services, management and financial models in view, ethical issues such as permits and taxes.

Generally, the financial analysis of the business is of prime importance in the business architecture. The volume of capital to start off with and to inject along the line; the flow of cash in and out, the projected profit and losses, labor costs, and preview of maintenance and expansion costs may all be captured in the plan.

Circle of Business Projection

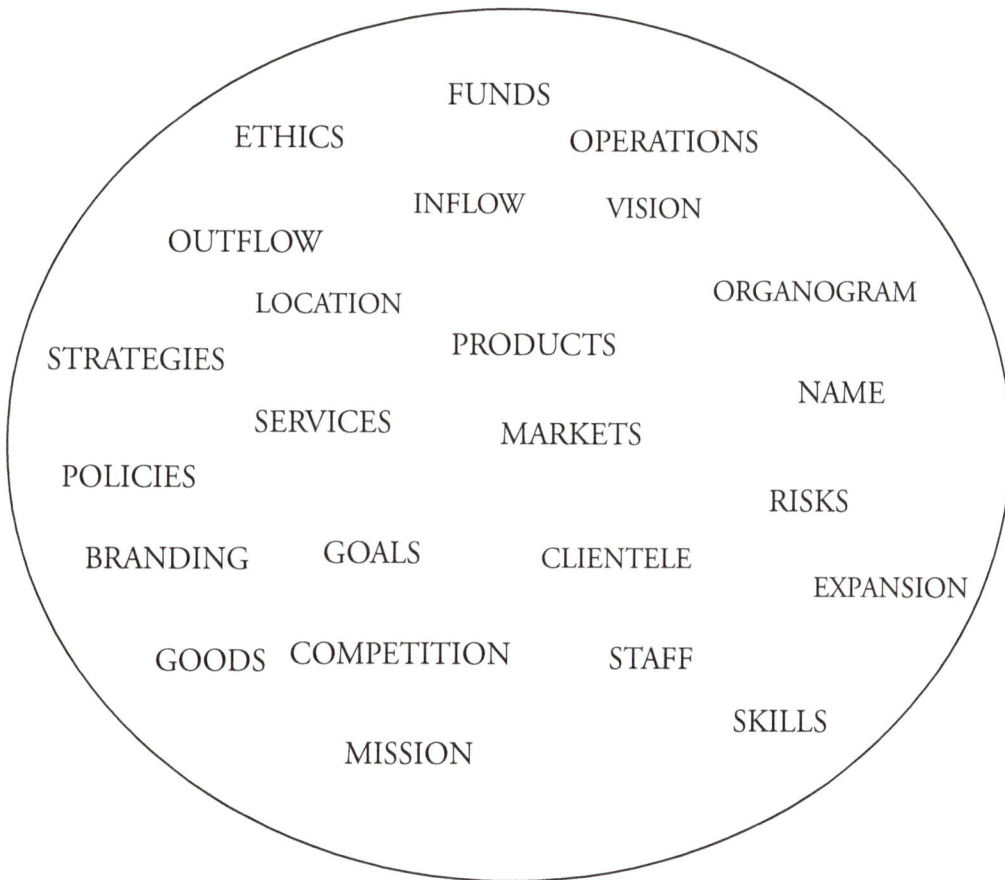

3.0 Knowledge of the Industry

Every economy operates sectorally. The skill acquisition and development is an emerging emphasis or a reinvention under labor as a factor of production and the drive to ensure food, water, products, services, housing, etc., match the growing human population.

Any promoter of a skill training program must settle the question of how the industry operates; the dynamics of labor operations in terms of needs, quality, quantity, levels, and outcomes. For example, beyond providing job potentials to trainees, the skill acquisition plan also has the "empowerment" catch for vulnera-

ble populations. Globally, the industry is trending either with regular personnel going for skill diversification or skilled people seeking high levels of competence.

The industry and its operationalities have to be mastered by the promoter according to the purpose and goals. There appears to be a blending of goals in the skill sector with actors seeking to have knowledge in particular fields and others wanting to operationalize new technologies.

4.0 Operational Guides

Every business set-up must function under specific and predictable guide covering a number of areas or dimensions such as these.

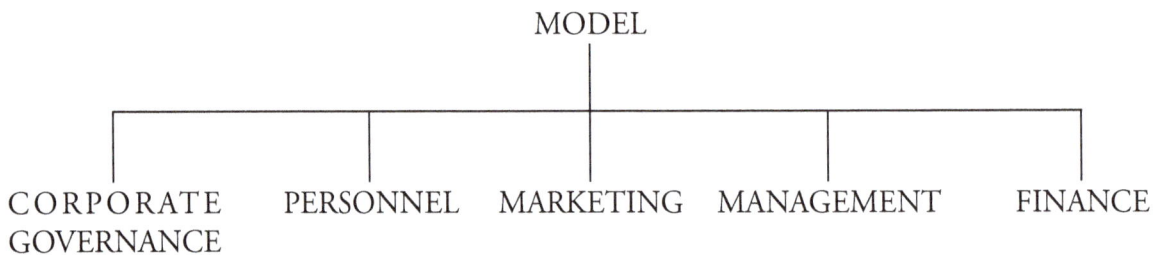

```
                              MODEL
                                |
   _____|_____
   |            |               |               |            |
CORPORATE   PERSONNEL       MARKETING      MANAGEMENT      FINANCE
GOVERNANCE
```

Corporate governance stipulates the ranks and their functions in the establishment. These include the directors, managers, trainers, evaluators, marketers, etc. This specification confines stakeholders to their boundaries. The personnel index marks the number of employees, their duties, discipline, rewards, holidays, entitlements, emolutions, and pensions. The market guide must be analyzed where a skill acquisition program produces certain goods, where will they be sold considering that the trainees may not consume all their products.

Also there must be a financial modules that spells out the books and their entries such as cashbook, ledger, payrolls, sales, and purchase journals, etc.

5.0 Equipment, Modules and Materials

These three entries are at the core of any skill acquisition/development center or program. Most skills are technology driven and such require equipment for demonstration, production, services, etc.

Modules may include syllabuses, curricula and time-tables for specific activities and durations. Modules may also include "questions and answers," step-by-step outline of processes and manuals for technical operations. Materials can include raw inputs and consumables, readymade items and combinations of existing products.

The teaching/learning nature of skills make instructional materials extremely important. Trainees need to see, touch and feel the equipment and structures they will use for the training and post training sessions. Their evaluation may require operationalize some of the equipment by themselves under the supervision of an assessor. Therefore, a promoter of skill acquisition must first put in place all the materials required for the training. This, at times, could cost a fortune. They have to be secured against theft, destruction, and loss.

6.0   Strategic Planning

In addition to the business plan, written to showcase germane issues concerning the skill program a project, there is need for a well thought out body of strategies constituted to provide problem-solving mechanisms in the areas of financial management, decision making process, location, expertise deployment, technology, source of energy and market. The essence of this planning is to serve as a rule for efficiency that needs to be followed by the grandaunt—trainees upon finishing the training. The strategic plan also outlines the duration of the training, the training costs and materials cost.

A strategic plan is usually an out of the box thinking competencies. It contains a predictable matrix that should be constantly previewed. The pretraining, training and post training components will be delineated for appropriate follow-through. There must be a strategy to deal with difficult trainees, slow learners and no-cooperating trainers/trainees.

A strategic plan easily caters for the coalescing of workers and trainees into teams and functional groups which will deliver fluently by complying with the demands of working together.

7.0   Ethical Considerations

Any business that operated with the regard to ethical compliance will head for the rocks. This is because it is in the interest of field operators, stakeholders and managers to be subject to rules, regulations and objective standards. Matters of registration, licensing, auditing, branding, evaluation, professional association, taxation reporting, safety, and security cannot be handled in a compromising manner.

Every trade has its canons, ethics and code of operations that make for effectiveness. There is the place of professional guards to every sector to create stability, decency and sustainability.

Ethical issues arise in skill training from the dimensions of teacher/student relationships, field actors/ government regulations, due diligence and due process, protection of the vulnerable trainees (minors, women, physically challenged, stigmatized people, etc.)

The legal codes as well as information processing and management are key issues to monitor. Often, there are terms and conditions of engagement that apply and must be monitored for due compliance. The entire gamut of the test/evaluation, assessment and reporting must be jealously guided to avoid abuse, favoritism, for different trainees. The process must be strict and objective.

Ethics of business in skill acquisition creates moral obligation and compliance index of the key actors and participants. Everyone is expected to inculcate the qualities of loyalty, respect, honesty, punctuality, responsibility and trust. No training can be successful in an atmosphere of untrustworthy leader, director, trainer, etc. No serious learning can take place where trainees want to cut corners, gloss over serious lines of duty and pose disobedience to the trainer. No trainee can pose to be more knowledgeable than trainer. Like the case of some students failing in mathematics because of their hatred to their teachers, the skill trainee must like their trainers so as to gain the knowledge.

The trainers cannot afford to hoard knowledge, conceal vital information, hold back helping hands or deceive the trainees as this breach will boomerang in the future. A teacher's pride is in producing better student. Therefore no trainer will do well in envying a bright trainee.

In the aspect who provides the training materials, it must be stated clearly so that trainees do not suffer material charges that become a burden. Finally, the entre process of assessment and offer of final qualification declaration must be absolutely transparent.

8.0 Conclusion

In this chapter, we reviewed skill acquisition as a business template based on the enterprise characteristics and operational principles. We outlined various business parameters with emphasis on the business plan as a compass to effective structuring, management and control (evaluation) of the training. We proceeded to state the importance of the promoters being knowledgeable about the industry, procuring and putting in place the right equipment, modules and materials under a strategic plan to deliver in human and nonhuman dimensions under due ethical compliance system.

Chapter Fifteen

Skill Acquisition, Entrepreneurship, and Enterprise: A Symbiotic Relationship

OUTLINE

1.0   Introduction
2.0   Features of Skill Acquisition
3.0   The Entrepreneur as a Labor Factor
4.0   Functions of the Entrepreneur
5.0   Enterprise: Forms of Businesses
6.0   Skillful Entrepreneur in Business
7.0   How to become a Skillful Entrepreneur
8.0   Conclusion

1.0   Introduction

There are three generally accepted factors production: land, capital, and labor. An entrepreneur is a person who deploys business techniques to run an outfit (enterprise) with the goal of making profit. The entrepreneur acquires land and capital and goes ahead to constitute different levels of labor or workers (low-skilled, middle-level, and high-skilled) to do the business with him and for him. To that extent, an entrepreneur must acquire a reasonable level of business or enterprise skills or knowledge to be able to run his business.

For example, an entrepreneur should know the types of business or enterprise structures (the sole proprietorship, company or partnership, and cooperative society), how they are formed, regulated and managed. If he chooses an enterprise that he alone can manage without any other worker, he needs to multitask. If he decides to run a complex enterprise that requires other workers (e.g. drivers, machine operators, accountants, secretaries, receptionists, cleaners, security, etc.), then he has to decide further, which to employ on what terms and which to outsource. Upon his decision to employ, then he has need for relevant skills among his employees, including those he will employ and sponsor to develop more skills for higher efficiency.

Therefore the tripartism of skill acquisition/development, enterprise, and entrepreneurship can be demonstrated thus:

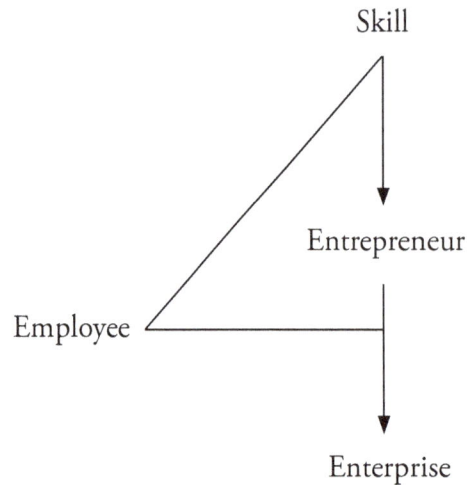

2.0 Features of Skill Acquisition

Skill acquisition relates to the possession of special talents, abilities, capabilities and problem solving strategies. It is therefore characterized BY INFORMATION, LEARNING, TEACHING, KNOWLEDGE, TECHNIQUES, EQUIPMENT, EVALUATION, AND COMPETENCIES.

Some of these features such as information, techniques, equipment, evaluation and competences are relevant both in enterprise and entrepreneurship. Information is a cornerstone in any economic activity. Without information, a skill trainer cannot impart knowledge to the trainee. The entrepreneur cannot function in a particular field and the businessman will flutter in his enterprise.

Information is derived from personal experiences or experiences of others which may be gained through training, learning, teaching or verbal and nonverbal communication.

Techniques constitute strategies deployed for any successful venture. The skill acquisition trainer requires techniques for his training. The entrepreneur must have his trade secrets and the business person must operate with techniques to thrive or sustain his business. A typical class of techniques is found in marketing of services and products. Advertising and publicity can be used positively to impact a skill acquisition program, an entrepreneurship outfit or a business concern.

Equipment also cuts across all the three domains. The skill trainer works with relevant equipment and machinery. This also goes for an entrepreneur and a business person in production. All the three engagements must be periodically evaluated to draw down areas of strengths and failures or challenges that must be overcome. Finally, skill training, entrepreneurship and enterprise depend largely on the competences of the actors.

3.0 Entrepreneur as a Labor Factor

The entrepreneur falls within the labor factor in the production or economic parameters. The other factors are land and capital. In this regard, the entrepreneur may function largely alone to drive his business as a sole trader or sole proprietor. He may be a managing director working for the company's shareholders and

Board of Directors. The Board may also be taken collectively as a corps of entrepreneurs who come together to promote, establish or run a going concern.

Below are the descriptions of these three sets of entrepreneurial templates:

Sole Trader

Is referred to be a person competent to start up a sole trade business. This type of business is a one man show and the capacities of that person may certainly be limited. It is also called an individual entrepreneurship. Here, the sole trader is responsible for risk of failure and profit. He/she is also responsible for the management of the business.

According to S. R. Davar, "the sole-trader is a person who carries on business of his own, that is, without the assistance of a partner. He brings in his own capital and uses all his labor. He also gets himself assisted by others to whom he pays a salary by way of remuneration." David also posited that a sole-trader uses his resources only and does not get the help of a partner. With the increase in work, he may employ some persons for his help who get salary for their work. The adding of a partner will even change the form of organization because it will become a partnership concern then.

Notes on the Legal Contents of Sole Trading

a. The sole-trade business will be subject to the general laws of the land. If there is a provision of getting a license for setting up a particular business, then the sole trader will also get the license before setting up such a business.
b. The liability of the sole trader is unlimited. If a business is dissolved then no distinction is made between business and private assets and business and private loans of the sole trader.
c. There is no specific law under which this business requires registration, etc. A sole trade business is not governed by any statue. The business can be started and dissolved at the discretion of the owner without reference to any statutory provisions.
d. The sole trader and his/her business are one and the same thing. The business exists only with the sole trader. If he/she disappears from the scene because of death or some other reason, the business will also be dissolved (https://www.yourarticlelibrary.com/business/sole-trader-definition-characteristics-and-other-details/42036, accessed August, 2021).

Managing Director

A managing director is a person who oversees a day-to-day operations of an organization or company. The role of managing director includes

- The responsibility of the performance of the company as directed by the board's overall strategy.
- He/she is to direct and control the company's operations and to give strategic guidance and direction to the board to ensure that the company achieves its mission and objectives.
- Establish and maintain effective formal and informal links with major customers, relevant government departments and agencies, local authorities, key decision-makers and other stakeholders generally, to exchange information and views and ensure that the company is providing the appropriate range and quality of services.
- Prepare, gain acceptance and monitor the implementation of the annual budget to ensure that budget targets are met, that revenue flows are maximized and that fixed costs are minimized.

- Develop and maintain Total Quality Management system throughout the company to ensure that the best possible products and services are provided to customers.
- Develop and direct the implementation of policies and procedures to ensure that the company complies with all health and safety and other statutory regulations (https://www.iod.com/news/news/articles/what-is-the-role-of-the-managing-director, accessedccccccccczSeptember,2021).

Shareholders

A shareholder can be a person, company, or organization that holds stock(s) in a given company. A shareholder must own a minimum of one share in a company's stock or mutual fund to make them a partial owner.

Roles of a Shareholder

- Making decisions on instances the directors have no power over, including making changes to the company's constitution.
- Deciding on how much the directors receive for their salary.
- Checking and making approvals of the financial statements of the company.
- Brainstorming and deciding the powers they will bestow upon the company's directors, including appointing and removing them from office.

Types of Shareholders

There are two types of shareholders, namely:

1. **Common Shareholders:** They are those that own a company's common stock. They are the more prevalent type of stockholders and they have the right to vote on matters concerning the company. They have the right to file a class-action lawsuit against the company for any wrongdoing that can potentially harm the organization because they have control over how the company is managed.
2. **Preferred Shareholders:** They own a share of the company's preferred stock and have no voting rights or any say in the way the company is managed. They rather are entitled to a fixed amount of annual dividend, which they will receive before the common shareholders are paid their part.

Board of Directors

Board is an all-in-one decision-making platform which combines Business intelligence tools with corporate performance management, stimulation, and predictive analytics capabilities. Its coding-free, drag-and-drop interface enables users to build self-service analytics and planning applications with ease to meet the ongoing decision-making requirements of their organization.

Board allows the creation of dashboards, reports, and analyses which are fully integrated with enterprise planning and simulation processes, bringing together financial and operational data for complete visibility of the relationship between output, performance and financial results (https://www.board.com/en#gref, accessed September 2021).

4.0   Functions of an Entrepreneur

An entrepreneur is defined as an individual or a person who organizes or operates a business(es). The functions of an entrepreneur is as follows:

1. **An Entrepreneur is a risk taker:** Here, he/she bears any risk in starting up and sustaining his/her business(es). An entrepreneur assumes every responsibility that might come up in the course of the business which might be caused by either change in time or quality.
2. **An Entrepreneur is a leader:** He/she must be at the forefront of his/her business at least during the startup. He/she must possess the ability to attract smart people and build a great business team.
3. **An Entrepreneur must be able to identify and solve problem:** An entrepreneur should be quick to identify any problem facing his/her business and immediately proffer a solution. He/she should be able to trace any challenge and resolve as soon as possible to avoid future setbacks in the business(es).
4. **An Entrepreneur must be a good sales person:** An entrepreneur should be responsible for marketing and advertising his/her products or services. An entrepreneur that cannot sell is bound to fail. He/she must provide goods and service and is not qualified to enjoy financial fortune.
5. **An entrepreneur must be a goal getter:** Entrepreneurs do not only set goals but also thrive so much to achieve their goals. He/she should set big goals that will be scary to an ordinary man.
6. **An Entrepreneur should be a decision maker:** An entrepreneur should decide and maintain the potential investors or financiers of the enterprise and also manages the funds available. He/she makes sure that his/her business venture is in good relationship with public authorities and society, and also decides the market for his/her product or services. Entrepreneurs determine the objectives of their business and they should know what is suitable per time (https://thetotalentrepreneurs.com-who-is-an-entrepreneur-2/, accessed September 2021).

5.0   Enterprise: Forms of Business

Business organization is the single-most important choice that entrepreneur will make regarding his/her company. There are four main types of business organization, namely:

a.   Sole proprietorship
b.   Partnership
c.   Corporation
d.   Limited liability company

- **Sole Proprietorship:** This is a business owned and manage by someone for their own benefit. It is the simplest and most common form of business ownership. The business' existence is entirely dependent on the owner's decision, so when the owner dies, the business also dies.

Merits of Sole Proprietorship

- Owners have total flexibility when running the business.
- All profits are subject to the owner.
- It requires very little capital for the starting of the business.
- There is very little regulation for proprietorships.

Demerits of Sole Proprietorship

- Ownership of proprietorship is difficult to transfer.
- Equity is limited to the owner's personal resources.
- Owner is one hundred percent liable for business debts.
- No distinction between personal and business income.

- **Partnership:** There are two types of partnership, general and limited. General partnerships, both owners invest their money, property, labor, among others, to the business and are both one hundred percent liable for business debts. This type of partnerships do not require a formal agreement, partnerships can be verbal or even implied between the two business owners.

Limited partnerships require a formal agreement between the partners. The must also file a certificate of partnership with the state. Limited partnerships allow partners to limit their own liability for business debts according to their portion of ownership or investment.

Merits of Partnership

- Each partner shares the total profits of the company.
- Inexpensive to establish a business partnership, formal or informal.
- Shared resources provide more capital for the business.
- Similar flexibility and simple design of a proprietorship.

Demerits of Partnerships

- Selling the business is difficult, it requires finding new partner.
- Partnership ends when any partner decides to end it.
- Each partner is one hundred percent responsible for debts and losses.

- **Corporations:** These are for tax purposes, separate entities and are considered a legal person. This means among other things, that the profits generated by a corporation are taxed as the "Personal Income" of the company. Then, any income distributed to the shareholders as dividends or profits are taxed again as the personal income of the owners.

Merits of a Corporation

- Profits and losses belong to the corporation.
- Personal assets cannot be seized to pay for business debts.
- Limits liability of the owner to debts or losses.
- Can be transferred to new owners fairly easily.

Demerits of a Corporation

- Starting a corporate business requires complex paper-work.
- Establishing a corporation is costly.

- With some exceptions, corporate income is taxed twice.
- Corporate operations are costly.

- **Limited Liability Company (LLC):** It provides owners with limited liability while providing some of the income advantages of a partnership. Essentially, the advantages of partnerships and corporations are combines in limited liability company, mitigating some of the disadvantages of each.

Merits of Limited Liability Company (LLC)

- The profits of limited liability company is shared by the owners without double-taxation.
- Limits liability to the company owners for debts or losses.

Demerits of Limited Liability Company (LLC)

- Beginning an LLC has high costs because of legal and filing fees.
- Owners are limited by certain state laws.
- Agreements must be comprehensive and complex.
  (https://www.rifkindpatrick.com/Blog/2015/November/The-4-Major-Business-   Organization-Forms.aspx-Accessed-September,2021).

6.0 Skillful Entrepreneur in Business

Entrepreneurial skill is an individual's ability to turn ideas into action. It includes creativity, innovation and risk-taking, as well as the ability to plan and manage projects to achieve target goals.

Entrepreneurial skills can encompass a broad range of various skill sets like technical skills, leadership and business management skills and creative thinking. This is because entrepreneurial skills can be applied to many different job roles and industries. Examples of entrepreneurial skills include

- branding, marketing and networking skills
- financial skills
- technical skills
- communication and listening
- business management skills
- teamwork and leadership skills
- strategic thinking and planning skills
- customer service skills
- time management and organizational skills
- critical thinking skills
- analytical and problem-solving skills

- **Branding, Marketing and Networking Skills:** Being able to implement successful branding and marketing strategies can be an essential aspect of becoming an entrepreneur. Entrepreneurs may spend the majority of their time marketing and networking with other professionals to promote and grow their brands.

- **Financial Skills:** An entrepreneur can develop financial skills by learning from a financial planner, reading financial guidebooks and using financial software to help him/her organize and keep track of the financial processes in his/her business.
- **Technical Skills:** It can be extremely beneficial to develop your technical skills as an entrepreneur. This is because of the availability of software programs for financial analysis, planning, marketing and other business processes. Entrepreneurs with efficient technological skills can use software and other digital approaches for managing projects, tracking sales, revenue and measuring the performance of business growth.
- **Communication and Listening:** Effective communication can translate to how an entrepreneur promotes awareness of his/her brand. Business owners and entrepreneurs should develop effective communication skills. Active listening also is relevant to discussions during meetings, being able to communicate effectively can help an entrepreneur work with others to build his/her awareness.
- **Business Management Skills:** Developing your business management skills as an entrepreneur can mean building up your ability to multitask, delegate responsibilities to subordinates and making decisions regarding the wealth and profitability of your business. Successful entrepreneurs will most often rely on their business skills to manage and run a business or brand.
- **Teamwork and Leadership Skills:** Being a business owner means you will most likely act as both a supervisor and as part of a team, and you will need to rely on effective leadership skills to help motivate your team. Becoming a successful entrepreneur can also mean taking on leadership roles and working as part of a team.
- **Strategic Thinking and Planning Skills:** To become successful as an entrepreneur, it takes planning and being able to think strategically to allow you find ways to beat out your competition, grow your market reach or implement effective strategies to reach your goals. Critical thinking can also translate into strategic thinking skills. Entrepreneurs who have built brands and business most likely applied their strategic planning skills to develop strategies for growing and developing their business.
- **Customer Service Skills:** Effective customer service skills can help entrepreneurs to connect with their customer base and ensure their brand is providing the products and services their market needs, from talking with potential clients to discussing opening partnerships. No matter the industry an entrepreneur venture into, he/she may still need to develop effective customer service skills.
- **Time Management and Organizational Skills:** Are also important skills for entrepreneurs to have strategies that can help develop these skill sets include breaking down tasks into manageable to-do lists and setting deadlines and achievable objectives for his/herself and for the team. Implementing technology to help keep business files organized or employ an office assistant to help an entrepreneur keep paperwork, business records and customer file organized is an additional skill.
- **Critical Thinking Skills:** Critical thinking skills can be necessary for strategic planning and evaluating the approaches and entrepreneur is using to make changes or improve his/her business strategies as needed. Critical thinking skills like analytical skills can be necessary for developing his/her overall entrepreneurial skills. Being able to look at problems, situations, projects and operations from different perspectives can help in decision-making and problem solving.
- **Analytical and Problem-Solving Skills:** Successful entrepreneurs may also have exceptional analytical and problem-solving skills. This is because there can be many aspects of building a brand or business that can require difficult decisions, finding solutions to obstacles and using creative thinking to develop plans and strategies that will help him/her achieve his/her business goal (http://www.indeed.com/career-advice/career-development/entrepreneurial-skills/, accessed September 2021).

7.0 How to Become a Skillful Entrepreneur

- **Creativity and Incentiveness:** Creativity is the ability to see things differently and proffer solutions where there are gaps. To build your creativity skill as an entrepreneur, try something new intentionally. Try talking to people that are out of your circle of comfort. Do something that other would not do.
- **Learning through Experience:** Try to learn something new through experience by starting your own business. This will make you learn from the mistakes you have made and you will get the opportunity to grow your skills such as business planning negotiation, sales and marketing.
- **Perseverance:** To build perseverance, create a goal or challenge that is meaningful and do not give yourself time to quit. Alternatively, give yourself a deadline to aim toward.
- **Delay Gratification:** Entrepreneurs have to get used to countless failures and almost zero rewards until they finally hit it. To train yourself to be able to delay gratification.

An aspirant to becoming a skillful entrepreneur must study basic book-keeping to have the competence for basic accounting processes. This financial literacy also includes awareness of the relevant tax regime that is operational in the area of business.

It is also important for the person to prepare for leadership which entails special abilities in communication as well as readiness to mentor and be mentored generally but specifically in salesmanship and partnerships/synergies as the hallmark of teamwork with peer entrepreneurs.

Finally, they would be skilled entrepreneur must be a problem-solver to keep the enterprise going.

8.0 Conclusion

This chapter focused on the inter-relatedness of skill acquisition, entrepreneurship and enterprise. In examining the features of skill acquisition, we found out the basis of the tripartite relationship from the viewpoint of information, techniques and evaluation. We proceeded to x-ray the functions of entrepreneur in the light of skilled labor and concluded that both entrepreneurship and enterprise demand skill for effective delivery. The last lines in the chapter has suggested how an entrepreneur promoter can become a skillful entrepreneur.

Chapter Sixteen

Achieving Career Growth Through Skill Acquisition

1.0   Introduction

Over the years, there has been the need and profound yearning for skill acquisition, culminating into career growth and expansion. Achieving career growth through skill acquisition can be undertaken through making findings for career opportunities, growing such career through volunteering adapting new technologies to work, setting new for career development, seeking specialization in a skill area, undergoing higher performance tasks in skill, engaging in professional mentorship, leveraging on more practice in addition to the fact that an individual needs to be interested to explore the possibilities inherent in skill acquisition, establish short-term goals, company options, establishing long-term objectives, and providing access to create a planning process which will allow such individual to set up everything, exactly how goals can be tracked and achieved.

2.0   Making Findings for Career Opportunities

The goal of skill acquisition as an educational endeavor is unachievable without its incorporation into some form of long term career or lucrative activity, which may or may not be geared toward financial gain.

Many theorists in the field thus identify entrepreneurship as the virtual endpoint of skill acquisition, as it is via entrepreneurship that the learner is able to apply the skills acquired to render services to all or certain aspects of society. However, we must beat in mind that entrepreneurship itself unfurls into a systematic continuum of ever-evolving processes which have to be tapered to suit the needs of those being served, which as well change drastically. It is then realized that only the fittest may survive in the jungle of service provision, which is even more difficult, given the pan-African challenges. The monopoly held by preexisting mogul's forces emergent and "novices" (not in the sense of competency here. See C. Dreyfus and Dreyfus, 1980) to redraft ideas and in the very rare exception, such new entrepreneurs manage to topple the erstwhile giants, and the cycle repeats itself. Opportunities thus become gold. Many former skill-acquisitors who have gained mastery in their respective endeavors jump at barely any sight of career opportunities. Many, but quite smaller in comparison, however, jump into active scouting for these opportunities. The manner in which the entrepreneur makes findings for career opportunities tends to determine how long his/her career would hold for, if at all he succeeds in his quest for one.

Making findings for career opportunities involves certain steps which include the following:

- **Establishing Relationships**

    Before findings can be made as to career opportunities, some form of social connection must be put in place to informalize the process where possible, and as well eliminate bureaucratic obstacles that usually surface when attempting at extracting information from sources with whom one is not acquainted. This is not endorsing behind-the-scene backhandedness nor favoristic indulgence, but it is easier to obtain information and by extension career opportunities from well-acquainted social contacts.

- **Knowing Where to Look**

    One may not attempt at finding a career opportunity in a bakery if he/she has a "mainstay" skill in tailoring and textile, for obvious reasons. However, on further observation, one may attempt to do so on the pretext that the bakers in the bakery have to put on clothes or aprons as the case may be. By finding this "link," such a person has uncovered an opportunity to easily seen by logically stringent individuals.

    Therefore, it is important to find such links to obtain a myriad of opportunities. Knowing where to look is beyond walking into a drug store for the pharmacist, or the workshop for the engineer. It extends into reading every job advertisement and making links as to how your skill can come in the picture.

- **Knowing What to Look For**

    Pursuant to the section above, it is important to know with specific precision what career opportunities are being sought after, and which of course must be in line with the skills or knowledge acquired. One must safeguard against haphazard descriptions in job search attaches. These descriptions (such as those one encounters on job search websites on the internet) should not be vague or hazy resumes of the individual, and as well should not impose brick borderlines or limitations as to the view of his/her capabilities. It is however sad that many people synchronize broad spectrum ability as an immensely valuable job criterion. Nonexistent or unnecessary points thus surface in the curriculum vitae of the career-seeking individual, which, soon enough, becomes a fiery harbinger of doom, both to the individual and to his employer or benefactor as the case may be. This can only be avoided by knowing specifically what one wants and consequently going for it.

- **Sources for Making Findings for Career Opportunities**

    The following are sources by which findings could be made for career opportunities:

    - **Broadcast media:** Advertisements of vacancy placed on radio and television.
    - **Outreach media:** Newspapers, posters, bills, letters, magazines, etc.
    - **Social media:** Internet websites, social media applications, etc.
    - **Resource media:** Official statements, files of contract, etc.

3.0   Growing a Career Through Volunteering

In the preceding section, making findings for career opportunities, certain rigmarole was established as concerns skills acquisition for lucrative purposes. Under this heading, we examine how one may grow a career through volunteering, which the Oxford Lexicon defines as:

"[offering] to do something without being forced to do it or without being paid for it"

Volunteering may have had its roots in early religions such as Hinduism, where pious individuals alleviated the suffering of the poor and enslaved by doing their work for them without payment (Rampa, 2000). In modern history, volunteering however came to have a military knack to it, as throughout the 20th Century, volunteering was a first-resort alternative in mobilizing armies to serve in various theatres of conflict across the globe since the First World War. Nevertheless, volunteering still occurs in peace-time through the National Youth Service Corps Program, which is argued to be a pseudo-volunteering activity, though.

Hence, having given a background for the term, how then can a career be harnessed via volunteering? A summary declassified into three parts is provided forthwith.

1. **Experience Acquisition**

    In a scenario where more than one person had the same skill, a usual ranking standard is that of experience. Rather than while away in activity, volunteering enables one rack up experience into his/her cache, and this buttresses his/her chances of being selected for job holdings in the future.

2. **Peculiar Accessory Status**

    In certain scenarios, volunteers are accorded with special status, and may have unrestricted access to otherwise unobtainable facilities as the case may be. This in turn adds to experience gained.

3. **Recommendation**

    The successful volunteer would be recommended by his/her detractors and this is a huge leap toward job acquisition. Certificates may as well be issued for the same purpose. Thus volunteering places one to be recommended for further engagement.

    However, it is disheartening that most times, the benefits listed above are far outweighed by the colossal losses incurred by the volunteers both physically and financially. Nevertheless, volunteering still serves as an important factor in growing a career when employment is delayed.

4.0   Upgrading Knowledge through Further Education

Knowledge is limitless and unquantifiable. Educational achievement is nevertheless the closest thing to be a benchmark by which we can measure how much knowledge a person has in a particular field, or rather, to what extent such knowledge as acquired by a person is sufficient for the tasks in his/her field of study.

As times goes on, certain methods and processes become obsolete, and are replaced with newer innovations. This heightens the need to further oneself to upgrade knowledge. It is as well necessary in providing one with more professional solutions to the same problems, leading to variety and overall versatility. Further education as well is a priority that must be undergone if an individual wishes to teach or impart knowledge acquired to subsidiaries and apprentices.

Moreover, further education does not necessarily entail "wholesome" absorption into tertiary education, which is facilitated by distance education schemes (see National Policy on Education, 2007), but is inclusive of all other processes aimed at increasing self-competence and relevance in the field, such as acquisition and

digestion of literary material, attendance of seminars, lectures and workshops, occasional participation in training schemes, etc. Where formal, further education aids to bolster ones credentials in certificate-emphatic organizations, where one's salary is a direct function of his/her educational achievements. Owing to this fact, holders of doctorate degrees (PhD, ThD, LLD, etc.) are employed and maintain positions far up the organizational ladder than baccalaureates (BSc, BEd, BA, etc.). While this ensures that highly intuitive individuals oversee the activities of the organization, it has led to loopholes and discrepancies, such as the outweighing of diplomas by degrees, and as well cut out the chances of youth who are not so educated but exercise practical dexterity in the field.

To that effect, it is this imperative that the skill acquisitor further his/her self educationally at any window of opportunity. As this only aids to propel his/her career beyond menial constraints. The knowledge thus upgraded would prove to be of vast utility in the field, and cushion against any disasters that could arise because of ignorance or unacquaintance with the conditions of things.

5.0   Adapting New Technologies to Work

Different tasks require different approaches. The manner of approach made use of depends on its durability, convenience and efficiency. Old hackneyed methods have had to give way for new, more effective ones. And unheeding individuals who refuse to adapt to the changes made over time give way with it, sadly. It is probably in retrospect of this that many modern organizations do put innovatory and technological units in place so as to avoid being swept away by the wave of change. For the skill acquisitor, however, adapting to advancements in technology may be a mild issue, as well, it could be severe. This is in the sense that, to adapt one may only have to learn a few additional "updates," or may have to unlearn in part or in whole, what has already being learnt.

Nevertheless, these are minor setbacks compared to what would likely occur if changes are passively responded to. Having clarified the why of the subject matter, some discourse is equally necessary as to the how aspect.

- **How New Technology may be Adapted to Work**
  Early on, the concept of online skill training was discussed in detail. That is a classic example of technology being adopted to carryout training, for skill acquisition.

New technology may be adapted to work through the following ways:

- **Using Technology-Driven Methods to Solve Problems**
  Technology aims at making life easier so complex, intricate problems may be attacked using technology-driven perspectives.

- **Using Technology to Facilitate Work**
  Advancements in technology may be used directly in work to facilitate financial transaction, social and public communications, etc.

- **Generating Work Patterns that are Compatible with Technology**
  Methods of working that easily allow for use of technology to alleviate tedium should be promoted, while traditional methods which exert considerable strain should be scrapped altogether. The recent switch from analog to digital broadcasting by some mass communication corporations is a fine example of traditional methods giving way to more efficient work patterns.

- **Acquiring Technical Knowledge**

    The term "tack of technical knowhow" is a frequent runner-up on disadvantage lists, but can be surmounted by effortful acquisition of technical knowledge, via formal education or informal indulgence, as may be possible.

6.0   Setting New Goals in Career Development

Over time, the monotony of maintaining a career after gaining mastery of a skill becomes overwhelming, and nothing seems new anymore. Stress eventually sets in, the apparent lack of enthusiasm that follows therefore signals a crash in such an endeavor. The scenario described may be catalyzed by general lack or absence of competition in the field, which causes many entrepreneurs to be localized at various plateaux of career development. This stagnation leads to several setbacks such as

- lack of innovation and creativity
- resource wastage
- lack of enthusiasm
- loss of efficiency, etc.

As a result, the entire skill acquisition process is jeopardized. Setting new Goals aids to ensure that redundancy is reduced, and innovation is encouraged. These goals may be long-term or short-term goals, or as well be continuous, with each goal achieved leading into the next.

- **What Is a Goal?**

A goal is "an end towards which an effort is directed" (R. Allen et al., 2003). It is a predetermined objective that is worked at. The goal(s) must be clear-cut and well defined. Shabbily drawn up goals are invariably unattainable. Hence, before attempting to achieve goals, they must first of all be set to an expedient degree of precision. One must be able to quickly visualize how the creative ideas behind the goal(s) might be used (Meredith, 1987).

Perspectives in Goal Setting for Career Development: A Treatise

When setting goals for career development, certain angles must serve as standpoints for viewing such goals. A self-centered approach may likely not serve the needs of others, and achieving goals set that way would more or less be an exercise in futility. Mbat (2010) identified three (3) of such perspectives:

Perspective 1: The Entrepreneur

The entrepreneur most certainly must consider his personal gains and constraints when setting goals, as he/she is the one to bear them.

The entrepreneur must envisage, clearly the scope and size of such a goal, and it's feasibility as a whole. This is done by reckoning of one's account and capital resource, which serve as a foundation to build upon.

The experiences of others undertaking similar goals should also be surveyed and counter-weighed, toward setting clear goals that would not impose strain on the entrepreneur.

Perspective 2: The Market/Consumer

Career development is impossible without positive input and review by the consumers. The entrepreneur should develop goal setting patterns that conform to consumer opinions. Goals may not be achieved if they are set to the contrary of popular trend, or below consumer standards. Therefore, the entrepreneur should view his/her goals from the standpoint of the market square, and streamline them accordingly. This may be done via market surveys, questionnaires, pilot survey polls, etc.

Perspective 3: The Investor

Too often, the goals set by career-pursuing individuals are usually of the capital intensive kind. And thus it is not uncommon for entrepreneurs to solicit for third-party funding or investment. Unfortunately, this proves to be a "who will bell the cat" scenario, and eventually such goals never see the light of day if investment is absent or inadequate. The investors, on the other hand, are only after profitable shares and dividends, and of course would not sow seed on arid, nondescript soils. It is therefore necessary that the entrepreneur make sound financial projections as to the market value and prospect of his/her goal.

Role playing is important here, as the entrepreneur undergoes self-assessment and self-evaluation by asking questions like: "Does the idea make sense?" "What do I need?" "Who are customers?" "Can I manage the goal to completion?" etc. This process enables the entrepreneur plan ways to avoid such obstacles.

- Reasons for failure of goals
- The goals set are untenable and not feasible
- The goals set are not kept track of
- The entrepreneur does not make total commitment toward the business.
- Lopsided perspective when setting the goal.
- Unforeseen circumstances leading to procrastination.

7.0 Seek Specialization in a Skill Area

Skills acquired may suffice for solving a broad spectrum of problems on the surface. Further incision would reveal different competency levels in the various aspects/areas that comprise the skill. Although these competencies is an implied function of the rank correlation of the distribution of the various aspect competencies which may be mensurated as scores, grades, etc. Rests them show which aspects are easily understood and grasped by the skill acquisitor—who may decide to go in-depth once more and gain specialized mastery in that aspect.

In the case of formal education, specialization is a necessary criterion for becoming an authority on an aspect of a skill or subject as the case may be. There can as well be "specialization within specialization," and although the academia may impose certain "jurisdictory classifications," they are however vague and for titulatory or naming purposes, and specialization tends toward infinity (i.e., specialization could be carried out consecutively an infinite number of times). Under this heading we examine why specialization is important for career growth, and how specialization can be done. We also pinpoint benefits of specialization and it's alternatives as well.

- **Why Specialize?**
  1. Specialization leads to professional approaches to skills and tasks: The added information gleaned from specialization programs or processes enable the entrepreneur apply professional touches to his/her career work. This is due to the emphasis on basic measures to prevent accidents, mishaps and failures in the advanced (and sometimes technical) tasks usually reserved for specialists only. Such measures may include the following:
     - Usage of personal protection equipment
     - Public relations training
     - Etiquette and professional ethics
     - Troubleshooting, etc.
  2. The overall efficiency of your career can be increased to maximal proportions by specialization, as complex tasks become singular components of more complex ones, and as such can be handled without much exertion of resources.
  3. **Endorsement and Licensing**

     In many fields, specialists are licensed and endorsed by governing bodies of the field. This confers a referral status on the specialist, recommending him/her as an authorized and recognized skillsman or entrepreneur. This of course increases the market reach of the entrepreneur.

- **How to Specialize**

  Because of the intricate nature of the specialist career or job, specialization may only be undertaken within the auspices of specialist bodies or organizations, to provide a universal standard of trustworthiness, and safeguard against fraudsters and quacks who may poise as specialists. (Meyers, 1997)

  Therefore, to specialize in a given area,
  - ascertain the body overseeing the field,
  - make findings as to specialization programs or exams,
  - apply for such programs to be certified.

  However, some bodies only offer certification without training, on the basis of theoretical or practical aptitude. In such a scenario, specialization may be carried out in the autodidactic, self-learn way—by acquiring material for specialist or advanced purpose and using them effectively.

- **When to Specialize**

  Although the choice of when to specialize oneself is solely that of the entrepreneur, it must be established that a solid understanding and competence in the field must first be maintained before seeking to absorb oneself into the intricacies of one or more aspects of the field.

8.0 Undergo Higher Performance Tasks in Skills

Higher performance tasks may be classified as tasks that require an input of greater effort, utility of more advanced approaches to accomplish. They are a necessary tool in career development because of the following reasons:

1. Undergoing higher performance tasks helps to ascertain ability limits. Many entrepreneurs swim in the euphoria of all round competence and infallibility, without ascertaining beforehand, their

limits. This leads to consumer disappointment when he/she having been assured earlier is told that his/her needs are beyond the ability of the entrepreneur, and as such, cannot be met.

2. Undergoing higher performance tasks readies the individual for specialization and self-advancement. By providing a glimpse of what is to be expected, undergoing higher performance tasks, the entrepreneur is familiarized with certain specialist obstacles and how to surmount them.

3. It also serves as a creativity test, as the entrepreneur is made to apply previous knowledge in attempting to solve current problems.

9.0   Engage in Professional Partnerships

Founder reknown of Apple Inc., Steven Jobs, in 1976 created his first computer, the Apple I (Davis, 1991). While he was quite successful with his innovation, it wasn't until he met a former manager who partnered with him, and invested $250,000, that he grossed over $2.7 million in 1977, and therefore established Apple Inc., as a telecom giant. By 1981, the revenue was upwards of $300 million, heading toward the $1 billion mark and beyond. This would have been undoubtedly impossible had he not entered into a partnership agreement with Stephen Woszniak.

Therefore, engaging in professional partnerships is an incredible tool toward making or marring one's career. The types of partnerships include the following:

a. **Innovatory Partnership**

   Here, the entrepreneur partners for the purpose of brainstorming, and idea generation.

b. **Financial Partnership**

   This type of partnership is for the purpose of funding an already outlined prospect. This type of partnership may entail marketing, funding or insurance. Shareholding is also a form of partnership.

Aims of Partnership

A partnership aims at the following:

1. **Providing Capital for the Venture**

   The required capital for a venture may be provided in part or in whole by partnership schemes under certain litigatory conditions and clauses.

2. **Providing Market Demand for Services**

   Effective partnership precipitates extensive market demand for services to be rendered by the entrepreneur.

3. **Providing Fresh Innovations**

   In certain scenarios, partnership is the machinery by which old perfunctory approaches to solving problems are scrapped altogether or recycled into more efficient ones, therefore guarding against egocentric ideas which do not serve the purpose(s) for which they are generated.

4. **Providing Synergy:**

The combined effort and communication of either the rise or failure of a business venture in the partnership scheme, exudes synergy, which is in sharp contrast to singular figure-headed schemes; the emotions and circumstances surrounding an individual are absorbed and countervened by the collective effort of partners. This is not possible in "one-man army" organizations.

10.0 Leverage on More Practice/Practicals

Education is a dualistic phenomenon, existing in both the facts of theory and practical, abstract and concrete (Enukoha *et al.,* 2010). The ratio in which these facets surface is determined by the subject matter, but there can never 100 percent of only one of the two. This is because while theory is broad and not limited to available circumstances, practical's actually simulate real life scenarios, which is actually the aim of skill acquisition—making use of one's skill to solve real life problems. But this does not also imply that practical's *ad solus* are ultimate and should be engaged in without prior theoretical acquaintance. In fact, the relationship existing between the two (theory and practice) is analogous to a logical bi-conditional, as theory must imply practice, and vice versa.

However, in skill acquisition processes involving vocational or technical aptitude, practical's become paramount toward ensuring understanding of the skill being acquired. For instance, an apprentice tailor, when asked if he/she *knows how* to sew, would likely respond in the affirmative, because he/she is well versed in the theory behind tailoring. However, if he/she is asked if he/she could sew, a contradictory response would be received. Note however that in Nigerian usage, the phrase "do you know how to…" is used interchangeably to refer to knowledge and physical capability.

Therefore, the need arises for skill acquiring processes to mount leverage on practicality. As stated earlier, practical's aid to provide a verisimilitude of everyday encounters, tasks, problems and strategies, providing the entrepreneur with an insight of what is obtainable in the field.

Setbacks to Practicals

1. Inadequate Supporting Infrastructure
   The infrastructure required to facilitate practical instruction is often absent or dilapidated beyond unity.
2. Lack of Instructors
   We realize, sadly, that the educational system is characterized greatly by theorism and other idealistic philosophies. This diminishes the number of available manpower to instruct in practical's. And often, instruction is provided by theoretic instructors, which is wrong.
3. Expense of raw materials
4. Distance education, etc.

11.0 Get Mentorship under a Pro:

Mentorship refers to the advice and help provided by a mentor to a less experienced person over a period of time, especially as part of a formal programs in a company, university (Oxford Advanced Learner's Dictionary, p. 981, 10th ed.). The right mentoring relationship can be a powerful tool for professional growth in a chosen career. It can lead to a new job. Mentorship is very vital in honing a person's specific skills

187

or to give him long-term career advice. In this case, the would-be skill acquisitor has the responsibility of driving the relationship to a positive result. Mentorship in skill acquisition goes a long way to supporting the individual when he or she is faltering, thereby keeping his goals on track. In the process of being mentored, an individual learns how to avoid common pitfalls and to stay focused and dedicated to mentorship process.

Mentorship is achievable when the skill learner gets relax and allows himself to be taught. This implies that the learner is expected to respect his mentor's opinion, considering everything they said carefully, and mainly bringing himself low, with humility. It is important to note that mentorship involves listening as the mentor expects his mentee (skill acquisitor) to be a good listener. In undergoing mentorship, it is important to realize that you are always going to be learning, and be willing to listen when advice is brought to the table.

Set a Consistent Meeting Schedule

It is possible that your mentor is sometimes very busy. However, be respectful of his time by scheduling each mentor meeting in whatever way is most convenient for him or her. Learners can get the most out of their mentorships by setting a consistent meeting time with those that give them experience and use every period of those meetings to the best of their interests. These could be done either through face to face activity, Skype, over the phone or any form of medium suitable for the trainee.

Another thing that is important to consider in mentorship process is for the mentee to know the right type of questions to ask his mentor. Young people during this process know they want a mentor but do not know what they want from it. Therefore a mentor must know the guiding questions to ask if he is to accomplish a successful relationship and career growth with his mentor. You should also learn why your mentor has made professional decisions. Learn the different ways in which your mentor has achieved professional success, including the kind of decisions he made before attaining such success. By doing so, the learner can apply a similar discerning thought process to his own professional choices.

When you follow your mentor piously and judiciously, you can be sure that your mentor's investment in you can and often does lead to real results.

12.0 Conclusion

Skill acquisition enhances career growth and expansion. For an individual to achieve career growth, he must be willing to make findings for opportunities to venture into a given career of interest to him. Such individual should be willing to grow a career through volunteering to offer career services related to such given occupation. Upgrade his knowledge of a particular career using education as a tool, set new goals that will facilitate the development of such career, be willing to seek specialization in that career area, and engage in professional partnership as well as undergo higher performance tasks in skills.

Chapter Seventeen

Government's Role/Impact in Skill Acquisition

1.0 Introduction

A role refers to the responsibility or the part that an individual plays, as a part of a group which will lead to the ultimate success of the goals and objectives of the group to which the individual belongs. The Cambridge Dictionary defines a role as "the position or purpose that someone or something has in a situation, organization, society or relationship; the duty or use that someone or something is expected to have."

Skill acquisition on the other hand can be defined as "the form of training by individuals or group of individuals that can lead to the acquisition of knowledge for self-sustenance. It involves the training of people in different fields of trade under a legal agreement between the trainers and the trainees for a certain duration and under certain conditions (Idoko, 2021). Ochiaga (1995 in Idoko, 2021) also defined that is related to some meaningful exercise, work or job. He maintains that for skill to be acquired, appropriate knowledge, attitudes, habits of thought and certain characters are learnt to enable the acquirer develop intellectual, emotional and moral character which prepares him or her for a brighter future.

The government is an art of governing. A body or a group of persons vested with the supreme power of the affairs of the state. The supreme power of the state lies in the hands of the government, thus giving it the authority to make and enforce laws and implement policies as well. The government has a vital role in the development of skill acquisition. One of the responsibilities of the government is to provide an employment opportunity for the unemployed members of the society. In reality, the government cannot employ all the unemployed members of the society, hence the need for the development of skilled labor and this is made possible through skill acquisition. The policies made by the government should first of all, allow for the establishment and training of the trainees. If the policy of the government does not make provision for this, then skill acquisition cannot thrive in such an environment or society. The population of the society which require these skill training programs are the youths and young adults. In many countries of the world, youth unemployment has always been an issue of great concern to parents, communities, and the governments. In a situation where these young people are left to themselves, they become tools in the hands of the destructive elements of the society such as political thuggery, terrorism, etc. They can as well become armed robbers and as such, constitute a nuisance to the society in which they exist. To develop and empower the youths for skill development, and acquisition, the government and other stakeholders must be involved in the business of youth empowerment by organizing youth programs that will help place them in a position where they can contribute meaningfully to the society in which

they live (Fatoki, 2019). He further explains that they skill acquisition programs, which are promoted by the government aim at

a. Stimulating the interests of youths in vocational trades through the provision of trainings at designated centers.
b. Training unemployed youths in simple vocations to make them self-reliant.
c. Encouraging productive entrepreneurial and small business skills.
d. Assisting in the development of the downstream industries.
e. Encouraging the adaptation to local technology.
f. Providing micro credit to the successful graduands of these skill acquisition centers.
g. Controlling the rate of rural-urban migration; and
h. Enhancing social peace and stability.

Ojikutu (1998 in Fatoki, 2019) believes that "youth empowerment is very crucial in the attainment of development because the transitional period from childhood to adulthood is unquestionably a challenge for many youths and for them to contribute their quota to national development, the government must help their transformation in this regard.

2.0 Registration of Skill Trainers

The major aim of the skill acquisition program is to train people, especially youths, to meet the standard of the labor market demand. In this regard, the skill acquisition centers should adopt various strategies to make their goal of producing skilled personnel a reality. The government also has a role to play in this regard. It is the duty of the regulatory body of the government to make sure that these skill acquisition centers are duly registered and that their trainers are well versed in the skill which they are training others. In doing so, their objectives should be the following, as explained in (Affiliation Norms for Training Service Providers).

a. To meet the challenge of skilling with speed and quality standards
b. To foster excellence in the skill acquisition center, building effectiveness in delivering competency based training, and to enable trainees and other stakeholders to make informed choices with regard to skill development centers.

Accreditation of Skill Development Centers

According to the American English Dictionary, accreditation is the process of, or the granting of approval to an institution of higher learning by an official review board after the school (training center) has met certain requirements. The accreditation process should focus on the employability of the trainees, after the period of their training and to ensure that the training centers pursue excellence in delivering the required skill to the trainers. The process of accreditation should take into cognizance the following factors according to Affiliation Norms for Training Service providers (n.d.).

1. **The management/institution:** The organization which requires to be accredited should have a written mission statement which shall guide the general operations of the training center. The institution should also
   a. have clearly defined objectives that will be helpful in establishing a vocational training system;

    b.   have documented processes and procedures covering the complete range of the vocational training, including the one's relating to continual improvement of these processes and procedures;

    c.   physically possess the resources or have a documented plan of owing the resources required to run and operate a vocational training system;

    d.   have a documented processes that will help the management to review the operational processes and procedures;

    e.   have a documented mechanism to ensure the applicability of the processes and procedures.

2. **Organization details:** The factual information of the institution wishing to be accredited should be provided as follows:

    a.   Details of the organization applying for the proposal

    b.   Prior exposure of the organization in skill development education

    c.   Educational qualification and experience of the management team

    d.   Key achievements of the management/project team in the area of skill development

    e.   Management committee shall identify all statutory and regulatory requirements for compliance

3. **Responsibilities and the authority of the operational teams**

    a.   The head of the institution or training center may be designated as director or principal. The head of the institution shall be empowered by the management committee to carryout day to day functioning of the institution. The management committee shall clearly describe the management structure. The head of the institution shall decide and implement the processes which support the development and deployment of the institution system. The responsibility for all personnel involved in key functional areas shall be defined and communicated within the institution.

    b.   The management committee shall appoint an existing senior staff members who, irrespective of other responsibilities, shall monitor to ensure that the requirement of these criteria are being implemented. The coordinator shall periodically report to the management committee on the compliance of criteria and the need for improvement. The coordinator shall ensure communication within the institution on the information related to the application and relevance of the criteria in training and support processes. The coordinator shall liaise with the board on other relevant matters.

4. **Existence of operations manual**

    The institution or skill acquisition center applying for accreditation should have an operations document covering the following aspects.

    a.   Background of the institution

    b.   Organizational structure

    c.   Details of other affiliations (if applicable)

    d.   Industry linkages

    e.   Profile of the management team members

    f.   Profile of trainers

    g.   Details of infrastructure, workshop, store, etc.

    h.   Process of internal evaluation

    i.   Placement cell and its placement record

    j.   Training courses/programs offered including a list of content and training materials available.

    k.   Quality assurance mechanism

    l.   Management information system of the institution (if any)

5. **Financial resources:** The institution shall provide resources which shall be capable of sustaining a sown vocational training program consistent with its stated mission and objectives for long term stability.

6. **Teaching process**
   a. Timetable
   b. Delivery plan
   c. Monitoring and evaluation process of students (i.e., continuous assessments)
   d. Management of student evaluation records
   e. Workshop exposure and its linkage to theoretical delivery
   f. Industry visits

7. **Training of trainers:** This will expose the trainers to strategies and methods for skill training for a high impact experiential learning, apart from their basic knowledge in the skill or vocation.

8. **Training material/syllabus:** The institution shall provide a training manual, which covers all the areas of knowledge which a trainee is expected to acquire. Assessment and practical workshop guide should be provided, in the case of technical courses.

9. **Continuous education:** The training center should adhere to the process of internal evaluation from time to time.

10. **Industrial interface:** The institution should engage experts from industries (guest industries) of the selected skill to expose the trainees to real life problems from industry with sample solution to the trainees.

11. **Assessment, internship and certification:** The training and assessment of the trainees should be done as spelled out in the assessment guide. The trainees should be sent for internship and those who are qualified should be certified accordingly.

3.0 Sponsorship of Trainings

The government at the federal, state and local level have a role in the sponsorship of skill acquisition programs. Many countries, states and local governments have a lot of young people who are out of school for one reason or the other. A good number of them are out of school because of their parent's and guardian's inability to fund their education. Some of them are out of school because they cannot cope with the rigors and demands of schooling. As such, they become school dropouts. Such young people, when they are not engaged in anything that keeps them busy, they tend to become a nuisance to the society. The government can include such funding's in their budgets so as to enable the sponsorship of the skill acquisition programs. This will further bring about economic development for the country and financial independence on the part of the young people. Deme, Franck, and Naqui (2005 in Bandopadhyay 2014) reveal that "if the government expenditure on education, training and skill acquisition is very large, the increased government expenditure on education, training and skill acquisition lowers urban unemployment and the urban formal sector expands, whereas urban information sector contracts."

However, it is not only the duty of the government to sponsor skill acquisition programs individuals, companies, and other well-meaning citizens of the country can sponsor such projects.

4.0   Regulation of Skill Training

Regulation, according to Britannica, is the promulgation of targeted rules, typically accompanied by some authoritative mechanism for enforcing compliance. The American English dictionary further defines it as a law or an administrative rule, issued by an organization, used to guide or prescribe the conduct of members of that organization; a type of law made by the executive branch of government, usually by the virtue of a statute made by the legislative branch, giving the executive the authority to do so. Education on the other hand involves the process of imparting skills and knowledge; which influences an individual socially, morally, intellectually and makes it possible for such an individual to fit into the society. It therefore means that for one to be able to fit into the society, he or she needs some level education, whether in a formal or an informal setting.

Vocational education, according to Okafor (2011), is "concerned with the qualitative technological human resource development which is directed towards a national pool of skilled and self-reliant craftsman in the technical and vocational fields." Otaigbe (2015) holds that "Craft vocations are usually based on manual or practical activities, traditionally nonacademic, related to a specific trade, occupation, or vocation. It is sometimes referred to as technical education and training (TUET). It is a type of education that prepares people for specific trades, craft and career at various levels from trade, craft, technician or professional positions in engineering, business, accountancy, nursing, medicine, architecture, office technology and management, etc. The vocational education is related to the age-old apprenticeship system of learning which may be designed for many levels of work from manual trade to high knowledge work.

A number of government policies tend to justify the claim that vocational education has come to be and it is a solution to some of the nation's economic and social problems. The recognition given to vocational education has led to its introduction at the primary, secondary, and tertiary levels of education.

Functions/duties of the regulatory bodies in skill acquisition and development

The regulatory body is made up of a group of persons, who are knowledgeable in a particular area, and are saddled with the responsibility of investigating, monitoring, evaluating the activities of the skill acquisition programs in the various training centers and acting as advisors to the government on what policy to make and implement so as to foster the activities of the skill acquisition.

The following are the responsibilities of the regulatory bodies in respect to the skill acquisition programs.

1. Advice the federal government of the nation on the activities of the skill acquisition programs and coordinate all aspects of technical and vocational education falling outside the universities curriculum.
2. Making recommendations on the national policy necessary for the training of technicians, craftsmen and other middle level skilled manpower.
3. Determining after consultation with the nation's manpower board, the industrial training fund and such other bodies as it considers appropriate, the skilled and middle level manpower needs of the country in the industry, commercial and other relevant fields for the purpose of planning training facilities and in particular, to prepare periodic master plans for the balanced and coordinated development of polytechniques. Such plans include
    a. the general programs to be pursued by the polytechniques to maximize the use of available facilitates and to avoid unnecessary duplication, while ensuring that they are adequate to the manpower need of the country;
    b. recommendation for the establishment and location of new polytechniques as and when considered necessary;

c. inquiry into and advice to the federal government on the financial needs, both the current and capital of polytechniques and other technical institutions to enable them meet the objectives of producing the trained manpower needs of the country;

d. receiving block grant from the federal government and allocate them to the skill acquisition programs in accordance with such formula as may be laid down by the federal government;

e. acting as the agency for channeling all external aids to training centers across the country or state;

f. laying down of standard skills to be attained and continually review such standards as necessitated by technological and national needs;

g. reviewing the methods of assessment of students and trainees and to develop a scheme of national certification for technicians with ministries and organizations having technical training programs;

h. undertaking periodic review of terms and conditions of service of personnel in polytechnic and other skill acquisition centers and to make recommendations there on the federal government;

i. collating, analyzing, and publishing information relating to technical and vocational education;

j. considering any matter pertaining to technical or technological education as may be referred to it from time to time by the ministry;

k. carrying out others of such activities as are conducive to the discharge of its functions.

The programs and activities of the regulating board constitute the main operational arm of the national board for technical education in executing its key function of quality assurance and maintenance of national standard of skill acquisition in vocational and technical training. Its functions include

1. laying down and reviewing as necessary the entry requirements, duration of programs and the skills gained in the technical and vocational institutions;

2. preparing guidelines on the curriculum and the course content and the procedure for the evaluation of the programs and the certification of technicians, craftsmen, and artisans;

3. proposing ways of encouraging technical and vocational subjects in the basic and secondary schools;

4. advising on ways of sensitizing the general public on the essence of vocation and technical education;

5. laying down guidelines for and advice on programs to be accredited in all polytechniques, technical colleges and other skill acquisition centers in the whole country for the purpose of awarding national certificates, diplomas, and for entry into national examinations in respect of such institutions.

6. To advise on ways and means of improving and developing the resources and materials for teaching and production in technical institutions and skill acquisition centers.

In its role of advising on all aspects of skill acquisition, the regulatory body also makes recommendations on how best to stimulate and encourage prevocational technical, agricultural, business and home economics education and such other additional subjects considered necessary by the authority, as the case may be in primary and secondary schools, not only as a basis for creating early technological awareness, but also to provide suitable orientation on further education and training in technology and direct practical skills for earning a living. Also, to advise on and take measures to improve the immediate and long-term prospects of technical and business education teachers of technical and business education teachers with respect to status and remuneration.

Finally, it can boldly be said that the regulatory bodies play a very vital role in the technical, vocational and skill acquisition programs within the national, state and local governments. They help to standardize

the activities of skill acquisition programs. The activities of the various regulatory bodies should be properly publicized to create the needed awareness on their activities. The bodies responsible for the evaluation of the skill acquisition programs should address the issue of extortion of the trainees and inadequate or ineffective training centers.

5.0   Harnessing the Informal Sector

"The informal sector represents a large workforce of semi-skilled or unskilled individuals in society. This caters for various skill areas that these men and women possess and competences they demonstrate, which assist them in their livelihoods. Most of their worksites are usually unplanned settlements that are eventually given recognition with time; where informal sector onsite training is carried out" (The Role of ODL in Improving Skills Acquisition in Zambia, 2019).

In most cases, the demand-driven skills training is mainly based on skills that are required by the formal economy but majority of the labor force is found in the informal economy; this might cause a reconsideration on whether the industry needs more of the formal or informal skills. Hence, the formal companies have a responsibility of "formalizing" these informal economy and harnessing them for the growth of the economy and harnessing them for the growth of the economy in general. The young entrepreneur in the informal setting requires experts in the field to help him or her promote his entrepreneurial skills. The government agencies and the regulatory bodies such as the chambers of commerce can stimulate this move by simplifying the rules and expectations from these informal economy and linking them up to standard companies.

In the economy, there are many young persons who have acquired such skills as electrical installations, catering, fashion designing, poultry farming, fish farming, arts and craft, etc. The government can establish industries where these skilled personnel can be gainfully employed. Such companies, which are now formal, can source for contracts and as such, the informal aspects of the economy can be harnessed for a better economic growth.

Etim and Daramola (2020) explain that generally, the informal sector, consisting of unpaid workers in family enterprises, casual wage employment, home-based worker or service providers, street vending are the means of survival for the poor and people exposed to natural disasters or acute urbanization from rural settings. Consequently, the widening output gap leads to inequality in income distribution. The inability of the government and the formal sector to cater for the migration surge leads to an increased economic activity in the informal sector, out of necessity and for survival. Companies can as well employ the services of these skilled workers to run smaller businesses, within the larger company.

ICLS (2003) defined informal employment more broadly to include small scale low income activities, whether in employment or self-employment, whether linked to registered firms or not. While some associate the informal sector with poverty, others view it as a transitory stage to a formal employment. Heintz (2012 as cited in developing the informal sector for inclusive growth 2015) explains three categories of informality, in respect to employment as follows

1.   **Enterprise based:** This approach distinguishes between the formal and the informal enterprise based on the size; registration status; employer/enterprise security contributions; legal form of organization and character of financial accounts; and legal entitlements and property rights.
2.   **Employment based:** This approach distinguishes an enterprise based on nature or status of the employees (whether formal or informal).
3.   **Focus on illegal activities:** Individuals that operate outside the law through, for tax evasion, violation of labor standards and laws; or trade and production of illicit goods and services. However,

there seem to be no perfect distinction between the formal and the informal business enterprises, as their activities are in most cases the same.

In the past, the informal sector was characterized by women and the youths. Nowadays, the informal sector has expanded and therefore meets the needs the people and plays a vital role in the economic growth of any nation.

Characteristics of the informal sector

According a CBN/NISER (2001 collaborative workshop, as cited in Onwe, 2013), the informal sector is one which operates without binding official regulations, as well as one who operates under official regulations that do not compel rendition of official returns on its operations or production process. The following are the characteristics of the informal sector as explained in Onwe (2013).

1. There is no proportion of workers.
2. It is labor intensive and no sophisticated technology.
3. Little or no literacy skill is required on the part of the owner/employee(s).
4. Their product are mostly homogenous.
5. There is a low working capital.
6. There is no personal insurance or social protection.
7. Employees consist of single street traders, cottage enterprises, subsistence farmers, small manufacturers, service providers, and distributors.

The traditional and modern views about the informal sector

Below are some of the traditional and current views about the informal sector, as explained as Onwe (2013).

Traditional views		Modern views
1.	The informal sector is the traditional economy that will wither away and die with modern, industrial growth.	The informal economy is increasing with modern, industrial growth-accounting for more than half of the jobs in Latin American and 80 percent of new jobs in Africa. In India, more than 90 percent of the labor force survive in it. It is a feature of economic transition as well as capitalist industrialization.
2.	It is only marginally productive.	Virtually everywhere, the informal economy is efficient and resilient, creating jobs. It is a major provider of employment, goods and services for lower-income groups. It contributes significantly to GDP.
3.	It exists separately from the formal economy.	It is linked to the formal economy—it provides for trades with, distributes for and provides services to the formal economy.
4.	It represents a reserve pool of surplus labor.	Much of the recent rise in informality reflects the decline informal employment associated with structural adjustment and global competition. It reflects not only the incapacity of formal firms to absorb labor, but also their willingness to do so.

5.	Most of those in the sector are entrepreneurs of illegal and unregistered enterprises seeking to avoid regulation and taxation.	It should not be equated with the criminal or illegal economy. It is made up of nonstandard wageworkers as well as entrepreneurs and self-employed persons producing legal goods and services, albeit through irregular or unregulated means. Most entrepreneurs and the self-employed are amendable to, and would welcome efforts to reduce barriers to registration and related transaction cost and to increase benefits from regulation. Most nonstandard workers should also welcome more stable jobs and worker's rights.
6.	Work in the informal economy is comprised mostly of survival activities and thus is not a subject for policy.	Informal enterprises include not only survival activities but also stable enterprises and dynamic growing businesses. All informal enterprises are affected by economic policies.
7.	It comprises mostly of street traders and very small-scale producers.	It is made up of a wide range of informal arrangements—both "resilient old forms" and "emerging new ones" (temporary and part time jobs plus home based work for high tech industries). It is two basic segments are informal enterprises and informal jobs.
8.	It comprises mainly of unregistered business.	It comprises not only of informal enterprises but also of informal jobs, including employees of informal firms, casual day laborers, and domestic workers as well as industrial outworkers and other nonstandard workers in both informal and formal firms.
9.	It is unregulated	Some informal enterprises—such as street vendors—are highly regulated so much so that regulations are impossible to enforce or comply with and are often not clear either to local authorities or to vendors. Regulations become a tool of harassment and control, not away to encourage economic contributions of street vendors. On the other hand, the employers of most informal workers often seek to avoid complying with labor legislation.
10.	Because it is unregulated and untaxed, many working in the informal sector are wealthy.	Average incomes are lower in the informal economy are micro entrepreneurs who live others. The poorest are typically, informal wageworkers, especially industrial outworkers.
11.	To regulate the informal economy is unnecessary interference with its workings.	In today's globalized economy, the active role of government is needed in the regulation of economic activities, including the informal economy. Clear rules and appropriate legislation are needed to regulate the relationship between governments, foreign investors, local enterprises, and the workforce.
12.	Street traders are to blame for crime in the inner sites.	Criminals are a threat to business interests of both formal and informal enterprises.
13.	It does not contribute to economic growth.	It contributes substantially to the economy and needs to be encouraged and facilitated.

How to Develop and Harness the Informal Sector

Aryetey (as cited in Developing the Informal Sector for Exclusive Growth 2015) explains the following strategic options for engaging the informal economy:

1. The government should make policies that are needed to deal with high unemployment, lawlessness and tax evasion, all of which are often associated with the informal economy. Countries must adopt explicit policies that encourage the development of the informal sector.
2. Private sector development is crucial for growth and employment creation in Africa and the world at large, also through tax revenues that enable more better public services.
3. Promotion of informal to formal economy linkages.
4. Provision of safety nets for informal workers.
5. Better measurement of informal production and employment and its contribution to economic growth.

6.0 Provision of Facilities for the Skill Acquisition Program

Facilities are structures and (or) equipment that makes the performance of the skill acquisition process a success. As important as it is to acquire a skill, the facilities needed for the acquisition of such skills helps or promotes the acquisition of the skill. Such facilities could include building. It has been observed that the speed of a nation's development is directly related to the quality of vocational skills possessed by its workforce. It should be noted also that without the necessary and relevant vocational training equipment, possession of quality vocational skills will be a mirage (Adebisi, and Oni 2012). Availability of equipment, machines and facilities for the purpose of vocational skills should mean that these training tools are provided in adequate quantity to a degree where it is possible for individual trainees to use during trainings in workshops (Umunadi, 2010 in Adebisi and Oni, 2012). Vocational training centers, workshops and the training environment should be well equipped to reach the standard of where trainees will work after training. After the training, the trainees should be provided with machines/equipment to establish them in their respective jobs after training. Availability of training equipment is as important as the skill acquisition itself. The government should device a way of assisting the trainers and training centers to procure necessary training facilities for proper impartation of employable skills into the trainees.

7.0 Approval of Institutional Curricula

Onwuka (1996) sees the curriculum as "a total experience with which the school deals in educating young people. It is a deliberate, systematic and planned attempts made by the school (training centers) to change the behavior of members of the society in which it situates. The curriculum is the life and program of the training center." Gbamanja (2002) further explains that it consists of all the knowledge, skills, attitudes and values that are designed to be studies by learners. It is an organization or a prescribed pattern of subject matter which addresses the needs, problems, desires, values and dreams of the society and is designed to be achieved through the school. It includes issues in the society about the trainee and knowledge, skill, attitudes and values needed to achieve set objectives.

Entrepreneurship is the capacity to harness the right quantity, quality and combination of resources that are consistent with profit making under risk and uncertainty. It is a dynamic and social process where individuals solely or in corporation identify possibilities and utilize them by transforming ideas into practical and

goal-oriented activities in a social, cultural or economic context. It involves educating learners through inculcation of a range of skills and attitudes, including the ability to think creatively, work in teams, manage risk and manage uncertainty. This is supported by the recognition that changing "mindset" is part of the entrepreneurial pipeline which starts in education and runs through research to running enterprises (Uwem 2012 in Achor, Agogo and Dodo, 2020). According to UNESCO (2002), the purpose of entrepreneurship education includes

1. educating individuals for and about business,
2. providing a continuous program of planned learning experiences designed to equip individuals to fulfil the following roles:
   a. Providing and distributing goods and services as workers
   b. Using the products as consumers
   c. Making wise socio-economic decisions as citizens
3. providing educational opportunities for students who are preparing for careers in professional field or discipline other than business, to acquire business knowledge and skills needed to function effectively in the world of work,
4. providing career information that helps individual students relate their interests, needs and abilities to occupation opportunities in business.

Strategies for Implementing Entrepreneurship Education Curriculum for Sustainable Development

The following are some of the strategies for the implementation of the curriculum of entrepreneurship, as explained in Danladi. To bridge the widening gap between the expected and the guarantee sustainable development, the following strategies should be adopted.

1. **Teaching for cooperative learning:** According to Okolodile (2009 in Danladi 2016), cooperative learning is a student-centered approach where trainees learn in small groups of five with the trainer as a guide. The trainees cooperate with one another to perform or complete a particular task. This kind of instructional strategy offers the trainees opportunity for effective interaction with one another, to make decisions and choices in their skill acquisition process, and to learn through greater knowledge of one another's needs.
2. **Relating the learning process to real life's experience:** The trainers need to explore the immediate environment of the trainee and take advantage of it for entrepreneurship skill acquisition.
3. **Training for the appropriate skills:** It is often seen that people acquire some skills which they later cannot utilize because of the lack of relevance. Teaching in the skill acquisition setting should be such that learning activities have direct relevance and applicability to the learner's daily life. Trainers are generally not interested in acquiring knowledge just for the sake of it. They would like to see a relationship between what they study in the training centers and what they would achieve after the skill acquisition process.
4. **Using field trips as resources for teaching/learning:** The management and the trainers should adopt the field trip as a resource for learning. The trainer can organize trips to companies where such skills are practiced. This will give the students an opportunity to ask questions from experts and express their feelings about the skill. It develops the student's interest in the learning process.
5. **Internship:** Sending trainees on internship will give them an opportunity to practice with a small business organization, with a view of exhibiting the skill they have learned in the skill acquisition center. The trainers can be paired for internship with local entrepreneurs. This builds a bridge between the skill acquisition program and the business world.

6. **School seminars and workshops:** Seminars and workshops on entrepreneurship skills and attributes which are needed by entrepreneurs to succeed in business should periodically be organized for students. Here, successful entrepreneurs and financial experts could be invited to deliver lectures on entrepreneurship practices. This would broaden the trainee's minds, knowledge and horizon.

8.0 Enacting Ethical Order

Ethical development is understood as the successive improvement of a person's ability to solve moral problems which he/she encounters in his/her real life. (Kavathatzopoulos 1994) Piaget (1932 in kavathatzopoulos 1994) explains that an individual can use two methods in his/her effort to solve a moral problem: the heteronomous or the autonomous one.

Anyaogu (2008 in Ukala and Nwabueze 2016) defines ethics as "the science that places value on human conduct. It is a reflective study of what one ought to do and how he ought to live. It is not about compliance but about doing what is right, good, just, virtuous and proper in our everyday living." It is not about the way things are but about the way things ought to be. Ukala and Nwabueze (2016) further define ethics as the principles of obligation, ends, motive and virtue that distinguish us for how we should determine right from wrong, good from bad, proper from improper, and virtuous from vicious. Also, Okele (2004 in Ukala and Nwabueze 2016) defines ethics as a code of conduct based on universal moral duties and obligations, which indicate how professionals should behave. It deals with the ability to distinguish good from bad, right from wrong, and propriety from impropriety.

The skills needed by individuals at work place, according to Ukala and Nwabueze (2016) include the following: information literacy skill, innovative and creative skills, problem solving skill, communication skills, interpersonal skill, team working skill and information technology skill.

a. **Information literacy skill:** Promotes the ability of the individual to identify sources of information, organize the relevant information and make effective use of media for disseminating information.
b. **Problem solving skill:** Helps them to identify problems and ways of resolving them without stress.
c. **Communication skill:** Involves the ability to communicate ideas clearly, fluently and confidently both orally, by giving presentations, and in writing, via the production of essays and reports.
d. **Interpersonal skill:** Promotes understanding and sensitivity to the views and roles of others, gaining their confidence at the right time.
e. **Team working skill:** Entails combining with others to achieve a task or goal, recognizing and respecting their views and opinions. Most employees have to work together to meet organizational objectives. An employee with a high sense of teamwork helps a team meet its goals and deliver quality work. These employees respect their peers and help them where they can, making collaborations for effective work delivery.
f. **Information technology skill:** Involves the ability to use a variety of software to store, analyze, process and present information and data conveniently.

Work ethics are skills and values based on hard work and diligence in a skill acquisition program. Dreyfus and Dreyfus (1980) summarize the five stages of skill acquisition as follows:

1. **Novice:** Normally, the instruction process begins with the instructor decomposing the task environment into context-free features that the beginner can recognize with the benefit of experience.

The beginner is then given rules for determining actions on the basis of these features, much like following a computer program.

2. **Advanced beginner:** As the novice gains experience and actually coping with real situations, he or she begins to note, or an instructor points out, perspicuous examples of meaningful additional components of the situation. After seeing a sufficient number of examples, the student learns to recognize them. Instructional maxims now can refer to these new situational aspects.

3. **Competence:** With an increased experience, the number of features and aspects to be taken into account becomes overwhelming. To cope with this information explosion, the performer learns to adopt a hierarchical view of decision making. By first choosing a plan, goal or perspective that organizes the situation, and by their examining only the small set of features and aspects that he or she has learned are relevant given that plan, the performer can simplify and improve his or her performance

4. **Proficiency:** As soon as the competent performer stops reflecting on problematic situations as a detached observer and stops looking for principles to guide his or her actions, the gripping, holistic experiences from the competent stage become the basis of the next advance in skill. Having experienced many emotion-laden situations, choosing plans in each, and having obtained vivid emotional demonstrations of the adequacy involved in the world of the skill notices, or is struck by, a certain plan, goal or perspective. No longer is the spell of involvement broken by detached conscious planning.

   Because there are generally far fewer ways of seeing than ways of acting, after understanding without conscious effort what is going on, the proficient performer will still think about what to do. During this thought process, elements that present themselves as salient are assessed and combined by rule and maxim to produce decisions.

5. **Expertise:** The proficient performer, immersed in the world of skillful activity, sees what needs to be done but must decide how to do it. With enough experience with a variety of situation's, all seen from the same perspective but requiring different tactical decisions, the proficient performer seems gradually to decompose this class of situations into subclasses, each of which shares the same decision, and action. This allows an immediate intuitive response to each situation.

9.0 Conclusion

Skill acquisition is the acquisition of knowledge for self-sustenance. It is a conscious effort from an individual to acquire such knowledge. However, the government has a role to play in the effective impartation of such skill. It is the duty of the government to set up a body that oversees, monitors and audits the activities in the skill acquisition centers, and to make sure that their goals and objectives are properly carried out. The government on their part can as well sponsor the skill acquisition process by providing facilities and learning equipment in the skill acquisition centers. The skills acquired by these trainees in turn will bring about the development of the economy of the nation.

Empowerment Through Skill Acquisition

1.0 Introduction

Skill acquisition is the ability to be prepared on a particular task or work and becoming an expert in it (Okolocha, John-Akamelu and Muogbo, 2020). Isaac (2011 in Okolocha, John-Akamelu and Muogbo, 2020) adds that skill acquisition is a major tool for extreme poverty eradication and hunger with the aim of creating an avenue for jobs and wealth creation which will bring self-reliance and sufficiency in contributing to the growth and development of the economy in the nation. The aim of every skill acquisition center is to

a. provide the form of training that gives the trainees the chances of obtaining skills that are appropriate for reachiness in a field or trade for beneficial business;

b. provide the distinct skill that relates to each trade that makes on an expert in one field rather than the others. There are different skills that can be acquired and such include animal husbandry, poultry farming, bead making, wood carving, fashion, designing. However, at the end of the acquisition of these skills, most of these trainees do not have the means to set up themselves in the business world, hence the need for empowerment.

2.0 The Concept/Meaning of Empowerment

The American English Dictionary defines empowerment as the achievement of political, social or economic power by an individual or group; the process of supporting another person or persons to discover and claim personal power or the state of being empowered. Empowerment is also defined as an intentional ongoing process centered in a local community, involving mutual respect, critical reflection, caring and group participation, through which people lacking an equal share of valued resources gain greater access to and control over these resources; or a process by which people gain control over their lives, democratic participation in the life of their community, and a critical understanding of their environment. (Perkins and Zimmerman 1995 in Perkins 2010). The common features in the two definitions above are the empowerment.

i. It is a process.
ii. It occurs in communities or organizations.
iii. It involves an active participation, awareness and understanding.
iv. And it provides an access to and control over important decisions and resources.

More so, it is the process of increasing the strength of individuals, teams or communities. It covers spiritual, political, social, as well as economic strength; it can also be developing confidence in one's own capacities, encouraging people to gain skills and knowledge that will allow them to overcome obstacles in life or work environment and ultimately help them to develop within themselves in the society. Empowerment can also be defined as an interactive process through which people gain or experience personal and social change enabling them to take decisions to achieve influence over the organization and instruction which affects their lives and the communities in which they live. It includes encouraging and developing the skill for self-sufficiency in the individual or a group to do their jobs magnificently with a focus on eliminating the future needs for charity or welfare (Blanchand, 2003 and Whitmore 1988 in Ikwegwe *et al.,* 2004). All the above definitions of empowerment point to the fact that humans, whether as individuals or as a group or community, have potentials hidden in them. The empowerment process makes it possible for them to look inwards and harness that hidden potentials in them, to the betterment of their individual lives and the communities in which the live.

3.0 Empowerment: A Global Phenomenon

All around the world, people talk a lot about empowerment. It is not limited to one's local environment or community. So many national, state, local, and nongovernmental organizations view empowerment as an ongoing process, if the people are to fully utilize their potentials. People are given birth to daily and as they grow, there are certain level of knowledge that they are expected to possess, so as the better their lives. When such knowledge is acquired by the individual, it makes it possible for them to fully maximize their potentials. Many governments have devised means to empower their people while some nongovernmental organizations come together to pull their resources together to develop a particular area, country or continent. In the recent years, most of the moves made at empowering people have been focused on women and the youths. To the women, a lot of societies do not give the women equal rights with the men socially and economically. They are sometimes seen as lesser humans, hence the need to empower the women. To the youths, lack of opportunities and the right level of knowledge could turn them to tools in the hands of politicians or make them to become societal miscreants. Therefore empowerment is necessary to harness their potential and create an area where they can channel their energies into. In 2019, the Global Empowerment Movement (GEM) hosted the fifty-seventh session of the Commission for social development with the theme "Activating and Strengthening Women Empowerment through Economic and Social Inclusion: Empowerment as a link to poverty eradication and sustainable development. The main objectives of that summit was to highlight how women and youth inclusiveness, economic and equality empowerment could be used to eradicate poverty, curb human trafficking and to achieve sustainable development goals. To achieve these goals, they discussed on the barriers surrounding poverty, economic and gender equality, and education. Apart from the GEM, there are other nongovernmental organizations that aim at making the lives of individuals better, such as the Economic Community of West African States (ECOWAS); United Nations (UN), World Health Organization (WHO), to mention but a few. Hence, we can confidently conclude that empowerment is a global phenomenon, and not just limited to local communities. The voluminous attention to the empowerment theory and research has been concentrated in the United States than in any other country. However, applications of empowerment concepts, and the study of those applications, have spread widely throughout the globe. As empowerment is a response to oppression, it is not surprising that scholars and community and resistance leaders in the many troubled parts of the world have begun to borrow and adapt empowerment ideas to their own circumstances. Outside the United States, Latin America has provided the greatest wealth of literature on the concept of empowerment Serrano-Garcia (1984 as cited

in Perkins 2010) describes a community development intervention that used empowerment strategies and tactics to facilitate residents ideological and skill development. Although participants were empowered at an ideological level, she concluded that empowerment was only an illusion in that the dominant culture and its institutions were still conservative, capitalist, individualistic and pro-United States, and that participants remain part of that culture and are having influenced by its values.

Empowerment has become a core principle of the international community development. Friedman (1992 in Perkins 2010) sees poverty in terms of social, political and psychological powerlessness and then views empowerment as an alternative to the over emphasis of international development agencies and many national governments on purely economic policies, which have been found wanting. Development interventions, as he proposes, should empower and mobilize poor households and communities for political participation on a wider scale. The idea of research and application of the theory of empowerment in a less developed and conflict countries is essentially important but often faced with difficulties.

4.0 Purpose of Empowerment through Entrepreneurship Education

The following are the main purposes of empowerment through entrepreneurship education as highlighted by Paul and Nwalado (2005/2012 as cited in Undiyaundeye and Otu 2015):

1. To provide the young graduates adequate training that will enable them to be creative and innovative in identifying great business opportunities
2. To offer functional education to the youth to enable them to be well empowered and self-reliant people in their own right
3. To serve as a catalyst for economic growth and development
4. To offer tertiary institution graduates with adequate training in risk management to make learning outcome feasible
5. To reduce the high rate of poverty and insecurity and violence
6. To create job and employment opportunities to the citizenry
7. To reduce rural-urban migration
8. To provide the young graduates with enough training skills and support that will enable them to establish a career in small and medium size business
9. To incubate the spirit of perseverance in the youth and adults which will enable them to persist in any business venture they embark on
10. To create a smooth transition from traditional to the modern industrial economy
11. To stimulate the interest of youth in vocational trades through the provision of trainings at designated centers and the provision of micro credit to successful graduands in those centers

5.0 Types of Empowerments

The following are the types of empowerment, according to Kelvin-Iloafu, Igwe, and Enemuo (2019).

a. **Psychological empowerment:** Enhances an individual's consciousness, belief in efficacy, awareness and knowledge of problems and solutions and of how individuals can address issues that harm their quality of life. This type of empowerment aims to create self-confidence and give the youths the skills to acquire knowledge.

b. **Community empowerment:** This focuses on enhancing the community through leadership development, improving communication, and creating a network of support to mobilize the community to address concerns.

c. **Organizational empowerment:** This aims to create of resources for a community, including voluntary organizations, unions and associations that seek to protect, promote, and advocate for the powerless.

d. **Economic empowerment:** This is the capacity of the people to participate in, contribute to and benefit from growth processes in ways which recognize the value of their contributions, respect their dignity and make it possible to negotiate a fairer distribution of the benefits of growth. Economic empowerment increases people's access to economic resources and opportunities including jobs, financial services, property and other productive assets, skills development and market information. It further teaches entrepreneurial skills, how to take ownership of their assets, and how to have income security.

e. **Social empowerment:** This teaches youths and women about social inclusion and literacy as well as helping them find the resources to be proactive in their communities.

f. **Cultural empowerment:** This aims at recreating cultural practices and redefining rules and norms for the men, women and children. Through these dimensions of empowerment, programs can work on empowering the women and the youths in one aspect of their lives or the other.

6.0 Factors that Promote Empowerment

According to O'Neil, Domingo and Walters (2014) the following are some of the factors that promote empowerment.

a. **Legal reform and institutional change:** Constitutions and laws establish the formal rules of the game about how a society allocates and uses power and resources. They are therefore important determinants of access to power and resources. Legal and institutional reforms can involve incremental changes to existing laws.

New constitutions that advance civil rights and political rights, including equality and women's rights, are often the most tangible markers of post-conflict or democratic transitions, whether violent or peaceful. In respect to women, laws and policies that affirm women's rights and open potential pathways for women's empowerment are not in themselves sufficient to change women's lives. Real change depends on other social and economic structures, such as access to welfare and other basic services, economic markets, socio-cultural norms and the quality of the civil society. Since women make up a greater percentage of the world's population, employment law and women's political rights, including affirmative action to increase the representation of women's public life, are two such areas, but there has also been important gains for women in more socially controversial areas that have been traditionally viewed as private matters, such as family law, land and inheritance rights and violence against women.

b. **Social and economic policies and the reallocation of resources:** Improved access to education, healthcare and employment are frequently found to facilitate empowerment, among women and the youths. Research has revealed and supported the claim that education facilitates changes in cognitive ability and that this, in turn supports critical awareness and the ability of the individuals to question and reflect on their lives. In comparison to those who are less educated, educated individuals are likely to participate in a wider range of the decision-making processes at the household, community and with the outside world, including engaging with public officials and service providers. Access to the labor market on the part of the woman can increase women's capacity

to have a wider social and political engagement and also be involved in collective action. The pathways (2011 as cited in O'Neil, Domingo and Valters 2014) reveals that whether education or employment empowers women depends heavily on their interaction with the social and economic conditions and therefore varies across time and place.

c. **Organizations and movements:** Organizations and movements which individuals belong to play a vital role in the people's collective organization, reflection and action. There is an evidence to prove that women's movements have been the key factor in both driving and ensuring the implementation of women's rights and sustaining changes in gender norms and relations.

First, in all the countries, when the women and the youths come together to share and reflect on their common experiences, it brings the development of critical consciousness about unjust social practices and structures against them and a redefinition of their identities. This is necessary and critical because the psychological dimension of women's empowerment is the cornerstone of other dimensions. Women and youths (who are mostly affected) who individually stood up to challenge oppression and abuse were usually made to face humiliation and were castigated for their audacity. When these people come together, they draw strength from being part of a cause, which contributes to a sense of self-worth and agency.

Secondly, women's organizations also contribute to the gradual reshaping of community, traditional-indigenous or religious law and other sociocultural norms that shape women's everyday experiences, capabilities and choices.

Moreover, women and youth organizations provide a platform for them to gain leadership skills and act as a steeping-stone for them to take on leadership positions in politics and public life.

d. **International politics and new social norms:** International factors, including developments in international law and assistance, have also been important contextual and enabling elements for progress on women and youth empowerment globally and at the country level. In some cases, women activists were able to use the United Declaration of Human Rights (UDHR) and the United Nations machinery as a platform to negotiate, lobby for and develop international law guaranteeing women's rights, culminating in the convention on the Elimination of all forms of Discrimination against Women (EDAW) in 1979. CEDAW has legitimized women's struggles for equality and provided focus for both women's mobilization and efforts to hold states accountable for the protection and promotion of women's rights. Along with the International Bill of Rights, it has also provided a focus for women's advocacy and action around the United Nations Conferences that have taken place since the 1990s. These conferences have helped to ensure that aid-agencies fund gender-related programs, through support to women's organizations and to the health and education of women and girls.

The international human rights framework has therefore provided a common set of standards and language for international diplomacy and multilateral and bilateral forums on women's rights and other issues. The transnational women's movement has been indispensable, both in pushing for changing norms at the international level and in providing technical, financial and moral support to women's struggles at the national and community levels—including to make effective use of emerging international norms. The importance of transnational mobilization of this kind cannot be overemphasized. This includes providing support to national processes of empowerment, using political leverage at the international level to cajole states into some degree of compliance with their international commitments, and internal lobbying and advocacy to push for legal change at the international and global levels.

At the same time, while international norms are important, women's empowerment, particularly for all women and on a sustained basis, depends on changes in socio-cultural norms and practices within national polities and communities.

7.0 Benefits of Empowerment

The benefits of empowerment to the society cannot be overemphasized.

The Benefits of Empowerment to the Women

In every nation of the world, women form a good number of the population. In a situation where these women are not empowered, the burden of the family falls on the men, hence the need for the empowerment of the women. The following are the benefits of empowerment to the women.

i.   Women's economic empowerment is central to realizing women's rights and gender equality. Women's economic empowerment includes women's ability to participate equally in existing markets; their access to and control over productive resources, access to decent work, control over their own time, lives and bodies; an increased voice, agency and meaningful participation in economic decision-making at all levels from the household to international institutions.

ii.   Empowering women in the economy are key to achieving the sustainable developmental goals. It brings about food security, promotes good health and reduces the issue of gender inequalities.

iii. Women empowerment brings about economic growth and development. When women are empowered economically and are successful, it boosts productivity, increases economic diversity and income equality, in addition to other positive developmental outcomes.

iv.   Women, when empowered can create employment opportunities for other women, thereby reducing the challenge of unemployment on the part of the government.

v.   Women's educational empowerment makes it possible for women to be gainfully employed. Research has shown that companies whose leadership include women tend to do better than their contemporaries. This further increases the organizational effectiveness and economic growth.

vi.   When women are gainfully employed, it reduces the financial responsibility on the part of the men and will better the living standard of the members of the family.

vii. Women who are educated and economically empowered tend to make better plans for their children's future than their counterparts who are less educated.

7.1 The Benefits of Youth Empowerment

Ojikutu (1998) asserts that youth empowerment is very crucial in the attainment of development because the transitional period from childhood to adulthood is unquestionably a challenge for many youths and for them to contribute their quota to the national development, the government must help their transformation in this regard. Skill acquisition bring about economic empowerment and this is beneficial to the youth's in the following ways, according to Olusola (2019).

1. **Poverty eradication:** Youth empowerment can curb the rate of poverty to a large level. One of the keys to empowering the youth is with skill development. When a youth is equipped with the essential skills, he or she can utilize them to feed, assist others and even invest for future use, aiding the nation economically. This will in-turn contribute to the increase to the employability and add to the GDP of the nation.

2. **Improved standard education:** Empowerment can help the youths to understand the importance of education which leads to the social improvement of the country. The empowered youths can donate educational facilities to primary, secondary and even to tertiary institutions. Empowering

the youths academically accelerates the spirit of patriotism in the educational sector and helps to place more value on education on the part of the youths.

3. When the youths are empowered, the masses are empowered as well and this leads to a better future for the youths. The empowered youth will grow up with a sense of responsibility and indebtedness to the individual or society that empowered him. This youth will someday reciprocate the same to other youths and this will bring about greater development.

4. **Crime reduction and national security:** Youth empowerment ensures that youths have the necessary skill to sustain a livelihood, preventing them from adopting the criminal lifestyle. It also gives the youths an opportunity to reflect on their quality of life and to dream bigger, thereby attaining greater heights. Many youths who are into crime today were not exposed to empowerment, hence the have little or no regard for human life. So with proper moral, academic and economic empowerment, the youths will be taken off the streets and this will bring about a greater security.

5. **Creation of employment opportunities:** When the youths are empowered, they go on to build businesses or companies which may require the services of other young people. Thus, the empowerment of youths creates employment opportunities to others in their society. It also reduces the dependency on the government for job creation. Any nation that typically wants to solve unemployment issues should first of all empower the youths.

6. **Technological development:** Youth empowerment increases and improves technological standards, as agreed by technophiles. Development in machines and other important discoveries occurs when the youths are fully empowered. They take their time to dig into science, reason out some important things and make them real. Many inventions of the world today came to be as a result of empowerment. When this is done, other nations of the world will buy either the machines or the technology and this will lead to economic growth for such a country.

7. **Security:** Many nations of the world have more youths in the military and other paramilitary bodies. This is because the youth are full of life and strength. They are not easily defeated in the challenges of life; they usually find their way. When the youths are empowered, it builds the spirit of patriotism in them. When the youths are trained on security skills, they protect their immediate environment and the nation at large.

8. **Economic growth:** When the youths are empowered and they become successful in their ventures, it brings about economic growth through the payment of taxes. These taxes which are paid by the youths are in turn used to build roads, hospitals, schools and also improve on the agricultural sector. This further leads to the betterment of the lives of the people in such a society.

In conclusion, no society or nation will grow without empowering her citizens. Understanding the importance of empowerment and promoting it leads to the achievement of the economic goals of such a society, government or nation.

8.0 Challenges to Empowerment Programs

The following are some of the challenges to economic empowerment through skill acquisition, according to Kelvin-Iloafu (2019).

1. **Political instability:** Political instability refers to a constant and an irregular change in government. These changes in government also bring about change in policies which greatly affects economic empowerment in the country. It affects the program in the following ways:

a. **Migration:** This refers to the movement of people to areas in search of greener pastures. Many people, especially the youths and the intellectuals, migrate from areas of political conflict and instability. Most of them arrive at their destination. While some may succeed, may find it difficult to fit in and they become wasted over there. Others, in the process of trying to escape lose their lives in the high seas and in the harsh weather conditions of the desserts. Some of the youth (girls) are sold into prostitution in such counties where they migrate to.

b. **Political thuggery:** Many of the politicians, to survive the political situation turn to political things and they introduce the youths into it, such that even when the political situation of such a country is settled, the politicians and those youths whom they had integrated still become a nuisance to their society.

c. **Unplanned strike:** When there are agitations from a particular aspect of the workforce, as a result of unfavorable, government policies, it halts or hinders any activity toward empowerment

2. **Economic meltdown:** Whenever there is an economic meltdown or recession, there is always untold hardship to the citizens. The companies may not be able to operate, as they seem to incur losses and that as well may lead to an increased level of unemployment or retrenchment. Foreign investors who would have come in to establish businesses would not want to take such risks and this affects youth, who would have been employed in such companies.

3. **Agitation in some geo-political zones:** When there are instances of agitation, such as terrorist activities, military, etc.; it hinders empowerment in such areas. As such, social instability, poor governance, competition for economic resources and environmental degradation takes its toll on such areas.

4. **Failed health facilities:** When the health facilities in the country are not properly managed or are not functioning well, it leads to the death of the citizenry and this can greatly impede economic empowerment.

5. **Lack of basic infrastructure:** In the developing countries of the world, lack of basic infrastructures can greatly affect the empowerment of the citizens. Without the basic infrastructures such as constant electricity, pipe borne water and good road networks, economic empowerment will be slow. Power, water and good road network helps in the processing and the distribution of agricultural produce from where they are produced to where they are needed.

6. Inadequate or lack of access to finance can impede economic empowerment. Many who do not have collateral may not have access to loans and as such, may not be able to empower themselves, even if they have the needed skills.

7. Family responsibilities and cultural norms can greatly hinder economic empowerment on the part of the women. A woman who has many children or whose culture does not permit to inherit properties may not be able to empower herself and even if she does, may not complete with her male counterparts who are less burdened with family life and taking care of the children.

9.0 Overcoming the Challenges of Empowerment

1. **Stability in government policies:** Policies adopted by the government should emphasis on pro-empowerment programs. The policy objective for empowering the poor and vulnerable members of the population, of which women and youth form a major part of, has always been to increase opportunities of livelihood for the poor through job creation, easy access to credits, provision of infrastructure, enhancement of business incentives, and increased participation in wealth creation. For these purposes, budgetary allocations are made annually. Yet the outcome falls short of the expectation. It should create an enabling environment for youths and women to be empowered.

2. **Land law reforms:** This reform is necessary in empowering all the marginalized segments of the population through social campaigns, advocacy and reorientation. This will change the people's value system and enable the women and youths to have access to land and this encourage agricultural activities.

3. **Formation of cooperative societies:** Cooperative societies serve as an effective community development vehicle. They build economic self-reliance and civil society. The benefits of cooperative organizations accrue to the larger society, because they create jobs, reinvest locally, emphasis on education and skill acquisition.

4. **Improvement and the provision of basic infrastructure:** When the basic infrastructures are provided or are improved upon, economic activities will be encouraged. Companies and small business will develop in such areas and the good road networks will promote the distribution of such products and services.

5. **Improvement and the provision of quality and well equipped health facilities:** The government and the civil societies should try as much as possible to improve upon the health facilities. This will reduce the mortality rate of the populace.

10.0 Recommendations

Perkins (1995), Ikegwu (2014) and Kevin *et al.* (2019) offer the following recommendations to policy-makers, program planners and researchers into empowerment-oriented programs and policies as follows:

1. Attention should be paid to all levels of empowerment, beyond individual to community, with an aim at solving the immediate needs of the people.

2. Identify those who can make or affect empowerment policies; determine their interests; find information relevant to their interest; and provide that information in the most valid, clear and compelling ways.

3. Policy makers need to establish an enabling environment that will facilitate access to financial services for women entrepreneurs, through the development of a supportive legal and regulatory framework and the development of educational and vocational training opportunities that are more aligned with the specific needs of those in need of the empowerment.

4. The role of young entrepreneurs as agents of positive change and creators of jobs in their communities must be recognized and a need to support these entrepreneurs and to increase the opportunities open to them is mandatory.

5. Skilled women and youths are more likely to access finance more easily. It is therefore necessary for the government to enhance funding for them, to ensure an upscale of their leadership, technical, entrepreneurial and managerial skills.

6. Since a good number of the vulnerable are women and girls, the government should increase the enrollment across all levels of education. It is also necessary to build the capacity of the financial institution to serve female entrepreneurs, as well as the men, so as to serve them better.

7. The educational system should be reappraised to move away from the theory-based learning to more practical (hands-on) learning.

8. The knowledge of entrepreneurship should promote productivity, with an aim at proffering solutions to some basic needs in the society.

9. Apprenticeship schemes should be formalized in the country so as to enable those pursuing skills acquisition through that medium have a sense of belonging.

11.0 Conclusion

Skill acquisition plays a vital role in empowerment. Since empowerment is aimed at developing and encouraging one's confidence and competence in a particular area, the trainees then apply the skills to better their lives and their economy. There are types of empowerment such as economic, psychological, community, among others. However, there are many challenges that can impede the successful implementation of a skill acquisition program. Such challenges include political instability and the instability of government policies, economic recession, terrorism as well as lack of basic infrastructure. These challenges can be overcome if the government and civic organizations make an effort at reaching the people. The government should also create an enabling environment for the empowerment programs to be actualized. With these, the trainees and the vulnerable will greatly benefit from the skill acquisition programs and will be empowered as well.

Chapter Nineteen

Curriculum Development for Skills Programs

1.0   Introduction

Curriculum development for skill is a lay down career which aid learners in completion of their tasks curriculum content described what is to be taught in a formal and nonformal school.

2.0 describes curriculum knowledge, experience and content, criteria for selecting learning experience and organizational criteria for learning experience and content.

3.0 explains curriculum development and planning, curriculum development model, curriculum planning, stages in curriculum planning, reasons for planning curriculum, curriculum planning techniques, needs and importance of curriculum development and principles of curriculum development.

4.0 deals with tools for developing curriculum and types of curriculum.

5.0 elucidates curriculum development process and organization, stages in the process of curriculum development, curriculum organization and steps for organizing curriculum.

6.0 illustrates a sample curriculum for skill acquisition context, significance of a good curriculum, vision of curriculum, and an example of curriculum for skill acquisition context.

7.0 details evaluation as a curriculum context, objectives of curriculum evaluation, types of curriculum evaluation, significance of curriculum evaluation, and criteria for curriculum evaluation.

8.0 summarizes and concludes curriculum development for skills.

2.0   Curriculum: Knowledge, Experience and Content

Curriculum in skill acquisition is described as a defined and lay down career design which learners/trainees must accomplish to proceed a certain level of skill training.

Knowledge is described as the circumstance or condition of apprehending truth or fact through reasoning (Merriam Webster Dictionary, accessed September, 2021).

Knowledge is also seen as specifiable actuality or facticity of constituent parts. A knowledge assertion will frequently include essential, annunciating or definite knowledge.

Skill is described as the ability to use one's knowledge effectively and readily in execution or performance (Merriam Webster Dictionary, accessed September 2021) in the context of curriculum. Skill can also be described as the employment of compound knowledge. A skill comment will frequently include implicit, procedural and relating to a particular field of study cognition.

Curriculum knowledge is defined as the acquired proficiency to employ diligently hypothetical comprehensive and fundamental law and behaviors combined with planning, implementing and evaluating the curriculum in distinguishing (differentiating) profession of teaching (instruction), and in accentuating the competency for sensitiveness to the social milieu and dynamics of the trainee/leaners context.

Curriculum Experience

Curriculum experience can also be referred to as learning experience. Learning experience refers to any interaction courses, skill program or other experience in which learning takes place, whether it occurs in traditional school setting (classrooms) or nontraditional school setting (outside of classroom or outdoor environment). According to Tyler, learning experiences are the interactions between the leaner and external conditions in the environment to which he/she can react.

Criteria for Selecting Learning Experience

1. **Validity:** Learning experience is valid when it related objectives are in any of the three domains; cognitive, affective and psychomotor, the learning experience must be holistic to involve all the domains.
2. **Suitability:** Learning experience must be suitable for the age or level of the learners and for the content which it is meant for it must not be too simple or complex.
3. **Relevance to life:** Learning experience must be relevant to real-life situations in school and in the society to help learners understand their society and proffer solutions to some problems of the society. Experience in real content and situation bring realism to teaching and learning.
4. **Variety:** Learning experience must help learners comprehend. This is because leaners are different and learn in different ways base on their interest and ability.
5. **Comprehensive:** Learning experience must cover all the stated objectives in a lesson; it must range from the simplest-learning experiences to the most complex, covering all the domains of learning.

Each experience reinforces and extends the previous one. Curriculum practices in the arrangement of sequence of learning experiences usually based according to one of the following; chronological order, logical order and difficulty.

Curriculum Content

Curriculum content is described as the totality of what is to be taught in a school system. The content component of teaching-learning situation refers to the important facts, principles and concepts to be taught. These contents must be in line with the learning experiences and there must be clear cut objective to be achieved by the end of each respective lesson. It can be in form of knowledge, skills, attitude and values that leaners are exposed to. Content involves subject matter drawn on the bases of problems, topics cutting traditional subjects and skills.

Criteria for Selecting Curriculum Content

1. **Self-sufficiency:** The criterion helps leaners attain maximum self-sufficiency at the most economical manner of content selection. This is done when the leaners/trainees are given the opportunity to experiment, observe and carryout field study.

2. **Validity:** The content of the curriculum is valid if it promotes the outcome that it is intended to promote. It is also the authenticity of the subject matter or content selected, to make sure the topics are not obsolete, for this to be achieve, there should be a regular check on the curriculum content and replace it if necessary.

3. **Significance:** The content is significant if it is selected and organized for the development of learning activities, skills, processes, and attitude that will help in solving the problem of the country. It also develops the three domain of learning and considers the cultural aspect of the learners particularly, if the learners come from different cultural background and races then the content must be cultural sensitive.

Organizational Criteria for Learning Experience and Content

The organization of learning experience content is based on the cumulative development behavior the learner's exhibit and gradually experience during teaching and learning process.

Content and learning experience are organized into two relationships bases; namely: vertical and horizontal relationship.

- Vertical organization is the arrangement of learning experiences and content over a time sequence access classes in the same subject/skill. Here, contents are arranged in hierarchical order, from the lowest level to the highest level. The arrangement of subject or skill outline becomes cumulative as knowledge continues to build up over time. This knowledge building starts from simple to complex in the subject progressively.

- The horizontal organization occurs when the learning in one subject enhances the knowledge, skill and attitude in another subject within the same class.

Here are criteria's in organizing learning experience and content:

- **Integration:** This refers to the relationship among learning experiences which brings about a unified view, and behavior is a horizontal relationship which cut across several subjects and the areas of learner's life one subject should buttress the other.

- **Continuity:** It is the recurring emphasis on the learners experience on a particular element or kind of activities, until mastery is achieved. With mastery, learners develop progressively, systematically and naturally, with new knowledge building on earlier acquired knowledge and thus learners can gain competencies.

- **Sequence:** It is related to continuity as well as progressively moving from lower to the higher level of knowledge and from simple to complex. In sequence, each successive experience goes more deeply and broadly into the subjects.

- **Interest:** This criterion is true to be learned centered curriculum. The interest of the learners should be considered in selecting content because learners learn best if the subject matter is meaningful to them. It becomes meaningful if they are interested in it. But if the curriculum is subject centered, teachers have no choice but to finish the facing schedule religiously and teach only what is in the book, this may explain why many fail in subject sometimes.

- **Learnability:** Teachers should apply theories on psychology of learning to know their subject are presented sequentially and organized to maximize the learning capacity of the learners. The content should be what the learners can learn and it should be within their experience.

Utility: It is more important in skill or procedural knowledge, whereby learners can put what they have learnt into practice. This is the usefulness of the content in solving problems at present and in future (https://hyattractions.wordpress.com/2016/12/07/the-meaning-of-curriculum-content-and-learning-experiences/, accessed September 2021).

3.0   Curriculum Development and Planning

Curriculum development is the stages of generating and upgrading a course taught at a school or training center. It is the advancement by which an instructor or institution designs or embraces that ambition for a course.

Curriculum Development Model

The curriculum development model begins when an issue, concern, or problem needs to be addressed (i.e., if education or training a segment of the population will help solve the problem), then it becomes a priority to support an educational effort with human and financial resources allocated.

Forming curriculum development team: The team makes systematic decisions about the target audience (learner characteristics), intended out-comes (objectives), content, methods, and evaluation strategies. Draft curriculum products are developed, redesigned, tested, and evaluated with input from the curriculum development team if necessary. When the final product is produced, volunteer training is conducted.

The Curriculum Development Model below shows a circular process where volunteer training provides feedback for new materials to the existing curriculum.

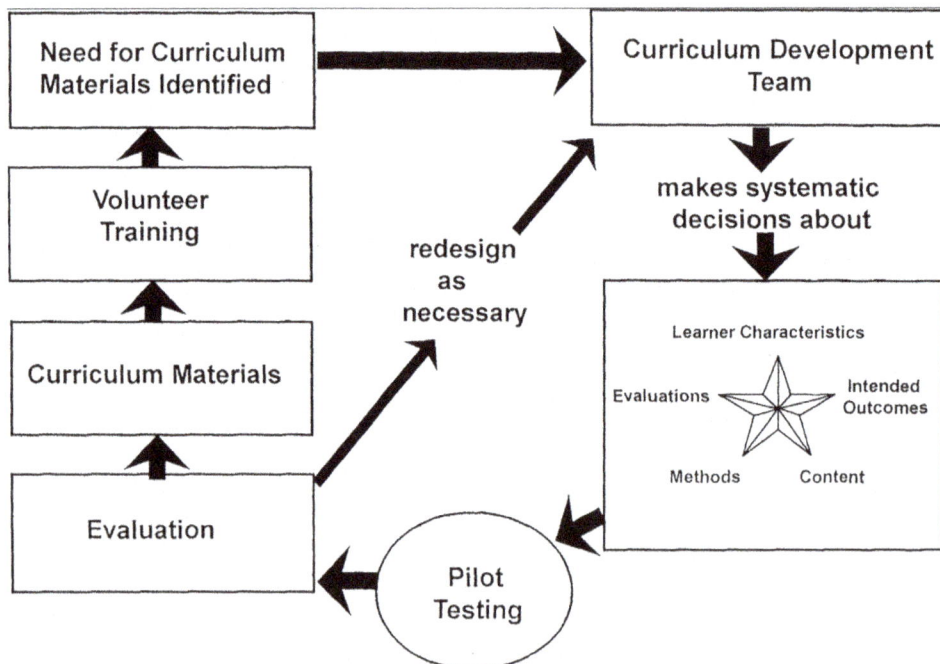

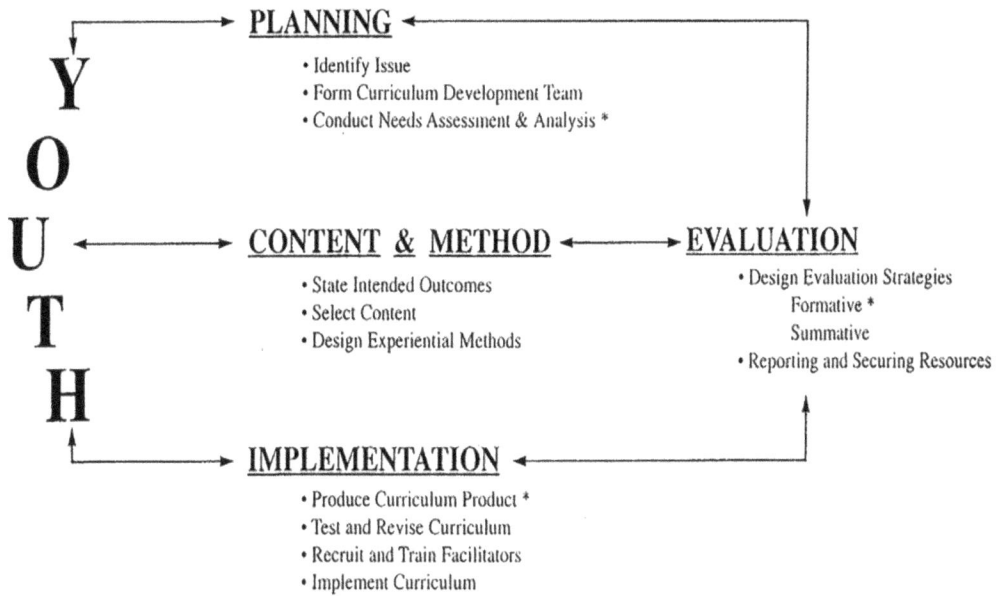

The essential phases of the curriculum development process involve:

i.   Planning
ii. Content and methods
iii. Implementation
iv. Evaluation and reporting

- **PHASE I: PLANNING:** This phase lays the foundation for all of the curriculum development steps. These steps include the following:

    a. **Identify issues/problem/need:** This section explores some of the questions that need to be addressed to define the issues and to develop a statement that will guide the selection of the members of a curriculum development team. The issue statement also serves a broadly identify, the scope (i.e., what will be included) of the curriculum. The need for curriculum development usually emerges from a concern about a major issue or problem of one or more target audience.

    b. **Form curriculum development team:** Once the nature and scope of the issue has been broadly defined, the members of the curriculum development team can be selected. Selected topics include the following:
        - The roles and functions of team members.
        - A process for selecting members of the curriculum development team.
        - Principles of collaboration and teamwork.

    The goal is to obtain expertise for the areas included in the scope of the curriculum content among the team members and develop an effective team.

    c. **Conduct needs assessment and analysis:** The needs assessment process has two phases:
        - Conducting a needs assessment is the first procedures. Here, a number of techniques are aimed toward learning *what* is needed and by *whom* relative to the identified issue.

- Knowledge, attitude and practice survey; focus groups, and environmental scanning are the techniques that covered in this section.
- Analysis described techniques on how to use the data and the results of the information gathered. It is the second part of needs assessment step. Other techniques included are: ways to identify gaps between knowledge and practice; trends emerging from the data; a process to prioritize needs; and identification of the characteristics of the target audience.

- **PHASE II: CONTENT AND METHODS:** This phase determines intended outcomes (i.e., what learners will be able to do after participation in curriculum activities), the content (i.e., what will be taught), and the methods (i.e., how it will be taught). The steps include the following:
  - **State intended outcomes:** An intended outcome states what the learner will be able to do as a result of participating in the curriculum activities. This section includes
    - a definition of intended outcomes,
    - the components of intended outcomes (condition, performance, and standards),
    - examples of intended outcomes,
    - an overview of learning behaviors.

  - **Select content:** Selecting content will make a real difference in the lives of the learner and ultimately society as a whole. The primary questions at this point are:

    > "If the intended outcome is to be attained, what will the learner need to know? What knowledge, skills, attitudes, and behaviors will need to be acquired and practiced?"

  - **Design experimental methods:** This step is to design activities (learning experiences) to help the learner achieve approximate intended outcomes. An experimental learning model and its components (i.e., experience, share, process, generalize, and apply). Additional topics include
    - learning styles and activities appropriate for each styles,
    - a list of types of activities (with description),
    - an activity design worksheet for facilitators,
    - brief discussions on learning environments and delivery modes.

- **PHASE III: IMPLEMENTATION:** Steps involved in this phase begin one the content and experimental methods have been agreed upon. The steps include
  - **Produce curriculum product:** This section involves
    - suggestions for finding and evaluating existing materials
    - evaluation criteria
    - suggestions for producing curriculum materials.

  - **Test and revise curriculum:** This step includes suggestions to select test sites and conduct a formative evaluation of curriculum materials during the production phase. Here, a sample evaluation form is provided.
  - **Recruit and train facilitators:** Suggestions for recruiting appropriate facilitators are provided with a sample three-day training program. This is because if adequate training is not provided for facilitators to implement it, the resources to develop curriculum materials will be a waste.

- **Implement curriculum:** Strategies to promote and use the curriculum are discussed in this step. Effective implementation of newly developed curriculum products is unlikely to occur without planning.

- PHASE IV: EVALUATION AND REPORTING: Evaluation is a phase in the curriculum development model as well as a specific step. The steps involved in this phase include the following:
  - **Design evaluation strategies:** This step reviews evaluation strategies and suggest simple procedures to produce valid and reliable information. Two types of evaluation are used during curriculum development, there are formative and summative evaluation.
    - Formative evaluations are used during the needs assessment, product development, and testing steps.
    - Summative evaluations are undertaken to measure and report on the outcomes of the curriculum.

    Series of questions are posed to guide the summative evaluation process and a sample evaluation format is suggested.

  - **Reporting and securing resources:** In this step, suggestions for what and how to report to key shareholders, especially funding and policy decision makers, are provided and a brief discussion on how to secure resources for additional programming. The final element in an evaluation strategy is "delivering the payoff (i.e., getting the results into the hands of people who can use them)" (www.fao.org/3/ah650e/A+1650E10.htm-accessed-September-2021).

Curriculum Planning

Curriculum planning is the process that is involved with decisions-making about what to learn, and the manner in which the learning will take place and how to systematically arrange the teaching and learning process and taking into the existing account of the requirement of curriculum and the available resources.

"Curriculum planning is a continuous process which involves activities characterized by interrelationships among individuals and groups as they work together in studying, planning, developing and improving the curriculum which is total environment planned by the school."

Stages in curriculum planning

- Set up or introduce a value base for the program.
- Create a theoretical structure.
- Decide the program goals.
- Construct the program.
- Set up assessment procedures for the program.
- Execute the program.

Reasons for planning curriculum

- To become familiar with the major problems involved in curriculum implementation
- To critically reflect on some common approaches that has been used in schools to support the process of curriculum implementation

- To share understandings and a common language in the school community
- To give learners the opportunity to develop deep understanding
- To eliminate repetition of learning activities without depth or breadth across levels
- To understand the implications of the ideas of fidelity of curriculum implementation and adaptation in curriculum implementation
- To cause continuity of learning between domains across ones levels (www.edufruit.blogspot.com/2017/03/88-importance-of-curriculum-planning.html?m=1, accessed September 2021).

Curriculum Planning Techniques

a. **Curriculum laboratory:** This is a place or workshop where curriculum materials are gathered or used by teachers or learners of curriculum.

b. **Progressive school:** It conceives the curriculum as something flexible based on areas of interest. It is learner-centered, having in mind that no two persons are alike. Its factor of motivation is individual achievement believing that persons are naturally good. The role of the teacher is to stimulate direct learning process. It uses a life experience approach to fit the learner for future social life.

c. **Essential school:** Its approach is authoritative and the teacher's role is to assign lessons and to recite recitations. It is book-centered and the methods recommended are memory work, mastery of facts and skills, and development of abstract intelligence.

Constant revisit ion of aims and experimental techniques of teaching and learning are imperatives in curriculum development to create independent thinking, initiative, individuality, self-reliance, self-expression and activity in the learner (www.bchmsg.yolasite.com/curriculum-development.php, accessed September 2021).

Needs and Importance of Curriculum Development

1. **It helps in the selection of learning experiences:** Curriculum development is needed for appropriate selection and organization of learning experiences. It helps in the selection of study matter and other activities so that learners are able to acquire goals and objectives of teaching/training.

2. **Continuous assessment and improvement of quality:** The curriculum followed by an institution/training school should be reviewed regularly to maintain its effectiveness in regards to the changing needs of the society as a whole valid and reliable assessment of the curriculum is necessary.

3. **Making strategy in teaching and learning:** Curriculum development helps in suggesting suitable teaching-learning strategies, teaching/training methods, instructional materials, and the likes. It helps in providing for the proper implementation of curriculum on the part of teachers/trainers and learners or trainees.

4. **Clear purpose and goals:** The goals and objectives are specified in considerable detail and in behavioral language. Curriculum construction provide written circular goals which are nothing but intended learner development outcomes.

5. **A rational sequence:** In a curriculum educational/skill, activities are carefully ordered in a developmental sequence. This developmental sequence aids to form a well-planned or coherent curriculum based or intended goals and outcomes of the curriculum and its constituent courses.

Principles of Curriculum Development

a. **The principle of the comprehensive curriculum:**
- The curriculum must have the necessary details (i.e., list of topics to be covered).
- Both teachers and learners should know clearly what is expected of them, what is the beginning and what is the end of the topic for the particular class or team.
- Instructional materials, tools, activities, life situations, etc., should be listed in the curriculum.

b. **The principle of availability of time and other resources:** Developing curriculum should be executed by experts and they should also keep the implementation of curriculum developed in mind. And they should be aware of the conditions of the schools/training centers and possible availability of time and resources available.

c. **The principle of practical work:** Curriculum should be designed in such a way that it provides maximum opportunity to the leaner for a practical work with the help of concrete things.

d. **The principle of suitability to the age and mental level of the learners:** What is to be given to the learners in the form of learning experiences at a particular age and grade level should suit their age and mental development.
- The capacity for understanding, how learners cope with the content of study in any skill/subject should be formed to suit their mental ability.

e. **Principle of flexibility:** Curriculum should show the sign of flexibility and not rigidity. The organization of the curriculum should be on the basis of individual differences as every learners is different from the other. The curriculum must be flexible enough to address the needs as aspirations of the society. This is because the society is undergoing change.

f. **The principle of environmental centered:**
- The content of the learning experiences should be linked with the learner's needs of the environment in which they live.

g. **The principle of joint venture:** It is necessarily a joint venture where various experts are involved like educational psychologists, educational technologists, curriculum specialists, evaluation specialists, teachers, subject matter experts, etc.

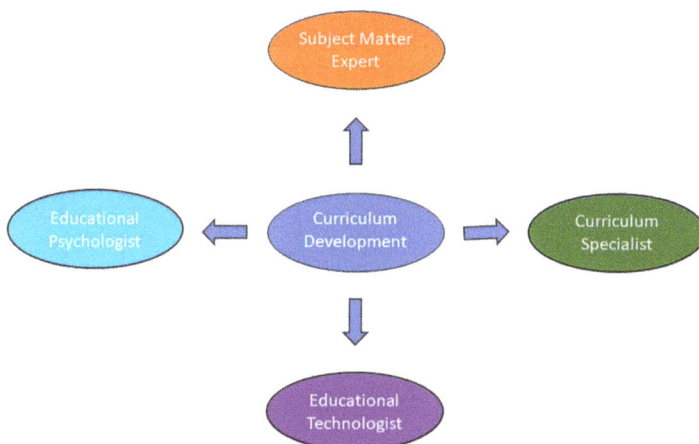

The principle of correlation: The curriculum should be such that all the subject are correlated with each other. It must be kept in mind that the subject matter of various subjects has some relation to each other, so that they help the leaner eventually.

h. **The principle of forward-looking:** This principle asks for the inclusion of those topics, content, and learning experiences that may prove helpful to the learners in leading their future life in a proper way.

i. **Principle according to the specific interests of learners:**
- Leaners will be able to learn better in fields where they have special tastes and inclination of the mind.
- Leaners have different interest patterns at different stages of age groups.

- Their interests also change according to circumstances and situations.
- Therefore learning experiences should be designed to suit the interests and tastes of the age group of learners.

j. **The principle of consultation with teachers:** Teachers play a key role in the implementation of the school curriculum of any grade or stage. It is therefore quite essential to seek the proper involvement of the teachers in the construction and development of the school curriculum (**Error! Hyperlink reference not valid.** https://physicscatalyst.com/graduation/principles-of-curriculum-development/, assessed September 2021).

4.0 Tools for Developing Curriculum

Curriculum tools are the aims, goals and objectives. Every curriculum must have an education philosophy. Aims must be linked to the country education philosophy. Every curriculum is aimed at developing the leaners certain competencies or abilities. The curriculum process must identify the aims that the curriculum is intended to achieve.

- Aims are broad statements which cover all of the experiences provided in the curriculum.
- Goals are tied to specific subjects or group of contents within the curriculum.
- Objectives describe the more specific outcomes that can be attained as a result of lessons or instruction delivered at the classroom (www.bchmsg.yolasite.com/curriculum-development.php, accessed September 2021).

Types of curriculum

i. **Taught curriculum:** Taught curriculum refers to how teachers/trainers actually teach/train. This is a less predictable and less standardized type of curriculum because how an educator delivers material can vary from one to the next. It can also change based on the types of tools a teacher has at his/her disposal. This can include experiments, demonstrations and other types of engagement through group work and hands-on activities. Taught curriculum is extremely critical for learners in special education or those who require another kind of specialized support.

ii. **Recommended curriculum:** Recommended curriculum focuses on the content, skill sets and tools educators should prioritize in the classroom/workshop. It stems from what experts in education suggest. This type of curriculum can come from a variety of different sources, including nationally recognized researchers, policy makers and legislators, and the likes.

iii. **Assessed curriculum:** It refers to quizzes, test and other kinds of methods to measure leaner's success. An assessed curriculum is also known as a tested curriculum. This can encompass a number of different assessment techniques, including presentations, a portfolio, a demonstration as well as state and federal standardized tests.

iv. **Written curriculum:** A written curriculum is what is formally put down in writing and documented for teaching/training. These materials come from the school itself. These materials can include an educators instruction documents, films, text and other materials needed for the implementation of instructions. Frequently, they contract or employ a curriculum specialist to develop a plan that meets specific goals and objectives.

v. **Learned curriculum:** A learned curriculum refers to what learners walk away with from a course. This includes the subject matter and knowledge they learned from a course, but it can also include

additional changes in attitude and emotional wellbeing. Teachers need to shrink the gap between what they expect learners to learn and what learners actually do learn.

vi. **Supported curriculum:** This type of curriculum involves the additional tools, resources and learning experiences found in and outside a classroom. These include textbooks, field trips, technology and software, in addition to other innovative new techniques to engage learners. Teachers and other individuals involved with the course are also a component of the supported curriculum.

vii. **Excluded curriculum:** It refers to what content is not taught in a course. It is also known as null curriculum. Often an educator or curriculum specialist believes that a certain skill or concept is less important or does not need to be covered. Sometimes what is left out, intentionally or unintentionally, can shape learners as much as what is included.

viii. **Hidden curriculum:** This type of curriculum is not always communicated or formally written down and includes implicit rules, unmentioned expectations, and the norms and values of a culture. It is often challenging for learners from diverse background or cultures, who can struggle to adjust or feel negatively judged. A hidden curriculum can also be influenced by how money, time and resources are allocated within a school. It is not planned, but it has a significant impact on what learners learn (https://counseling.education.wm.edu/blog/8-types-of-curriculum, accessed September 2021).

5.0   Curriculum Development Process and Organization

Curriculum development is a process in which different components such as formation of curriculum policy, curriculum research, curriculum planning, its implementation and its evaluation play an important role.

The impact of the school curriculum is so crucial for national and state policies that in most of the countries in the world this responsibility is shouldered by various government and national level organizations and agencies. Curriculum development process cannot be ignored by any country.

States in the Process of Curriculum Development

There are basically four stages of curriculum development:

- Formulation of objectives
- Selection and organization of appropriate learning-material
- Selection of suitable learning experiences
- Selection of suitable material for evaluation of curriculum

- **Formulation of objectives:** The objectives of teaching mathematics formulated and determined in behavioral terms. While formulating and determining objectives following points should be kept in mind:
  a. That the set objectives formulated should indicate both the desired behavior and the type of situation in which it is to occur.
  b. An objective should be expressed in terms of desired pupil behavior rather than of teacher behavior.
  c. An objective should be specifically stated so that it is possible to infer some appropriate learning activities.

- **Selection and organization of appropriate learning material:** The selection of suitable content depends to a great extent on the extent on those basic considerations that underlie in the formulation of objectives. The example above of the objectives recognize four significant aspects of mathematical learning:
  - Contents or meanings
  - Computational skills
  - Problem-solving (reasoning)
  - Mathematical attitudes

  Concepts play an important role in the reasoning and also facilitate the learning of computational skills. Great emphasis should be placed upon those basic concepts and skills of mathematical thinking and problem-solving that most people should know to function intelligently as members of society.

- **Selection of suitable learning experiences:** The concept of learning-experience as it emerges from the thinking about the learner and the learning principles accepted as the basis for objectives, can be broadly described as a desired change in the mental makeup of a child and it can be brought about through, "Activities leading to the discovery of connections, relationships and meaning which have significance in the directing or ordering of conduct."

  Learning experience, envisaged here, place great importance on the learner and the learning situation, instead of on the leather and the content. The proper organization of learning experiences depends upon a number of factors such as
  - age, needs, and previous experiences of the learner;
  - needs of a particular community;
  - attention and interest of the leaner;
  - facility available in the school;
  - ability of the learners;
  - readiness, maturity and capability of the learner.

  Each teacher should feel free to adjust the objectives, content and activities to suit his or her requirements. However, the following criteria should be kept in view while selecting and organizing learning experiences:
  - They should be adequate and effective.
  - Leaning experiences should be appropriate to behavior changes defied under objectives.
  - They should be practicable.
  - They should be suitable for the content area.

- **Selection of suitable material for evaluation of curriculum:** Evaluation and curriculum are regarded as closely related parts of the same educative process, not as distinct and separate functions.

  No curriculum can therefore, be said to have been planned without laying down some basic principles of evaluation. Evaluation comes in at the planning stage when objectives are identified. The needs, interests, attitudes and abilities of learners should be kept in mind while selecting suitable material for the evaluation of the curriculum.

  National agencies like the National Council of Educational Organization and the Council of Boards of School Education need to undertake the following tasks:

  i. Organizing training programs for paper setters of different boards

ii. Developing conceptual materials and proto-types on learner-centered, activity-oriented, and competency-based

iii. Laying down the expected levels of attainment in each curricular area of all the stages of school education

iv. Generating various kinds of tests, which could be meaningfully employed for assessing cognitive and noncognitive learning outcomes, making them available to the state agencies (https://examwinners.com/school-curriculum-development/stages-process-of-curriculum-development/, accessed September 2021).

Curriculum organization

Curriculum organization is the process of selecting curriculum elements from the subject, the current social life and the learner's experience, then designing the selected curriculum elements appropriately so that they can form the curriculum structure and type (https://www.academia.edu/25237982/patterns-of-curriculum-organization, accessed September 2021).

Steps for organizing curriculum

a. Determine your vision and intention for the curriculum.
b. Outline your overarching topics.
c. Review any current curriculum to determine what to keep and what to retire.
d. Organize your standards based on the topics and timeline.
e. Write the lessons to provide a comprehensive learner learning-experience.
f. Create or attach a variety of assessments to the lessons.
g. Determine what materials and resources you will need.
h. Pull it all together (https://artsintegration.com/2018/07/01/how-to-write-a-curriculum-from-start-to-finish/, accessed September 2021).

6.0   A Sample Curriculum for Skill Acquisition Context

Skill acquisition curriculum is described as an accurate component of training/learning of educational characteristic which is purposeful for trainers and trainees in the actualization of an intended outcome. Since, skills have been considered as the universal currentness in this era.

"A training curriculum is a comprehensive set of learning objectives, content, materials and methods for evaluating participant attainment of the training goals. Training materials are items used during the training and can comprise or accompany various features of a training" (https://www.vawamei.org/tools-resources/faq/what-is-the-difference-between-training-curricula-and-training-materials/, accessed September 2021).

Curriculum is described as the academic content and lessons in a particular program. It also refers to the range of cognition and a learned or developed abilities which includes the training objectives that the trainees are expected to meet, these includes the training materials, videos, presentations, and readings used in training course, the units and lessons that the trainers train, the tests, assessments, the assignments and projects given to the trainees and learners, among others.

Curriculum is the total effort of the school to bring about desired outcomes in school and out-of-school situations. It is also defined as a sequence of potential experiences set up in school for the purpose of disci-

plinary children and youth in group ways of thinking and acting. Curriculum can be defined "as a dense and flexible contract between politics/society and teachers."

Significance of a Good Curriculum

1. It makes learning (and teaching) consistent.
2. It helps teachers/trainers align.
3. It opens the doors for collaboration.
4. It keeps up with a changing world.
5. It provides measurable targets.
6. It both creates and reflects culture and identity.
7. It saves schools money.

Vision of curriculum

- It is a diversity of learning processes to achieve quality education.
- The curriculum is a political and technical issue that is well embedded in the complex interfaces between politics, society and education.

An example of curriculum for skill acquisition context

Things to put into considerations:

- Mission and philosophy consistency
- Short-range and long-range goals
- Theory and research
- Engagement of the learners
- Variety and meaningful content
- Learner's active engagement
- Opportunities to make choices, explore, and experiment
- Foundation for future learning
- A daily schedule that is functional
- The value of social interaction and peer learning on social development
- Approach to providing a psychologically safe environment

- **Mission and philosophy consistency:** This curriculum mission and philosophy is written to incorporate the learner's mission and philosophy. Learners (children and youth/adult) should grow, learn and flourish in a well-designed, learner-centered environment that is completely made through the implementation of a good training plans that would assist them.
- **Short-range and long-range goals:** Here, the training managements and instructors provide adequate planned and emergent activities and experiences that promote skill acquisition for all age level, independence, self-help skills, motivation for learning, and self-control, which put learners/trainees in a proper state of mind for the accomplishment of their training program and years of training ahead. The planned environment is the tools for utilization and organization of the short term and long term goals, daily lesson plans, activities that emerge from learner's modernistic competencies and interest are tools the implementation of curriculum.

The preparation of curriculum for skill training should provide a forceful underpinning structure for the learner's life success through fostering appropriate self-confidence, independence and social skills.

- **Theory and research:** Appropriate learner's curriculum developmental age are the foundation of development theory and scientific research. These aspects inform decision making, influence the trainers/instructors view of learners/trainees, and should be the guides to use when planning lessons and the environment should be considered as well. Skill acquisition curriculum for trainees/learners should reflects on modern publications. It should also be influenced by the works of great theorist like Jean Piaget, Maria Montessori, Howard Gardner, Levvygotsky, and Erik Erickson (This is applicable to children's curriculum. *Names of great theorist from the above chapters should be used here like Wan Palov* and the likes for youth and adult motivational theories.

  Appropriate written training/lesson plans should be designed to follow the learner's lead, developmentally combined with age appropriate learning materials in a careful designed environment, which are tools that should be used to promote each learners growth, development, and positive behavior.

- **Engagement of the learners:** Curriculum is designed to facilitate tall areas of development. Training planned environment, daily schedule, written curriculum materials and individualized training/lesson plans promote development in the following areas:
  - Language development
  - Social development
  - Cognitive intellectual development
  - Emotional development
  - Physical development

- **Variety and meaningful content:** The learning environment, combined with curriculum and written lesson/training plans allow learners/trainers to participate in a wide variety of experiences each day that range from simple to complex. Materials and lesson plans are evaluated to assure that content and incorporation is meaningful to the lives and interests of learners/trainers and to the world. There is classroom management to arrange the learners/trainees into their different skill training/learning centers. For example:
  - Fashion and design center
  - Cosmetology center
  - ICT center, among others

- **Learner's active engagement:** This curriculum has been developed for how trainees/learners learn with the foundation of Developmentally Appropriate practices. For learners, play is the primary mode of learning. This is because lesson/training plans and the environment are designed around the learners, you will find learners that are actively engaged in activities and experiences that meet their needs and interests. Extra materials are available for rotation as to maintain interest and promote further skill acquisition.

- **Opportunities to make choices, explore and experiment:** Learners have daily opportunities to make choices and participate in self-guided activities; which makes their endeavors more successful. Learners are provided with open-ended opportunities and materials that promote experimentation and exploration in a safe and secure environment that is built around their development and individual needs.

- **Foundation for future learning:** Implementation of age appropriate techniques, lessons, and emergent experiences pave a way for future learning in different areas of skill acquisition.

- **A daily schedule that is functional:** Daily schedule provides large blocks of time for learners to actively engage in discovery and learner initiated learning activities. This schedule is also designed

226

to provide a balance of active and quiet; individual, small group and large group activities and indoor/outdoor times. This carefully designed schedule aids to meet the various and changing needs of learners in their whole approach.

- **The value of social interaction and peer learning on social development:** Trainers/teaches encourage learners to interact with their peers, which promotes social development in learners. This curriculum values the importance of multi-age grouping, which provides an opportunity for learners to learn from and teach each other.

  The trainers/instructors view inappropriate behaviors as opportunities to promote more socially acceptable skills. Social emotional development is promoted by the trainers or instructors through consistency, kindness and modeling of appropriate behavior.

- **Approach to providing a psychologically safe environment:** Studies have proven that creating a psychologically safe environment fosters intelligence learner-centered approach helps learners feel safe, and important. Warm and mutual understanding provides learners with the basis for all types of learning (https://kidsworldnm.com/curriculum/, accessed September 2021).

7.0   Evaluation as a Curriculum Context

Curriculum is referred to as the total of all experiences, which are to be provided in an educational institution. Tanner and Tanner (1975) defined curriculum as the planned guided learning experience and intended learning out-comes formulated through a systematic reconstruction of knowledge and experiences under the learner's continuous and willful growth in academic, personal and social competence.

The term "evaluation" generally applies to the process of making a value judgment. In education, the term "evaluation is used in reference to operations associated with curricula, programs, interventions, methods of teaching and organizational factors. Curriculum aims to examine the impact of implemented curriculum on learner achievement so that the official curriculum can be revised if necessary and to review teaching and learning processes in the classroom/workshop.

Curriculum evaluation establishes:

- critical information for strategic changes and policy decisions,
- specific strengths and weaknesses of a curriculum and its implementation,
- indicators for monitoring,
- inputs needed for improved learning and teaching.

Curriculum evaluation may be an internal activity and process conducted by the various units within the education system for their own respective processes. Curriculum evaluation may also be external or commissioned review process (www.ibe.unesco.org/fileadmin/user_upload/COPs/pages-documents/Resource_Packs/TTCD/sitemap/Module_8/Module_8.html, accessed September 2021).

Objectives of curriculum evaluation

a. To help in future development of the curriculum material for continuous improvement
b. To determine the outcomes of the program
c. To ascertain the need for the revision of the course content
d. To improve methods of teaching and instructional techniques
e. To help in deciding whether to accept or reject a program

Types of curriculum evaluation

There are three main types of curriculum evaluation according to Screven, namely,

- Formative evaluation
- Summative evaluation
- Diagnostic evaluation

- **Formative evaluation:** It occurs during the course of curriculum development. Its purpose is to contribute to the improvement of the educational program. The merits of a program are evaluated during the process of its development. The evaluation results provide information to the program developers and enable them to correct flaws detected in the program.
- **Summative evaluation:** In summative evaluation, the final effects of a curriculum are evaluated on the basis of its stated objectives. It takes place after the curriculum has been fully developed and put into operations.
- **Diagnostic evaluation:** Diagnostic evaluation is directed toward two purposes either for placement of learners properly at the outset of an instructional level, or to discover the underlying cause of deviancies in learner learning in any field of study.

Significance of curriculum evaluation

It is to determine the value of the curriculum itself. Thus, it poses these questions:

- Is the curriculum appropriate for the particular group of learners with whom it is being used?
- Are the materials recommended for instructional purpose appropriate and the best available for the purpose envisaged?
- Is the content the best that could be selected?
- Are the instructional methods selected, the best choices in the light of the objectives sought? (www.studylecturenotes.com/curriculum-evaluation-meaning-importance-objective, accessed September 2021).

Criteria for curriculum evaluation

There are four criteria for accessing the workability of the curriculum:

i.   Subject
ii. Skills
iii. Experiences
iv. Attitude and values

i.   **Subject:** In curriculum, various subject are included such as: English, psychology, history, sociology, among others, while in skill curriculum, type of training include the following: fashion and design, cake baking, cosmetology skill acquisition, and the likes. The structure of content of these subjects and training skills is determined for the curriculum development.
ii. **Skills:** Some curriculum provides the situations for developing skills or psychomotor activities: Languages reading writing, speaking, observation, perception use of different type instrument in

the workshops and field works communication skills, craftwork, verbal and nonverbal communication skills. It is related to psychomotor objectives.

iii. **Experiences:** The curriculum provides the following type of experiences to the learners, geographical (time and place sense) physical, historical, social, political, religious, civic senses, spiritual and relative experiences, expression of ideas fact and events.

iv. **Attitude and values:** This type of curriculum provide the experiences for developing affective domain of the learners. It develops self-confidence, sensitivity, morality, honesty, sincerity, objectivity, character and adjustment (https://onlinenotebook.wordpress.com/2020/02/04/criteria-for-currculum-evaluation, accessed September 2021).

8.0　Conclusion

Curriculum is the means to realize the outcomes of the educational objectives of the school. Implementation of the curriculum is equally important as curriculum construction. Curriculum is grouped into various concepts namely; curriculum as the content and knowledge in school (i.e., curriculum here is seen as orderly or regular course of study accepted by a learner in or beneath the aegis of school/training centers, college or university). Curriculum as discipline or subject, curriculum in this concept is seen as a written document that constitutes an outline or rundown of the subject matters to be taught. Curriculum as all the learning experiences; in the learning experiences of curriculum, it is seen as an orderly arrangement or designed experience offered to the learner under the guidance of the school or the content of the school curriculum to needs, interests and the experiences of the learner as well as the necessarily and importance of the society curriculum as school experience and culture; this is perceived as alternation from culture which circumfuses way of life, specific categories of knowledge, specific attitudes and relative worths regarded as so important that their transmission to the next generation is not left to chance or as the summation of what educational system attempt to do to accomplish predetermined objectives.

Learning experiences are not tailored for various distinct domains of instructional objectives. Therefore, it is compulsory to plan for learning experiences that will afford and stipulate for the three domains as method of technique for making learning. When learning experience is said to be comprehensive, it should involve cognitive, affective, and psychomotor domains of learning.

Chapter Twenty

Practical Issues in Skill Acquisition and Development

1.0   Introduction

This chapter offers simple but vital elements that can drive the skill acquisition and development deal. Irrespective of all the technical and nontechnical issues exposed in this text, if these basics are missing, the decision to acquire a skill or develop a career stagnates. It is incontrovertible fact that everything about decision making lies in the mind choices, will power, resolution, acceptance and determination dwell in the mind. Thus a success is skill acquisition must first be conceived in the mind before translation into reality.

Once one makes up his mind, the next question should be: what are the ways and means to go about carrying out the decision. What time is available? What support structures are available? Where and how is the market to sell the skill for income?

2.0   Mental Setting: Purpose Driven

> Can success change the human mechanism so completely between one down and another? Can it make one feel taller, more alive, more handsome, more uncommonly gifted and indomitably secure? Yes, it can and it does. (Moses Hart)

Success, that feeling of genuine accomplishments in life pursuits appears to be everyone's desire. Failure is an orphan. Everyone radiates toward the sun of success. The quest for success is a product of the mind. It is a decision, a determination and a resolution. Its purpose is compelling: to change completely from a state of disaffection and dissatisfaction to a place where life is worthier of living, were the talents are expressed, where life problems are solved and everyone has something to bring to the marketplace of life.

A key component of success is mental-setting or resetting. When a purpose is established, action follows and results abound. The primary essence of setting one's mind is to place it on the drive gear by taking a decision to be free, better in competence or becoming an expert, a champion, a thorough professional, a marketable brand or sort after problem solver.

The mind is associated with the dream factor. One who creates a purpose of living a rewarding, satisfying and enjoyable lifestyle, holds a dream which needs to be translated into reality. One way to achieve this transformation is to explore the FORCE within that compels action. Transformation is a change movement from an unemployed, unskilled person to a self-employed, efficient employee status via potential development.

One of the most sort empowerment where security: that feeling of self-empowerment where one is sure that lack, want, penury and neglect have been driven away by acquiring an experience that supports solutions to life challenges from personal knowledge and confidence. Here is the formula for success and security:

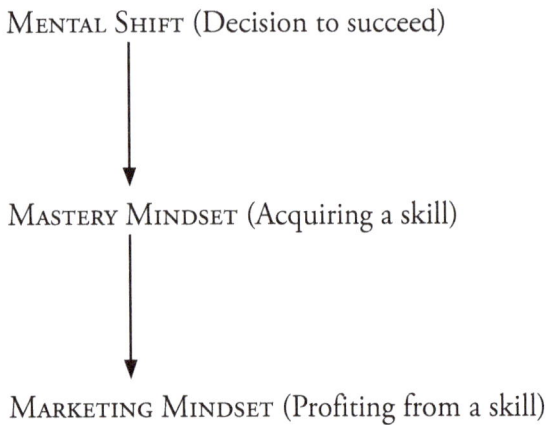

MENTAL SHIFT (Decision to succeed)

↓

MASTERY MINDSET (Acquiring a skill)

↓

MARKETING MINDSET (Profiting from a skill)

3.0 Awareness of Approaches

After the decision to create success by undertaking a skill capacity or attaining higher heights in the skill ladder, one must sit down and engage what is popularly called the SWOT Analysis:

STRENGTHS E.g.	WEAKNESSES	OPPORTUNITIES	THREATS
• Time	• Zero-capital	• Identified goal	• Laws
• Health	• Illiteracy in technology	• Counselling	• Location
• Literacy	• Lack of motivation	• Stratagem	• Fear

The most important awareness is a construction of the SWOT sheet. In the example above, an unemployed youth should be able to understand his strengths in terms of having ample time to engage a change of life-style by finding a skill to acquire. If he is healthy and basically literate (ability to read and write) then these are additional and available strengths. Weaknesses may include zero-access to capital or fund to even pay for the skill and inability to use any technological device like a cell phone which can be used to obtain information or object lack of motivation to take a decision or make a move for accomplishments.

Fortunately, in the face of weaknesses or challenges, there can still be opportunities or approaches to overcome or solve problems. Therefore, a would-be skill trainee must be aware of the opportunities to leverage on. In the above template, it is considered a big opportunity to be able to identify a goal (need to have a skill) and to drive for it. It is also important to speak with an expert or a professional in the desired trade or specialization who will provide information, advice, hope, preknowledge and prospects in the area. Also, reading books or publications can reveal strategies to adopt in acquiring or developing a skill.

Life may still through up challenges, some of which may be unpredictable. Government's regulations can hamper success. The location a person finds himself, say in an undeveloped rural setting may be a challenge or the person may even be a victim of the fear to step out.

In all, the SWOT record can provide a starting point in revealing awareness of the entire spectrum of transformation through skill acquisition and development.

4.0   The Time Factor

Life and success are measured by time. Everyone has twenty-four hours a day to utilize for activities. These hours culminate into weeks, months and years of life subject to many factors including the inevitable and divinely defined end in death. Therefore, time cannot be separated from life. Some of the most valued things of life are FREEDOM (ability to take charge of one's life), CHOICES, and RESPONSIBILITIES.

These three issues are time-bound. The decision to be financially free needs to be taken at the right time. For example, the secular education which is the basis for personal awareness is preprimary and primary education. If there is an opportunity to proceed to the high school or college, CHOICES come into place, up to what one wants to become in life or a life-style to adopt.

Choices enable one to look inwards in terms of identifying natural gifting's or talents which one does effortlessly and with joy and satisfaction, not necessarily for monetary rewards. The time of this realization and commencement of the goal or pursuit is equally important. A popularly African proverb says that it is difficult to learn left-handness in the forties. Once a choice is made, the choice-maker has responsibilities to work out the preference for appropriate results. This concept can be diagrammatically presented thus:

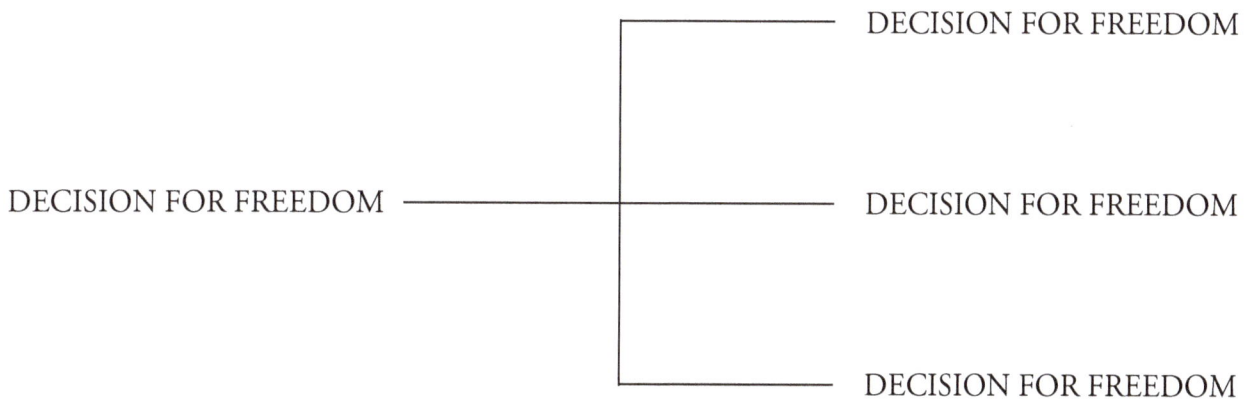

DECISION FOR FREEDOM

DECISION FOR FREEDOM

DECISION FOR FREEDOM

DECISION FOR FREEDOM

Time determines the results of these indicators. If the decision to be free and secure in life is taken at the right time, it gives allowance for considering the choice of the parameters, methodologies, strategies and potentials to adopt in obtaining the freedom. For example, a person who wants to become a lawyer must consider, and in time, the university or legal establishment to attend as well as the professional institution and chamber to follow through in developing the lawyering skills.

Thereafter, he needs to responsibly manage the time of his life, available resources, legal necessities and character contents to attain his destination.

5.0   Leveraging on Potentials

The most potent credential of anyone is the SENSE of PERSONAL RESPONSIBILITY, the idea that no matter the situation of life, there are things that a person must decide for himself and take responsibility for the decision. This power for decision and action is called the WILLPOWER.

A lot of factors account for a person's will power and its exercise. Some of these elements are as follows: curiosity, creativity, motivation, determination and result. The first four are potentials while the last is the end. Curiosity is an inner propensity to ask questions, seek information, desire revelations and develop inter-

est. A curious person will ask, Why is my life like this? What can I do to make a better life? What are my problems and where can I get solutions to them?

Curiosity leads to creativity which provides answers to the questions and solutions to the problems. The quest for actualization and the expectation of rewards constitute the motivation for the pursuit of goals. At times, the motivation can go beyond mere search for survival to the desire for doing something that provides satisfaction, sense of self-worth and joy of living.

Motivation alone may not sustain the drive for results or attainment of goals. Discouragement may set in or seemingly unsurmountable challenges may emerge on the path of progress. Determination will be required in good dosage to sustain the drive and increase the tempo of commitment. Determination is the never-say-die spirit; that inner will power to jump hurdles and overcome obstacles; that depth of never giving up; that strength to stand up after a fall or falls; that restoration of the hope grid.

The result lies at the end of our life pursuits. Results are the outcomes of our efforts. When we set out to learn a skill to have a better life-style, earn income, pay our bills and realize our aspirations, we create options of routes that will take us there. We sustain the search with a motivational drive for success. We key into the spirit of determination and our results arrive. At last, we move from unemployed person through a trainee to an expert, then a pro in the field.

6.0   The Money Factor

In most human endeavors, including skill acquisition and development, money places a role, indeed a big role. Unfortunately, as a means of exchange and measurement of wealth, money is scarce and hardly enough to solve all human problems and needs.

Jerry Gillies, in the book *Money-Love* states thus:

> Money is a vehicle to take you to your desires. Its' an extension of your personality. So-called money problems are not problems at all, but results that are dissatisfying. If you get results that don't satisfy you, it is because you are doing something to achieve those results. Many people want to solve their money problems without changing what they are doing to achieve those results. You have to change what you are doing if you want to change the results.

The above long quotation is a justification for both looking for money to pay for a skill training or career rising program and using the result of the training/setting up a career to improve on one's financial capacity.

Getting start off money to pay for skill training may require some personal sacrifices, such as:

- Checking ones expenses on the track
- Cutting down on unimportant bills
- Setting out "stuff" that are not needed
- Be your coach/mentor on capital raising
- Take up a part time job to make some money
- Think creatively about money-making
- Consider problem-soling services you can do
- Consult experts in money raising
- Accept borrowing as the last resort only.

Once you have pulled together enough resources to sustain and undergo a training, put in all the management techniques to ensure your mission is not frustrated by external forces outside your control. This is when a mentor or helper will play a significant role.

Beyond the training, it is expected that the deployment of the skill in a post-training era will be an easy way to raise money and establish a business. There are hindsights in this book on establishing a business or making income from training for skills.

7.0   A Matter of Priority

Decide what you want, decide what you are willing to exchange for it. Establish your priorities and get to work.

H. I. Hunt

Everyone appears to be choked by several activities in life. There are timing demanding engagements such parenting, struggling for livelihood, social activities and hobbies. In the midst of these, it is important to draw up a scale of preference for time.

Researches have revealed that a small proportion of any activity produces a majority of the results tagged the 80/20 formular, it is stated that you can analytically identify the 20 percent activities that you need to accomplish 100 percent results while putting off the 80 percent time wasters. Pinning down the 20 percent activity is aligning progress with purpose. When devoted to getting a skill training, it is necessary to put down many other activities which constitute distractions so as to concentrate or focus on the skill training and obtain maximum results in the right time.

These three steps are helpful to take while deciding on skill acquisition.

1.   Clear your mind of clogging items
2.   Use a personal time organizer to stipulate your activities.
3.   Align specific tasks with time in a time to task schedule.

8.0   Networking and Marketing

Networking is a concept of pulling together resources, ideas and facilities to achieve a particular purpose or task. Certainly, nobody has a monopology of knowledge or information. In every meaningful endeavor including skill acquisition, there is a place for networking. The following are some of the key benefits of networking:

1.   Sharing of information and techniques
2.   Advancing career skills through contacts
3.   Obtaining fresh ideas on getting things done
4.   Getting professional supports and leveraging
5.   Building personal confidence at work
6.   Getting access to more opportunities through building more relationships.
7.   Building trust in the business transactions.
8.   Learning how to handle challenges through shared experiences and strategies.

9. Attending professional events with others can be a valuable way to boost one's personal profile.
10. Staying abreast with latest developments in the industry through advice, supports, publications, and diverse perspective.

Marketing is a powerful way of generating attention to business situation. In the skill acquisition situation, there is need for the trainees to be acquainted with diverse marketing strategies which will be deployed during and after the training, as applicable.

Generally, the following approaches are viable marketing mechanisms:

1. Attendance of industry events.
2. Holding conversations with practitioners in the industry, especially the experts.
3. Using the search engines for information netting.
4. Using the social media and viral marketing platforms.
5. Exploring moderate paid media ads.
6. Direct selling of training products.
7. Customization and branding of products, services, ideas, etc.
8. Attracting the attention of customers through interesting websites with knowledgeable prospects.
9. Creating a customer relationship management and content system for synergy of perspectives.
10. Generating high visibility by adopting multiple markets to diverse audiences.

9.0 Technological Resources

In today's world, technology is the in-thing. This latest global wonder has permeated all dimensions of human activities including skill acquisition and development. Indeed, it is a great deficit to effective functioning without technological know-how. The following constitute the basic advantages of technological knowledge and deployment:

1. Access to massive volume of information within a very short time, thus saving valuable time for accomplishing much more deliveries.
2. Easy movement of persons and materials through various technology-based machines and components.
3. Cost efficiency and results maximization as so much can be done with a short time and with fewer hands as against the analogue and manual operations.
4. Education, learning, teaching and skill impartation can all be done now with better technology-based techniques and well-thought out innovations.
5. Enhancement of communication which is the life-wire of modern engagements through instant messaging, photo-sharing, videos and audio transmissions.
6. Storage and access to money through conventional and innovating banking and financial services have made businesses, skill acquisition and career development very easy and interesting. While on a particular training, the trainees can now purchase their materials online and even pay their fees without carrying cash around.
7. With technology today, disabled and physically challenged persons can still take advantage of learning skills which were thought as impossible. With artificial foot, brails, smart sticks and hearing aids, learning is how available to all.

8. The advancement in artificial intelligence which is coming on-stream is a new revolution which will make for high growth in human capabilities.
9. Trainees, employees can now achieve high productivity and flexibility at work by easily connecting with the best resources regardless of distance and deployment of computer-aided activities.
10. The final and most important benefit of technology is its every growing in leaps and bounds thus providing the windows for skill trainees to syn into latest developments in the industry and to get easily updated.

10.0 Conclusion

This is obviously one of the most important chapters in this compendium. It foregrounds areas of success in any activity, that are usually under-rated, assumed and neglected, yet which matter the most. Here we have emphasized the need for the appropriate mindset in engaging in skill acquisition and development with a purpose driven psyche. Anything done out of identified purpose cannot be meaningfully accomplished.

Awareness of approaches in pursuing a dream and accomplishing an intention is crucial to lead to success in time and resources management as evidence of leveraging on potentials and capabilities. The money factor has also been examined as a key issue that can make or mar a decision to acquire a skill. It is proposed that with the attitude of understanding priorities in life, training can be achieved. The importance of networking, marketing and deployment of modern technologies in easing and facilitating trainings and career developments has been properly exposed here for a successful skill training decision.

Chapter Twenty-One

Designing Modules for Skill Acquisition Programs

1.0 Introduction

In recent years, there has been an increasing emphasis in skill acquisition training and development among potential entrepreneurs particularly in recounting to employability. The purpose of this module is to understand the fundamental skill acquisition and the methods of implementing some discussed skills, how training can be enhanced. Each of the discussed skills will comprise of theoretical and practical equipment trainee's interaction, curiosity and parley.

Formal workshop training sessions will further foster understanding of the area in different skills with a focus of applying thorough practical in the real classroom. It is very crucial to keep in mind the kind of skill you would like to venture in to as a trainee, for example, cosmetology skill acquisition, baking, fish farming (aquaculture skill acquisition), fashion and designing skill acquisition, photography and video coverage skill acquisition, and welding and fabrication skill acquisition, among others.

2.0 Vision/Mission Statements

Vision:

To be the preeminent center in Entrepreneurial and to stimulate or arouse learners or trainees in the training centers in theory and practice.

Mission:

To develop, enrich and nurture entrepreneurial skills and knowledge that would enable beneficiaries of various skills to be wealth creators by applying global best entrepreneurial practices and providing relevant entrepreneurial skills for accelerated labor productivity globally.

3.0 Aims and Objectives

Aims

- To introduce trainees or learners to theories, concepts and opportunities available in entrepreneurship and innovation, enunciate activities following effective and efficient models guiding the discipline
- To be the best center for the entrepreneurial training in the society, in theory and in practice
- To make every potential competent trainee from the training school to be expert and complete through the entrepreneurial skill acquisition

Objectives

The training will provide the trainees with the basic understanding of the various ventures of the skill acquisition. Hence acquaints the trainees with knowledge and creativity to solve common problems with ease.

4.0 Philosophy of Learning

The philosophy of learning is the culture of training people to be inspired and encouraged from the practical hints and meaningful insights contained in the concepts and theories guiding the discipline to enrich knowledge of truth and wealth. The program has as its goal to redirection of trainees toward creativity, abilities, innovation and competences such that they would better understand and function in different ways bringing to light something unique, which represents value in the sight of a given target audience.

5.0 Contents Description

- **Introduction to entrepreneurship and skill development:** This introductory of entrepreneurship and skill development is designed to expose the novice minds to entrepreneurship and skill development mix in line with discipline, intuition, art, attitude and experience. The course/content also aids the trainees to understand the difference between entrepreneur, entrepreneurship, entrepreneurism, being entrepreneurial as well as examining the significance of entrepreneurship to skill development.
- **Entrepreneurship theory:** Entrepreneurship theory exposes the advanced beginner to development of entrepreneurship, the global entrepreneurial environment, innovation and creativity, business opportunity and evaluation, as well as the ability to draw a business action plan.
- **Entrepreneurship practical skills:** Practical skills enable the trainees to acquire various skills such as cosmetology, fashion and design, baking (domestic skills). Catfish farming (aquaculture skill). Photography and video coverage (creative skills). Welding and fabricating (technical skills) among others. The enlisted skills equip the competent trainees to be job creators at graduation instead of job seekers. It further enhances their research ability using best practice in business environment. The aforementioned skills enable the competent trainees use the four entrepreneurial mix (4Ps)—process, products, person, and place for product/service development and management. Entrepreneurship practical training skills expose trainees to varieties of research opportunities in all areas using best practices.

Domestic Skills

- **Cosmetology skill acquisition:** This is a lucrative skill because there is no household, offices, especially in this COVID-19 pandemic era that do not use either liquid or bar soap for washing, cleaning and bathing. Trainees who undertake this skill should be able to understand and explain various ingredients involved in the production of cosmetology product.
- **Fashion and design skill acquisition:** Fashion designing is the application of design and aesthetics to clothing and accessories. It is influenced by cultural and social attitudes and has varied over time and place. It has today evolved into a thriving, global multibillion dollar industry. As an entrepreneurial skill, it prepares trainees for a successful career.
- **Baking skill acquisition:** Baking is one of the method of cooking. It is the cooking of food by dry heat in an oven in which the action of the dry convection heat is modified by steam.

Aquaculture skills: Aquaculture plays a vital role in employment and national economic development by providing nutrition and earning revenue.

Photograph and video coverage skill acquisition: A camera or video is a device for taking still or motion pictures, it could be analog or digital. A digital camera is similar to the analog camera, but captures image digitally, when you take a picture the image is recorded by sensor called a charged coupled device (CCD) and save the photo in the digital memory called the memory card, but some cameras have inbuilt memory, the digital camera have many advantage over analog camera.

Technical Skills

- Welding and fabricating: Welding is the prepared metal from fabrication process is then welded together applying a range of techniques and procedures. While fabrication of metal refers to the building of metal structures. This is done using a various processes such as bending, cutting, profiling, welding and assembling.

6.0   Equipment, Facilities, and Raw Materials

Cosmetology

Equipment used in liquid soap production are

- Fermenting tank
- Measuring instrument like spoon, scale, unit, etc.
- Mixer or stirring rod
- Hydrometer gauge

Liquid soap production: It is a liquid substance made up of some acidic and nonacidic chemicals.

Raw materials (chemical) used in liquid soap production includes

- Sulfuric acid
- Soda arch

- Formalin
- Texapon
- Caustic soda
- Color
- Natrosol or Antisol
- Sodium lan sulphate (SLS)
- Industrial perfume
- Sodium triphosphate (STPP)

Texapon and sulfuric acid: These are foamy agent. There are mixed with other chemicals during production.

Soda arch and caustic soda: These are acidic chemicals and cleansing agents used in production of liquid soap.

Color: This adds beauty to the soap.

Natrosol and Antisol: These are the thickening agents used in production of liquid soap. Antisol ferment in water for twenty-four hours while Natrosol ferment immediately.

Sodium lan sulphate (SLS): This is used to boost the foamy agent to bring out more foam and bubbling during production.

Industrial perfume: This adds sweet fragrance to the soap during and after production.

Sodium Tripolyphosphate (STPP) and formalin: These are preservative agent that come in powder and liquid form in its natural state.

Method of Production

Step I: Pour Natrosol or Antisol into some liters of water and mix or stir with a stirring rod.

Step II: Pour Texapon into a bowel and use sulfuric Acid to dissolve it.

Step III: Measure some table spoons caustic soda and soda arch into water and stir. Set aside for fementation.

Step IV: Pour some kg of water and mix, keep for some minutes for fementation.

Step V: Measure STPP and ferment in water and keep aside.

Step VI: Ferment color into 50–75cl of water and keep aside.

Step VIII: Add sulfuric acid to step 1 and stir properly.

Step IX: Add step 3 and 4 into step 1 and stir properly.

Step X: Add step 5 and 6 to step 1 before adding perfume and stir it properly and leave it to settle down.

Bleach production: Bleach is a type of liquid soap used for the removal of stubborn dirt and stain. It is used for washing of white materials and adding to liquid soap for cleaning of dirty floor and tiles.

Raw materials or chemical used in bleach production are

1. caustic soda (sodium hydroxide)
2. soda arch (sodium carbonate)
3. sodium hypochloride (HTH)

Method of Production of 20 Liters of Bleach

Step 1: Dissolve half (1/2) cup of caustic soda with 20 liters of water and stir for 15–20 minutes.

Step 2: Add one (1) cup of soda arch to the mixture and stir for 10–15 minutes.

Step 3: Add 1½ cup of sodium hypochloride to the mixture and stir for 15–20 minutes and leave it to settle down for 24 hours. Then filter it and package.

Tablet Soap Production

Laundry soap: This is also known as bar or tablet soap. It is a substance made up of oil and some acidic chemicals such as sodium hydroxide (caustic soda) and sodium carbonate (soda arch).

Equipment's used in tablet soap production include the following:

- Fermenting tank
- Measuring instrument
- Mold
- Stampling machine
- Mixer or stirring rod
- Cutting or slicing machine
- Boiler
- Hydrometer gauge

Raw materials or chemicals used in tablet soap production include the following:

- Soda arch
- Formalin
- Sodium silicate
- Caustic soda
- Color
- Sodium Triphosphate (STPP)
- Palm kernel oil (PKO)
- Industrial perfume

Soda carbonate (soda arch): This is found in light and dense form. Like caustic soda, it need to be fermented into liquid soluble before use.

Sodium silicate: This comes in liquid form. It plays a vital role in formation of soap. It is foamy, binding and shining agent. This must be added to other chemicals according to specification.

Sodium hydroxide (caustic soda): It comes in two forms in its natural state, that is solid and peals form and it must be fermented before use.

Color: This is two types of color, oil soluble and water soluble. It is advised that in tablet soap production, oil soluble should be used.

Sodium Triphosphate (STPP): This is commonly referred to as STPP. It is one of the most preservative agent. It comes in a powder form which has to be fermented into liquid before used for production.

Palm kernel oil (PKO): This is oil extract out of palm kernel fruit. It is best and ideal oil for soap production compare to animal fat.

Industrial perfume: This comes with different aroma and in liquid form. It give soap the desired scent the producer want.

Sodium sulphate: It reduces chemical reaction of some corrosive chemicals

Method of Production:

Step 1: **Fermentation:** Provide two tanks and ferment caustic soda in one and soda arch in the other. Take a full measurement of each chemical and pour them in a separate tanks or base and use that same measurement to add three (3) parts of water to each of the tanks and stir properly. The two chemicals should be allowed to ferment for at least 48 hours or more, because they are too harsh.

Step 2: **Hydrometer reading:** Check the concentration of the caustic soda and soda arch soluble with hydrometer gauge. The range for caustic soda and soda arch is 12.75–13.00m. When it is higher than this range, it will burn the skin and when it is lower than this range, the soap will be too soft.

Step 3: **Ferment STPP:** Use little quantity of water to ferment STPP and keep it aside.

Step 4: **Production Start:** Put on your boiler, measure PKO into boiling vessel or pot and place it in your boiler or stove and warm or bleach the PKO after 5 minutes.

Step 5: Measure fermented caustic soda into mixer, mixing base add PKO, fermented soda arch to it.

Step 6: Add ferment STPP.

Step 7: Add industrial perfume to your taste and stir it properly.

Step 8: Measure silicate with tablespoon and add to it and finally pour it into mold for setting unit for two (2) or three (3) hours.

Fashion and Designing:

Fashion and designing is the conscious use of skill acquired by experience, study or observation and creative imagination especially creating trendy, exclusive or fashionable attire or apparel.

Fashion and designing equipment

- Sewing machine
- Sewing machine oil
- Tape measure
- Table
- Scissors
- Hand needle
- Tailor's chalk
- Iron and ironing board
- Mannequin (dummy)
- Sewing thread (different colors)
- Dress maker
- Pincushions and magnetic pin holders
- Sewing seam rippers
- Sewing box
- Sewing needles threader
- Sewing gauges

How to use a sewing machine and other equipment

i. **Sewing machine:** It is a machine with a mechanically drive and needle used to stitch or sew fabric and other material together using thread.

How to use a sewing machine

- Select straight stitch and a medium stitch length.
- Practice on some scrap materials.
- Line up the fabric under the needle.
- Lower the presser foot onto the fabric.
- Hold the loose ends of both thread.
- Press the foot pedal.
- Find the reverse button or lever and try it.

How to maintain sewing machine

- Remove the throat place bobbin, a bobbin case.
- Use small lint brush to dust under the feed dog around the bobbin area.
- Spray tension under feed dog and around bobbin area with compressed air to remove any excess lint and thread.

ii. **Sewing machine oil:** This oil is used to lubricate the sewing machine else the machine will be stiff and difficult to operate.

iii. **Tape measure:** It is a nonstretchable flexible strip usually marked with inches on one side and centimeter on the other. It is a must have tool for sewing.

iv. **Table:** A table is one of the essential tools of fashion designing. It can be used for ironing. It is also where fabric is kept during cutting. It has multiple function.

v. **Scissors:** This is used for cutting fabric accurately. It is the key to having piece fit together.

vi. **Hand needle:** It is use in all types of hand sewing, the most commonly used hand sewing needle are called sharps. Sharps have a medium length in comparison with all available needles, have a round eye for the thread. Hand needle is used to make the correct choice when choosing to eliminate damaging fabric when sewing with hand needle.

vii. **Tailor's chalk:** Is used to sketch the measurement on the fabric for each cutting.

viii. **Iron and ironing board:** Is used for ironing garment after sewing to help bring out the beauty of the finished product.

ix. **Mannequin (Dummy):** This is one of the fashion design draping tools or decorating tools used in show-casing garment after sewing.

x. **Sewing thread:** This is a trim which ensures the functional properties of a garment by securing the seams. It is a special type of yarn which is used for sewing but not for weaving or knitting.

xi. **Dress maker:** This is used for holding two seam together during sewing.

xii. **Pincushions and magnetic pin holders:** A pincushion holds the straight pins needles while a fashion designer is working to prevent accident.

xiii. **Sewing seam rippers:** This is used to remove unwanted stitches. The fine tip of a seam ripper allows a fashion designer to pick out single threads, decreasing the likelihood of cutting the fabric that the stitches are attached to.

xiv. **Sewing box:** It is used for putting nonessential and spare items such as thread and spare scissors, etc., together

xv. **Sewing needles threader:** A needle threader is usually a wire, bent into a diamond shape that is attached to a handle. The wire easily passes through the eye of a needle, opens allowing a large opening for the thread and is then pulled back through the eye of the needle. Its function is to make threading a sewing needle faster and easy.

xvi. **Sewing gauges:** These are hand tools used for measuring small areas as you are sewing. Gauges are available in variety of forms.

Baking Skill Acquisition

Baking is a method of preparing food that uses dry heat (oven) but it can also be done in hot ashes or on hot stones.

Baking Equipment

- **Oven:** For baking
- **Mixing machine:** For mixing pastry or dough
- **Scale:** For measuring flour, butter, sugar, etc.
- **Cylinder:** For gas.
- **Cake pan:** For putting the cake mixture for baking.
- **Sieve:** To sieve the flour before using.
- **Bread pan:** For putting the dough for baking.
- **Cutting board:** For cutting onion, leaves, carrot, etc.
- **Meat blander:** For grinding meat.
- **Icing set or piping tube:** For decorating of cake.
- **Knife:** For cutting
- **Spoon (tablespoon):** For measuring baking powder, sugar, etc.
- **Meat pie cutter:** For cutting meat pie dough.
- **Doughnut cutter:** For cutting the dough for frying.
- **Frying spoon:** For packing snacks from the oil
- **Baking sheets:** For putting the dough's for baking.
- **Washing hand bowl:** For washing of meat, carrot, onion, etc.
- **Measuring cups:** For measuring flour, water, sugar, etc.
- **Irish potatoes cutter:** For cutting potatoes for meat pie.
- **Pastry brush:** For glazing unbaked dough.
- **Mixing bowl:** For mixing dough.
- **Egg mixer or whisker:** For beating of egg.
- **Cake board:** For placing the cake for decoration.
- **Wooden spoon:** For creaming of butter and sugar for cake making.
- **Strainer or filter:** For putting the hot snacks from the oil.
- **Frying pan:** For frying
- **Bread table:** For kneading of dough.
- **Rolling pin:** For rolling the dough before cutting.

Baking Ingredients

Ingredients for meat pie (filling and dough)

- Flour
- Margarine or butter
- Vegetable oil
- Salt
- Irish potatoes
- Eggs
- Meat
- Onion
- Water
- Curry
- Thyme
- Carrot
- Bouillon cubes
- Flavor
- Baking powder
- Cabbage

Ingredients for cake

- Flour
- Margarine or butter
- Baking powder
- Salt
- Lemonade
- Dry fruit or mix fruit
- Preservative
- Sugar
- Browning
- Nutmeg
- Flavor
- Egg

Ingredients for icing

- Glucose gum
- Gelatin
- Coloring
- CMC
- Icing sugar
- Corn flour
- Glycerin

Ingredients for buns, chin-chin, and eggroll

- Flour
- Margarine or butter
- Oil (vegetable)
- Water
- Sugar
- Baking powder
- Nutmeg
- Milk
- Egg
- Flavor
- Salt

Ingredients for bread

- Flour
- Vegetable oil
- Preservative
- Salt
- Dry fruit
- Margarine or butter
- Yeast
- Water
- Sugar
- Nutmeg
- Flavor
- Milk
- Egg
- Browning

Aquaculture Skill Acquisition

- **Catfish farming:** Catfish farming is a specialized sector of aquaculture. It is a form of aquaculture in which fishes are raised in enclosures to be sold as food.

Equipment needed for catfish farming

- **The pond:** It is used for housing the fishes during rearing. The pond is either an above ground pond made from plastic, block or concrete or dugout pond. It is the first and most important equipment needed for catfish farming.
- **Plumbing and water pumps:** The water pump is very important because the fish farmer needs an easy mechanism to perform water change functions. The water pump is either solar pump or electric pump for better performance and easy maintenance. The plumbing works require plastic or iron pipes located at the let or outlet. The pipe is connected to the water pump for easy filling and evacuation of waste.

- **Aerators:** Aerators come in different shapes, performance and functionality depending on the size of the pond and number of fishes. Aerators helps the fish to grow faster and healthier in a relatively short period. Other types of aerators include the following: waste water, aerator, air/oxygen aerator and filter medium, etc.
- **Automatic fish feeder:** The automatic feeder feeds the fish at predetermined times. The fish feeder can only work properly if the water is mechanically recycled. This is because if the fish feeder continues to feed the fish while the water is saturated and dirty it can kill the fish. This equipment eliminates hand reading and it is quite effective.
- **Dip nets:** The nets are useful when catching catfish for weighing or sales. The fish farmer needs different sizes of dip nets to perform different functions.
- **Water quality tester:** This is used to test the quality and Ph level of the water.
- **Generator:** This is used to supply light in the farm.
- **Fish transporter:** This is used for transporting fishes to long distance. Transporting fishes is a difficult task, so this equipment is fitted with devices that keep the water and environment conducive.
- **Handling and grading equipment:** This is used to handle fishes during sorting, artificial insemination and extraction of eggs.
- **Seine reels:** Seine reels sink to the bottom of large ponds and are used to collect fish.

Other tools are measurement scale, wheelbarrow, knife, cutlasses, among others.

Photography and Video Coverage Skill Acquisition

Photography and video coverage is the amount and kind of footage shot used to capture a scene in film making and video production (https://en.m.wikipedia.org/wiki/carema-coverage, accessed October 2021).

Types of Cameras

- Film cameras
- Smart camera
- View camera
- Digital camera
- Point and shoot or compact cameras
- Specialty cameras
- Rangefinder/Viewfinder camera
- Single lens reflex camera (SLR)
- Twin lens reflex camera (TLR)

Welding and Fabrication

Welding is the process of fusing two metals while fabrication is the process of cutting, bending and assembling of metals to form a specific structure (https://www.precgroup.com/welding-fabrication-terms, accessed October 2021).

Equipment used for welding and fabrication:

- Beginners MIG welders equipment
- Best—Millermatic 211

- Better—Multiprocess welder
- Good—Affordable flux core welder
- Power Tools
- Angle grinder with a paddle switch
- Sawzall (optional)
- Metal band saw
- Consumables
- Shielding gas
- Welding wire
- Angle grinder wheels
- Steel
- Clamping, measuring and marking
- Soapstone
- Squaring tools
- Scribe
- Permanent markers
- Welding magnets
- Welding clamps
- Hand Tools
- Hack saw
- Welding pliers
- Steel wire brush—specifically a steel brush, not a stainless steel or aluminum brush.
- Personal safety
- Welding jacket
- Safety glasses
- Welding helmet
- Work shoes
- MIG welding gloves
- Ear protection
- Face mask
- Grinding visor
  (https://www.instructables.com/Welding-Tools-and-Materials, accessed October 2021).

7.0 Modes of Evaluation

Trainees are assessed by:

a. **Theory (through training/teaching):** This type of assessment approach to teaching and learning creates feedback which is then used to improve trainee's or learner's performance in summative test and examination. Summative assessment: essay in uncontrolled conditions, coursework, portfolios, trainer assessment are informal, while tests, examinations, and essays in controlled conditions are formal assessment under summative.

b. **Practical skill acquisition:** Practical skill acquisition assessment are a form of coursework which enable trainers or instructors to see how well instructions have be followed and also reflect on the

trainee's attention to detail how well they are able to apply the knowledge gained from the course to a practical situation.

c.   **Examinations:** Examination should be consistent with your learning outcomes for the course. As a trainer,

- Use the topics list provided in the course outline.
- Skim through your training notes to find key concepts and methods.
- Review chapter headings and subheadings in the assigned readings.

8.0   Conclusion

Designing modules for Skill Acquisition Programs is an important aspect to be considered. This is because it serves as a guide in stimulating potential entrepreneurs to be conscious minded in theory and practice. It also forge, enhance and foster entrepreneurial skills and cognition that would enable the trainees to be wealth creators by applying global best entrepreneurial practices.

Chapter Twenty-Two

Instructional Materials and Resources in Skill Training

1.0   Introduction

Instructional material are used in assessment and lively modification of a behavioral tendency by exposure or experience. These are sources of support to aid a trainer/teacher in an effective teaching of a lesson. The instructional materials are classified into groups, because different courses/subjects has different methodology of teaching/training, so also is instructional material. For example, language arts classrooms always have literature textbooks, vocabulary, writing textbooks and spelling workbooks, supplemental reading materials include novels or poems outside of the textbooks. In skill training, cosmetology skill acquisition, the trainer and the trainee should note that their instructional materials to be used include the following: industrial perfume, soda arch, Natrosol or Antisol, caustic soda, color, sodium lan sulphate (SLS), formalin and the likes in the production of liquid soap.

Furthermore, instructional materials varies in teaching and training. What is applicable in classroom teaching may not be applicable in training workshop. Therefore, in training, a trainer should rummage what specific outcomes he/she wants.

What is Instructional Material?

Instruction is utmost of importance for education, as it is there consign of learning from one person to another. Any time is asked or told how to do something or is given directions, he/she is receiving instruction. Instruction is an exercise that disclose cognizance or skills.

Material is defined as the physical components of something to relevant facts, to jokes or items that are part of a performers' routine, or to the things required to build something or accomplish a task (www.yourdictionary.com/material, accessed September 2021).

"Instructional materials are defined as resources that organize and support instruction. It can also be referred to the human and nonhuman materials and facilities that can be used to ease, promote and improved teaching and learning" (www.igi-global.com/dictionary/relevance-of-the-use-of-intructional-materials-in-teaching-and-pedagogical-delivery/48956, accessed September 2021).

The term "instructional materials" should include printed materials and multimedia materials, and should include materials habituated in the classroom and accessible in the libraries.

2.0   The Importance of Instructional Materials

The significance of instructional materials is to enhance trainee's knowledge, competences, and skills, to keep track of their process of receiving new facts or responding to information, and to play a significant part to their overall development and upbringing. It also expound important notions to stimulate and keep up unfamiliar learning, assist in making learning more stable.

- **Training cogitation:** Instructional materials offers trainees the chances to carryout cogitations and expound a commodity that illustrates their magnitude of comprehension. When training on or learning unfamiliar skill, it is very pivotal to heed to prototype and exercise cognizance instantaneously.
- **It engross and train trainees:** Instructional materials permit the trainer to engross trainees by corroborating concepts through the use of multimedia, which includes interactive games, sound clips, video, hands-on-experience and images. It is because there are various kinds of trainees like visual and auditory trainees, these instructional materials diversify in presentation to assist extend all trainees.
- **It stipulate an actual occurrence and communication of information:** Instructional materials stipulate a profusion of knowledge in all relevant subject contents, contributing in-depth information based on facts. It also provides trainees background on the subject content. It provide a start off point to begin training unfamiliar information.
- **Assessment of knowledge:** Those products are then applied to assess trainee's knowledge accordingly. Instructional materials permit the trainer to assist trainees with modifying levels of ability and fundamental skills by giving additional aid. These materials include quizzes and tests.

Advantages of Instructional Materials

1. Instructional materials should provide 'step-by-step' instruction.
2. It should be used to update instruction and content easily.
3. It should be accessible.
4. It should not be too expensive.
5. It should serve the purpose of learning.

Disadvantages of Instructional Materials

1. Some of the instructional materials provide step-by-step instruction.
2. Trainers do not know how to use/manipulate them effectively.
3. Trainers do not provide helpful instructional materials for beginners.
4. Instructional material recommended for each skill training are not accessible in some environment or in the country.
5. The instructional materials are too expensive.

Things to consider when selecting instructional materials

- Instructional materials should be designed to motivate learners to examine their own attitudes and behaviors and to comprehend their own duties, rights, responsibilities, and privileges as participating citizens in a pluralistic society.
- Instructional materials should have aesthetic, cultural, literary, or social value.

- Instructional materials should be diverse with respect to levels of difficulty, reader appeal, and should present a variety of points of view.
- Instructional materials should support the educational philosophy, goals and objectives of the curricular offering in which the materials will be used.
- Instructional materials should meet high standards of quality in factual content and presentation.
- Instructional materials should encourage learners to utilize higher order thinking skills and to become informed decision-makers, to exercise freedom of thought and to make independent judgments through examination and evaluation of relevant information, evidence and differing points of view.
- Instructional materials should foster respect for men, women, the disabled, and minority groups and should portray a variety of roles and life styles open to people in today's world. It should foster respect for cultural diversity.
- Instructional materials should be appropriate for the age, emotional and social development, and ability level of the learners for whom the materials are selected (https://www.urbandaleschools.com/policy/article-600-educational-program/627-instructional-materials-selection-inspection-and-reconsideration, accessed September 2021).

3.0 General Learning Resources

Learning resources are those devices and procedure that assist to make teaching and learning more interesting, more stimulating, more reinforcing and more effective.

Teaching and learning resources referred to in the guidelines include any spoken, written or visual text or activity used or conducted by schools or training centers to aid the effectiveness of teaching-learning. These resources include

- Performances
- Plays
- Textbooks
- Multimedia
- Films
- Digital learning resources which include video, audio, images and animations text, among others.
- Radio programs
- Speeches
- Novels
- Lectures
  (https://www2.education.vic.gov.au/pal/selecting-suitable-teaching-resources/policy, accessed September 2021).

Principles of selecting learning resources

Appropriate and wise selection of learning resources are required from teacher's side as these resources are helpful for achieving teaching objectives. Principles that help to select learning resources include

- **Principle of learner centeredness:** Learning resources should suit the age, maturity, intellectual level, motives, and social environment of the learners.

- **Principle of relevancy and suitability:** Relevant, suitable and appropriate learning resources makes the trainee's to grasp the reasonableness of or technical acquaintance of the topic. It provide the purpose of teaching in most effectiveness.
- **Principle of educational value:** Learning resources should recreate or provide variety in teaching-learning situations. They should not be employed for the same of name.
- **Principle of accuracy:** This principle states that learning resources should be accurate and properly maintained to provide better learning.
- **Principle of interest and motivation:** Learning resources must be interesting, it must attract the attention of learners/trainees, it must be motivating for the learners for getting fully absorbed in learning.
- **Principle of size:** Learning resources should be prepared considering the size of a class. It should serve the whole class.
- **Principle of simplicity:** Learning resources should be simple enough so that learners can understand it and enhance their learning.
- **Principle of availability of resources:** Financial budget, trained teacher/trainer, ability and skills in a teacher/trainer to handle aid material are things to be considered while selecting learning resources.
- **Principle of realization of objectives**: Learning resources must be capable and meaningful for the proper realization of teaching-learning objectives.
- **Principle of means to an end**: Learning resources are made to assist teachers to provide better and not to treat end means in themselves (https://www.slideshare.net/sarishtigarg/learning-resources-46775217, accessed September 2021).

4.0 Reading Materials, Handbooks, and Syllabuses

Reading materials is described as list of books, stories, articles, etc., that need to be look at and understand (printed or written words or other signs) for one's studies.

Types of reading materials

Knowledge or information can be obtained from investigation, study or instruction or virtually anywhere; for example: books, journal and magazine articles, newspapers, etc.

- **Books:** Books cover virtually any topic, fact or fiction. For research purposes, an individual will probably be looking for books that synthesize all the information on one topic to support a particular argument or thesis.

Examples of books:

- Udofot and Bassey, PhD. *A Comprehensive English Course: For School and Colleges*, 2004.
- Smith, J. T. *Roman Villas: A study in social structure*, 1997.
- Silverstone, Roger, ed. *Visions of Suburbia*, 1997.

Uses of books

a. It is used to find historical information.
b. It is used when looking for lots of information on a topic.
c. It is used to find summarizes of research to support an argument.
d. It is used to put ones topic in context with other important issues.

• **A journal:** This is a collection of articles usually written by scholars in an academic or professional field. Although, there is an academic journal. An academic journal is an editorial board reviews articles which is to decide whether they should be accepted. Articles in journals can cover very specific topics or narrow fields of research. Examples of journals are Journal of Historian, Lancet, Journal of Communication and Journal of the American Medical Association.

Uses of journal

a. It is used to find out what has been studies on one's topic.
b. It is used when doing scholarly research.
c. It is used to find bibliographies that point to other relevant research.

• **Magazine:** A magazine is a collection of article and images about diverse topics of popular interest and current events. Usually these articles are written by journalists or scholars and are geared toward the average adult. Magazines may cover very "serious" material and to find consistent scholarly information. Examples of magazines includes Efik gong, *National Geographic*, *Sports Illustrated*, etc.

Uses of magazine

a. It is used to find general articles for people who are not necessarily specialists about the topic.
b. It is used to find information or opinions about popular culture.
c. It is used to find up-to-date information about current events.

• **Newspapers:** A newspaper is a collection of articles about current events usually published daily. It is a great source for local information, since there is at least one in every city. For example, *Chronicles, Vanguard,* the *Nation, Dailytime, New York Times*, etc.

Uses of news-papers:

a. It is used to find editorials, commentaries, expert or popular opinions.
b. It is used to find current information about international, nation and local events. (https://courses.lumenlearning.com/engcomp1-wmopen/chapter/outcome-types-of-writing-1-1, accessed September 2021).

Handbooks

A handbook is a type of reference work, or other collection of instructions, that is intended to provide ready reference. It is applied to a small or portable book containing information useful for its owner (https://en.m.wikipedia.org/wiki/handbook, accessed September 2021).

A handbook is about supporting quality teachers. It is presented as a companion to the book qualities of Effective Teachers (Stronge, 2002). Handbook for qualities of Effective Teachers is to provide a tool for teachers as they seek to improve their effectiveness in delivering high-quality, productive learning experiences for all learners (https://www.ascd.org/books/handbook-for-qualities-of-efective-teachers?chapter=intoduction-maximizing-your-use-of-the-handbook-for-qualities-of-effective-teachers).

Application of the Handbook

- Teacher conductors who are committed in tutoring and cooperative school wide enhancement.
- School executives who direct and assess teachers.
- Teachers who yearn for to accentuate their own achievement through recollection and usage of tools for enhancing accomplishment.
- Policy makers and their staffs who are answerable for developing equipment and methodology for section teacher development and assessment furtherance.
- Teacher and administrator educators who can engage the book's research and operation approaches in their teacher training and instructional leadership programs in the given order.

Syllabuses

Syllabuses is described as a summary outline of a discourse, treatise, or course of study or of examination requirements. It is also known as "Headnote" (Merriam Webster Dictionary, accessed September 2021).

A syllabus is an outline and summary of or comprehensive subject of a discourse to be covered in an education or training career. A syllabus always comprises accurate facts or information about the subject of a discourse, such as information on how, where, and when to connect the teacher/trainer and assistant instructors; a rundown of what will be covered in the discourse; an agenda of assessment dates and the appropriate dates for assignments; how to assign grade to trainees/learners; accurate classroom criterion; etc. Thereby numerous courses end in an examination.

A syllabus is usually either prescribed by an examination board, or arranged by the professor or professional who oversees or regulates the course quality. It may be provided in hard copy (paper) form or soft copy (online). It is always given to each leaner/trainee during the first training class section so that the objectives and expected value of acquiring them are clear.

Syllabuses are employed to guarantee persistency between schools (training schools) and that every teachers/trainees understand what must be trained/taught and what is not needed. Examination can only test cognizance or knowledge based on facts included in the syllabus.

5.0 Multimedia Components

Multimedia is a combination of two words, 'Multi' and 'media'. Multi means many and media means material through which something can be transmitted. Multimedia is a medium through which the information can be easily transmitted from one place to another. It combined all the media rudiments like graphics

and text to make the information more effective, attractive and relevant. Multimedia is used in various fields like in education, business, training, etc. (https://www.indiastudychannel.com/resources/151966-Multimedia-Components-Application.aspx, accessed September 2021).

The various components of multimedia include

1. Edmodo
2. Socrative
3. Project
4. Thinglink
5. TED-Ed
6. Ck-12
7. ClassDojo
8. Educlipper
9. Storybird
10. Animoto
11. Kahoot

- **Edmodo:** This is an educational tool that connects teachers and students, and s assimilated into a social network. Teachers can create online collaborative groups, administer and provide educational materials, measure student performance and communicate with parents/guidance, among other functions with this digital tools.
- **Socrative:** This is a system that allows teachers to create exercises or educational games which students can solve using mobile devices, like smartphones, laptops, or tablets. Teachers can see the results of activities and depending on these, modify the subsequent lessons to make them more personalized. This educational tool was designed by a group of entrepreneurs and engineers passionate about education.
- **Project:** This is a tool that allows an individual to create multimedia presentations, with dynamic slides in which someone can embed interactive maps, links, online quizzes, twitter timelines, and videos, among other options. During a class session, teachers can share with students' academic presentations which are visually adapted to different devices.
- **Thinglink:** This allows educators to create interactive images with music, sounds, texts and photographs. These can be shared on other websites or on social networks, such as Twitter and Facebook. Thinglink offers the possibility for teachers to create learning methodologies that awaken the curiosity of students through interactive content that can expand their knowledge.
- **TED-Ed:** This website allows democratizing access to information for teachers/instructors and students/trainees. This kind of educational platform allows creating educational lessons with the collaboration of teachers, students, animators. Generally, people who want to expand knowledge and good ideas can have an active participation in the learning process of others.
- **cK-12:** This platform has an open source interface that allows creating and distributing educational material through the internet, which can be modified and contain videos, audios, and interactive exercises. It can also be printed and comply with the necessary editorial standards in each region. The books that are created in K–12 can be adapted to the needs of any teacher or student.
- **ClassDojo:** This tool helps to improve student/learner behavior. It provides real-time notifications to students, like "well done, David!" and "ti," for working collaboratively. Teachers provide their students with instant feedback so that good disposition in class is 'rewarded' with points, this will make students to have a more receptive attitude toward the learning process.

- **eduClipper:** It provides the opportunity for teachers to organize a virtual class with their students/learners and create a portfolio where all vital works are carried out. References and readable educational material can be share and explore by learners and teachers. eduClipper offers the possibility to manage more academic work found online, improve research techniques, and have a quality digital record of what the learners achieved during their course of training and learning.
- **Storybird:** This tool helps teachers to create interactive and artistic books online through a simple and easy use of interface. The aim also include promoting writing and reading techniques in learners/trainees through storytelling. Storybird also enable teachers/instructors to create projects, give constant feedback, and organize classes and grades with students. The stories created can be embedded in blogs, sent by email, and printed, among other options.
- **Animoto:** It is a friendly and practical interface which allows instructors/teachers to create audiovisual content that adapts to educational needs. This digital gadget enables an individual to create super-quality videos in a short time and from any mobile device, inspiring students and helps in improving academic training lessons.
- **Kahoot:** It promotes game-based learning, which increases student engagement and creates a dynamic, social and fun educational environment. It is an educational platform that is based on games and questions. This tool can enable teachers to create questionnaires, discussions, or surveys that complement academic lessons. This material is projected in the classroom and questions are answered by leaners/students which playing and learning at the same time. (https://elearningindustry.com.digital-education-tools-teachers-students, accessed September 2021).

Criteria for the Selection of Multimedia Components

The trainer/teacher should consider:

i. The appropriateness media to the materials.
ii. The financed or affordability of the materials.
iii. The easiness of using the teaching/training aids (media too).
iv. The availability of hardware to facilitate the training.
v. The quality of the teaching/training aids.
vi. The suitability to the trainees'/learners' intelligence level.
vii. The alignment to standards and depth of knowledge.

6.0   Tools and Equipment

Instructional tools are the tools used in teaching and learning or training in educational lessons, which involves active learning, test and evaluation. It also aid a teacher or trainer to teach/train his/her leaners'. These are examples of instructional tools:

a. Class content and lecture delivery tools
b. Collaborative tools
c. Communication tools
d. Homework/Assignment activity tools
e. Feedback/Polling tools
f. Examination/Assessment tools.

- **Class content and lecture delivery tools:** These tools content can be delivered synchronously (operating at exactly the same periods) or asynchronously (not simultaneous). A teacher/trainer should have in mind that asynchronous delivery of content can be applied in courses/training that primarily has to do with face-to-face meeting as a way of setting aside in-class time for learners' discussion. This will depend on one's course/training goals.

- **Collaborative tools:** Collaborative simply means working jointly with others or together especially in an intellectual endeavor. Here, many of the available educational technology tools can be implemented to accommodate collaboration in all instructional modes. There are many number of ways to facilitate collaboration among learners both during face-to-face and asynchronously online.

- **Communication tools:** There are many communication tool options available to power for both synchronous and asynchronous communication with learners. It is critical for instructors/trainers to keep in contact with their learners/trainers in any course/training. As a trainer, make sure that you talk to your trainees about your preferred communication tool so that they can understand where to go and find messages about your course/skill and how to contact you if needs arises.

- **Homework/Assignment activity tools:** Educational technology tools can make homework/assignment management and collection more efficient for both learners and instructors. Some educational tools provide features that streamline collection, grading and feedback for traditional paper-based class homework while other tools help expand beyond traditional homework by opening up more submission options.

- **Feedback/Polling tools:** Feedback and polling tools can foster inclusivity by being used as a mechanism for learners to provide input on topics and activities they would like to engage with as part of your course or skill. Collecting feedback from learners is a great way to measure learner's comfort and understanding both during class and between classes.

- **Examination/Assessment tools:** Educational technology tools can be used to organize examinations and assessments. Whether the examination is standard research/essay style examination or a multi-question examination, multi-choice style examination, there are tools that can be used to organize collection, grading and feedback (https://poorvucenter.yale.edu/strategic-resources-digital-publications/instructional-tools, accessed September 2021).

Instructional Equipment

Instructional equipment expenditures are eligible if the equipment, library material, or technology is for classroom instruction, learner instruction or demonstration, or in the preparation of learning materials in an instructional program. Examples include

- **Equipment and furniture:** Instructional equipment and furniture for primary use by learners in instructional or training programs.

   i. Classroom/laboratory equipment (this is applicable in an online classroom and formal classroom settings)
      - Whiteboard
      - Projector screen
      - Projector, etc.

   ii.   Instructional furniture (this is applicable in classroom settings)
- Desks, tables, podium, etc.
- Chairs, etc.

- **Information technology:** Instructional/information technology equipment for learner use in classroom or laboratories:
  - Desktops, laptops
  - Printers
  - Monitors
  - Servers
  - Network/wireless infrastructure
  - AV/TV
  - Multimedia
- **Software:** Software licenses are allowed but only the initial year is permitted. Other software that are permitted are those that are used in excess of one year and software modifications that add capacity or efficiency to the software that defers obsolescence and results in an extension of the useful life of the software.
  - Registration
  - Counseling
  - Student/trainee services
  - Learning management systems for learner use
- **Adaptive equipment:** ADA/OCR learners are allowed to assist them in a learning environment.
- **Library material**
  - Databases
  - Books, periodicals, videos, etc.
  - Online subscriptions
- **Other instructional equipment:** Examples include
  - Video cameras
  - Laptop computers
  - Slide projectors
  - Document cameras
  - Portable data projectors
  - Audio cassette players
  - Overhead projectors
  - Portable TV/VCR
  - Video projector (https://www.washburnlaw.edu/library/services/equipment.html, accessed September 2021).

Online Instructional Tools

Online instructional tools for teachers/trainers provide the option to both create and keep a grade book. Here, teachers can upload assignments and keep track of their learners' attendance. It also let teachers share grades with parents. Learners will have access to the class resources in any location they find themselves, since the syllabus and assignments are online and they can attend classes anywhere the teacher (or student) wants it to be.

Online instructional tools guide trainers/teachers through the process of creating a grade book, making information available to parents and learners, uploading content. The online instructional tools include

a. **Teacher tube:** Teacher tube is a video site for educators. Teachers can upload instruction videos, which can be viewed by anyone anywhere in the world. Videos can show classroom instructions on different topics. There are no limits on the content. Teacher Tube also lets learners showcase their work. Learners display their artwork, engagement in classroom activities, or show off their special talents to the web.

b. **Blackboard:** Blackboard is one of the most capable teaching tools in the space. Educators can upload grades, monitor student performance, and administer tests. Teachers can also input assignments and manage their syllabus. It can also allow learners access all the information their teachers add to their class page, check their grades and complete assignments.

c. **Engrade:** Engrade provides learners with a place to monitor grades and see how they have performed on tests. Information, here, is provided by the teachers, who can also customize their engrade grade books, input scores from anywhere they have web access, and create instruction plans for learners to download. It is a powerful tool that is easy to use for both learners and teachers. Engrade is free, unlike most other services in the market.

d. **Classroom 2.0:** It is a social network for teachers. Educators can chat, send messages, and exchange ideas on how to best educate learners. Many of the educators discuss ways to use the Web to enhance classroom instruction. Classroom 2.0 is an ideal place for teachers to find best practices to create a more effective educational environment.

e. **MyGradeBook:** This is an impressive utility. It has the option to create online assignments, manage grade books, administer quizzes, communicate with parents and provide access to learners. Once the teacher buys a license, he/she will find one of the most powerful teaching utilities on the Web (https://www.cnet.com/how-to/five-tools-for-the-worlds-best-teacher, accessed September 2021).

7.0 Customized/Improvised Resources

Customized instruction is designed to give learners multiple ways to approach a single new concept. It is also known as differentiated instruction. Customized or differentiated instruction permits the teacher to acclimatize their lessons to a variety of learning styles and needs giving their learners the best chance for expansion.

In customized instruction, learners are given a chance to exhibit their potencies while also enduring to develop weaker areas. This is because learners are dynamic, and each one comes to the classroom with various needs, different areas for growth and different strengths, customized instruction serves as a favorable juncture for learner and teacher equally to draw near the classroom with rejuvenated effort or energy and excitement.

Elements of customized or differentiated resources

- **Content:** What the learner needs to learn or how the learner will get access to the information;
- **Process:** Activities in which the learner engages to make sense of or mater the content;
- **Products:** Culminating projects that ask the learner to rehearse, apply and extend what he or she has learned in a unit;
- **Learning environment:** The way the classroom works and feels.

- **Product**
  i. Using rubrics that match and extend learners' varied skills level.
  ii. Encouraging learners to create their own product assignments as long as the assignments contain required elements.
  iii. Giving learner's options off how to express required learning (e.g. create a puppet show, write a letter, or develop a mural with labels).
  iv. Allowing learners to work alone or in small groups on their products.

- **Learning environment**
  i. Setting out clear guidelines of independent work that matches individual needs.
  ii. Providing materials that reflect a variety of cultures and home settings.
  iii. Helping learners understand that some learners need to move around to learn, while others do better sitting quietly.
  iv. Making sure there are places in the room to work quietly and without distraction, as well as places that invite learner collaboration.
  v. Developing routines that allow learners to get help when teachers are busy with other learners and cannot help them immediately (Tomilson, 1995, 1999; Winebrenner, 1992, 1996).

- **Content**
  i. Putting text materials on tape.
  ii. Using reading buddies.
  iii. Using reading materials at varying readability levels.
  iv. Presenting ideas through both auditory and visual means.
  v. Meeting with small groups tore-teach an idea or skill for struggling learners or to extend the thinking or skills of advanced learners.
  vi. Using spelling or vocabulary lists at readiness levels of learners.

- **Process**
  i. Providing interest centers that encourage learners to explore subsets of the class topic of particular interest to them.
  ii. Offering manipulatives or other hands-on supports for learners who need them.
  iii. Using tiered activities through which all learners work with the same important understandings and skills, but proceed with different levels of support, challenge, or complexity.
  iv. Varying the length of time a learner may take to complete a task to provide additional support for a struggling learner or to encourage an advanced learner to pursue a topic in greater depth.

Examples of Customized or Differentiated Resources

i. **Creating literature circles:** It sounds like an English concept, but it can be applied in any class where the teacher can group learners with leveled texts. Learners could all be reading different text that is at their reading level.

ii. **Grouping learners by their learning styles:** Here, learners who are auditory learners will work better together because they probably have similar styles of communication.

iii. **The classroom is to have learners work in groups to move through several stations around the room:** Learners can work together on skills that everyone needs to know on their own. Here, the teacher can work with individual groups at one of those stations, so learners get individualized lessons designed for what they need to learn in the unit.

iv. **The classroom should be leveled with graphic organizers and worksheets:** Here, teachers can assign struggling learners a task where they have to identify the problem and solution of a text. An

LMS is a very beneficial kind of example. The middle group of learners would not only have to identify the problem and solution within the story/text, but also create a different solution of their own. The group of learners who are ready for extensions would identify the problem and solution as well as create two different solutions and explain why they might not work in solving the problem. The teacher can assign each of these individual so that learners may not even know that they are learning different aspects of the same skill. (https://www.schology.com/blog/differentiated-instruction-definition-examples-and-strategies, accessed September 2021).

Importance of Customized Resources

i. **Learners can learn new skills comfortably:** Menu boards and flexible grouping activities may be designed to challenge learners to step outside of their own comfort. It provides a safe atmosphere for learners to improve upon their weaker areas while they still fall back on what they are good at in doing this.

ii. **It enable learners to learn at their pace:** Customized resources help the learners gain more confidence in the subject matter. It also keeps them learning at a pace that is sensible for them. This is because they learn the material more quickly and are able to apply and expand their knowledge upon it.

iii. **Customized resources is beneficial to both the teachers and learners:** Customized resources make it easier for teachers to identify when learners are struggling with a concept (as opposed to a method of instruction). When learners enjoy learning and the learning feels customized to their individual needs, it becomes more enjoyable. Because of this, they are more likely to achieve at a higher level and remember the content over and again. This gives the instructor clues about when a topic needs to revisited or a learner may need more support.

iv. **It allow teachers/trainees to be more flexible:** Customized resources allow the teachers to be more flexible and make classroom more dynamic. For instance; allowing learners a choice of visual, auditory, or hands-on method of approaching the topic. This means that customized resources make simple adjustments to the lesson and provide a new way of fun to approach lesson planning. These activities tend to be more open-ended and inquiry focused, allowing the teacher to step into a facilitator role. When learners' are engaged in activities designed to meet them where they are, they are more likely to enjoy the topic even better (https://tenneyschool.com/differentiation-customized-instruction-necessary, accessed September 2021).

Improvised Instructional Material

Improvisation is the capacity of bringing existing fragments and combine them sequentially in a modern combination for a set goal. Teachers or learners utilize methods to these fragments in a very flexible nature.

Advantages of Improvisation

- It brings out ones playful side.
- It helps an individual to become a team player.
- It allows one to be a more positive person.
- It makes one a better listener.
- It helps one enjoy the moment.

- It makes one more creative.
- It helps an individual make big choices.
  (https://www.playyourwaysane.com/blog/advantages-of-improvisation, accessed September 2021).

Disadvantages of Improvisation

- Adult learners do not get enough chance to play.
- It is abstract; this is because your team decides what the exercises mean.
- It is risky or threatening.
- It is pleasurable.
- It is unprecedented.
- It is conceptual.
- It is on the spot.

Importance of Improvisation in Learning

i.   Learners are more creative.
ii.   Learners listen better.
iii. Learners collaborate better.
iv.   Learners have fun.
v.   Learners get more comfortable with taking risks.
vi.   Learners write more.
vii. Learners are less judgmental and more open to other perspectives.

8.0 Consumables and Machinery

Consumables are educational products that the learner will use up completely and therefore the product cannot be used by another learner. While nonconsumables are educational items that can be used again by another learner. (https://creativehomelife.com/the-ultimate-consumable-idea-list-for-charter-school-funding/, accessed September 2021).

Consumable materials are also known as supplies, which are distributed to teachers and learners for the implementation of the instructional program. Supplies include paper, clay, chalk, string, scissors, markers, pencils, artistic materials, adhesive tape, soap, and the like (https://www.vtsd.com/vtsd-pol-regs/instructional-supplies, accessed September 2021).

Examples of consumable products

i.   Educational items
  - Printer papers
  - Envelops
  - Batteries
  - Whiteboard markers
  - Calculators
  - Computer cables

    ii.   Classes

    iii. Subscriptions

    iv. Field trips

    v.   Memberships

    vi. Information packets

    vii. Workbooks

Examples of nonconsumable products

These are educational items in which learners can borrow, rent or check out, such as a regular library. This is where he/she can borrow educational materials like

- Projector
- Computers
- Instrument
- Chairs
- Electronic equipment
- Books, and the likes

Importance of consumables during classroom

    i.   It allows learners to do what consume the text and own its content.

    ii. It allows learners' to annotate, talk, highlight, question, and even sketchnote or booksnap the text, without penalty.

    iii. Consumable serve as a reference guide to refresh learning.

    iv. Consumable aid the learners to understand, create, apply, remember, analyze, and evaluate their readiness in career choice.

Machinery

Machinery is a system by which something is kept in action or desired result is obtained (Merriam Webster Dictionary, accessed September 2021). Machine is described as a mechanically, electrically, or electronically operated device for performing a task (Merriam Webster Dictionary, accessed September 2021). Having known what machinery and machine is, we want to critically explain how machine is significant and appropriate or compatible with learning. Pairing the two words we have what is called "Machine Learning." What is machine learning will ever be in the mind of those who have not heard or come across this word, or one may think that it is a new topic but history has it that this concept existed since 1950, these was when Alan Turing published a paper answering the question "can machines think?"

Frank Rosenblatt designed the first neural network for computers in 1957, which is recently and commonly called the perception model.

Diagram illustrating types of machine learning

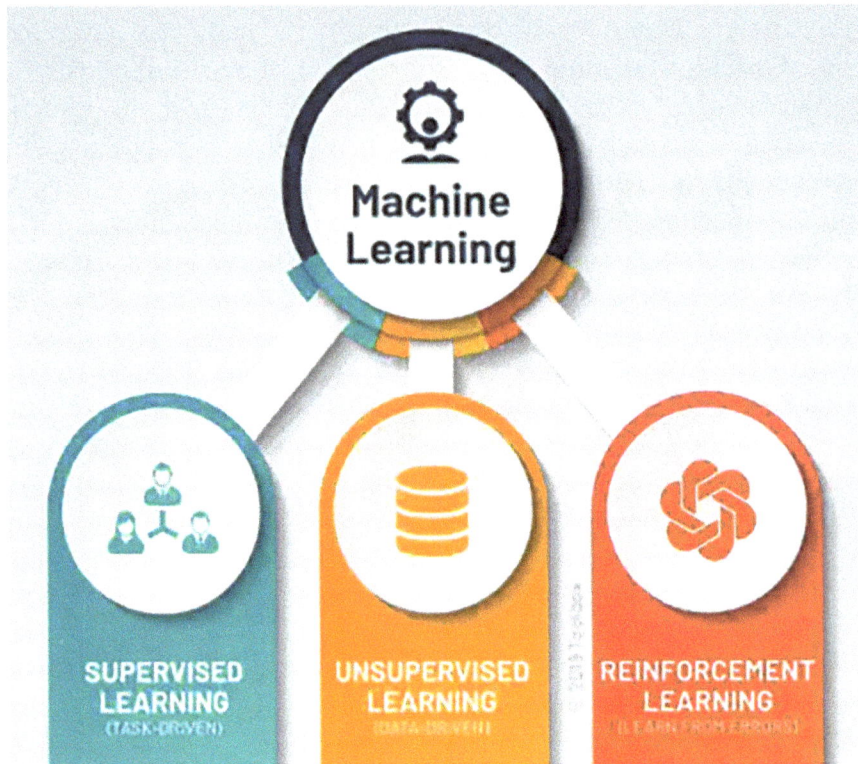

https://www.verzero.com/blog-what-is-machine-learning, accessed September 2021.

Bernard Widrow and Marcian Hoff created two neural network models canned Adeline in 1959 that could detect binary patterns and Madeline that could eliminate echo on phone lines. The Nearest Neighbour Algorithm was written that allowed computers to use very basic pattern recognition in 1967. Gerald DeJonge introduced the concept of explanation-based learning in 1981, in which a computer analyzes data and creates a general rule to discard unimportant information.

Work on machine learning shifted from knowledge-driven approach to a more data-driven approach during 1990. In this era, scientists began creating programs for computers to analyze large amounts of data and draw conclusion or "learn" from the results. Which finally overtime after several developments formulated into the modern age of machine learning. Machine learning is the circle of computer science which constitute the machine suitable for learning on its own without being specifically predetermined.

"Machine learning is defined as the study of computer programs that leverage algorithms and statistical models to learn through inference and patterns without being explicitly programmed. Machine learning field has undergone significant developments in the last decade" (https://www.potentiaco.com/what-is-machine-learning-definition-types-applications-and-examples/accessed-September,2021).

Types of machine learning

Machine learning is divided into three main areas, namely:

- Supervised machine learning
- Unsupervised machine learning
- Reinforcement machine learning

- **Supervised machine learning:** This type of machine learning means training the machine learning model just like a coach trains a batsman. In this learning, the machine learns under the guidance of labeled data (i.e., known data). This known data is fed to the machine learning model and is used to train it.

- **Unsupervised machine learning:** It means the MI model is self-sufficient in learning on its own. In unsupervised machine learning, the training data is unknown or unlabeled. This unknown data is fed to the machine learning model and is used to train the mode. The mode tries to find patterns and relationships in the dataset by creating clusters in it.

- **Reinforcement machine learning:** Here, the machine learns from a hit and trial method. Whenever the model predicts or produces a result, it is penalized if the prediction is wrong or rewarded if the prediction is correct. Based on these actions the model trains itself. (https://www.verzero.com/blog-what-is-machine-learning-accessed-September,2021).

Uses of machine learning

i.   It is used for predictive analytics.
ii. It is used for statistical arbitrage.
iii. It is used for translation of speech (speech recognition).
iv. It is used for medical diagnosis.
v.   It is used for extraction.
vi. It is used for facial recognition within an image. (https://www.salesforce.com/eu/blog/2020/06/real-world-examples-of-machine-learning.html, accessed September 2021).

Advantages of machine learning

- Wide range of applications.
- Automation for everything.
- Trends and patterns identification.
- Continuous improvement.

Disadvantages of machine learning

- Time-consuming.
- Highly error-prone.
- Data acquisition.
- Algorithm selection. (https://ivyproschool.com/blog/advantages-and-disadvatages-of-machine-learning-in-2020, accessed September 2021).

9.0 Conclusion

In this chapter, we have the importance of instructional materials as it relates to skill training, advantages and disadvantages of instructional materials, things to consider when selecting instructional material. We proceeded to discuss the general learning resources, reading materials, handbooks and syllabuses. We

went further to analyze multimedia components, tools and equipment, customized/improvised resources, consumables and machinery.

Instructional materials/resources should be seen as a source from which the trainer/trainee will benefit and accomplish their activity and achieve their set goals. The trainer should not just purchase instructional materials but should improvise (teacher-made resources). Improvise or teacher-made resource include anything the teacher/trainer creates and are useful for training/learning of any given topic which it was created for. It must meet the standard of the learning outcome.

Chapter Twenty-Three

Inclusive Skill Training

1.0 Introduction

Inclusive skill training is the type of education which trainees/learners with disabilities or impairment are merged with regular or general learner population in the same classroom and are trained with the same curriculum. These persons have been excluded because of their gender, race, sexuality or ability, down syndrome, autism spectrum, learning delays, among other disabilities.

The contents of this chapter are carefully selected and arranged to meet the purpose of inclusiveness in skill training.

2.0 gives an overview of philosophy of inclusiveness (skill is a right).

3.0 treat the dynamics of inclusive learning.

4.0 deals with the value of inclusiveness, values that promote a diverse and inclusiveness in skill training.

5.0 traces relevant methodologies in inclusive skill training, importance of inclusive training/teaching.

6.0 detailed the similarities and differences in inclusiveness, integration and mainstreaming.

7.0 elucidates UN convention on the rights of persons with disabilities.

8.0 explains inclusive practices or approaches while 9.0 concludes with the overview of inclusive skill training.

2.0 Philosophy of Inclusiveness: Skill Is a Right

Inclusive simply means including everyone especially allowing and accommodating people who have historically been excluded (as because of their race, gender, sexuality, or ability). "Inclusive" as related to education refers to including learners with disabilities and learners without severe disabilities to learn side-by-side. It helps to undo the stigma associated with special education. (Merriam Webster Dictionary accessed, October, 2021.

The general learner's population are taught the same curriculum. Learners with special needs are given occupational therapy inside the classroom instead of being pulled out. 'Inclusion' in education has become the term used to describe the right of parents and children to access mainstream education alongside their peers, where parents what it and children's needs can be met.

Inclusion is seen as a universal right which aim to embrace all people irrespective of race, gender, disability, medical or other need. It is about giving equal access and opportunities and getting rid of discrimination and intolerance (https://www.inclusion.me.UK/news/what-does-inclusion-mean, accessed October 2021).

Inclusive skill training is referred to as providing workshops or places that special need learners/trainees and normal learners can use for training various skills. These places or workshops should be designed to affect both learner's ability to move, hear, see and communicate effectively.

Inclusive skill training aims to eradicate the obstructions that hinder undue effort and separation. Trainees are able to participate confidently equally and independently in their day-to-day activities.

The Principles of Inclusivity

1. Acknowledge individuals have unique and particular needs in the learning and working environment.
2. Promote inclusitivity by reasonably adjusting procedures, activities and physical environments.
3. Serve all with sensitivity, respect and fairness.
4. Respect each individual's right to express and present themselves relative to their religion, sexual orientation, culture, gender-identity, ethnic background, physical and mental ability.
5. Be inclusive in all forms of communication.
6. Focus on the capability of the individual without assumptions or labels.
   (https://uwaterloo.ca/organizational-human-development/learning-development-programs/inclusivity-series/principles-inclusivity, accessed October 2021.

Inclusive educators are those who draw on the knowledge and experiences of their learners. They are flexible and ready for a challenge; they also embrace diversity in their workshop or classroom.

Steps to Inclusion in Skill Training

1. **Training management should be sure about the administration of training center they may intend to apply:** This has to do with the organization of training centers, schools and workshops, the training methodologies that should be used during training and the evaluation method. This step also view learner's/trainee's dependability, punctuality, participation and the outcomes of training across the curriculum. It involves the moral responsibility on those trainees who may be at risk are statistically and carefully monitored (i.e., the trainer must be vigilant in watching careless trainees).

2. **Training management/instructors should expound a shared means of communication of training/learning:** Here, trainers or instructors should create time and chance to visit another colleague while training to monitor and develop more inclusive practices. They can help each other through shared experiences and to articulate they experience during their visitation. This will triggered language of practice about detailed aspects of their practice.

   This means that there should be a collaborative process of experts in different fields of training coming together as a group to design the training plan and notes, which they will implement by each trainer (turn taking) and their colleagues observing how the trainees reach or respond. Micro-training should be arranged between each trial of training.

3. **Apportion of obligation for instructors:** This requires schools with an inclusive culture to characterized and present leaders who are committed to inclusive value and leadership style in a hierarchical structures to function as team. This requires new thinking and practices among them to encourage movement in an inclusive direction. They must also place a strong emphasis on the use of inquiry to stimulate experimentation with new ways of working.

4. **The application of subsist skills and knowledge:** This allows effective practices to be identified and shared while, at the same time, draws attention to ways of working that may be create barriers

to participation and learning of some learners. Teaches who are effective in responding to learner diversity use a range of teaching/training approaches, from which they choose that they judge to be appropriate for a particular lesson. These decisions take account of a range of inter-connected factors, such as the subject to be taught, the age and experience of the class, the environmental conditions of the classroom and the available resources. In schools that make progress on their inclusive journey, teachers help one another to improve their skill in improvisation. This involves sharing practices and working together to find better ways of reaching hard to reach learners. The use of such practices can be effective means of supporting the involvement of those learners who are new to a class, learners from different cultural backgrounds, and those with disabilities.

5. **Encourage esteem regard for diverseness:** When schools are successful in moving in a more inclusive direction, there is usually a degree of consensus among adults around values of esteem regard for diverseness and commitment to offering all learners access to learning opportunities.

Furthermore, there is likely to be a high level of staff collaboration and joint problem-solving, and similar values and commitments may extend into the learner body, and among families and other community stakeholders associated with the school. The key factor is the emphasis placed on tracking and supporting (https://www.eduforics.com/en/steps-to-inclusion-in-schools, accessed October 2021).

3.0 Dynamics of Inclusive Learning

The teaching-learning process is an inherently social act, and as instructors, they need to be mindful of the quality of the social and emotional dynamics in the course they teach, because they impact learning and performance.

There are a number of strategies instructors can implement to create a productive and inclusive climate. These strategies include

Source: Inclusive Learning Environment Strategies, by the Center for Excellence in Learning and Teaching (CELT) at Lowa State University is licensed under creative commons BY-NC-SA 4.0

(https://www.celt.iastate.edu/teaching/creating-an-inclusive-classroom/creating-an-inclusive-learning-environment, accessed October 2021).

- **Class dynamics:** Classroom dynamics involve the interaction between learners and teachers or instructors in a classroom community. Classroom dynamics assist the instructors on how to set up a positive classroom atmosphere where learners feel comfortable learning and communicating with other learners and with the trainer/teacher. Components of classroom dynamics involve discipline, gender, participation and motivation.

- **Discipline:** Instructors should inform learners from the beginning of the class what their behavioral expectations are for them. This is because every classroom needs a behavioral code to maintain order. Learners will never feel comfortable to express themselves in a classroom without rules. It helps if they also have a discussion to get feedback from the learners about the rules and to clarify any confusion. When a learner breaks a rule, it is important that the teachers follow through with the predetermined consequences.

- **Gender:** Proper classroom dynamics will include both genders and be mindful of their different needs. Some classes isolate, embarrass or exclude a particular gender from the classroom by the activities or by the discussions.

- **Participation:** Good classroom dynamics will include all learners in its activities and discussion. Instructors must show an interest in every individual learner and encourage him or her to participate in the classroom. Classroom participation is not, however only about the learners. The teacher/trainer has to be willing to participate fully in class discussions and activities to create lively and dynamic classroom dynamics. A teacher that merely goes on teaching the material without noticing whether the learners are understanding it has a major problem with classroom dynamics.

- **Motivation:** Every classroom must out of necessity have slightly different dynamics because they all consist of different learners. Each learner has his or her own interests and talents, so each classroom should be flexible enough to accommodate the individuality of its learners. Some learners are not naturally motivated to learn within the constraints of a classroom, while some are more motivated when they feel that the classroom dynamics focus on their goals and interests. (https://classroom.synonym.com/classroom-dynamics-7946454.html-accessed-October,2021).

- **Examine your curriculum:** Neglecting some issues implies a value judgment (hooks 1994), which can alienate certain groups of learners. This means that there are certain perspectives systematically not represented in your course material that is very crucial to teaching-learning. For example; a course on family focusing only on traditional families, or a course on public policy ignoring race issues.

- **Establish ground rules for interaction:** This will assure that other learners are also being inclusive and respectful. To generate maximal buy-in into the ground rules, an instructor can involve the learners in the process of establishing them, and will still need to enforce the ground rules and correct learners for the occasional noninclusive or disrespectful comment.

- **Examine your assumptions as an instructor:** It is very common for instructors to assume that learners shares their own background, but this is not necessarily so. Do you find yourself as an instructor, addressing learners as if they all share social identities with you?

- **Use multiple and diverse examples:** Multiple examples increase the likelihood of learners relating to at least one of them. Take care of include examples that speak to both sexes or gender and that work across cultures.

- **Learn to use learner's names:** As an instructor, you can start building up to know your learner's names even in large classes. At the very least, let learners know that you are making an effort to do so.

- **Strive to be fair:** Perceptions of unfairness can induce feelings of learned helplessness (Peterson *et al.,* 1995), which are highly demotivating for learners. It is crucial to be perceived as fair, both in grading and in implementing course policies, especially in courses with multiple sections and teaching assistants.

- **Do not ask people to speak for an entire group (team):** Learners of underrepresented identities often report either feeling invisible in class or sticking out like a sore thumb as the token member. This experience is heightened when they are addressed as spokespeople for their whole group and can have implications on performance (Lord and Saenz, 1985).

- **Be mindful of low ability cues:** Some instructors inadvertently send mixed messages in their efforts to help learners. These clues encourage attributions focused on permanent, uncontrollable causes, which diminish learner's self-efficacy. Instead, it is more productive to focus on controllable causes, such as effort.

- **Model inclusive language:** When an instructor, uses United States English idioms, explain them for the benefit of nonnative English speakers. For instance, avoid using masculine pronouns for both males and females.

- **Provide accommodations for learners with disabilities:** Instructors are required by law to provide reasonable accommodations to learners with documented disabilities.

4.0 Value of Inclusiveness

There is an emphasis on value of inclusiveness in an organization, education, and in the corporate culture. But we cannot over look diversity, when we are discussing inclusiveness. This is because they are core values of any organization, education, and the likes. Let us discuss what it means to value diversity and how diversity and inclusiveness can be implemented as a core value.

Impacting inclusion as a core value requires maintaining a state of feeling respected, supported, and valued, focusing on the individual needs of learners, and ensuring the right conditions for learners to achieve their full potential. This core value differences and offers respect for every learner in terms of words and actions, allowing them to bring their entire, authentic selves to learn.

A diverse education means a variety of talents, skills, culture, and values coming together as one. It can be a major challenge to be in the same learning environment with people where they have different beliefs, ideas, and values different from yours. These differences can lead to resistance and changes. However, the benefits of a diverse education outweigh these challenges.

To impact diversity as a core value, trainers/teacher should respect and appreciate differences in gender ethnicity, physical abilities, race, religion, education among others. Instructors should be empowered as individuals and trusted to make the decisions that are in the best interest of teaching and learning.

Value of Diversity and Inclusion in Skill Training

Diversity and inclusion have risen ahead, when done correctly affects the skill training directly below line. It is more pivotal and critical than ever before to ensure that the skill-training center utilizes and embraces diversity and inclusion.

Regardless of the background and characteristics of the learners, it is important that they are supported and included in team work for their personal success as well as for the success of the group. Inclusive characters in learning allow the instructor to unlock the innovative potential to increase their cognition (https://www.emexmag.com/diversity-as-a-core-value/accessed-October,2021).

Values That Promote Diversity and Inclusiveness in Skill Training

1. **Value of diversity:** This is described as respecting a variety of cultures and behavior or characters. As an instructor, you should exhibit the value of diversity by respecting other cultures and behavior. You should take an interest in learning about different cultures and learners' behavior and you will be aware of how cultural differences affect behaviors.

2. **Value of fairness:** This is referred to as treating people and being treated fairly. The trainer/instructor should thrive on openness, honesty and transparency. Life may not always be fair, but you should never use that as an excuse to treat others unfairly. The trainer should believe that others on the team should be included in decision making, also in execution of task, and should approachable.

3. **Value of teamwork:** As an instructor, when you value teamwork, cooperation and collaboration that simply means that you value every learner working together toward a common goal and unique talents. A diverse set of learners with different points of view make better outcomes.

4. **The value of courage:** When it comes to building a diverse and inclusive skill training, having the courage to embrace what may not be familiar to you and the courage to embrace differences, as an instructor, you will also exhibit the courage to examine yourself to be more self-aware, welcome, and engage the differences of learners.

Also have the courage to change and grow where necessary to create a diverse and inclusive skill that will take the learners to the next level (https://corporatesolutions.johnmaxwell.com/blog/values-that-drive-a-diverse-and-inclusive-culture/accessed-October,2021.

5.0 Relevant Methodologies in Inclusive Skill Training (Instructional Principles) P. 91

Inclusive teaching strategies refer to any number of teaching approaches that address the needs of learners/trainers with a variety of backgrounds, learning modalities, and abilities. These strategies contribute to an overall inclusive learning/training environment in which learners feel equally valued.

Inclusive Classroom Methodologies or Strategies

Building or creating a safe space for different learning instructions; learning styles, racial, religious and ethnic backgrounds, genders and the likes should be put into considerations. Here are some strategies for inclusive classroom:

- **Get to know your leaners and let them get to know you:** It takes time to establish a bond with learners. As an instructor/trainer, think about what can work, something you can do consistently to connect with each learners. Create opportunities for learners to share their interests, struggles and aspirations with you and you have to motivate and encourage them by sharing yours with them to build a connection that will eventually grow.
- **Create a safe space for learners to share:** Reinforcing social-emotional skills like empathy and compassion in your classroom fosters positive interactions between learners. Learners also need explicit time to establish connections with their peers. As a trainer, split learners regularly into new small groups and use the "I see, I think, I wonder" strategy to digest something they have learned about or a current event that may be on their minds. By modeling how this should work and creating group norms, learners can have fruitful conversations that build empathy and share different opinions in a respectful way.
- **Instructions should be deliver in diverse ways:** There should be increasing evidence that shows that gamified lessons positively influence learner engagement. To appeal to different learning styles, reimagine existing lessons, especially those that feel lecture heavy, with fresh videos, books, and gamified digital activities.

    Varied learning content that appeals to different learner interests is just as essential as the instruction style. Provide learners the chance to learn about a social justice movement, history or current events through different mediums and have the unit culminate in a team-based project.
- **Choose relevant literature:** Part of culturally responsive teaching includes providing learners with literary works that highlight the human experience. Include indigenous, African American and refugee stories, as well stories that include characters with a physical or learning disability.
- **Invite guest speakers to share their stories:** When learners can identify with a trainer or instructor or guest speaker's racial or ethnic background they are more likely to perform higher and be more engaged as they see a potential role model or mentor in that person. By inviting a guest speaker. As an instructor, you are providing your leaners access to an authentic learning experience they may never otherwise have (https://everfi.com/blog/k-12/inclusive-classroom-strategies/accessed-October,2021.

Importance of Inclusive Teaching/Training

- Learners feel comfortable in the classroom environment to voice their ideas/questions.
- Trainers/instructors can connect and engage with a variety of learners.
- Learners connect with course materials that are relevant to them.
- Learners are more likely to be successful through activities that support their learning modalities, abilities and backgrounds.
- Trainers/instructors are prepared for "hot moments" that may arise when controversial material is discussed.

Source: Amrbose, S. A; Bridges, M. W., Dipietro, M., and Lovett, M. C. (2010). How learning works: seven research-based principles for smart teaching. San Francisco, CA: Joossey Bass. (https://teaching.cornell.edu/teaching-resources/building-inclusive-classroom/inclusive-teaching-strategies-accessed-October,2021).

6.0 Inclusiveness, Integration and Mainstreaming: Similarities and Differences

Inclusion refers to the merging of special education and regular education with the belief that all learners should have access to the same curriculum. It states that all learners are different, so they should learn differently. The involved barriers get removed so that every learners can get equal value and fully participate in the curriculum. It uses different techniques and accepts the diversity of learners to benefit every learners.

An integrated classroom refers to a setting where the learners suffering from disabilities learn with other standard learners. Extra support is used to implement learning so that learners can adapt to the regular academic curriculum. Subsequently, separate education programs are also started within the classroom for motivating the learners with disabilities (https://www.irelandassignmenthelp.com/samples/difference-between-integration-and-inclusion/accessed-October,2021).

Mainstreaming is the practice of educating learners with special needs in regular classes during specific time period, based on their individual skills (https://www.calstatela.edu/academic/CCOE/programs/cats/mainstreaming/accessed/October,2021).

• Inclusion focusses on every learner in the classroom.	Integration focusses on only those learners who are suffering from special needs.	Mainstreaming is the practice of placing learners with special education during specific time periods based on their skills.
• Inclusion states that learners with disabilities do not adjust to a fixed education structure, instead, the structure gets altered, so the learning styles of every learner get fulfilled.	Integration improves social skills and exposes the learners to adapt typical classroom structure.	Mainstreaming classroom expects learners to perform and maintain comparable pace with learners who do not have disabilities (normal learners).

• In inclusion, the system changes to assist the education procedure of the learners.	Integration is a matter which varies according to the requirements of special needs learners.	Mainstream is suitable for disabled learners who could perform to near average of the regular classroom learners.
• The main objective of inclusion is to improve the overall development of the learners in the classroom activities instead to fit the learner according to the education system.	Integration aims to meet the learners with special needs in the education system.	Mainstreaming focuses on learners with special needs having a right to equal opportunity in the regular classroom, regular environment, and stimulation of typical peers to gain functional life and work skills and to develop social relationship.
• Inclusion is the process of educating the learners so that they can participate in classroom event.	Integration is the process in which children with special education needs have to adjust according to the mainstream education system.	Mainstreaming is provided as a supplement to primary placement in special education where specific social and academic opportunities are targeted.

7.0   UN Convention on the Rights of Persons with Disabilities (Un, 2006): A Review

The purpose of the present convention is to promote, protect, and ensure the full and equal enjoyment of all human rights and fundamental freedoms by all persons with disabilities, and to promote respect for their inherent dignity.

Persons with disabilities include those who have long-term physical, mental, intellectual or sensory impairments which in interaction with various barriers may hinder their full and effective participation in society on an equal basis with others.

For the purpose of the present convention:

"Communication" includes languages, display of text, Braille, tactile communication, large print, accessible multimedia as well as written, audio, plain-language, human-reader and augmentative and alternative modes, means and formats of communication, including accessible information and communication technology;

"Language" include spoken and signed languages and other forms of nonspoken languages.

"Discrimination on the basis of disability" means and distinction, exclusion or restriction on the basis of disability which has the purpose or effect of impairing or nullifying the recognition, enjoyment or exercise, on an equal basis with others, of all human rights and fundamental freedoms in the political, economic, social, cultural, civil or any other field. It includes all forms of discrimination, including denial of reasonable accommodation;

"Reasonable accommodation" means necessary and appropriate modification and adjustments not imposing a disproportionate or undue burden, where needed in a particular case, to ensure to persons with disabilities the enjoyment or exercise on an equal basis with others of all human rights and fundamental freedoms;

"Universal design" means the design of products, environments programs and services to be usable by all people, to the greatest extent possible, without the need for adaptation or specialized design. "Universal design" shall not exclude assistive devices for particular groups of persons with disabilities where this is needed.

General Principles

The principles of the present convention shall be:

- Respect for inherent dignity, individual autonomy including the freedom to make one's own choices, and independence of persons;
- Nondiscrimination;
- Full and effective participation and inclusion in society;
- Respect for difference and acceptance of persons with disabilities as part of human diversity and humanity;
- Equality of opportunity;
- Accessibility;
- Equality between men and women;
- Respect for the evolving capacities of children with disabilities and respect for the right of children with disabilities to preserve their identities;

General Obligations

- States parties undertake to ensure and promote the full realization of all human rights and fundamental freedoms for all persons with disabilities without discrimination of any kind on the basis of disability. To this end, states parties undertake:
  a. To adopt all appropriate legislative, administrative and other measures for the implementation of the rights recognized in the present convention;
  b. To take all appropriate measures, including legislation, to modify or abolish existing laws, regulations, customs and practices that constitute discrimination against persons with disabilities.
  c. To take into account the protection and promotion of the human rights of persons with disabilities in all policies and programs;
  d. To refrain from engaging in any act or practice that is in consistent with the present convention and to ensure that public authorities and institutions act in conformity with the present convention;
  e. To take all appropriate measures to eliminate discrimination on the basis of disability by any person, organization or private enterprise;
  f. To undertake or promote research and development of universally designed goods, services, equipment and facilities, which should require the minimum possible adaptation and the least cost to meet the specific needs of a person with disabilities, to promote their availability and use, and to promote universal design in the development of standards and guidelines;
  g. To undertake or promote research and development of, and to promote the availability and use of new technologies, including information and communications technologies, mobility aids, devices and assistive technologies, suitable for persons with disabilities, giving priority to technologies at an affordable cost;
  h. To provide accessible information to persons with disabilities about mobility aids, devices and assistive technologies, including new technologies, as well as other forms of assistance, support services and facilities;
  i. To promote the training of professionals and staff working with persons with disabilities in the rights recognized in the present convention so as to better provide the assistance and services guaranteed by those rights;

- With regard to economic, social and cultural rights, each state party undertakes to take measures to the maximum of its available resources and, where needed, within the framework of international cooperation, with a view to achieving progressively the full realization of these rights, without prejudice to those obligations contained in the present convention that are immediately applicable according to international law.
- In the development and implementation of legislation and policies to implement the present convention, and in other decision-making processes concerning issues relating to persons with disabilities, states parties shall closely consult with an actively involve persons with disabilities, including children with disabilities, through their representative organizations.
- Nothing in the present convention shall affect any provisions which are more conducive to the realization of the rights of persons with disabilities and which may be contained in the law of a state party or international law in force of that state. There shall be no restriction upon or derogation from any of the human rights and fundamental freedoms recognized or existing in any state party to the present convention pursuant to law, conventions, regulation, or custom on the pretext that the present convention does not recognize such rights or freedoms or that it recognizes them to a lesser extent.
- The provisions of the present convention shall extend to all parts of federal states without any limitations or exceptions.

Equality and Nondiscrimination

i) States parties recognize that all persons are equal before and under the law and are entitled without discrimination to the equal protection and equal benefit of law.

ii) States parties shall prohibit all discrimination on the basis of disability and guarantee to persons with disabilities equal and effective legal protection against discrimination on all grounds.

iii) To promote equality and eliminate discrimination, states parties shall take all appropriate steps to ensure that reasonable accommodation is provided.

iv) Specific measures which are necessary to accelerate or achieve de facto equality of persons with disabilities shall not be considered discrimination under the terms of the present convention.

Women with Disabilities

1. States parties recognize that women and girls with disabilities are subject to multiple discrimination, and in this regard shall take measures to ensure the full and equal enjoyment by them of all human rights and fundamental freedoms.

2. States parties shall take all appropriate measures to ensure the full development, advancement and empowerment of women, for the purpose of guaranteeing them the exercise and enjoyment of the human rights and fundamental freedoms set out in the present convention.

Children with Disabilities

- States parties shall take all necessary measures to ensure the full enjoyment by children with disabilities of all human rights and fundamental freedoms on all equal basis with other children.
- In all actions concerning children with disabilities, the best interests of the child shall be a primary consideration.

- States parties shall ensure that children with disabilities have the right to express their views freely on all matters affecting them, their views being given due weight in accordance with their age and maturity, on an equal basis with other children, and to be provided with disability and age appropriate assistance to realize that right.

Awareness-Raising

1. States parties undertake to adopt immediate, effective and appropriate measures:
    a. To raise awareness throughout society, including at the family level, regarding persons with disabilities, and to foster respect for frights and dignity of persons with disabilities;
    b. To combat stereotypes, prejudices and harmful practices relating to persons with disabilities, including those based on sex and age, in all areas of life;
    c. To promote awareness of the capabilities and contributions of persons with disabilities.
2. Measures to this end include
    a. Initiating and maintaining effective public awareness campaigns designed:
        i) To nurture receptiveness to the rights of persons with disabilities.
        ii) To promote positive perceptions and greater social awareness toward persons with disabilities;
        iii) To promote recognition of the skills, merits and disabilities of persons with disabilities, and of their contributions to the workplace and the labor market;
    b. Fostering at all levels of the education system, including in all form of early age, an attitude of respect for the rights of persons with disabilities;
    c. Encouraging all organs of the media to portray persons with disabilities in a manner consistent with the purpose of the present convention;
    d. Promoting awareness-training programs regarding persons with disabilities and the rights of persons with disabilities.

Accessibility

1. To enable persons with disabilities to live independently and participate fully in all aspects of life, states parties shall take appropriate measures to ensure to persons with disabilities access, on an equal basis with others, to the physical environment, to transportation, to information and communications, including information and communications technologies and systems, and to other facilities and services open or provided to the public, both in urban and in rural areas. These measures, which shall include the identification and elimination of obstacles and barriers to accessibility, shall apply to, inter alia:
    a. Building, roads, transportation and other indoor and outdoor facilities, including schools, housing, medical facilities and workplaces;
    b. Information, communications and other services, including electronic services and emergency services.
2. States parties shall also take appropriate measures:
    a. To develop, promulgate and monitor the implementation of minimum standards and guidelines for the accessibility of facilities and services open or provided to the public;
    b. To ensure that private entities that offer facilities and services which are open or provided to the public take into accounts all aspects of accessibility for persons with disabilities;
    c. To provide training for stakeholders on accessibility issues facing persons with disabilities;

d. To provide in buildings and other facilities open to the public signage in Braille and in easy to read and understand forms;

e. To provide forms of live assistance and intermediaries, including guides, readers and professional sign language interpreters, to facilitate accessibility to buildings and other facilities open to the public;

f. To promote other appropriate forms of assistance and support to persons with disabilities to ensure their access to information;

g. To promote access for persons with disabilities to new information and communications technologies and systems, including the internet;

h. To promote the design, development, production and distribution of accessible information and communications technologies and systems at an early stage, so that these technologies and systems become accessible at minimum cost.

Right to Life

States parties reaffirm that every human being has the inherent right to life and shall take all necessary measures to ensure its effective enjoyment by persons with disabilities on an equal basis with others.

Situations of Risk and Humanitarian Emergencies

States parties shall take, in accordance with their obligations under international law, including international humanitarian law and international human rights law, all necessary measures to ensure the protection and safety of person's armed conflict, humanitarian emergencies and the occurrence of natural disasters.

Equal Recognition before the Law

1. States parties reaffirm that persons with disabilities have the right to recognition everywhere as person before the law.

2. States parties shall recognize that persons with disabilities enjoy legal capacity on an equal basis with others in all aspects of life.

3. States parties shall take appropriate measures to provide access by persons with disabilities to the support they may require in exercising their legal capacity.

4. States parties shall ensure that all measures that relate to the exercise safeguards to prevent abuse in accordance with international human rights law. Such safeguards shall ensure that measures relating to the exercise of legal capacity respect the rights, will and preferences of the person, are free of conflict of interest and undue influence, are proportional and tailored to the person's circumstances, apply for the shortest time possible and are subject to regular review by a competent, independent and impartial authority or judicial body. The safeguards shall be proportional to the degree to which such measures affect the person's rights and interests.

5. States parties shall take all appropriate and effective measures to ensure the equal right of persons with disabilities to own or inherit property, to control their own financial affairs and to have equal access to bank loans, mortgages and other forms of financial credit, and shall ensure that persons with disabilities are not arbitrarily deprived of their property.

Access to Justice

1. States parties shall ensure effective access to justice for persons with disabilities on an equal basis with others, including through the provision of procedural and age-appropriate accommodations, to facilitate their effective role as direct and indirect participants, including as witnesses, in all legal proceedings, including at investigative and other preliminary stages.
2. To help to ensure effective access to justice for persons with disabilities, states parties shall promote appropriate training for those working in the field of administration of justice, including police and prison staff.

Liberty and Security of Person

1. States parties shall ensure that persons with disabilities on an equal basis with others;
   a. Enjoy the right to liberty and security of person;
   b. Are not deprived of their liberty unlawfully or arbitrarily, and that any deprivation of liberty is in conformity with the law, and that the existence of a disability shall in no case justify a deprivation of liberty.
2. States parties shall ensure that if persons with disabilities are deprived of their liberty through any process, they are, on an equal basis with others, entitled to guarantees in accordance with international human rights law and shall be treated in compliance with the objectives and principles of the present convention, including by provision of reasonable accommodation.

Freedom from Torture or Cruel, Inhuman, or Degrading Treatment or Punishment

a. No one shall be subjected to torture or to cruel, inhuman, or degrading treatment or punishment. In particular, no one shall be subjected without his or her free consent to medical or scientific experimentation.
b. States parties shall take all effective legislative, administrative, judicial or other measures to prevent persons with disabilities, on an equal basis with others, from being subjected to torture or cruel, inhuman or degrading treatment or punishment.

Freedom from Exploitation, Violence, and Abuse

- States parties shall take all appropriate legislative administrative, social, educational and other measures to protect persons with disabilities, both within and outside the home, from all forms of exploitation, violence and abuse, including their gender-based aspects.
- States parties shall also take all appropriate measures to prevent all forms of exploitation, violence and abuse by ensuring inter alia, appropriate forms of gender-and-age-sensitive assistance and support for persons with disabilities and their families and caregivers, including through the provision of information and education on how to avoid, recognize and report instances of exploitation, violence and abuse. States parties shall ensure that protection services are age-gender-and disability-sensitive.
- To prevent the occurrence of all forms of exploitation, violence and abuse, states parties shall ensure that all facilities and programs designed to serve persons with disabilities are effectively monitored by independent authorities.

- States parties shall take all appropriate measures to promote the physical, cognitive and psychological recovery, rehabilitation and social reintegration of persons with disabilities who become victims of any form of exploitation, violence or abuse, including through the provision of protection services. Such recovery and reintegration shall take place in an environment that fosters the health, welfare, self-respect, dignity and autonomy of the person and takes into account gender-and age-specific needs.
- States parties shall put in place effective legislation on policies, including women-and child-focused legislation and policies, to ensure that instances of exploitation, violence and abuse against persons with disabilities are identified, investigated and, where appropriate, prosecuted.

Protecting the Integrity of the Person

Every person with disabilities has a right to respect for his or her physical and mental integrity on an equal basis with others.

Liberty of Movement and Nationality

- States parties shall recognize the rights of persons with disabilities to liberty of movement, to freedom to choose their residence and to a nationality, on an equal basis with others, including by ensuring that persons with disabilities:
  a. Have the right to acquire and change a nationality and are not deprived of their nationality arbitrarily on the basis of disability;
  b. Are not deprived, on the basis of disability, of their ability to obtain, possess and utilize documentation of their nationality or other documentation of identification, or to utilize relevant processes such as immigration proceedings, that may be need to facilitate exercise of the right to liberty of movement;
  c. Are free to leave any country, including their own;
  d. Are not deprived, arbitrarily or on the basis of disability, of the right to enter their own country.
- Children with disabilities shall be registered immediately after birth and shall have the right from birth to a name, the right to acquire a nationality and, as far as possible, the right to know and be cared for by their parents.

Living Independently and Being Included in the Community

States parties to the present convention recognize the equal right of all persons with disabilities to live in the community with choices equal to others, shall take effective and appropriate measures to facilitate full enjoyment by persons with disabilities of this right and their full inclusion and participation in the community, including by ensuring that

i)   persons with disabilities have the opportunity to choose their place of residence and where and with whom they live on an equal basis with others and are not obliged to live in a particular living arrangement;
ii) persons with disabilities have access to a range of in-home, residential and other community support services, including personal assistance necessary to support living and inclusion in the community, and to prevent isolation or segregation from the community;
iii) community services and facilities for the general population are available on an equal basis to persons with disabilities and are responsive to their needs.

Personal Mobility

States parties shall take effective measures to ensure personal mobility with the greatest possible independence for persons with disabilities, including by:

a. Facilitating the personal mobility of persons with disabilities in the manner and at the time of their choice, and at affordable cost;
b. Facilitating access by persons with disabilities to quality mobility aids, devices, assistive technologies and forms of live assistance and intermediaries, including by making them available at affordable cost;
c. Providing training in mobility skills to persons with disabilities and to specialist staff working with persons with disabilities;
d. Encouraging entities that produce mobility aids, devices and assistive technologies to take into account all aspects of mobility for persons with disabilities.

Freedom of Expression and Opinion, and Access to Information

States parties shall take all appropriate measures to ensure that persons with disabilities can exercise the right to freedom of expression and opinion, including the freedom to seek, receive and impart information and ideas on an equal basis with others and through all forms of communication of their choice, including by:

i. Providing information intended for the general public to persons with disabilities in accessible formats and technologies appropriate to different kinds of disabilities in a timely manner and without additional cost;
ii. Accepting and facilitating the use of sign languages, Braille, augmentative and alternative communication, and all other accessible means, modes and formats of communication of their choice by persons with disabilities in official interactions;
iii. Urging private entities that provide services to the general public, including through the internet, to provide information and services in accessible and usable formats for persons with disabilities;
iv. Encouraging the mass media, including providers of information through the internet, to make their services accessible to persons with disabilities;
v. Encouraging the mass media, including providers of information through the internet, to make their services accessible to persons with disabilities;
vi. Recognizing and promoting the use of sign languages.

Respect for Privacy

a. No person with disabilities, regardless of place of residence or living arrangements, shall be subjected to arbitrary or unlawful interference with his or her privacy, family, home or correspondence or other types of communication or to unlawful attacks on his or her honor and reputation. Persons with disabilities have the right to the protection of the law against such interference or attacks.
b. States parties shall protect the privacy of personal, health and rehabilitation information of persons with disabilities on an equal basis with others.

Respect for Home and the Family

1. States parties shall take effective and appropriate measures to eliminate discrimination against persons with disabilities in all matters relating to marriage, family, parenthood and relationships, on an equal basis with others, so as to ensure that:
   a. The right of all persons with disabilities who re of marriageable age to marry and to found a family on the basis of free and full consent of the intending spouses is recognized;
   b. The rights of persons with disabilities to decide freely and responsibly on the number and spacing of their children and to have access to age-appropriate information, reproductive and family planning education are recognized, and the means necessary to enable them to exercise these rights are provided;
   c. Persons with disabilities, including children, retain their fertility on an equal basis with others.
2. States parties shall ensure the rights and responsibilities of persons with disabilities, with regard to guardianship, wardship, trusteeship, adoption of children or similar institutions, where these concepts exist in national legislation; in all cases, the best interests of the child shall be paramount. States parties shall render appropriate assistance to persons with disabilities in the performance of their child-rearing responsibilities.
3. States parties shall ensure that children with disabilities have equal rights with respect to family life. With a view to realizing these rights, and to prevent concealment, abandonment, neglect and segregation of children with disabilities, states parties shall undertake to provide early and comprehensive information, services and support to children with disabilities and their families.
4. States parties shall ensure that a child shall not be separated from his or her parents against their will, except when competent authorities subject to judicial review determine, in accordance with applicable law and procedures, that such separation is necessary for the best interests of the child. In no case shall a child be separated from parents on the basis of a disability of either the child or one or both of the parents.
5. States parties shall, where the immediate family is unable to care for a child with disabilities, undertake every effort to provide alternative care within the wider family, and failing that, within the community in a family setting.

Education

- States parties recognize the right of persons with disabilities to education. With a review to realizing this right without discrimination and on the basis of equal opportunity, states parties shall ensure an inclusive education system at all levels and lifelong learning directed to:
  a. The full development of human potential and sense of dignity and self-worth, and the strengthening of respect for human rights, fundamental freedoms, and human diversity;
  b. The development by persons with disabilities of their personality, talents and creativity, as well as their mental and physical abilities, to their fullest potential;
  c. Enabling persons with disabilities to participate effectively in a free society.
- In realizing this right, states parties shall ensure that:
  i. Persons with disabilities are not excluded from the general education system on the basis of disability, and that children with disabilities are not excluded from free and compulsory primary education, or from secondary education, on the basis of disability;
  ii. Persons with disabilities can access an inclusive, quality and free primary education and secondary education on an equal basis with others in the communities in which they live;

283

    iii. Reasonable accommodation of the individual's requirements is provided;

    iv. Persons with disabilities receive the support required, within the general education system, to facilitate their effective education;

    v. Effective individualized support measures are provided in environments that maximize academic and social development, consistent with the goal of full inclusion.

- States parties shall enable persons with disabilities to learn life and social development skills to facilitate their full and equal participation in education and as members of the community. To this end, states parties shall take appropriate measures, including:

- Facilitating the learning or Braille, alternative script, augmentative and alternative modes, means and formats of communication and orientation and mobility skills, and facilitating peer support and mentoring;

- Facilitating the learning of sign language and the promotion of the linguistic identity of the deaf community;

- Ensuring that the education of persons, and in particular children, who are blind, deaf or deaf-blind, is delivered in the most appropriate languages and modes and means of communication for the individual, and in environments which maximize academic and social development.

- To help ensure the realization of this right, states parties shall take appropriate measures to employ teachers, including teachers with disabilities, who are qualified in sign language or Braille, and to train professionals and staff who work at all levels of education. Such training shall incorporate disability awareness and the use of appropriate augmentative and alternative modes, means and formats of communication, educational techniques and materials to support persons with disabilities.

- States parties shall ensure that persons with disabilities are able to access general tertiary education, vocational training, adult education and lifelong learning without discrimination and on an equal basis with others. To this end, states parties shall ensure that reasonable accommodation is provided to persons with disabilities (https://www.un.org/development/desa/disabilities/convention-on-the-rights-of-persons-with-disabilities/article-35-reports-by-states-parties.html/accessed-October,2021).

8.0　Inclusive Practices or Approaches (P. 89 of Text)

Inclusive practice is a process of identifying, understanding and breaking down barriers to participation and belonging. It is also referred to as teaching/training approach that recognizes the differences between learners and uses this to ensure that all learners can access educational/training content and participate fully in their training and learning (www.highspeedtraining.co.uk).

Successful inclusive education happens primarily through accepting, understanding, and attending to learner differences and diversity, which can include physical, cognitive, academic, social and emotional.

Inclusive education is largely based on an attitude toward educating learners with special needs. Inclusive education is about educating all learners, alongside same-age peers and peers with varying abilities, in a general education classroom.

It is reliant on learner access to curriculum schools/training centers must create opportunities using activities, space and materials so that all learners can learn.

Types of Instructional Approaches

- **Technology:** Technology is vital to the twenty-first-century classroom. It provides accessibility to the curriculum for learners with special needs. Technology can play various roles in the inclusive classroom, whether it be a computer, iPad, audio/visual equipment or assistive devices. It can offer educational software, provide an accessible curriculum to learners with special needs and help differentiate lessons. Highly engaging, technology appeals to most groups of learners and support inclusion in numerous ways.

- **Visual aids:** Visual aids are very important items in the inclusive classroom. They attract learners' interest, explain an idea or assist learner understand a lesson. Visual aids come in many forms and there should be a variety available in a classroom to facilitate inclusion. Some examples include the following: diagrams, schedules, posters, graphic organizers, number lines, charts and different types of paper such as lined, plain or graph. A visual aide can also be a SMART Board, television, or iPad. Inclusive classrooms always have numerous types of visual aids handy to help deliver, accommodate or modify a lesson.

- **Learner information binder:** An inclusive class welcomes learners of all abilities, it is extremely important that trainers/instructors track the strengths and needs of each learner. Important data such as assessments, IEPs, observations and notes can be kept together in one place. The trainer/instructor can use this information to ensure that all learners are included and participating in the classroom into a Learner Information Binder which will support the implementation of an inclusive curriculum.

- **Job chart:** A job chart helps keep the classroom running smoothly. Secondly, it enlists the help of the learners and makes the workload lighter. Most importantly and finally, it allows all learners to contribute to the successful operation of the classroom. A job chart serves several purpose in a classroom. Class jobs are usually rotated weekly with learners participating in the best way they can for the betterment of the group. Often overlooked, yet very effective, a class job chart can include every learner in the classroom in numerous ways.

- **Manipulatives:** Manipulatives can be easily grouped, placed into plastic containers and put on shelves around the room. It can support this process by allowing learners to demonstrate their knowledge, develop new levels of understanding and explore deeper concepts. Inclusive classrooms provide curriculum for different types of learners. For some leaners, they prefer a "hands-on" approach to help them understand lessons useful for all ages, manipulatives are an easy way to make a classroom more inclusive.

- **Games:** Games such as card games, board games and classroom games are often used by trainers/instructors to reinforce a new concept. However, they also play a large role in teaching and training learner's social skills and team work. This is because game choices are endless, they provide many different ways in which a learner can participate. Most importantly, games can allow learners to relax in the learning environment, enjoy one another's company and form relationships.

- **A large table:** The table is usually placed in a prominent area of the room, and facilitates many opportunities of learners to be members of a group. Having a table allows the trainer/instructor to bring learners together and provide them with various types of instructional programming that meet the needs of the group. In addition, learners can meet at the table to work together on projects, have discussions or use as an alternate work space. There is no piece of furniture more important in an inclusive classroom than a table large enough for small groups of learners.

- **High-Interest Leveled Books:** Inclusive classrooms recognize that learners learn in different ways in different rates. Not only do trainers/instructors want to provide lessons that address the varying

abilities, but also provide classroom materials that all learners can use. As well as textbooks, an inclusive classroom should also provide books that can be read for enjoyment. Offering books (or audio books) that are age-appropriate, interesting and can be read by readers at different levels are an important way of making a classroom more inclusive.

- **Popsicle sticks:** Trainers/instructors need to have a method of choosing learners for classroom-based activities in a fair manner. There are many strategies for this, but one simple and easy way that ensures all learners in the classroom have an opportunity to be included is called Popsicle Sticks. This method involves putting each learner's name on a Popsicle stick (found at craft stores) and placing all the sticks in a jar. Whenever the trainer requires learners to make teams, complete a task, or answer a question, a Popsicle stick is randomly chosen from the jar. This strategy ensures that every learner in the classroom has a chance of being asked to complete the task and done so in an unbiased manner.

- **Positive behavior management system:** A positive behavior management system can support and maintain a safe, optimal learning environment. It allows the instructor/trainer to highlight and reinforce the strengths of individual learners. In addition, it provides learners with cues to good behavior. Supporting learner behavior, maintaining a clam learning environment and providing predictable routines assist in giving all learners optimal learning conditions. For a detailed description of a positive behavior management system used in inclusive classrooms (https://www.friendshipcircle.org/blog/2014/02/21/10-items-that-can-make-your-classroom-more-inclusive/accessed-October,2021).

Inclusive practice aims to ensure that all learners can flourish in education, in spite of any challenges they face in their daily life. A trainer should use a variety of training methods and must be flexible.

Types of Training Methodology

- Working in pairs, ability grouping and individually
- Reading books
- Working on computers and out of books
- Role play
- Musical activities
- Sporting activities
- Story writing
- Making posters and other creative books
- Inclusive practice ensures that learner's diversity is accepted and championed, rather than discriminated against.

Benefits of Inclusive Practice

- It provide teachers/trainers with additional ways to incorporate problem-solving, teamwork, and collaboration into their lessons.
- It develops leaners empathy and sensitivity to people who are different from themselves.
- It promotes parental confidence that their wards are being accepted and can be successful in the school/workshop settings.
- It improves friendships, confidence, and self-image.
- It aids in training/teaching leaners about diversity and equality (https://www.highspeedtraining.co.uk).

9.0 Conclusion

Inclusive skill training allows learners of all backgrounds to train/learn and grow side by side with regular or normal learners to the benefit of all. It is the real training opportunities for those children who have been traditionally excluded from acquiring formal education. It is the most effective way to opportune all children with a fair chance to attend school, learn and develop the skills they need to explore in their environment. This type of training is not only for children with disabilities, but speakers of minority languages too, but the progress comes slowly. "At the school level, teachers must be trained, buildings must be refurbished, and learners must receive accessible learning materials. At the community level, stigma and discrimination must be tackled and individuals need to be educated on the benefit of inclusive education. At the national level, governments must align laws and policies with the convention on the Rights of persons with disabilities, and regularly collect and analyze data to ensure children are reached with effective services, this is because inclusive systems require changes at all levels of society" (https://www.unicef.org/education/inclusive-education-accessed-October,2021).

Setting Up a Skill Acquisition Center

1.0 Introduction

Acquiring a skill is very important to the individual, as it adds value to the individual who acquires it. "Skill acquisition is a well-designed procedure of acquiring new ways and methods of carrying out specialized functions" (Chudi-Ofi 2013 in Fatoki, 2019).

Donli (2004 in Idoko 2014) in a similar view holds that "skill acquisition is the manifestation of idea and knowledge through training which is geared toward instilling in individuals, the spirit of entrepreneurship needed for meaningful development." However, the skill acquisition program cannot be carried out in space or a vacuum. There are centers that are built for the skill acquisition programs. A skill acquisition center is a place that is built and equipped with the aim of impacting certain skills on the trainees. These centers serve as an indigenous skills acquisition and knowledge transfer centers (Crafts Development and Skills Acquisition Centers 2017). In a similar view, Agboola (2010 in Enweani 2021) views an entrepreneurship or skill acquisition center (within the framework of the polytechnic) as a unit that is saddled with the mission of ensuring sufficient acquisition of entrepreneurial skills by students (trainees) so that they can be self-reliant and self-employed after graduation.

2.0 What Is Skill Acquisition Center?

Skill acquisition center is where skills and talents are given the needed platform to be discovered, developed, and improved.

Importance of Skill Acquisition

There are many reasons for skill acquisition and some advantages attached to them. In respect of this, skill acquisition in every sector is considered essential. That is due to some importance to the individuals and the community at large. The importance of skill acquisition are

- better financial management,
- improved strategic planning,
- crisis-management capabilities,
- better decision-making ability, and
- improved communication with stakeholders.

What Is the Difference between Skill and Skill Acquisition?

Skill and skill acquisition are related teams.

A *skill* can be defined as the technique or ability to do something well. Skills, as reiterated, are usually learned and acquired instead of talent, often considered innate. Skill, as a concept, is as simply defined as above. The only difference between skill and skill acquisition is getting or gaining the skill. Thus, a skilled artist is a person who has acquired either drawing, painting, or any other art related to a particular skill.

Skill acquisition, in short, requires effort, discipline, and constant practice.

The importance of skill acquisition outside the four walls of the classroom cannot be overemphasized in today's world. This is due to the heightened need for primarily technical skills, which are sometimes not taught in schools. Thus, sourcing knowledge, talent, and skilled workers becomes necessary.

3.0   Types of Skill Acquisition Centers

Skill acquisition centers are built and equipped based on the type of skill that is taught in such a center. However, there are some skill acquisition centers that offer more than one skill. The types of skill acquisition centers are labelled based on the type of skill program(s) offered in such centers.

Setting up a Skill Acquisition Center

Setting up a skill acquisition is a herculean task, especially for those who want to set up a private skill acquisition institution. One needs to be well prepared, as well as develop a passion for teaching or training. Such an individual would need to seek counselling from professionals in the field.

The following are things to consider before the establishment of a skill acquisition center (Roy, P.)

1. **Get to know the skill or vocational gaps in the industry or society:** It is necessary to understand the need of skilled and trained manpower required by the local industry and the rate at which the local industry is growing. An understanding of the attributed factors in the industry and the pressure it is creating on the demand and supply circle and its analysis will give a fair understanding of the need to train people for the entry and supervisory workforce for the region and country.

2. **Assessment of requirements:** Once the demand and industry analysis is complete, an assessment of requirements needs to be done in terms of facility, location and staff. The location in terms of the city and its connection with the industry is of prime importance. Centers can be located either in the source markets where the people migrate to work for the industry or in the industry clusters where there is a sizable presence of the industry in multiple formats.

3. **Capacity analysis and size of the center:** The size of a skill training center will depend on the number of students that can be mobilized over a period of five years. It will also depend on the types and number of courses that can be offered in relation to the industry requirement and interests of the community that will use the center.

4. **Funding and financial implications:** Every owner needs to understand the source of funds and its cost (in terms of loans) to calculate the return on investment of the learning center. It is essential to relate the ROI to the project demand and the ability of the prospective students to pay the training fees. Vocational programs may also be able to attract cheaper funds or even grants from the local government agencies who would be keen to skill their population and make them employable.

5. **Marketing services:** Marketing is an essential part in the daily operations of a training center and will include a proper plan of action to successfully run the training center. This can be done through
   a. The recruitment of the best marketing trainers.
   b. Creation of ready-to-launch school website and lead generation platform.
   c. Marketing audit and recruitment acceleration
   d. Marketing collateral design, etc.

   The skill training institution may need to have their own team to mobilize the prospective trainees, counsel them and help them take the decision to apply. This is a year-long process as it helps create a sizable pipeline of students for multiple entry circles in the center one must remember that it takes sometime before the center becomes strong on self-generating leads for the admission. Until leads are self-generating, all efforts should be targeted at strengthening the pipeline.

6. **Human resources:** The success of a training center is in a large part defined by the faculty who conduct the theory and practical classes. Qualifications and credentials of the manpower are extremely important to the successful running of the center, thus some activities become crucial such as
   a. Creation of job posts
   b. Recruitment and interviews
   c. Payroll
   d. Guidance on appraisals
   e. Design of an organizational structure
7. Provision of facilities
8. Placement of the student/student services
9. Operationalizing of the center
10. Maintaining the quality of industry standards

Registering a Skill Acquisition or Vocational Training Center

The skill acquisition center, like any other business, is aimed at making profit, apart from the fact that it creates an empowerment opportunity for members of the community. In many countries of the world, the registration of business are regulated by the Corporate Affairs Commission. The purpose for the registration of any business is to get the business venture recognized and to be free to operate. However, not all vocational training centers are profit oriented. In the process of registration, it is however necessary to specify if the skill acquisition center is a business or nonbusiness organization.

A business organization is one that is formed strictly for making profit but a nonbusiness organization is one whose aim is not for business or to make profit. Such organizations are usually for charitable or humanitarian services. Such organizations enjoy certain tax exemptions. Moreover, the purpose of the vocational training registration is so as to enhance vocational training quality management of the training establishments to ensure that the training activities. Comply with the law (on Vocational Training Registration 2008).

Requirements for Skill Acquisition Center Registration (Regulation on Vocational Training Registration 2008)

Chapter 1—General Provisions

Article 1. Scope of the regulation

This Regulation prescribes the order and procedures to register vocational training activities and grant vocational training certificates; additional registration of vocational training activities; and withdrawal of vocational training registration certificates.

Article 2: Subjects of application

1. This regulation applies to:
   a. Public, private and foreign-invested Vocational colleges, Vocational intermediate schools and vocational training centers;
   b. Universities, colleges, professional secondary schools and other educational institutions engaged in vocational training (below collectively referred to as educational institutions);
   c. Enterprises, cooperatives and production, business and service establishments (below collectively referred to as enterprises) engaged in elementary-level vocational training.
2. This Regulation does not apply to enterprises that enroll vocational trainees and apprentices for free training to work for these enterprises.

Article 3: Purposes of Vocational Training Registration

Vocational training registration aims to enhance vocational training quality management of vocational training establishments to ensure that vocational training activities comply with law.

Article 4: Vocational training registration requirements

1. Vocational training establishments specified in clause 1, Article 2 of this Regulation may enroll trainees after they are granted vocational training registration certificates by competent state agencies.

Chapter 2: Order and Procedures for Registration and Grant of Vocational Training Registration Certificates

Article 5: Vocational training registration order

The order of vocational training registration involves the following steps:

1. Submission of vocational training registration dossiers;
2. Receipt and evaluation of vocational training registration dossiers;
3. Grant of vocational training certificates.

Article 6: Vocational Training Dossiers

1. For public and private vocational colleges and intermediate schools and vocational training centers, a vocational training registration dossier comprises.
    a. An application for vocational training registration (made according to Form No. 1 attached to this Decision [the decision to register the vocational training center])
    b. A copy of the decision on establishment of the college, school or center;
    c. A report on the applicants' current conditions to guarantee the training of registered trades (made according to Form No. 2 attached to this Decision). Such repot covers the following contents:
        i. General information on material foundations, equipment, administrators and trainers of the college, school or center, which covers basic information such as overview of material foundations, works and general classrooms; total number of full-time and visiting trainers; and list of trainers teaching general subjects at the college, school or center;
        ii. Existing material foundations, equipment, trainers, curricula, and training manuals and documents for trades registered for training;
        iii. A report on material foundations, equipment and trainers of trades registered for training at the applicant's branches/other training establishments, if any;
    d. A copy of the charter of the Vocational College or vocational intermediate school or the regulation of the vocational training center approved by a competent agency or organization;
    e. Curricula for trades registered for training;
    f. Papers evidencing the conditions specified in article 8 of this Regulation.
2. For foreign-invested vocational colleges and intermediate schools and vocational training centers, a vocational training registration dossier shall be made comprising.
    a. An application for vocational training registration (made according to Form No. 1 attached to this Decision).
    b. A copy of the investment license or decision on establishment of the college, school or center.
    c. A report on the applicant's current conditions to guarantee the training of registered trades under point C, clause I of this article;
    d. A copy of the charter of the vocational college approved by the Director General of Vocational Training; or the charter of the vocational intermediate school or the regulation of the vocational training center approved by the chairperson of the people's committee of the province or centrally run city where the college, school or center is headquartered;
    e. Curricula for trades registered for training;
    f. Papers evidencing the conditions specified in article 8 of this regulation.
3. For educational institutions and enterprises specified at points b and c. Clause 1, article 2 of this regulation, a registration dossier comprises:
    i. An application for vocational training registration;
    ii. A copy of the establishment decision;
    iii. A copy of the decision to appoint or recognize the head of the educational institution or enterprise;
    iv. A report on the material foundations, equipment, trainers and administrators; curricula and training manuals for trades registered for training (made according to Form No. 3 attached to this decision) such report covers the following major contents:
        i. General information on material foundations, equipment, administrators and trainers of the establishment, which must cover basic information such as material foundations, works and general classrooms: total number of full-time and visiting trainers; and list of trainers teaching general subjects and the general training scale of all current training levels;

    ii. A report on the material foundations, equipment and trainers of trades registered for training at the applicant's branches/other training establishments, if any;

    iii. A copy of the charter or organization and operation regulation approved by a competent agency;

    iv. Curricula for trades registered for training

    v. Paper evidencing the conditions specified in Article 8 of this regulation

4. For training of jobs in medicine and pharmacy sector; drivers of road motor vehicles; steersmen of inland waterway and seagoing ships, train drivers; and bodyguards, in addition to the requirements specified in clauses 1, 2, and 3 of this article, a vocational training registration dossier must contain the relevant ministry's written certification of eligibility for training in those jobs.

Article 7. Order and Procedures for Registration and Grant of Vocational Training Registration Certificates

1. Vocational colleges, colleges and universities engaged in vocational training.
   a. Vocational colleges, colleges and universities shall submit vocational training registration dossiers to the vocational Training Directorate.
   b. Within twenty working days after receiving complete and valid dossiers, the vocational Training Directorate shall evaluate dossiers and grant vocational training registration certificates (made according to Form No. 4 attached to this Decision); in case of refusal, it shall issue a written reply clearly stating the reason;
   c. Within 10 working days after granting a vocational training registration certificate, the vocational training directorate shall send a copy of this certificate to the Labor and Productivity Department.
2. Vocational intermediate schools, vocational training centers, professional secondary schools, other educational institutions and enterprises shall submit vocational training registration dossiers to Labor and Social Affairs Departments of the provinces or cities where they are headquartered.
   a. Within 15 working days after receiving complete and valid dossiers, the Labor and Social Affairs Department shall evaluate dossiers and grant vocational training registration certificates. In case of refusal, they shall issue a written reply clearly stating the reason.

Article 8: Conditions for Obtaining Vocational Training Registration Certificates

1. For jobs trained at intermediate and collegial levels
   a. Jobs registered for training must be on the list of jobs for training promulgated by the Ministry of Labor and Social Affairs.

       For jobs which are not on the list, schools shall report thereon to relevant line ministries which shall propose in writing to the Ministry of Labor and Social Affairs to add them to the list before they registered for training.
   b. Material foundations must be suitable to trained jobs and the training scale and levels and built according to Vietnam construction standard for vocational training schools, promulgated under the Construction Minister's Decision No. 21/2003/QD-BXD of July 28, 2003. Specifically,
   - Having sufficient lecture rooms matching the training scale under regulations. The number of students per lecture class must not exceed thirty-five.
   - Having practice rooms and workshops meting requirements under vocational training programs. The number of students per practice class must not exceed eighteen.

    c. Having sufficient teaching aids suitable top trained jobs and the training scale and levels. Main teaching aids must match technological levels of current production and services; and be sufficient to meet requirements on trained jobs and the training scale as registered.

    d. Having sufficient trainers and administrators suitable to the trained job structure and training levels who meet criteria and requirements on professional qualifications and skills and vocational training skills to ensure the achievement of vocational objectives and programs.

- The ratio of students equivalent to trainers is maximum twenty students/trainer;
- The ratio of full-time trainers is at least 70 percent, for public vocational colleges, universities, colleges and vocational and professional secondary schools; 50 percent, for private vocational colleges, universities, colleges and vocational intermediate and professional secondary schools. Schools must have full-time trainers for each trained job.

    e. Having sufficient curricula in compliance with the framework curriculum promulgated by the Ministry of Labor and Social Affairs.

2. For jobs trained at elementary level:

    a. Having material foundations and equipment suitable to trained jobs and the elementary training scale and level. The area of a lecture room must ensure at least 1.3nr/student equivalent; and a classroom for practice, at least 2.5nr/equivalent student;

    b. Having trainers meeting criteria and requirements on professional qualifications and skills and vocational training skills under law; ensuring the ratio of student's equivalent to trainers not exceeding 20 students/trainer; having full-time trainers of trainers of trained jobs.

    c. Having sufficient vocational training curricula under regulations.

Article 9. Competence to Grant Vocational Training Registration Certificates

1. The vocational Training Directorate, the Ministry of Labor and Social Affairs may grant vocational training registration certificates to vocational colleges, colleges and universities.

2. Provincial—level Labor and Social Afairs Departments may grant vocational training certificates to vocational intermediate schools, vocational training centers, professional secondary schools and other educational institutions and enterprises.

Chapter 3: Additional Registration of Vocational Training and Withdrawal of Vocational Training Certificates

Article 10: Additional Registration of Vocational Training

1. Vocational training establishments specified in Clause 1. Article 2 of this Regulation that have obtained vocational training certificates shall make an additional registration of vocational training in the following cases:

    a. Adding trained jobs;

    b. Changing training levels;

    c. Raising the training scale by at least 20 percent (twenty percent) per year (including training association activities;

    d. Relocating headquarters or branches/other training establishments to other places;

    e. Having additional training functions and tasks under decisions of competent agencies or organizations;

    f. Establishing new branches or training establishments.

2. A dossier of additional registration of vocational training comprises:
   a. A copy of the granted vocational training registration certificate.
   b. An application for additional registration;
   c. A written explanation on additional registration and the current conditions of material foundations, equipment, trainers and administrators; curricula and training manuals to guarantee such additional registration.
3. The registration order and procedures and conditions for obtaining, and competence to grant, certificates of additional registration of vocational training shall comply with Articles 7, 8 and 9 of this Regulation. Certificates of additional registration of vocational training shall be made according to Form No. 8, attached to this Decision.

Article 11: Withdrawal of Vocational Training Registration Certificates

1. When terminating operation, vocational training establishments which have obtained vocational training registration certificates shall return these certificates to the certificate granting agencies.
2. Certificate granting agencies specified in Article 9 of this Regulation may withdraw granted vocational training registration certificates when vocational training establishments administratively violate regulations on vocational training under the law on administrative sanctioning in the vocational training domain.

Chapter 4: Organization and Implementation

Article 12: Responsibilities of the Vocational Training Directorate

1. To guide and recognize the vocational training registration.
2. To inspect and examine the vocational training registration.
3. To receive and evaluate registration dossiers, to grant and withdraw registration certificates under Clause 1, Article 7; Clause 1. Article 9; and Articles 10 and 11 of this Regulation.

Article 13: Responsibilities of provincial—level labor and Social Affairs Departments

1. To guide and organize the vocational training registration in their localities.
2. To receive and evaluate registration dossiers, to grant and withdraw registration certificates and additional registration certificates under Clause 2, Article 7; Clause 2, Article 9 and Articles 10 and 11 of this Regulation.
3. To biannually and annually review and report on the vocational training registration in their localities to the Vocational Training Directorate;
4. To inspect and examine activities of vocational training establishment which have obtained vocational training registration certificates in their localities.

Article 14: Responsibilities of Ministries and Branches

Ministries, ministerial—level agencies, government attached agencies and central agencies of socio-political organizations having vocational training establishments shall:

1. Direct vocational training establishments under their management to register vocational training activities;
2. To examine activities of vocational training establishments under their management.

Article 15: Responsibilities of Vocational Training Establishments

1. Vocational colleges, and vocational intermediate schools and vocational training centers shall register vocational training activities within 24 months or 12 months respectively, after obtaining establishment or establishment permission decisions or investment certificates;
2. Educational institutions and enterprises specified at Points b and c. Clause 1. Article 2 of this Regulation which meet vocational training requirements under this Regulation shall register vocational training activities.

NOTE: The skill acquisition registration process given above is in line with the Vietnam Regulation on Vocational Training Registration. It is only used here as a sample. Registration processes or procedure vary as per country. Anyone wishing to register a skill acquisition program(s) should consult the Corporate Affairs Commission of any other body saddled with such responsibility in his/her country for guidelines.

Accreditation of a Skill Acquisition Center

Accreditation is the process of gaining recognition. The American English Dictionary defines accreditation as "the granting of approval to an institution of higher learning by an official review board after the school has met certain requirement." It is further defined by Brumbaugh (1949) as "the procedure employed by educational associations, professional groups, or special agencies to determine the eligibility of a secondary school, college, university, or professional school for membership, or eligibility for other forms of recognition, on the basis of previously established standards or criteria." In a similar view, it is seen as "the process by which a (nongovernmental or private body evaluates the quality of a higher education institution as a whole or of a specific educational program to formally recognize it as having met certain predetermined minimal criteria or standards (Vlasceanu, Grunberg and Parlea 2007). Thus, an institution or a skill acquisition center that has passed through the process of accreditation is approved or licensed to practice. Although a program or an institution goes through the process of accreditation one, there is always on occasional accreditation survey. The accreditation process is usually carried out by the government or a body set aside by the government.

The process of accreditation "a specific level of quality according to the institution's mission, the objectives of the program(s) and the expectations of the different stakeholders, including students and employers. The process usually results in the award of a recognition status (a score on a multiple scale, a combination of letter grade and score, an operating license, or conditional deferred recognition) for a limited period" (Sanyal and Martin 2006).

Purpose of Accreditation

The following are the purposes of accreditation according to Brumbaugh (1949)
1. To promote and maintain a high standard of skill training in the student's program choice.
2. To promote and maintain standards of preparation for service in the chosen skill.
3. To protect the society against incompetent professional practitioners.
4. To maintain an adequate supply of qualified personnel in the professions.
5. To guide prospective trainees and their sponsors in the selection of a training center of recognized standing.
6. To encourage the trainees to engage in experimentation and self-evaluation.
7. To aid the institutions of skill training in securing experienced trainers, staff and facilities needed to produce competent trainees/graduates.

8. To protect the institutions from undue political interference.
9. To protect the society against fraudulent trainers.

The Procedure of Accreditation

The process or the procedure of accreditation begins with assessment. This involves the gathering of both qualitative and quantitative information "in view of judging the instructional effectiveness and the circular adequacy of the skill center or institution and its training programs. It implies the evaluation of the core activities of the higher education institution to validate a formal accreditation decision" (Vlasceanu, Grunberg and Parlea 2007).

The following are the general criteria for the accreditation of a (skill) training institution, according to Sanyal and Martin (2006).

1. Established institutions of skill acquisition should already be offering the programs to be accredited and the new institution should be recognized by the relevant authorities and should already have been offering a training program for a specified period of time.
2. The skill training institution should be able to demonstrate that they have considered all available strategic options for academic development and that they are committed to continuing improvement in their training programs.
3. Institutions should be able to demonstrate that they meet the requirements of a quality audit, that, they have established systems for internal review and for reporting the skill training activities, including the means to self-evaluate and commit to effective improvement plans, and they are prepared to be externally evaluated by experts in that area.

Below are the specific criteria for the accreditation of a skill acquisition center (Eligibility Criteria 2019).

1. The entrepreneurship skill training institution must be duly registered with the Corporate Affairs Commission or be a public-sector institution.
2. The institution must have been in existence for a minimum of three (3) years with the evidence of past trainees.
3. It must have a qualified faculty in the functioning areas listed on the attached.
4. It must have at least five (5) workshops and five (5) classrooms well equipped for training.
5. The skill training center must provide training modules with a robust curriculum which should include vocational, skill acquisition and entrepreneurship training.
6. It must demonstrate with proof, track record of mentioning and training small and medium enterprises (SMEs).
7. It must have at least two (2) years audited financial records
8. The center must provide tax identification number and Bank Verification Number (BVN) of the entrepreneurship development center and its promoters.
9. It must provide evidence of tax payments.
10. The center must provide a minimum of three (3) months training for start-up businesses in the identified functional areas on the attached list. However, existing businesses could be less.

In addition to the already mentioned, and as an integral part of the quality assessment, the skill training center should meet the following conditions. Sanyal and Martins (2006).

Mission: The skill training institution should be able to demonstrate the existence of a mission statement with strategic objectives and a mechanism for reviewing and updating it.

Governance and administration: The organizational, structure and skill training leadership should ensure that the policies, systems and practices are effective, be responsible to changing priorities and emerging needs, and be able to transform the institution into a standard and world-class skill acquisition center.

Human resources: Detailed information should be available on the staff members (both the trainers and the nontrainers). The institution should be able to demonstrate that they are capable of meeting the institution's objectives and explain staff development policies and practices for meeting emerging challenges.

Training programs: Institutions should clearly define the quality of their training programs. They should ensure that the bodies responsible for reviewing their programs have clearly defined roles. Their monitoring procedures should ensure that students are achieving training outcomes in accordance with the benchmark standards. Institutions should provide detailed statistics on the number of training programs, number of registered program; identify cases where graduates performed better and worse. In the case of worse performances, the institution should suggest possible solutions. The institution should also give details on each of the programs' structure, both theoretical and practical; and the duration of such a program.

Training standards: The skill training institution should ensure the achievement of training standards with reference to the benchmark; the effectiveness of the trainees' assessment procedures; the relevance of the training program in the society (employability) and the external evaluation of trainee's performance.

Community involvement: The institution should have a clear policy for community services and mechanisms for measuring the real needs of the community and related stakeholders. It should provide information on the number of community service units within the institution; for instance workshops and seminars, conferences, technical consultation and services and other related activities. It should have a mechanism for evaluating the quality of services provided and increasing their quality and quantity. It should also have a proposal for an action plan with clearly stated responsibilities and a time frame.

Quality of learning opportunities: The institution should ensure that their facilities and resources are adequate

1. To achieve the intended training outcomes and enable the trainees to participate in all aspects of life;
2. To enable socially and physically challenged trainees to acquire the required skills in their program of choice.

The Role of the Government (State) in the Accreditation of Skill Training Centers (Recommendation)

The government or state should understand that when the citizens, especially the youths are gainfully employed, it will reduce the crime rate and at the same time, boost the economy of such a state. Hence the government has a role to play.

1. The government should have a national accreditation policy.
2. Governments should facilitate the establishment of accreditation mechanisms for quality assurance of their skill acquisition programs.
3. The government should establish a rigorous monitoring system and an effective public information mechanism (Sanyal and Martin 2006).

5.0 Preparing the Training Curriculum

Entrepreneurship education involves the acquisition of skills that enables the trainee to be self-sufficient and independent on the government for job opportunities. Just like in any other educational activity in the formal setting, the curriculum is also necessary in the skill training programs.

Tanner and Tanner define the curriculum as "the planned and guided learning experiences and intended learning outcomes formulated through the systematic reconstruction of knowledge and experiences under the auspices of the school, from the learners' continuous and willful growth in personal and social competence (Tanner and Tanner 1980 in Achor, Agogo and Dodo 2020). In a similar view, Gbamaiya (2002 in Achor, Agogo and Dodo 2020) explains that the curriculum consists of all the knowledge, skills, attitudes and values that are designed to be studied by learners. It is an organization of a prescribed pattern of subject matter which addresses the needs, problems, desires, values and dreams of the society and is designed to achieve through the school. It includes issues in the society about the child and knowledge, skill, attitudes and values needed to achieve set objectives." This curriculum when prepared should promote the chances for "economic growth and self-reliance especially with the changing societal needs (Okolo and Ekesionye 2011). The graduates of these skill training centers need to be confident of the fact that what they are taught are relevant to the economy and the society in which they live. If this is not achieved, the aim of the acquisition of such a skill is defeated, hence the need for the preparation of a proper curriculum which caters for the students, in relation to the demands by the labor market.

The Features of the Curriculum Guide

A curriculum guide is a structured document that delineates the philosophy, goals and objectives, learning experiences, instructional resources and assessment that comprise a specific educational program. Additionally, it presents an articulation of what students should know and be able to do and support teachers in knowing how to achieve these goals. It helps and functions as a guide in planning and performing an educational or training program. Therefore a good curriculum guide should

i. Establish a clear philosophy and set of goals that guide an entire program and the decisions that affect each aspect of the program;

ii. Establish sequences both within and between levels and should assure a coherent and articulated progression from one level to another.

iii. Outline the basic framework for what to do, how to do it, when to do it, and how to know if it has been achieved.

iv. Allow for flexibility and encourage experimentation and innovation within an overall structure;

v. Promote interdisciplinary approaches and the integration of curricula when appropriate;

vi. Suggest methods of assessing the achievement of the program's goals and objectives.

vii. Provide a means for its ongoing revision; and

viii. Provide direction for procurement of human, material and fiscal resources to implement the training program (A Guide to Curriculum Development: Purposes, Practices, and Procedures).

Functions of the Training Curriculum

1. The training curriculum provide the trainers with a framework for the training period so they know which skills and knowledge the trainers need before the training period elapses.

2. It helps the trainers to align with one another so they know which concepts to build up on.

3. The curriculum acts as a map, directing the teacher or trainer on what to do, what the aim of the activity is and the expected outcome. Thus, it helps both the trainer and the trainee to get to the desired destination.
4. It decides what kind of developmental being developed, how the skill, capacity and concepts of the learners can be developed, in relation to the trainee's skill of choice.

The management of the skill acquisition center is saddled with the responsibility of developing the curriculum for the different skills, in relation to the period or duration of such a skill acquisition program. The management is expected to consult professionals in the field to assist in the preparation of the curriculum for the skill program(s) offered. The management should equip the training center with the adequate training materials and qualified trainers.

Preparation of the Curriculum Objectives—Its Advantages

The following are the advantages of the preparation of the curriculum objectives, according to Skilbeck (1971).

1. The preparation of objectives is one way in which we can begin to think clearly and critically about the educational process and our own particular contribution to it.
2. The formulation of curriculum objectives are means of selecting a practical and defensible set of learning tasks and materials from the very wide range of content, source material and forms of treatment available for use.
3. The formulation of objectives also helps teachers or trainers to take decisions about the sequence in which material is presented, a point which is particularly important when time for teaching is extremely limited.
4. Without clearly formulated and precise objectives, it is difficult to prepare valid tests and other forms of assessment. This point is of great significance to the student, who is entitled to know, in advance, at least the general outlines of what it is he or she is expected to do to perform adequately. The existence of clear and detailed objectives is a help both to the teachers and students in judging progress toward attainment of a goal.
5. Having a clear idea of objectives enables the teacher in the classroom to pick out the highly structured teaching-learning situations which are now so common (e.g., projects, case studies, discussions, etc.), elements of potential significance, ad to build on these. This is very important in discussion classes where it might be argued that much shallow talk takes place because the teacher is not sure of what he or she is intending to achieve.

Recommendations on Preparing a Skill Acquisition Curriculum

In a study carried out by Achor, Agogo and Dodo (2020), the following recommendations are given in respect to the preparation of the skill training curriculum.

1. A formal curriculum for entrepreneurship centers should be developed by the government for the harmonization of their content for uniformity. This would enable the learners or trainees within the same trade areas to acquire the same skills just as it is obtainable in the formal education setting. The government, as well as other well-meaning agencies should properly recognize these entrepreneurship centers by way of giving them financial support to boost their production as this could encourage the learning and productivity among students.

2. Curriculum planners and developers should adopt internship training strategy and introduce it into the entrepreneurship education curriculum, especially in teaching prevocational studies.
3. Entrepreneurship education teachers should use internship training strategy to teach entrepreneurship education to improve the trainee's skill acquisition interest.

Steps to Developing a Vocational Training Curriculum

The following should be considered when developing the training curriculum

1. Definition of the training objective or the purpose of the training.
2. Topics to be covered.
3. Strategies—course activities designed to achieve the specified objectives; defined by using such action verbs as organize, design, contract, implement, repair, build and finish.
4. Instructional materials needed to be prepared before the training session, such as materials, machines, homes for installation and agreements with house owners, entrepreneurs willing to accept a trainee for short practical lessons, etc.
5. Time frame for the course.
6. Feedback.

It is also necessary to consider the pretraining entrance level skills of the trainees. Their skill level will determine to a large extent the content of the curriculum. Trainees with little practical experience need more time to master new machines, tools and resource materials. The following steps will assist in the preparation of the skill training curriculum.

1. Define the teaching objective.
2. **List the topics to be covered:** This should be done in a chronological order. Begin with the basic theory and gradually build up the required knowledge to achieve the following objective.
3. List the learning aims for each topic.
4. Detail the training objectives of each training aim. A training objective is the specific knowledge and skills that the trainees are to gain as a result of the training activity. An objective is usually measurable. By defining objectives in a measurable way, you describe a desired behavior and will later be able to offer better feedback. Note that the attitudinal goals are often not measurable. The detailed training objectives are divided into three separate parts:
   a. Performances: This should give detailed statements of what the artisan will be able to do at the end of the training session.
   b. Conditions: The conditions under which the performances will be executed during the training sessions. The training is usually realized in the workshop of the training institute. The following conditions should be considered.
      i. **The range of problems:** This depends on the local working conditions of the artisan and the equipment he owns.
      ii. **Tools and equipment:** It is useful to educate a trainee on the use of both electrical and manual tools and equipment. In a situation where there is no power supply, the trainee can still perform the task, and it creates room for versatility.
      iii. **Manuals and job aids:** Where manuals are available, the trainee can always make reference to the manual where and when necessary.

    iv. **Special physical demands:** For house construction type of jobs, the artisan must be physically able to carry or lift building materials, work on heights and under hot or cold climate conditions.

  c. **The standards:** These are the quality standards of the performed work. Quality standards of construction work are strongly related to the strength and durability of the product. Only when a good quality or standard product is produced will the client be satisfied and so help to advertise the product or service. Standard can be viewed in four angles:

    i. Accuracy—the precision in which the work is performed.

    ii. Speed—how soon or fast the work can be performed.

    iii. Quality of the materials and finishing.

    iv. Satisfaction by the client about the work performed.

5. **Make lesson plans for each topic:** The benefits include the following:
   - Helping the trainer to prepare in advance.
   - Reminding the trainer of key points during the session.
   - Providing the trainer with a written record of the lesson, which can be critiqued.
   - Providing materials for future use by other trainers.

This planning of the lesson can be done by doing the following:

  a. Plan each training topic daily schedules.

  b. Decide on a timeframe—how much time to be spent on each topic component.

  c. Decide on what training methods to use e.g. demonstration by the trainer of the product in manufacturing and finishing.
   - Theory lecture with samples and drawings.
   - Practical exercises on machines and in houses.
   - Role playing e.g. client—entrepreneur relationship. Since the vocational trainee needs to deal with clients later on, practical role-playing exercises should be developed between the artisan and the client.

  d. **Trainer preparation work:** List the items that need to be prepared and ready for the training, such as the training environment, audio-visual equipment, notebooks and models

  e. **Practical exercises:** Sufficient materials, tools and other equipment or space should be available for the practical sessions. The group should be split into smaller units when the equipment are available. In a situation where the equipment are insufficient, the group can still be split, such that while one group study the theoretical aspect, the other group can study the practical aspect of the training (Culled from Nienhuys 2011).

6.0   Raising Capital for the Skill Acquisition Center

Capital may be seen as a source of funding for a business or any other venture. The Investopedia online Dictionary defines capital as "anything that confers value or benefit to its owner, such as a factory and its machinery, intellectual property like patents, or the financial assets of a business or an individual." It can also be seen as the "measurement of wealth and a resource for increasing wealth."

Skill acquisition or vocational training is very important in economic development. However, little attention is paid to the financing of skill acquisition programs. Individuals and groups who are interested in training the youths have to source for funds to promote the skill training programs. Before sourcing for the

funds, it is necessary for the manager at such a center to analyze the needs of the skill acquisition center. The following points are to be taken into consideration:

1. The type of skill acquisition program(s) which the institution is aimed at offering;
2. The number of skilled trainers per skill acquisition program;
3. The type of facility that would promote the success of the skill training program;
4. The equipment needed for the successful implementation of the training program;
5. The number of anticipated trainees per training session, etc.

Also, if the skill acquisition center is privately owned, then it is assumed that such a skill center may be out to make profit but if it is owned by a company, then such a skill center only trains individuals according to the needs of the company. In the case of a privately owned skill acquisition center, the following are the sources of funds or means of raising capital for the skill center.

1. **Personal funding:** Personal funding of a training center could be in the form of savings. When an individual has saved up enough money and may not have need of it in the nearest future, such can be channeled into the establishment of the skill acquisition center. The manager can also apply for soft loans from banks and other lending enterprises.
2. **Training fees:** Any individual who is interested in acquiring a particular skill may be made to pay a particular amount of money. This also acts as a source of income for the skill training center.

However, if the skill training is owned by a company or it is state owned, such a center can be funded through the following according to Ideman (2016)

1. **Earmarked training levies:** These training levies are usually levied on the payrolls of enterprises. They are used to fund the training of individuals in skill acquisition by the public sector.
2. **Development partner support:** The government can source for funds from the multilateral and bilateral donor institutions; either to the government or to individual training institutions. In some countries, donor funding may play a central role in both initiating and building training capacities. However, the government should not depend totally on donors for skill training development. This is because these donor countries will not continue to donate their resources to a particular country, yet there is a need for sustainability in the skill training programs.
3. **Imposition of training fees:** The skill training center can also generate capital by imposing fees on the trainees for the acquisition of the skills in the different areas. This reduces the financial weight on the public sector. The imposition of fees that has its own advantages. The first is that, the individual trainees who have paid so much to acquire a particular skill will show a higher level of seriousness to the training as against those who do not. This will also encourage the training providers to develop a more dynamic, and aggressive approach to exploiting the potential of the local market environment. The adverse effect of this is that, those who cannot afford to pay the fees will not benefit from the training programs. Thus, limiting the access to opportunities of the poor, minorities, rural popularities and other disadvantaged groups.
4. **Income from production and services:** The funds that are generated from the goods and services offered by the trainees can generate an additional income to the training institution. It is seen as one of the benefits of the training process. It is possible to utilize available skills and facilities to produce output for sale in the local market. This can as well lead to a more relevant, market oriented training. However, when the skill training center is more interested in the generation of

funds, the other aspect of the training (i.e., the impartation of the required skill may suffer). This therefore calls for a balance in the source for funds and the quality of skill training provided.

5. **Promotion of private training:** When there is an upsurge in the number of privately owned skill acquisition centers, the weight of the funding will be reduced on the part of the government. The government can then subsidize the fee for some of the skills, thereby making it accessible to almost everyone who is interested in the acquisition of such a skill. The government can promote the establishment of private training by

   i. Making policies that prevent the over charing of trainees in the acquisition of certain skills.
   ii. Subsidizing the cost of some of the skills that are very expensive.
   iii. Creating an enabling environment that allows for the establishment and smooth running of such skill acquisition centers, without the unnecessary encroachment of the government in its activities.

6. **Co-financing:** In most cases, training institutions have been financed mainly from a single funding source (i.e., by the state). Some of trainees are given on-the-job training that are either funded by the state and companies or a combined effort of both. This can be achieved through the following means, according to Ziderman (2016).

   a. **Cost reimbursement:** Firms receive pay grants on a cost-incurred basis, for certain forms of training (both off and on-the-job). The purpose of such scheme is to reimburse the companies for the training expenditures incurred so as to encourage the companies to do more.

   b. **Cost redistribution:** This is designed particularly to deal with the ill-effects on training supply of the poaching of skilled workers by nontraining firms. Training companies may receive grants in excess of the amount of levy paid, providing strong incentives for firms to train.

   c. Levy-exemption: Levy-exemption allows firms, adequately meeting their training needs, to withdraw from the levy-grant system or at least to benefit from reduced levy assessments. This frees the companies from levy payments and subsequent grant claims.

7.0   Certifying and Graduating Trainees

Certification, according to the American English Dictionary, is the formal attestation or confirmation of certain characteristics of an object, person or organization. In a similar view, it is seen as the process of issuing a certificate, diploma or title formally attesting that a set of learning outcomes (knowledge, skills and competences) acquired by an individual have been assessed and validated by a competent body against a predefined standard (Cedefop, 2008).

Certification in skill or vocational training can be carried out in two ways

1. **Cumulative:** Here, the trainee is made to carryout series of tests and the results of such tests (whether practical or theoretical) form the basis of the certification.
2. **Final certification:** In this case, a trainee enrolls in a particular skill training program for a particular period of time. At the end of the training session, the trainee is given a particular task to perform. The performance of the trainee at this point determines the quality of the result which is given to the trainee.

It is also worthy to note that certification is not a guarantee that an individual is qualified to practice the skill for which he or she has been certified. Certification can as well be a license to practice a particular skill acquired, with the hope that constant practice on the part of the graduate will lead to proficiency in that aspect of skill.

Chapter Twenty-Five

Online Skill Training

1.0 Introduction

Online training takes place in twenty-first-century classroom also known as the internet or online learning environment. This is the type of learning environment where the child acquire information or skills, values, beliefs and knowledge from the internet through social networking. The term learning environment refers to an aspect of the field in which an individual functions. The home, the school, the peer group, the classroom tone, the totality of an individual's upbringing including the provision of his tissue needs, and his spiritual needs constitute an environment. It greatly contributes to a learner's learning in unique ways.

Online skill training often bolster and encourage the child's motivation to learn the skill of networking social media platforms such as WhatsApp, Facebook, Twitter, 2go, Baddoo, Imo, Telegram. Their skillfulness of providing new information online is greatly improved based on their level of interest and constant practice of the computer, smart phones and other forms of online information provision.

2.0 Definition and Scope of Online Skills

Even for a simple straightforward phrase like online skills training, we are quickly entangled with rhetoric grammatical and logical tentacles as concerns its definition. Online skills training as a subject of online or distance learning is a form of learning where students are educated in a virtual environment via the internet or corporate intranet communication system. It is a form of education where learners are removed in time and space from the teacher (National Policy on Education, 2004).

Online learning may also be defined as the learning process undergone partially or wholly in a virtual environment and with teaching instructions relayed via internet-based communications. Online skill training though a form of distance learning requires an emphasis on internet-based instruction. I will further reiterates that while distance learning involves a learner who is removed in time and space from a teacher, online training eliminates the time factor, as interactions between the teacher and student are possible in real time. This distinguishes the online method from other forms of skill acquisition media.

3.0 Online Training: Background Issues

In several consecutive pan-African societies, the advance in technology has been received in a manner which may more or less be referred to as dining with the devil but with a long spoon. The argument of neo-socialist and grossly anti-capitalist have even gone as far as to label such advancement as "inhuman" (C.

P. Alozie, *et al.,* 2009:486). When "we relate this to the major changes brought to skill acquisition by technology, we find to be diluted the venom of such arguments, whose themselves have in one way or the other adopted to keep up with the pace of technology." This brings about a philosophical and political analysis of the online method.

In online skill training, the learner must be acquainted with the online skills to produce an effective and productive training exercise. Online skills are those skills the learner must be familiar with so as to manipulate online information or messages. In the course of acquiring online skills, the online skill acquisitor has to take into consideration the online approaches to adopt, its challenges, pedagogical factors, role playing, his psychological state of mind, merits or benefits he will derive from such online learning program such considerations will enable him to have a footing that will enable him make good use of his online program effectively and efficiently.

4.0   Merits of Online Training

Having had the concept of online skill training clearly defined and its background issues lucidly expatiated, it is necessary that we now carefully outline its merits and demerits in an all-encompassing analysis. In comparison to traditional method of skill acquisition, online skill training is actually cost efficient, though initial fundamental costs may be overtly expensive. This barrier, however, has been surrounded by various subsidies in technological commerce. Therefore, the online method of skill acquisition holds forth in terms of socio-economic stability. In addition to the contrary positions held by many who believe that online methods are pseudo-educational, and quasi-effective, the average online skill acquisition meets the criteria for any learning center as poised by Udofia and Chigbo (2005) and also fosters to a high level the concept of individualistic instruction, as is lacking in many real life institutions of learning (Ibid, p. 12).

Furthermore, while maintaining such a high level of individuality, online skill training allows for improved interaction that is not vaguely demarcated by geographic and linguistic barrier, as opposed to one four-walls-of-the classroom experience. Another aspect in which the online method of skill training scores a point is in the area of evaluation, tests and educational measurements. The computer-based interface ensures a comprehensive design for data collection, location, procession, interpretation and utilization, which is wholly in conformity with the second principle of Educational Measurement and Evaluation as emendated by M.J Joshua (2005) and in turn derived from preceding works by Gronhund (1985) and Denga (1987). In fact, the computerized process yields an evaluation system that is free from any sort of prejudicial disposition or material-oriented encumbrance and eradicates the chances of malpractice to a small value. The realization of this fact enables more effort to be put into the skill acquisition process and is a great counter measure to guard against one pernickety of underqualified skills persons in the society.

Moreover, online skill training which also known as online learning process is has the merit of greatly synergizing and brings to the grasp of the student audio-visual access to information and enhancement of abstract concepts by learners. A good of this is in the aviation industry. In the early years of aviation, the cost of becoming a licensed pilot was enormous as real plans had to be used in providing tutelage. Now simulators are used to recreate in striking details, flight conditions and paraphernalia, greatly reducing the cost of the career. The continuous use of ICT methods in skill acquisition creates an inclination toward ICT-enabled processes. The resultant merit effect of this is that individuals become increasingly technologically enlightened. This is good for the future as more citizens become technologically oriented, thus negating the accusations of the society being ruled by a handful of aristocratic technocrats in the near future (Alozie, *et al.,* 2009:487). This further justifies the position of online skill training in the philosophical and ethical light, and serves to make at even more appealing to the skill acquiring layman. Online materials may be con-

densed versions of a longer sequence of in activity where the virtual nature of training may fail to guarantee efficiency in the psychomotor domain of skill learning.

We can then summarize the importance of skill acquisition via the online method as follows:

i. Increased productivity
ii. Enhanced efficiency
iii. Broader outreach for marketing
iv. Consistency with current friends
v. Increased statistic accuracy
vi. Increased reliability of information
vii. Better storage of information for future referencing

5.0 Demerits of Online Training

Just as online skill training is accompanied by its various merits so does online skill training is associated with numerous pitfalls.

Therefore one of the major demerits of online training method is the vulnerability to cyber-attack and unwanted infiltration into an individual's privacy. In this case, cyber-attack becomes common as computer users can easily find access to people's private information, financially and otherwise. Regrets is inscribed on the individual victim because of the fraudulent and financial loss he encounters, and it only follows that he or she feels a sense of foreboding when encountering any online measure in the future, thus clogging the wheel of ICT induced enhancement.

Another ethical demerit is that of the associative distraction that is brought about by the pro-advertisement nature of the web. This prevents individuals from the course of skill acquisition, and results in a longer time for skill acquisition to be completed or even complete abandonment. Most individual's in the sub-Saharan societies have little or no preliminary knowledge of ICT and refrain themselves from online method which they consider as unfamiliar waters to sail in. In the course of maintaining individualism also, the basic social interaction is nearly abolished, as individual's spend more time peering into screens with virtual companions and eventually lose enthusiasm for real conversation and thus loses the communication skills that are so necessary in twenty-first century entrepreneurship. More so, there is an increased reliance on computerization of processes. This results in what can be termed cognitive laziness. An induced effect of computerization of activities ordinarily is carried out by the brain. The virtual nature of training may fail to guarantee efficiency in the psychomotor aspect, as online materials may be condensed versions of a longer sequence of an activity.

In addition, there may be no good internet connection by the school on its website. This could lead to argument and misleading of information between teachers and parents. Therefore, parents are prone to taking another school which may have better internet facilities. Online training may require more time than on-campus classes. Online courses require good management skills for them to be meaningfully imparted to learners for maximum productivity and efficiency. Another disadvantage of online training is that it may create a sense of isolation of students. This means that it causes social isolation, in addition to the demerit that e-learning feedback is usually limited in nature. Ekzatalks.com>online-education>ad...streamed other disadvantages of online training to be.

1. It has less face-to-face interaction
2. It involves more work
3. It produces low quality programs

The same vein, **Error! Hyperlink reference not valid.** Sees online learning to be disadvantageous in terms of the fact that it lacks accreditation and of low quality. While **Error! Hyperlink reference not valid.** Opined that online training does not have self-discipline, **Error! Hyperlink reference not valid.** Buttress the above assertion by saying that online learning requires self-discipline and time management skills. This means that learners usually find it uneasy to be patient in learning and acquiring information and knowledge on the net even as they also find it difficult to have the skills of successfully in the process of trying to access information or acquire learning online.

6.0   Use of Technology in Online Training

Technology is continually changing the way we work and play, create and communicate. So it is natural that advancements in digital technology are also creating game changing opportunities in the world of education. Therefore one of the ways technology can be used to realize online training sessions is education. For teachers, technology is opening up new possibilities to enrich and stimulate young minds. With the innovation and practicability of emerging new technology, software and platforms such as the cloud, video streaming, argument reality, virtual reality, block chain, flip grid, interactive videos, automation, there rechanges in the ways students and teachers learn permanently when used in the e-learning classroom. These had in recent time resulted to a growing excitement around the potential for assertive technology, high-tech collaboration tools, gratification, podcasting, blogging, 2D printing, artificial intelligence, personalized learning and the likes. The use of technology in education has led to a concept known as "education technology." Education technology refers to the theory and practice of educational approaches to learning (Sandiego.edu). It is also viewed as the technological tools that assist in the development and communication of knowledge. Another definition of educational technology focuses on the theory and practice of utilizing new technology to develop and implement innovative educational approaches to learning and achievement of student.

Behind all the high-technological tools, the digital bells and whistles, are the teachers who possess the skill and the inspiration to use these new technologies to expand educational world of their students. According to a report by the international Society of Education ("11 Hot Edutech Trends to Watch"), the most compelling topics among educators who embrace technology for learning and teaching are not about the technology at all, but about the students.

Benefits of technology in online training of students include expanded opportunities for personalizing learning, more collaborative classrooms and new strategies such as the so-called "flipped learning" in which students are introduced to the subject material outside the classroom, often online, with classroom time then being used to deepen understanding through discussion and problem solving activities with peers. For teachers who aspire to make an impact in this area of study, obtaining a master's degree in educational technology is clearly about learning new tools, strategies and practices but it is also about understanding the supportive structures that must be in place to ensure most successful outcomes. These according to grees.sandiego.edu include the following:

1. Policy and legal issues
2. Ethical issues such as a student's privacy.
3. Funding grants and budgets
4. Real-world applications—this include the world of work, partnership opportunities, etc.
5. Networking basis hardware, learning management software.
6. Equity between community and school's access and assets, student access.
7. Ability to compare a school or distract needs assessment and site technology survey analysis.

Technology can also be used for school purposes such as e-learning through the computer. For example, during Covid-19 pandemic period, schools used e-learning so that they can be able to keep up with their regular teaching and learning terminal session. This prevents their students from being idle during the period. Another importance of technology in online training is that it can be used for business purposes. In this case, vide calls can be used to reach a company's clients or the client may send a list of goods he wants to buy from wither through WhatsApp or Facebook before such goods can be delivered to them through the post office. Business interviews can as well be conducted by private or public establishment toward intending workers online. This implies that through the internet, interviews are conducted on form of chats, discussions where questions are asked regarding the objectives, ideas of interviews as well as their inputs they intend to make on the business if employed into their business establishment.

In addition, concurring technology's use in school, **Error! Hyperlink reference not valid.** That e-learning makes good use of database and Content Management System (CMS). These two work hand in hand to ensure a viable. Others include media resources, phig-ins, Demos, course templates like multimedia Educational. Technology is used in the classroom to enhance teaching and learning. In the school system, digital readers and tablets, smart cards, are used to replace the bulkier hard-copy textbooks. The romanticized view of technology is that its mere presence in schools will enhance student learning (**Error! Hyperlink reference not valid.**). Technology contribution for instructors to review the frequency of student contribution and watch videos that will facilitate learning. This corroborates with the reality that technology in online training links teachers to their students and to professional content, resources, and systems to help them improve teaching and learning processes online. There are numerous technologies available to improve the quality of materials produced by teachers. Some of them include web based training, online education, instructor, internet based learning, virtual education.

In light of the above discussion, it believes in us to emphasize that the use of technology cannot be over-emphasized.

7.0 Approaches to Online Training

These has to do with various methodologies employed to gain knowledge and access information through the internet. Training which is synonymous with learning refers to skill or knowledge acquired through study, experience or being taught. **Error! Hyperlink reference not valid.** Outlines some of the best online training approaches to include the following:

1. Rapid learning
2. Blended learning
3. Mobile learning

While egyamkosh.ac.in>bitstream discusses online training approaches to include the constructive and mixed approaches, e-student.org>types-of-e-learning highlights ten different distinguished types of online training to be:

1. Computer Managed Learning (CML)
2. Computer Assisted Instruction (CAI)
3. Synchronous Online Learning
4. Asynchronous Online Learning
5. Fixed E-learning

6. Adaptive E-learning
7. Linear E-learning
8. Interactive Online Learning
9. Individual Online Learning
10. Collaborative Online Learning

It is now very important that the above online learning types be explained succinctly for better understanding of the topic.

1. **Computer Managed Learning (CML):** This is also known as Computer-Managed Instruction (CMI). Here, computes are used to manage and assess learning processes. Computer-managed learning systems operate through information databases. These databases contain bits of information which the student has to learn, together with a number of ranking parameters which enable the system to be individualized according to the preferences of each student and the.

   As a result of two-way communication between the student and the computers, determinations can be made as to whether the student achieved their learning goals on a satisfactory level. If not, then the process can be repeated until the student has achieved their desired learning goals. Also, educational institutions use computer-managed learning systems for storing and retrieving information which aids in educational management. This could imply that information such as lecture information, training materials, grades, curriculum information, and enrolment information.

2. **Computer Assisted Instruction (CAI):** Acronomised as CAI, computer assisted instruction also known as computer assisted learning, is an e-learning approach which uses computers together with traditional teaching. This could mean interactive software for the students or the kind of training software used by Patrick Suppes of Standard University in 1966. This online training method uses a combination of multimedia such as text, graphics, sound, and video to enhance learning. The main value of computer assisted instruction is interactivity-as it allows students to be active learners instead of passive learners, by utilizing various methods such as quizzes and other computer assisted teaching and testing mechanisms. Most online and traditional schools recently use different kinds of computer-assisted learning to facilitate the development of skills and knowledge in their students.

3. **Synchronous Online Learning:** This type of online training approach enables groups of students to participate in a learning activity together at the same time, from any place in the world. Real-time synchronous online learning often involves online chats and video-conferencing as those allow training participants and instructors to ask and answer questions instantly while being able to communicate with the other participants. This kind of community-oriented online learning has been made possible with the rapid development of online learning technologies. Before the invention of the computer networks in the 1960s, synchronous learning was practically impossible to implement. Nowadays, synchronous e-learning is considered to be highly advantageous as it eliminates many of the common disadvantages of e-learning such as social isolation and poor teacher-to-student and student-to-student relationships. Synchronous e-learning is currently one of the most popular and quickest growing types of e-learning.

4. **Asynchronous Online Learning:** In this approach to online training, groups of students study independently at different times and locations from each other without real-time communication taking place. Asynchronous e-learning methods are often considered to be more student-centered than their synchronous counterparts, as they give students more flexibility.

   For these reasons, this approach is often preferred by students who do not have flexible schedules, because it allows them to utilize self-placed learning. They can set their own time frames for

learning, and they are not required to learn at specific time intervals together with other students. Before the intervention of the Plato Computer System, all e-learning was considered to be asynchronous, as there were no methods of computer networking available.

5. **Fixed E-learning:** "Fixed" in this context implies that the content used during the learning process does not change from its original state and all the participant students receive the same information as all the others. The materials are predetermined by the teachers and do not adapt to the student's preferences. This type of learning has been standard in traditional classrooms for thousands of years, but it is not ideal in e-learning environments. That is because fixed e-learning does not utilize the valuable real-time data gained from students inputs. Analyzing each student individually through their data and making changes to the materials according to this data leads to better learning outcomes for all students.

6. **Adaptive E-learning:** This is a new and innovative type of e-learning which makes it possible to adapt and redesign learning materials for individual learner. Taking a number of parameters such as student performance, goals, abilities, skills and characteristics into consideration, adaptive e-learning tools allow education to become individualized and student-centered than ever before.

   Adaptive e-learning can be used for mathematical sequencing of student's data. When done correctly, this could mean a new period education science. While this type of e-learning can be more difficult to plan and accomplish than traditional teaching methods. Its potential value of effectiveness is, however, often understood.

7. **Linear E-learning:** When referring to human-computer interaction, linear communication means that the information passes from sender to receiver without exception. In this case of e-learning, this becomes a very limiting factor as it does not allow two-way communication between teachers and students. This type of e-learning does have its place in education, although it is becoming less important with time. Examples of linear e-learning approach is ending training materials to student through television and radio.

8. **Interactive Online Learning:** Interactive e-learning allows sender to become receivers and vice versa, effectively enabling a two-way communication channel between the groups involved. From the messages sent and received, the teachers and students can make changes to their teaching and learning methods. For this reason, interactive-learning is considerably more popular than linear, as it allows teachers and students to communicate more freely with each other.

9. **Individual Online Learning:** Individual learning in this context refers to one number of students participating in achieving the learning goals rather than the student-centeredness of the material. This type of learning has been in traditional classrooms for thousands of years. When practicing individual online learning, the students study on their own. This type of learning is not ideal for developing communicational skills and teamwork abilities in students, as it largely focuses on student's learning independently without communication with other students. Therefore a more modern approach is necessary to replace the communication of skills and abilities.

10. **Collaborative Online Learning:** Collaborative e-learning is a modern type of learning method through which multiple students learn and achieve their learning objectives together as a group. Here, students have to work together and practice teamwork to achieve their common learning objectives. This is done through the formation of effective groups, where each individual student has to take into account the strengths and weaknesses of each other student. This boots the communication skills and team working abilities of the students. Collaborative e-learning expands on the ideas that knowledge is best developed inside a group of individual's where they can interact and learn from each other. While this type of learning is more often used in traditional classrooms than in online courses, it is still a valid type of e-learning which can be lightly effective if done correctly.

8.0   Online and Offline Training: A Contrast

Students tend to lack concentration on what is being taught by their teacher during online learning training sessions compared to offline or face-to-face training periods. This is largely because of some distractions such students often at home or wherever they may be face. But when teachers and students have face to face training sessions, it becomes easier for teachers to assess their level of understanding thereby affecting appropriate instructions and corrections where necessary. This assessment is often achieved through monitoring of the student by the teacher. In this case offline training gives room for face-to-face monitoring and correction of student's mistakes. Students monitoring usually deepen motivation and encouragement to work harder.

Also, online learning method, tête-à-tête interaction is not encouraged. The change of maligned disposition and prejudice are completely removed but in offline training situation, two persons could be involved in some kind of private discussion and sharing of individuals.

9.0   Challenges of Training Online

There are often difficulties associated with training online. One of such visible challenges is that some learners will showcase a carefree attitude to such online training due mainly to the in lack of basic electronic devices whole others will get easily distracted when such online lessons are going on.

Another glaring challenge of online training session is that training online fees may be very expensive and almost unaffordable by students. High cost of training online fees and other charges can discourage learners from showing interest in acquiring knowledge and assessing information online.

According to eLearning industry.com, several challenges of online training include the following:

1. **Negative public perception:** The perception often associated with online training do militate against its training program. Sometimes, those who are employed may have participated in many unencouraging online training courses in the past that they expect more of the same in the present online course they may have been undertaking. The online trainers are expected to provide them with online contents that will entertain, engage and personalize them. In this way, online trainees will be spurred and actively involved, thereby giving them the power to apply their skills and acquire practical experience.

2. **The time flaws:** Mature learners tend to be busier than school-aged children. They do have the jobs but they also have their families, their personal lives, and their hobbies. This way, it becomes difficult for them to find time to study. Hence many of the online learners disengage themselves. This usually happens even with compulsory online training and can therefore get employees off their online engagement. But the online trainer can make it easier for them to manage their time better by dividing online training modules. Alternative study formats like podcasts, videos or info-graphics should be used to eliminate this online challenge. This allows cooperate learners to study as they commute or read through their headphones while they get in their morning activities.

3. **Limited interaction with online peers:** For many leaners, the value of school is in the people. It is true that people like talking with each other in class, talking to interesting teachers or networking or involving themselves in catching an after school game. Those extra-curricular activities that accompany any curricular activity such as staff seminar is very important. Online learners miss out on a lot of this activity. Also, teleconferencing and messaging applications have come a long way and the Covid-19 crisis has forced many organizations to resort to meetings online. A forum or

chat room should be built in the online training course. This will allow corporate learners to hang out remotely.

4. **Inconsistent internet access:** It is assumed that all virtual classes take place online, so corporate learners are used to missing assignments or falling behind. Web connections that are spotty to be nightmares of every learner. For many online trainees, Wi-Fi is not a given, and that is one of the worst online training challenges they could face. Phone data bundles are very expensive. Even in developed countries of the world, not everyone has internet connection at home. In the course of buying or designing your online training classes, of reliance on live web access should be accessed. They will need to be connected when they are uploading homework or chatting with online instructors. But the rest of the time, preloaded offline modules should be designed so that online students can study anywhere, anytime, regardless of internet status.

5. **Translation into the real world:** One of the two online training challenges is that my type of training risks being remote. If learners focus on regurgitating crammed facts and passing, they will get no practical benefits from their studies. The trainer needs to frame factual lessons in real-world scenarios so that your corporate learners do not just know the answers, but they know how to use then too. The trainer can teach situational analysis and critical thinking.

6. **Motivation is in short supply:** Online learners also known as trainees do not sometimes have motivation to see the online training course through to completion. A good knowledge of what your online training offers and how employees are expected to participate should be gotten. Long term goals should be broken into small milestones so that their progress can be tracked. The trainer also needs to consider adding game mechanics to your online training strategy such as rewarding employees with badges or points to encourage their motivation. Leaderboards, however, can be used to create friendly competition and motivate disinterested employees.

7. **Lack of personalization:** The online training sessions aligns with objectives of an organization but it lacks the personal touch. Employees are expected to participate in the same online training activities and modules regardless of their job duties, responsibilities or personal preferences. In this case turn the tides by incorporating online training paths. This often helps corporate learners the ability to choose their own online training activities and support resources, as well as go at their own pace. For instance, learners can pick online training tools that will care for their learning preferences which also the learners engagement and allows them to bridge gaps, thereby increasing workplace productivity.

Therefore, it is important to create online discussions so that co-trainees can interact. The trainer should design his online training course with offline access and use lots of simulation to offer context. Corporate learners should be awarded for their diligence and hard work.

10.0   Pedagogical Factors in Online Training

Educational institutions are increasingly adopting planning and implementing courses whether done face-to-face education or with e-learning environments deals a lot with pedagogical issues. Learning is influenced by a couple of factors such as learner's prior knowledge, cognitive learning and learning styles, intellectual abilities constitutional status, etc. E-learning can be considered to be highly related to learning and teaching as stated in (Jain *et al.,* 2020). Therefore, pedagogy and didactivism are important aspects for all the facets of e-learning, reading from the creation of the courseware and the application of an e-learning system to the evaluation of the learning process.

Ped Knowles *et al.* (1998) posited that education can be understood as activity undertaken or initiated by one or more agents that is designed to effect changes in the knowledge, skill and attitudes of individuals, groups or communities. The term learning, however, emphasizes the person in whom the change occurs or is expected to occur. Thus, learning comprises that act or process by which behavioral changes, knowledge, skills and attitudes are acquired. In the learning process, factors are important. These are attention, motivation, emotion, and experience of the learner. The focus of attention determines if a student mentally follows a lesson and their fore if the intended behavioral change affects a learner at all. Particularly, e-learning requires a strategy for getting and keeping the learner's attention. Thus, it is necessary to consider cognitive processes such as the learner's selection of incoming information into the sensory memory, organizing and integrating this data by building connections in short-term memory and encoding it by transferring it to long-term memory. It is therefore necessary to apply particular standards for instructional design.

Secondly, the motivational state of the students are of high importance when questioning how the stimuli given by the teacher promotes the learning process. Brashford *et al.* (2000) states that motivation affect the amount of time that people are willing to devote to learning. Yet the willingness to learn is caused by different motives beginning with the intention of achieving something over completing against colleagues or helping other people up to emotional factors such as anxiety. Entiwistle (1981), categorized three orientation styles of motivation to be meaning-oriented, reproducing-oriented and achieving-oriented motives. Considering motivation aspects for e-learning is mainly dependent on the learning context itself, for example, by pointing out the relevance for an instruction or including interactive elements such games and simulations.

Furthermore, it is advantageous to create competition within a learner group and adapt to preknowledge in the subject. In the third place, emotions have in the same way the motivation, a strong impact on the online learning process. It is true that student's performance depends on anxiety, in particular tests anxiety and proposes special methods for dealing with such problems. Emotion is an unconscious arousal system that alerts us to potential dangers and opportunities. Therefore, addressing a learner's emotion channel can be seen as an important cognitive process for transferring data into short or even long-term memory with the e-learning situation, the improvement of the learning process can be realized through emotions, for example, by storytelling, provocations, emotional figures and animations, group works, enabling confidence in the learning or learning process.

In the fourth place, knowledge transfer can be improved if learners can tie up to prior knowledge either in the same domain or in a similar context. Anderson (1995) states that interference happens when information gets mixed up with, or pushed aside by other information. At the beginning the degree of mastery of the original subject influences the learning process. In particular, an adequate level of initial learning is required. Then learners can construct new understanding by trying up to previous experiences which may not have been activated before. In this case, learners become capable of conceptual changes, which may not have adopt knowledge concerning their culture or and even improve their thinking abilities. After all, the higher the level of one's prior within a domain or a content, the less instructional support is required to accomplish a task (Tobis and Ingber, 1976). Tobia (1994) vehemently relates prior knowledge to one's interest in a given subject.

Other pedagogical factors that are important in online training are learner characteristics. In this case, each learner has a distinct and unique profile of intellectual abilities which can be characterized by various kinds of cognitive or mental abilities. Education deals with the theory multiple intelligence in two ways. Firstly, teachers device curricular addressing different intellectual capabilities of learners and secondly where educators focus on the development of specific intelligence such as intra and inter-personal skills.

11.0   Role Playing in Online Training

For online training to be effective, it clearly requires at least a two-party relationship existing between the online instructor and the skill acquisitor also known as the online leaner. Therefore separate online roles are to be filled only by the separate individual entities.

The role of the instructor: An instructor is a person whose job is to teach somebody a practical skill (Oxford Advanced Learner's Dictionary, 6th ed.). The instructor is the supplier of the information necessary in skill acquisition. In the classroom situation, the instructor may be one who already the skill acquisition process, and has been able to achieve an expert level of competence in that particular area of study. In the peer-to-peer interactive setting, the learner who has carried out good amount of research in a topic peculiar to him or her is usually the instructor in that situation. But the fact to be established here is that the instructor must exercise expertise in the field both in practice and in theory. The virtual curtain, however, between for pedagogical maneuvers usually required in tackling gender discrepancies within the mixed real-time system (Kruse, 1999).

Furthermore, the instructor may be assumed by a nonhuman entity, specifically an artificial intelligence. This ensures an error-free instructional activity, though less engaging. Here, the computer functions as a primary instructor and gives material it is programmed with by a human expert, who serves as the secondary instructor. The "persona" factor of the instructor may as well be totally eliminated, as instructor may be in form of self-help textual or audio-visual information. Therefore, one can see that the trainer-trainee relationship may vary from one-to-many to many-to-one. This will go a long way to ensuring maximum efficiency in the process of skill acquisition.

The role of the student: In contrast to the role of the instructor being a job the student actually may pay to access the instructions necessary to achieve proficiency in the given field. Hence his or her role is to clearly follow the stated instructions provided by the instructor. The online training method conversely may provide more information on the student to the instructor, and is usually not shielded as is the case with the instructors. Although this negatively affects the anti-prejudicial advantage of the online skills training process, it must be taken into cognizance that in most models of online training, biometric information of students is for administrative processes only, and therefore out of reach of the instructor thereby preserving its unbiased efficacy.

Role-playing and Online Training

Role-playing can be seen as an educational concept toward skills acquisition is defined by Louise Cohen and Lawrence Manion (1994) as participation in simulated social situations that are intended to throw light upon the role/rule context governing real life episodes. Hamilton (1976) identified and declassified various role-play methods in terms of passive-active distinction in certain scenarios, or expressively do so by acting it out in mock scenes. Their responses in such situations are taken to be typical and eventually used as stereotypes in researches that are educationally oriented.

Role-play may as well as be seen as a form of simulation studies and is widely accepted by educationists. Role-playing, however, may merge as a form of gaming or computer simulation which is one of the important aspects of the online training methods. The role-playing method may be either absolute, adaptive or assessor. Role-playing, is therefore very necessary because it helps learning to be performed based on experience. This certainly levels the base of the complementary pyramid as acquiring learning and experience can be carried out at the same time and so bridge the gap between the learning state and the stage of Ie.

12.0   A Survey of Online Applications (APPS)

There is no doubt the fact that a solid online survey tool will allow one to build a survey that uses logic such as branding. Survey is important because it provides feedback from people or ideas. Even if someone wants to know what his customers think about his product, he needs ideas from his team for an upcoming supply of goods, or wants to research public opinions for a project he is working on, survey is important to get that feedback from them.

In all the online survey applications, the most widely used online application software is the survey monkey which is used by millions of businesses globally. It provides its users with fifteen different types of survey questions such as multiple choice, open comments, and Likert scales.

However, a list of several online survey applications can be x-rayed below:

1.   Survey planet
2.   Survey monkey
3.   Typeform
4.   Questionpro
5.   Quick tap survey
6.   Yesinsights
7.   Surveybot
8.   Survey sparrow
9.   Forms.app
10. SoGo survey

It is now very important for us to have a discourse on each of them

1.   **Survey planet:** This is an excellent survey application for beginners to enable them create a survey. It offers over ninety survey templates with prewritten questions that the beginner can use. As an individual builds his survey, you can view a live copy as you edit right in the same window. The panel is a thin column on the left side of the screen and in the course of adding your survey title, you can choose a question from multiple choice to an image-based questions.

      Also, a survey planet makes editing fast in other ways. For any question you enter, you will see one text field below it to type in a response.
2.   **Survey monkey:** This is one of the biggest names in survey applications. Survey monkey also offers one of the earliest ways to create surveys even when you are mobile. While most survey applications just let you collect responses on mobile, survey monkey allows you to create, edit, gather responses and analyze results in your smartphone or tablet and anything you do on mobile will sync with your desktop account and vice versa. It often automatically creates surveys on a phone or tablet.
3.   **Typeform:** This type of online application does a lot of things very smartly, including having a wide library of some of the best-looking themes that are found and chatbot-style surveys. But a unique feature of this kind of online survey software is that it visualizes logic branches. Typeform allows a person to see question branches visualized on a map while most application platforms use dropdown dialogs or lists of conditions. Through this survey application, users are able to easily search a library of icons for the perfect visuals without ever leaving the survey application. It also helps to preview how visual images will look as you build your survey. It helps to build an embeddable chatbot or craft complex logic paths. When an automated typeform that overflows with zapier is created, it can result to creating new email subscribers and add items to your to-do list.

4. **Questionpro:** This type of online survey application is often used for advanced survey logic and scripting which usually makes for greater flexibility if the user have an understanding of its usage. For instance, a user can create a script that creates a good number of questions and then randomly selects a few of those questions to show to various people. This is useful in testing or to reduce survey bias. Survey fatigue, for instance often takes place when respondents get tired of answering questions. In this case, survey question order can be randomized to help reduce this kind of bias from being focused on specific questions.

5. **Quick tap survey:** This online application offers one of the best means of building offline surveys. In this survey application, one can create his own survey or choose from more than 50 customized templates based on category of the survey, like an employee exit survey or post-event feedback survey which shows one question at a time or a mobile form that allows you to run mobile-only surveys and shows all questions in a list. Once your survey is completed, you are required to check "publish" before logging into the Quick Tap Survey application on your smartphone or tablet and download your newly published survey to collect feedbacks. The survey can be filled out offline and synced back to your account automatically when you are offline. By connecting Quick tap survey to the other applications you use, you can automatically crate new leads from survey responses, share responses with your team in a chat application, etc.

6. **Yesinsights:** This type is often used for one-click surveys. It enables one to keep things simple by allowing you to create one-question survey that respondents can answer with just one click. This is because you can only create surveys with one question which allows you to collect very precise feedbacks.

   Nevertheless, if a person chooses to distribute his survey via email, he or she can create a landing page that respondents see after they click their answer or set up a triggered follow-up email. In the course of distributing your survey and selecting your email service from more than 35 options, yesinsights will help you provide the plain text for you to copy and paste into your email client. Also survey results from Yesinsights are used to power activities in other applications.

7. **Surveybot:** For one to get responses to his surveys, he needs to be able to reach the right audience, which surveybot often facilitates. This implies that surveybot enables you to distribute surveys to an already-established audience on Facebook by contacting them via Facebook Messenger of Facebook workplace. When you sign up for surveybot, you either sign up using Facebook Messenger or Facebook workplace, or create an account manually and connect your Facebook account later. If you have a Facebook page, you have a variety of options for distribution. When you reach the period of campaign for surveyor's editor, you can choose to automatically message users with your survey when they comment on a post or click on your ad. Once users begin to answer your surveys with surveybot, they will automatically be added to a "panel," a segment inside surveybot that shows all previous or earlier respondents. When you have enough users in your panel, you could send a direct message over Messenger about your new survey.

   And you can trigger surveys to launch when someone completes another survey, when a respondents enters a panel segment, or by calling the surveybot API.

8. **Survey sparrow:** This survey software helps in creating websites that have chatbots popping up in the corner to help new visitors. It is done by crafting a survey that takes the form of a helpful chatbot and ask particular questions to your users in a conversational way. It is one of the few services found to offer not only chatbot survey styles but also included them on the free tier. When creating a survey using this software application, the user can choose from a few templates and see how they would play out in a simulated chat. This approach allows on to craft surveys that feels less formal and might likely get answers from the audience.

While the surveys are structured like a chatbot, they are more robust than Facebook Messenger. Custom buttons, scales, multiple choice answers can be created, in addition to open-ended text responses. This gives it more flexibility than survey Bot although one will need to distribute the survey yourself through links or gets embedded in your own website.

Survey sparrows offers a robust array of traditional surveys with designs that are attractive. In this case, one can customize the templates or creates his own surveys from scratch with branching logic and even export your data to CVS, PDF, and Excel formats in the free tier. When survey sparrow is connected to Zapier, you will get notifications for new responses, automatically add respondents to your email marketing application, or send event feedback survey to all attendees.

9. **Forms.app:** This form of online application helps to stick to the users company's branding or even just get people to stay engaged long enough to finish your survey. In that way, forms.app does better than any other survey application. The service offers a huge library of dozens of themes with distinct patterns of colors and even animated backgrounds.

Once a theme is picked, you can customize it to a good level. You can also change the fonts used in the form, the primary and accent colors, the shape of the boxes around the answers where buttons are positioned and a bunch of other factors. The text can be tweeted so as to read from right to left if you are creating surveys in language that read that way. You can even customize the appearance of your survey using CSs even on the free version of forms.application. This is often a paid feature of other survey tools. This service is a traditional form application hence if a user have a need to connect surveys, and also gather form data, using one service is very good. Even if you do not need form features, few other services will offer your audience better-looking or more customizable surveys than formsapplication. One will automatically send emails, create tasks and more whenever there are new survey submissions, when you connect forms.app to Zapier.

10. **SoGo survey:** This survey helps to build a bigger library of questions to quickly build surveys, security features to ensure that only certain people are able to access the survey or more powerful data analysis. For beginners, while creating surveys, SoGo has a great amount of question bank with ready-made template questions. There are about two hundred questions mainly in corporate-oriented categories like employee satisfaction, compensation, and work-life balance. Personal custom bank of all the questions can be created. When it is time to distribute your survey, one can create his single-use links so each person can only submit one answer, or multi-use links so that many people can submit responses from the same link. You can also, add a password to the survey to keep people from outside your organization from submitting the survey.

Higher tiers of SoGo survey helps you to create custom branching logic, gives you total control over the theme of your survey including adding your own company to branding and can even automatically create contacts, tasks and notifications whenever there are new survey responses.

However, other great online survey tools include form builder applications such as survey templates, marketing automation tools including email marketing applications like construct contact which often include survey builder. If you are working in a large enterprise that has more advanced needs from your survey, you might find tools like Qualtrics, Adobe Marketing Cloud, or Zoho Survey to have more features you need.

13.0 Assessment of Performances Online

Joshua (2005) identified various categories of tests used in the measurement of the cognitive domain of an individual, as follows:

i. **Achievement Tests:** These tests that are used to measure learning that has taken place recently.
ii. **Aptitude Tests:** These refer to those tests that assesses the ability of an individual to acquire the certain skills or behaviors if given the appropriate training with regard to the future.
iii. **Ability Tests:** These kind of test measures or assesses one's power to perform a certain task or role.
iv. **Intelligence Test:** The category of tests usually aim at assessing a learner's general intellectual capacity. It is important to note that the above four types of assessment can be administered via channel.

However, online training sites tend to favor achievement tests in terms of usage, and only make use of ability tests as a form of retrospective assessment tool at intervals that are cumulative. A typical example situation is one in which Mr. A watches an online tutorial in computer programming on the first day, he is introduced to computer programming and when he finds the tutorial, he asked questions on what programming means: the second to the sixth day go on in that similar way, each having questions based on what Mr. A. has learnt for that day. At day 7, however, Mr. A is asked questions comprising of topics learnt from day 1 to 7. One can see that this conforms to the achievement ability test cycle-model. This is the model mostly found in online training sites. This actually summarizes the assessment method in online training.

Nevertheless, critics of educational tests and measurements have stipulated that the answers given by learners in the online environment may not be true reflectives of their cognitive ability in that area, since the online method allows users to minimize and cheat the test, a far cry from a classroom test will stringent surveillance by the instructor. It is on this basis that some sites have decidedly put clock-timers and destroyers which shots down the application in case a user tries to cheat one system. However, people who are literate internet-wise have always produced means to warp their way around such blockades. Therefore, the reliability of classroom tests outcomes that are of the online methods. It must be stated that the online method is more upbeat in terms of consistency, since there is an absence of class fatigue and other humanisms.

Joshua (2005) earlier cited also declassified the range of assessments in education into three domains of knowledge namely the cognitive, affective and psychomotor. But the first two domains do not apply to the virtual space that is online training. This is because there is the absence of stimuli and other education phenomena that trigger the affective responses to be assessed. This means that without stimuli, there can be no affective or psychomotor association or response.

On that note, a major demerit of online training as it relates to assessment measurement and evaluation is that it falls short of a holistic resume in all the three domains of assessment. In the technical educational system, much emphasis is placed on the handling of tools and equipment and one ratio of practical to theoretical teaching is disproportionate toward the former, it then follows that tests of practical ability follow the affective and psychomotor evaluation measures. This makes online training handicapped in this area.

To solve this problem, undoubtedly, many online training programs are only utilized as secondary teaching tools, or as an alternative to textbooks or oral lectures. While others have been able to adopt their programs to become capable of holistic evaluation by creating online classrooms, where the individuals learning can see and interact with each other, and the end of the period, each individual is affectively assessed via the peer-appraisal technique (Joshua, 2005). But it must be realized that the appraisal so obtained may be vogue and spatial in context, as the peers do not have insight of an individual's capabilities outside the virtual space.

Another method is the make-a-video method, where the online trainee makes a video of his/herself performing a specific skill from where he/she is assessed. Yet, this method has often proved to be an exercise in vain, as many individuals may doctor such videos especially where the needed apparatus is not even available to the individual. Hence, the training process must be tapered to meet the needs of the learner in terms of testing, measurement and evaluation.

14.0 Psychological Factors in Online Training

As a field of study, psychology investigates the state of the wind and how it influences behavior individuals activity and overall behavior originates from and is coordinated by the mind or what educators referred to as the affective domain.

Therefore, it is acknowledged that any behavioral activity must be properly coordinated to produce optimal results. Learning and skill acquisition are behavioral activities in the sense that they are carried out over time for the purpose of instilling certain skills in a person for them to become unconscious reflective activities. It therefore becomes necessary for us to ascertain the psychological ends of the skill acquisition methods used in training activities, thus setting a reference standard for training methods with regard to psychological concerns.

Online skill training and psychology are interrelated in several ways as one cannot do without the other, to some extent especially with regard to synchronous and asynchronous types of online training. In synchronous learning, the individual students learn in real time, though they are separated by distance. But in asynchronous kind of training, the learners learn at their own pace of time and make use of pre-prepared materials to gain proficiency in their various fields of study.

Furthermore, synchronous and asynchronous training often produce certain psychological advantages as well as psychological stresses and strains. In general the psychological stresses usually occurring in the classroom learning environment are ambiguously reduced while some of such stresses are worsened by the method.

The psychological factors of the online training session include the following:

1. **Anxiety:** The virtual nature of online training produces a sense of anxiety that is claustrophobic in the learner. The feeling of being separated in space and time is been created in the learner because of anxiety.
2. **Stress:** All physically draining activities tend to create stress and tiredness on the individual undertaking such activities. Thus, online learning is inclusive of such stressful activities.
3. **Virtual learning fatigue:** At times, learners may become bored or fatigued with the monotony of staring into the scree for hours and become distraught with the whole process.
4. **Control:** In the asynchronous form of online learning, the learner acquires at his or her own pace and time which gives him a sense of control and self-esteem.
5. **Depression:** The stringent and unconsidering form of assessment used during online training classes may lead to depression in the individual.
6. **Reticence:** Continuous use of the online training method seems to create some kind of reticence in the individual learner hence such learner becomes introvertically reclined. This situation experienced by the learner majorly changes into a sense of loneliness, inwardness and severe pains, which may be dangerous for one's health.

15.0 Conclusion

Online skills training has over the years given learners the opportunity to acquire knowledge in way that is different from the usual face-to-face classroom setting. It is, however, very important for the online skills acquisitor to have a good awareness of the different issues involved in online training. They include its merits and demerits, approaches to online training, its various challenges, pedagogical factors in online skill training, different applications surveys, role-playing in online training as well as the psychological factors in the acquisition skills online.

Chapter Twenty-Six

Skill Development in Sports

1.0 Introduction

It is important that I begin this analysis by defining key words in this topic, namely skills, development and sport before further analysis of this entire subtopic Chambers Universal Learner's Dictionary (p. 690) defines a skill as cleverness at doing something, resulting either from practice or from natural ability. It is a job or activity that requires training and practice. It is also the capacity to do something well. Skills are usually acquired or learned, as opposed to abilities, which are often thought of as innate. Skills are the result of training the whole body to coordinate property. Individual increase their ability to master certain skills as they grow older. This is known as maturation, which is best learned by playing tennis, football or all other sports. Skills coordination are learned mostly through trial-error plus imitation. In this case, mistakes which are integral part of all learning, are bound to be made, for they can be no end result without initial attempts. Since young sportsmen learn sports skills largely by imitating others and practicing what they see them do, the most productive teachers of sports know how to perform a number of skills well.

On the other hand, development involves the process of horizontal increase in size or expansion in a thing or an individual. Oxford Advanced Learner's Dictionary (p. 400) defines development as the gradual growth of something so that it becomes more advanced, stronger, etc. Therefore development is often used synonymously with growth. Sports is an activity that uses physical exertion or skills competitively under a set of rules that is not based on athletics. They are seen as games or competitions involving physical activity organized for the entertainment of the people taking part or of spectators. They are synonymously used with games such as football, basketball, rugby, hockey, tennis, javelin, relay, short put, hammer hockey, tennis, etc. In the same vein Oxford Advanced Learner's Dictionary (p.) sees sports as can be described as amusements, funs, outdoor exercises or recreation activities.

However, skill development in sports gives academics coaches, students and sportsmen and women the rigorous and wider grounding and understanding in the rules, ethics and principles associated with the field. Developing other's skills in sports involves training, both physical and mental physical training consists of specifically selected exercises designed to develop and maintain the physique or body appearance of an individual. It is the daily exercises which individuals do either at school or outside school to give them an all-round development of the body. For example, a laborer who is cutting grass in the field is doing a physical exercise and is therefore likely to develop the muscles of his arms more than those of the other parts of the body. Similarly, a child who walks to school every morning takes exercise which develops the muscles of the feet more than any other muscles in the body. Therefore an individual needs all-round development of his body, and the exercise provided by day-to-day tasks does not always encourage balance muscle development.

Sports reflect the culture in which there exist and take a form that is consistent with such culture. As the culture changes, so do sports programs change. Many factors in a culture may affect sports programs such

as social, political, educational and religious beliefs. Sports provide opportunities for the individual for the participant and the group to learn from skilled personnel activities which are refreshing, invigorating, funny, exciting hence leading to positive physical, social, mental, and emotional th.

2.0   Developing Skills in Sports

Sports means a particular form of exercise such as athletics, swimming, boxing, wrestling or a game such as football or tennis. Sports is not just good for children's body, it is good for their minds also. It is common place that sports has psychological benefits for children, adolescents and teach them important life skills. Organized sports has many psychological and social benefits for children even more than the physical activity during play. This according to researchers is because children benefit from the social side of being in a team, and from the involvement of other children and adults.

www.healthdirect.gov.com all presents several benefits of sports to individual participants.

These include the following:

1. **Developmental benefits of sports:** Development from sports goes beyond learning new physical skills. Sports help children to develop better ways to cope with the challenges of life. Playing sports helps children learn to control their emotion and channel respective feelings in a positive way.
2. **Emotional benefits:** Physical activities do stimulate chemicals in the brain that make you feel better. So playing sports regularly improves one's overall emotional being. Research had shown that there is a connection between playing sports and self-esteem in children. Children feel better about themselves when they hear kind words from their coach, support from their team, or when they achieve success personally.
3. **Social benefits of sports:** Playing in a team helps children to develop many of the social skills they will need for life. It teaches them to cooperate to be less selfish and to listen to other children, as well as gives them a sense of belonging. It helps them to make new friends and build their social circle outside school.

An important aspect of playing in a team is accepting discipline. Playing sports means that children are require to follow certain rules that are associate in them, accept decisions and understand that they could be penalized for bad behavior. It greatly teaches them to take direction from their coach, referee and other adults during the exhibition of their sports skills. The above items are all part of physical education which is one of the basis for developing sports skills physical education is mainly concerned with education with the person in a particular sport being educated and with its parts in the care for that person as an individual, and as a part of the society as a whole. At times this could imply that a school child who is talented in a sporting activity, might have been protected from the demands of adult sport. Munrow (1972:22) is of the assertion that children should be insulated but not isolated. They should be involved and given good opportunity to participate instead of being looked down upon and be sidelined. As a matter of fact, talented children need to be protected from some external pressures, such as the worst aspects of professional sport attitudes and practices. In the process of developing a child's skill, it is possible that a child might have to be advised by either a coach or any physical educationist not to pay much attention to sports in contrast with other aspects of education during certain important periods.

Physical education as an important basis for skills development in sports has the following aims in it's curricular as outlined by Andrews John (1979:25)

1. The promotion of cognitive development
2. The promotion of aesthetic development
3. The promotion of moral development
4. The promotion of social development
5. The promotion of education for leisure
6. The promotion of fitness for positive living.

This means that in the course of acquiring and developing sports skills, the individual needs to have cognitive, moral, social, mental attributes and behaviors to enable him excel in such skill development. It therefore implies here that sports as a physical exercise is beneficial to participate in physical activities to

1. Cope with the physical emergencies and the excess strain which a person may face on a regular basis.
2. Allow a person undertake chosen leisure activities with maximum enjoyment.
3. Become fit and help control obesity and prevent adverse changes because of aging.
4. Obey rules and decisions made by coach and other physical educations.

3.0 Types of Skills to Master in Sports

Different sports often have their corresponding skills exhibited for the cognitive, moral, social, educational, psychological and health advancement of a sport athlete.

1. **Basketball:** Advanced skills in basketball include footwork, arm work, ball handling, dribbling, passing, shooting, defense (man to man or zonal) and team defense. To acquire/develop skills in footwork, the player must be able to
   a. Maintain balance on the foot.
   b. Make a short but sharp burst of speed and practice changing of direction.
   c. Keep feet close to the ground.
   d. Pivot by keeping one foot in place.
   e. Do reverse pivot by keeping one foot in place and rotating the other backward in a semi-circle.

For effective arm work, the player must be able to keep the arm moving when attacking; for defense, keep the hand up, to prevent shooting by opponent; use the arm to block shots.

Another skill to develop in basketball is known as ball handling. To develop such skill the player is expected to catch and receive the ball with his eyes on the ball; attempt short, snappy passes and follow through; use fingertip controls, cup his hands to receive the ball; and always go for the ball and not to wait for it; ensure the ball is passed in good direction with good speed to the earmarked colleague.

To dribble in basketball, the player must develop the skill of using wrist and fingers; keep the body low for protection while the head is held up; his/her palms are kept off the ball and only the fingers push the ball into the ground; control the ball in front of the athlete; keep the ball low, and below the waste, avoid a big bounce dribbling; practices dribbling without looking at the ball; and practices fast dribbling down the

court. An important skill to playing good basketball is "passing." The ability to move the ball, control and handle it quickly will ensure a successful game.

Types of passing include

1. **The chest or push passing:** This is where the ball is held with both hands, elbows close to the body finger spread with thumb pointed inward, and the ball is whipped with a strong wrist and elbow snap forward and follow through.
2. **The baseball pass:** This is where the ball is shifted in front of the waist to the throwing hand, the player also turns to the opposite side of the body in the direction of the pass, and he whips the ball as in field throw, steps toward the receiver and throws the ball with a full arm motion.
3. **The two-hand overhead pass:** Here, it is used particularly when passing over a smaller/shorter player.

Another skill to be developed in the game of basketball is shooting. Shooting is of different types depending on whether the player poise and hold the ball, chin high with both hands (the two-hand set shot) or where he holds the ball with both hands and his waist high, takes off with the left foot, leap high into the air, transferring the ball to the shooting hand as high as possible, and in front of the head in zonal defense, each man in the team marks an area of the playing court. While in man-to-man defense, player closely marks a player is in possession of the ball, the player attempts to place himself always between the opponent and his own basket.

In the sport of football, its corresponding skills to be acquired/developed are passing dribbling, heading goalkeeping, spinning the ball, chesting penalty kicking, and even defense. Various skills of passing include the long pass which has to do with the ball being kicked to a player in the other position of the football field away from the player in possession of the ball. But in a short pass, the ball is often kicked to the player who is at close distance with his teammate handling the ball. We also have the wall pass where a player kicks the ball to another who returns it without stopping the ball. That is, the ball bounces off the receiver-player's legs. This is like playing the ball against a wall, hence the name "wall pass." But in the chip pass, the foot stabs the ball close to the ground making the ball spin and rise in the needed direction. In "the lofted" pass, the ball is kicked in such a way that it rises above the players' heads. Examples of this type of pass is the corner kick and the free kick.

In the throw pass, skill needed to be developed is that the ball is kicked into space for another player of the same side to run and take possession. The kick must be timed appropriately by the player for the ball to be collected by the player for whom it was meant.

Dribbling is yet another skill in the game of football that can be acquired/developed by players. A forward player should be a good dribbler. Good dribbling depends on the ability to control the ball, burst or turn fast and cut in turn quickly without any form of interception by other players. But in heading, skills to be exhibited are actually in form of sport rules which include the following:

1. Do not let the ball hit you.
2. Go out to meet the ball.
3. Contact the ball frontally with your forehead.
4. Do not close your eyes but watch the flight of the ball until the moment of impact when it is possible to head it (Oduyale 1991:20).

Every coach, athlete, fan and every skill instructor of the knowledge that the fundamental element of sports is skill. Therefore skills form the fulcrum by which sporting activities are performed. Kicking and

passing in football, throwing and catching in cricket and baseball, dividing, turning and finishing in swimming, tackling and passing in rugby, passing and shooting in basketball and netball, learning, practicing and mastering the basic skills of sports is one of the foundations of coaching sports performance and athletic training.

In addition, www.healthdirect.gov.au streamlined seven sports skills every sportsman or athlete must master.

1. **Perform the skill:** This is the first and unfortunately for most athletes the last step in their skills learning program. Coaches come up with a drill while athlete learn and perform.
2. **Perform the skill very well:** Skill mastery comes from regular mastery combined with quality feedback from coaches and many incorporate the use of video and other performance analysis technology.
3. **Perform the skill very well and at speed:** Technically, perfection at slow speed may look great for the textbooks but unless the skill can withstand competition levels speed then it is not competition ready.
4. **Perform the skill very well at speed under fatigue:** Think of the danger zone in competition sports. Many competitions came down to the quality of skills execution during the last five percent of time and being able to perform fundamental skills when tired, dehydrated and suffering from neuromuscular fatigue is a winning edge in all sports.
5. **Perform the skill very well at speed under fatigue and under pressure:** This involves the number of times athletes missing targets or drop balls or makes errors at critical moments in competitions. Undoubtedly, emotional stress and mental pressure affect the ability of the athletes to perform skills with quality and accuracy.
6. Perform the skill very well, at speed, under fatigue and under pressure consistently. Being able to perform the skill under competition condition once could be lock, but being able to do it consistently under competition conditions is the sign of a real champion. Consistency in skills exhibition in competition comes from consistency in training standards. Such training standards include adopting a no-compromise approach to the quality of skill executed at training is a sure way to develop a consistent quality of skills execution in competition conditions.
7. **Perform the skill very well at speed, under fatigue, under pressure consistently in a competition condition:** The real factor on what makes a champion athlete is their capacity to perform consistently in competition condition. Performing a basic skill well is not difficult but adds the fatigue of seventy five minutes of competition, the pressure of knowing the whole season is on the line with one kick, the expectation of the board, the coach, the management, team mates and tens of thousands of fans and all of a sudden, that basic skills are not so basic.

   In light of the above, it therefore implies that the fundamental element of all sports is "skill." This is reemphasized by wgcoachng.com>sports-skills that the fundamental movement skills to be developed through Health and Physical Education include locomotive and nonlocomotive skills which include rolling, balancing, sliding, jogging, running, leaping, jumping, hopping, galloping and dodging.

   We also have object controlled skills examples of which include bouncing, throwing, catching, kicking, striking.
8. **Balance skills:** These has to do with movements where the body remains in one place but moves around its horizontal and vertical axes.
9. **Ball skills:** The skills here are as follows—catching, throwing, kicking, underarm roll, and striking.

By mastering fundamental movement skills, individual sportspersons will find it easier to learn fundamental sports skills. Depending on the type of sports a player or an athlete is engaging himself in, there is a specific set of skills he needs to master to do well in that particular area of sport that such individual performer involves himself in. However, basic skills are often generic to many sports. Sports people need to master basic skills before they can attempt more complex ones. But before they master such basic sports skills, it is incumbent on the sportsmen to understand motor learning stages. This is because understanding motor learning stages usually improve skills development and mastering. In developing sports skills also, the use of kinetic perception is very important. As an athlete tries to develop his skills of movement during sports exercises, he needs to perceive the direction of his movement for better game success. Thus kinetic perception is a factor that is relevant to the skills being developed or acquired. This would literally imply that there is a correlation between movement perception and football engineering ls.

4.0   The Role of Effective Practice

Practicing sports enables the player, athlete any sportsman to set goals and achieve them, whether they look and feel better about yourself or become a better player and teammate. Repetitions of skills during practice also enables one to learn from mistakes and become a more confident player. A sport practice is confined to a specific moment, shared by a particular group of people, all pursuing a common sports goal.

In sports, coaching, play and practice are said to be two of the important variables that influence skill acquisition in sports and sporting activities as stated by www.pheamerica.org.thefoundation.

However, they are four key elements that are responsible for developing an effective sports practice.

1.   Establishing standards of performance.
2.   Designing activities with a purpose.
3.   Creating a serene learning environment.
4.   Communicating clearly.

The above key variables are fundamental in running an effective practice.

The topic of skill acquisition, motor learning, skill transfer and best practice is a hot and complex topic. This is because as coaches continue to teach athletes on various skills common in sports, they usually face certain difficulties with regard to concepts involved in such sports. They often face the element of pressure in skills practices during such teaching and training sessions and ensure that training is more challenging and more demanding than the competition itself (wgcoaching.com>sports>skills).

Also, mountain biking is also a sport involving a skill component that is worth practicing. In road racing, the start alone is a skill worth practicing. Learning practicing and mastering the basic sports skills is one of the foundations of coaching, sports performance or athletic training. Athletes do not fail because their ability to perform the skill in competitions conditions is poor and that is a coaching issue.

In performance practice, an athlete has to train the way he wants to perform, how to learn and master a skill so that he can embrace his performance under competitive conditions. Performance practice is a logical, systematic seven-step process that takes athletes from the execution of the basic skills to being able to perform it under competition conditions.

Also, athletes should be taught to perform better visual and kinesthetic images. This involves the role of kinesthetic perception in supporting the acquisition of skills in sports.

5.0   Role Playing in Sports

Role playing refers to the duty assigned to a coach or player to support a team to perform very well. A role player refers to a player who plays a supporting role on his team and does it well and willingly. A role player could either be a bench player. In basketball, a role player could be either a bench player who is reserved by a coach to later replace another player or a player who is already in the basketball pitch performing his assigned sporting roles during a match. A role player in basketball is a player on the team who plays a supporting role on the roster. This player usually comes off the bench.

In role playing, each player has a role to play in any given sport be it football, basketball or any other kind of sports activity individuals often engage themselves in. each athlete within a team will often have both formal and informal roles to perform. Formal roles are those which are prescribed by the group, organization or team and are directly established to group members blog.innerdrive.co.uk>sports). Examples of formal roles in a sport context include the positional responsibilities held by athletes and the leadership role of a captain.

An example of role playing in sports is when you pretend that your friend is your boss and you have a practice conversation in which you ask for a raise. Another example is when you and your spouse pretend to be out on a first date, even though you have been married for ten years.

Individuals are they players or athletes in a sporting event do play different roles and are not simply to perform the same role. Sports usually receive an inordinate amount of attention and has attracted the interest of varieties of views, fans and supporters of different sporting clubs and activities. This attests to the fact that sports plays vital roles in today's global community irrespective of ethnic background, country of origin, race, gender, social standing or educational attainment of those involved in them either directly as participants or sponsors or indirectly as viewers and supporters of clubs. Irrespective of the kind of sports involved, role playing is common and is often performed by various categories of persons. For example, in the game of football, specific roles are often common to sports authorities to oversee. The coach, referee, linesmen, the players and the goalkeepers are expected to perform specific roles that are uniquely assigned to them to ensure that the success of the sport at a given point in time is realized.

In the game of wrestling and boxing, for example, the umpire's specific roles of overseeing a wrestling or boxing match that do issued between opponent contenders. The umpire ensures the rules and regulations set out by the sports authorities are succinctly adhered to by such fighting opponents. This means that role play also has to do with not only setting out rules by sports boards and authorities nor does sports sponsors having the willful responsibility supporting clubs financially but also implies that coaches and players/athletes have to seriously involve themselves in obeying those rules during the actual performance of physical exercise. Physical could be in form of training or actual sporting play in either a physical pitch. Physical exercise which is an important ingredient of sports is beneficial to participants in physical activities and the acquisition of physical fitness.

However, Andrews (1979) states categorically that such physical exercises are beneficial to sports participants in the following ways:

1.   To cope with the physiological demand of daily work without undue fatigue.
2.   To allow a person undertake chosen leisure activities with maximum enjoyment.
3.   To cope with physical emergencies and the excess strains which a person may face from time to time in life.
4.   To play the role of preventing malfunction of the various systems of the body.
5.   To help in the control of obesity and to help prevent adverse changes because of aging.

6.0   Kinetic and Physiological Issues

It is pertinent at this point that before discussing on this subtopic, the two key words, namely kinestic and physiological be clearly x-rayed.

While "kinestic" undoubtedly has to do with movement or motion of bodies, objects or things, *physiological* is "a derivative of physiology and it involves the way in which living bodies work." (Chambers Universal Learner's Dictionary: p. 533). Physiology itself refers to the study of the way in which living bodies. Therefore kinetic and physiological issues as they relate to skill development in sports has to do with how particular body parts of athletes/players perform certain sports actions in terms of their positional movements. Movement position is very vital in the physical movement training of athlete: success in sports performance depends on how effective the performers detect, find and use relevant sensory information. The source of sensory information are eksteroceptive and proprioceptive. The organs of eskteroceptive information source is eskteroceptive which is rooted in "vision" and "hearing" while the source of proprioceptive includes proprioceptive sensory receptor, specifically in muscles, tendons, joints and vestibular apparatus. Proprioceptor also called kenaesthetic perception or kinaesthetic senses which means the sensory input that occurs in the body that serves as feeling responsible for the correction of a movement. This means that the better the kinaesthetic perception is, the better the skill in football techniques vice versa. A runner may imagine how legs feel while performing the running action. However kinaesthetic imagery can also encompass other bodily feelings including body movement. Many young athletes should be encouraged to train in terms of sporting competitions from an early age. A major problem for elite athletes is to deal with the feeling of choking when performing sports.

7.0   Stages of Skill Acquisition in Sports

Skill acquisition and development remains the most critical element in the successful performance of an athlete. A strong, well-conditioned athlete with a poor skill level is akin to a high performance race car with flat tires. Any athletic skill is actually a motor skill, which can be defined as an act or task that has a goal to achieve and requires voluntary body or limb movement to be properly performed. Many times, however, the terms skills and ability has been used interchangeably to mean the same.

However, any young sportsperson who undergoing the process of acquiring and developing talent and the coach imparting learning into such youngster must as a matter of necessity be aware that such skills can be developed or imparted through a number of three distinct stages. They are outlined by tscienceinsider. com as follows:

    i.   The cognitive stage
    ii. Associative stage
    iii. Autonomous stage

    1. **The Cognitive Stage of Skill Acquisition**

This is the skill acquisition stage of mental processing of information knowing, learning and understanding things. It is closely associated with a performer's or an athlete's introduction to a skill set or activity involving awkwardness, errors and confusion. While in this stage, practitioners must realize the type of exercise and coaching behaviors that are most appropriate to provide athletes with the best possible foundational beginning. An informative and positive continuous

feedback should very importantly be used in facilitating both confidence in and an understanding of a given task in sports.

Also tasks in sports should be structured in such a way as to ensure that a high degree of early success is witnessed, ensuring that a performer's feelings of their own inherent competence grows. As the first phase in skill acquisition, the cognitive stage is also referred to as "the novice phase of learning." This stage has to do with painting the correct picture of how a skill or task is to be completed. Here, a platform of functional movement skill should be ensured for a performer to graduate out of this stage. Functional movement skill produces the base from which specific movements in sports later grow, hence their importance cannot be underestimated. This is important for both coaches and teachers of those from less socially fortunate backgrounds to understand.

However, when an athlete or player seems to be displaying a full-fleshed understanding and execution of a skill void from conscious mechanical thought, their journey to the associative has just started. Here, the theory of cognitive stage of skill acquisition/development fix in the athlete/player the idea/thought to work out what to do. The theory states that learners attempt to cognitively understand the requirements and parameters of movements. Imagine an athlete learning to serve in tennis. To begin with, the novice athlete has to concentrate very hard, attending to many, if not all aspects of the serve. In this case, the amount of information being processed in his mind can be any or all of the following questions:

1. Do I hold the racket?
2. Where should my feet be?
3. How should I move my arm?
4. How do I time the movement?
5. Where am I hitting to?

The above questions highlight the self-talk that might be going on inside the head of the athlete when learning to serve. Mistakes will inevitably be made by the athlete at this stage while actively taking part in problem-solving and trying to make sense of the task.

2. Associative Stage of Skill Acquisition

The stage is characterized by much less verbal information, smaller gains in performance, conscious performance, adjustment making, awkward and disjointed movement and taking a long time to complete. Once an individual can execute a skill to a basic level and understand proper technique, instruction can then progress to the associative stage (us.humankinetics.com>Excerpts). The associative stage of skill acquisition and development is when the athlete has progressed from thinking about what they are doing to thinking about how they are doing it.

The associative stage of skill acquisition is also seen as a stage in learning skills when the learner refines movement by defecting and correcting errors. Here, the performer or individual begins to understand the requirements of the skills and becomes more consistent. He is learning how to perform the skill well and how to adapt the skill. This means that this stage is intensified by an emphasis on practice. This is also known as "the practice phase." Here, the learner having acquired an idea of what the skill is, needs to repeat the movement to enhance performance result. In this stage, there is less self-talk and the athlete can perform chunks of the skill with less thoughts but performing the movement as a whole requires cognitive thought and problem solving (tscienceinsider.com). The associative stage of learning can continue for varying periods of time, depending on the complexity of the task and volume of practice. Some performers may never progress beyond this stage if they do not invest heavily in skill development.

3. **Autonomous stage of skill acquisition**

In this stage, the skill is almost automatic to produce and requires small amount of thought. Athletes require less conscious control of movements and the actions produced often feel effortless. Thus, less attention is required to allow the performer focus more on perceptual question, such as where their opponent is within the court. At this stage, athletes can also produce the movement alongside other demanding tasks, as their attentional capacity is no longer needed to control the action, for example, where they needed to move to after their service to be prepared for the return shot. Being able to perform automatically spells out learning success. Here, the beginner is expected to continue to practice this basic step skills so that the step skills are automatically understood, enabling him to connect the dots of the complex skills combinations and become a skilled or experienced step participant.

On the whole, autonomous stage is achieved when the learner has mastered all subparts of a skill and are able to combine them to perform the whole sequence automatically with precision. This implies that they are able to perform with full awareness while also identifying and correcting errors quickly and independently. They can also easily process and adapt to external feedback. A person at the stage can confidently execute a skill while focusing on multiple factors at the same time. A rugby player passing the ball in game play is a goal example. Not only do have to receive the ball but also need to be spatially aware of the location of opposition player trying to tackle them, their own support players and decide who to pass the ball to, while still throwing the ball with accuracy, perfect timing and optimal tactical advantage. This may take place in just two to three seconds. When a sportsperson can execute a skill effortlessly without stress, he is most likely at the autonomous e.

8.0 Conclusion

Skill development in sports is necessary for all-round development of an individual. But the performer should be willing to record success in acquiring skills by undergoing its three different stages of acquisition. From there he will have to master different skills in his nature-oriented sports activity which will enable him to play his role effectively taking into cognizance his body movement for successful sporting.

Chapter Twenty-Seven

Communication Skills Development

1.0 Introduction

There is no meaningful project, program or business that can be successfully executed without communication. Communication "maintains and animates life. It is also the motor and expression of social activity and civilization, it leads people and people's from instinct to inspiration, through variegated process and systems of enquiry, command and control; it creates a pool of ideas, strengthens the feeling of togetherness through exchange of messages…communication integrates knowledge, organization and power and runs as a thread linking the earliest memory of man of his noblest aspirations through constant striving for a better life" (MacBride, 1980:3).

The UNESCO publication edited by MacBride (1980) says further that "Communication has become a vital need for collective entities and communities. Societies as a whole cannot survive today if they are not properly informed about politic affairs, international and local events, or weather conditions, etc. (pp. 14–15)." Communication also refers to a process by which information is exchanged between or among individuals through a common system of symbols, signs or behavior. As a process, communication involves sending and receiving messages or exchange of messages using written or spoken form of language and sometimes through nonverbal means as facial expression, gestures and even voice qualities (Iyorza, 2015). From the above, communication is not simply broadcasting or sending out. Information, but involves a two-way process which is sending and receiving information and therefore requires both speaking and listening and most importantly an understanding of the information being transmitted and received.

Good communication skills can enhance the way you operate through life, making you have a trouble-free relationship with others. Poor communication skills, on the other hand can sour relationships from business to personal, and make one's life significantly difficult. Looked at from a more practical perspective, an individual without the means of effective communication in the society is not in full existence in that society. Communication functions to meet both the material and nonmaterial needs of man. Man does not live by bread alone; the need for communication is evidence of an inner urge toward a life enriched by cooperation with others (MacBride, 1980). One of the most effective means or tool of communication is language. According to Babatunde (2002:1), language is the divine benevolence of man that is so inexorably tied to the effective existence of man in the society that any meaningful discussion of man must begin with it (it steers the course) and it ends the discussion. The end and purpose of language is the enhancing of communication.

Language not only distinguishes man from other animals, it equally helps man socialize with other humans. So, human existence and development depends largely on the existence and development of language for communication. It can be clearly stated that MacBride's statement quoted about expresses the essence of communication which mainly depends on the existence and development of language. Language skills are what make up the ability to comprehend incoming information and articulate outgoing messages.

For development plans to be embraced, they must be articulated and channeled through commination. Communication is broadly divided into two namely: verbal and nonverbal communication. Verbal communication is further divided into oral (the use of human speech organs in producing meaningful sounds that represent meanings) and written (the use of symbols, alphabets or some form of signs that represent peculiar meanings). While nonverbal communication involves the use of body movement, distance or para-language for information transmission purposes (Iyorza, 2015).

This chapter intends to look at communication skills development in skill acquisition. Employers demand people who can listen, comprehend and make work cooperatively with others because "… 4the scientific and technological environment have changed as such good communication skills are necessary, you can't survive without them." (Chambers, 2001).

2.0   Receptive Skills

In communication, a receptive capacity for decoding any language and content of the message is a skill which can be trained and developed through teaching. Receptive skills are the ways in which people extract meaning from the discourse they see or hear. Receptive skills comprise listening and reading. Reves and Levine (1988) indicated that listening and reading are distinct but similar skills sharing commonalities in integrated and holistic comprehension of the message.

Further research studies have suggested crossover and overlap between listening and reading abilities beyond their unique trait of skill operation and function (Bae and Bachman, 1998).

Listening

Being a good listener is one of the best ways to be a good communicator. Listening ability lies at the very heart of all growth, from birth through the years of formal education, the better learning skills are developed, the more productive our learning efforts (Vennum, 1987). Listening is consensual activity and cannot be enforced. It is considered an ability to identify and understand what others say or speak. This involves understanding a speaker's accent or pronunciation, grammar, vocabulary and gauging the meaning. Listening represents "a kind of human behavior that almost everyone thinks important" (Weaver, 1972, p. 24). It is perfectly possible to hear, but not listen. Hearing denotes a capacity to discriminate characteristics of one's environment through aural sense perception while listening is a relationally oriented phenomenon, it "connects and bridges" (Lipari, 2012, p. 233). To listen thus involves skill sets that go beyond the physiological requirements to perceive sound.

Abilities to comprehend, understand, and reflect spoken language are universally recognized to help foster professional success and personal happiness alike. Active listening which involves paying close attention to what the other person is saying, asking questions and rephrasing what the person says to ensure understanding has additionally been linked to academic motivation and achievement and a higher likelihood of upward mobility in the workplace (Sypher, Bostrom, and Seibert, 1989). Adding to the importance of listening, research finds that natural decrements in the ability to process speech can negatively impact individual and relational health and well-being (Villaume, Brown and Darling, 1994). Several professions are built on listening such as therapists, social workers, customer service specialists, and healthcare providers. Even more businesses and occupations rely on listening to survive. Good listening is thus perhaps the quintessential positive interpersonal communication behavior (Bodie, 2012).

Judgments of listening competency are based on the degree to which a listener is perceived as attentive, understanding, responsive, friendly, and able to sustain conversational flow (Bodie *et al.,* 2012). How then

can one know if listening is taking (or has taken) place? Through the responses that listeners enact while engaging in a discussion.

Reading:

Another receptive skill is reading. Reading is a very complex process involving many physical, intellectual and emotional relations. Physical variable which is the visual perception is a prerequisite to accurate and rapid reading. However, many people think that reading merely involves the ability to sound the words printed on a page (Al-jawi, 2010). Reading is versatile in nature and thus, a reader must be skilled to derive meaning from printed text accurately and efficiently. Reading as a skill intensifies one's knowledge, understanding and intelligence. "Reading any material is expected to make the reader more competent and give him more knowledge and insight" (Gangula and Eliah, 2015).

Reading is one of the resources of knowledge, therefore one must know the drive and intent. Also, as an active process, a reader can understand a text only when he actively puts to use his mental facilities. According to Al-jawi (2010), reading involves the following:

1. **Knowledge of certain reading mechanism:** The direction in which a text is to be read which varies from one language to another. For instance, English is read from left to right where as Arabic is read from right to left. Another mechanism is the eye movement drill and the way meaning is represented in print which also varies from language to language.
2. Understanding the meaning or message the words are intended to carry.
3. **Understanding the language that is written:** This is the first requirement of reading. One needs prior knowledge of the language in which a text is written to derive sense.
4. **Reading involves thinking process:** It is the attempt of the reader to understand as nearly as possible the thinking of the writer.
5. **Reading is an interactive process:** The reader interacts in a less obvious way. Ones reaction to any text is determined by many things—previous knowledge, attitudes and beliefs about the content.
6. **Reading is a life-support system:** One needs to read reference books, journals and textbooks to get information necessary for day to day living.

Some of the reading strategies proffer by Shikha (2012).

1. Recognizing the script of a language.
2. Deducing the meaning and use of unfamiliar lexical items.
3. Understand explicitly stated information.
4. Understand conceptual meaning.
5. Understand the communicative value of sentences and utterances.

Another important factor about reading is that while reading, each reader tries to understand what he reads from his own perspective in the context of his past or present knowledge of the text. Thus while reading, a reader interacts with a text, decodes it and constructs meanings in the process. What he constructs depends on not only what the writer writes but also what the reader brings to the text (Gangula and Eliab, 2015). The main ways or reading are:

1. **Skimming:** Helps the reader get a general surface idea of a text.
2. **Scanning:** Helps the reader get a specific piece of information by quickly going through a text.

3. **Extensive reading:** Constitutes reading of longer texts for the reader's own pleasure.
4. **Intensive reading:** Helps a reader to extract specific information, an in-depth, hidden or symbolic meanings from a text. A good reader varies his speed of reading depending on the purpose of his reading (Gangula and Eliab, 2015).

3.0 Expressive Skills

Expressive skills are also called productive or actual skills, means the dissemination of information that a user yields. These skills are crucial as they give students opportunity to practice real life activities in the classroom. Expressive language skills can be defined as the skills necessary to form thoughts and express them using appropriate word and grammar combinations. This may also include gesturing and facial expressions, especially in childhood (Kulman, 2015). The main forms of communication people think about when discussing expressive language are speaking and writing. This section shall focus on speaking and writing as a form of expressive language skills which are used for producing and conveying information. Speaking and writing are communicative tasks and imply an audience. Therefore the message must be organized so that it is communicated effectively.

Speaking

Saduku (2015) put it thus, that speaking is all special; when words are read, ideas written and thoughts heard, all that would be needed will be the expression of one's speaking ability. When sounds are projected wrongly or weakly, the listener misses out and may regard the speaker as incompetent.

Burns and Joyce (1997) and Luoma (2004:2) define speaking as an interactive process of constructing meaning that involves producing, receiving and processing information. Its form and meaning are dependent on the context in which it occurs, including the participants themselves the physical environment, and the purposes for speaking. Communication through speaking has many assets, such as facial expressions, gestures and even body movements. Such factors facilitate communication (Elmenoufy, 1997:10; Widdowson, 1998 and Burns, 1998). The purpose of speaking can be either transactional or interactional. In transactional discourse, language is used primarily for communicating information. Accurate and coherent communication of the message is important as well as confirmation that the message has been understood. Language serving this purpose is message-oriented rather than listener-oriented (Nunan, 1989:27).

Interactional or interpersonal use of language is used for establishing or maintaining a relationship. Examples of interactional uses of language are greetings, small talks and compliments. The language used here is listener-oriented (Dornyei and Thurrell, 1994 and Richards, 1990).

Sheth (2016) highlighted three sub-skills of speaking which are:

1. **Vocabulary:** The body of words used in a particular language. The development of new vocabulary is an activity that spans all the skills of language.
2. **Structural accuracy:** This has to do with the correct usage of sentence structure either in dialogue or writing.

    Developing structural accuracy in speaking is a process that should be accompanied by classroom activities (Sheth, 2016).
3. **Phonological accuracy:** Understanding how to correctly pronounce words is another important element of speaking skills.

Similarly, Florez (1999) also highlighted the following skills underlying speaking:

a. Using grammar structure accurately.
b. Assessing characteristics of the target audience, including shared knowledge, status and power relations, or differences in perspectives.
c. Selecting vocabulary that is understandable and appropriate for the audience.
d. Applying strategies to enhance comprehensibility.
e. Paying attention to the success of the interaction and adjusting components of speech.

It can be observed from the above mentioned speaking skills that speaking is a complex mental activity which differs from other activities because it requires greater effort of the central nervous system (Bygate, 1998:23). It includes processes and planning. First the speaker has to retrieve words and phrases from memory and assembles them into syntactically and propositionally appropriate sequence (Harmerr, 2001:269-270).

Writing

Nunan (1991) defined writing as an extremely complex cognitive activity in which the writer is required to demonstrate control of variables simultaneously. Writing is one of the four skills (listening, speaking, reading and writing) in language. It is the system of written symbols, representing the sounds, syllabus or words of language, with different mechanisms—capitalization, spelling and punctuation, word form and function (Durga and Rao, 2013). The writing skill is the 'hard copy' of your intellectual level or the level of your expression (Sadiku, 2015). A person with good writing skills is always victorious at expressing oneself.

Generally, writing is very important because communication is transmitted more through writing than any other type of media. Written communication is influenced by the vocabulary and grammar used, writing style, precision and clarity of the language used. Another reason why written communication is important is because the message written down is for posterity. One can read it whenever one likes, especially for research purposes. Written communication can also serve as a form of acknowledgement—(recognition of achievement). And sometimes helps to clarify thoughts and thinking processes. Written document can help you stay up to date with development in whatever project you are involved in.

Durga and Rao (2018), highlighted the importance of writing skills

1. In searching and obtaining a job.
2. To write technical documents, research papers, and put forth the right facts and information.
3. To make presentations and reports, etc.
4. For improving communication skills.
5. For improving creativity, exploration, and essential for self-understanding.

4.0 Verbal Communication Skills

Verbal communication is any communication that uses words to share information with others. Verbal communication is the most common way people relay messages and these messages should be conveyed respectfully. It can therefore include both written and spoken language, though many people use the term to describe only spoken language. People with hearing impairment consider sign language to be another form of verbal communication (Kabir, 2017).

Verbal element of communication is all about the words one chooses and how these words are heard and interpreted. For instance, the choice of words you use when communicating with a young child is quite different from a conversation with an old friend. A conversation with a friend is equally different from a business discussion. Under these circumstances, one uses simple and short sentences to talk with the child; informal language to chat with an old friend and more technical language when discussing with a colleague. Written and spoken language have been extensively handled in the sub-section of expressive skills. This section shall look at why verbal communication is important.

McKay, Martha and Patrick (1995) view that verbal communication helps one meet various needs through one's ability to express oneself. Through verbal communication, one can ask questions to get specific information; describe things, peoples and ideas; one can also inform, persuade and entertain others which are considered the general purposes of public speaking.

Barnard (2021) underscores the importance of verbal communication in the following areas:

a. **Managerial role:** Oral communication skills are essential for many areas of management. Through this skills, one can command respect from colleagues while building a strong team-spirit. One can also be able to handle unexpected crisis.
b. **Workplace success:** One needs strong communication skills to be able to talk to clients, customers, team members, request information and discuss problems.
c. **Secure a new job:** An employer needs an employee that will be able to speak clearly, concisely and confidently.

Verbal communication as already mentioned is the communication that uses words to share information with others. To ensure that what you have heard and understood is what was intended, two techniques are used which are reflection and clarification. "Reflection is the process of paraphrasing and restating what the other person has just said, to check that you have understood. While clarification is the process of seeking more information to inform your understanding, for example, by asking questions" (Skills you Need, 2017).

5.0 Nonverbal Communication

A substantial portion of communication is nonverbal. It is sending and receiving messages in variety of ways without the use of verbal code (word)s (Ben-nun, 2014). It involves those nonverbal stimuli in a communication setting that are generated by both the source (speaker) and his or her use of the environment and have potential message value for the source or receiver (Samovar, Porter and McDaniel, 2009). Nonverbal communication is both intentional and unintentional. It includes touch, glance, eye contact (gaze), volume, vocal nuance, proximity, gestures, facial expression, pause (silence) intonation, dress, posture, smell, word choice and syntax, and sounds (paralanguage), Ben-nun (2014).

Nonverbal communication can be understood best in relation to the settings in which it occurs. Settings are defined both in terms of the varying roles taken by actors within societies and the diverse cultures in which expressions and gestures are learned (Gordon and Druckman, 2019). Gesture as a medium of communication co-ordinate with vocal and written language by Fancis Bacon (1884; in 1st ed.). He suggested that "as the tongue speaketh to the ear, so the hand speaketh to the eye" (quoted in Kendon, 1981, p. 155).

Knapp (1972) suggested seven dimensions that describe the major categories of nonverbal behavior research as related to communication:

1. **Kinesis:** Commonly referred to as 'body language'. This includes posture, body movements, gestures, eye behaviors and facial expressions. Posture and movement can convey a great deal of information.

2. **Paralanguage:** This is defend as content-free vocalizations and patterns associated with speech such as voice pitch, volume, frequency, stuttering, filled pauses (for example, "ah"), silent pauses, interruptions and measures of speech rate and number of words spoken in a given unit of time. A tone of voice can have effect on the meaning of a sentence. A strong tone of voice may be interpreted to mean approval and enthusiasm. The same words said in a hesitant tone of voice may be interpreted as disapproval and a lack of interest (Kendra, 2014).

3. **Physical contact:** Communicating through touch is another important nonverbal behavior. Touch can be used to communicate affection, familiarity, sympathy and other emotions.

4. **Proxemics:** Involves interperson spacing which is an important type of nonverbal communication. The amount of distance needed and the amount of space perceived as belonging to a person is influenced by factors such as social norms, situational factors, personality characteristics and level of familiarity.

5. **Physical characteristics:** This includes one's appearance; such as skin color, body shape, body odor.

6. Related to physical characteristic is the category of artefacts or adornment such as perfume, clothes, jewelry, and wigs. Appearance can alter physiological reactions, judgments and interpretation (Ben-nun, 2014).

7. Environmental factors makeup the last category and deal with the influences of the physical setting in which the behavior occurs—a classroom, an office, a hall-way or a street corner.

Knapp's seven dimensions help depict the breadth of nonverbal communication. It is observed by Gordon and Druckman (2019) that physical characteristics, adornment and environmental factor categories do not involve an overt nonverbal expressions, but rather information about the actor that is communicated nonverbally. An important distinction in viewing nonverbal behavior as communication is that between the encoder and the decoder. The encoder is the person who develops and sends the message while the decoder is receiver of the message. Within the context of the encoder—decoder distinction, a major concern is that of intention and whether intended and unintended messages obey the same rules and principles of communication (Dittmann, 1978).

One of the model of nonverbal communication presented by Ekman and Friesen (1969) is distinction between the three characteristics of nonverbal behavior which are

1. Usage
2. Origin and
3. Coding

1. **Usage:** Refers to the circumstances that exist at the time of the nonverbal act. It include the physical setting (office, school), role relationship (supervisor-employee) and emotional tone of the interaction (formal and informal, stressful or relaxed). It also involves the relationship between verbal and nonverbal behavior. For instance, nonverbal acts may serve to support or substitute for verbal behaviors.

2. **Origin:** Some nonverbal behaviors are rooted in the nervous system such as reflex actions; while some are learned and used in dealing with the environment.
3. **Coding:** The meaning attached to a nonverbal act. For example, a thumbs-up sign for signaling that everything is ok.

Another distinction made by Ekman and Fresen (1969) to categorize the nonverbal behavioral acts are:

a. **Emblems:** These are nonverbal acts that have verbal translation and can substitute for words. Examples include waving the hands in a greeting or frowning to indicate disapproval, also emblems that depicts religion or religious acts. Gordon and Druckman (2019) added that the most survival based emblematic expressions which shows degree of universality is the emblems representing, attitude and responses of "yes," "no," and "I don't know."
b. **Illustrators:** These are movements that are tied directly to speech and serve to illustrate what is verbalized. An example is holding the hands a certain distance apart to indicate the length of an object.
c. **Regulators:** These nonverbal acts serve to regulate conversation flow between people. Regulators may be subtle indicators to direct verbal interaction. Such as head nods, body position shifts and eye contact.
d. **Adaptors:** Are behavioral habits and are triggered by some feature of the setting that relates to the original need. Examples, scratching the head and arm-folding.
e. **Affect displays:** These consist primarily of facial expressions of motions which may include happiness, sadness, anger, surprise, fear, disgust and interest (Ekman, 1994).

Every day, one respond to thousands of nonverbal cues and behaviors. Nonverbal communication is one of the key aspects of communication and especially important in a high-context culture. It can seriously undermine the message contained in one's words if one is not careful to control it.

6.0   Benefits of Effective Communication Skills

Leaders who know how to communicate effectively with those around them will see better productivity and improved relationships in every aspect of their lives.

According to CLIMB Professional Development and Training (2019), some benefits of effective communication one sees in and outside the office are as follows:

1. **Building trust:** Effective communication fosters trust with others.
2. **Preventing or resolving problems:** The ability to communicate effectively plays a large role in resolving conflicts and preventing potential one's from arising.
3. **Providing clarity and direction:** With effective communication skills, one is able to deliver clear expectations and objectives for one's team.
4. **Creates better relationships:** Good communication improves relationships: good communication improves relationships, both withy employees and in one's personal life with friends and family members.
5. **Increases engagement:** By prioritizing effective communication, one can increase engagement and also boost satisfaction among team members.

6. **Improves productivity:** When team members understand their roles, the roles of others and their expectations, they can focus more on their work and less on workplace issues.

7. **Promotes team building:** With improved communication, team members will be able to rely on each other. And this may leads to division of labor which may encourage positive feelings and relationships between team members.

Similarly, Bodla (n.d.) looked at the benefits of communication in business from the following points.

1. **Healthy organizational environment:** The activities of the management and the employees in any business organization are governed by social as well as psychological laws. If the management has to keep the healthy organizational environment and healthy relations with the individuals from outside, other business houses, government authorities, etc., it must use the communication channels and media effectively.

2. **Management-employee relations:** As organizations need people and people also need organizations, people can use organization and organization can use people to reach their objectives by communicating properly with each other. The employees and the management should develop the link of communication for better mutual understanding and encourage each other to achieve their self-interests.

3. **The external and internal communication network:** Every business finds it necessary to maintain both the internal and external communication. The communication between the management and the workers is an internal communication. The management must be well-informed about the internal activities of the organization. Especially those businesses that are spread over different places in the country. These divisions and branches maintains a link (through communication) with the management of the central organization. In some of the multinational corporations, the directors and the managers spend their time in maintaining communication links. The dynamics of the internal system influence the activities of the external system.

4. **Functionalization:** This is the division of work into different kinds of duties. Functionalization naturally leads to specialization. There are specialists who acquire a vast knowledge and experience in their limited subject. This specialized knowledge, training and experience will be useless if it is not communicated. So, experts in different field must be able to communicate their knowledge to the management and the employees, and the company may derive benefit from the advice, suggestions and information provided by these experts.

5. **Trade unions-labor problems:** The businessmen are mostly after productivity gains and other economic and technical benefits. Sometimes, this tendency of the businessmen comes in conflict with the problems, which are primarily human. The employees are now more conscious of their rights and are now organized into trade unions, which continuously demand the rights of the employees, better working conditions and dignity of labor. The employers are convinced that there ought to be some ways of effective communication between the management and the workers to develop better employee's satisfaction and a sense of security.

6. **Competitors:** Businessmen seek to obtain profit from the sale of their goods and services and the consumers seek the satisfaction of their wants by buying them in the market. The products of common consumption are available in the market in many brands and the buyers are free to buy any of them. A businessman who wants to survive in this world of free competition should know how to communicate better. A good salesman should be efficient.

Apart from the above points, developing communication skills can help all aspects of one's life, from ones professional life to social gatherings and everything in between.

7.0 Barriers to Communication

Communication is a complex process involving shared and unspoken agreements between individuals. Several types of barriers prevent us from transmitting our ideas meaningfully and these may occur at any stage in the communication process. It is hard to identify these barriers, but with the aid of feedback one can partially know if communication has succeeded or failed (Bodla, [n.d.]).

The following are categorization of barriers to communication (Skills you Need, 2017 and Bodla, [n.d.])

1. **Language and semantic barriers:**
   These barriers are caused by the following:
   a. **Lack of common language:** Every language has its own vocal symbol and its own grammatical structures. If the communication and the receiver belong to different language groups, the lack of a common language will be a barrier to communication between them.
   b. **Semantic barriers:** A word may have a variety of meanings associated with it. The meaning attributed to a word by the communicator may not be the same as that which the receiver attribute to that same word. A word can have different meaning to different people at different occasions.
   c. **Poor vocabulary:** Poor vocabulary makes one's message more complicated. Poor vocabulary does not allow the communicator to write or speak effectively. It does not allow the receiver to understand the message clearly and completely.
   d. **Poor knowledge of grammar and punctuation:** Poor knowledge to grammar and punctuation is a barrier to verbal communication. An understanding of grammatical structures provide excellent basis for effective writing, speaking and reading skills. And also, a knowledge of punctuation is essential for effective communication.
2. **Organizational barriers:** These are caused by the following factors
   a. **Hierarchical barriers:** In an organization, communication transmission must flow through certain formal channels which are established by the organizational hierarchy. The employees are expected to contact their superiors and their subordinates through their immediate superiors or subordinates. This often results in hardship and difficulties in maintaining free flow of communication because the subordinates find it hard to communicate their problems to their superiors.
   b. **Increasing specialization of the workforce:** Increasing specialization of the workforce is posing a serious barrier to effective internal communication in large-size business organizations. The tasks are specified and the procedures are structured in such a way that the workforce can communicate with people in other functional groups.
   c. **Wrong choice of medium:** The various media of communication (oral, written or nonverbal are suitable for communicating at different times and for different purposes. Therefore, it is essential to think about their merits and limitations, before selecting one of the media for communication. For instance, the sales manager must think over if it would be better for him to hold a face-to-face talk with the prospective buyer than talking to him on the phone.
   d. **Length and complexity of messages:** The length of the message received by the receiver is one of the major barriers to communication. In a busy organization, a person who is connected with all the formal and informal channels of communication, is bound to be very busy in receiving and imparting the messages rather than a person who is supposed to receive the mes-

sages through a single channel. Communication under-load can also be a barrier to communication. An employer who is under-communicated gets bored because of his noninvolvement.

3. **Physical barriers:** Physical barriers are caused by the following factors:

   a. **Noise:** Noise is quite often a barrier to communication. It interferes with the transmission of the signals. The disturbance is usually in the form of sounds, visual, audio-visual, written, physical or psychological form. For instance, in manufacturing organization, oral communication is rendered difficult by the electronic noise like blaring noise of the stereo and such other noises which often interferes in communication.

   b. **Time and distance:** Time also act as barriers to the smooth flow of communication. If the employee does not communication with his superior for a long time, or if husband and wife stay away from each other for a long time, it may create a communication gap between them which may affect their relationship

   Distance between the transmitter and the receiver becomes a mighty barrier. Faulty sitting arrangement in the office can create a kind of communication gap which can be eliminated by adjusting the distance.

   c. **Age and educational background:** The age, maturity, educational background and the eras in which a person grows up make a generation which inevitably comes in the way of human communication. The generation gap between becomes obvious in their use of vocabulary and style of speeches and the values of life which they adhere.

   d. **Sex:** When men and work together in a group, men tend to be more assertive, self-confident and aggressive than the woman. The sex stands as a barrier to a direct, honest and appropriate expression of a female's thought opinions and beliefs.

4. **Socio-psychological barriers:** These barriers are caused by social and psychological status and are as follows:

   a. **Status barrier:** Status is a position or social rank of a person in a group. Status consciousness exists in every organization and is one of the major barriers to effective communication status reflects the degree of power, authority, importance and responsibility placed on an individual by other people in the organization. The subordinates are usually afraid of communicating unpleasant and unfavorable information to the high-status people. This status consciousness is harmful in the process of upward communication.

   b. **Attitudes and values:** Personal attitudes and opinion often act as barriers to effective communication. Message are interpreted by the people in terms of their attitudes and values which may be different because of their different backgrounds.

   c. **Abstracting:** This may be defined as the process of focusing attention on some details and omitting others. Language is used to communicate ones experience and feelings, but one cannot communicate every detail of his experience to others. Attention is being focused on some details and the rest is forgone.

   d. **Bad listening:** Some people often become inattentive while receiving a message. A poor listener always feel that the thought in his mind is more interesting than what the speaker is saying. For instance, a college student involves himself in thinking about his girl-friend rather than listening to the lecture of his professor. Or an employee may get engrossed in worrying about the sickness of his child rather than listening to the instruction given by his manager. The lack of interest in the message contents is a strong barrier to communication.

   e. **Emotions:** Emotions are our feelings about the world around us. The positive emotions such as joy, love or affection do not interfere with communication, but the negative emotions act as strong barriers to effective communication. Emotionally excited communicator cannot orga-

nize his message properly. His nervous state of mind does not allow him to think clearly and ends up expressive his blurred thoughts with gesticulations and keeps on repeating the same words.

    f.   The source of communication (halo effect)

            Trust is an essential dimension of all human encounter (Bodla, n.d.). What two people say to each other and how they interpret it depends on the level of trust between them. Distrust distorts mutual understanding and takes away pleasurable and acceptable aspects of communication. If one trust the speaker, his attitude may easily change according to what the speaker proposes.

5.   **Physiological barriers:** Physiological barriers to communication may result from the receiver's physical state. For example, a receiver with reduced hearing may not fully grasp the content of a spoken conversation especially is there is significant background noise. And also a receiver with poor eyesight may not be able to see the speaker's nonverbal signal.

6.   One must be educated to use the written form of communication as well as the skill of reading.

8.0 Maximizing Communication Skills

Effective communication is very important in every aspect of human life. Therefore developing an effective communication skill plays a vital role. The following are ways by which communication can be maximized or improved.

1.   Learners should be exposed to more communication skills and in different methods.

2.   They should encouraged to communicate in the target language frequently in their day to day lives. This acquaintance with the language will help them to develop their confidence.

3.   Learners should be encouraged to develop reading habits to minimize their communication problems; they should be constantly encouraged to make use of the dictionary for their enhancement.

4.   Involving the learners and making them to play roles in the team projects helps to motivate them toward engaging themselves in such team works, which will lead to vocabulary development, enhancement of communication skills, through their interaction with their peers.

5.   Moreover, since communication involves two persons, groups or parties, the listener also has a part to play in the improvement of the communication process.

The listener can do the following to improve the communication process between the two parties.

1.   **Be an active listener:** Being an active listener does not necessarily mean intermittent disruption of the communication process or the interruption of the speaker. One can actively listen by using nonverbal clues like a nod, a raise of the eyebrows, a wink, or raising the hands in support or objection.

2.   To participate in communication effectively, the listener has to put away distracting thoughts and try as much as possible to pay attention to both the speaker's verbal and body language. Constantly calling on the speaker to repeat his/her statement hinders the flow of communication.

3.   One can express emotions such as surprise, dismay and disappointment where necessary. This is a form of feedback to the speaker that one is "following" the communication process.

4.   During the communication process, the listener may not totally be in support of the speaker's viewpoint. The listener is expected to defer his judgment to the end of the communication process.

It is not advisable to interrupt with counter argument. When such is done it may degenerate to an argument.

5. Appropriate response is a model for respect and understanding. Providing an honest response and asserting one's opinions respectfully will make the speaker to accept one's viewpoints, even when they are contrary to his/her views.

9.0 Conclusion

It is hard to think of a single, activity that does not involve communication. Skill Acquisition Programs involve communication because communication is an essential part of every business. Communication, as explained earlier, is the process of transmitting information. It therefore requires both the transmitter and the receiver but also and perhaps more crucially, developing a shared understanding of the information being transmitted and received.

In the present chapter, we have described some of the skills of communication; these skills can be grouped differently: reading and listening are receptive skills as they are used in receiving information, while writing and speaking are expressive or productive skills as they are useful for producing and conveying information. Verbal and nonverbal communication skills were also looked at. The sender should use the right nonverbal cues to convey a positive message, while the receiver should learn to look for unintended messages conveyed by nonverbal communication. Benefits and barriers of communication were addressed as well as way of maximizing communication skills.

The businessman who wants to survive in the competition that surrounds business has to develop his communicating skills. The ability to communicate information accurately, clearly and as intended is a vital life skill and something that should not be overlooked.

Selected Skills in Arts and Humanities

1.0 Introduction

This chapter leads the tripartism of skills in arts/humanities and science and technology. There is an insight into the array of the overriding skills which appear to be domiciled in the arts domain. This is justified in the sense that skills in sciences and technology are outcomes of man's quest to understand and manage himself vis-à-vis his universal system created by God in nature. Technology is man's creation to enable him advance knowledge, ease task and attain effectiveness in tasks.

In section 3.0 we have outlined the values of the arts-based skills, seven in number. The relevance of communication and lawyering skills can be appreciated in the prevalence of these two domains. Man must communicate and man needs the law to guide him in all aspects of his dealings with fellow man.

2.0 Broad Components of Skills

In contemporary world of work and human relationships where effectiveness and harmony are desired, skills for survival come in three broad categories: arts/humanities, science and technology. Arts are insights into human creative and will power as well as behavior. Science is man's attempt at explaining the relationships between humanity and nature. Technology came at the tail of science as an applied tooling to enhance man's activities.

In economic analogy, the factors of production are akin to the above dimensions of skills. The Arts-based skills relate to man (the labor) and his natural gifting's in enhancing the creation. Land relates to science while capital is similar to technology. These three components lead to production. Similarly, man seeks the fluency of knowledge and information in these three areas (faculties) of Arts, Science and Technology.

Arts/Humanities, which are human-centered provide five basic essentials in the spectrum of skills. These can be portrayed as follows: Thinking, Communication, Teamwork, Leadership and Management

3.0 Values of Arts-based Skills

Based on the table above, one can easily appreciate how the arts-based skills dominate the scale of basic intra- and inter-personal skills. Seven values are palpable in this system of values:

i) **Self-awareness and Acquired Knowledge**

The human civilization and progress sit on how humans engage in intrapersonal communications, curious thinking, creative thinking, analytical thinking, imaginative thinking; which have resulted in understanding oneself and others through languages, histories and cultures.

ii) **Communication and Sharing of Meaning**

Consequent upon building thoughts and images through imagination, man skillfully transfers or shares the outcomes with others using language as well as the receptive (listening, reading) and expressive (speaking and writing) motors.

iii) **Education and Information Transfer**

In the process of communication of experiences acquired through sharing of meaning in diverse ways, humans have structure methodologies to transfer the gains of knowledge, discoveries, inventions and problem-solving mechanisms to others through education and skill acquisition/development. Education in the arts, sciences and technology is largely an artistic skill. Thoughts and analysis in the arts have only attracted tests and verifications from the sciences and enhancement from the world of technology.

iv) **Teamwork and Collaboration**

Humans only survive in communities, groups and societies, not in isolation. Personal differences, idiosyncrasies, preferences and independent discretions tent to erupt disharmonies in human relationships. A major skill in working effectively with others through the tenets of justice, equality before the law, adaptability to differences, cooperation and good attitudes is sin-quo-non. As individuals get motivated by diverse deploy their labor so as to carry out the right performances for appropriate results. Thus, a footballer will play well to score goals and gain rewards. A carpenter will construct well to sell his products in exchange for money.

v) **Leadership and Entrepreneurialism**

In multitask settings with many hands set in for accomplishments, leadership skill is of a great essence. Where a number of persons seek knowledge, skill or information under a competent hand, that hand is the leader (teacher, instructor, lecturer) in that context. A leader is an entrepreneur whose duty is to harness all other inputs for effectiveness. He must be a democrat with the right empathy, moral standing, experience, trustworthiness and confidence to be able to provide inspiration and supervision. To achieve his task, a leader must be flexible but firm, critical but brilliant, independent but adaptable to teaching his followers and also learning from them since nobody has monopoly of knowledge.

vi) **Management and Organization**

Research has indicated that the global fastest growing economies are anchored on education, creativity, law, finance, information/communication and public administration. In all these fields, management is key. An education system requires a good manager to thrive. The creative artists/

entertainers demand separate managers to organize their productions, tours and finances. A good lawyer must institute an office manager for schedules and filings. The financial houses cannot do without trained managers in their boards and staffment. The gamut of information and communication systems require good management for control and results. Both private and public concerns can only be effectively administered by a core management in place.

vii) **Problem-Solving**

A manager is at once a thinker, a team player, and a leader. He is a problem-solving. To succeed in this ultimate task, he must be savvy in decision-making process, time management, goal-setting in vision/mission statements, etc. Problem solving skill thrives in a humble and honest heart that accepts genuine mistakes and seeks changes for correction. The keys to solving any problem are to lay out a dependable plan and to have the willpower to drit.

4.0 Prevalence of Communication Skills

In the first place, communication refers to the exchange of ideas between persons, organizations, establishment or institutions for the purpose of achieving a common goal. It is the means of linking people together in a setting to achieve a common purpose. It is a means of conveying a desired message to two or more people that are involved. For students, the purpose of being in school is to acquire knowledge and skills. To communicate means to interact or send ideas/information for a desired purpose.

Therefore, developing communication skills is a shared responsibility of not only government but also teachers and other communication skills practitioners. The government on their part is much aware of the vitality of communication in learning and has made provision for it as enshrined in the National Policy on Education. In this case the policy seriously emphasizes the indispensability of the four language skills namely: listening, speaking, reading and writing. Uwatt (2015) buttresses that the policy envisages that the leaner will acquire through training, the ability to listen with understanding, read with comprehension, speak fluently and write efficiently.

The idea that communication skills are only relevant in the learning situation is an error. This is because the communication skills of listening, speaking, reading and writing are necessary for the sustenance of life in the family, politics, commercial, workplace/office, and in the culture of a set of people.

Receptive Skills

From a communicative or educational point of view receptive skills which consists of listening and reading is a unit of the two groups of skills that learners are expected to communicate with, aside the productive or expressive skills of speaking and writing.

Receptive skills are those that are associated with the receiving of information, idea or knowledge by a learner either from a text, a communication gadget or through face to face interaction with other persons.

However, two categories of receptive skills include

1. listening
2. reading

Listening

Listening is the first and most important primary component of any communication situation be it at the family level, work place, religion, commercial, cultural, socio-political and even within the academic environment. It is a very important skill for communication and interactive purposes within a setting. Uwatt (2015) sees listening as an active mental exercise whereby a partner in a verbal communication situation receives sounds and signals and makes a conscious effort to generate meanings by pitching such sounds and signals against a language background, past experiences, events, objects or situations to enhance the generation of meanings. According to her, effective listening thrives on the effective mobilization of the rich vocabulary and the alert, unbiased and receptive mind of the listener. Before an individual can read or write, he must be able to listen. Listening involves the use of sounds to detect meaning.

Acquiring and applying listening skills does not only enhance one's learning capabilities but also quicken our ability to perform their social, political, academic, economic, and religious functions in the course of influence, persuading and negotiating with others. To listen effectively, the receptive mind of the speaker must be effectively mobilized regarding his rich vocabulary. It is very common that in particular settings, both the young and adult listeners are often perceived and easily diverted with many though patterns are hindered. The receptive skill of listening expects a person to be self-disciplined and focus on the contents of a message. Listening transcends mere hearing. The listening process proceeds from the reception of sounds to the creation and production of meaning from the sounds and signals been received and the critical of thought patterns to produce understanding, hence react appropriately to the message been transferred. Listening as a language skill helps humans to healthily share knowledge, fears and feelings.

It is not only the lexical and syntactic meaning of words that a listener has to understand. He also has to extract additional meanings, moods, undertones, overtones, from the gestures, facial expressions, pauses variations of pitch of voice, of stress and intonation of the speaker. The total personality of the speaker is involved when speaking. Therefore the active listener has to make meanings out of the total personality of the speaker, including his appearance, posture, etc. The active purposeful listener listens to know the purpose of the message of a talk, whether it is to inform, to entertain, to persuade or dissuade, to express opinions or value judgments. First, he recognizes the kind of speech whether it is a monologue as an address to the staff and students by a school principal, or a dialogue, a talk by two individuals, each trying to understand the thinking-going-on in the speaker's mind before responding or even interrupting.

In a debate, seminar or any form of public speaking, monologues are common and turn-thinking is faced. In this case, the main speaker is not to be interrupted until he has exhausted his speech. As he speaks, the active listeners respond and give him feedback which may be in for of smiles, laughter, nods, frowns, applause, hand-shaking, grumbling, shoulder-shrugging, hisses, ear-scratching, pater rustling, gazing out of the window or at worst booing, which is very common when listeners think the manifesto or promises of a politician are empty.

Other forms of dialogue a person may listen to are television conversations, husband-wife dialogues, co-workers' discussions and manager's interview of an applicant, discussions at seminars, conferences and symposia. Furthermore, the purposeful listener at the beginning has to find out the relationships of speaker-message, listener which may in turn make a speech either informal, personal, close, warm and casual or formal, impersonal, businesslike, cold and distant. For example, a dialogue between a husband and wife or mother and child will often sound informal and personal, but the manager's interview is of an applicant or a staff for promotion may not only be formal but also tensed and frozen.

Factors Affecting Efficient Listening

The first important factor in efficient listening is "listening readiness." Listening readiness means that the child is mentally and psychologically prepared to begin a listening assignment in a state of mind which will promote learning. It is this mental and psychological preparedness which will crucially affect the listening process. Listening readiness in turn is affected by their factors such as physiological and psychological, the home environment, individual ability, experiential background, interest, listening environment and purpose for listening. Physiological factors has to do with how adequate the child's listening organs and brain functions for listening to take place. Psychological factor implies how stable the child's emotional state is for listening to be done. If he is anxious, resentful, insecure, angry that such an individual may not be in the best frame of mind to listen well. The home environment and the amount of communication that exists between the parents, siblings and other relations and the child is equally important. Individual ability of the listener is another factor affecting reading readiness; hence, the teacher should be sensitive to this in setting goals. Experiential background as an important factor in listening has to do with the fact that a child's background knowledge about the content of a text or information to which he listens affects what is eventually comprehended. So exposure to a variety of content and experiences may aid listening.

In addition, if a topic is of interest to a person, he will profitably listen to what is being said. If a listener is in a quiet, relaxed atmosphere with minimal distracting noises, he is likely to concentrate and to follow readily his listening material. And finally, a clearly set purpose for reading can enhance efficient listening. When a listener sets his listening purpose clearly, at the beginning of listening exercise, it will enable him to concentrate and to allocate his attention to information relevant to his purpose.

Types of Listening

It is the purpose of listening that determines the degree of attention, and both purpose and degree of attention will provide the classification for specific listening situations.

However, four types of listening are often identified, to be

1. **Attitudinal listening:** This involves facts which affect listening be it environmental or individual factors. When the factor is environmental, it has to do with the place where the listening takes place. The place could be noisy or quiet, comfortable or uncomfortable. Such considerations unfailingly affect the level of efficiency in listening.

2. **Informational listening:** As the most common type of listening; it has to do with listening for a message, for instruction about how to do certain things; how to operate a gadget, etc. Students listen to lectures and take note of important points which they may develop later into full note.

3. **Appreciative listening:** This type of listening requires more than merely getting general information from a speech event. The appreciative listener is able to decipher the mood of the speaker from the speech situation. He is able to see how the speaker makes his words to add effects to the meaning intended. Uwatt (2015) states that appreciative listening has its inclination toward pleasure. Here, the recipient takes special delight in the artistic organization and presentation of content, the choice and ordering or words, the effective use of words, gestures, images sceneries, mental pictures, images and other literary devices in communicating meaning content.

Uwatt (2015) highlights the following guidelines relevant to appreciative listening

1. Acquire extensive vocabulary to function effectively in the listening situation.
2. Utilize grammatical functions and literacy devices normally used in embellishing speeches to derive meaning and joy.
3. Endeavour to see how the network of the various characters story themes, passage of time and key issues are developed, put in place and used to appeal to your sense of beauty.
4. Observe how consistent the presentation and coordination of story line, character roles and scenarios are effectively integrated in terms of established flow of ideas, level of language, use of imageries and other notable markers to convey information clear undistorted manner.

Reading

Geoffrey Roberts (1969) defines reading as a matter not so much of knowing what a sequence is, but rather of seeing the insignificance of what sequence, when applied to letters and words, in terms of spoken language. He further reiterated that reading is not merely a mechanical response to symbols. It is a process whereby symbols are interpreted and placed within the wider structure of language. Uwatt, L. E. and Nta, G. E. (2010) defines reading as a purely mental exercise which involves the perception of the written symbols, giving meaning to the message and synthesizing the knowledge into cognitive structures for its realization and recall.

When oral language is reduced to written form, it becomes coded in silent symbols which must be interpreted by the reader to produce the message. In this case, reading involves the ability of an individual to interpret graphic symbols through speech. The concept of speech has to do with the fact that sounds are accurate by articulated to make meaning. It involves saying the words clearly in sentences. It is the process of decoding the relationship between the written symbols and the spoken words Uwatt (2015).

In Eyisi (2005), reading should be more of reasoning involving the meaningful interpretation of words, phrases, sentences requiring all types of thinking such critical, evaluative, judgmental and problem solving. It also involves gaining meaning from a written text. Nuttal (1982:5) in Uwatt (2015:47) believes reading to mean "getting out of text as nearly as possible the meaning that the writer puts into it. Here, reading is portrayed as an exercise whereby the reader extracts information from a given text. The ability to get meaning from a text is nurtured from an early stage to maturity where a learner can independently mobilize appropriate reading skills for various reading purposes. When we talk about reading, Shapiro (2000) says that we are interested in the final outcome, which is literacy. Literacy here implied the use of oral and written language as well as other sign systems such as mathematics and art, to make sense of the world and communicate with others (Halliday, 1978).

However, the process of reading involves knowledge of books and texts, knowledge of the alphabetic system and its relationship to the sounds of a language, general language skills, general knowledge, and specific knowledge of material discussed in a text.

Benefits of Reading

According to Shapiro (2000), a good book is more than just something to pass time. For children, it can be a portal to distant lands or ancient history. However, the benefits of/purpose of reading include the following:

1. **To avoid danger:** An individual who knows how to read is able to see, for example, an indication of danger in printed form on a drug. This drug is not recommended for children between 18 years. Such a child does not need any other person to explain that is dangerous to use the drug.

2. **To stay healthy:** There are some publications that one can read to maintain a good health without going to the doctor. A child who can read enjoys the benefits of being involved about health instructions, how to take drugs regarding the number of doses involved.

3. To increase the frontiers of knowledge.

4. To gather information about places that are not where we are. For example, a child can know a lot about Russia without going there at all.

5. **To solve academic problems:** It is through reading that a lot of academic problems are solved. Children read and find solutions to their academic problems.

6. **For association and relaxation:** People can read to forget their worries and increase their happiness. When children read to act in a play, a game or do a puzzle, it brings about entertainment and relaxation.

7. **For update in current issues:** When children read, they need not ask question about the current position of issues around them or even issues for away from them. Reading acquaints them with such facts.

However, the main purpose of reading is to comprehend the ideas in the materials/written text, but some people read without understanding, hence reading becomes a wasted exercise. Pressley (2001) asserts that skilled comprehension requires fluid articulation of all these processes of individual letters and their associated sounds, to word recognition to text processing competences, beginning with the sounding out and recognition of individual words, to the understanding of sentences, in paragraphs or part of much longer text. A reader reads for the purpose of following directions. In this case, specific details need to be noted and utilized. For example, the reader reads to follow health instructions such as which drug to take and not to take to be healed of a particular disease such as malaria.

Moreover, people read to question issues, sharpen focus, making influences and evaluating issues as he interpret with texts. Issues to be questioned in this case include the authenticity of the texts, the author's area of specialty and the ability to handle the issues raised in the text. Uwatt (2015) asserts finally that another purpose for reading may be for pleasure. Reading for pleasure often comes from the search for the relaxation of the mind and body and therefore do not require the rigorous as experienced in critical reading. The reading searches for the beauty in the storyline; the aesthetics in the use of language and use effective prowess in touching the emotions/feelings of the reader.

Knowing the reason for reading and doing so before the commencement of any reading exercise get the reader mentally prepared to interact with the text. The reader at the end of the reading exercise makes use of the set goals to assess the reading attainment.

Oral and Silent Reading

Individual's literate acts emerge from their wealth of experience with oral language and the attempts to enter the rewarding world of print. Oral reading implies that the graphic symbols are interpreted by the mouth or relay it just to the brain and the mind without saying anything aloud or even whispering it. The first is called oral reading or reading aloud while the second is known as "silent reading."

Oral reading helps us in achieving the following:

1. To share information
2. To emphasize discussion
3. To prove a point
4. To join in choral reading
5. To narrate in the reader's theatre experience

The above uses of oral reading are known as end-uses.

However, the sub-skills or oral reading from which the general and specific objectives can be worked out are:

1. Ability to recognize and combine letters and read words.
2. Ability to read phrases
3. Ability to read sentences
4. Ability to use stress at word level
5. Ability to use phrasing (stress at group level).
6. Ability to use intonation in reading.
7. Ability to combine all the features above appropriately to give the correct meaning and mood of what is being read.

Since communication involves the sender, the message and the message, the sender of classroom communication/teacher must possess the skill of the knowledge/content he intends to transmit to his receivers/learners. Such knowledge will help to guide the instruction in the selection of content and the suitable method to adopt.

Silent Reading

Most times, we read silently more than we read aloud. In terms of needs, we use the skill of silent reading more than that of oral reading or reading aloud. When we buy a newspaper to read or to go to the library to read, or pick some drugs in the medicine shop, we adopt silent reading as we do not often read such materials aloud. A teacher can read a story to a class, a public speaker can read his lecture to an audience, and a priest can read his sermon to his congregation. In all these situations, it is one person doing the oral reading while the audience ranging from ten to thousands listen. This example is necessary to illustrate the fact that in real life, silent reading is commonly used more than oral reading.

Therefore, the emphasis and real training should be toward comprehension of reading materials, which can only be sufficiently achieved through silent reading.

Expressive Skills

Apart from receptive skills of listening and reading, communication can be undertaken through the expressive skills of speaking and writing. This seriously implies that language can be expressive through the communicative skills of speaking and writing. There are types of human language:

Speaking: Volume and Clarity

Uwatt (2015) sees speaking as a form of communication (mainly in the verbal form) whereby ideas, etc., are shared among communicators using the sound system of a given language. Speaking skills are, therefore, techniques used in the presentation of message in an oral communication setting to a given group of people called "audience." When an individual is trained and well groomed in these techniques, he is empowered to speak effectively. Speaking otherwise known as speech-making is often referred to as the thinking-going-on in the mind of the speaker.

Speaking skills consist of a complex set of skills. Such skills are naturally acquired, though not automatically, during the first three years of a child's life. The rate and efficiency of the acquisition of speaking skills

is different from one person to another, depending on how enriched the language environment in which a child grows is. A child left to himself without language, especially talking going on around him, may no talk in his own good time.

Speaking consists of the use of human vocal organs such as the tongue, lips, roof of the mouth, teeth and the larynx as well as the use of language and bodily actions, such as smiling, frowning, nodding, shoulder-shrugging, etc. Speech is therefore a three-in-one medium. Just as the actual words of a language convey meaning, so do the voice volume including the pitch and tone are clear enough to convey meaning as expressed by the speech performer/speaker. At the same time, the bodily actions which accompany the words do also convey or produce additional meanings to the words.

For example, a speaker may say "You may, take it," in response to someone's request. "Can I take this?" But the speaker may convey his willingness or hesitation to allow the taking. He may also convey his approval or disapproval or complete lack of interest, by his smile or frown, respectively. In other words, the same sentence structure and the same vocabulary items may be used by the same speaker on two or more different occasions, for different purposes and for different effects.

A lot of noise compete with the mind during the thinking process. Noise here means any distracting elements, even in the mind of the speaker or intended talker. For example, the boy who after saying, "I sir," gets up to a false start or goes into complete silence has had his thinking disturbed by noise from within him. In the same vein a listener to a talk may also have his learning disturbed by the noise around or even within him. The external noises stated above can hinder him from accurate and purposeful listening. At the same time or sometimes, the noise within him in form of absent-mindedness, self-debating and detouring may prevent him from getting an accurate message.

A typical illustration of the above discourse is where a steward, to whom one gives simple instructions such as "Go now and warm the rice," but who thirty minutes later, still tells you:" I never start, madam. When asked why he did not warm the rice earlier, he stupidly said

"I no hear, Madam. I sorry.

This may sound funny but it is a daily feature of some homes in the country. If you are interested to know why these belated stewards and stewardesses show these behavioral patterns, the answer in this sociolinguistic short-comings. Most of the time, they are self-debating and detouring in their minds while you talk to them. Moreover, some of them are drop-outs from primary education, before they reach the "mastering phase" of English. In a communication situation where speaking is a skill, a communicator must intentionally speak audibly and clearly; he must be understood by the information he conveyed to his listening audience. In this case, he is expected to speak out such that each individual can listen and derive meaning from what is being said.

Speech: Time Audience, Context Relationships

There is no doubt the fact that speech do vary even on the same ideas, in different social contexts, to different listeners, and at different times regardless of the fact that speech is the thinking-going-on in the mind of the speaker. When an effective speaker talks, he observes the reactions of his listeners and seeks to make his speech suit his listening audience. For example, if a mother scolds a son and he is noncaring to face, she raises her voice and sometimes her arm to smack him, in addition to the use of harsher words. This reaction is the use of harsher words. This reaction is known as nonverbal and verbal feedback to the speaker.

Speech Rhythm

In connected speech, the tendency is for the good speaker of English to give attention the significant syllables or words in the sentence. This is performed so regularly that the speaker achieves rhythm in his

speech through the action. This implies that stressed syllables occur at fairly equal intervals of time, the number of unstressed syllables in between them notwithstanding. In real fact, the more numerous the unstressed syllables occurring between the stressed syllables, the more rapid the delivery of the unstressed syllables.

Technically, a stressed syllable and all the unstressed coming after it, that is, excluding the next stressed syllable, usually form a "foot." In connected speech, the same time is spent on each foot irrespective of the same number of unstressed syllables in each foot.

Here are some examples:
'Go to the/shop and/'buy/me
'Play the/'match with vigor
Stay a/'way/or'p her/'money

As seen above, each column constitutes a foot, and to achieve rhythm, equal time has to be spent in each column.

Oral Communication

Speaking skills find expression in oral communication. While various animals have different ways of expressing facts, ideas, opinions, requests, and feelings known to members in their group, humans do often communicate through the medium of language, which is by far more complex than any other systems of animal communication. As communication, language can therefore be viewed as the human vocal sounds or the arbitrary graphic representation of these sounds in writing used systematically and conventionally by speech community for purposes of communication. Human communication therefore operates at the level of sound (speech) and of the level of graphic representation. The meaningful combination of the vocal sounds form oral communication, while the graphic representation forms "writing."

Writing

As a communication skill, writing can be described as the graphic representation of vocal sounds of a language. It is an expressive communication skill that uses the meanings placed on written symbols of a given language for the purpose of sharing thoughts, feelings, fears, opinions and so on. Uwatt (2015) opines that writing is also called a productive communication because the communicator initiates the process of giving or perceiving the ideas to be shared, identifying the audience, deciding the much to be given and in what ways it will be shared. Every human being has the desire to communicate effectively. Communication through expressive mode of writing involves or requires the ability to creatively compose and transfer the meaning clearly while at the same hold or sustain the interest of your listeners during the process of communication. This can surely be achieved through the careful deployment of communication skills both in the verbal and nonoral form (written form) of communication setting. When such skills are attained and mastered, it would reduce the many inhibitions or challenges often associated with communication in the written form.

Perception: An individual needs to see things and note the specific features of such things before he can describe them. This means that the starting point in training a child to write is to train him to look at shapes, sizes and lengths. This could be done by means of oral questions and answers. In the school environment, learners should be made to compare objects of pictures, drawings, etc., in terms of shape, size and length. For example, a piece of chalk is usually shorter than a pen just as a pen is generally shorter than a ruler. A situation or game in which a child is asked to pick the shortest out of a piece of chalk, a pen, and a ruler

will make the learner focus attention on the three objects and take a mental measurement of their lengths to determine the shortest one. The above example helps to explain what perception is. Objects, pictures, and drawings that have greater similarities than what we have in the above example can definitely be used. As an instructor, you can for example, ask learners to pick out the odd shape out of the following:

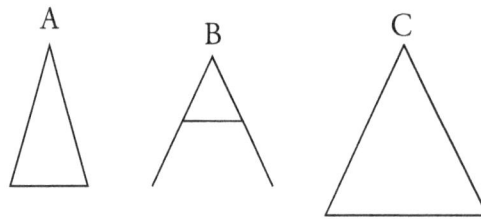

A child who sees shape (B) as the odd one has been able to perceive the difference. There are various games of this type that academic instructors can use to focus learner's attention on differences and similarities. Such activities will keep children active and lively in class, if the activities are well managed. At this stage, learners could give their responses in their mother tongue if they cannot use the English Language. However, your focus of attention here is to prepare them for writing, not speaking. But if the learners can use English, responses in English should be encouraged to enhance fluency in oral language.

Motor skills: Motor skills involve the use of the hand to make various strokes, slants and shapes. A beginning could be made by asking pupils to do some writing in the air or on paper, chalk board, or even on paper. The emphasis in this case the mobility of the child's hand after you have ensured a proper holding of the pencil. The first thing to do here is to ensure that the learners can demonstrate three finger grasp near the end of the pencil. After that, the child is taught to move the hand in various directions. From left to right, from top to bottom, in a semi-circle or complete circle to the left or the right, etc.

Letter Formation and Word Writing

Letter formation is one of the first steps in the performance of actual writing exercise especially at the primary school level. It is in fact, basic to the art of writing since words are made up of letters, and written compositions are made up of written words. This is why it is very necessary to master the technique of letter formation properly. After learners have been trained in moving their hands in various directions and making different shapes, verbal instructional technique can be used to direct the movement of the hand to form specific letters. For example, in forming letter 'e', you can instruct your pupils to carry out the following instructions:

i.   Draw a short line from left to right.
ii. From the right end of the line, draw parts of a background circle (to the right) to make contact with the let end of the line.
iii. Continue the background circle down beyond the line.
iv. Let the circle curve below the line and step a little distance from the right end of the line.

Another useful technique is the "watch-me-as-I-do-it" application. After they must have watched you do it on the white marker board, you would ask them to do the same thing on their papers. The following figures provides an illustration.

Good handwriting requires that individual letters should be well formed and legible. Sometimes when we have individual's letters in rather long contexts, we may not be able to decide easily whether all letters are

well formed or not. A method of ascertaining this is by cutting a hole a little larger than a single letter in the center of a small card. An illegible or a poorly formed letter will stand out clearly. You will then be able to focus the attention of your learners on such poorly formed letters for intensified practice.

Developing Punctuation Skills

Punctuation marks provide the means of conveying written ideas clearly to readers. Since a writer is not in a face-to-face situation with the reader he cannot use gestures and other signals which a speaker can use to make his meaning clear. The only techniques available to the writer are the punctuation marks. And if punctuation marks are well used, they can make meaning a writer is trying to convey to the reader clearly. This is making you see the potentials of punctuation marks and to learn to recognize the meaning attached to each punctuation mark. Punctuation marks such as the full stop, comma, colon, apostrophe, the dash, semi-colon, exclamation mark, the bracket, the inverted comma, ellipsis, the hyphen, etc. Such punctuations could be used in the middle (middle punctuation) or at the end (end punctuation) of a communicative structure. We also have word punctuations which are marks at work level. They help to indicate whether certain combination of letters should be regarded as one word or two words; whether the word has possessive function or whether special meanings are attached to the words, etc.

Nonverbal Cues

Different aspects of nonverbal cues include body language, eye contacts, movements as well as gestures.

1. **Body language:** Body language as a nonverbal cue goes a long way to generating meaning through the use of body movement, movement of all or some parts of the human body. Body language as a nonverbal cue involves gestures such as frowns-facial expressions of frowning, smiling, whistling, wincing, scratching the leg on the floor and other forms of attitudes facilitated by body language.
2. **Eye contacts:** This can also be referred to as eye fixation and retrogression. Eye contacts is one of the skills used during reading. In this case, the reader is taught how to use eye peripheral vision concept and in symbols in meaningful units. Uwatt (2015) believes that this helps to facilitate the establishment of contextual relationship for meaningful and effective generation of meanings. The reader is discouraged from reading individual words which will reduce the speed of reading and twist the accurate generation of meaning in the sentence.

   Reading involves mainly the use of eyes. The gift of sight is an indispensable endowment for human beings. Before a person can read, he has to be able to see things, to look at objects, places, people and things around him. But seeing for reading is more than merely looking at or just conscious of appearance. The eye must be able to discriminate between objects and things, people in terms of their shapes, sizes, and color patterns. The eyes see and send signals to the brain to register the forms and patterns associated with such persons, objects or things.

   Reading therefore begins with visual discrimination/eye contact with the content of the material being read. Although the eyes can see most things, not every seer can discriminate between shapes, forms. Through eye contact to printed materials, learners can make distinctions in colors, shapes, symbols, sizes and directions. Their contact with printed text is necessary in actual reading situations.

   On the whole, poor eye sight can prevent people from learning to read. The training in visual discrimination helps the teacher in the school setting to detect a child having eye problem.

3. **Movements:** Movement is a nonverbal cue used to generate meaning in a nonverbal communication situation. While reading, eye movement, body and limb movement, including facial expressions are often exhibited especially in children.

    In the act of reading, the reader must make some movement of the eye. This movement follows a particular direction. It is usually from left to right of the printed page. This movement has been described by expert observers as a "sweep." The eyes themselves are naturally made in such a way that they can make tactile movements. Try and fix your head firmly in one position and then let your eyes rove to try to see some object positioned to the left or right of that central point. The eyes are capable of roving to the let or to the right up to a limit. The sweep from left to right of the printed page is therefore like the floor of a river. It moves in spans, giving birth to a reading concept known as eye span. Eye span refers to the extent which your eye focus covers when you fix your eyes on a particular position. This can be illustrated in the diagrams below

    As seen above, each point of the arrow represents the limit of your eye span. To see clearly and sharply what is contained in the next unit of arrow point, the eyes must naturally shift focus. Even though objects to the left or right of the span are visible to the eyes they are not as sharply seen as the ones at the center of the eye span.

4. **Gestures:** A gesture is another nonverbal cue often employed in communication situations. As used in this context, gestures imply a movement of the limb or body, especially one made to emphasize a speech. It is an element of nonverbal communication where meaning is derived through some kind of silent responses to certain language communication settings. Gestures could be in form of shrugging of shoulders, frowning of face, wincing of the eyes, nodding of the head, etc. They are usually used to show approval or rejection. As a nonverbal cue, it is used by a speaker to drive home his point.

Sharing Feedback

Feedback is an important requirement for a successful oral communication, the others being the sender, the message and the receiver. Communication simply means the exchange of ideas between two or more persons or entities. It is the means of sending a desired meaning of message to two or more people that are involved to elicit feedback. Some striking features of communication is that is regulative and need focus; it is innovative and intended to change attitude or action of a receiver, purposeful and directional.

In a communication setting, be it classroom, public and private sector, feedback is an indispensable tool in the communication process. For example, when a football match is in progress, if the referee blows the whistle, he expects the players to stop playing immediately. The feedback he receives is the stoppage of the match in oral communication, when a speaker sends out his message, the receiver responds in one or more of the following ways depending on the demands of the message.

*   Verbal response
*   Facial expression
*   Concrete action
*   Complete silence

As shown above, any of the responses selected by the receiver amounts to a feedback for the sender/encoder of the message. The sender of the message is also known as "the encoder" while the receiver is also called "the decoder" and the back is referred to as the "response." In oral or verbal communication, however, feedback is necessary for the following reasons:

1. 1It signals understanding or lack of it on the part of the receiver.
2. It gives the green light to the sender to continue to encode further messages.
3. It informs the sender that he needs to choose other language forms that are more appropriate.
4. It informs the sender that the receiver is no longer interested in the message because he is getting bored. Whenever there is a target receiver, feedback is always needed for a meaningful oral communication

On the whole, feedback is an unavoidable element of communication. There is hardly any communication situation that does not have feedback. Even in one way communication setting, for example, during seminar exercise where one person addresses an audience, there is usually a resultant response from the audience. Such response either takes the form of asking questions or nodding of heads by the target audience to indicate an approval or acceptance of what the speaker said by the audience. Even among members of an organization, communication is an integral part of their existence. Therefore in the course of interacting with one another, feedback is often ensued.

Methods of Effective Communication

For any communication to be effective between persons or group of persons, the following glaring methods must be unfailingly adopted:

1. Confidence
2. Calmness
3. Consistency
4. Assertiveness
5. Empathy
6. Clarity
7. Audibility
8. Precision

Now let use look at them one after the other

Confidence: As a method of effective communication confidence is needed for a speaker to clearly state and expatiate the idea or purpose for communication. There can be no meaningful and effective communication situation where confidence is not available on the part of the speech presenter. An air of confidence on the part of the encoder will help him pass on his message effectively and audibly and clearly to the overall understanding of his listening audience. If at the verge of communication an individual intends to address the public segment of the society, it is vital that he first of all stands up, then take a deep breath or clear his throats. This will give him a good amount of confidence without confidence a communicator can never convey his information/message to the admiration and approval of his audience.

Calmness
An individual who intends to communicate with others must adopt the communicative method of calmness. In this case, he needs to remain focus without exhibiting any trait of fear. Instead of

fidgeting, the communicator needs to create an atmosphere of confidence around him. This is why it is important for him to stand up, clear his throat and even look at his audience's faces in a confident and bold manner.

Consistency: If a speaker is to be effective, and understood by his listeners, he or she has to be consistent in the occasion of speech performance. This would mean that such speaker should not, for example, use the speech style of the religious language to address the law courts, otherwise the communication situation will not make any kind of meaning to his audience.

Assertiveness

This is the quality of being self-assured. Oxford Advanced Learners English Dictionary views assertiveness as it implies not saying what you do not know. You should not say more or less than is necessary during a speech event. Whatever you say must be firm and relevant to the speech occasion. Finally, the speaker should not elaborate more than is needed to convey what he intends to say.

Clarity

There is a strong concern over the issue of clarity in speakability. The choice of a given language to be used for communication, such as religious language must pay careful attention to the fact that its main use is in the corporate public worship either by a group of people speaking together or aloud or by individuals speaking to a congregation. The need for clear cues as to how such language should be spoken and the avoidance of unnecessary difficulties of pronunciation of words will definitely produce the intended meaning of the message to be communicated to a given set of audience.

Audibility

This method of effective communication concerns itself with the ability of a speaker to pronounce words, phrases, and make sentences audibly to the listening of an audience. It involves reading aloud by the speaker for his audience to grasp and understand the content of his communication which would in turn elicit the needed feedback. Most of the time, audibility is the product of confidence. This strongly implies that when a speaker has some good level of confidence during interaction with others, he is bound to speak and pronounce words loud enough for the listening of the audience.

Precision

This method of effective communication has to do with the exactness and appropriateness of language used during communication setting, though there are often strong pressures from popular attitudes toward the appropriateness and intelligibility of the language to be used. When one is creating a new form of language for a large number of persons, say in a context such as that of religion, one must try to choose a language which the majority of the would-be listeners do not revolt at. This would mean that too intellectual, obscure or unintelligible language should be avoided just as a variety of language that is too colloquial and informal would equally be an anathema.

Sample Communications

This topic, sample communications will be discussed under the following headings

- Job interviews
- Project documentations
- Project proposals
- Report writing
- E-mails
- Memos

Now, let's discuss them one after the other.

Job Interviews

Job interview is a structure conversation where one participant asks questions, and the others provide answers. The one who asks questions is known as the "interviewer" while the participant who answers questions is known as the "interviewee."

In common parlance, however, interview refers to a one-on-one conversation between an interviewer and an interviewee. An interviewer may also transfer information in both direction. Great communication skills are key to workplace success for almost any position, but particularly for any type of communication job. In your interview, you can expect to field questions about the intricacies of your ability to communicate, such as:

1. Tell about your greatest accomplishment.
2. What skills do you have that have prepared you for work in the communications field?
3. Where do you see yourself five years from now?
4. Tell me about a time of conflict and how you resolved it.
5. What efforts will you put forth to ensure you will excel in your new communication role
6. Have you ever worked with the media or written press release?
7. How do you work effectively within a budget?

Project Documentation

In the first place, a project, as used in this context refers to a planned endeavor, usually with a specific goal and accomplished in several steps or stages.

Project documentation is the implementation of a streamlined, efficient and uniform process for producing the key documents that are required to implement a new project successfully. For example, these documents might include business cases, project status reports and project requirement sheet.

Project Proposals

Project proposals is the initial document used to define an internal or external project. The project includes sections such as title, start and end dates, objectives and goals, requirements, and a description of the proposed solution. Inclusive in project proposals are financial terms and amount intended to be used in the execution and completion of projects.

Report Writing

Nwachukwu-Agbada (1994), Ekpa (1997), Brusaw *et al.* (1976), Eka (1993), Little (1978) in Udofot and Ekpenyong (2001) point to the definition of report to be an account of something seen, heard or examined with the aim of providing adequate information on it. Report is required on a daily or regular basis for ideas and information to be attained. Reports may, however, be oral or written, academic or business, formal or informal, routine or special historical, scientific, legal reports, etc.

The main purpose of report according to Ikpe (1993:164) quoting Gartside (1975) in Udofot and Ekpenyong (2001:216) is to provide information, submit opinion and ideas, report findings and the conclu-

sion drawn from them and to make recommendations. Reports require information for proper functioning of all spheres of human endeavors.

However, features of report writing may include

Precision: A report needs to be precise to add meaning to information being communicated. Udofot and Ekpenyong (2001:217) are of the opinion that a report writer should restrict himself to the terms of reference or the framework for the report. To achieve the above assertion then it is incumbent on the report writer to possess and maintain an objective point of view, and that sentences should be coherently linked as they carry ideas that are central to the communication situation. However, www.forecast.app/faqs sees report as a concise document based on research that typically analyzes a situation and sometimes makes recommendations.

Clarity and readability: The language of a report need to be simple, avoiding cumbersome expressions. When good expression of language is employed, a report becomes clear, understandable and easily readable.

Competences: A report is complete when it has the three vital components of introduction, body and conclusion. Udofot and Ekpenyong (2001:27) asserts that a report is complete when it has achieved its purpose. In this case, facts, opinions, findings and recommendations are separately presented to ensure adequate attention of what is being communicated.

Different formats of reports writing are:

1. **The letter format:** This is where the report is presented or official letter writing. Examples of reports under this format are Police Reports, Feasibility Studies, Accident Reports, etc.
2. **The memo format:** This type of report format is mainly used in proposals writing. In some establishments, standard memo sheets are provided for this report. Its structural composition include the writer, the receiver, date, the subject, the body and signature of the writer.
3. **Schematic format:** This usually follows a pattern of key headings followed by their sub-headings arranged in an orderly manner. The major headings of a schematic report format need to be centralized fully capitalized and properly underlined.

Though there are some reports which do come with other patterns as specified by authorities. Some establishments, for example, have designed formats for staff appraisals, routine reports and feasibility studies.

In addition, some institutions of higher learning has produced required formats for the final year reports of their students. They include long essays, term papers, or projects, thesis and dissertation.

Types of Reports

Various types of report as indicated by Little (1978:159) in Udofot and Ekpenyong (2001:219) include routine and special report, short and full reports, eye-witness, work and investigation reports, Brusaw *et al.* (1976:405) in Udofot and Ekpenyong (2001:219) lists reports types to include Progress Reports, Business Report, and the Memorandum. Similarly Ekpa (1997:141) in Udofot and Ekpenyong (2001:219) sees reports types to include evaluation, feasibility, business, financial, project, investigative, laboratory, medical, budget, end-of-year and routine reports.

However, some of the common types of reports in vogue are: minutes, book review, etc.

E-mails

E-mails are known as electronic mails are messages distributed by electronic means from one computer user to the one or more recipients via a network.

An example of an email is a happy birthday message a person sends from their yahoo account to their mother Gmail account (www.yourdictionary.com/email).

Memos

A memo is a short official note that is sent by one person to another within the same company or organization. It is also a message or other information in writing sent by one person or department to another in the same business (dictionary.Cambridge.org/dictionary). The word memos, which is derived from memoir, is also known as memorandum (singular) or memoranda (plural) meaning a reminder.

Therefore memorandum is a piece of writing used in reminding someone about something. It can be defined as a note to help the memory (Peter Little 1965:95). Consequently, the memorandum (memo) is a business communication which is intended to disseminate information about a particular event to members of an institution, business organization or enterprise communication within such establishments are performed through the memo.

5.0   Basics of Lawyering Skills

1. **Networking/Teamwork**

   Lawyering involves meeting, relating with and engaging a large variety of people: colleagues/partners in the firm/practice, clients, court officials (clerks, magistrates, registrars, bailiffs and judges), legal trainees/pupils, witnesses, etc. A lawyer must be socially savvy to be able to keep good customer and working relationships with all. To success in this, a lawyer should be very polite, friendly, confident and firm. These qualities are requirements for career growth in the legal profession. There is no successful lawyer who is aloof in the industry. From the law firm, to the court, and other places of inspection, the lawyer encounters various shapes of individuals and groups.

2. **Communication Analysis**

   Communication skills are the keys to effective lawyering. All the four cornerstones of community are important to a lawyer:
   - Ability to listen to a client so as to take down facts/briefs/narratives during consultation.
   - Ability to write or draft all types of legal document using the right structuring, words and expressions.
   - Ability to read through volumes of law reports, precedents, judicial decisions, briefs, etc., and to sift out facts and principles.
   - Ability to speak audibly, fluently, confidently and convincingly in arguing cases, negotiating issues and explaining the workings of the law.

   A lawyer must have a balancing in these four aspects of communication as they are all equally important for the practice of law.

3. **Research and Analysis**

   The law career is an analytical research career. Sailing through the ocean of information in books, reports, documents, evidence, articles, drafts, laws, and other resources to extract meaningful and relevant facts in advancing cases and arguments can be very demanding. The strength of a lawyer lies in the ability to find out and deploy a superior evidence, argument, facts and principles with which to vitiate inferior positions of the opposing party. In lawyering, volumes of documents and sheets are exchanged and must be very painstakingly studied because in them lie the facts principles for the advancement of cases and arguments. A lazy lawyer with shallow resources will lose cases no matter how eloquent. Law thrives on information and facts.

4. **Financial Literacy and Commercial Awareness**

   The bulk of legal matters: contracts, trusts, estates, etc., involve financial calculations and commercial or business components. Not only should a lawyer maintain a clear and transparent accounting system, to earn the trust of the client, he must exhibit awareness of the business world locally, nationally and internationally.

   A lot of business dealings and transactions attract legal attention leading to litigations, legal drafting's, interviewing, fact-finding and problem solving which can only be effectively implemented through basic financial record-keeping and interpretation of the motions in the commercial arena and corporate world.

   Nowadays, almost all businesses are regulated by Government in the form of registration, licensing, tax entries and compliance with due process in founding and folding up business. A lawyer must guide his client in all these.

5. **Management and Organizational Techniques**

   The office and court activities are important parts of lawyering. The management of case files, taking briefs from clients, attending court sessions, storing and retrieving information, managing relationships, dealing with colleagues and employees can be very tasky but must be properly done. In most cases, lawyers are entrusted with projects by the clients and so projects can entail procuring high profile estates and managing them for the client. In cases like this, a lawyer must understand the dynamics of estate management as well as organizational issues.

6. **Problem-Solving through Capacity Building**

   Lawyering is a very demanding profession. The lawyer holds out a claim to the public in the order of a capacity to solve very sensitive and critical problems at times bordering on finances, life and reputation.

   In a lawyer should be practical in common sense and in problem solving by earning a special capacity for communication, mediation, drafting, advocacy, inter-personal relationship and analytical research. Through experience, resilience and confidence, the lawyer can beam insights into cases, developments, situations, issues and scenarios and come out with workable answers to questions, suggestions to complex situations and the way forward for grey areas.

   The key area for a lawyer to excel in problem solving of sorts is in the art of opinion writing based on experience, research and analysis.

7. Using Emerging Technologies

   Lawyering has gone digital in many ways. There are volumes of e-resources at the disposal of a lawyer who is ICT savvy. Interviewing/conferencing can now be done via zoom. The e-law libraries holds on the spot and latest law reports that are needed in effective litigation and advocacy.

   Minutes, reports and opinions can now be constituted and shared online in matters of minutes. Negotiations can now be done using ICT technologies. Court rooms now operate with electronic gadgets for audibility, clarity, and replays. Many jurisdictions have now adjusted their

practice procedures to incorporate computed mediated evidences. Jurists can now have their voices automatically transcribed on pages. Volumes of laws can now be accessed by citizens. Today, truly, ignorance of the law is not an excuse. Legal education and the law professional training have increased tremendously because of availability of technology-enhanced methodologies and techniques.

6.0 Conclusion

This chapter focused on three key areas: the values of arts-based skills in juxtaposition to the skills highlighted in science and technology in chapters 29 and 30 respectively; the reechoing of communication skills which leverage most skill acquisition and developments; and the basics of lawyering skills which are also useful for nonlawyers who are interested in the workings of the law and how to relate with or what to expect from their lawyers.

One thing that is common among the submits of this chapter is communication. Every aspect of developing communication skills follows that there must be a sender/giver of an information, there must be an information or idea to communicate and finally, there must exist an individual who need to decode or receive such information for the performance and attainment of a specific goal.

Therefore, communication skills, ranging from those of receptive to expressive, nonverbal, as well as sharing feedback, adopting proper methods for effective communication to exploring several sample communications must of necessity be adequately developed to attain certain communication purposes/goals.

Chapter Twenty-Nine

Selected Skills in Sciences

1.0 Introduction

Despite the clamor for self-reliance and job creation in Nigeria, the planning of basic science education in the country has not given enough attention to quality, relevance, and functionality of education. This is evident in students that have graduated from the junior secondary schools that are not yet self-reliant and cannot even do anything for themselves (Double Gist, 2017). Second, although it is basic science education that prepares the students for post-basic and tertiary education, the planning of education for job creation has been shifted to the last two levels of education (the post-basic and tertiary levels). Consequently, the need to investigate the innovative and entrepreneurial skills integrated into basic science education; see how the skills are being imparted to the students for job creation; and hence the need for the groundwork on skills acquisition and development project.

Skill acquisition as a means of empowerment has caught government's globally for decades. This is so because it is believed that exposure in skill acquisition programs will reduce unemployment and enhance self-sustenance. In view of this therefore, the Groundwork on skills acquisition and development project examines different and related skills in basic sciences. The project also makes recommendations such as the establishment of skill acquisition centers to make the program accessible, the recruitment of competent and experienced instructors to make these programs more viable and the reformation of the skill acquisition programs to make them effective for the benefits of the unemployed and others. Skill acquisition in this perspective can then be defined as the form of training by individuals or group of individuals that can lead to acquisition of knowledge for self-sustenance. It involves the training of people in different fields of trade under a legal agreement between the trainers and the trainees for certain duration and under certain conditions. Ochiagha (1995) defined skill acquisition as the process of demonstrating the habit of active thinking or behavior in a specific activity.

He further stated that skill acquisition is seen as the ability to do or perform an activity that is related to some meaningful exercise, work or job. He maintains that for skill to be acquired, appropriate knowledge, attitudes, habits of thought and qualities of character are learnt to enable the acquirer develop intellectual, emotional and moral character which prepares the person for a brighter future. Similarly, Donli (2004) is of the view that skill acquisition is the manifestation of idea and knowledge through training which is geared toward instilling in individuals, the spirit of entrepreneurship needed for meaningful development. He stressed that if individuals are given the opportunity to acquire relevant skills needed for self-sustenance in the economy, it will promote their charisma in any work environment. He further maintains that skill acquisition increases competition and cooperation among people. Accordingly, Magbagbeola (2004) posited that skills acquisition requires the accumulation of different skills that enhances task performance through the integration of both theoretical and practical forms of knowledge.

The Federal Republic of Nigeria recognized the immense role of the development of entrepreneurial skills at the basic school level when it noted that basic education should provide science and technological

skills for economic development (FRN, 2004). Therefore, the quality of instructional delivery should be oriented toward inculcating the right type of value and attitude in the students. In addition, the acquisition of appropriate skills and the development of mental, physical, and social abilities/competencies were necessary for the individual to live in and contribute to the development of the society. Basic science education is that aspect of education that lays the foundation for sustaining lifelong learning.

It involves the acquisition of innovative skills and application of the knowledge of science that leads to particular occupations and for the improvement of man's environment (Onwuachu and Okoye, 2012). This includes workforce training in professional areas such as engineering, pharmacy, agriculture, business, and home economics. One of the pillars of the Nigeria National Economic Empowerment and Development Strategy (NEEDS) is "growing in the private sector." Consequently, Nigeria like other nations has accepted this market-driven or private sector-led economy as the model to achieve rapid economic growth and development, efficient resource allocation, and utilization. It was also recommended by the World Economic Forum (2011) that governments should improve their entrepreneurial ecosystem by bringing entrepreneurship to the classroom so that every student in the basic, secondary, and tertiary level of education should learn entrepreneurial principles, welcome new ideas, and give support to all types of entrepreneurs.

The initiative taken by the Nigerian government to encourage entrepreneurial activity includes the infusion of entrepreneurship education into the basic education curriculum and developing up trade subjects in the post-basic education curriculum, of which senior secondary school students must learn at least one of them before graduation. To this effect, all institutions in the country are required to incorporate entrepreneurship programs into their curriculum and provide young people the opportunity to acquire an entrepreneurial orientation and skills. This infusion of entrepreneurial studies into basic science education is meant to provide the young science and technical students the mind-set for creating and sustaining innovations. Such an infusion might also produce the necessary hub for job creation, poverty reduction, and possibly launch Nigeria into the production market. The 17th Commonwealth Conference of Education Ministers in 2009 led to the restructuring of school curriculum jointly by the Universal Basic Education Commission and the Nigeria Educational Research and Development Council to reflect these community needs and aspirations. Even the curriculum review for primary and secondary schools reflects the government's reforms as spelt out in the NEEDS, which has its focus on poverty reduction, wealth creation, and employment generation.

2.0   Features of Skills in Sciences

The main features or characteristics of science are as follows:

- Objectivity
- Verifiability
- Ethical Neutrality
- Systematic Exploration
- Reliability
- Precision
- Accuracy
- Abstractness and
- Predictability
- Empirical
- Provisional results

2.1 Objectivity

The scientific method is objective. It relies on facts and on the world as it is, rather than on beliefs, wishes or desires. Scientists attempt with varying degrees of success to remove their biases when making observations. Science provides a way of thinking about and solving problems in the world. It is used to explain the behavior of both people and atoms alike. Scientists set out to answer questions by creating experiments that test their ideas about how something works. Objectivity is therefore necessary to get an accurate explanation of how things work in the world. Ideas that show objectivity are based on facts and are free from bias, with bias basically being personal opinion. In science, even hypotheses, or ideas about how something may work, are written in ways that are objective. This means that experiments may prove a hypothesis false if the data does not support it. Scientists will alter hypotheses and theories when new knowledge is developed. Scientific knowledge is objective. Objectivity simple means the ability to see and accept facts as they are, not as one might wish them to be. To be objective, one has to guard against personal biases, beliefs, wishes, values and preferences. Objectivity demands that one must set aside all sorts of the subjective considerations and prejudices. Scientific objectivity is a property of various aspects of science. It expresses the idea that scientific claims, methods, results, and scientists themselves, are not, or should not be influenced by particular perspectives, value judgments, community bias or personal interests. Objectivity in science is an attempt to uncover truths about the natural world by eliminating personal biases, emotions, and false beliefs. It is often linked to observation as part of the scientific method. It is thus intimately related to the aim of testability and reproducibility. To be considered objective, the results of measurement must be communicated from person to person, and then *demonstrated* for third parties, as an advance in a collective understanding of the world. Such demonstrable knowledge has ordinarily conferred demonstrable powers of prediction or technology. Objectivity is important in science because scientific studies seek to get as close to the truth as possible, not just prove a hypothesis. Experiments should be designed to be objective and not to get the answers that scientists want.

Results are a part of scientific studies where it is important to remain objective. Scientific knowledge builds on itself; one discovery leads to another. For example, it is known that two scientists, James Watson and Francis Crick, discovered the structure of DNA. However, they would not have been able to discover the structure without the work of other scientists. Rosalind Franklin's initial experiments showed that the structure of DNA was a double helix and not a triple helix. Another scientist who necessarily followed from Watson and Crick's discoveries about the structure of DNA was Erwin Chargaff. Chargaff did experiments to show how the different molecules in DNA strands pair together. If either Rosalind Franklin or Erwin Chargaff had not been objective about their results, Watson and Crick may not have made any significant progress with their ability to understand the structure of DNA.

2.2 Verifiability

Scientific knowledge is supposed to be verifiable. Replications promote verifiability in several ways. Most straightforwardly, replications can verify empirical claims. Replication research also promotes dissemination of information needed for other aspects of verification; creates meta-scientific knowledge about what results to treat as credible even in the absence of replications; and reinforces a broader norm of scientists checking each other's work. The proof established by a scientific test must have a specific form, namely, repeatability. The issue of the experiment must be a statement of the hypothesis, the conditions of test, and the results, in such form that another experimenter, from the description alone, may be able to repeat the experiment. Nothing is accepted as proof, in psychology or in any other science, which does not conform to this requirement (Dunlap 1926). The ability to systematically replicate research findings is a fundamental feature of the scientific process. Indeed, the idea that observations can be recreated and verified by independent sources is usually seen

as a bright line of demarcation that separates science from nonscience (Dunlap 1926). A defining feature of science is that researchers do not merely accept claims without being able to critically evaluate the evidence for them (Lupia and Elman 2014). In broadest terms, scientists seek a systematic organization of knowledge about the universe and its parts. This knowledge is based on explanatory principles whose verifiable consequences can be tested by independent observers. Science encompasses a large body of evidence collected by repeated observations and experiments. Although its goal is to approach true explanations as closely as possible, its investigators claim no final or permanent explanatory truths. Science changes, evolves and verifiable facts always take precedence. Verifiability is a broad idea that can be applied to every step in the derivation of a scientific claim, and it is the basis for many current norms, practices, and expectations in scientific discourse. Science rests upon sense data, i.e., data gathered through our senses: eye, ear, nose, tongue and touch. Scientific knowledge is based on verifiable evidence (concrete factual observations) so that other observers can observe, weigh or measure the same phenomena and check out observation for accuracy. Others should be able to independently replicate or repeat a scientific study and obtain similar, if not identical, results.

2.3 Ethical Neutrality

Neutrality means that scientific theories make no value statements about the world; they are concerned with what there is, not with what there should be. The fundamental relationship among science, technology, and ethics is often claimed to be one of neutrality. After all, science and technology can be put to good or bad uses by good or bad people; they are thus value-neutral. Put simply, science does not express itself in moral declarations. It is neutral in the very way in which neutrality is seen to be a good thing in a free liberal society: science does not tell us what to do. It takes as its guides, the needs and desires of human beings, and not assumptions about good and evil. Science is ethically neutral. It only seeks knowledge. How this knowledge is to be used, is determined by societal values. Knowledge can be put to differing uses. Knowledge about atomic energy can be used to cure diseases or to wage atomic warfare. Ethical neutrality here means that the Scientists must not allow values to distort the design and conduct of researches. The conventional wisdom about the practice of science is that it is value-free in the senses: that science discovers facts, but there can be no scientific investigation of values; that the only value recognized by the scientist is that of knowing the truth; and that the applications of scientific knowledge can, and should, be democratically decided by society as a whole.

Thus, scientific knowledge is value-neutral or value-free. The term neutrality implies that an inquiry is free of bias or is separated from the researcher's perspectives, background, position, or conditioning circumstances. Science is the impartial search for truth without regard for the interests of those affected.

2.4 Systematic Exploration

Scientific method is systematic; that is, it relies on carefully planned studies rather than on random or haphazard observation. A scientific research adopts a certain sequential procedure, an organized plan or design of research for collecting and analysis of facts about the problem under study. Generally, this plan includes a few scientific steps: formulation of hypothesis, collection of facts, analysis of facts (classification, coding and tabulation) and scientific generalization and predication.

2.5 Reliability

This section examines the importance of reliability of scientific knowledge, for the scientific community and for society. Reproducibility is one criterion for reliability of scientific knowledge. Reliable science includes an experiment with proper observation, careful reading, gathering the proper information and modeling

with a justifying conclusion. Scientific knowledge must occur under the prescribed circumstances not once but repeatedly. It is reproducible under the circumstances stated anywhere and anytime. Reproducibility, the extent to which consistent results are observed when scientific studies are repeated is one of science's defining features. In principle, the entire body of scientific evidence could be reproduced independently by researchers following the original methods and drawing from insights gleaned by prior investors.

2.6 Precision

Precision refers to how close measurements of the same item are to each other. Precision in scientific investigations is important to ensure we are getting the correct results. Since we typically use models or samples to represent something much bigger, small errors may be magnified into large errors during the experiment. Precision is also important to ensure our safety. The characteristics of a precise system are repeatability and reproducibility. Precision requires giving exact number or measurement. Instead of saying "most of the people are against love marriages," a scientific researcher says, "Ninety per cent people are against love marriages."

2.7 Accuracy

Accuracy simply means truth or correctness of a statement or describing things in exact words as they are without jumping to unwarranted conclusions. Scientific knowledge is accurate. A physician, like a common man, will not say that the patient has slight temperature or having very high temperature but after measuring with the help of thermometer, the physician will pronounce that the patient is having 101.2° F temperature.

2.8 Abstractness

Abstract as an adjective is contrasted with concrete in that, whereas the latter refers to a particular thing, the former refers to a kind, or general character, under which the particular thing i.e., the "instance" falls. Thus, war is abstract, but World War I is concrete; circularity is abstract, but coins, dinner plates, and other particular circular objects are concrete. The term abstract is sometimes used to refer to things that are not located in space or time; in this sense, numbers, properties, sets, propositions, and even facts can be said to be abstract, whereas individual physical objects and events are concrete. The capacity for making and employing abstractions is considered to be essential to higher cognitive functions, such as forming judgments, learning from experience, and making inferences.

2.9 Predictability

Scientists do not merely describe the phenomena being studied, but also attempt to explain and predict as well. It is typical of social sciences that they have a far lower predictability compared to natural sciences. The most obvious reasons are the complexity of the subject matter and inadequacy at control.

2.10 Empirical Observation

The scientific method is empirical. That is, it relies on direct observation of the world, and disdains hypotheses that run counter to observable fact. These contrasts with methods that rely on pure reason including that proposed by Plato, and with methods that rely on emotional or other subjective factors.

2.11 Provisional Results

Results obtained through the scientific method are provisional; they are (or ought to be) open to question and debate. If new data arise that contradicts a theory, that theory must be modified. For example, the phlogiston theory of fire and combustion was rejected when evidence against it arose.

3.0 Science Process Skills

One of the important objectives of education in our day is to bring into the pupils the scientific thinking skills and the science process skills. In the recent years, many countries put emphasis on the scientific thinking and the science process skills in their curricula. Cepni *et al.* (1997) defined the science process skills as the core skills that guide in research means and methods, that enable the easy learning and persistency of sciences, and that provide the pupils to be responsible and active in their own learning. Arslan and Tertemiz (2004: 4), articulated the science process skills as 'the developer of self-responsibility in pupils' learning that enable easy learning in classes and that supplies the pupils to be active and structure their knowledge.' Based on these definitions, it may be suggested that the science process skills involve means and methods to reach scientific information and thus allow the pupils to think scientifically.

The science process skills involve skills that require more complex experiences such as the ability to observe that we develop and utilize naturally even in our very early ages, in addition to comparison skills, data gathering, data interpretation and ability to hypothesize. Tan and Temiz (2003) approached the science process skills as observation, classification, quantification, correlating number and space, forecasting, data recording, data using and modeling, data interpretation and making inferences, determining variables, changing and controlling variables, hypothesizing and testing and experimentation skills. Arslan and Tertemiz (2004) investigated science process skills also from the affective perspective. In cognitive aspect, there are the skills that enable to observe, forecast, explain, hypothesize, ask questions, conduct researches, plan and produce, and communicate. In affective aspect, there are the skills that enable to adapt to reality, respect proof, be curious, be flexible, think critically, take risk and question.

Science process skills are comprised of many skills groups from basic to complex. In many resources (Padilla, 1990; Martin, 1997; Kilic, 2006), this skills group is classified as core and consolidated science process skills. The core science process skills involve observation, comparison, classification, inferring, forecasting, communication and quantification skills. The consolidated science process skills, however, involve determining and control of variables, hypothesizing and testing, data gathering and interpretation, operational definition, experimentation and modeling skills. The basic science process skills are considered as the prerequisite of integrated science process skills. In this respect, the integrated science process skills may involve utilizing many basic level skill areas (Sen and Nakiboglu, 2012). This multidimensionality requires presenting the science process skills to pupils that are appropriate to their levels and guide them to utilize these skills in every sphere of life (Ango, 2002). To keep pace with the scientific and technological developments in the world and to adapt to environment, the science process skills of individuals should be developed. By this means, it may be possible to find solutions to problems that will be faced during change and produce genuine products (Celep and Bacanak, 2013).

Science is a general way of understanding the natural world. Science process skills include observing qualities, measuring quantities, sorting/classifying, inferring, predicting, experimenting, and communicating. Science is one of the important subjects in school education. However, really the traditional teaching methods are challenged for their inability to foster critical thinking, holistic learning environment among children. The science subject must develop science process skills where children, observe, measure, classify, process

information, interpret, think on solving problems, analyze, synthesize, formulate conclusions and perform applications that lead to a holistic understanding of the concept. These skills are best taught through hands-on activities and experiments. The skills at the top of the list are the easiest to master and can be introduced to young learners through nature studies. The more challenging skills can be inculcated by using successively more difficult experiments over time. While not all skills may be taught at once, a good science lesson will incorporate several of these skills. As an instructor, one should always move from material that is concrete or familiar, to material that is more complex or abstract, start with observing and move toward predicting a result, interpreting what happened, or forming a conclusion. These skills can be reinforced on a regular basis.

Successfully integrating the science process skills with classroom lessons and field investigations will make the learning experiences richer and more meaningful for students. Students will be learning the skills of science as well as science content. The students will be actively engaged with the science they are learning and thus reach a deeper understanding of the content. Finally active engagements with science will likely lead students to become more interested and have more positive attitudes toward science.

3.1 Observation

Observing is the fundamental science process skill. We observe objects and events using all our five senses, and this is how we learn about the world around us. The ability to make good observations is also essential to the development of the other science process skills: communicating, classifying, measuring, inferring, predicting, innovations and forming conclusions. The simplest observations, made using only the senses, are qualitative observations. For example, the leaf is light green in color or the leaf is waxy and smooth. Observations that involve a number or quantity are quantitative observations. For example, the mass of one leaf is five grams or the leaves are clustered in groups of five. Quantitative observations give more precise information than our senses alone.

Not surprisingly, students, especially younger children, need help to make good observations. Good, productive observations are detailed and accurate written or drawn descriptions, and students need to be prompted to produce these elaborate descriptions. The reason that observations must be so full of detail is that only then can students increase their understanding of the concepts being studied. Whether students are observing with their five senses or with instruments to aid them, we can guide them to make better more detailed descriptions. We can do this by listening to students' initial observations and then prompting them to elaborate. For example, if a student is describing what can be see, they might describe the color of an object but not its size or shape. A student might describe the volume of a sound but not its pitch or rhythm. We can prompt students to add details to their descriptions no matter which of the five senses they are using. There are other ways that we can prompt students to make more elaborate descriptions. For example, if something is changing, students should include, before, during, and after appearances in their observations. If possible, students should be encouraged to name what is being observed.

3.2 Communication

As implied already, communication, the second of the basic science process skills, goes hand in hand with observation. Students have to communicate to share their observations with someone else, and the communication must be clear and effective if the other person is to understand the information. One of the keys to communicating effectively is to use so-called referents, references to items that the other person is already familiar with. For example, we often describe colors using referents. We might say sky blue, grass green, or lemon yellow to describe particular shades of blue, green, or yellow. The idea is to communicate using descriptive words for which both people share a common understanding. Without referents, we open the door to misunderstandings. If we just say hot or rough, for example, our audience might have a different

idea of how hot or how rough. If a student is trying to describe the size of a pinecone they might use the size of his or her shoe as a referent. The pinecone could be either larger or smaller than his shoe.

This skill touches every other one. Students must be able to transmit information through words, charts, diagrams, and other mediums. Emphasize is on the importance of using correct language when communicating with an audience. Discuss with them, also, the importance of using accurate supporting mediums (charts, diagrams, etc.).

3.3 Measuring Skill

The additional science process skill of measuring is really just a special case of observing and communicating. When we measure some property, we compare the property to a defined referent called a unit. A measurement statement contains two parts, a number to tell us how much or how many, and a name for the unit to tell us how much of what. The use of the number makes a measurement a quantitative observation. One can start by teaching young students how to use a ruler and a measuring cup. As they grow older, they will acquire more complex measuring skills using mathematical equations and advanced equipment.

3.4 Sorting/Classification

Students in the early grades are expected to be able to sort objects or phenomena into groups based on their observations. Grouping objects or events is a way of imposing order based on similarities, differences, and interrelationships. This is an important step toward a better understanding of the different objects and events in the world. There are several different methods of classification. Perhaps the simplest method is serial ordering. Objects are placed into rank order based on some property. For example, students can be serial ordered according to height, or different breakfast cereals can be serial ordered according to number of calories per serving. Two other methods of classification are binary classification and multistage classification.

In a binary classification system, a set of objects is simply divided into two subsets. This is usually done on the basis of whether each object has or does not have a particular property. For example, animals can be classified into two groups: those with backbones and those without backbones. A binary classification can also be carried out using more than one property at once. Objects in one group must have all of the required properties; otherwise they will belong to the other group. A multi-stage classification is constructed by performing consecutive binary classifications on a set of objects and then on each of the ensuing subsets. The result is a classification system consisting of layers or stages. A multi-stage classification is complete when each of the objects in the original set has been separated into a category by itself. The familiar classifications of the animal and plant kingdoms are examples of multistage classifications. A useful activity for younger children could be to create a multi-stage classification of some local animals using physical or behavioral similarities and differences.

This skill builds upon observation. Students can learn to separate and sort objects based on properties. Younger students can learn to sort using a single factor (e.g., number of legs: spiders have eight and insects have six), while older students can classify using several factors at once. Teaching classification is also a great time to introduce new vocabulary words. Students can be encouraged to practice using these words by writing them in a science notebook, or for younger students, by memorizing a song or poem using the nerds.

3.5 Inference

Unlike observations, which are direct evidence gathered about an object, inferences are explanations or interpretations that follow from the observations. For example, it is an observation to say an insect released a dark, sticky liquid from its mouth, and it is an inference to state, the insect released a dark, sticky liquid from

its mouth because it is upset and trying to defend itself. When we are able to make inferences, and interpret and explain events around us, we have a better appreciation of the environment around us. Scientists' hypotheses about why events happen as they do are based on inferences regarding investigations.

Students need to be taught the difference between observations and inferences. They need to be able to differentiate for themselves the evidence they gather about the world as observations and the interpretations or inferences they make based on the observations. We can help students make this distinction by first prompting them to be detailed and descriptive in their observations. Then, by asking students questions about their observations we can encourage the students to think about the meaning of the observations. Thinking about making inferences in this way should remind us that inferences link what has been observed together with what is already known from previous experiences. We use our past experiences to help us interpret our observations.

Often many different inferences can be made based on the same observations. Our inferences also may change as we make additional observations. We are generally more confident about our inferences when our observations fit well with our past experiences. We are also more confident about our inferences as we gather more and more supporting evidence. When students are trying to make inferences, they will often need to go back and make additional observations to become more confident in their inferences. For example, seeing an insect release a dark, sticky liquid many times whenever it is picked up and held tightly will increase our confidence that it does this because it is up-set and trying to defend itself. Sometimes making additional observations will reinforce our inferences, but sometimes additional information will cause us to modify or even reject earlier inferences. In science, inferences about how things work are continually constructed, modified, and even rejected based on new observations.

Inferring is to use logic to draw conclusions from what is observed. As for defining operationally, Martin et al. (2009) stated that it is to describe what works; explain how to measure variables in an experiment, relationships between observed actions to explain phenomena and to explain relationships by generalizing to other events not observed. According to Curriculum Development Center (2002), it is to give interpretations of a concept by stating it in terms of what to be done and observed. Inference skill refers to the ability to engage in the process of reasoning the conclusions based upon available information or evidence that is implicit and not explicitly stated (Bryce *et al.*, 1990). This skill is particularly relevant to scientific understanding and investigations, and it is one major component of science process skills (National Research Council, 2011). Espoused in many countries' science curriculum framework and syllabuses, inference skill is more cognitively demanding as compared to direct information recall. While students can be provided with information to memorize, science inference skills can only be developed through exposure to diverse cases, scenarios, and events requiring students to draw relevant contextual information and prior knowledge to explain the observed phenomena.

3.6 Prediction

Making predictions is making educated guesses about the outcomes of future events. We are forecasting future observations. The ability to make predictions about future events allows us to successfully interact with the environment around us. Prediction is based on both good observation and inferences made about observed events. Like inferences, predictions are based on both what we observe and also our past experiences the mental models we have built up from those experiences. Predictions based on our inferences or hypotheses about events give us a way to test those inferences or hypotheses. If the prediction turns out to be correct, then we have greater confidence in our inference/hypothesis. This is the basis of the scientific process used by scientists who are asking and answering questions by integrating together the six basic science process skills.

This skill derives from learners being able to spot patterns in past experiments or existing evidence. Predicting is an educated guess about what's likely to happen when one introduces changes. Before perform-

ing any experiment, learners could be asked for what they think would happen and have them write down their guesses. Guide younger students by asking questions such as: How many are in the jar? How much does this weigh? What will happen if we add something else? Advanced students will be capable of more in-depth predictions or hypotheses, based on what they know already.

3.7 Innovative Skills

Innovativeness is the ability of introducing or using new ideas or ways of doing things. The process of innovation involves thinking creatively: Using imagination to manipulate instruments or variables, to formulate models, to discover possibilities, and to construct objects and images that never existed before. Innovation can be a change made in established laws and practices by the introduction of something new, with the purpose of improving quality, quantity, output, or procedures. Mbanefo and Chiaha (2013) stated that innovative learning environments focus on the facilitation and utilization of new knowledge acquisition modes, adoption of problem-solving strategies, integration of knowledge from diverse sources, utilization of self-directed learning, and knowledge extension through elaborate creative expression.

3.8 Experimenting

Experimenting is being able to conduct an experiment, including asking an appropriate question, stating a hypothesis, identifying and controlling variables, operationally defining those variables, designing a "fair" experiment, conducting the experiment, and interpreting the results of the experiment.

3.9 Forming Conclusions

This skill is connected to interpreting. Scientists cannot make conclusions hastily; they must be reached through careful reasoning. When forming conclusions, they look back at their predictions and compare them with the actual results. Make sure they take all the information they gathered into account as they draw a conclusion.

4.0 Technical Issues in Sciences: Challenges and Perspectives

Our societies are dominated and even driven by ideas and products from science and technology. It is very likely that the influence on science and technology on our lives will continue to increase in the years to come. Scientific and technological knowledge, skills and artifacts invade all realms of life in our modern society. The workplace and the public sphere are increasingly dependent on new as well as the more established technologies. So are also the private sphere and our leisure time. Knowledge and skills in science and technology are crucial for most of our actions and decisions, as workers, as voters, as consumers, etc. Meaningful and independent participation in modern democracies assumes ability to judge evidence and arguments in the many socio-scientific issues that are on the political agenda.

In short, modern societies need people with science and technology qualifications at the top level as well as a general public with a broad understanding of science and technology contents, methods and as a social force shaping the future. Science and Technology are major cultural products of human history. All citizens, independent of occupational needs, need to be acquainted with this part of human culture. Science and Technology are important for economical well-being, but also seen from the perspective of a broadly based liberal education.

One might expect that the increasing significance of Science and Technology should be accompanied with a parallel growth in the interest in these subjects as well as increasing understanding of basic scientific ideas and ways of thinking. This does, however, not seem to be the case. The evidence for such claims are in part based on hard facts, in part on large comparative studies and in part based on research and analysis of trends in our societies. The situation is described briefly and analyzed in the following.

4.1 Falling Enrolment and Increasing Gender Gap

In many countries, the recruitment to science and technology studies is falling, or at least not developing as fast as expected or planned for. This lack of interest in science often manifests itself at school level at the age where curricular choices are made. In many countries there is noticeable decrease in the numbers of students choosing some of the sciences. This trend is further enlarged in the enrolment to tertiary education. A similar trend occurs in some areas of engineering and technology studies. It should, however, be noted that there are large and interesting differences between the various countries and between the different areas of science and technology. The fall in recruitment has in particular hit the harder parts of science and technology, in particular physics and mathematics. In many countries, one also observes a growing gender gap in the choice of science and technology subjects in schools as well as at the tertiary level. The teacher is the single most important source of variation in the quality of learning (Hattie, 2003). The supply, development, and retention of good science teachers is therefore of paramount importance. Studies show that the proportion of undergraduates willing to consider teaching seriously has broadly declined over the last decade. Despite this decline, potential teachers' judgments on the character of the job are comparatively stable. Students are often central to the attraction of becoming a teacher. The possibilities of making a difference, of enthusing students and of working with people, rather than with money or things, are important motivations to teach. Undergraduates often cite the influence of their own teachers on them as students. This shows that there is a large pool of goodwill available.

The concern about unsatisfactory enrolment is voiced from many interest groups. Industrial leaders are worried about the recruitment of qualified work force; universities and research institutions are worried about the recruitment of new researchers; educational authorities are worried about the already visible lack of qualified science and technology teachers. In some countries, the grave situation for the recruitment of new students as well as for the substitution of those who retire has caused great national concern. This concern is often based on comprehensive reviews of the current situation in the education sector and the labor market. The concern is not only about the actual numbers, but also about a more or less identifiable fall in the quality of the newcomers. A weaker quality may of course be a consequence of the fact that very few candidates compete to get places at institutions where the entrance qualifications previously were very high. Many tertiary science and technology institutions are unable to fill their study places with students.

The evidence for claims about problems in recruitment stems from objective and uncontroversial educational statistics concerning enrolment. Statistical data and most surveys do, however, shed much light on the underlying causes why science and technology apparently lost its attraction among young people. Unless one has some ideas about this, intervention programs to increase the interests in science and technology are not likely to have success. The following points are attempts to suggest explanations, although some of claims can be backed up with research evidence.

4.1.1 Disenchantment with Science and Technology

It is not easy to understand what causes the difficult situation for the recruitment to science and technology. Reasons for the doubt in and dissatisfaction with science and technology have to be found in the youth culture and in society at large. The decline in recruitment must be understood as a social and political

phenomenon that occurs in many highly industrialized countries. This means that the current situation can hardly be explained fully by events or reforms in each individual country. One should seek for more general and common trends found in different countries. The following is an attempt to suggest underlying reasons for the present situation. The listing is tentative, and it needs critical scrutiny and modification in each country. The first point refers to schools, the other are related to wider social trends.

i. **Outdated curriculum**

Many studies show that pupils perceive school science as lacking relevance. It is often described as dull, authoritarian, abstract and theoretical. The curriculum is often overcrowded with unfamiliar concepts and laws. It leaves little room for enjoyment, curiosity and a search for meaning. It often lacks a cultural, social and historical dimension, and it seldom treats the contemporary issues.

ii. **Science: Difficult and untrendy**

Scientific knowledge is by nature abstract and theoretical. It also often contradicts common sense. It is also often developed through controlled experiments in artificial and unnatural and idealized laboratory settings. Learning science often requires hard work and intellectual efforts, although school science should be tailored to better meet the needs and abilities of the pupils. Concentration and hard work is not part of present youth culture. In a world where so many channels compete about the attention of young people, such subjects become untrendy.

iii. **Lack of qualified teachers**

Science and Technology are often poorly treated in teacher preparation for the early years. Moreover, the students who choose to become primary school teachers are often those who did not take or did not like science themselves in school. The present decline in recruitment of science teachers is now being felt also in secondary schools.

iv. **Anti and quasi-scientific trends and alternatives**

In many Western countries there is an upsurge of "alternative" beliefs in the metaphysical, spiritual and supernatural. These movements are often labeled "New Age" and comprise a rich variety of world-views and therapies. They include beliefs in astrology and several forms of healing. A common denominator is often the rejection of scientific rationality, often characterized as mechanistic, reductionist, etc. Although most "alternatives" reject science, some do however also base their ideas on misinterpretations of ideas taken from modern science, like quantum mechanics.

v. **Postmodernist attacks on Science and Technology**

This may be seen as the more serious and academic version of the critique imbedded in the above mentioned alternative movements. Many postmodernist thinkers reject basic elements of science, and reject notions like objectivity and rationality. The more extreme versions assert that scientific knowledge and claims say more about the researcher than about reality, and that all other stories about the world have the same epistemological status. Notions like reality and truth are seldom used without inverted commas. These postmodernists attacks on scientific thinking has even been called "Science War" and book titles like "The flight from science and reason" and "Higher superstition" indicate the tone of the 'debate' and how these trends have been met by the scientific community.

vi.   **Stereotypical image of scientists and engineers**

Many research projects indicate that the perceived image of the typical scientist and engineer is stereotypical and problematic. The image of the "crazy scientist" is widespread, possibly supported by cartoons, plots in many popular movies and in media coverage. Scientists especially in the hard, physical sciences are by pupils often perceived to be authoritarian, closed, bored and somewhat crazy. They are not perceived to be kind or helping and working to solve problems of humankind.

vii. **Disagreement among researchers perceived as problematic**

Scientists debate and disagree on many contemporary socio-scientific issues like causes of global warming, effects of radiation, possible dangers of food processing techniques, etc. Such discussions are the normal processes for the healthy development of new scientific knowledge. Recently, such debates are also taken to the mass media and are not as before confined to professional conferences and journals. The disagreement in public may, however, confuse and disappoint people who are acquainted with "school science," where scientific knowledge is presented as certain and uncontroversial.

viii. **Problematic values and ethos of science**

The traditional values of science are meant to safeguard objectivity, neutrality, disinterestedness and rationality. Taken to the extreme, however, these values may seem to justify absence of ethics, empathy and concern for the social implications of science. The search for universal laws and theories may lead to an implied image of science as abstract and not related to human needs. For many people, science is cold and lacks a human face.

ix.   **Dislike of an overambitious science**

The achievements of science may call for admiration, but also unease. Many people dislike the image and ambitions of modern biotechnology. They have emotional and rational fear about scientists who are "tampering with nature," and "playing God." Similarly, many people react emotionally when physicists talk about their quest for "the final theory," also called "the theory of everything" or the search for "the God particle" (the title of a book by Nobel laureate Leon Lederman). Such perspectives may attract some young people, but it is not unlikely that these ambitions of modern science will scare others. Many people feel that science is intruding areas that they consider sacred, and they do not want a world where science can explain everything. Many people like to think of Nature as sacred and mystical, not as explainable, controllable and rational.

x.   **The new image: Big Science and techno-science**

Science used to be seen as a search for knowledge driven by individual curiosity. Scientists have historically rightfully been described as radicals and revolutionaries who often challenged religious and political authorities. Present science is different in fundamental ways. We have in the last decades seen a fusion between science and technology into what is called techno-science and Big Science (NASA, CERN, Human Genome Project, etc.). The scientists and engineers of today often work close to industrial or military interests. The earlier image of scientists being dissidents and rebels has been replaced with a less exotic image of scientists being loyal workers in the service of power and authority. Scientists and other 'experts' are often on the pay-roll of industry, military or the State. Hence, their role as neutral defenders of objectivity and truth is questioned by many scholars, and also pupils in schools.

xi. **Scientists and engineers: No longer heroes**

Not very long ago, scientists and engineers were considered heroes. The scientists produced progressive knowledge and fought superstition and ignorance, the engineers developed new technologies and products that improved the quality of life. This image is, however, 'history' by now. For many young people in rich, modern societies, the fight for better health and a better material standard is an unknown history of the past. They do not see the fruits of science and technology, but are more able to see the present evils of environmental degradation, pollution, global warming, etc. Forgetting the victories of the past, many put the blame of the current problems on science and technology. The heroic status of scientists and engineers has faded.

xii. **The new role models: Not in Science and Technology**

We live in a world that is in part created by the media. Football players and pop artists are exposed and earn fortunes. The lives of journalists and other media people seem interesting and challenging. Although few young people can obtain such careers, the new role models on either side of the camera create new ideals. The young people also know that lawyers and people at the stock exchange earn more money than the physicist in the laboratory. They also know that lack of physics knowledge is no hindrance to such careers. A white-coated hardworking and not very well paid scientist in a lab is not the role model of young people of today. This social climate does not create an atmosphere where it is easy to convince young people that they should concentrate on their science learning!

xiii. **Communication gap between scientists and the public**

The science and technology establishment is often confused and annoyed when met with critique. In the past, they have enjoyed enormous popularity, increasing budgets and excellent recruitment. They are not used to face distrust, and they have not been in need to justify their research in public debates. The immediate reaction to the new situation is the search for scapegoats, often found in the schools and in the media. The problematic situation is often seen by the science and technology establishment as a problem of information. Critique and skepticism are often interpreted as based on misunderstandings and lack of knowledge from the public. In some cases this may, of course be justified, but the new situation does call for a form for self-critique within the science and technology community. Communication works both ways and a lack of mutual understanding cannot only be blamed on one part only.

4.2 Contradictory and Optimistic Trends

It is evident from the points raised above that the situation has many dimensions. Some of the recent trends are also contradictory. From the falling enrolment, one may deduce that there is a falling interest in science and technology. On the other hand, young people are more than ever interested in using all sorts of new technology. It is a paradox that the countries which have the most problems with recruitment to science and technology are also the countries with the most widespread use of new technologies among the young people. There seems to be an eagerness to use the new technologies, but a reluctance to study the disciplines that underlie the very same products.

Skills and knowledge in science and technology are learned and acquired in many different contexts, not only in formal settings like schools. The media, museums of various kinds, the workplace and even everyday life provide other learning contexts. Most of the impressive skills that young people have in handling personal computers, internet, cellular phones and all sorts of electronic devices are acquired in informal

out-of-school settings. Besides, young people have often developed more advanced skills in such areas than their teachers at school, although their understanding of the underlying physical principles may be totally lacking. Young people as well as many older persons demonstrate an impressive ability to learn and to pick up new skills that they deem to be of relevance for their daily life. Educational authorities might learn important lessons from these arenas of learning. They should also seek ways to support such learning, also to avoid possibly growing inequalities in the area of new technology based on gender or economical and social background.

4.3 Public Understanding of Science and Technology: An International Concern

The situation that has been described above (a growing importance but increasingly problematic status of science and technology in many countries) is the obvious background for a growing political concern about science and technology in schools, higher education, media and the general public. Phrases like 'scientific illiteracy' are used, more or less rightfully, to describe the situation. Acronyms like PUST (public understanding of science and technology) have become expressions for the growing concern about the situation. Academic journals are devoted to these issues (i.e., public understanding of science) and several research institutions study these challenges. In many countries, the situation has attracted public attention, and in many countries projects and counter-measures are planned or put in operation. The Portuguese Ciencia Viva is an example of such national program. Some of these national programs have also initiated research, discussions and other efforts to increase the understanding of the problematic situation.

4.4 Ways Forward

As indicated above, the problem or technical issues in sciences have many dimensions, and different interest groups may understand and conceive the challenges in widely different terms. The perspectives of industrial leaders are often different from those of the environmental activists. It has also been argued that the problems related to the interests in and attitudes to science and technology can not only be perceived as educational challenges. They have to be understood and addressed in a wider social, cultural and political context. Hence, solutions may be as different as the way in which the challenge is understood. One can, however, argue that there may be broad agreement about some reforms and innovations in spite of different reasons for concern. Agreement can be reached about the need to stimulate and maintain young children's' curiosity about natural phenomena and how things work. There can also be agreement that everybody will benefit from a broad base of knowledge about key ideas in science and basic principles in technology. Everybody should also understand and appreciate the key role played by science and technology in contemporary society. An understanding and appreciation of scientific theories and ideas as major cultural products of humankind is probably also uncontroversial. This list could be continued, and is an indication that different groups should be able to work together to achieve what is often called "scientific and technological literacy."

Finally, if one accepts that the problems of recruitment to and attitudes to S&T are embedded in a wider social context, one will also need a broader approach than only to address school reforms, curriculum reform, reforms in teacher training and in higher education. If the challenges are of a deeper social and cultural nature, as argued here, then there is no easy one-shot solution. One will need to look beyond the education system, and involve different stakeholders. There is a need for reforms that are context specific, that require multiple approaches and are implemented of long periods of time. Initiatives will also have to be monitored, and the development and results will need continuing discussions, informed by evidence and careful analysis.

5.0 Social Dimensions of Scientific Development

Social dimensions of scientific knowledge and development encompass the effects of scientific research on human life and social relations, the effects of social relations and values on scientific research, and the social aspects of inquiry itself. Scientific knowledge can improve the quality of life at many different levels: from the routine workings of our everyday lives to global issues. Science informs public policy and personal decisions on energy, conservation, agriculture, health, transportation, communication, defense, economics, leisure, and exploration. It contributes to ensuring a longer and healthier life, monitors our health, provides medicine to cure our diseases, alleviates aches and pains, helps us to provide water for our basic needs—including our food, provides energy and makes life more fun, including sports, music, entertainment and the latest. Science generates solutions for everyday life and helps us to answer the great mysteries of the universe. In other words, science is one of the most important channels of knowledge. It has a specific role, as well as a variety of functions for the benefit of our society: creating new knowledge, improving education, and increasing the quality of our lives.

Science must respond to societal needs and global challenges. Public understanding and engagement with science, and citizen participation in science are essential to equip citizens to make informed personal and professional choices. Governments need to make decisions based on quality scientific information on issues such as health and agriculture, and parliaments need to legislate on societal issues which necessitate the latest scientific knowledge. National governments need to understand the science behind major global challenges such as climate change, ocean health, biodiversity loss and freshwater security. To face sustainable development challenges, governments and citizens alike must understand the language of science and must become scientifically literate. On the other hand, scientists must understand the problems policy-makers face and endeavor to make the results of their research relevant and comprehensible to society. Challenges today cut across the traditional boundaries of disciplines and stretch across the lifecycle of innovation: from research to knowledge development and its application. Science, technology and innovation must drive our pursuit of more equitable and sustainable development. Science has made human life much more convenient and more accessible by saving labor, time, and much more with new technologies. Indeed, its series of discoveries has helped understand the nature of the world and has improved for the betterment of society.

Education in the area of scientific social inquiry includes the application of social scientific theories, concepts, research findings and methods in identifying and comprehending broad societal trends and important events. Science as an enterprise has individual, social, and institutional dimensions. Scientific activity is one of the main features of the contemporary world and, perhaps more than any other, distinguishes our times from earlier centuries. As a social activity, science inevitably reflects social values and viewpoints. Scientific work involves many individuals doing many different kinds of work and goes on to some degree in all nations of the world. Men and women of all ethnic and national backgrounds participate in science and its applications. These people: scientists and engineers, physicians, mathematicians, technicians, computer programmers, librarians, and others, may focus on scientific knowledge either for its own sake or for a particular practical purpose, and they may be concerned with data gathering, theory building, instrument building, or communicating. Science goes on in many different settings. Scientists are employed by universities, hospitals, business and industry, government, independent research organizations, and scientific associations. They may work alone, in small groups, or as members of large research teams. Their places of work include classrooms, offices, laboratories, and natural field settings from space to the bottom of the sea. In view of the social nature of science, the dissemination of scientific information is crucial to its progress. Some scientists present their findings and theories in papers that are delivered at meetings or published in scientific journals. Those papers enable scientists to inform others about their work, to expose their ideas to criticism by other scientists, and, of course, to stay abreast of scientific developments around the world. The

advancement of information science (knowledge of the nature of information and its manipulation) and the development of information technologies (especially computer systems) affect all sciences. Those technologies speed up data collection, compilation, and analysis; make new kinds of analysis practical; and shorten the time between discovery and application.

Science is organized into content disciplines and is conducted in various institutions. Organizationally, science can be thought of as the collection of all of the different scientific fields, or content disciplines. From anthropology through zoology, there are dozens of such disciplines. They differ from one another in many ways, including history, phenomena studied, techniques and language used, and kinds of outcomes desired. With respect to purpose and philosophy, however, all are equally scientific and together make up the same scientific endeavor. The advantage of having disciplines is that they provide a conceptual structure for organizing research and research findings. The disadvantage is that their divisions do not necessarily match the way the world works, and they can make communication difficult. In any case, scientific disciplines do not have fixed borders. Physics shades into chemistry, astronomy, and geology, as does chemistry into biology and psychology, and so on. New scientific disciplines (astrophysics and sociobiology, for instance) are continually being formed at the boundaries of others. Some disciplines grow and break into sub disciplines, which then become disciplines in their own right.

Universities, industry, and government are also part of the structure of the scientific endeavor. University research usually emphasizes knowledge for its own sake, although much of it is also directed toward practical problems. Universities, of course, are also particularly committed to educating successive generations of scientists, mathematicians, and engineers. Industries and businesses usually emphasize research directed to practical ends, but many also sponsor research that has no immediately obvious applications, partly on the premise that it will be applied fruitfully in the long run. The federal government funds much of the research in universities and in industry but also supports and conducts research in its many national laboratories and research centers. Private foundations, public-interest groups, and state governments also support research. Funding agencies influence the direction of science by virtue of the decisions they make on which research to support. Other deliberate controls on science result from federal (and sometimes local) government regulations on research practices that are deemed to be dangerous and on the treatment of the human and animal subjects used in experiments.

Scientists participate in public affairs both as specialists and as citizens. Scientists can bring information, insights, and analytical skills to bear on matters of public concern. Often they can help the public and its representatives to understand the likely causes of events (such as natural and technological disasters) and to estimate the possible effects of projected policies (such as ecological effects of various farming methods). Often they can testify to what is not possible. In playing this advisory role, scientists are expected to be especially careful in trying to distinguish fact from interpretation, and research findings from speculation and opinion; that is, they are expected to make full use of the principles of scientific inquiry. Even so, scientists can seldom bring definitive answers to matters of public debate. Some issues are too complex to fit within the current scope of science, or there may be little reliable information available, or the values involved may lie outside of science. Moreover, although there may be at any one time a broad consensus on the bulk of scientific knowledge, the agreement does not extend to all scientific issues, let alone to all science-related social issues. And of course, on issues outside of their expertise, the opinions of scientists should enjoy no special credibility. In their work, scientists go to great lengths to avoid bias—their own as well as that of others. But in matters of public interest, scientists, like other people, can be expected to be biased where their own personal, corporate, institutional, or community interests are at stake. For example, because of their commitment to science, many scientists may understandably be less than objective in their beliefs on how science is to be funded in comparison to other social needs.

6.0   Careers in the Sciences

Science is a core field of study that everyone should be interested in, however, careers for one to apply or build science knowledge are relatively uncommon. The careers list shows realistic opportunities for a science career. Generally, they rely on doing specialist postgraduate study after a general science degree. For the purposes of the careers listed, emphasis is limited to those interested in careers in the natural and physical sciences, apart from technology, engineering and mathematics disciplines. The main job roles in a science career are:

- Researcher—expand the frontiers of scientific knowledge
- Technician—physically carry out tests and experiments
- Applied scientist—apply science knowledge for practical uses
- Science-based profession—such as pharmacy and veterinary practice and
- Educator—teach science at a school or university.

6.1 Environmental Science

Career in Environmental science is devoted to the study of the environment and development of plans and policies for the protection of the components of the environment, including its air, water, fauna and flora. People may find employment directly participating in practical conservation efforts. In this case, one would be working a great deal in an outdoor setting. An alternative is to work in the area of environmental policy development. If one already has an undergraduate science degree, environmental science postgraduate education programs are also pertinent. Job titles in this field include the following: air quality consultant, contaminated land scientist, ecologist, environmental scientist—contaminated land, environmental scientist/engineer, environmental scientist/planner, environmental scientist (wetlands), principal environmental engineer/scientist, project environmental scientist/engineer, senior aquatic ecologist/environmental scientist, senior environmental engineer/scientist.

6.2 Pharmacy

If one is detail-oriented and strong at the sciences, perhaps the person should consider a career in pharmacy. To become a pharmacist, a Bachelor of Pharmacy degree is needed. If one already has a science degree, Master of Pharmacy degree programs are also pertinent. Once have a pharmacy degree is gotten, the fellow have to register with the Pharmacy Board of Nigeria and complete a one-year internship with a registered pharmacist. Workplaces for pharmacists include retail pharmacies, hospitals and pharmaceutical companies. Job titles include the following: cancer care clinical pharmacist, clinical pharmacist, community pharmacist, dispensary pharmacist, director of operations—clinical trials, drug safety associate, emergency medicine pharmacist, pharmacist, pharmacy clinical research coordinator, pharmacist senior, pharmacist—technical consultant, production pharmacist, senior clinical pharmacist, specialist clinical pharmacist.

6.3 Medical Laboratory Science

For a person who is detail-oriented and observant with outstanding analytical skills, a career in medical laboratory science might be right. Medical laboratory scientists do advanced tasks in medical laboratory settings, including, for example, the study of disease and pathologies of the human body. Examples of duties might include studying and testing blood, growing organisms that lead to disease (such as viruses, bacteria,

and fungi) for diagnosis and study, and examining DNA and RNA. For a career in this field, one needs an accredited degree in Medical Laboratory Science. Job titles include the following: medical laboratory scientist, medical laboratory scientist—molecular genetics, medical scientist—anatomical pathology (cytology), laboratory supervisor, scientist—histopathology, senior scientist, and senior scientist—immunohistochemistry, senior scientist (coagulation).

6.4 Science Education

If one pictures self as teaching young people and thriving in that career, then if so, consider becoming a high school science teacher or a professor in the sciences at university level. If one thinks a career as a secondary school science teacher is the right path, then one will need to earn a degree in Education (Secondary). If one already has a Bachelor of Science degree, enrolling in a Master's program is also necessary. If one prefers teaching at the university-level (and deeply enjoys research), getting a PhD degree in the chosen science subject field is eminent. Job titles include the following: biology and mathematics teacher, biology teacher, chemistry and science teacher, classroom teacher—science/VCE biology, head teacher—science, instructional leader—science, mathematics/science teacher, lecturer, lecturer in biomedical science, lecturer/senior lecturer in animal ecology, lecturer/senior lecturer in chemistry, mathematics and science teacher, physics/mathematics, physics teacher, postdoctoral research fellow, robotics and STEM teacher, science teacher, science teacher (biology and chemistry), science teacher chemistry, science teacher (secondary), senior lecturer in biomedical science, STEM program team leader, teacher of biology and chemistry, teacher of mathematics/science, teacher (science), teacher—secondary (chemistry), teacher—secondary mathematics and science, teacher—secondary physics and chemistry.

6.5 Geology, Geophysics and Hydrogeology

If one is fascinated by the earth and what lies beneath the surface of the ground, a career in this area could be considered. The geologist's focus is the earth and everything that lies beneath, studying structure, composition and nature. Geologists are often needed to provide advice on mineral extraction and land rehabilitation. Geophysicists gather measurements from beneath the earth's surface by using magnetic, seismic, electrical and gravity methods of data collection. To be a geologist, one will need a degree in geology or geosciences. Geophysicists are usually required to have a degree in geophysics. If a career as a hydrogeologist—in which case one would be specifically studying bodies of water, getting a degree in that the discipline could help set an individual up for success. Job titles include the following: drilling geologist, engineering geologist, exploration geologist, geologist, geophysicist data processor, graduate geologist, graduate hydrogeologist, hydrogeologist, imaging geophysicist, junior hydrogeologist, junior rig geologist, project geologist, mine geologist, principal consultant (geology), project exploration geologist, resource geologist, rig geologist, senior exploration geologist, senior geologist, senior geotechnical engineer, senior hydrogeologist, senior mine geologist, senior resource geologist, senior staff geophysicist.

6.6 Veterinary Science

If a person has natural love for animals and is good and strong at the sciences starting a career in veterinary science could be advised. To become a veterinarian, one will be required to complete an accredited degree program at a university. Once one has graduated with a degree in veterinary science, one will have to register with the veterinary registration board to be licensed to practice. If one would prefer becoming a veterinary nurse, the person will require a minimum of specific certificate-level education and training.

Job titles include the following: associate veterinarian, ECC veterinarian, emergency and critical care vet, emergency veterinarian, graduate veterinarian, head veterinarian, head veterinary nurse, lead veterinarian, locum veterinarian, senior veterinary officer, senior veterinarian, specialist—small animal medicine, specialist—small animal surgery, veterinarian, veterinary cardiologist, veterinary director, veterinary officer, veterinary nurse, veterinarian—internal medicine specialist, veterinary director, veterinarian—specialist surgeon, veterinarian (small animal medicine), veterinary surgeon, wildlife veterinarian, wildlife vet nurse.

6.7 Life Sciences

There are numerous different career paths available in the life sciences, which are the study of human, animal, and plant life. To pursue work in this field, one will need an undergraduate degree at the very least. Many positions will require graduate education (frequently to the PhD level) as well and one could be working in a university environment. Other workplaces include, for example, medical research institutes and hospitals. Jobs in industry are also available, such as in pharmaceutical companies. Advanced observation and analytical skills are critical in this field. Job titles include the following: biochemist, bioinformatician, botanist, environmental consultant, exercise physiologist, field applications specialist, microbiologist, microbiologist—veterinary diagnostic, microbiology analyst, molecular biologist, postdoctoral research associate, postdoctoral fellow, postdoctoral research fellow in biotechnology, quality control technician (microbiology), quality manager, research assistant—biologics lead antibody discovery, rehabilitation consultant, research assistant—antibody technologies, research assistant—molecular biologist, research fellow—molecular and cell biology, research officer, research scientist, senior technical officer (plant science).

6.8 Agricultural Science

A career in agricultural science means that the individual is involved in studying, researching and analyzing plants and animals involved in agriculture. The person also examines cultivation methods to improve agricultural productivity. The person would probably work with farmers and other stakeholders, such as food manufacturers and government regulators. Attention to detail, analytical skills and resourcefulness are required for success in this field. Just some of the types of tasks one will be carrying out include data collection (for example, the collection of soil, feed, produce, and water samples), analysis, project management (including equipment management, staff supervision and budget management), and research. A degree focusing on agricultural science will help one get started on this career path. Job titles include the following: agronomist, postdoctoral fellow in soil science/agronomy, research fellow, research scientist cropping systems modeling, sales agronomist, senior agronomist, senior scientist (research).

6.9 Chemistry

A Chemist works in the laboratory, making new discoveries, and has strong scientific aptitude. Chemists determine the composition of materials by studying their chemical and physical properties. To succeed in this field, one will need to be observant, detail-oriented and patient. Even more importantly, one must have an inquiring and curious mind. One will need to earn a graduate degree (for positions with universities, often a PhD) in chemistry to become a chemist. Job titles include the following: application development scientist—food safety division, chemist, development chemist, formulations chemist, junior laboratory analyst, laboratory manager, laboratory safety officer—chemistry, offshore chemist, postdoctoral research fellow, process chemist, quality control chemist, research and development chemist, research scientist, senior chemist, vitamin analysis chemist.

6.10 Forestry Science

Forestry scientists must be versatile and observant, with high-level analytical and problem-solving skills. Managing forests requires the ability to embrace a multi-disciplinary vision and approach. One will probably be working with professionals from other disciplines, such as the social sciences and commerce. As a forestry scientist, one might be required to understand how to manage land that combines natural forest and agricultural activity. This is sometimes referred to as farm forestry. A university-level science education with a focus on forestry is needed for a career in this field. Job titles include the following: consultant—natural resource management, senior ecologist, senior lecturer in forest science and management, senior team leader native forest policy and programs, urban forestry officer.

7.0   Templates/Models for Developing Skills in Sciences

The main types of scientific models or templates are visual, mathematical, and computer models. A scientific model is a representation of a particular phenomenon in the world using something else to represent it, making it easier to understand. A scientific model could be a diagram or picture, a physical model like an aircraft model kit you got when you were young, a computer program, or set of complex mathematics that describes a situation. Whatever it is, the goal is to make the particular thing you're modeling easier to understand. When we do that, we're able to use it to predict what will happen in the future. For example, predicting what will happen as our climate changes would be easy if we could make a fully accurate model of the atmosphere.

7.1 Visual Models

The use of visual representations (i.e., photographs, diagrams, models) has been part of science, and their use makes it possible for scientists to interact with and represent complex phenomena, not observable in other ways. Despite a wealth of research in science education on visual representations, the emphasis of such research has mainly been on the conceptual understanding when using visual representations and less on visual representations as epistemic objects. In this project on groundwork on skills acquisition and development, we posit that by positioning visual representations as epistemic objects of scientific practices, science education can bring a renewed focus on how visualization contributes to knowledge formation in science from the learners' perspective. During the last decades, research and reform documents in science education across the world have been calling for an emphasis not only on the content but also on the processes of science (Bybee 2014; Eurydice 2012; Duschl and Bybee 2014; Osborne 2014; Schwartz *et al.,* 2012), to make science accessible to the students and enable them to understand the epistemic foundation of science. Scientific practices, part of the process of science, are the cognitive and discursive activities that are targeted in science education to develop epistemic understanding and appreciation of the nature of science (Duschl *et al.,* 2008) and have been the emphasis of recent reform documents in science education across the world (Achieve 2013; Eurydice 2012). With the term scientific practices, we refer to the processes that take place during scientific discoveries and include among others: asking questions, developing and using models, engaging in arguments, and constructing and communicating explanations (National Research Council 2012). The emphasis on scientific practices aims to move the teaching of science from knowledge to the understanding of the processes and the epistemic aspects of science. Additionally, by placing an emphasis on engaging students in scientific practices, we aim to help students acquire scientific knowledge in meaningful contexts that resemble the reality of scientific discoveries.

Visual templates or models are things like flowcharts, pictures, and diagrams that help us educate each other. They are the ones nonscientists have most experience with. Visual modeling is the graphic representation of objects and systems of interest using graphical languages. Visual modeling is a way for experts and novices to have a common understanding of otherwise complicated ideas. By using visual models complex ideas are not held to human limitations, allowing for greater complexity without a loss of comprehension. Visual modeling can also be used to bring a group to a consensus. Models are a mentally visual way of linking theory with experiment, and they guide research by being simplified representations of an imagined reality that enable predictions to be developed and tested by experiment. Models help effectively communicate ideas among designers, allowing for quicker discussion and an eventual consensus. In science, visual models are often useful as educational tools, say in a classroom or from a scientist to a colleague. For example, a visual model can show the main processes that affect what the atmosphere is made of. No matter how clever and educated you might be, diagrams are extremely helpful in explaining how the world works. They can describe abstract concepts, and show things that would be too tiny or too gigantic to see with our own eyes. In an office you might create a flowchart that describes the work that you do. Maybe orders come in by phone, and that information gets transferred to both the warehouse and the membership department. If you include every input and output, that flowchart is an example of a visual model.

Schematic, pictorial symbols in the design of scientific instruments and analysis of the perceptual and functional information that is being stored in those images have been areas of investigation in philosophy of scientific experimentation (Gooding *et al.,* 1993). The nature of visual perception, the relationship between thought and vision, and the role of reproducibility as a norm for experimental research form a central aspect of this domain of research in philosophy of science. For instance, Rothbart (1997) has argued that visualizations are commonplace in the theoretical sciences even if every scientific theory may not be defined by visualized models.

Visual representations (i.e., photographs, diagrams, tables, charts, models) have been used in science over the years to enable scientists to interact with complex phenomena (Richards 2003) and might convey important evidence not observable in other ways (Barber *et al.,* 2006). Some authors (Ruivenkamp and Rip 2010) have argued that visualization is as a core activity of some scientific communities of practice (e.g., nanotechnology) while others (Lynch and Edgerton 1988) have differentiated the role of particular visualization techniques (e.g., of digital image processing in astronomy). Visualization in science includes the complex process through which scientists develop or produce imagery, schemes, and graphical representation, and therefore, what is of importance in this process is not only the result but also the methodology employed by the scientists, namely, how this result was produced. Visual representations in science may refer to objects that are believed to have some kind of material or physical existence but equally might refer to purely mental, conceptual, and abstract constructs (Pauwels 2006). More specifically, visual representations can be found for: phenomena that are not observable with the eye (i.e., microscopic or macroscopic); phenomena that do not exist as visual representations but can be translated as such (i.e., sound); and in experimental settings to provide visual data representations (i.e., graphs presenting velocity of moving objects). Additionally, since science is not only about replicating reality but also about making it more understandable to people (either to the public or other scientists), visual representations are not only about reproducing the nature but also about: functioning in helping solving a problem, filling gaps in our knowledge, and facilitating knowledge building or transfer (Lynch 2006).

Using or developing visual representations in the scientific practice can range from a straightforward to a complicated situation. More specifically, scientists can observe a phenomenon (i.e., mitosis) and represent it visually using a picture or diagram, which is quite straightforward. But they can also use a variety of complicated techniques that are either available or need to be developed or refined to acquire the visual information that can be used in the process of theory development (Latour and Woolgar 1979). Furthermore, some

visual representations need decoding, and the scientists need to learn how to read these images; therefore, using visual representations in the process of science requires learning a new language that is specific to the medium/methods that is used and then communicating that language to other scientists and the public.

There are much intent and purposes of visual representations in scientific practices, as for example to make a diagnosis, compare, describe, and preserve for future study, verify and explore new territory, generate new data (Pauwels 2006), or present new methodologies. According to Latour and Woolgar (1979) and Knorr Cetina (1999), visual representations can be used either as primary data or can be used to help in concept development, to uncover relationships and to make the abstract more concrete. Therefore, visual representations and visual practices, in all forms, are an important aspect of the scientific practices in developing, clarifying, and transmitting scientific knowledge (Pauwels 2006).

It is important to stress, however, that visual representations are not used in isolation, but are supported by other types of evidence as well, or other theories. More importantly, this finding can also have implications when teaching science as argument (Erduran and Jimenez-Aleixandre 2008), since the verbal evidence used in the science classroom to maintain an argument could be supported by visual evidence (a model, representation, image, graph, etc.). For example, in a group of students discussing the outcomes of an introduced species in an ecosystem, pictures of the species and the ecosystem over time, and videos showing the changes in the ecosystem, and the special characteristics of the different species could serve as visual evidence to help the students support their arguments (Evagorou *et al.,* 2012). Therefore, an important implication for the teaching of science is the use of visual representations as evidence in the science curriculum as part of knowledge production. Even though studies in the area of science education have focused on the use of models and modeling as a way to support students in the learning of science (Dori *et al.,* 2003; Lehrer and Schauble 2012; Mendonça and Justi 2013; Papaevripidou *et al.,* 2007) or on the use of images (Korfiatis *et al.,* 2003), with the term using visuals as evidence, we refer to the collection of all forms of visuals and the processes involved.

The implication of these norms for science teaching and learning is numerous. The classroom contexts can model the generation, sharing and evaluation of evidence, and experimental procedures carried out by students, thereby promoting not only some contemporary cultural norms in scientific practice but also enabling the learning of criteria, standards, and heuristics that scientists use in making decisions on scientific methods. As here demonstrated, visual representations are part of the process of knowledge growth and communication in science. Additionally, visual information, especially with the use of technology is a part of students' everyday lives. Therefore, we suggest making use of students' knowledge and technological skills (i.e., how to produce their own videos showing their experimental method or how to identify or provide appropriate visual evidence for a given topic), to teach them the aspects of the nature of science that are often neglected both in the history of science and the design of curriculum. Specifically, what we suggest in this project is that students should actively engage in visualization processes to appreciate the diverse nature of doing science and engage in authentic scientific practices.

7.2 Mathematical Models

Scientific models are often mathematical models, where one uses mathematics to describe a particular phenomenon. For example, one might notice that the force of gravity on an object is equal to its mass multiplied by the strength of the gravity field. When one puts all the gravity equations together, one gets an overall model of gravity that was first created by Newton. A mathematical model usually describes a system by a set of variables and a set of equations that establish relationships between the variables. The values of the variables can be practically anything; real or integer numbers, Boolean values or strings, for example. The variables represent some properties of the system, for example, measured system outputs often in the form

of signals, timing data, counters, event occurrence. The actual model is the set of functions that describe the relations between the different variables. Often when engineers analyze a system to be controlled or optimized, they use a mathematical model. In analysis, engineers can build a descriptive model of the system as a hypothesis of how the system could work, or try to estimate how an unforeseeable event could affect the system. Similarly, in control of a system, engineers can try out different control approaches in simulations.

A mathematical model is an abstract model that uses mathematical language to describe the behavior of a system. Eykhoff (1974) defined a mathematical model as "a representation of the essential aspects of an existing system (or a system to be constructed) which presents knowledge of that system in usable form." Mathematical models can take many forms, including but not limited to dynamical systems, statistical models, differential equations, or game theoretic models. These and other types of models can overlap, with a given model involving a variety of abstract structures. Mathematical models are used particularly in the natural sciences and engineering disciplines (such as physics, biology, and electrical engineering) but also in the social sciences (such as economics, sociology and political science); physicists, engineers, computer scientists, and economists use mathematical models most extensively.

7.3 Computer Models

Computational modeling is the use of computers to simulate and study complex systems using mathematics, physics and computer science. A computational model contains numerous variables that characterize the system being studied. Simulation is done by adjusting the variables alone or in combination and observing the outcomes. Computer modeling allows scientists to conduct thousands of simulated experiments by computer. The thousands of computer experiments identify the handful of laboratory experiments that are most likely to solve the problem being studied. Today's computational models can study a biological system at multiple levels. Models of how disease develops include molecular processes, cell to cell interactions, and how those changes affect tissues and organs.

Examples of computational modeling include weather forecasting models make predictions based on numerous atmospheric factors. Accurate weather predictions can protect life and property and help utility companies plan for power increases that occur with extreme climate shifts. Flight simulators use complex equations that govern how aircraft fly and react to factors such as turbulence, air density, and precipitation. Simulators are used to train pilots, design aircraft, and study how aircraft are affected as conditions change. Earthquake simulations aim to save lives, buildings, and infrastructure. Computational models predict how the composition and motion of structures interact with the underlying surfaces to affect what happens during an earthquake.

Computational modeling can also be utilized to improve medical care and research. Computational models are being used to track infectious diseases in populations, identify the most effective interventions, and monitor and adjust interventions to reduce the spread of disease. Identifying and implementing interventions that curb the spread of disease are critical for saving lives and reducing stress on the healthcare system during infectious disease pandemics. Computational models intelligently gather, filter, analyze and present health information to provide guidance to doctors for disease treatment based on detailed characteristics of each patient. The systems help to provide informed and consistent care of a patient as they transfer to appropriate hospital facilities and departments and receive various tests during their course of treatment. In addition to these, computational models are also engaged in predicting drug side effects. Researchers use computational modeling to help design drugs that will be the safest for patients and least likely to have side effects. The approach can reduce the many years needed to develop a safe and effective medication.

8.0 Conclusion

Scientific knowledge is the common heritage of humankind. It is the only treasure of humankind that can provide a possible remedy to conquer inequality and to bring about an acceptable quality of life and a purpose, for a majority of the people of the world. A case should be made for science and science education in the developing world, a case for optimal support for science and education even in the poorest and the least-developed of the countries of the world. The relevance of science to the future of society is likely to be considerably more far-reaching than its influence on human affairs in the past. Some of the pressing problems of society today are related to the rapid decline in the quality of global environment, depletion of natural resources, increasing poverty, hunger and illiteracy in many countries and regions of the world. Solutions based on science and technology is likely to provide remedial measures to some of these problems, and yet science and technology as we understand today, are not available to a vast human population. It is essentially in the advanced world that science and technology have contributed to individual fulfillment, the well-being of communities, and to the health of nations.

A high percentage of the human population does not understand science or its utility, and its potential for economic and social development. There is a tendency to get impressed with certain products of technology that may bring in superficial prosperity, but a proper understanding of technological innovation and of the way science and technology are related to society is important for real progress of all countries, particularly the developing ones. Such an understanding is retarded today by the barriers impending the sharing and the use of scientific and other knowledge necessary to make decisions and choices, and hence this project on the Groundwork on skills acquisition and development.

Chapter Thirty

Selected Skills in Technology

1.0 Introduction

Technical skills are hard skills that are necessary to perform specific job-related tasks. It involves specialized knowledge and expertise in information technology, computers, engineering, research, analytics, programming, marketing, design, and security and computer science. These practical skills help one achieve in technology careers and careers that value technology-related knowledge and often include training in mechanics, mathematics, science and information technology. Technical skills are the abilities and knowledge needed to perform specific tasks. They are practical, and often relate to mechanical, information technology, mathematical, or scientific tasks. Some examples include knowledge of programming languages, design programs, mechanical equipment, or tools. While technical skills are often most important for jobs related to information technology (IT) and other fields in the sciences, many other industries also want employees with at least some technical skills. In addition to the technical skills that are needed in the workplace, ones command of job-specific skills can help ensure one gets hired or promoted.

If a person is looking to secure a job in technology, it's helpful to acquire relevant technical skills. There are many different tech skills that are applicable to technology-related careers or jobs that use technology. Knowing the different skills and how to use them to make one desirable for particular jobs can help the person in preparing the resume, perform well in an interview and start ones career in technology, and hence highlighting this topic in this Groundwork on skills acquisition and development project. Technical skills are important for a number of reasons. They can help one work more efficiently, boost ones confidence and make the fellow a more valuable candidate for employers. Candidates who have a technical skill are often more confident when applying to certain industries than those who don't.

In addition, employees with a technical skill are often better at multitasking in a challenging and complex role. With sufficient technical ability, one will be able to speak to colleagues and clients more confidently using specialist expertise. Graduates who take the time to learn a technical skill often receive higher pay. Businesses are always on the lookout for knowledgeable staff, as their clients expect to work with highly skilled teams who they have confidence in to deliver the results they need. Technically skilled graduates can also save employers money, as they don't require so much training to get to a particular level. Plus they can prevent technical issues from occurring, increase customer satisfaction and reduce technical problems before they arise. There's no doubt that proficiency of technical skills will make one stand out.

2.0 Selected Skills in the Technology Sector

To apply for a role in the technology sector, one will need to have a few basic skills Firms recognize that many undergraduates will not have the specific technical skills the sector needs but computer science, electronics, mathematics or similar graduates are sought after in areas where technical expertise is paramount. However, most firms are also interested in recruiting graduates from both information technology IT and software and non-IT software backgrounds for other technical areas. As a general rule, firms are looking for evidence of solid academic achievement, along with the right combination of technical and business skills. Here presented are the top six skills that recruiters look for to give our readers an idea of where one could fit in.

2.1 Strong interest in Technology/IT/Computing

To do well in any job, one needs to find it interesting. Top employers, want to see their Technology Consultant graduates have an interest in their sector and talk about the latest developments and trends with enthusiasm. No one is expecting every job seeker to be a world-class expert, but an awareness of what is happening in the ever-changing world of technology will certainly stand the fellow in excellent stead with recruiters.

2.2 Problem Solving

You must love a challenge, even more so where there are no specific answers, and you have to have persistence to seek out solutions. Perhaps you're a fan of games, puzzles or chess and love the complexity of logic and reasoning problems. If either of the latter, you could be rather good in this sector.

2.3 Good with Numbers

If one likes logical problem solving, the chances are that the fellow will probably rather be confident when it comes to handling numbers. No one needs you to be a mathematical genius but one will need to be comfortable with dealing with them as part of your job.

2.4 Commercial Awareness

Ideally you'll have an awareness of the role technology plays in business. You don't need to know the level of detail which is expected of strategy consultants and investment bankers, but being commercially astute will only enhance ones credibility among employers. It will also serve you well as you progress in your career and become more senior.

2.5 A willingness and Openness to Learn

This is a sector that is consistently innovating. You'll need to be someone who can adapt to change and show openness to new ideas and concepts. You'll like learning about new innovations that can improve the lives of a business or consumer, and you're happy to stay across trends to keep you on your toes.

2.6 Ability to Work Independently and in a Team

Depending on your role, you might find yourself completely ensconced on a project that might require quite a lot of independent work. Equally, there will be times when you'll form part of a team and be required

to adapt to a different working environment. In an ideal world, you'll be someone who thrives in both environments.

3.0   Difference between Science and Technology

Closely intertwined, that their difference is many a time ignored. Science is all about acquiring knowledge of the natural phenomenon along with the reasons for such phenomenon. When this knowledge is put to practice, to solve human needs or problems, it is termed as technology. Still further, science refers to the process of exploring new knowledge methodically through observation and experiments. It focuses on ethical process of gathering data. In science the goal is achieved through corresponding scientific process. It is a continuous process of exploring knowledge. It is always useful. If we will see science always focuses on understanding natural phenomena. Investigation in science results advance science knowledge and discovery. Some examples of branches of science included biology, chemistry, physics, mathematics, geology, human behavior, etc. Technology refers to the process of applying scientific knowledge in practical applications for various purposes. It focuses on ethical effect of taking action. In technology the goal is achieved through corresponding scientific process. It is a continuous process of implementing knowledge. It can be useful or harmful. If we will see technology always focuses on understanding the made environment. Technological design advances standard of living in societies by making human life more comfortable.

3.1 Definitions of Science and Technology

The word science is explained as a system of obtaining knowledge, through experimentation and observation, so as to elucidate natural phenomena. It is a methodical and rational approach to exploring: What are the objects present in the universe? How do they work? Etc. It is a discipline that has several branches like physics, chemistry, biology, geology, botany, psychology and so on. In simple terms, science is the set of knowledge gained by way of analysis about all the things existing around us. The knowledge is based on facts and evidence, relating to the subject, rather than opinions and personal choices. And so, the statements and laws generated by science cannot be challenged, as they are well observed and tested. Science can be used in the development of latest technology, cure diseases and solve many other problems. Research is continuously made, to expand our scientific knowledge, which leaves a room of question for further investigation.

Technology on the other hand is a combination of technique, skills, processes, design, products, etc., which is dedicated to creating instruments or gadgets or to complete scientific investigation. It is a set of knowledge that has practical application in the creation, designing and utilization of products for industrial, commercial or everyday use. Humans are surrounded by things that are created with the help of certain technology (i.e., whether we work, communicate, travel, manufacture, and secure data), business, and almost everywhere. Most people use technology, to simplify their work and also to extend their abilities. It also ensures a solution to various scientific problems.

Difference between Science and Technology

1. Science can be defined as an organized way of gathering knowledge on a subject, through various observations and experiments. Technology is the practical usage of the laws of science for different purposes.
2. Science is nothing but a process of exploring new knowledge, whereas technology is putting scientific knowledge into practice.

3. Science is very useful to gain knowledge about a natural phenomenon, and their reasons. On the contrary, technology can be useful or harmful (i.e., technology is both a boon and bane), such that if it is used in the right way, it can help humans in solving a number of problems, however, if it is put to wrong uses, it can cause destruction of the whole world

4. Science can be defined as an organized way of gathering knowledge on a subject, through various observations and experiments. Technology is the practical usage of the laws of science for different purposes

5. Science is used to make predictions whereas technology simplifies the work and fulfil the needs of people

Table 1
Difference between Science and Technology

S/N	Sciences	Technology
1	Science refers to the process of exploring new knowledge methodically through observation and experiments	Technology refers to the process of applying scientific knowledge in practical applications for various purposes
2	It focuses on ethical process of gathering data.	It focuses on ethical effect of taking action
3	Science refers to a continuous process of exploring knowledge.	Technology refers to the continuous process of implementing knowledge
4	It is based on conceptualized process.	It is based on optimized process
5	Science is always useful.	Technology can be useful or harmful
6	The motto of science is knowing something.	The motto of technology is doing something
7	Science does not change continuously	Technology changes continuously.
8	It always gives emphasize on discovery	It always gives emphasize on invention
9	Science is used to make predictions	Technology simplifies human life, work/activities and fulfils the need of people
10	Scientific investigation results advance science knowledge and discovery.	Technological design can advance standard of living in societies by giving more comfortable to human life.
11	Academic, experimental, analytical and logical skills are required for science	Planning, design, developing, problem solving, decision making and interpersonal skills are required for technology.
12	Some examples of branches of science included Biology, Chemistry, Physics, mathematics, geology, human behavior, etc.	Some examples of branches of agriculture, applied physics, engineering, biotechnology, etc.

Table 2
Chart Comparing Science and Technology

Basis for Comparison	Science	Technology
Meaning	Science is a methodical way of gaining knowledge on a particular subject, through observation and experiments.	Technology alludes to the practical application of the scientific knowledge for various purposes.
What is it?	It is the process of exploring new knowledge	It is the use of laws of science to create new products.
Effect	It is useful	It can be useful or harmful
Change	Does not change	Changes continuously
Stresses on	Discovery	Invention
Deals with	Study of structure and behavior of natural and physical world, to create premises.	Putting those premises into practice.
Method of evaluation	Analysis, deduction and theory development	Analysis and synthesis of design.
Use	Used to make predictions	Simplify the work and fulfill the needs of people

6. Science is nothing but a process of exploring new knowledge, whereas technology is putting scientific knowledge into practice.

7. Science is very useful to gain knowledge about a natural phenomenon, and their reasons. On the contrary, technology can be useful or harmful (i.e., technology is both a boon and bane), such that if it is used in the right way, it can help humans in solving a number of problems, however, if it is put to wrong uses, it can cause destruction of the whole world.

8. Science remains unchangeable; only additions are made to further knowledge. Conversely, technology changes at a rapid pace, in the sense that, improvement in previous technology is made constantly.

9. Science stresses on discovery, like facts and laws of nature. Unlike technology, focuses on the inventions, such as the development of latest technique, to ease the work of humans.

10. Science is the study of structure and behavior of natural and physical world, to create premises. In contrast, technology deals with putting those premises into practice.

11. Science is concerned with analysis, deduction and theory development. On the other hand, technology is based on analysis and synthesis of design.

To sum up, we can say that science is knowing, but technology is about doing. When it is about solving of problems both the two disciplines work together. Science has helped us in gaining knowledge of the things existing in the universe and also to make predictions on future outcomes. Technology, on the other hand, has helped us in simplifying our work by providing us various products that helps us to get better results in less time. However, it has some negative uses too, so it should always be used positively.

4.0   Deployment of Technology in the Production Sector

A manufacturer can be innovative in various ways beyond the use of technology. Technology does support and drive innovation. Technological advancements can allow manufacturers to create higher quality goods faster than before; with less expense and help them realize more efficient operations to become more competitive. In particular, technology is used to maximize product quality and reduce production costs. Technology was identified as the most important area of manufacturing process decision making, followed by quality assurance and control.

Technology benefits businesses as it allows them to produce higher quantities, make products more consistent and be more cost-effective. This both reduces costs and improves employee health. Productivity—using machinery to mechanize or automate parts of the production process leads to an increase in productivity. Businesses compete with rival businesses. Production costs must be kept low so that products can be priced competitively. The ability to do this is affected by production methods and technology. Technology has a big impact on businesses and the production sector, in terms of both updating existing products and finding new ways of manufacturing products.

Technology drives innovations for every industry, changing business for the better, and hence improves manufacturing and production. Manufacturing is the reason that we are able to use many of the products as well as enjoy all the services that we have today. However, the introduction of technology into the manufacturing industry has helped take it to an entirely new level. Not only has it made it more interesting in terms of innovation, but it has also enabled quicker and more efficient ways of operating which is key. Once seen as a blue-collar industry, things have quickly changed in manufacturing as a response to technological advancements. In light of this, we are going to present few ways that technology can improve manufacturing and production businesses in this project

4.1 Maximizing Efficiency

One of the first ways that technology can improve production business is by maximizing efficiency. This means that technology is able to ensure time is used in the best manner possible by cutting down production times and automating tedious as well as time-consuming tasks. An example of technology that could improve business is 3D printing. This technology is transforming the manufacturing industry as it can reduce design to production time, reduce manufacturing lead time, reduce waste, and ensure greater flexibility in production. There are many areas of manufacturing business that be made efficient. You can, for example, automate emails (as long as they're personalized), and even invest in an HR system that allows employees to fill out their own personal data, apply for vacation time and work in real-time so that the HR department doesn't have to deal with minuscule tasks.

4.2 Managing Data

As a production company, it's likely that you manage mass data. As with any data, it can become problematic if you don't have adequate knowledge regarding how to manage it. Seeing as better data management is said to improve the profitability of a manufacturing business, it is in your best interest to find more effective ways of doing so which is where technology comes in. Organizations such as Bytes, for instance, specialize in helping to support your cloud management which could help ensure your mounds of data are all securely in one place. You should also think about finding effective data management software that's capable of helping you both sort and make sense of the data that you're collecting.

However, with managing data comes great responsibility. Data is incredibly valuable, and so you need to ensure you're taking appropriate measures when it comes storing the data of your clients and customers.

You should encrypt your data, back it up in the case of cybercrime and ransom ware, and have the proper anti-malware protection in place. Furthermore, you need to educate yourself and your employees on how to keep their computers safe through password protection and good judgment of links and untrustworthy emails. While you may not consider the manufacturing industry a hotbed for cybercrime, in actual fact, smaller businesses and those that are considered less at risk are, in fact, also threatened. Cybercriminals are looking for industries that may be more lax in their data protection, so you need to ensure you're doing everything possible when it comes to keeping your data protected.

4.3 Increasing Productivity

Productivity is key when running a manufacturing business as the greater the productivity, the more you can produce and the quicker you can produce it. Technology also plays a major role in productivity, so looking for software solutions may be ideal for your business. You could, for instance, make time to find software solutions that help with scheduling, inventory, and monitoring workflow. Considering automation is also a good idea as it can help reduce the risk of error which can also affect your productivity levels as it often creates setbacks. It has been forecasted that machine learning will reduce supply chain forecasting by 50 percent and reduce lost sales by 65 percent. This reflects how technology can help improve your bottom line when used in the right way. There is always room for improvement in business, and this is especially true in the manufacturing industry. Seeing as it can be relatively technical as well as consist of repetitive tasks, technology can contribute to helping streamline processes to help ensure maximum productivity. By doing so, you should find that your business can reach greater heights and you're able to meet your business objective much more easily.

5.0 Types of Manufacturing and Production Technologies

Manufacturing technology is a term that can refer to a number of modern methods of science, production, and engineering that assist in industrial production and various manufacturing processes. There are many modern manufacturing technologies, most of them specifically relevant to the fourth industrial revolution, associated with automation, data exchange, digital technology, artificial intelligence and machine learning, and the 'Internet of Things'. Therefore, a lot of the manufacturing technologies innovating production and industry are also relevant to this fourth wave of technological advancement.

5.1 Smart Factories

Smart factories are environments that are highly digitized for manufacturing to take place more efficiently through connected systems. Through innovative manufacturing technology, machines and systems can, through automation and self-optimization, learn and adapt to situations with increased productivity. Facilities in France, Ireland, China, and the Czech Republic were named the most productive and powerful smart factories in the world by the World Economic Forum in 2019. Able to produce goods on a large scale, smart factories are useful not just for manufacturing jobs but also for processes like planning, supply chain logistics, and product development.

5.2 Cyber-Physical Systems

Cyber-physical systems are those which integrate computer, networking, and physical processes, in which embedded computing technologies control and monitor processes in real time. The combination of

cyber and physical industries is crucial to this manufacturing technology; the computer system monitors the process and identifies areas where change is required, and the physical system reacts accordingly. Cyber-physical systems are often considered one of the main advancements of Industry 4.0 software.

5.3 Additive Manufacturing

3D printing, also known as additive manufacturing, is a computer controlled process in which three-dimensional objects can be created by materials deposited in layers. Using computer aided design (CAD) or 3D object scanners, components, parts, or any other object can be made without the use of machining or any other techniques, and therefore less surplus material.

5.4 Big Data

Today data is collected constantly in systems, sensors, and commonplace electronic items like mobile devices, and the amount of data to be stored is growing every day. 'Big data', a collection of global data from various sources, can be a useful component in manufacturing technology. Industry is in the process of developing methods to interpret and analyze data to use in production. These potential productive uses include risk management, manufacturing products to a customer's specific tastes or order, improving quality, tracking production, and logistics, among others.

5.5 Augmented Reality

Augmented reality (AR) technology displays digital content in the real world, allowing visualization of products or superimposing data or plans onto physical components and machinery. In manufacturing, AR could be used to overlay text, statistics, such as showing the running temperate of a piece of equipment without touching it, or virtual health and safety training without requiring an individual to involve themselves in something potentially harmful. Augmented reality glasses are predicted to reach around 19.1 million units by 2021, and when combined with virtual reality devices, could hit 59.2 million units.

5.6 Numerical Control

Machining tools or items used in manufacture, such as 3D printers, can be regulated and controlled remotely using CNC—computer numerical control. A CNC machine processes a piece of material to key specifications, following a coded programmed instruction and without the need for a manual operator. Modern CNC systems, through high tech computer programming, allows the design and manufacture of a mechanical part to be highly automated. Processes like laser cutting and additive manufacturing rely on numerical control to efficiently and remotely create products.

5.7 Robotics in Manufacturing Technology

Robotics is a field of technology which has seen huge technological advancements, which have had many impacts on manufacturing. Robots are able to perform tasks repetitively and tirelessly, and with precision, high efficiency, and very little error. Many of the examples already discussed are bolstered by the use of robotics. For example, the data analytics and technology insights essential to the smart factory can be bolstered by robotics, and numerical control can be carried out efficiently by a piece of robotic technology. One of the main changes this means for the world of manufacturing technology is a shift in jobs. Rather

than being about production and manufacture, now people specialized in robotics to oversee the machinery doing the manufacturing are sought after by this industry.

6.0 Economic Values of Technology

Technology has deeply affected the global economy and its usage has been linked to marketplace transformation, improved living standards and more robust international trade. Technological advances have significantly improved operations and lowered the cost of doing business. Currently, as an example, just a few technicians controlling robotic systems can operate an entire manufacturing plant, and innovative inventory systems are capable of supplying needed parts within a short time for assembly. Advancements in the computer industry, coupled with advancements in telecommunications, have increased job opportunities and strengthened economic growth.

All physical barriers to communication over distances have been properly overcome by the internet. In a similar way, manufacturing and consumer goods companies have developed online links to their suppliers and customer support. Suppliers can keep track of production line efficiencies through automated systems and can more efficiently ship parts and materials to the required locations, reducing inventory and downtime. In addition to that ecommerce and online banking capabilities have also helped reduce the cost of doing business. Within this new context, and given the fast-paced emergence of disruptive products and business models, as well as the transformative power of digital technologies on business and society, executives must become masters of the global "technology economy," being capable of detecting the economic impact of such fast technological changes and respond with similar speed and foresight.

6.1 The impact of Technology Economy

The impact of technology economy in the market is very significant, infusing even the measurement of the market economy. Some of the largest indexes known in the market, such as the Dow Jones Industrial Average (DJIA) and the S&P 500, have changed. Technology powerhouses like Apple, Google, and Amazon, whose stocks are valued much higher than those of many long-time industrial members, are replacing large industrial super companies. Apple, with its high market capitalization, accounts for such a large share of the DJIA, for example, that any hiccup in its quarterly earnings can move the entire index, situation that was once done by other large corporations such as GM and Caterpillar.

Technology has an amazing power to permeate companies. An important measurement of the technology economy is observing the Worldwide IT spending volume, which is regarding the corporate spending for hardware, software, data centers, networks, and staff, both internal and outsourced IT services. Currently, this volume is close to USD6 trillion per year. To put this number on a more illustrative perspective, if we were to consider the global technology economy a country and its yearly spending its GDP, it would be ranked as the world's third largest economy, between the economies of China and Japan and more than twice the size of the UK economy. Technology spending, gross margins and economic growth have a strong relationship when measured by productivity and GDP. A good example is that executives can predict with some accuracy the impact on the overall economy of a decline in technology spending. Whenever companies cut back on discretionary spending to improve profits during a downturn, they slash their investments in technology. Soon afterward, GDP falls dramatically, and, within a few years, labor productivity across the economy falls, as technological innovation is an important component of productivity. The drop in technology intensity that results from a decline in technology spending causes the labor force to decrease, which shows up in productivity up to three years later because productivity is a "stickier" measure.

As a matter of fact, whenever considering a company's productivity, it possible to observe not only a connection between technology intensity and gross margins but also a strong correlation, which means that technology intensity and gross margins tend to rise and decline together, one as a consequence of the other. It's possible to set as a recent example of this effect before and after the recent world economic crash that started in 2007, when companies were investing more and more heavily in technology relative to revenues and operating expenses, and gross margins were rising. That trend accelerated through 2008 and until 2009, when companies belatedly realized the magnitude of what had happened and began to cut technology investment dramatically. After that, technology intensity dropped precipitously along with gross margins. Within most companies around the globe, in every single industry, technology investment is growing faster than revenues and, in many cases, faster than the GDP of any country. It is clear to all companies that technology is vital to the successful operations of companies and, mainly, to the global economy, but being able to manage technology spending properly within a few years ahead will require an increasingly sophisticated way of looking at the world and at a company's performance.

With that in mind, it is essential for companies to control, adapt, and optimize investments in real-time according to market conditions and on the basis of new forms of market data. Companies need to consider all inputs and outcomes and look at technology economically to gain competitive advantage before competitors do. Finally, if executives understand it and look at technology investments this way, it will not only matter, it will make all the difference for the their companies and for the global economy

6.2 Technology's Role in Economic Development

Technology encompasses a huge body of knowledge and tools that ease the use of economic resources as a way to produce goods and services efficiently and innovatively. Technological progress is essential to economic growth and development, and the more advanced the technology available, the more quickly the local and global economy can improve. Technology's role in economic development is further broken down below.

6.2.1 Time is Money

Technology can save the time it takes to produce a good or deliver a service, contributing to the overall profits of a business.

6.2.3 Efficiency

Technology can contribute to the efficiency of a business's output rate, allowing for larger quantities of products to be moved or of services to be rendered.

6.2.4 Specialization

Technology has led to an increase in the division of labor and specialization of jobs within a business, further contributing to the efficiency with which a business is able to run.

6.2.5 Natural Resources

Technology has a huge effect on the ability of businesses and governments to access natural resources and use them in the most effective ways possible to benefit both the business and the economy.

6.2.6 Industrial Expansion

Thanks to the increased efficiency of labor with the ever-improving state of technology, businesses are able to increase total output, which in turn leads to higher profits and greater economic development.

6.2.7 Research

Better technology has led to further research into nearly every sector of business and science, meaning businesses can benefit from all sorts of technological advancements.

6.2.8 The Internet and International Trade

Information technology is the single most important element in the success and growth of international trade and job market growth, allowing businesses to share information and conduct trade in less time than the blink of an eye.

7.0 Patterns of Learning Technology

A learning pattern is conceptualized as a coherent whole of learning activities that learners usually employ their beliefs about learning and their learning motivation, a whole that is characteristic of them in a certain period of time. It is a coordinating concept, in which the interrelationships between cognitive, affective, and regulative learning activities, beliefs about learning, and learning motivations are united. The learning patterns framework is firmly rooted in two research traditions in the late 1970s and early 1980s. The first is the work on approaches to learning and conceptions of learning, which later became known as the Student Approaches to Learning (SAL) tradition. In this tradition, student learning was mainly conceptualized in terms of cognitive strategies and motivation (e.g. Biggs 1987; Entwistle and Ramsden 1983; Marton and Säljö 1984; Pask 1988; Schmeck 1988). The second pillar was the early work on metacognition (Brown 1987); which later developed into a tradition known as Self-Regulated Learning (SRL). In this line of work, scholars were interested in children's metacognitive knowledge and beliefs and their self-regulated learning strategies.

In the learning patterns theoretical framework, four components of student learning are discerned: cognitive processing strategies, metacognitive regulation strategies (metacognitive) conceptions of learning, and learning motivations or orientations. Processing strategies are those combinations of cognitive learning activities that students employ to process subject matter and that lead directly to knowledge, understanding, and skill. Regulation strategies are those combinations of metacognitive learning activities that students use to plan, monitor, steer, and evaluate their cognitive learning processes and which indirectly lead to learning outcomes. Conceptions of learning are the metacognitive views and beliefs students hold about learning, teaching, and related phenomena. Learning motivations or orientations encompass the aims, goals, motives, and worries of students in relation to their studies, and they represent the motivational-affective component of the model. The learning strategies that students employ to process subject matter are regulated by metacognitive strategies, which are in turn influenced by students' conceptions of learning and learning motivations. These learning patterns lead to learning outcomes, and are influenced by various personal and contextual factors. Learning outcomes may constitute input for new learning processes. If the context changes, learning patterns may change as well (Vermunt and Vermetten 2004).

We conceive a learning pattern definitely not as a hard-to-change human trait, but as the result of the interplay between personal and contextual influences (Coffield et al. 2004). Research on student learning

in higher education has repeatedly identified four qualitative different patterns in the way students learn: *reproduction-directed learning*, *meaning-directed learning*, *application-directed learning*, and *undirected learning* (Lonka *et al.*, 2004). In *reproduction-directed learning*, students try to remember the learning contents to be able to reproduce them on a test. They memorize the learning materials and go through the study materials in a sequential way, step by step, without thinking much about relations between larger units. They pay a lot of attention to the regulation provided by teachers, study materials, and other external agents. Their motive for learning is to pass the test or to test their capabilities. They view learning mainly as the intake of knowledge from an external source to their own head, keeping it as closely as possible to the original. This learning pattern is defined by the ILS scales stepwise processing (consisting of the subscales "memorizing and rehearsing" and "analyzing"), external regulation (with subscales referring to learning processes and outcomes), intake of knowledge as learning conception, and certificate directed and self-test directed learning orientations.

Students who learn in a *meaning-directed* way adopt a deep approach to learning: they try to understand the meaning of what they learn, try to discover relations between separate facts or views, structure the learning material into a larger whole, and try to critically engage to what they learn. They learn in a self-regulated way, not limiting themselves to the prescribed materials. They view learning as their own construction of knowledge for which they are mainly themselves responsible. Often they are motivated through personal interest for the topics of their studies. This learning pattern is defined by the ILS scales deep processing (with subscales 'relating and structuring' and 'critical processing'), self-regulation (with subscales referring to learning processes/outcomes and learning contents), construction of knowledge as learning conception, and personal interest as learning orientation. Students who learn in an application-directed way try to discover relations between what they learn and the world outside.

They try to find examples of what they study and think about how they would be able to apply what they learn in practice. Both more self-regulated and externally regulated variants of this pattern exist. What is common, however, is the great value these students attach to learning to use the knowledge they acquire; knowledge they cannot use is of much less value to them. Vocational motives often underlie this pattern: students want to prepare themselves for a profession or they want to become better in their current job. This learning pattern is defined by the ILS scales concrete processing, the learning conception use of knowledge, and a vocational learning orientation.

Students who learn in an undirected way do not know well how to approach their studies. This pattern can often be seen with students who are in transition from one form of schooling to another, for example from secondary to higher education, from undergraduate to graduate studies, or students coming from another country with different pedagogical practices (Biemans and Van Mil 2008). They try to adopt the approach they are used to previously, realize that this approach is not adaptive in the new circumstances, but do not know well how to learn in a better way. They often experience a lack of regulation, doubt whether they are able to cope with the demands of the new learning environment, and attach great value to fellow students and teachers to offer the direction and hold they miss so much. This learning pattern is defined by the ILS scales lack of regulation, the learning conceptions emphasizing stimulating education and cooperative learning, and an ambivalent learning orientation (Vermunt and Vermetten 2004).

Research on student learning has shown that several personal and contextual factors influence the learning patterns that students adopt. Among the personal factors are age, knowledge of subject matter, and educational experience. Important contextual factors influencing students' learning are for example the teaching methods used, type of assessment, and opportunities to collaborate with other students. Students' learning processes also prove to be related to the learning outcomes they attain. Research has for example shown that exam results are often positively related to many features of the meaning-directed learning pattern (students' relating and structuring activities, self-regulation, critical engagement) and analytical processing. Exam results show consistent and negative relations with students' lack of regulation and ambivalent learning orientation, two features of the undirected learning pattern (e.g., Vermunt and Vermetten 2004).

8.0 Templates on Teaching and Learning Information Communication and Technology ICT Skills

S/N	Skill	Activities	Learning Objectives
1.	Master the work environment	Effectively use a workstation	Have a clear mental picture of how a workstation functions Use the educational institution's shared workstation through the network. Process, save and classify information
		Use a computer in a responsible and autonomous manner Use ICT in an ethical, socially responsible and secure manner	Independently learn to use new software or new online resources. Independently accomplish online learning activities. Organize the working environment so that it is comfortable, Personal computer maintenance. Make sure electronic information, resources and transactions are secure and confidential.
2.	Search for information	Perform a documentation search	Analyze the subject before launching a query on a computer. Identify the resources and tools needed to find what is required. Develop and carryout effective search strategies.
		Evaluate search results	Evaluate the search results as a responses to the research question. Evaluate the quality of the information found.
		Use a transmit information in a legal and ethical manner.	Understand copyright law as it applies to users and the sources being used. Cite sources correctly. Write a mediagraphy according to standard rules.
3.	Process information	Organize information	Manage files. Decode the extensions and icons for files as well as applications. Use software to compress and decompress files. Organize sources of information so they are easily found. Use format converters to convert files. Create tables for processing qualitative data.
		Process qualitative data Process quantitative data (using a spreadsheet).	Master the main elements of the spreadsheet interface: workplace, options and menus. Manipulate data to organize information. Develop formulas to process the data from a group of cells. Create data list to standardize the presentation.

4.	Present information	Create a document with a word processor	Master the basics of word-processing: workspace, options and menus. Use a glossary, a guide, reference material and writing tools. Format a document Design the page layout of a document Incorporate objects into a document. Print a document Format a long report
		Present data using a spreadsheet	Master the spreadsheet interface Manipulate the data to organize information Format cells in a way that highlights the information they contain Create a chart to present data. Format a spreadsheet to prepare it for printing.
		Make a computer-assisted presentation.	Master the principal elements of presentation software: workspace, options and menus. Plan a presentation to make it relevant, structured and engaging. Incorporate objects into a presentation. Make a presentation dynamic View and show a presentation Export a presentation to different storage devices. Use a multimedia projector to show a presentation. Write for the Web.
		Publish on the Web	Distinguish the different characteristics of Web publication tools and make the appropriate choice. Master the principal elements of the chosen Web publication tool: workspace, options and menus. Publish online using a simplified Web 2.0 page editing tool. Plan out a Web publication. Incorporate elements into a Web publication. Post a Web publication online.
		Produce audio and visual material	Produce audio and video material for good technical quality. Use image processing software to modify images. Produce a podcast with audio content. Make a video.

5.	Communicate and collaborate on the Internet	Use the educational institution's portal.	Use a username and a password for identification to access the institution's portal. Consult the academic calendar and course schedule. Perform various transactions to register or reregister.
		Use the educational institution's platform	Use a username and a password for identification to access the institution's training platform. Master the principal elements of the training platform's interface (workspace, options and menus). Master the main functions of the educational institution's platform (sometimes called a portal). Communicate with colleagues and teachers via e-mail. Consult and participate in a forum. Communicate in an ethical manner.
		Use basic communication and telecollaboration tools	Use an online document repository. Organize work with an electronic agenda or calendar and a task planner. Communicate in real time (i.e., in synchronous mode). Participate in tasks through exchanges that are not immediate (i.e., in asynchronous mode)
		Use advanced communication and telecollaboration tools	
6.	Project evaluation	Build an electronic learning portfolio	Explain the concept of a learning portfolio Put together a learning portfolio

9.0 The Future of Technology

With the advent of Industry 4.0, advances in technology such as robotics and the increase in use, storage, and recording of data mean that digitalization is reinventing manufacturing. Smart technology and other new methods are not simply increasing the efficiency and quality of production, but are changing the shape of the manufacturing industry. Manufacturing business systems are constantly being revolutionized and digitized. Jobs in this area are becoming more about computing and Artificial Intelligence and concepts like smart factories should continue to expand in function and become fully realized into the future. It is likely that we have only scratched the surface of Industry 4.0. The breadth and complexity of opportunities in this sector means that robotics, AI and data will probably continue to revolutionize production and manufacturing.

The existing technologies have already paved the way for further innovations into future technologies that would certainly have the potential of changing lives even more, make lives easier and rethink the ways we go about our daily existence. At any given moment, scientists and engineers are redesigning future technology, for which the rate of progress over the last half century has been astounding in fields as broad as computing, medicine, communications and materials science.

9.1 Lab-Made Dairy Products

A growing number of biotech companies around the world are investigating lab-made dairy including milk, ice-cream, cheese and eggs. Compared with meat, milk isn't actually that difficult to create in a lab.

Rather than grow it from stem cells, most researchers attempt to produce it in a process of fermentation, looking to produce the milk proteins. Some products are already at market in the United State, from companies such as Perfect Day, with ongoing work focused on reproducing the mouth feel and nutritional benefits of regular cow's milk. Beyond that, researchers are working on lab-produced mozzarella that melts perfectly on top of a pizza, as well other cheeses and ice-cream.

9.2 Digital Twins Health Tracker

The Q Bio Mark I self-driving, whole-body scanner—the fastest, most accessible scanner developed, and the first scanner optimized for proactive care. The Mark I scanner collects information based on current health and personal risks, adapting in real time to changes in an individual's anatomy and biochemistry that are weighted by lifestyle, medical history, and genetic risk factors. Capable of scanning the whole body in 15 minutes or less without radiation, breath holds, or claustrophobia, the scanner provides individuals with maximum comfort in an open space, including the option to stand, sit, or lie down. The Mark I offers faster and more precise medical scanning without the use of artificial intelligence or machine learning, avoiding issues with bias and "hallucinations." The company's technology, which is based on advanced computational biophysics, has been shown to be at least 10x faster than conventional MRI scans without the loss of diagnostic quality, and allows for the construction of dramatically cheaper hardware, with rapid deployment and reduced operational costs. "Until now, no existing technology has been able to develop a digital twin in a cost-effective way that combines an individual's genetics, chemistry, anatomy, lifestyle, and medical history over time, with integrated tools that make it easy to correlate between quantitative changes and an individual's risk factors," said Jeffrey Kaditz, founder and CEO of Q Bio.

Human beings can walk into the medbay and have their entire body digitally scanned for signs of illness and injury. Doing that in real life would, say the makers of Q Bio, improve health outcomes and alleviate the load on doctors at the same time. The US Company has built a scanner that will measure hundreds of biomarkers in around an hour, from hormone levels to the fat building up in the liver to the markers of inflammation or any number of cancers. It intends to use this data to produce a 3D digital avatar of a patient's body—known as a digital twin—that can be tracked over time and updated with each new scan. Q Bio Chief Executive Officer Jeff Kaditz hopes it will lead to a new era of preventative, personalized medicine in which the vast amounts of data collected not only help doctors prioritize which patients need to be seen most urgently, but also to develop more sophisticated ways of diagnosing illness. Q Biotechnology Company's "digital twin" platform would capture and monitor comprehensive baseline patient health in a scalable virtual model. In addition, the company announced a program to develop and expand access to its proprietary platform and breakthrough whole-body scanning technologies that enable data-driven, proactive, and more affordable preventive care for all.

9.3 Bio-Cremation and Green Funerals

Most alternative ways of disposing of our bodies after death are not based on new technology; they're just waiting for societal acceptance to catch up. Another example is alkaline hydrolysis, which involves breaking the body down into its chemical components over a six-hour process in a pressurized chamber. It's legal in a number of US states and uses fewer emissions compared with more traditional methods. From coffins made of recycled cardboard to saying no to embalming chemicals that seep into the soil, people are increasingly searching for ways to make their final resting place a more environmentally friendly one.

Cremation, the choice today of a third of Americans and more than half of Canadians, is getting a green make-over. A standard cremation spews into the air about 400 kilograms (880 pounds) of carbon dioxide,

a greenhouse gas blamed for global warming, along with other pollutants like dioxins and mercury vapor if the deceased had silver tooth fillings. On top of that, each cremation guzzles as much energy, in the form of natural gas and electricity. Bio cremation, a chemical body-disposal process uses one-tenth the natural gas of fire-based cremation and one-third the electricity. Carbon dioxide (CO_2) emissions are cut by almost 90 percent and no mercury escapes as fillings and other metal objects, such as hip or knee replacements, can be recovered intact and recycled.

The Pittsburgh, Pennsylvania-based company that makes caskets and other funeral products is planning the world's first commercial launch of human alkaline hydrolysis. In alkaline hydrolysis the body is submerged in water in a stainless steel chamber. Heat, pressure and potassium hydroxide, chemicals used to make soap and bleach, are added to dissolve the tissue. Two hours later all that's left is some bone residue and a syrupy brown liquid that is flushed down the drain. The bones can be crushed and returned to the family as with cremation.

9.4 Artificial Eyes

Bionic eyes have been a mainstay of science fiction for decades, but now real-world research is beginning to catch up with far-sighted storytellers. A raft of technologies is coming to market that restore sight to people with different kinds of vision impairment.

In January 2021, Israeli surgeons implanted the world's first artificial cornea into a bilaterally blind, 78-year-old man. When his bandages were removed, the patient could read and recognize family members immediately. The implant also fuses naturally to human tissue without the recipient's body rejecting it. Likewise in 2020, Belgian scientists developed an artificial iris fitted to smart contact lenses that correct a number of vision disorders. And scientists are even working on wireless brain implants that bypass the eyes altogether. Researchers at Montash University in Australia are working on trials for a system whereby users wear a pair of glasses fitted with a camera. This sends data directly to the implant, which sits on the surface of the brain and gives the user a rudimentary sense of sight.

9.5 Airports for Drones and Flying Taxis

Our congested cities are in desperate need of a breather and relief may come from the air as opposed to the roads. Plans for a different kind of transport hub—one for delivery drones and electric air-taxis—are becoming a reality, with the first Urban Air Port receiving funding from the UK government.

It's being built in Coventry. The hub will be a pilot scheme and hopefully a proof of concept for the company behind it. Powered completely off-grid by a hydrogen generator, the idea is to remove the need for as many delivery vans and personal cars on our roads, replacing them with a clean alternative in the form of a new type of small aircraft, with designs being developed by Huyundai and Airbus, among others. Infrastructure is going to be important. Organizations like the Civil Aviation Authority are looking into the establishment of air corridors that might link a city center with a local airport or distribution center.

9.6 Energy Storing Bricks

Scientists have found a way to store energy in the red bricks that are used to build houses. Researchers led by Washington University in St Louis, in Missouri, US, have developed a method that can turn the cheap and widely available building material into "smart bricks" that can store energy like a battery. Although the research is still in the proof-of-concept stage, the scientists claim that walls made of these bricks "could store a substantial amount of energy" and can "be recharged hundreds of thousands of times within an hour"

The researchers developed a method to convert red bricks into a type of energy storage device called a super capacitor. This involved putting a conducting coating, known as Pedot, onto brick samples, which then seeped through the fired bricks' porous structure, converting them into "energy storing electrodes." Iron oxide, which is the red pigment in the bricks, helped with the process, the researchers said.

9.7 Sweat powered smart watches

Engineers at the University of Glasgow have developed a new type of flexible super capacitor, which stores energy, replacing the electrolytes found in conventional batteries with sweat. It can be fully charged with as little as 20 microliters of fluid and is robust enough to survive 4,000 cycles of the types of flexes and bends it might encounter in use. The device works by coating polyester cellulose cloth in a thin layer of a polymer, which acts as the super capacitor's electrode. As the cloth absorbs its wearer's sweat, the positive and negative ions in the sweat interact with the polymer's surface, creating an electrochemical reaction which generates energy.

"Conventional batteries are cheaper and more plentiful than ever before but they are often built using unsustainable materials which are harmful to the environment," says Professor Ravinder Dahiya, head of the Bendable Electronics and Sensing Technologies (Best) group, based at the University of Glasgow's James Watt School of Engineering. "That makes them challenging to dispose of safely and potentially harmful in wearable devices, where a broken battery could spill toxic fluids on to skin. "What we've been able to do for the first time is show that human sweat provides a real opportunity to do away with those toxic materials entirely, with excellent charging and discharging performance.

9.8 Self-Healing "Living Concrete"

Scientists have developed what they call living concrete by using sand, gel and bacteria. Researchers said this building material has structural load-bearing function, is capable of self-healing and is more environmentally friendly than concrete—which is the second most-consumed material on earth after water. The team from the University of Colorado Boulder believes their work paves the way for future building structures that could "heal their own cracks, suck up dangerous toxins from the air or even glow on command.

9.8 Living Robots

Tiny hybrid robots made using stem cells from frog embryos could one day be used to swim around human bodies to specific areas requiring medicine, or to gather microplastic in the oceans. "These are novel living machines," said Joshua Bongard, a computer scientist and robotics expert at the University of Vermont, who co-developed the millimeter-wide bots, known as xenobots. "They're neither a traditional robot nor a known species of animal. It's a new class of artifact: a living, programmable organism."

9.10 Internet for Everyone

We can't seem to live without the internet, but still only around half the world's population is connected. There are many reasons for this, including economic and social reasons, but for some the internet just isn't accessible because they have no connection. Google is slowly trying to solve the problem using helium balloons to beam the internet to inaccessible areas, while Facebook has abandoned plans to do the same using drones, which means companies like Hiber are stealing a march. They have taken a different

approach by launching their own network of shoebox-sized microsatellites into low Earth orbit, which wake up a modem plugged into your computer or device when it flies over and delivers your data. Their satellites orbit the Earth 16 times a day and are already being used by organizations like The British Antarctic Survey to provide internet access to very extreme of our planet.

9.11 Heart Monitoring T-shirt

Wearable sports bands that measure heart rate are nothing new, but as numerous studies have shown, the accuracy can vary wildly. Using a single lead ECG printed into the fabric, this new T-shirt from smart materials company KYMIRA will accurately measure heart beats and upload them to the cloud via Bluetooth. Once there, algorithms process the data to accurately detect irregular heartbeats such as arrhythmia heart beats, which could prove lifesaving. "The possibilities this product offers both sportspeople and the general public is astonishing," says Tim Brownstone, CEO and founder of KYMIRA. "We envisage developing this product to be used for clinical applications to allow those who may already suffer with heart conditions enough warning of a heart attack."

9.10 Drown Forest Fires in Sound

Forest fires could one day be dealt with by drones that would direct loud noises at the trees below. Since sound is made up of pressure waves, it can be used to disrupt the air surrounding a fire, essentially cutting off the supply of oxygen to the fuel. At the right frequency, the fire simply dies out, as researchers at George Mason University in Virginia recently demonstrated with their sonic extinguisher.

9.11 The Artificial Intelligence (AI) Scientist

Cut off a flatworm's head and it'll grow a new one. Cut it in half, and you'll have two new worms. Fire some radiation at it, and it'll repair itself. Scientists have wanted to work out the mechanisms involved for some time, but the secret has eluded them. By analyzing and simulating countless scenarios, the computer was able to solve the mystery of the flatworm's regeneration in just 42 hours. In the end it produced a comprehensive model of how the flatworm's genes allow it to regenerate. Although humans still need to feed the AI with information, the machine in this experiment was able to create a new, abstract theory independently—a huge step toward the development of a conscious computer, and potentially a landmark step in the way we carry out research.

9.12 Car Batteries that Charge in 10 Minutes

Fast-charging of electric vehicles is seen as key to their take-up, so motorists can stop at a service station and fully charge their car. But rapid charging of lithium-ion batteries can degrade the batteries, researchers at Penn State University in the US say. This is because the flow of lithium particles known as ions from one electrode to another to charge the unit and hold the energy ready for use does not happen smoothly with rapid charging at lower temperatures.

However, they have now found that if the batteries could heat to 60°C for just 10 minutes and then rapidly cool again to ambient temperatures, lithium spikes would not form and heat damage would be avoided. The battery design they have come up with is self-heating, using a thin nickel foil which creates an electrical circuit that heats in less than thirty seconds to warm the inside of the battery. The rapid cooling that would be needed after the battery is charged would be done using the cooling system designed into the

car. Their study, published in the journal Joule, showed they could fully charge an electrical vehicle in ten minutes.

9.13 Self-Driving Trucks

We've almost gotten used to the idea of driverless cars before we've even seen one on the roads. The truth is, one might well see a lot more driverless trucks. They'll be cheaper to run than regular rigs, driving more smoothly and so using less fuel. Computers never get tired or need comfort breaks, so they'll run longer routes. And they could drive in convoys, nose-to-tail, to minimize wind resistance. Companies like Mercedes and Peloton are already exploring these possibilities, and if the promised gains materialize, freight companies could upgrade entire fleets overnight. On the downside, it could put drivers instantly out of work, and even staff at the truck stops set up to service them, but many companies have said the trucks will still need a human passenger to ensure their cargo is safe.

9.14 Artificial Neurons on Silicon Chips

Scientists have found a way to attach artificial neurons onto silicon chips, mimicking the neurons in our nervous system and copying their electrical properties. "Until now neurons have been like black boxes, but we have managed to open the black box and peer inside," said Professor Alain Nogaret, from the University of Bath, who led the project. "Our work is paradigm-changing because it provides a robust method to reproduce the electrical properties of real neurons in minute detail. "But it's wider than that, because our neurons only need 140 nanowatts of power. That's a billionth the power requirement of a microprocessor, which other attempts to make synthetic neurons have used. Researchers hope their work could be used in medical implants to treat conditions such as heart failure and Alzheimer's as it requires so little power.

9.15 Floating Farms

The UN predicts there will be two billion more people in the world by 2050, creating a demand for 70 per cent more food. By that time, 80 per cent of us will be living in cities, and most food we eat in urban areas is brought in. So farms moored on the sea or inland lakes close to cities would certainly reduce food miles.

But how would they work? A design by Architect Javier Ponce of Forward Thinking Architecture shows a 24m-tall, three-tiered structure with solar panels on top to provide energy. The middle tier grows a variety of vegetation over an area of 51,000m², using not soil but nutrients in liquid. These nutrients and plant matter would drop into the bottom layer to feed fish, which are farmed in an enclosed space. A single Smart Floating Farm measuring 350 × 200m would produce an estimated 8.1 tonnes of vegetables and 1.7 tonnes of fish a year. The units are designed to bolt together, which is handy since we'll need a lot of them: Dubai, for instance, imports 11,000 tonnes of fruit and vegetables every day.

10.0   Conclusion

Information Communication Technology ICT refers to our everyday use of communicative and data processing technologies. Whether it's using our laptop to send an e-mail, our phone to make a video call, or simply surfing through the internet—all such activities rely on basic ICT skills and related devices to perform successfully. With most transactions and social connections now formed in the digital world, ICT expertise

has become an increasingly valuable commodity. As technologies advance, so does demand for those capable of managing, maintaining, and implementing them in the modern workplace (as well as spurring further innovation and development). A core element of the Information Communication and Technology ICT field is the ability to seek, develop, manage and process data with the right digital tools. After all, data plays a key role in communicating results, trends, and consumer patterns within a business; and serves as the backbone of web and app development. Through studies in ICT, one will discover the best software, practices, and the required programming languages to boost data management and processing efficiency. Students will explore crucial tools from basic programs such as Microsoft Excel to more specialized, analytical platforms. With sharp data management and processing skills, aspiring ICT professionals can help minimize operational errors, aid decision-making, improve compliance and keep in time with changing market needs and technological advancements within their business.

Review of ICT Skills

1. **Cloud Computing**

   Cloud computing has become a digital mainstay across industries nationwide. Its emergence in IT has boosted ICT technologies with its ability to streamline collaboration, improve customer service, and allow for flexible or remote work practices. Acquiring cloud computing skills can help one increase the efficiency of cloud migration among businesses, enhance cloud security, optimize automation tools, and integrate their platform's machine learning and artificial intelligence capabilities into everyday operations or suited work projects.

2. **Web development**

   Social media, instant messaging, teleworking and online research—these daily communications (and plenty more) are owed to the specialized efforts of web developers and designers. Without their skills in website creation, configuration, and maintenance; we wouldn't have the World Wide Web as we know it today. With interactions and transactions dominating the online realm, web development is a popular subject in ICT education. Undertaking a specialized course allows you to hone the necessary skills to build engaging, dynamic websites that convert potential consumers and offer user-friendly viewer experiences.

3. **Online collaboration**

   Studying ICT can sharpen your knowledge of the available tools, software, and platforms for streamlining online collaboration with other teams and employees. Such tasks can be as simple as adding meetings or events to a shared work calendar; or involve more complex, ongoing activities such as projects accessed through Google Drive. Understanding and training yourself in crucial collaborative technologies can effectively boost communication, operational efficiency, and mobility in the workplace. For aspiring or current managers, optimizing these tools can help you seamlessly enact telecommuting opportunities—as they maintain clear, precise delegation of tasks and interaction among workers despite geographical location.

4. **Programming**

   With rapid developments and growth in technology, businesses are growing increasingly reliant on coding expertise. It's the "language of the modern world"; the skills that enable regular use of the smart devices, internet platforms, and digital communication tools we currently take for granted. Without programming knowledge, the ICT field—as we know it today—would cease to

exist. AI-powered machines and automated technologies are expected to replace a significant percentage of employees in the coming decades; making programming skills a must in future-proofing careers. Learning the language of tech innovation can help you ride the changing, ever-digitized tides—regardless of your industry.

5. **Cyber Security**

   With much of our communication performed over the web, cybercrime is an imminent threat. Ransom ware, malware, phishing scams, and plenty more—all such tactics run rampant on the World Wide Web, with hacker methods growing in sophistication by the day. Identity theft and fraud are just two of the most common types of cybercrime. With the notoriety of online crime, cyber security has garnered high priority among businesses nationwide. Acquiring skills in network protection, malware analysis, programming and intrusion detection can help in pursuing a lucrative cyber security career, with plenty of courses now available among ICT education providers.

6. **Hardware Skills**

   Pursuing studies in ICT can familiarize one with basic computing and communications hardware. This can include the use of everyday smart devices and computer equipment (such as printers, scanners, projectors, and internet modems)—to more technical skills such as driver configuration and network maintenance. Hardware management skills are particularly valuable for those seeking computer technician roles, though are generally beneficial to any worker, regardless of profession. With our reliance on computers and digital devices, the ability to troubleshoot, maintain, and update them can help create a more seamless, secure, and efficient workplace experience.

7. **2D/3D Animation**

   This skill requires one to create animated images like *South Park, The Simpsons,* etc. You will have to draw different images with a slightly different pose till you have 24 frames a seconds. There are limited to what you can do with 2D animation. In the other hand, 3D gives you the control of your objects, they can be control 360 degree and you can move to any angle you wish is the best for viewers.

8. **Graphic Designer**

   A graphic designer is a visual communicator, someone who creates visual concepts by hand or by using computer software. They communicate ideas to inspire, inform, or captivate consumers. These skills are very important in an organization that deals with product marketing. As a graphic designer you work with software's like Adobe Photoshop, Adobe Illustrator, Adobe InDesign or Light Room. You are required to be creative and also think outside the box.

9. **Web Designer**

   Web design encompasses many different skills and disciplines in the production and maintenance of websites. The different areas of web design include web graphic design; interface design; authoring, including standardized code and proprietary software; user experience design; and search engine optimization. Often many individuals will work in teams covering different aspects of the design process, although some designers will cover them all.

10. **Database Management System**

A database-management system (DBMS) is a computer-software application that interacts with end-users, other applications, and the database itself to capture and analyze data. A general-purpose DBMS allows the definition, creation, querying, update, and administration of databases. This skill allows you to work with big organization or company for storage of data and other relevant information about staffs, etc.

11. **Java Programmer**

Java is a general-purpose computer programming language that is concurrent, class-based, object-oriented, and specifically designed to have as few implementation dependencies as possible. It is intended to let application developers "write once, run anywhere" (WORA), meaning that compiled Java code can run on all platforms that support Java without the need for recompilation. Java programming skills are always needed by company to help them create java application or any java program. This skill is very easy to learn when you have access to some good tutorial videos online.

12. **Networking**

Computer network technology can prepare you for a variety of careers, such as computer and information systems management, computer systems analysis, network and computer systems administration and computer network architecture. In computer networks, networked computing devices exchange data with each other using a data link. The connections between nodes are established using either cable media or wireless media.

13. **Video Editing**

Video editing is the manipulation and arrangement of video shots. Video editing is used to structure and present all video information, including films and television shows, video advertisements and video essays. Video editing has been dramatically democratized in recent years by editing software available for personal computers. This skill is high in demand with the increase in movie production, animation, music video, documentary, etc.

14. **Ethical Hacking**

An ethical hacker (also known as a white hat hacker) is the ultimate security professional. Ethical hackers know how to find and exploit vulnerabilities and weaknesses in various systems—just like a malicious hacker (or a black hat hacker). In fact, they both use the same skills; however, an ethical hacker uses those skills in a legitimate, lawful manner to try to find vulnerabilities and fix them before the bad guys can get there and try to break in.

References

Ackerman, P. L. (1988). Determinants of individual differences during skill acquisition: cognitive abilities and information processing. Journal of Experimental Psychology: General, 117(3), 288–318. doi:10.1037//0096-3445.117.3.288.

Anderson, J. R. (1982). Acquisition of Cognitive Skill. Psychological Review, 89(4), 369–406. doi:10.1037//0033295x.89.4.369.

Auerbach, E. R. (1986). Competency-based ESL: one step forward or two steps back? TESOL Quarterly, 20(3), 411–415.

Bowden, J. A. (2004). Competency-based learning. In S. Stein and S. Farmer (Eds.), Connotative Learning: The Trainer's Guide to Learning Theories and their Practical Application to Training Design (pp. 91–100). Dubuque, IA: Kendall Hunt Publishing.

Dekeyser, R. (2007). Practice in a second Language: Perspectives from Applied Linguistic and Cognitive Psychology. New York: CUP.

Dekeyser, R. M. (1998). Beyond focus on form: Cognitive perspectives on learning and practicing second language grammar. In C. Doughty and J. Williams (Eds.)

Dekeyser, R. M. (2007b). Skill acquisition theory. In B. Van pattern and J. Williams (Eds.), Theories in second language acquisition: An introduction (pp. 97–113). New Jersey: Lawrence Eribaum Associates, Inc.

Ellis, R. (2009). Implicit and explicit learning, knowledge and instruction. In R. Ellis, S. Loewen, C. Elder, R. Eriam, J. Philip and H. Reinders (Eds.), implicit and explicit knowledge in second language learning, testing, and teaching (pp. 3–26). Levedon: Multilingual Matters.

Fitts PM, Posner MI. Human Performance. Brooks/Cole Pub. Co; Belmont, CA: 1967. https://www.ncbi.nlm.nih.gov/pmc/articles/PMC4330992/(accessed August 2021).

FITTS, P. M. and POSNER, M. I. (196). Human Performance. Oxford, England: Brooks and Cole. https://www.brianmac.co.UK/tech.htm (accessed August 2021).

Guskey, T. (2005).Mapping the road to proficiency. Educational Leadership, 63(3), 32–38.

http://www.valamis.com/documents/10197/783138/cognitive-learning-loop.png, accessed July, 2021).

https://drowningintheshallow.wordpress.com/2016/03/14/what-is-a-constraints-led-approach/, accessed August 2021.

https://slideplayer.com/side/5812428/19/images/7/closed+loop+theory+stimulus+input+memory+trace+initiates+MP.jpg, accessed August 2021.

https://www.ai.rug.n11-nicks/publications/CSRpublished.pdf, accessed July 2021.

https://www.jbe-platform.com/content/books/9789027272225-aals.9.07ch4, accessed August 2021.

https://www.oxfordreference.com/view/10.1093/oi/authority.20110803095618867 (accessed August 2021).

https://www.prezi.com/ozzgozm4igljl/dekeyser-skill-acquisition-theory1?frame=97e16f1b-8f7789a131e96b0179941, accessed July 2021.

https://www.sciencedirect.com/topics/engineering/loop-theory, accessed, August 2021.

Jones, B., Valdez, G., Nowakowski, J., and Rasmussen, C. (1994).Designing Learning and Technology for Educational Reform. Oak Brook, IL: North Central Regional Educational Laboratory.

MACKENZIE, B. (1997) Skill Development [www] Available from https://www.brinmac.co.uk/tech.htm (accessed August 202}].

Merriam-Webster Dictionary (accessed July, 2021).

Miyake, A., and Shah, P. (1999). Models of working memory: Mechanisms of active maintenance and executive control. Cambridge: Cambridge University Press. http://www.researchgate.net/publication/233446680-The-role-of-working-memory-in-sport#pf9, accessed August 2021.

Richards, J. and Rodgers, T. (2001).Approaches and Methods in Language Teaching. New York, NY: Cambridge University Press.

Smith, J. and Patterson, F. (1998). Positively Bilingual: Classroom Strategies to promote the Achievement of Bilingual Learners. Nottingham: Nottingham Education Authority.

Speelman, C. (2005). Skill acquisition: History, questions, and theories. In C. Speelmanand K. Kinser (Eds.) Beyond the learning curve: The construction of mind (pp. 26–64). Oxford: Oxford University Press.

Speelman, C. (2005). Skill acquisition: History, questions, and theories. In C. Speelmanand K. Kinser (Eds.), Beyond the learning curve: The construction of mind (pp. 26–64). Oxford: Oxford University Press.

Sturgies, C. (2012). The art and science of designing competencies. Competency Works Issue Brief. Retrieved August 19, 2014 from http://www.nmefoundation.org/getmedia/64ecl32d-7d12-482d-938f-ce-9c4b26993b/competencyWors-IssueBrief-DesignCompetencies-Aug-2012.

Taatgen, N. A. (2002). A model of individual differences in skill acquisition in the Kanfer-Ackerman air traffic control task. Cognitive systems Research 3, 103-112. Retrieved October 30, 2013, from https://www.ai.rug.n11-niels/publications/CSRpublished.pdf, accessed July 2021.

Vapatten, B., and Benati, A. G. (2010).Key terms in second language acquisition. New York: continuum International publishing Group.

www.enactionschool.com/resources/papers/02-Speelman-chap02.pdf, accessed July 2021.

www.mextesol.net/journal/index.php?page=journal/id-article=519, accessed July 2021.

www.valamis.com/hub/cognitive-learning, accessed July 2021.

www.verywellmind.com/piagets-stages-of-cognitive-development-2795457-accessed July, 2021).

Zeeman, A. (2019). Dreyfus Model of Skill Acquisition. Retrieved (accessed July 2021) from toolshero: https://www.toolshero.com/human-resources/dreyfus-model-of-skill-acquisition/.

References

A. S Hornby, *et al.,* Oxford Advanced Learner's Dictionary. Oxford University Press, London.

Amesi, J., Akpomi, M. and Okwuanaso (2014). Teaching Strategies in Business Education for Sustaining Information and Communication Technology Learning in the Niger Delta. Global Journal of Arts Humanities and Social Sciences. Vol. 2; No. 3, pp. 10–21.

Basil, A. (2004). Organizational Theory and Management. Lecture notes on EDU 722. Imo State University-Calabar Study Center-Calabar.

Crompton, R. (n.d.) Evaluation: A Practical guide to Methods. Retrieved from www.lcbl.hw.ac.uk/ltdi/implementing-it/eval.htm.

Damilola, O. (2017). Communication: A Management Function.

Dekeyser, R. (2007). Introduction: Situating the Concept of Practice in R. M. Dekeyser (Ed.), Practice in a Second Language: Perspectives from Applied Linguistics and Cognitive Psychology (pp. 1–18). Cambridge: Cambridge University Press."

Designing Effective Monitoring and Evaluation of Education Systems of 2030: A Global Synthesis of Policies and Practices (2016)—A Draft.

Disha, M. (n.d.). Evaluation in Teaching and Learning Process/Education. Retrieved from www.yourarti-clelibrary.com/statistics-2/evaluation-in-teaching-and-learning-process-education/92476

Elmore, L. (n.d.) Role Play: Research on Activity Types. Retrieved from www.ablconnect.havard.edu.

Erwin (1991). Assessing Student Learning and Development: A Guide to the Principles, Goals and Methods of Determining College Outcomes.

Essentials for Effective Evaluation (2016). Retrieved from www.cese.nsw.gov.au/publications-filter/5-essentials-for-effective-evaluation.

Esu, A., Enukoha, O. and Umoren, G. (2016). Curriculum Development in Nigeria for Colleges and Universities. Calabar: Stiffaith Prints.

Fisher, M. (n.d.) Student Assessment in Teaching and Learning

Formative vs. Summative Assessment: 15 key Differences and Similarities (n.d.). Retrieved from www.formpl.us/blog/formative-summative-assessment.

Gagnon, D. (2019). 10 Qualities of a Good Teacher. Retrieved from www.snhu.edu/about-us/newsroom/2017.

Gray, K. (2021). Assessing Data on Student Learning in Cognitive and Affective Domains. Retrieved from www.study.com/academy/lesson/assessing/data-on-student-learning-in-cognitive-affective-domains.

https://articles.bplans.com/11-questions-to-help-your-business-start-off-on-the-right-foot/-AccessedAugust,2021.

https://bmmagazine.co.uk/in-business/advice/importance-business-registration-licensing. Accessed August 2021.

https://businessjargons.com/licensing.html. Accessed August 2021.

https://dictionary.cambridge.org/us/dictionary/english/qualification. Accessed August 2021.

https://docs.oracle.com/cd/A60725_05/html/comnls/us/ota/ota05a.htm. Accessed August 2021.

https://en.w.wikipedia.org/wiki/self-regulation-theory. Accessed August 2021.

https://louischew.medium.com/josh-kaufman-how-to-learn-anything-from-scratch-cb53d70c36ec. Accessed August 2021.

https://www.yourarticlelibrary.com/business/sole-trader-definition-characteristics-and-other-details/42036. Accessed August 2021.

https://www.iod.com/news/news/articles/what-is-the-role-of-the-managing-director. Accessed September 2021.

https://www.board.com/en#gref//. Accessed September 2021.

https://thetotalentrepreneurs.com-who-is-an-entrepreneur-2/. Accessed September 2021.

https://openlib.umn.edu/principlesmanagement/.

https://outward.fandom.com/wiki/skill-combinations. Accessed August 2021.

https://searchsofwarequality.teachtarget.com/definition/testing. Accessed August 2021.

https://thekindergartenconnection.com/secrets-developing-measuring-skills/. Accessed August 2021.

https://vervoe.com/skill-testing/#1. Accessed August 2021.

https://www.business.com/articles/7-tips-for-young-entrepreneurs/. Accessed August 2021.

https://www.ecoursesonline.iasri.res.in/mod/page/view.php?id=49598. Accessed August 2021.

https://www.employmentcrossing.com/article/9000218971/skill-identification/. Accessed August 2021.

https://www.igi-global.com/dictionary/is-entrepreneurship-a-bio-social-phenomenon/92105. Accessed August 2021.

https://www.igi-global.com/dictionary/pre-training-principle/23203. Accessed August 2021.

https://www.indeed.com/career-advice/career-development/conceptual-skill. Accessed August 2021.

https://www.indeed.com/career-advice/career-development/improve-your-personal-development-skills. Accessed August 2021.

https://www.insightassessment.com/article/interpretation. Accessed August 2021.

https://www.learningsolutionsmag.com/articles/1570/brain-science-pre-training-is-essential-to-a-complete-training-package. Accessed August 2021.

https://www.managementstudy.com/strategy-definition.htm

https://www.marketing91.com/licensing/. Accessed August 2021.

https://www.ncbi.nlm.nih.gov/pmc/articles/pmc5024935/. Accessed August 2021.

https://www.nidirect.gov.uk/articles/key-skills-qualifications. Accessed August 2021.

https://www.prospects.ac.uk/postgraduate-study/professional-qualifications. Accessed August 2021.

https://www.psychology.iresearch.com/sports-psychology/motor-development/skill-acquisition/. Accessed August 2021.

https://www.researchgate.net/publication/339640947.com

https://www.shiftelearning.com/blog/the-importance-of-pre-training-engagement. Accessed August 2021.

https://www.talentlms.com/blog/essential-skills-training-tools-for-trainers/. Accessed August 2021.

https://www.thecompetencygroup.com/competency-services/skill-certification/. Accessed August 2021.

https://www.understood.org/articles/en/trouble-with-self-regulation-what-you-need-to-know. Accessed August 2021.

https://www.westminister.edu/about/accreditation-assessment/definition.cfm. Accessed August 2021.

Irukaku, D. and Mary, N. (2018): Strategies for Effective Skill Acquisition by Business Education Students: Implication for Sustainable Human Capital Development Nigeria Journal of Business Education (NIGJBED) vol. 5 No. 2. url: http://www.nigjbed.com.ng.

Joshua, M. (2005). Fundamentals of Test and Measurements in Education.

Karni, A. (1996). The Acquisition of Perceptual and Motor Skills: A Memory System in the Adult Human Cortex. Brain Research Cognitive Brain Research, 5(1–2), 39–48. https://link.springer.com/reference-workentry/10.1007 percent2F978-1-4419-1428-6-852.

Kasilingam, G., Ramalingam, M. and Chinnavan, E. (2014). Assessment of Learning Domains to Improve Students' Learning in Higher Education in *Journal of Young Pharmacists* 6, 4 www.dx.doi.10.5530/jyp.2014.1.5.

Kitsantas, A., Robert, A. and Doster, J. (2004). Developing Self-Regulated Learners: Goal Setting, Self-Evaluation, and Organizational Signals During Acquisition of Procedural Skills. In the Journal of Experimental Education 269–287. http://dx.doi.org/10.3200/JEXE.72.4.269.287.

Marston, R. (2020). The Daily Motivation: A Strong Sense of Responsibility. Retrieved from www.greatday.com/motivate/200502.html.

Merriam-Webster (n.d.) Trainer. In Merriam-Webster.com dictionary. Retrieved Aug. 2021 from https://www.merriam-webster.com/dictionary/trainer.

Mgbekem, S. J. (2002). Essentials of Employee's Task Motivation in the Work-Environment. NIVS in conjunction with IBEPS, Calabar.

Mgbekem, S. J. (2004). Management of University Education in Nigeria. University of Calabar Press.

Miller, D. (2020). Importance of School Monitoring and Evaluation Systems.

Ndebbio, J. E. (2000). "Planning and Execution of Development Programmes." Paper presented at the National Seminar on Development Strategies, Labour Research Services, Unilag, Lagos.

Ndebbio. J. (2007). Project Planning, Analysis and Evaluation: Theory and Practice. University of Calabar Press.

Nyirenda, E. (2018). Monitoring and Evaluation (M&E) in the Education Sector. Retrieved from www.academia.edu/41058055UNESCO(2016).

Palomba, and Banta (1999) Assessment Essentials: Planning, Implementing and Improving Assessment in Higher Education.

Prachi, J. (2015). Strategy-Definition and Features.

Principles of Management (2010). Retrieved from Role Playing (2020). Retrieved from https://serc.carleton.edu/58460

Role-Play: Approach to Teaching and Learning (2014). Retrieved from www.blogs.shu.ac.uk.

Solesi, A. *et al.* (2014). An Appraisal of Skill Acquisition Centers in Nigeria. Research and Curriculum Development Department (R&CDD). Industrial Training Fund (ITF), Jos.

Spacey, J. (2017). 51 Examples of Management Strategy https://www.simplicable.com.

Swell, L. (2013). Role Playing in the Context of Learning Theory in Casework Teaching in *Journal of Education for Social Work*. https://doi.org/10.1080/00220612.1968.10671800.

The Assessment Process. Retrieved from www.missouristate.edu/assessment/the-assessment-process-htm.

The Importance of the Assessment Process (2013) in Special Education Guide: Retrieved from www.specialeducationguide.com/pre-k-12.

The Three Domains of Learning-Cognitive; Affective; and Psychomotor (CAPS)—It's Application in Teaching and Learning.

Thompson, J. (2019). What are Management Strategies? Reviewed by Michelle Seidel https://bizfluent.com/info-7737312management-strategies.html.

Thompson, S. (n.d.). Strategic Management vs. Strategy. Retrieved from https://smallbusiness.chron.com/strategic-management-vs-strategy-66207.html.

Understanding of Production and Operations Management (n.d.). Retrieved from www.magementstudghq.com.

What is Management? Definition, Concept, Features (n.d.). Retrieved from https://www.edunote.com.

Wilson, L. (n.d.) Three Domains of Learning-Cognitive, Affective, Psychomotor.

www.ilo.org.wcms.171329.

www.merriam-webster.com/dictionary/control. Accessed August 2021.

www.yourarticlelibrary.com/human-resource-development/training-meaning-definition-and-types-of-training/32374. Accessed August 2021.

Yambi, T. (2020). Assessment and Evaluation in Education. Retrieved from www.researchgate.net.

Zaidi, N., Rani, M., and Rahman, Z. (2017). Challenges in Performing Role-Play as an Assessment: Student's Views. In *International Journal of Academic Research in Business and Social Sciences*. 7:17 Retrieved from http://dx.doi.org/10.6007/IJARBSS/v7-112/3604.

Zall, J. and Ray, C. (2004). Ten Steps to a Risult-Based Monitoring and Evaluation System: A Handbook for Development Practitioners. The World Bank, Washington DC.

Zimmerman, B. J. (2001). Theories of Self-Regulated Learning and Academic Achievement: An Overview and Analysis. https://cehs.unl.edu/secd/self-regulation/. Accessed Augusst 2021.

References

(2008). On Vocational Training Registration. Sourced from https://www.thuviewphapluat.vn/archieve

(2015). Ensuring the Quality of Certification in Vocational Education and Training. European Center for the Development of Vocational Training CEDEFOP.

(2017). Crafts Development and Skills Acquisition Centers. Sourced from www.ncac.gov.ng/projects/crafts-development

(2019). Eligibility Criteria/Checklist for Selection of Entrepreneurship Development Centers under the AGSMEIS. Sourced from https://www.cbn.gov.ng/out/2019/dfd/eligibility

(2021). Definitions and Purposes of Accreditation. Sourced from https://www.ada.org

(n.d.) A Guide to Curriculum Development: Purposes, Practices and Procedures. Sourced from https://www.portal.ct.gov.curguide-generic

(n.d.) What is the Importance of Curriculum in Education? Sourced from https://www.quora.com

A. S. Hornby, *et al.* Oxford Advanced Learner's Dictionary. Oxford University Press. London.

Achieve. (2013). *The Next generation science standards* (pp. 1–3). Retrieve from http://www.nextgenscience.org

Achor, E., Agogo, P. and Dodo, E. (2020). Curriculum Content of Entrepreneurship Program and its Impact on Basic Students' Skills Acquisition in Entrepreneurship in Benue State Nigeria. In *International Journal of Vocational and Technical Education Research,* 6(1).

Achor, E., Agogo, P. and Dodo, E. (2020). Curriculum Contents of Entrepreneurship Program and Its Impact on Basic Student's Skills Acquisition in Entrepreneurship in Benue State Nigeria. In *International Journal of Vocational and Technical Education Research.* Vol. 6(2). Pp. 11–34.

Adebisi, and Oni, C. (2012). Availability of Vocational Training Facilities for the National Directorate of Employment (NDE) in Nigeria. In *International Journal of Development and Sustainability.* Vol. 1(3). 889-902 sourced from www.isdsnet.com/ijds.

AL-Jawi, F. d. (2010). Teaching the Receptive Skills: Listening and Reading Skills.

Alozie, Princewill *et al.* (2009): History and Philosophy of Science (6th ed.). Tavich Oil Ltd, Lagos.

Andrew, J. (1979): Essays on physical education and sports. Stanley Thomas Ltd, England.

Arslan, A. G., and Tertemiz, N (2004). Mastery of Science Process Skills and Their Effective Use in the Teaching of Science: An Educology of Science Education in the Nigerian Context. *Online Submission,* 16(1), 11–30.

Audu, R., Umar, I. and Idris, A. (2013). Facilities Provision and Maintenance: Necessity for Effective Teaching and Learning in Technical Vocational Education in IOSR Journal of Research and Method in Education (IOSR-JRME) 3(1). Sourced from www.researchgate.net

Babatunde, s. and Adeyanju, D. (2002). Language, Meaning and Society: "Papers in Honour of E. E. Adebija at 50." Haytee Press and Publishing Co. Nig. Ltd.

Bacon, F. (1947). The New Atlantis. New York; NY: Russell F. Moore.

Bae, J. and Bachman, L. F. (1998). A Latent Variable Approach to Listening and Reading: Testing Factorial Invariance across Two Groups of Children in the Koran/English Two-way Immersion Program. Language Testing, 15, 380–414.

Bandopadhay, T. (2007). Skill Acquisition and Economic Development—Some Comments. Sourced from https://mpra.ub.uni.muenchen.de./1759/MPRA

Barber, J, Pearson, D, and Cervetti, G. (2006). *Seeds of science/roots of reading*. California: The Regents of the University of California.

Barnard, D. (2021). How to Develop Effective Verbal Communication Skills: https://virtualspeech.com/blog/verbal-communicationskills.

Barnier, B. (2021). What is Capital? Sourced from https://www.investopedia.com/terms/c/capital.asp

Ben-nun, L. (2014). Nonverbal Communication Skills. Publish B. N. Publication House Israel.

Ben-Nun, L. (2015). Verbal Communication Skills. B. N. Publication House, Israel.

Biemans, H., and Van Mil, M. (2008). Learning styles of Chinese and Dutch students compared within the context of Dutch higher education in life sciences. *Journal of Agricultural Education and Extension, 14*, 265–278. doi:10.1080/13892240802207700.

Biggs, J. (1987). *Student approaches to learning and studying*. Melbourne: Australian Council for Educational Research.

Biggs, J., Kember, D., and Leung, D. Y. P. (2001). The revised two-factor study process questionnaire: R-SPQ-2F. *British Journal of Educational Psychology, 71*, 133–149.

Bodie, G. D. (2012). Listening as Positive Communication. In I. Socha and M. Pitts (Eds.), The Positive Side of Interpersonal Communication (pp. 109–125). New York, NY: Peter Lang.

Bodie, G. D., St. Cyr, K., Pence, R., Rold, M., and Honeycutt, J. (2012). Listening Competence in Initial Interactions I: Distinguishing Between What Listening is and What Listeners Do. International Journal of Listening, 26, 1–28, DOI: 10.1088/10904018.2012.639645.

Bodla, B. S. (n.d.) Barriers to Communication Lecture Note on Business Communication CBBA-206.

Broughton, G. (1978). "Teaching English as a Foreign Language." London: Routledge and Kegan Paul.

Brown, A. L. (1987). Metacognition, executive control, self-regulation and other more mysterious mechanisms. In F. E. Weinert and R. H. Kluwe (Eds.), *Metacognition, motivation and understanding* (pp. 65–116). Hillsdale: Erlbaum.

Brumbaugh, A. (1949). The Significance of Accreditation in *Sage Journals*. Sourced from journals.sage.pub.com/doi/abs/10.1177/00027162492650

Bucher, C. A. (1975): Administration and Education Dimensions of Health and Physical Education Program including Athletes (6th ed.). St. Louis the C.V Mosby Co., New York.

Burns, A. (1998). "Teaching Speaking." Annual Review of Applied Linguistics. Vol. 18, n. 3, pp. 102–123.

Burns, A. and Joyce H. (1997). Focus on Speaking. Sydney: National Center for English Language Teaching and Research.

Bybee, RW. (2014). NGSS and the next generation of science teachers. *Journal of Science Teacher Education, 25*(2), 211–221. doi:10.1007/s10972-014-9381-4.

Bygate, M. (1998). "Theoretical Perspectives on Speaking." Annual Review of Applied Linguistics. V.18, n.1, pp. 20–42.

Cambridge Dictionary (n.d.) Role Play Definition. Retrieved from https://dictionary.cambridge.org/dictionary/english/role

Chambers, H. (2001). "Effective Communication Skills for Scientific and Technical Professional," New York: Basic Books, p. 9.

CLIMB Professional Development and Training (2019).

Coffield, F., Moseley, D., Hall, E., and Ecclestone, K. (2004). *Learning styles and pedagogy in post-16 learning: a systematic and critical review*. London: Learning and Skills Research Center.

Curriculum Development Center (2002). Secondary School Integrated Curriculum for Physics Form 5. Kuala Lumpur: Ministry of Education of Malaysia.

Danladi, S. and Okon, C. (2016). Entrepreneurship Skill Acquisiton Education in Nigeria's Senior Secondary School: A Source of Youths Empowerment. In *Journal of Resourcefulness and Distinction,* vol. 13(1). Sourced from www.globalacademicgroup.com.

Denger, D. I. (1987). Educational Measurement, Continuous Assessment and Physiological Testing. Rapid Educational Publishers, Calabar.

Dittman, A. T. (1978). The Role of Body Movement in Communication. In A. W. Siegman and S. Feldsten (Eds.) Nonverbal Behavior and Communication. Hillsdale, NJ: Lawrence Erlbaum.

Dori, YJ, Tal, RT, and Tsaushu, M. (2003). Teaching biotechnology through case studies—can we improve higher order thinking skills of nonscience majors? *Science Education, 87*(6), 767–793. doi:10.1002/sce.10081.

Dornyei, Z. and Thurrell, S. (1994). Teaching Conversation Skills Intensively. Course Content and Rational. ELT Journal, V. 48, n. 1, pp. 46–49.

Double Gist. (2017), Adolescent Problems and their Counselling Strategies in Enugu State. Available from: http://www.doublegist.com/adolescent-problems-counseling-strategies-enugu-state. [Last accessed on 2017 Oct 05].

Douli, J.G. (2002), An Overview of Nigeria's Economic Reforms. Central Bank of Nigeria; Economic and Financial Review, 42(4).

Dreyfus, H. and Dreyfus, S. (1980). The Ethical Implications of the Five-stage Skill Acquisition Model. In Bulletin of Science, Technology and Society. DOI. 10.1.1.940.31365(1) sourced from www.researchgate.net/publications.

Dunlap, Knight (1926). The method and problems of social psychology. Psychological Review 47(6):471-48 DOI: 10.1037/h0057527

Durga, S. and Rao, S. (2018). Developing Students' Writing Skills in English—A Process Approach. In Journal for Research Scholars and Professionals of English Language Teaching. Vol. 2, n. 6 https://www.jrspelt.com

Duschl, R., Schweingruber, H. A., and Shouse, A. (2008). *Taking science to school.* Washington DC: National Academies Press.

Duschl, RA, and Bybee, RW. (2014). Planning and Carrying out Investigations: An Entry to Learning and to Teacher Professional Development around NGSS Science and Engineering Practices. *International Journal of STEM Education, 1*(1), 12. Doi: 10.1186/s40594-014-0012-

Effiong, J. Etuk and David, O. Mbat (2010). Entrepreneurship Development (for students and practitioners). University of Calabar Press, Calabar, Nigeria.

Ekman, P. (1994). Strong Evidence for Universals in Facial Expressions: A Reply to Russell's Mistaken Critique. Psychological Bulletin, 115, 268-287.

Ekman, P. and Friesen, W. (1969). The Repertoire of Nonverbal Behavior: Categories, Origins, Usage and Coding, Semiotica, 1, 49–98.

Elmenoufy, A. (1997) "Speaking: The Neglected Skill." New Directions in Speaking Proceedings of the Fourth Efl Skills Conference Under the Auspices of the Center of Adult and Continuing Education, the American University in Caro, pp. 9–18.

Encyclopedia Britannica Dictionary (n.d.) Definition of Regulation of Regulation.

Entwistle, N. J., and Ramsden, P. (1983). *Understanding student learning.* London: Croom Helm.

Entwistle, N., and McCune, V. (2004). The conceptual bases of study strategy inventories. *Educational Psychology Review, 16,* 325–345. doi:10.1007/s1064800400030.

Enukoha, O. I. *et al. (*2010): Philosophy of Education: An Introduction. University of Calabar Press, Calabar.

Enweani, U. (2021). Influence of Entrepreneurship Centers on Acquisition of Entrepreneurial Skill in International *Journal of Research and Innovation in Social Science* 5(1). Sourced from www.rsisinternational.org.

Erduran, S, and Jimenez-Aleixandre, MP (Eds.). (2008). *Argumentation in Science Education: Perspectives from Classroom-Based Research*. Dordrecht: Springer.

Etim, E. and Daramola, O. (2020). The Informal Sector and Economic Growth in South Africa and Nigeria: A Comparative Systematic Review in *Journal of Open Innovation: Technology,* Market and Complexity.

Eurydice. (2012). *Developing key competencies at school in Europe: challenges and opportunities for policy—2011/12* (pp. 1–72).

Evagorou, M, Jimenez-Aleixandre, MP, and Osborne, J. (2012). "Should we kill the grey squirrels?" A study exploring students' justifications and decision-making. *International Journal of Science Education, 34*(3), 401–428. doi:10.1080/09500693.2011.619211

Excerpted from: Tomlinson, C. A. (August, 2000). Differentiated of instruction in the Elementary Grades. ERIC Digest. ERIC clearinghouse on Elementary and Early Childhood Education. (https://www.readingrockets.org/article/what-differentiated-instruction-accessed-September,2021).

Eyisi (2005). The Mechanics of Reading Comprehension and Summary Writing. Rex Charles and Patrick Limited, Nimo.

Eykhoff, P. (1974). System identification: Parameter and State Estimation. London: John Wiley and Sons.

Fatoki, O. (2019). The Skill Acquisition Program and Youth Empowerment in Ondo State of Nigeria: An Empirical Study in *Global Journal of Human-Social Science: Arts and Humaities-Psychology-19:6.*

Fatoki, O. (2019). The Skills Acquisition Program and Youth Empowerment in Ondo State in Nigeria: An Empirical Study in *Global Journal of Human—Social Science: An Arts and Humanities—Psychology.* 19(6).

Federal Government of Nigeria (FRN). (2004). National Policy on Education. Lagos: NERDC Press.

Federal Republic of Nigeria (2004): National Policy on Education. 4th edition, NERD press, Lagos.

fkfh.sportsmanitoba.ca>basic-skills

Florez, M. (1999) "Improving Adult English Language Learners' Speaking Skills" ERIC Digest (ERIC Document Reproduction Service No. ED: 435204.

Frank, M. and Shaw, A. (2016). Evolution and Nonverbal Communication. In D. Matsumoto, H. C. Hwang, and M. G. Frank (Eds.) APA Handbook of Nonverbal. Communication (pp. 45–76, Chapter XXIV, 626 pages. Washington, D. C. American Psychological Association. http://dx.doi.org.libpdb.d.umm.edu.2048/10/037/14669.003

Fried, A. E. and Koontz, T. Y. (2005). *Teaching science to children: An inquiry approach* (6th ed.). New York: McGraw-Hill

Gabrielatos, C. (1998). "Receptive Skills with Young Learners" In: Gika, A. S. and Berwick, D. (eds.) Working with Young Leaners. A Way Ahead. Whistable, Kent: IATEFL.

Gangula, A. and Eliah, P. (2015). "The Art of Effective Reading for Professional Success" www.ijelh.com/papers/

Gbamanja, S. (2002). *Essential of Curriculum and Instruction: Theory and Practice*. Port Harcourt: Paragraphic.

Glenn, S. (n.d.). Importance of Curriculum to Teaching. Sourced from https://www.classroomsynonym.com/professional-standards-teacher-evaluation

Gooding, D, Pinch, T, and Schaffer, S (Eds.). (1993). *The Uses of Experiment: Studies in the Natural Sciences*. Cambridge: Cambridge University Press.

Gooding, D. (2006). From phenomenology to field theory: Faraday's visual reasoning. *Perspectives on Science, 14*(1), 40–65.

Gordon, R. and Dnickman, D. (2019). Nonverbal Behavior as Communication: Approaches, Issues and Research. In O. Hargie (Ed). The Handbook of Communication Skills (4th ed.). (pp. 81–134, Chapter 3, 641 pages)) New York, NY: Routledge. Retrieved from http://search.proquest.com/ibpdb.d.com.

Gronlund, N. E. (1985): Measurement and Evaluation in Teaching (5th ed.). Macmillan Publishers New York.

gs.usafootball.com

Halliday, M. A. K. (1978). Language and Social Semiotic Edward Arnold. London.

Hamilton, V. L. (1976): Role play and Deception: A Reexamination of the Controversy. Journal for the theory of Social Behavior (p. 233–50).

Harmer, J. (2001). The Practice of English Language Teaching. Edinburgh: Pearson Education Limited.

Hornby, A. S. (2021): Oxford Advanced Learner's Dictionary of Current English (10th Edition). Oxford University Press, United Kingdom.

https://classroom.synonym.com/classroom-dynamics-7946454.html-accessed-October,2021.

https://corporatesolutions.johnmaxwell.com/blog/values-that-drive-a-diverse-and-inclusive-culture/accessed-October,2021.

https://counseling.education.wm.edu/blog/8-types-of-curriculum-accessed-September,2021

https://courses.lumenlearning.com/engcomp1-wmopen/chapter/outcome-types-of-writing-1-1/accessed/September,2021.

https://creativehomelife.com/the-ultimate-consmable-idea-list-for-character-school-funding/accessed-September,2021.

https://elearningindustry.com.digital-education-tools-teachers-students-accessed-September,2021.

https://en.m.wikipedia.org/wiki/carema-coverage-accessed-October,2021.

https://en.m.wikipedia.org/wiki/handbook-accessed-September,2021.

https://examwinners.com/school-curriculum-development/stages-process-of-curriculum-development/accessed-September-2021.

https://hyattractions.wordpress.com/2016/12/07/the-meaning-of-curriculum-content-and-learning-experiences/accessed-Septmber-2021.

https://ivyproschool.com/blog/advantages-and-disadvantages-of-machine-learning-in-2020/accessed-September-2021.

https://kidsworldnm.com/curriculum/accessed-September-2021.

https://onlinenotebank.wordpress.com/2020/02/04/Criteria-for-curriculum-evaluation/accessed-September-2021.

https://physicscatalyst.com/graduation/principles-of-curriculum-development/accessed/September-2021.

https://poorvucenter.yale.edu/strategic-resources-digital-publications/instructional-tools-accessed-September,2021.

https://sup[port.skillscommons.org/home/contribute-manage/metadata-and-apprendices/learning-resource-material-types/accessed-September,2021.

https://teaching.cornell.edu/teaching-resources/building-inclusive-classroom/inclusive-teaching-strategies-accessed-October,2021.

https://tenneyschool.com/differentiation-customized-instruction-necessary/-accessed-September,2021.

https://uwaterloo.ca/organizational-human-development/learning-development-programs/inclusivity-series/principles-inclusivity-accessed-October-2021.

https://www.calstatela.edu/academic/CCOE/programs/cats/mainstreaming/accessed/October,2021.

https://www.celt.iastate.edu/teaching/creating-an-inclusive-classroom/creating-an-inclusive-learning-environment/accessed-October,2021.

https://www.cnet.com/how-to/five-tools-for-the-worlds-best-teacher/accessed-September,2021.

https://www.eduforics.com/en/steps-to-inclusion-in-schools/accessed-October,2021.

https://www.emexmag.com/diversity-as-a-core-value/accessed-October,2021.

https://www.friendshipcircle.org/blog/2014/02/21/10-items-that-can-make-your-classroom-more-inclusive/accessed-October,2021.

https://www.highspeedtraining.co.uk.

https://www.inclusion.me.UK/news/what-does-inclusion-mean-accessed-October-2021.

https://www.indiastudychannel.com/resources/151966-multimedia-components-application. aspx-accessed-September,2021.

https://www.instructables.com/Welding-Tools-and-Materials/accessed-October,2021.

https://www.irelandassignmenthelp.com/samples/difference-between-integration-and-inclusion/ accessed-October,2021.

https://www.playyourwaysane.com/blog/advantages-of-improvisation-accessed-September,2021.

https://www.potentiaco.com/what-is-machine-learning-definition-types-applications-and-examples/ accessed-September-2021.

https://www.precgroup.com/welding-fabrication-terms/accessed-October,2021.

https://www.salesforce.com/eu/blog/2020/06/real-world-examples-of-machine-learning. html-accesed-September-2021.

https://www.schoology.com/blog/differentiated-instruction-definition-examples-and-strategies-accessed-September,2021.

https://www.slideshare.net/sarishtigarg/learning-resources-46775217-accessed-September,2021.

https://www.un.org/development/desa/disabilities/convention-on-the-rights-of-persons-with-disabilities/ article-35-reports-by-states-parties.html/accessed-October,2021.

https://www.unicef.org/education/inclusive-education-accessed-October,2021.

https://www.urbandaleschools.com/policy/article-600-educational-program/627-instructional-materials-selection-inspection-and-reconsideration/accessed-September,2021.

https://www.vawamei.org/tools-resources/faq/what-is-the-difference-between-training-curricula-and-training-materials/accessed-Sseptember-2021.

https://www.verzeo.com/blog-what-is-machine-learning-accessed-September-2021.

https://www.vtsd.com/vtsd-pol-regs/instructional-supplies/accessed-September,2021.

https://www.washburnlaw.edu/library/services/equipment.html-accessed-September,2021.

https://www2.education.vic.gov.au/pal/selecting-suitable-teaching-resources/policy-accessed-September,2021.

https://wwwascd.org/books/handbook-for-qualities-of-effective-teachers/chapter=introduction-maximizing-your-use-of-the-handbook-handbook-for-qualities-of-effective-teachers-accessed-September,2021.

Hye, K. (2012). A Model for Receptive and Expressive Modalities in Adult English Learner's Academic L$_2$ Skills. PEARSON.

Idoko, C. (2014). Skill Acquisition and Youth Empowerment in Nigeria in *Global Journal of Commerce and Management Perspective* 3(1). Sourced from www.researchgate.net.

Idoko, C. (2021). Skill Acquisition and Youth Empowerment in Nigeria. Sourced from https://www.researchgate.net/publication/350344460.

Ikwegwu, E. *et al. (*2014). Human Empowerment through Skills Acquisition: Issues, Impacts and Consequences—A Nonparametric View. In Journal of Poverty, Investment and Development 5. Sourced from https://www.researchgate.net/publication/344191691.

Iyorza, S. (2015) Social and Behavior Change Communication: Principles, Practices and Perspectives. B$_2$ Publication.

Joshua, M. T. (2005): Fundamentals of Test and Measurement in Education, University of Calabar Press, Calabar.

Kabir, S. M. (2017). Communication Skills. Retrieved from https://www.researchgate.net/publication/325844168

Kavathatzopoulos, I. (1994). Training Professional Managers in Decision-Making about Real Life Business Ethics Problems: The Acquisition of the Autonomous Problem-Solving Skill. In *Journal of Business Ethics* 13(5) pp. 379–386. Sourced from https://www.jstor.org/stable/25072541

Kelvin-Iloafu, L., Igwe, N. and Enemuo, J. (2011). Women's Economic Empowerment. Sourced from www.icrw.org.uploads

Kelvin-Iloafu, L., Igwe, N. and Enemuo, J. (2018). Facts and Figures: Economic Empowerment—Benefits of Economic Empowerment. Sourced from www.unwomen.org/en/what-we-do

Kelvin-Iloafu, L., Igwe, N. and Enemuo, J. (2019) Activating and Strengthening Women Empowerment through Economic and Social Inclusion. (Concept Note) sourced from www.social.un.org./csocd

Kelvin-Iloafu, L., Igwe, N. and Enemuo, J. (2019). Managing the challenges of Women and Youth Empowerment Programs in Nigeria. In Global Journal of Human-Social Science: Interdisciplinary 19:5 sourced from www.researchgate.net/publication/335773098

Kendon, A. (1981). The Study of Gesture: Some Remarks on its History. In J. N. Deely and M. D. Lenhart (Eds.) Semiotics. New York, NY: Plenum Press.

Kendra, C. (2014). Types of Nonverbal Communication. Available 16 May 2014 at Psychology.about.com/…/nonverbal communication/…/nonverbal types.html.

Kirkpatrick, E. M. (ed.) 1980: Chambers Universal Learner's Dictionary. Chambers Harrap Publishers Ltd., Edinburg.

Knapp, M. L. (1972). Nonverbal Communication in Human Interaction. New York, NY: Holt, Rinehart and Winston.

Knorr Cetina, K. (1999). *Epistemic cultures: how the sciences make knowledge*. Cambridge: Harvard University Press.

Korfiatis, KJ, Stamou, AG, and Paraskevopoulos, S. (2003). Images of Nature in Greek Primary School Textbooks. *Science Education, 88*(1), 72–89. Doi: 10.1002/sce.10133.

Kottacheruvu, N. (2014). Listening as a Basic Skill of Communication. Journal of Business Management and Social Sciences Research (3.4) 31-32.

Kruse, A. M. (1999): Single-sex Settings: Pedagogy for Girls and Boys in Danish Schools. Learners and Pedagogy pp. 210-220. Paul Chapman Pub. Ltd, London.

Kulman, R. (2015). What are Expressive Language Skills? https://southcountrychildandgamily.com

Latour, B, and Woolgar, S. (1979). *Laboratory Life: The Construction of Scientific Facts*. Princeton: Princeton University Press

Latour, B. (2011). *Visualization and Cognition: Drawing Things Together* (pp. 1–32).

Lehrer, R, and Schauble, L. (2012). Seeding Evolutionary Thinking by Engaging Children in Modelling its Foundations. *Science Education, 96*(4), 701–724. Doi: 10.1002/sce.20475.

Little, P. (1978). Communication in Business. Longman, London.

Lonka, K., Olkinuora, E., and Makinen, J. (2004). Aspects and prospects of measuring studying and learning in higher education. *Educational Psychology Review, 16*, 301–331.

Louis Cohen and Lawrence Manion (1994): Research Methods in Education. Routledge Press, London.

Luoma, S. (2004). Assessing Speaking. Cambridge: Cambridge University Press.

Lynch, M. and S. Y. Edgerton Jr. (1988). 'Aesthetic and Digital Image Processing Representational Craft in Contemporary Astronomy', in G. Fyfe and J. Law (eds), *Picturing Power; Visual Depictions and Social Relations* (London, Routledge): 184—220

Lynch, M. (2006). The Production of Scientific Images: Vision and Revision in the History, Philosophy, and Sociology of Science. In L Pauwels (Ed.), *Visual Cultures of Science: Rethinking Representational Practices in Knowledge Building and Science Communication* (pp. 26–40). Lebanon, NH: Darthmouth College Press.

MacBride, S. (ed.) (1980). Many Voices, One World. Paris: The UNESCO Press.

Magbagbeola, N. O. (2004), Theoretical and Conceptual Issues in Economic Sector. Central Bank of Nigeria: Economic and Financial Review, 42(4)

Martin, D. J. (1997). Elementary Science Methods: A Constructivist Approach. (Ed: Erin J. O'Conner and Timothy Coleman). *Delmar Publishers: New York.*

Marton, F., and Säljö, R. (1984). Approaches to learning. In F. Marton, D. Hounsell, and N. Entwistle (Eds.), *The experience of learning* (pp. 36–55). Edinburgh: Scottish Academic Press.

Marton, F., Wen, Q., and Wong, K. C. (2005). 'Read a hundred times and the meaning will appear...'. Changes in Chinese university students' views of the temporal structure of learning. *Higher Education, 49,* 291–318.

Mbanefo, M. C. and Chiaha, G. T. (2013). Curriculum Innovations in Science and Technology for Quality, Relevance Sustainability in Teacher Education in Nigeria. In: Onyegaegbu N and Eze U. (Eds.), Teacher Education in Nigeria: Quality, Relevance and Sustainability. Nsukka: Institute of Education, UNN. Pp. 74-85.

Mbanefo, M. C. (2015). Developing Creative Thinking Skills in Basic Science Students: Prospects and Challenges. Journal of Science Teachers Association of Nigeria. 50(1), 207-216.

McArthur, L. Z. and Baron, R. M. (1983). Toward an Ecological Theory of Social Perception. Psychological Review, 90, 215-238.

McKay, M., Martha, D. and Patrick F. (1995). Messages: Communication Skills Book, 2nd ed. Oakland, CA: New Harbinger Publications.

Meaning of Government. Sourced from https://nigerianscholars.com/tutorials/introduction-to-government/meaning-and-scope-of-government.

Mendonça, PCC, and Justi, R. (2013). An instrument for Analyzing Arguments Produced in Modelling-based Chemistry Lessons. *Journal of Research in Science Teaching, 51*(2), 192–218. Doi:10.1002/tea.21133.

Meredith, G. C., Nelson, R. E. and P. A. Neck (1987): The Practice of Entrepreneurship, UNILAG Press, Lagos, Nigeria.

Michael Mayers (1997). At Certification, COMPTIA Publishers, New York.

Mundhe, G. (2015). Teaching Receptive and Productive Language Skills with the Help of Technique. An International Journal in English Vol. 1. Iss. 2. www.punresearch.com

Munrow, A. D. (1972): A Discussion of Principles; Physical Education. Boel, London.

National Research Council (2000). *Inquiry and the National Science Education Standards*. Washington DC: National Academies Press.

National Research Council (2011). *National Science Education Standards*. Washington, DC: The National Academic Press.

National Research Council (2012). *A Framework for K-12 Science Education*. Washington DC: National Academies Press.

Nienhuys, S. (2011). Curriculum Development Framework for Vocational Training Modules. Sourced from https://www.researchgate.net/publications/231182877

Nunan, D. (1991). Language Teaching Methodology: A Textbook for Teachers. Edingburgh, Harlow, England: Longman.

Nunan, D. (9189). Designing Tasks for the Communicative Classroom. New York: Cambridge University Press.

Nuttal, C. (1982). Teaching Reading in a Foreign Language: Practical Language Teaching No. 59). Great Britain Heinmann.

O'Niel, T., Domingo, P. and Valters, C. (2014). Progress on Women's Empowerment: From Technical Fixes to Political Action. Sourced from www.researchgate.net/publication/335773098

Ochiagha, C. C. (1995), Theory and Practice of Career Development. Enugu: Snaap Press Limited.

Ojikutu, A. (1998). Community Participation Development of Secondary School Building in Irele Local Government Area, Ondo. Unpublished M.Ed. Thesis, University of Ibadan, Nigeria.

Okafor, E. (2011). The Role of Vocational and Technical Education in Manpower Development and Job Creation in Nigeria in *Journal of Research and Development* 2(1), 152-157.

Okolo, A. and Ekesionye, E. (2011). Curriculum Development and Implementation: An Imperative for Prouction of New Distance and Nonformal Education Teachers for Nigerian Journal of Curriculum Studies, 18(2).

Okolocha, C., Muogbo, U. and Jihn-Akamelu, C. (2020). Effect of Skill Acquisition on Youth Employability in Nigeria. In International Journal of Research in Finance and Management 3:1, pp. 33–37. DOI. 3-1-10-19(1). Sourced from https://www.researchgate.net/publication/339352867

Okwuagbala, U. (2020). Importance of Youth Empowerment. Sourced from www.discover.hubpages.com/politics/importance-of-youth-empowerment

Olusola, L. (2019). Importance of Youth Empowerment in the 21st Century. Sourced from www.m.guardian.ng/features/importance-of-youth-empowerment

Onwe, O. (2013). Role of the Informal Sector in Development of the Nigerian Economy: Output and Employment Approach. In *Journal of Economics and Development Studies.* Vol. 1(1). 60-74.

Onwuachu, W. C. and Okoye, P. O. (2012). Relevance of Basic Science Curriculum for Entrepreneurship Skill Acquisition. Knowledge Review, 26(4), 6-13.

Onwuka, U. (1996). Curriculum Development for Africa. Onitsha: African Fed Publishers Ltd.

Osborne, J. and Dillon, J. (2008). *Science Education in Europe: Critical Reflections.* London: Nuffield Foundation.

Osborne, J. (2014). Teaching Scientific Practices: Meeting the Challenge of Change. *Journal of Science Teacher Education, 25*(2), 177–196. Doi: 10.1007/s10972-014-9384-1.

Otaigbe, O. (2015). Evaluation of Vocational Education in Nigeria: A Review of the Roles of the Regulation Bodies. In *Global Journal of Interdisciplinary Social Sciences.* 4(3) 16-21.

Padilla, M. J. (1990). The Science Process Skills. *Research Matters-to the Science Teacher, 9004.*

Papaevripidou, M, Constantinou, CP, and Zacharia, ZC. (2007). Modeling Complex Marine Ecosystems: An Investigation of Two Teaching Approaches with Fifth Graders. *Journal of Computer Assisted Learning, 23*(2), 145–157. doi:10.1111/j.1365-2729.2006.00217.x.

Pask, G. (1988). Learning strategies, teaching strategies, and conceptual or learning style. In R. R. Schmeck (Ed.), *Learning strategies and learning styles* (pp. 83–100). New York: Plenum Press.

Pauwels, L. (2006). A Theoretical Framework for Assessing Visual Representational Practices in Knowledge Building and Science Communications. In L Pauwels (Ed.), *Visual Cultures of Science: Rethinking Representational Practices in Knowledge Building and Science Communication* (pp. 1–25). Lebanon, NH: Darthmouth College Press.

Perkins, D. (2010). Empowerment. Sourced from https://www.researchgate.net/publication/316451077_EmpowermentProcess

Radovic Markovi, M. and Aid, S. (2018). The Importance of Communication in Business Management. Retrieved from: https://www.researchgate.net/publication/328630849.

Radovic Markovi, M. and Omolaja, M. (2009). Information Management-Concepts, Analysis and Applications, Himalaya Publishing, Delhi, India.

Reves, T. and Levine, A. (1988). The FL Receptive Skills: Same or Different System, 16, 327-336.

Richards, J. (1990). The Language Teaching Matrix Cambridge: Cambridge University Press.

Robert, E. Allen, *et al. (*2003). Penguin English Dictionary (2nd Edition). Penguin Books Ltd, London, the U.K.

Roberts, Geoffrey R. (1969). Reading in Primary Schools. London: Routledge and Kegan Paul Ltd.

Rothbart, D. (1997). *Explaining the growth of scientific knowledge: metaphors, models and meaning.* Lewiston, NY: Mellen Press.

Roy, P. (n.d). Vocational Training Centers can be a Prosperous Investment.

Ruivenkamp, M, and Rip, A. (2010). Visualizing the Invisible Nanoscale Study: Visualization Practices in Nanotechnology Community of Practice. *Science Studies, 23*(1), 3–36.

Sadiku, M. (2015). The Importance of Four Skills Reading, Speaking, Writing, Listening in a Lesson Hour. European Journal of Language and Literature: Vol. 1. Nol. 1

Samovar, L. A., Porter, R. E. and McDaniel, E. R. (2009). Communication between Cultures-engage Learning Social Sciences.

Sanyal, B. and Martin, M. (2006). Quality Assurance and the Role of Accreditation: An Overview. Sourced from https://www.core.ac.UK./display/4178615

Schmeck, R. R. (Ed.). (1988). *Learning strategies and learning styles.* New York: Plenum Press.

Schrodt, P., Wheeless, L. R., and Ptacek, R. M. (2000). Informational Reception Apprehension, Educational Motivation and Achievement. Communication Quarterly, 48, 60-73. DOI: 10.1080/01463370009385580.

Schwartz, RS, Lederman, NG, and Abd-el-Khalick, F. (2012). A Series of Misrepresentations: A Response to Allchin's Whole Approach to Assessing Nature of Science Understandings. *Science Education, 96*(4), 685–692. Doi: 10.1002/sce.21013.

Schwarz, CV, Reiser, BJ, Davis, EA, Kenyon, L, Achér, A, Fortus, D, *et al. (*2009). Developing a Learning Progression for Scientific Modeling: Making Scientific Modeling Accessible and Meaningful for Learners. *Journal of Research in Science Teaching, 46*(6), 632–654. Doi:10.1002/tea.20311.

Şen. A. Z., and Nakipoğlu, C. (2012). Analyze Of High School Chemistry Textbooks In Terms Of Science

Shapiro, H. (2000): New Research on Reading America.

Sheth, T. (2015). Receptive Skills—Listening and Reading: A Sin qua non for Engineers. In International Journal of English Language, Literature and Humanities. Vol. III. ISS III. https://www.ijellh.com.

Sheth, T. (2016) Expressive Communication Skills in English: A Criterion for Nonnative L$_2$ Students. https://www.researchgate.net

Shikha, S. (2012). "Communication Skills for Engineers in Global Arena." International Journal in Arts, Management and Humanities (11) 1-6.

Skilbeck, M. (1971). Preparing Curriculum Objectives. In the Vocational Aspect of Education 23(54). https:doi.org/10.1080/03057877180000011

Skills you Need (2017). https://www.skillsyouneed.com/lps/verbal-communication.

Stake, R. E. (2005), "Qualitative case studies," in N. K. Denzin and Y. S. Lincoln (eds.), The Sage Handbook of Qualitative Research(3rd Ed.), Thousand Oaks, CA: Sage Pub.

Sypher, B. D., Bostrom, R. N., and Seibert, J. H. (1989). Listening, Communication Abilities, and Success at Work. Journal of Business Communication, 26, 293-303. Doi: 10./177/002-194368902600401.

Taylor, J. L and Walford, R. (1972): Simulation in the Classroom. Penguin Books. London.

The American English Dictionary (n.d.) Definition of Regulation of Regulation. www.trovami.altervista.org.

The top that Glossary: www.taphet.com/definitions

Tobias, S and Ingber, T (1976): Achievement Treatment Interactions in Programmed Instruction. *Journal of Educational Psychology (43-47).*

Tobias, S. (1994): Interest, Prior Knowledge, and Learning. Review of Educational Research 64(1) 37-54.

Torky, S. A. (2006). The Effectiveness of a Task-Based Institution Program in Developing the English Language Speaking Skills of Secondary Stage Students. A PhD Thesis Submitted to the Department of Curricula and Methods of Teaching. AIN SHAMS UNIVERSITY.

tscienceinsider.com

Udofia, U. I and Chigbo, C. (2005): Resource Center Mgt. Lagos.

Ukala, C. and Nwabueze, A. (2016). Work Ethics for Skill Acquisition. In Ebong, J. and Asodike, J. (Eds.) Economics of Education: Trends in Nigeria. Pp. 7–99. Port Harcourt: Eagle Litograph Publishers. Sourced from www.researchgate.net/publication.

Undiyaundeye, F. and Otu, A. (2015) Entrepreneurship Skills Acquisition and the Benefits among the Undergraduate Students in Nigeria. In European Journal of Social Sciences, Education and Research 2:3, pp. 9–14. Sourced from www.researchgate.net/publications.

Upari, L. (2012). Rhetoric's other: Levinas, Listening, and the Ethical Response. Philosophy and Rhetoric, 45, 227-245. Doi: 10.5325/philrhet.45.3:0227.

Uwatt, L. (2015). Basic Communication and Study Skills. Stiffaith Prints and Supplies Co; Calabar.

Uwatt, L. E. and Nta, G. E. (2010). Study Skills for Human Cognitive Development from the Standpoint of Reading Skills in Literacy and Reading in Nigeria (Vol. 12, No.2) Reading Association of Nigeria.

Vennum, T. (1987). Technological Approach in English Language Teaching: New, Vol. 1. Issue 204. Accessed on 9 March 2015.

Vermunt, J. (1987). Learning styles and self-regulation. Paper presented at the annual Conference of the American Educational Research Association, Washington DC. ERIC Document ED 285 900 TM 870 481.

Vermunt, J. D. (1996). Metacognitive, cognitive and affective aspects of learning styles and strategies: a phenomenographic analysis. *Higher Education, 31*, 25–50.

Vermunt, J. D. (1998). The regulation of constructive learning processes. *British Journal of Educational Psychology, 68*, 149–171.

Villaume, W. A., Brown, M. H., and Darling, R. (1994). Presbycusis, Communication, and Older Adults. In M. L. Humert, J. M. Wiemann and J. F. Nussbawn (Eds.), Interpersonal Communication in Older Adulthood: Interdisciplinary Theory and Research (pp. 83–106). Thousand Oaks, C. A: Sage.

Vlasceanu, L., Grunberg, L. and Parlea (2007). Quality Assurance and Accreditation: A Glossary of Basic Terms and Definitions. Sourced from https://www.unesco-cepes

Wallace, A. (2020). The Difference between Receptive and Expressive Language. https://napacenter.org/receptive-vs-expressive-language/

Weaver, C. (1972). Human Listening. Process and Behavior. Indiana Polis, In: Bobbs Merrill.

wgcoaching.com>sports>skills

Widdowson, H. (1998). "Skills, Abilities and Contexts of Reality." Annual Review of Applied Linguistics, V. 18, n. 3, pp:323-333.

Williams Davis (1991). Innovations Penguin Publisher, New York.

www.bchmsg.yolasite.com/curriculum-development.php-accessed-September-2021

www.bchmsg.yolasite.com/curriculum-development.php-accessed-September,2021

www.edufruit.blogspot.com/2017/03/88-importance-of-curriculum-planning.html?m=1-accessed-September-2021.

www.fao.org/3/ah650e/A+1650E10.htm-accessed-September-so21

www.healthdirect.gov.ay

www.highspeedtraining.co.uk.

www.ibe.unesco.org/fileadmin/user_upload/COPs/Pages-documents/Resource_Packs/TTCD/Sitemap/Module_8/Module_8.html/acccessed/September,2021.

www.studylecturenotes.com/curriculum-evaluation-meaning-importance-objective/accessed-Sesptember,2021.

Ziderman, A. (2016). Funding Mechanisms for Financing Vocational Training: An Analytical Framework. Sourced from https://www.researchgate.net

American Psychological Association. (n.d.) APA Dictionary of Psychology. American Psychological Association. https://dictionary.apa.org

Ariani G, Kwon YH, Diedrichsen J. Repetita iuvant: repetition facilitates online planning of sequential movements (preprint). bioRxiv 819938, 2019.

Baczriska, A. K., Rowinski, T., and Cybis, N. (2016). Proposed core competencies and empirical validation procedure in competency modelling: confirmation and classification.

Bertelson P. Sequential redundancy and speed in a serial two-choice responding task. QJ exp psychol 13:19-102. 1961 doi:10.1080/17470216108416478.

Bloom (1956). Major categories in the cognitive domain of the taxonomy of educational objectives

Campion, M. A. Fink, A. A., Ruggeberg, B. J., Carr, L., Philips, G. M., and Odman, R. B. (2011). Doing competencies well: best practice in competency modelling. pers. psychol. 64, 225-262. doi:10.1111/j.1744-6570.2010.01207.x

Dai, G., and Liang, K. (2012). Competency modelling research in practice in China: a literature review. J. Chin. Hum. REsour. Manag. 3, 46-66. doi:10.1108/20408001211220566

Edwards M G. Humphreys GW, Castiello U. Motor facilitation following action observation: a behavoural study in prehensile action. Brain cogn 53:495-502, 2003. doi:10.1016/s0278-2626(03)00210-0.

Ericsson K. A., Krampe RT, Tesh-Romer C. The role of deliberate practice in the acquisition of expert performance. Psychol Rev 100:363-406.1993.doi:10.1037/0033-295x.100.3.363.

Goldberg L. R. (1993). The Structure of Phenotypic Personality Traits. American psychologist, 48(1), 26— Parks, L., and Guay, R. P. (2009). Personality, values and motivation. Personality and individual differences, 47(7), 675-684.

Griffiths D, Tipper SP. Priming of reach trajectory when observing actions: hand-centered effects. QJ Exp Psychol (Hove) 62:2450-2470, 2009. doi:10.1080/17470210903103059.

Hardwick RM, Edwards MG. Observed reach trajectory influences executed reach kinematics in prehension. QJ exp psychol (Hove) 64:1082-1093, 2011. doi:10.1080/17470218.2010.538068.

Hardwick RM, Forrence AD, Krakauer JW, Haith Am. Time-dependent competition between goal-directed and habitual response preparation. Nat Hum Behav 3:1252-1262, 2019. doi:10.1038/s41562-019-0725-0

Hatcher, R. L., Fouad, N. A., Campbell, L. F., McCutcheon, S. R., Grus, C. L., and Leachy, K. L. (2013). Competency-based education for professional psychology: moving from concept to practice.Train.Edu. Prof.psychol.7,225-234.doi:10.1037/90033765.

Kaslow, N. J. (2004). Competencies in professional psychology.Am.psychol.59,774-781. doi:10.1037/0003-066x59.8.744.

Kaslow, N. J., Rubin, N. J., Forrest, L., Elman, N. S., Van Horne, B. A., Jacobs, S. C., et al (2007). Recognizing, assessing, and intervening with problems of professional competence.prof.psychol.Res. pract.38,479-492.doi:10.1037/0735-7028.38.5.479.

Kenkel, M. (2009). Adopting a competency model for professional psychology: essential elements and resources. Train.Educ.Prof.psychol.3(4, suppl.) 559-562.doi:10.1037/90017037.

Leigh, I. R., Bebeau, M. J., Rubin, N. J., Smith, I. L., Lichtenberg, J. W., Portnoy, S., et al. (2007). Competency assessment models. Prof.psychol.Res.pract.38,463-473.doi:10.1037/90017037

Lichtenberg, J. W., Bebeau, M. J., Smith, I. L., Portnoy, S. M., Leigh, I. W., Rubin, N. J., et al. (2007). Challenges to the assessment of competence and competencies. Prof.psychol.Res.pract.38, 474-478. doi:10.1037/0735-7028.38.5.474

Magill RA, Anderson DI. Motor learning and control: concepts and Applications. New York: McGraw-Hill, 2013.

Maljkovic V, Nakayama K. priming of pop-out: 1. Role of features. Mem Cognit 22:657-672, 1994.

Maljkovic V. Nakayama K. Priming of pop-out:11. The role of position. Percept psychophys 58:977-991, 1996. doi:3758/BF03206826.

Mawase F, Lopez D, Celink PA, Haith AM. Movement repetition facilitates response preparation. Cell Reports 24:801-808, 2018. doi:10.1016/j.Celrep.2018.06.097.

McClelland, D. C. (1973). Testing for competence rather than for intelligence.Am.Psychol.28,1-14. doi:10.1037/hoo34092

Medium.com/self-starter/the-three-stage-model-of-skill-acquisition… (access July, 2021).

Mitrovic, S. (2021, May 4). 7 of the most common types and How to Identify Yours Mindvalley Blog. https://blog.mindvalley.com/types#headlines.

Mooradian, T. A. (2011). Personality, person-brand fit, and brand community: An investigation of individual's brands and brand communities. Journal of marketing management, 27 (9-10), 874-890.

Nash, J. M., and Larkin, K. T. (2012). Geometric models of competency development in specialty areas of professional psychology.Train.Educ.Prof.psychol.6,37-46.

Rodolfa, E., Baker, J., Demers, S., Hilson, A., Meck, D., Schaffer, J., et al. (2014). Professional psychology competency initiatives: implications for training, regulation, and practice. S. Afr.J.Psychol.44,121-135. doi:10.1177/008124631452271

Rodolfa, E., Bent, R., Eisman, E., Nelson, P., Rehm, L., and Ritchie, P. (2005). A cube model for competency development: implications for psychology educators and regulators. Prof.psychol.Res.pract.36, 347-354. doi:10.1037/0735-7028.36.4.347

Rodriguez, D., Patel, R., Bright, A., Gregory, D., and Gowing, M. (2002). Developing competency models to promote integrated human resource practices. Hum.Resour.Manage.41,309-324. doi:10.1002/hrm.10043.

S. R. (2016, August 1). Types, Development and Tools: Psychology. Psychology Discussion-Discuss Anything About Psychology. https://www.psychologydiscussion/types-development-and-tools-psychology/2058

Schippmann, J. S., Ash, R., Battista, A., Carr, M., Eyde, L., Hesketh, L. D., et al. (2000). The practice of competency modeling. Pers.psychol.53, 703-740.doi:10.1111/j.1744-6570.2000.tb0020.x

Schwartz BL, Hashtroudi S. Priming is independent of skill learning. J EXP Psychol Learn Mem Cong 17:1177-1187, 1991.

support.skillscommons.org/hom/com…accessed July, 2021

Tanaka Y. Shimojo S. Location vs feature: reaction time reveals dissociation between two visual functions. Vision Res 36:2125-2140, 1996. doi:10.1016/0042-6989(95)00272-3.

Thomas, J. (2018, February 18). The Difference Between Concrete vs Abstract Thinking. BetterHelp. https://www.betterhelp.com/advice/self-esteem

Voudouris, N. (2009). On defining competencies in the training of Australian psychologists.Inpsych 31, 32–33.

Voudouris, N. (2010). Toward assessment of professional competence in Australian psychology. Inpsych 32, 24–26.

www.frontiersin.org/articles/10.3389/feduc.2017.00054/full

www.lexico.com/definition/test

www.phychologydiscussion.net/learning/learning-meaning-nature-types-and-theories-of-learning1652

www.sociologygroup.com/types-of-thinking/

www.yourarticlelibrary.com/hum

Mr. Jacob Oroks is a dedicated professional. He is the president and chief executive officer of Iboto Empire LLC. Mr. Oroks is a pragmatic and well-articulated personality. He possesses the following skills: data analysis, master trainer, certified Google trainer, Microsoft certified trainer, software developer, and data manager.

Mr. Oroks bagged the following educational degrees as part of his portfolio: master of information systems management (MISM), bachelor of science in technical management (BSTM), and associates of Science Health Information Administration (ASHIT).

Mr. Jacob Oroks has the following professional certification: Six Sigma Certified, Project Management Professional (PMP), Lean Six Sigma certified (LSSC), Lean Culture certified (LCC), certified team supervisor (CTS), certified information security manager (CISM).

He has acquired tremendous experience as an IT specialist. This includes twenty-two years' technical experience, data modeling, data warehousing, data analysis, systems development, systems privacy and security, Microsoft Offices, Tableau, SAS, design, and implementation, electronics health record implementation and management, computer system repairs, installations, and upgrades, healthcare business analysis, data management, transformation, and achieving.

Mr. Jacob Oroks additional important information and personal history include twelve years with the County of Los Angeles as a health care data analyst and fourteen years with HIMSS (Health Information Management Systems Society).